Federalism and Legal Unification

IUS GENTIUM
COMPARATIVE PERSPECTIVES ON LAW AND JUSTICE

VOLUME 28

Series Editors

Mortimer Sellers
University of Baltimore

James Maxeiner
University of Baltimore

Board of Editors

Myroslava Antonovych, *Kyiv-Mohyla Academy*
Nadia de Araújo, *Pontifical Catholic University of Rio de Janeiro*
Jasna Bakšic-Muftic, *University of Sarajevo*
David L. Carey Miller, *University of Aberdeen*
Loussia P. Musse Félix, *University of Brasilia*
Emanuel Gross, *University of Haifa*
James E. Hickey, Jr., *Hofstra University*
Jan Klabbers, *University of Helsinki*
Cláudia Lima Marques, *Federal University of Rio Grande do Sul*
Aniceto Masferrer, *University of Valencia*
Eric Millard, *West Paris University*
Gabriël Moens, *Curtin University*
Raul C. Pangalangan, *University of the Philippines*
Ricardo Leite Pinto, *Lusíada University of Lisbon*
Mizanur Rahman, *University of Dhaka*
Keita Sato, *Chuo University*
Poonam Saxena, *University of Delhi*
Gerry Simpson, *London School of Economics*
Eduard Somers, *University of Ghent*
Xinqiang Sun, *Shandong University*
Tadeusz Tomaszewski, *Warsaw University*
Jaap de Zwaan, *Erasmus University Rotterdam*

For further volumes:
http://www.springer.com/series/7888

Daniel Halberstam • Mathias Reimann
Editors

Federalism and Legal Unification

A Comparative Empirical Investigation of Twenty Systems

Springer

Editors
Daniel Halberstam
Eric Stein Collegiate Professor of Law
University of Michigan Law School
Ann Arbor, MI, USA

Mathias Reimann
Hessel E. Yntema Professor of Law
University of Michigan Law School
Ann Arbor, MI, USA

ISBN 978-94-007-7397-4   ISBN 978-94-007-7398-1 (eBook)
DOI 10.1007/978-94-007-7398-1
Springer Dordrecht Heidelberg New York London

Library of Congress Control Number: 2013952745

© Springer Science+Business Media Dordrecht 2014
This work is subject to copyright. All rights are reserved by the Publisher, whether the whole or part of the material is concerned, specifically the rights of translation, reprinting, reuse of illustrations, recitation, broadcasting, reproduction on microfilms or in any other physical way, and transmission or information storage and retrieval, electronic adaptation, computer software, or by similar or dissimilar methodology now known or hereafter developed. Exempted from this legal reservation are brief excerpts in connection with reviews or scholarly analysis or material supplied specifically for the purpose of being entered and executed on a computer system, for exclusive use by the purchaser of the work. Duplication of this publication or parts thereof is permitted only under the provisions of the Copyright Law of the Publisher's location, in its current version, and permission for use must always be obtained from Springer. Permissions for use may be obtained through RightsLink at the Copyright Clearance Center. Violations are liable to prosecution under the respective Copyright Law.
The use of general descriptive names, registered names, trademarks, service marks, etc. in this publication does not imply, even in the absence of a specific statement, that such names are exempt from the relevant protective laws and regulations and therefore free for general use.
While the advice and information in this book are believed to be true and accurate at the date of publication, neither the authors nor the editors nor the publisher can accept any legal responsibility for any errors or omissions that may be made. The publisher makes no warranty, express or implied, with respect to the material contained herein.

Printed on acid-free paper

Springer is part of Springer Science+Business Media (www.springer.com)

Preface

If federalism means unity in diversity and diversity in unity, the uniformity of laws ought to be central to the discussion about whether federalism delivers on its promise. This groundbreaking book begins that conversation in earnest.

The International Academy of Comparative Law was innovative when in November of 2008 it convened at the Institute for Legal Research of the National Autonomous University of Mexico in Mexico City its first thematic congress entitled "The Impact of Uniform Law in National Law: Possibilities and Limits". For the first time, the Academy hosted a congress on a discrete theme, as opposed to the much larger multi-themed World Congresses of Comparative law traditionally held every 4 years.

Among the topics selected for this thematic congress was uniformity of law in federal systems. The conference thereby sparked the inquiry that led to this book. Professors Daniel Halberstam and Mathias Reimann have conducted a detailed comparative study yielding remarkably deep and precise understandings based on comparative empirical research across a range of legal systems, including Argentina, Australia, Belgium, Brazil, Canada, Germany, India, Italy, Malaysia, Mexico, the Netherlands, Russia, Spain, South Africa, Switzerland, the United Kingdom, the United States, Venezuela, as well as the supranational entity that is the European Union. These legal systems span the civil and common law worlds and are diverse in terms of age, size, structure, and population.

Professors Halberstam and Reimann chose these systems according to their working definition of a *federal system* as "a compound polity with multiple levels of government each with constitutionally grounded claims to some degree of organizational autonomy and direct legal authority over its citizens." They engaged national experts to prepare a national report for each system and to provide the information necessary for their own cross-cutting comparative analysis.

The resulting comparative investigation is divided into three distinct parts: the different modes of legal unification, the current level of unification across various systems and areas of law, and an analysis and explanation of the results.

The first part traces how unification or harmonization of law may stem from a variety of sources, including the exercise of coercive central government powers, various forms of voluntary coordination (which, in turn, involve component government initiatives and non governmental actors who draft restatements, principles or model laws), and national systems of professional education. Professors Halberstam and Reimann show the varying degrees to which these different factors contribute to legal unification. They conclude that the impetus for unification stems principally from central sources of power, especially central legislation, with other factors playing a less instrumental role. This conclusion alone will be both useful and sobering as some federal systems, such as the supranational European Union, contemplate different ways of increasing the uniformity of law within its system.

In the second part, the authors examine the level of unification that has been achieved across a variety of dimensions.

After considering uniformity by area of law and by federation, Professors Halberstam and Reimann consider several hypotheses about what drives unification. They evaluate and cautiously confirm the importance of "legislative centralization," consider and end up rejecting the independent significance of "structural centralization," and, to the surprise of those who thought that legal traditions no longer matter, cautiously confirm a "legal traditions" hypothesis. This latter finding will require comparative law scholars to rethink the currently fashionable conclusion that we live in a world that has escaped the significance of the civil v. common law divide.

This ambitious study provides by far the most comprehensive and systematic examination of legal unification in federal systems to date. No other study has attempted to consider more than one or two areas of the law and more than a small handful of legal systems.

Finally, the methodology of the research upon which the present volume rests is highly original. It complements the largely theoretical literature with an innovative effort at data collection and analysis. The work thus expands our appreciation not only of the particular subject at hand – legal unification in federal systems – but of the profound utility and continued promise of the comparative law method.

New York and Mexico City

George A. Bermann
Jorge A. Sánchez Cordero

Acknowledgements

This book is the result of a collaborative effort. We thank the National Reporters, whose individual reports may be found in Part II of this book, for their contributions. This project would not have been possible without them. We also thank the many additional experts, who are too numerous to mention here, for their time and effort to fill out scorecards as explained in Appendix 2.

We give special thanks to Jennifer Miller, a Ph.D. student in the University of Michigan Department of Political Science, and to Joanna Lampe, a J.D. student at the University of Michigan Law School, for outstanding research assistance, to Cynthia Bever and Pamela Tanner, our faculty assistants at the University of Michigan Law School, for extraordinary help in managing this project, and to Sarah Bullard and Martha Kreutzer for help in editing the national reports.

We are grateful to our colleagues Jenna Bednar, Steven Croley, John diNardo, Jim Hines, Ken Kollman, Rick Lempert, J.J. Prescott, Adam Pritchard, and Mark West for valuable comments and discussions. We also thank the University of Michigan Law School and the Cook Research Fund for support.

Three national reports are based on earlier publications. Jeffrey Kahn, Nikolay Balayan, and Alexei Trochev, "The Unification of Law in the Russian Federation," 25 *Post-Soviet Affairs* 310–346 (2009); Aline Grenon, "Unification of Laws in Federal Systems: The Canadian Model" in: Nathalie Vézina (ed.), *Uniform Law: Limits and Possibilities* 33–61 (Quebec: Carswell, 2009); and Louis F. Del Duca and Patrick Del Duca, "An Italian Federalism?—the State, its Institutions, and National Culture as Rule of Law Guarantor", 54 *American Journal of Comparative Law* 799–842 (2006). We thank those authors and publishers for their permission to use those materials here.

Finally, we thank the International Academy of Comparative Law, under whose auspices the first edition of this study was published last year.

Ann Arbor	Daniel Halberstam
June 1, 2013	Mathias Reimann

Contents

Part I Comparative Analysis

1   **Federalism and Legal Unification: Comparing Methods, Results, and Explanations Across 20 Systems** 3
    Daniel Halberstam and Mathias Reimann

Part II National Reports

2   **The Argentine Federal Legislative System**............................. 71
    Alfredo M. Vítolo

3   **The Australian Federation: A Story of the Centralization of Power** .. 87
    Cheryl Saunders and Michelle Foster

4   **Federalism and Legal Unification in Austria** 103
    Anna M. Gamper and Bernhard A. Koch

5   **Belgium: A Broken Marriage?** 121
    Alain-Laurent Verbeke

6   **Federalism and Legal Unification in Brazil**............................. 153
    Jacob Dolinger and Luís Roberto Barroso

7   **Unification of Laws in Federal Systems: The Canadian Model** 169
    Aline Grenon

8   **The European Union: A Federation in All but Name** 191
    Jan Wouters, Hanne Cuyckens, and Thomas Ramopoulos

9   **Unification of Laws in the Federal System of Germany** 237
    Jürgen Adam and Christoph Möllers

10 **India: From Political Federalism and Fiscal Centralization to Greater Subnational Autonomy**.. 255
    Sunita Parikh

11	**Emergence of the Italian Unitary Constitutional System, Modified by Supranational Norms and Italian Regionalism** .... Louis Del Duca and Patrick Del Duca	267
12	**Federalism and Legal Unification in Malaysia** .... Hean Leng Ang and Amanda Whiting	295
13	**Federalism and Legal Unification in Mexico** .... Oscar Echenique Quintana, Nadja Dorothea Ruíz Euler, and Ricardo Carrasco Varona	339
14	**How Federal Is the Russian Federation?**............................... Jeffrey Kahn, Alexei Trochev, and Nikolay Balayan	355
15	**Federalism and Legal Unification in South Africa**..................... Karthy Govender	391
16	**The Trend Towards Homogenization in the Spanish 'State of Autonomies'** .... Aida Torres Pérez	417
17	**Federalism and Legal Unification in Switzerland**...................... Eleanor Cashin Ritaine and Anne-Sophie Papeil	439
18	**The United Kingdom: Devolution and Legal Unification** .... Stathis Banakas	461
19	**United States Federalism: Harmony Without Unity**.................... James R. Maxeiner	491
20	**Venezuela: The End of Federalism?** .... Allan R. Brewer-Carías and Jan Kleinheisterkamp	523
Contributors		545
Index		551

Part I
Comparative Analysis

Chapter 1
Federalism and Legal Unification: Comparing Methods, Results, and Explanations Across 20 Systems

Daniel Halberstam and Mathias Reimann

1.1 Introduction

This study investigates the unification of laws in federal systems. It describes how such unification is pursued, states the degree to which it has been accomplished, and seeks to explain the respective differences among the systems covered.

1.1.1 The Need for This Study

This study fills a significant gap in the scholarly literature, especially in investigating the correlation between federal structures and degrees of legal uniformity. Many scholars have sought to make comparative assessments of the level of decentralization across federal systems. These valuable studies (mostly from political scientists) have examined such aspects as the nominal distribution of powers over policy areas, the relative distribution and expenditure of fiscal resources, the political interaction between the central and constituent governments and institutions, and the legal preservation of autonomy of constituent units or institutions of governance. Some projects (mostly by legal scholars) have examined legal convergence (usually with regard to single systems) in particular policy areas such as corporate governance, civil procedure, or tort liability. But ours is the first study that seeks to ascertain

---

D. Halberstam (✉) • M. Reimann
University of Michigan Law School, University of Michigan, South State Street 625, 48109 Ann Arbor, MI, USA
e-mail: dhalber@umich.edu

comparatively the level of legal uniformity within federal systems across a host of legal domains with a view to understanding better the relation between federal structure and legal uniformity.[1]

1.1.2 Federalism Defined

We define a federation as a compound polity with multiple levels of government each with constitutionally grounded claims to some degree of organizational autonomy and direct legal authority over its citizens. Obviously, this definition masks a welter of particular forms.[2]

Federal models can be distinguished along several lines. Some systems are classic state federations like Argentina, others *sui generis* entities like the European Union. Federations range from highly centralized systems like Italy to marginally integrated ones like The Kingdom of the Netherlands.[3] Some countries have "integrative" federal systems that resulted from the coming together of previously more or less sovereign states, like Switzerland, others constitute "devolutionary" systems that result from the decentralization of previously unified nations, like Belgium. There are "vertical" models like Germany in which executive, legislative, or judicial powers are vertically integrated, as well as "horizontal" models like the United States in which each level of government makes, executes, and adjudicates its own laws separately. There are federations in which all component states are constitutionally equal, like Mexico,[4] and asymmetric systems in which some components receive greater powers than do others, like Malaysia. And some countries formally acknowledge their federal nature, like Brazil, while others view themselves as by and large unitary, like the United Kingdom.

Furthermore, there are significant differences pertaining to the respective countries' political character and social make-up. Some federations have parliamentary systems, like Spain, while others have a presidential system, like Russia. Some

---

[1] Some noteworthy exceptions are the studies published in *Harmonization of Legislation in Federal Systems* (Ingolf Pernice, ed., Baden-Baden: Nomos, 1996); and *Harmonization of Legislation in Federal Systems* (George Bermann, ed., Baden-Baden: Nomos, 1997). These works, however, do not attempt a comprehensive comparative study of the level of unification within federal systems either.

[2] *See generally*, Daniel Halberstam, "Federalism: Theory, Policy, Law", in, *The Oxford Handbook of Comparative Constitutional Law* (M. Rosenfeld and A. Sajo, eds., Oxford: Oxford University Press, 2012).

[3] Note that the Kingdom of the Netherlands is a larger unit the Netherlands (in Europe) itself. The Kingdom of the Netherlands consists of a rather centralized European country and a few small islands in the Netherlands Antilles. These islands were former Dutch colonies and are now loosely associated with the mother country through a "Statute".

[4] The Federal District (Distrito Federal), i.e., Mexico City, has, like the District of Columbia in the United States, a somewhat special status as the seat of the federal government.

are soundly democratic, like Canada, while others are borderline authoritarian, like Venezuela. And some systems are characterized by deep ethnic, linguistic, or economic cleavages, like India, while other federations have largely homogeneous populations, like Austria.

Last, but not least, the federations of the world belong to different legal traditions. Most of them are part of the civil law world, like Spain, while others belong in the common law orbit, like Australia. And some have a mixed legal system, like South Africa.

We shall gloss over these differences as we describe the modes of legal unification and present data about the varying degrees of legal uniformity.[5] Yet, when we seek explanations for the differences in the various federations' degree of legal unification, we will resort to at least some of the distinctions mentioned; thus, we will ask, for example, whether these differences can be explained by reference to the structural features, legal traditions or socio-political characteristics of the respective federations.

1.1.3 Database and Method

This study covers 20 federal systems from six continents: Argentina, Australia, Austria, Belgium, Brazil, Canada, Germany, India, Italy, Malaysia, Mexico, The (Kingdom of the) Netherlands, Russia, Spain, South Africa, Switzerland, the United Kingdom, the United States, Venezuela, and the European Union.[6] In cooperation with the International Academy of Comparative Law we identified these 20 systems as major, more or less democratic federations from which we could reliably obtain data within a reasonable time.

The data we summarize, analyze, and interpret come from national reports authored by local experts on each of these systems. These reports were written in response to a detailed questionnaire, which is reproduced in Appendix 3. We asked about *The Federal Distribution and Exercise of Lawmaking Power*, *The Means and Methods of Unification*, and the *Institutional and Social Background*. In addition, the questionnaire contained a "Unification Scorecard" on which the national reporters assessed the degree of unification in their respective systems across nearly 40 areas of law. We also obtained an additional assessment of uniformity for each system from at least one other expert who also filled out the "Unification Scorecard". While

---

[5]Thus, for purposes of this study, the term federalism is used simply as an analytic tool to determine the inclusion or exclusion of the system as an object of study. Note that we use the generic terms "central" or "federal" to refer to the central level of governance and "component state", "member state", "component unit" or "member unit" to refer to the regional governments, be they "Member States" as in the European Union, "Provinces" as in Canada, "States" as in the United States, "Cantons" as in Switzerland, or "Regions" or "Communities" as in Belgium, etc.

[6]Nigeria was originally part of this study but we were ultimately unable to locate a competent national reporter.

we checked the reliability of their assessment through eight "control questions", the data obtained about degrees of uniformity remain inevitably subjective because they are the views of expert insiders. Our data-gathering and evaluation process is described in greater detail in the Methodological Appendix (Appendix 2).

A draft of this comparative chapter was presented to all national reporters to ensure the reliability of the conclusions we drew from their initial submissions. Many national reporters supplied us with extensive feedback which we incorporated.

1.1.4 Three Caveats

Three caveats are in order lest the scope and thrust of this study be misunderstood. They concern the meaning of legal unification and harmonization, the relationship between legal rules and actual outcomes, and the descriptive and analytic, rather than normative and programmatic, nature of this study.[7]

First, we consider both legal unification and harmonization. We take the former to mean (more or less complete) sameness and the latter to mean similarity.[8] We do not conceive of the difference between these two concepts as fundamental but rather as a matter of degree. In other words, unified and harmonized laws represent different points on a spectrum of likeness. To be sure, in examining the methods of unification and harmonization, we consider whether sameness results from simple takeover of an area by central authorities or from assimilation of the content of distinct laws across subunits. At bottom, however, the question of sameness is simple and generic. We ask how similar the law is across the subunits of a particular federation and how that level of similarity compares to the level of similarity found across the subunits of other federations.[9]

Second, this study examines the unification of legal rules, not of actual outcomes in concrete cases. While it looks beyond the law "on the books" and includes consideration of the respective rules' interpretation and application, it does not address the degree to which identical or similar disputes are actually decided

---

[7]Beyond the three limitations listed below, the study also limits itself to official (state) law. Thus, it does not deal with so-called "non-state" or "private" norms. Such norms are harmonized or unified through very different processes and often to a much greater degree than state law. They would require a study entirely in its own right.

[8]We are aware that there are other, more specific, understandings of these terms, as in Canada, for instance, where harmonization has special meaning in connection with so-called "harmonized bijural law," which takes both common and civil law traditions into account. For purposes of this report, however, we have communicated the understanding of these terms as laid out in the text to all participants as the operative understanding for purposes of this study.

[9]Consequently, this study is limited to the unification of law *within* federal systems. It does not address the question of uniformity across different federations, i.e., on the international level. We do, however, include the European Union in this study as a federal system.

identically or similarly. Measuring sameness or similarity on the level of actual outcomes would require a fundamentally different approach in the tradition of "common core" research.[10] Finding a high degree of legal uniformity in this study merely suggests, but does not guarantee, that like cases are actually treated alike throughout the system.

Third, the thrust of this study is descriptive and analytic. It summarizes and analyzes the data and seeks to explain them. It does not take a normative stance and thus does not ask to what degree legal uniformity is desirable, or how it can best be accomplished.[11] Perhaps lessons can be learned from our study in these regards but teaching them is not our goal.

1.1.5 What Lies Ahead

Beyond this Introduction, this chapter consists of three main parts, dealing, respectively, with the factors of unification, the current situation, and potential explanations for our findings.

Section 1.2 focuses on *the modes of legal unification*. It describes the factors that drive the process, looking at constitutions and legislation, court decisions and scholarly works, legal education and practice, and at the influence of international lawmaking projects. To do so, it summarizes and analyzes the national reporters' answers to the main part of the questionnaire.

Section 1.3 describes the *current level* of unification. It shows – inter alia through tables – the degree to which areas of law are unified as well as the degree to which the law within particular federal systems is uniform. The data here come from the assessments of legal uniformity in the "Unification Scorecards" filled out by the national reporters as well as by the respective second experts for each system.

Section 1.4 then seeks *explanations* for the differences noted in Section 1.3 by considering the findings in Sect. 1.2, but also by looking beyond to other factors. In this section, we offer a series of explanations which are mutually compatible and should be considered in concert. Its conclusions, however, remain tentative and leave several questions open.

While the three main parts build on one another, they can also be read separately. For example, a reader who is mainly interested in how much uniformity there

---

[10] For the classic study of this sort, see *Formation of Contracts – A Study of the Common Core of Legal Systems* (Rudolf Schlesinger, ed., 2 vols., 1968). A more recent, and much broader, enterprise of this nature is the Common Core of European Private Law project (often referred to as the "Trento Project"), *see* Mauro Bussani and Ugo Mattei (eds.), *The Common Core of European Private Law Project* (Cambridge: Cambridge University Press, 2004).

[11] See, e.g., Daniel Halberstam and Mathias Reimann, "Top-Down or Bottom-Up? A Look at the Unification of Private Law in Federal Systems," in Roger Brownsword et al. (eds.), *The Foundations of European Private Law* (Oxford: Hart Publishing, 2011).

actually is can fast-forward to Sect. 1.3, and a reader who is primarily interested in potential explanations can go straight to Sect. 1.4. The whole picture, however, only emerges from reading all sections together.

1.2 Modes of Legal Unification

In the process of creating (or working towards) legal unification (or at least harmonization) of law in federal systems, a variety of factors are usually at work. In particular, such unification can result from the exercise of central government power (infra 1.2.1); from formal or informal voluntary coordination among the component units (1.2.2); from non-state actors drafting restatements, principles, or model rules (1.2.3); from a nationwide system (or orientation) of legal education and legal practice (1.2.4); and from compliance with international law and participation in international unification efforts (1.2.5). The National Reports suggest that all these factors matter, albeit not always in all systems and often to substantially varying degrees.

1.2.1 Top-Down Unification: Central Government Power

Unification of law through the exercise of central government power is top-down. It regularly occurs in three principal ways: through central ("federal") constitutional norms, via central ("federal") legislation, and through the work of central courts creating uniform case law. Other means, such as centrally managed coordination among component units, play a more occasional and diffuse role.

1.2.1.1 The Constitution

All systems under consideration have a common (and in that sense "federal") constitution, although it may not be written in a single document (as in the United Kingdom), called a "constitution" (as in the European Union), or not reflect the reality of federalism (as in Venezuela). Since legal unification studies have traditionally focused on commercial and private law (and, to a lesser extent, criminal and procedural law), it is easy to overlook that these constitutions have a significant unifying effect in and of themselves. This effect has two dimensions.

First, constitutions promote legal unification by allocating certain lawmaking power to the center, especially in the form of legislative jurisdiction. By granting legislative jurisdiction over at least some areas to the central government, a constitution authorizes legislation and therefore unification in these areas of law. As we will see (infra Sect. 1.4), the allocation of legislative powers to the center has some regularity but it also varies considerably from one federation to another.

Of course, the actual strength of a constitution's unifying force depends heavily on the interpretation of the respective provisions – the commerce clause of the United States Constitution, for example, could have been read narrowly but was instead interpreted to allow a broad swath of uniform federal legislation often very tenuously related to actual commerce. For this and other reasons, constitutional texts can be deceptive. In particular, they sometimes suggest a high degree of decentralized lawmaking and thus diversity, while in reality, centralization and uniformity prevail, as in the cases of Argentina and Venezuela.

Second, constitutions often contain directly applicable norms that provide, sometimes within a margin of discretion accorded to local officials, for reasonably uniform law throughout the system. The most significant norms in this regard concern fundamental rights which are in one form or another part of almost all the constitutions we have examined (either as explicit catalogs incorporated in or appended to the constitution or implied in the constitutional text). Such fundamental constitutional rights are a significant force of legal unification because they typically require all public authorities, both at the central and component level of governance, to act (i.e., to legislate, execute, and adjudicate) in compliance with the same basic norms. This unifying force is at work in virtually all the federations under review here although its strength varies considerably. It depends mainly on four factors: the number, kind, and interpretation of basic rights guaranteed by the constitution; the extent to which they are voluntarily respected in practice; the degree of their enforcement by the courts; and the margin of discretion accorded local officials. Where the fundamental rights catalog is extensive and strong, respect for basic rights is high, and the courts exercise powerful judicial review with little tolerance of variation, the unifying force of fundamental constitutional rights is great. This is true in many federal systems, notably in Austria, Belgium, Canada, Germany, India, Italy, Mexico, Spain, South Africa, and the United States.[12] In other systems, the unifying force of central constitutional rights is weaker, either because the Constitution contains few constitutional rights, as in Australia, or because judicial review is less powerful or less extensive, as in the European Union, Malaysia, and the United Kingdom.

In addition, many constitutions contain (explicit or implicit) norms pertaining to the political character and legal structure of the subunits. This is the case, for example, in Belgium, Brazil, Germany, India, Malaysia, Mexico, Russia, Spain,[13] and the United States. The strength of these provisions and their impact on uniformity varies considerably.[14] As a general matter, however, these norms also

---

[12] In some of these countries, special procedures exist for the enforcement of constitutional rights on a broad basis, like the German *Verfassungsbeschwerde* and the Mexican *amparo*.

[13] In Spain, these norms pertain only to some of the component states, i.e. those that followed a certain fast-track procedure to autonomy.

[14] For example, in the United States, the Republican Form of Government Clause has little bite. Argentina's Article 6 of the Constitution, by contrast, which similarly authorizes the federal government to intervene in the territory of the provinces to guarantee a republican form of government, has had a dramatic effect on component state autonomy. The Argentine central

militate in favor of uniformity because they constrain the permissible variety of subunit structures. Thus, they make the structural political landscape generally more uniform – and thus also more likely to produce similar legal norms.

1.2.1.2 Central Legislation

In most systems under review, central legislation (including executive and administrative regulation) is reported to be the primary means of legal unification, and in all systems, it is heavily employed for that purpose. This is especially the case in the areas of commercial, private, and procedural law. Central legislation can promote unification in a variety of ways.

Most importantly, central legislation usually creates directly applicable norms which are thus *per se* uniform throughout the system.[15] In most federations, such directly applicable central norms are clearly the most powerful and effective means of unification. The reports for Brazil, Germany, Italy, Malaysia, Russia, and Venezuela emphasize this point in particular, but it is also true for Argentina, Austria, Belgium, India, Spain, and South Africa. In other systems, central legislation plays a somewhat less powerful, though still very substantial role, as in Australia and Switzerland. Finally, in a few federations, central legislation, while common and important, may not be the most dominant unifying force; one could say this about Canada, Mexico, and the United States, and it is also true for the European Union. In these systems, unification also occurs heavily through other means, especially through legislative models (in the form of federal laws, uniform statutes, EC directives, etc.).[16]

Beyond the enactment of directly applicable (uniform) rules, the central legislature can employ various other strategies of unification. These alternative legislative strategies appear only in a minority of systems. Still, where they are used, they can be powerful promoters of legal unification.

A small group of federal systems allow the center to enact legislation mandating that the member units pass conforming (implementing) rules. This strategy aims at legal harmonization rather than unification. It is particularly important in the

---

government has used this power repeatedly to, as the Argentine Report puts it, "strong-arm the provinces into complying with federal mandates in any situation it deemed necessary to do so."

[15]They are, however, not necessarily entirely uniform in interpretation and practical application. Different authorities (courts or executive officials) may interpret them differently. In Canada, federal legislation expressly provides that, due to the "bijuralism" of the legal system, federal rules may have to be interpreted differently in the common law contexts on the one hand and in the context of Quebec's civil law system on the other.

[16]In the latter three systems, part of the reason for this more limited unifying role of central legislation is the breadth of concurrent jurisdiction: even if the center legislates, the member units do not necessarily lose their competence to enact parallel, and possibly divergent, norms for their own territories. Of course, where the very point of central legislation is to create uniformity, the member units may lose that right, as in the case of *federal preemption* in the United States.

European Union. Here, the center has enacted hundreds of "Directives" (and many "Framework Decisions")[17] prescribing basic policies, principles, and rules which the member states must then, with some choice regarding the details, implement in their national legislation. Similar central legislation exists in Austria (though in limited areas only) and occasionally in the Dutch federation. It also used to play an important role in Germany but was abolished by constitutional amendment in 2006.[18]

Furthermore, in areas of concurrent jurisdiction, the center can also threaten to take over a field unless the states agree on uniform rules or follow the center's preferred path of regulation. This has happened, albeit only intermittently, for example, in Australia, the European Union, and the United States. In Malaysia, the center has induced the states by political means to hand over competences. And in India, the federal legislature has frequently used its power to enact laws (by a 2/3 majority) in the national interest even in the areas of exclusive state jurisdiction. These options for national legislative overrides thus promote legal unification either by coaxing the states into enacting uniform laws or, if they fail to do so, by creating legal uniformity at the central level.

Finally, in a small number of federal systems, the center promotes legal uniformity by what is, in effect, regulatory bribery, or, to put the matter more mildly: its capacity to incentivize. Thus the center provides financial incentives for the member units to enact rules conforming to centrally determined (but so far non-binding) standards. This strategy has been employed in Australia, Canada and the United States, and to a lesser extent in the European Union. In the United States, for example, rules ranging from speed limits to the minimum drinking age are (or at least were until recently) fairly uniform throughout the country not because the federal government had legislative jurisdiction over them, but because the states were required to adopt federal standards in order to secure federal money for roads and other public projects. Its sometimes questionable constitutionality notwithstanding, this exercise of the "power of the purse" can have a unifying effect in practice. This power can also be rather informal and yet very effective: where the central government raises most of the revenue and then distributes it to the states, it can have a powerful political influence on lawmaking on the local level, as, for example, in Mexico.

---

[17] A Eur-Lex search brought up over 2,000 directives and nearly 30 framework decisions. Many directives, however, are passed as amendments to earlier directives.

[18] In some systems, especially those marked by broad concurrent legislative power, central legislation does not strictly speaking require the member units to legislate, but allows, and indeed expects, them to do so. Here, the center enacts broad principles and rules while the member units fill in the details. In this manner, federal framework laws and member unit regulation end up working in tandem on different levels of specificity. Like EC Directives, this ensures uniformity regarding the broad outlines but at the same time allows for regional or local diversity regarding the particulars.

1.2.1.3 Central Court Jurisprudence

Top-down legal unification through the exercise of central governmental power is not necessarily limited to constitutional or legislative rules ("written law"). It can also occur judicially, i.e., if central courts, especially Supreme Courts, create uniform case law. This case law does not have to be strictly binding in the (common law) sense of precedent. It can also create uniformity if it is de facto authoritative, i.e., if lower courts and other legal actors routinely follow it in practice, as is the case today in most civil law jurisdictions. The extent to which judicial norms created at the center contribute to legal unification top-down is rather difficult to gauge because it varies significantly in two regards: the type of law involved and the system concerned.

On the *constitutional* level, central judicial norm creation plays a significant role in the vast majority of federations. Wherever central courts exercise judicial review power, they ensure legal uniformity throughout the federation in the sense of keeping law within constitutional boundaries. They do so by striking down legislation that is constitutionally out of bounds, by reversing judicial decisions that violate the constitution or by interpreting the law to conform to established constitutional principles. Despite the general prevalence of all these mechanisms as sources of legal harmonization and unification, there are (as noted in 1. above) considerable variations regarding the nature and strength of judicial review across federations.

On the level of subconstitutional *federal* law, central courts can, and usually do, produce uniform interpretation for the entire system. Yet, the degree to which they actually manage to ensure such uniformity varies significantly as well. It is high in countries with large Supreme Courts deciding hundreds or thousands of cases per year, as in Germany, Italy, or Russia. But it is much lower in jurisdictions where smaller tribunals hand down many fewer decisions in select cases, as in Canada or the United States. Especially the United States legal system is rife with so-called "intercircuit conflicts", i.e., conflicting interpretations of federal law among the various federal circuit courts (of appeal). Most of these conflicts will never be resolved by the Supreme Court because that tribunal has in recent times rendered fewer than a hundred fully reasoned opinions per year.[19]

On the level of *member unit* law, the picture is even more diverse. The main reason is that only some systems have a central court (or courts) with the jurisdiction to interpret the law of the member states authoritatively.[20] Where central courts do have such jurisdiction, they contribute significantly, and in some cases heavily, to legal unification by rendering authoritative and converging interpretations of subunit law. Interestingly, this is the case primarily in countries in the British orbit,

---

[19] Some conflicts may trigger central legislation or regulatory enactments.

[20] Based on the information provided in the National Reports as they currently stand, it appears only a minority of federations grant their central courts jurisdiction authoritatively to interpret member unit law.

i.e., the United Kingdom itself[21] and the former members (or close associates) of the British Empire, i.e., Australia, Canada, India, Malaysia,[22] and South Africa. It is true, however, also for Russia with its largely federal and thus unitary judiciary.[23] By contrast, where central courts do not have jurisdiction over member unit law, they cannot, of course, render authoritative interpretations of it; here, the member state courts have the last word.[24] This situation prevails in most civil law jurisdictions, both in continental Europe (e.g., Germany, Switzerland, the Kingdom of the Netherlands, and the European Union) and beyond (Brazil, Mexico). Note, however, that the United States with its full-fledged double (state and federal) hierarchy of courts also belongs into this category.[25]

Beyond the three levels of constitutional, federal, and member unit law lies yet another potentially unifying effect of central court jurisprudence, albeit one that is even harder to quantify: central (supreme) courts often contribute to legal uniformity by developing general principles or by emphasizing particular policies and values. These principles, policies, and values may not *bind* the other courts; they may thus not compel member state courts to interpret member state law in a particular fashion. But they can still exercise a heavy influence on the judiciary throughout the system, simply by setting examples and providing guidance. This is clearly the case in the United States where the guiding effect of US Supreme Court decisions can be very strong indeed, but also in Germany, India, Italy, Mexico, Russia, and Switzerland where the respective highest courts clearly set the tone for the judiciary throughout the country. Of course, such central court guidance does not guarantee uniformity of judicially created norms but it can work quite strongly in that direction.

---

[21] At least in theory, this is supposed to change when the latest judicial reforms enter into force in 2009.

[22] In Malaysia, where national courts have the general power to interpret component state law, there is a fierce jurisdictional debate over whether and to what extent national secular courts have the power to interpret sharia law.

[23] In Russia, the constitutional or charter courts of the component states (of which there are presently 16) have exclusive competence to resolve disputes concerning the interpretation of regional constitutions (or charters) and compliance of regional laws and regulations with those constitutions (or charters). In all other respects the judiciary in Russia is unitary.

[24] These courts may of course follow each other's jurisprudence but that is not an exercise of central (judicial) power top-down but a matter of voluntary cooperation which will be addressed infra. Sect. 1.2.2.2.

[25] Russia and the United States make it impossible to say that common law jurisdictions give their supreme courts power over member state law while civil jurisdictions do not: each does the opposite of what its group membership would require. Still, the line-up suggests that the common and civil law heritages are not unrelated to this allocation of powers. Different notions of judicial power (precedent-creating vel non) may lurk in the background here, and the idea of a "common law" (common, that is, to the whole system) may also play a role. A full exploration of these matters is, however, beyond the scope of this overview.

1.2.1.4 Other Centrally Controlled Means

In addition to central constitutional norms, legislation, and judicial lawmaking, there are various other centrally controlled means that promote legal uniformity in one form or another. Their variety is considerable, and we will only briefly mention the most important ones.

The only institution of this sort that is somewhat widely shared is a "Law Commission" (or "Law Reform Commission"). Such Commissions are part of the British legal tradition and exist in the former Commonwealth member countries, i.e., the United Kingdom itself, Australia, India, Malaysia, and South Africa. Such a commission also existed in Canada for several decades but has recently become defunct for lack of funding. Typically created by the central legislature or executive and working under the auspices of the ministry of justice or its equivalent, these Commissions are quasi-governmental institutions. Their primary role is law reform.[26] Yet, reform efforts coordinated by a single body sponsored by the center will often have a unifying effect on the legal system as a whole. The force of this unifying effect varies. In the United Kingdom it is reasonably strong, whereas in India such unification apparently occurs only slowly and on a piecemeal basis.

In many other systems, the central government has created a variety of bodies or mechanisms to coordinate central and member unit policies. They come in all forms, shapes, and sizes, and their effectiveness is difficult to evaluate from an outside perspective.[27]

Notably, however, many federal systems do not seem to maintain any such official coordinative bodies or mechanisms at the central level. None are reported

---

[26]In Malaysia, however, the primary role of such commissions is not to propose any substantial changes, but only to assist in such things as modernization of language.

[27]Such bodies and mechanisms exist in Austria with regard to the implementation of EU law; in Brazil where the federal legislature has created various national systems in select areas of law (such as environment and health) aiming at coordination within the federation; in Italy with its "Conference of State-Regions" and "Conference of State-Cities"; in Mexico, where the federal government constantly organizes and sponsors congresses, meetings, and publications to promote the uniformity of law; in Russia where the "State Council" (consisting of the heads of the subjects of the Russian Federation) assists the President in resolving disagreements with member units; in South Africa (in addition to the Law Commission) with the President's "Co-ordination Committee" which includes the provincial premiers, and several similar institutions; in Spain, where the central government has some "coordination power" over the states; in Switzerland, for example, through the Federal Commission for Coordination in Family Matters (COFF) and the Federal Commission for Coordination for Safety in Labor Matters (CFST); and in the EU where the Commission and Council monitor and work with the member states in search for common policies and strategies, more recently under the label of an "open method of coordination." In addition to these policy-oriented and coordinative bodies and mechanisms, the Russian central government also employs a more coercive means: the President has "envoys" (plenipotentiaries, "polpredys") in each of seven "federal district[s]," which are composed of 6–18 component states each. Reporting directly to the President, they protect his constitutional authority in these districts and check member unit law for conformity with (central) constitutional norms. In other words, the central executive keeps watchdogs throughout the system that ensure that nobody strays from the flock.

for Germany, the Netherlands, and the United States. Our tentative explanation for their absence is an institutional one. Most civil law countries have a tradition of professionally staffed ministries (of justice); here, the central bureaucracy handles law reform and unification efforts in-house, so to speak, obviating any need for a separate, British-style law (reform) commission. In the United States, distrust towards centralization has been strong and has thus militated against law (reform) institutions run by the federal government.[28] Of course, even in systems without unification efforts organized by the central government, legal unification can be pursued by the established political institutions, most notably by the legislature, and by the political parties, especially if one or two parties are dominant (see infra Sect. 1.4).

1.2.2 Coordinate Unification: Cooperation Among the Member Units

In quite a few systems, legal unification also results from the voluntary cooperation among the member units of the federation and is thus, in a sense, bottom-up. Here, we distinguish between cooperation on the legislative level, among the member units' judiciaries, and among the executive branches.[29] On the whole, the picture is, once again, quite diverse.

1.2.2.1 Cooperation on the Legislative Level

Only two systems are reported to have permanent institutions in which states come together to work towards legal unification. The prime example here is the US-American *National Conference of Commissioners of Uniform State Laws* (NCCUSL), which is now called (more simply) *The Uniform Law Commission* (ULC). It consists of commissioners delegated by the states. Since its inception in 1892, the NCCUSL has promulgated about 200 Uniform Laws, i.e., blueprints that have no force in and of themselves but are proffered to the states for adoption. The NCCUSL's record with regard to promoting the uniformity of US-American law is decidedly mixed. On the one hand, its showpiece, the Uniform Commercial

---

[28]Uniform law making in the United States by and large takes place on the coordinate (i.e., state) level, see infra. Sect. 1.2.2.1; the Administrative Conference of the United States is a federal institution but its goal is the "improvement of federal agency procedures", not the unification of administrative law on the state level, http://www.acus.gov./about/the-conference/ (last visited August 1, 2011)

[29]To be sure, in parliamentary systems so-called "executive" cooperation can take on a distinctly legislative character in light of the close connection between the government and the dominant coalition in the parliament. Nonetheless, for purposes of this report, we set out legislative and executive cooperation separately.

Code, has been adopted by all states (some parts excepted in Louisiana), and several other acts have been so widely adopted as to create virtual (legislative) uniformity throughout the country. In addition, states have occasionally followed a uniform law's lead without formally adopting it. On the other hand, only about 10 % of the acts promulgated have been adopted by 40 states or more. In addition, states often modify a uniform act in the legislative process and courts sometimes interpret them differently with no national tribunal available to resolve conflicts. As a result, uniformity in practice is sometimes an elusive ideal. On the whole, it can perhaps be said that the NCCUSL has managed (by and large) to unify (statutory) state law in a few select and, on occasion, highly important, areas but not across the majority of law in the manner originally envisaged.

The NCCUSL's Canadian counterpart is the *Uniform Law Conference of Canada* (ULCC) with representatives of the provincial governments. Since its foundation in 1918, the ULCC has adopted nearly 100 uniform acts. Despite limited funding, it has recently engaged in an ambitious project, the "Commercial Law Strategy". This "Strategy" aims to produce and promote a considerable variety of uniform acts in the areas of commercial law and enforcement matters, some of which have already been adopted by state legislatures.[30]

In some other systems, there is ad hoc legislative cooperation among the member units. In Australia, for example, states can jointly delegate legislative jurisdiction to the center which may then legislate in a uniform fashion. The Australian states may also "adopt" Commonwealth law as amended from time to time (generally pursuant to an intergovernmental agreement that gives them some say over its content). In Austria, states sometimes conclude formal agreements ("concordats") with each other or with the federal government in order to establish legal uniformity in particular areas. In Germany, the states have sometimes come together (through government representatives) to create model laws, some of which were then so generally enacted as to create almost complete uniformity among the states and often also harmonization between state and federal laws.

Finally, in many systems, including Australia, Belgium, Brazil, Germany, Spain, and the United States, the member units will closely consider, and often actually imitate, legislation passed by other member units. In other words, states tend to follow each other's example. At least in some cases, this spontaneous borrowing process can lead to considerable legal uniformity. This is also true in Mexico, albeit in a more peculiar fashion: the states often treat federal law as a model and thus follow its lead, again voluntarily establishing considerable uniformity in many core areas of law.

---

[30]In Italy, there is the "Conference of the Regions and the Autonomous Provinces" as well as a Conference of the State and Cities and Other Local Autonomous Entities. Their purpose, however, seems not primarily to be legal unification but rather coordination with respect to dealings with the national government. Similarly, in Belgium, various committees exist reflecting widespread cooperation among the federal government and the subunits as well as among the subunits themselves.

Still, in a surprising number of federal systems, there is no evidence of any significant interstate legislative cooperation at all. In some countries, like South Africa, Venezuela, and perhaps even Italy, this might be explained by the already high degree of centralization which leaves too little room for interstate unification efforts. This explanation has less force in other systems without such cooperation, notably Argentina, India, Malaysia, Russia, or Switzerland, although perhaps even here, centralized lawmaking weighs so heavily (at least *de facto*) that coordinate efforts are not considered worthwhile. The European Union is a different story. Governments already come together in the Council to decide upon Regulations (uniform legislation) or Directives (blueprints for harmonization) as a matter of EU law. These unification measures have already been quite far reaching in the last two decades. Unsurprisingly, there is little desire among many member states to push for even more Europe-wide legal unification through other intergovernmental cooperation. Such cooperation does exist, however, within particular regions, such as the Benelux countries and Scandinavia.

1.2.2.2 The Role of Component State Judiciaries

Do member state courts contribute to legal unification by looking to sister state court decisions when deciding cases under member state law? In other words, is there judicial "cooperation" on the horizontal level that fosters legal uniformity in federal systems?

In about a third of the systems under review, the question does not arise, at least not in this form, because there are no member state judiciaries. In the federations of Austria, Belgium, India, Italy, Malaysia,[31] Russia, Spain, South Africa, and Venezuela, there is (at least by and large) only one, unitary judiciary. A unitary judiciary should make it rather likely that courts located in one state decide matters of state law by considering pertinent decisions of courts sitting in other states, at least at the appellate level.

Where member state judiciaries actually exist, they do consider other member state courts' decisions. This is true not only in common law systems like Australia, Canada, the United Kingdom, and the United States. It also applies to civil law countries like Brazil, Germany, and Switzerland where court decisions are (with some exceptions) not binding *de jure* but treated as very nearly so in practice. In Mexico, state courts interpreting state laws often follow the decisions by federal courts interpreting (more or less) identical federal legislation. Similarly, in Argentina, courts in the provinces often take their lead from cases decided in the capital where most of the judicial prestige lies. On the whole, however, the degree to which state courts consider decisions from other jurisdictions seems to vary considerably. Notably, this difference does not seem to be directly related to

---

[31] In Malaysia, there is a unitary judiciary for secular matters only. In matters of sharia, however, there are separate and independent component state courts (without any coordinating high court).

the common v. civil law divide – German state courts, for example, take account of each other's decisions as routinely as do their US-American counterparts.

The European Union is, again, in a category apart. While it does happen that EU member state courts look at (and occasionally even follow) decisions from another country's judiciary, this is so rare that comparative lawyers note it with great interest when it occurs. This is not surprising: within the EU, we are dealing with *national* judiciaries which are not only ensconced each in its own legal culture but also separated by language barriers which range from merely inconvenient to the virtually insurmountable.

It is undeniable that mutual attention among member state courts contributes to legal uniformity, simply because it increases the chance (or reflects an aspiration on the part of the courts) that similar norms will be interpreted identically and that like issues will be decided alike. In some systems, as in Australia, Canada, Germany, Switzerland, and (with regard to federal court decisions) Mexico, this contribution can be quite significant. It is also undeniable that judicial promotion of legal uniformity on the coordinate level has severe limits. To begin with, it can work only where sufficiently similar cases come up before several member state judiciaries. Furthermore, pertinent decisions from other judiciaries have to come to the attention of the respective court, and that court has to be willing to follow them or consider them seriously in making its own decision. In addition, adopting another court's solution leads to uniformity only where member state courts of the system faced with the issue generally fall into line. And even then, it creates uniformity only with regard to single issues, not across whole fields of law.[32] This is not to belittle the importance of member state judicial "cooperation", but at least compared to the impact of constitutional norms, central legislation, and central supreme court jurisprudence, it can be only a minor factor in the unification of law.

1.2.2.3 Coordinate Action by the Executive Branches

In most federations, the executive branches of the member units have established platforms for coordination and cooperation. In many instances, these platforms involve the central executive as well, and therefore serve as a connecting link between the two levels of government. But in many other cases, the member state governments cooperate on a purely horizontal level.

Although unification may be promoted by horizontal executive coordination, this is apparently more the exception than the rule. In Germany, ministerial conferences on the *Länder* level have developed several model laws which were adopted either uniformly or at least so widely that they have by and large unified the law throughout the nation in certain areas (such as higher education and the police).

---

[32]In the United States at least, the virtually routine consideration of sister state court judgments has not overcome the diversity of law in most areas. In many instances, it has actually exacerbated the chaos of case law.

In Switzerland, the cantons often conclude *concordats*, i.e., treaties, which establish inter-cantonal cooperation and at times lead to uniform legislation. Similarly, in Australia, the Standing Committee of Attorneys General has occasionally developed uniform laws. There is an extensive network of ministerial councils, all of which can contribute to uniformity of law in the area concerned.[33] In some instances, a framework exists to permit cooperative legal unification on the member state level but it is rarely or never used for that purpose.[34]

Unsurprisingly, most executive cooperation between member units apparently concerns administrative and policy matters or serves to represent the member states' collective interests vis-à-vis the central government.[35] Administrative and policy oriented cooperation can of course also contribute to legal unification, e.g., with regard to administrative regulations and practices, but this effect resists measurement in any general way.

1.2.3 Unification Through Non-state Actors

In gauging the role of non-state actors in legal unification, one should distinguish between two kinds of activities: those that directly generate uniform norms and those that merely influence the creation of norms by other players.

1.2.3.1 Direct Uniform Norm Generation

Private actors sometimes directly generate uniform norms for adoption by, or at least to provide guidance to, state actors, especially legislators and judges. Such direct private norm generation occurs, however, only in very few federal systems. In saying this, we do not count the Law (Reform) Commissions that exist in various countries

---

[33] A unique case is presented by Russia. Here, the chief executives of the component units are now nominated by the federal President (they must then be confirmed by the regional legislatures), and they can also work in the federal civil service. They can thus contribute to legal unification on the subunit level as parts of the "unified system of executive power". Yet, since they are largely on the tether of the central executive, the top-down element is so strong here that this process cannot count as truly coordinate.

[34] In Spain, the federal constitution provides for "collaboration conventions" and "cooperation agreements" among the member units but few such conventions or agreements have ever been concluded in a multilateral fashion; as a result, that mechanism has played little or no role in the unification of law. In the United States, there are interstate compacts or various sorts, but they have, again, normally not concerned legal uniformity.

[35] This is the case, for example, in Austria with its meetings of the chief executives of the member states (called, by a wonderfully long German word, *Landeshauptmännerkonferenz*); in Canada in the meetings of the provincial premiers; in Italy with its variety of standing regional conferences; in Mexico with its National Conference of Governors; and in the United States with its National Governors Association.

as non-state actors since these Commissions are normally created by governments and work under their auspices.[36] We are also not counting non state law, i.e., norms created by private actors for the regulation of particular industries or commercial practices. These private norms often accomplish greater uniformity in practice than state law can provide (indeed, that is part of their attraction) but assessing unification of law attributable to "private ordering" would require a study in its own right.[37]

If we thus leave state created Law Commissions as well as private industry standards aside, the creation of uniform norms through private actors matter only in three of the systems here under review.

In the United States, private norm setting is longstanding and fairly prominent. Here, the *American Law Institute* (founded in 1923) has put together *Restatements of the Law* for almost a century. They cover about a dozen areas mainly of private law, and several are now in their third generation. They are often cited, especially abroad, as one of the most important unifying factors in US-American law. To some extent, this is true: Restatements do establish a set of principles and rules which can serve as a common reference point especially for courts and also for scholarship and law teaching. Still, the degree to which Restatements actually establish legal uniformity is limited for three reasons. First, they are by and large ignored by state legislatures which have now covered even the traditional areas of the common law with a dense network of statutory rules, mostly in deviation from the common principles enshrined in the Restatements. Second, even courts, to whom the Restatements were primarily addressed, often ignore them; in some areas (such as contracts or conflict of laws), the respective Restatement enjoys a lot of authority; in others, such as torts, only some sections are routinely consulted. Third, perversely, Restatements can have a *dividing*, rather than unifying, function. Thus, with regard to products liability, many courts have continued to adhere to the *Second Restatement of Torts* (1965) (especially § 402A) while others have switched to the newer *Restatement Third: Products Liability* (1998). On the whole, the unification of (private) law through Restatements is more apparent than real – and usually overrated by outside observers, probably because Restatements are the feature of US law that most closely resembles, in structure and tone, the codifications with which especially jurists from civil law countries are so familiar.

In the European Union, direct norm generation by private actors is more recent but has grown to impressive proportions over the last 20 years. It has arisen in the context of pursuing a common private law of Europe. This pursuit has been mainly an academic agenda but it has sometimes been endorsed and even financed by the European Community (especially the Commission) itself. Its origins lie in

---

[36]Thus their impact is addressed supra Sect. 1.2.2.1. Given their often considerable independence, one could plausibly consider them non-state actors, and many National Reports address them in this mode. In that case, non-state actors must be said to have a significant influence on legal unification in a considerable number of federal systems.

[37]To be sure, the lines are blurry here. Sometimes, privately created industry and other standards are sanctioned or even ratified by states and can thus take on an official character.

the *Commission on European Contract Law* (also known, after its founder and chairman, as the *Lando Commission*) which began its work in the early 1980s. Over a period of about 20 years, it compiled *Principles of European Contract Law* (*PECL*) in a *Restatement*-like fashion. Today, there is a veritable academic industry of proliferating follow-up projects, ranging from *The Study Group on a European Civil Code* (*von Bar Group*) and the *Academy of European Private Lawyers* (*Gandolfi Group*), to a host of study groups in individual areas such as contracts, torts, property, family law, trusts, and insurance, as well as the search for a *Common Core of European Private Law* (*Trento Project*). In addition, there is a semi-official project: the drafting of a *Common Frame of Reference* (*CFR*) for core areas of European private law by the *Joint Network of European Private Law*. This project is the result of the European Union's initiative and financial support. To be sure, none of the many works published by this entire law reform industry has the force of law, and to date, these efforts have not had much of a unifying effect in practice. But these endeavors may well become the foundations on which a future (more or less) common private law of Europe can be built.

Finally, since its creation in 2004, the *Mexican Center of Uniform Law* has worked towards harmonization and unification of law in the Mexican federal system (and beyond). It has cooperated with the NCCUSL in the United States and the ULCC in Canada. It is currently undertaking the project of a model contract law for the Mexican states, and it has played a significant role in putting together the *White Book* of the Mexican Supreme Court, which emphasizes the need for greater harmonization and uniformity in the Mexican federation.

1.2.3.2 Influencing Uniform Norm Creation

As several National Reports (in particular those on Austria, Italy, Malaysia, Mexico, and Spain) show, in many (and probably in all) federations covered here, private industry groups and other non-governmental organizations often lobby legislatures and regulators to adopt particular rules. Where such groups and organizations operate on a nationwide (and in the EU, Europe-wide) scale, they are likely to lobby for system-wide rules in their interest. Thus they push for legal uniformity, and where they succeed, help to establish it in an indirect fashion. The significance of this activity for legal unification is extremely difficult to gauge but possibly quite high.

Finally, as some National Reports indicate, the unification of law can be fostered by the academic literature. Especially in the civil law tradition, scholarly writings often offer important guidance for the courts as well as ideas for legislative reform.[38] Where authors of leading treatises, commentaries (on the major codes), and other

---

[38]This, of course, presumes a certain quality level of scholarly research and literature which may not exist everywhere. The National Report on Argentina, for example, laments serious deficits in this regard.

writings reach an agreement on a particular issue, they become the "prevailing opinion" (*herrschende Meinung*). Legislatures and courts are of course not bound by these views, but they will often adopt them. In European private law, a growing number of academic publications, such as Hein Kötz' *European Contract Law*[39] and the *Ius Commune Casebooks* published under the auspices of Walter van Gerven,[40] have sought to contribute to the unification of law by demonstrating the commonalities of the various European legal orders in particular areas. In the common law orbit, the authority of academic writings continues to be smaller, but even here it can be significant, and in some countries, notably in England, its influence has grown substantially in recent years.[41] In the United States, there is a small library of leading works that are frequently consulted and cited by courts.[42] Although the precise degree of their influence is hard to measure, they contribute to uniformity since they are usually written from a national perspective.

1.2.4 Legal Education and Legal Practice

Legal uniformity is not merely a matter of existing norms. It is also a matter of whether the legal profession thinks and operates on a system-wide level. To be sure, the character and outlook of the legal profession is itself shaped by the degree of legal centralization: unified law engenders unified training, a common legal consciousness and similarity of practice while diversity of law does not. But it also works the other way around: where legal education focuses on system-wide law, where exams test primarily central norms, and where the profession operates easily across member state boundaries, legal uniformity is fostered through a common body of professional knowledge, perspectives, and practices.

As we will see below, both legal education and legal practice in federations are usually more unified than the systems of law in which they operate. Both provide lawyers with a nationally oriented perspective. As a result, the bar should on balance be considered a pro-unification factor in virtually all federal systems, with the

---

[39]Hein Kötz, Axel Flessner, and Tony Weir, *European Contract Law* v. 1 (Oxford: Oxford University Press, 1998), German original: Hein Kötz, *Europäisches Vertragsrecht* I (Tubingen: Mohr, 1996). See also Christian von Bar, *The Common European Law of Torts* (2 vols., Oxford: Oxford University Press, 1998–2000) (German original: *Gemeineuropäisches Deliktsrecht*, 2 Bde., München 1996–1998); Thomas Kadner Graziano, *Europäisches Vertragsrecht* (Basel: Helbing Lichtenhahn, 2008); Peter Schlechtriem, *Restitution und Bereicherungsausgleich in Europa. Eine rechtsvergleichende Darstellung* (Tubingen: Mohr, 2001).

[40]See, e.g., Walter van Gerven et al., *Torts* (Oxford: Hart, 1999).

[41]See Alexandra Braun, *Guidici e Accademia nell'esperienza inglese. Storia di un dialogo* (Mulino: Bologna 2006).

[42]See, e.g., Dan Dobbs, *The Law of Torts* (St. Paul: West Group, 2001), Allan Farnsworth, *Farnsworth on Contracts* (3 vols., New York: Aspen Publishers, 2008); James J. White and Robert Summers, *Uniform Commercial Code* (4 vols., 5th ed., St. Paul: West Group, 2002).

probable exception of the European Union, where a system-wide bar has yet to develop. After all, lawyers with a system-wide perspective are likely to prefer, and push for, legal uniformity because it seems more natural and convenient to them than diversity among the member units.[43]

1.2.4.1 Legal Education

In most federations, legal education has a primarily nation-wide focus – with regard to the students as well as to the curriculum.[44] This is not surprising in systems where central law dominates anyway, as in Austria, Germany, India, Italy, Russia, and South Africa. But it is true also in others where lawmaking is more decentralized, as in Australia, Mexico, Switzerland, and the United States.

In the clear majority of systems, students at the various law faculties come from throughout the country. Even when students stay relatively close to home, as many do, this is mainly a matter of cost and convenience and usually not a function of jurisdictional boundaries within the federation. Elite law schools, in particular, recruit students from all over the system; this is most visible in Canada, India (at the graduate, i.e., LL.M. or Ph.D. level), Russia, the United Kingdom, and the United States, and is beginning to be the case in Australia. And law schools in dominant cities such as Buenos Aires, Caracas, Kuala Lumpur, Mexico City, Moscow, and Sao Paulo are similarly attended by students from the whole nation. In other words, in by far most federal systems, there is a largely national pool and body of law students trained in much the same way.

Our study identified only four exceptions. In Belgium, students from Wallonia and Flanders overwhelmingly stay in their home region. In Canada, there is a similar dividing line between the common law provinces on the one hand and civil law oriented Quebec on the other, although four Canadian law faculties now offer a "bijural" legal education covering both common and civil law and are thus attended by students from both areas.[45] In the United Kingdom, the exchange between England and Scotland is very limited, for very few English students study law in Scotland. The fourth, and most pronounced, exception is the European Union. While there is some cross-border student mobility, the vast majority obtain their law degree in their home countries. Given the cultural, language, and other barriers on the international level, this is only to be expected.

---

[43]In the United States, this statement must be handled with caution. There is, in some contexts, a truly national bar for which the statement is true. There is, however, also a more local bar which is often intensely tied to state or even municipal law; this local bar may actually be a force working against national unification because it often has an interest in keeping law local and idiosyncratic.

[44]This is true even where legal education is organized by the member units, as in Germany or Switzerland, and, with regard to both public and private universities.

[45]In both Belgium and Canada, the respective language barriers play a role in this. It also limits the mobility of students in Switzerland between the German and French speaking parts.

Perhaps even more important, the curriculum in most systems focuses mainly on national (i.e., central, uniform) law rather than on the law of the member units. That does not necessarily mean that member unit law is ignored. In some systems, especially where important areas of private law, criminal law, or procedure are left to the states, local law receives some attention; this is notably the case in Canada (especially between the common and civil law), Mexico, and Switzerland as well as Argentina (with regard to procedure). But even in these countries, subunit law does not dominate, and in most systems, it plays a distinctly marginal role.[46] This is perhaps most surprising in the United States where many (if not most) core areas of law are largely left to the states yet law schools mainly focus on law and legal issues common to the entire legal system.[47]

With regard to the curriculum, there are only three exceptions, and two of them are of limited significance. In Canada, the split between common and civil law translates into a partial split of the curricula between the anglophone provinces and francophone Quebec, mainly with regard to private law; even this partial split is overcome at the institutions providing a "bijural" legal education, such as McGill University in Montreal or the University of Ottawa. In the United Kingdom, English and Scottish universities do not normally teach the respective other law; yet, with the exception of criminal law, this does not much affect the core areas. The third exception, however, is significant: in the European Union, legal education focuses on the respective national laws. It is true that European law is now also taught virtually everywhere and that courses comparing various European legal orders are quite common. Still, legal education continues to be so overwhelmingly geared toward national law that a student can do very well with very little knowledge of anything that spans national boundaries.

Finally, there are a variety of institutions and practices involving post-graduate legal education which can have a considerable unifying effect. In some federations, special programs bring together law graduates from all over the system for academic training in central law, as in India (LL.M. and Ph.D. programs) and the European Union (College of Europe/Bruges, European University Institute/Florence, Europäische Rechtsakademie/Trier). Sometimes, graduates clerk for judges sitting on central courts; this is mainly the case in common law countries (Australia, Canada, India, and the United States) but also at the European Court of Justice. Elsewhere, as in Germany, India, and the Dutch Federation, judges are sometimes temporarily delegated to another court, inter alia to learn from their

---

[46]This is not the case in Australia, however, where the teaching of subjects that are controlled by state law (e.g. criminal law) will focus on the law of the state within which the law school is situated.

[47]In the United States, the degree to which this is true depends on the rank of the law school in the overall hierarchy. Elite law schools pay next to no attention to the law of the state in which they sit. As one descends the prestige ladder, passing the (state) bar exam is more important (as well as more problematic) so that teaching state law plays a greater role. Also, in Louisiana, legal education has to focus more than elsewhere on state law due to specific nature of its codified private law system.

colleagues dealing with a different docket. And some countries have special national training programs for members of the bench, as in Canada, Mexico, and Russia, or even a national school for judges, as in Spain.[48] Such system-wide platforms for post-graduate training will usually foster a system-wide legal consciousness and, more likely than not, a concomitant preference for legal uniformity.

1.2.4.2 Admission to the Bar and Legal Practice

In light of the largely system-wide student bodies and curricula, it is somewhat surprising that bar examinations (where they exist) and admission to the bar (where it is formally required) take place on the member unit level in a majority of federal systems. Yet, in most cases, one should not make too much of that. Even where bar examinations and admissions are run by states, provinces, cantons, etc., it is mostly quite easy to practice law in another subunit.[49] Still, in some systems, the boundaries between the subunits do constitute serious barriers.[50] Perhaps surprisingly, the *legally* most fragmented system of bar admission is no longer the EU, because European law now mandates far-reaching recognition of academic degrees as well as considerable mutual admission to practice among the member units. Instead, the system most ridden by legal barriers is the United States, where most states require lawyers licensed to practice in another jurisdiction to pass the local bar examination before being admitting to local practice. *In practice,* however, relocating to another member state is still easier in the United States than in Europe, not only because some states are willing to "waive in" lawyers from other jurisdictions with several years of experience,[51] but also because the cultural, language, and other practical obstacles are much less serious in the United States than within the European Union.[52]

Despite these administrative barriers in some federations, legal practitioners can, and frequently do, move throughout the system, although the degree of their

---

[48]Some systems also require, or at least offer, continuous legal education (CLE), especially for members of the bar. These programs may also have a national focus but they can just as well deal with member state law, as is often the case in the United States.

[49]Most of the respective systems either generally allow nationwide practice, as in Belgium, Italy or Switzerland, or at least have fairly generous rules about mutual recognition of bar exams and memberships, as in Australia and Canada.

[50]In Malaysia, for example, lawyers admitted to practice in the peninsula cannot easily practice in the East Malaysian states of Sabah and Sarawak.

[51]Also, US states' bar examinations now contain a "multistate" part, which covers areas of law that are uniform throughout the country. While candidates also have to take the state-specific part, in some states, passing the multistate section (or passing with a specified high score) can mean that the state-specific part will not be graded. This often leads candidates to concentrate particularly on the multistate section, i.e., uniform law.

[52]As a result, many American lawyers are admitted to the practice of law in more than one member state while such multiple admissions are still a rarity in Europe.

mobility varies considerably among the federal systems and the strata of the profession. More or less everywhere, many lawyers set up shop, or take a position, close to home while many others gravitate toward the big cities or otherwise move from one subunit to another. The National Reports strongly suggest that where geographic mobility is systemically hindered, it is not so much by jurisdictional boundaries than by cultural and linguistic barriers.[53]

The geographic mobility of legal professionals militates in favor of legal uniformity because greater mobility increases the transaction costs of diversity. To be sure, as the example of the United States vividly illustrates, a high degree of such mobility is by no means a guarantee for a high degree of legal uniformity. But it is almost certain that US-American law would be even less uniform than it is if lawyers in the United States were not as mobile as they are and if there was not, in addition to local practice, an essentially national bar.[54]

1.2.5 The Impact of International Law

So far, we have looked at the factors promoting legal unification from *within* the respective systems. Is unification also the result of factors operating from the *outside*, i.e., on the international level? Here, we should distinguish between *mandatory* compliance with international norms on the one hand and *voluntary* participation in international unification projects on the other.

1.2.5.1 Mandatory International Norms

Mandatory compliance with the supranational law of the European Union plays a large role for unification within Europe, of course, i.e., for Austria, Belgium, Germany, Italy, Spain, the Netherlands, and the United Kingdom. EU law is binding on the member states and supreme to, and within, their domestic legal orders.[55] Many provisions of the respective treaties and all Regulations are directly applicable, and Directives must be implemented in domestic law. The unification effect of EU law is twofold. First, it unifies (or, in case of Directives, harmonizes) the law *within the European Union* itself, i.e., among the member states. Second, EU law also frequently unifies the law *within the member states* because its direct

---

[53]These barriers are often daunting, of course, within the European Union but they also play a significant role in Belgium (except for the mix of lawyers practicing in Brussels) and Canada and, although in a much more attenuated fashion, in Switzerland and (despite the lack of a language barrier) the United Kingdom, i.e., between England and Scotland.

[54]The national organization of lawyers, the American Bar Association (ABA), also provides a platform for a nationwide discussion of legal issues among lawyers and often takes positions on law reform in its monthly publication, the *American Bar Association Journal (ABAJ)*.

[55]This is contested with regard to the member states' Constitutions only.

applicability and supremacy make it override even the law of the member states' subunits (Länder, Provinces, Regions, etc.). In other words, where EU law rules, both the member states and their parts must all march to the beat of the same drum. Since EU law has proliferated at a breathtaking pace over the last few decades, it now unifies significant amounts of law within Europe, especially in the areas of economic regulation, private law, private international law, and increasingly civil procedure.

Mandatory compliance also plays a role within the Council of Europe because all its members must abide by the European Convention on Human Rights (ECHR). This concerns all the states just mentioned plus Russia and Switzerland. Yet, the unification effect of the ECHR is much smaller than that of EU law because the basic rights listed in the ECHR are by and large already contained in the member states' domestic federal constitutions. To be sure, there are some differences, but instances in which the ECHR (as interpreted by the European Court of Human Rights) has overridden and thus unified the member states' subunit law are fairly rare exceptions. Still, the ECHR can have a unifying effect in some systems. It does so, for example, within Russia, as a more recent member of the Council of Europe, because compliance with the ECHR is still a work in progress; as the Russian report points out, the supremacy of treaty obligations under the ECHR has led to considerable harmonization and even unification of law. This could also be said for the United Kingdom, where the Human Rights Act of 1998 implemented the ECHR and thus codified a detailed fundamental rights catalog for the first time in the history of the UK.

On a worldwide level, the picture is much more mixed, and compliance with international law seems to have a unifying effect just occasionally. This may seem somewhat surprising because almost all systems considered here are, for example, members of the major United Nations human rights treaties[56] and thus subject to the same international law obligations.[57] But in many systems, these international norms have no direct internal effect (i.e., they are not "self-executing") and thus cannot themselves unify domestic law. And in most instances, international human rights obligations are, again, largely duplicative of federal constitutional provisions which are already uniform throughout the respective countries.

International law can, however, have a unifying effect in some more specific regards. For example, the center often has the power to make and then implement treaties even in areas falling (internally) under the jurisdiction of the subunits. Thus the center can create uniformity via international law where it otherwise could not.[58]

---

[56]All but the European Union, which is not a state in the international sense and thus cannot be a UN member, and Malaysia are members of the International Covenant on Civil and Political Rights (ICCRR); 16 of our 20 systems considered here are members of the International Covenant on Economic, Social and Cultural Rights (ICESCR), and 17 are members of the International Covenant on the Elimination of all Forms of Discrimination against Women (CEDAW).

[57]In addition, they are all subject to customary international law, of course.

[58]For example, in systems were procedural law is the domain of the member states, the center can still unify aspects of civil procedure by ratifying the Hague Convention on the Service Abroad of

In addition, domestic courts often interpret domestic law in light of international norms; this is reported particularly for Australia, India, Mexico, and South Africa but clearly also true for Canada, Germany, Italy, the United Kingdom, and, within narrower limits, the United States. The extent to which these powers and practices actually contribute to internal legal unification is, as the Canadian Report points out, hard to measure. It also varies a lot because the domestic legal actors' concern with international norm compliance can range from a sense of obligation to virtual disinterest.

One must also not overlook that international legal obligations can have both a unifying and a divisive effect at the same time. Perhaps the most illustrative case in point is the (Vienna) Convention on the International Sale of Goods (CISG) which has been ratified by 14 out of the 20 systems covered in this study. In systems in which the law of (commercial) sales is left to the subunits, such as Canada and the United States, the CISG, as a self-executing treaty with the rank of federal law, indeed unifies the law nationwide. But since it does so only for the transactions it covers, it also creates a new split: international sales fall under the CISG while domestic sales are still governed by the law of the respective subunits.[59] In short, unification via international law is often a double-edged sword and should be approached with caution. It creates full uniformity only where both international and domestic cases are treated alike, and such (in a sense, vertical) uniformity is often hard to accomplish.[60]

1.2.5.2 Voluntary Participation in International Unification Projects

The vast majority of systems covered in our study regularly participate in international unification efforts. All 20 are members of the Hague Conference on Private International Law,[61] 17 are members of the International Institute for the Unification of Private Law (UNIDROIT), 15 participate in the United Nations Commission on International Trade Law (UNCITRAL), and 12 belong to the Organization for Economic Cooperation and Development (OECD). Thus, the great majority are more or less constantly involved in the drafting of internationally uniform treaty or

---

Judicial and Extra-Judicial Documents in Civil or Commercial Matters (1965). When the United States ratified the Convention in 1976, it became "the supreme law of the land" (US Const. Art. 6 § 2), binding federal and state courts and litigants alike.

[59] An important unifying effect is also created by the wide (and voluntary) use of INCOTERMS (International Commercial Terms) in international sales transactions.

[60] In fact, such a split can even occur without concomitant unification benefit, namely where the subject covered by a treaty is already unified under federal law. For example, service of process in many European Union members states is governed by different sets of rules depending on whether such service is purely domestic (federal law), transboundary within the EU (Regulation on the Service of Process 2001) or international beyond it (Hague Service Convention).

[61] Even the European Union became a member in 2007 after the organization's statute had been specifically amended for that purpose.

model norms. As some reports (for Australia, Germany, Mexico, Russia, and Spain) mention, this involvement can have a unifying effect, e.g., where such models are adopted either on the federal level or by the member units.

Yet, while national participation in international unification projects certainly fosters the spirit of legal uniformity, the actual impact of these activities on the domestic level should not be overrated. The example of the UNICTRAL Model Law on International Commercial Arbitration illustrates the limits of this impact. While participation in UNCITRAL has sometimes led to the adoption of the Model Law and to (internal) legal unification, as in Australia, this is the exception, not the rule. To begin with, the Model Law has been adopted in only half of the systems under review here. Moreover, in most of these countries, like Austria, Germany, Mexico or Spain, its adoption amounted to a reform but did not cause (greater) uniformity, because the law of international arbitration had been federal already before. Finally, in the United States, where this area has been left to the member units, the Model Law was adopted only by a minority of component states – thus, again, the pursuit of international harmonization has fragmented the law on the domestic level.

1.2.6 Summary and Evaluation

It is clear that of the factors driving unification discussed in this chapter, the most powerful appears to be central constitutional and statutory law. This is especially so, of course, where federal law is exclusive and supreme. Unification through the central courts, i.e., case law, is already a more diverse phenomenon. It is strong at the federal constitutional level and significant in systems where central courts interpret both federal and member state law. But in many federations, the central courts have no jurisdiction over the law of the subunits and can thus not contribute directly to its unification.

Cooperation on the horizontal level, i.e., among the member units, to create legal uniformity exists in some systems but not in others. Uniform model laws play a role only in a small minority of federations, especially in the United States and in the countries with a law (reform) commission. Member state judiciaries (where they exist) do look to sister state case law but this seriously contributes to legal unification only in a few systems. Other coordination schemes exist here and there but play a very minor role in the grand picture.

Non-state actors contribute to legal unification mainly when they draft common norms, but this is a significant factor only in the United States (*Restatements*), the European Union, and, in an incipient fashion, in Mexico. Non-state actors may also prompt legal uniformity through system-wide lobbying efforts but the impact of these efforts varies greatly and is almost impossible to gauge.

Legal education and legal practice have a nationwide orientation in most countries; note that this is true even where lawmaking power is widely distributed and legal diversity is high. The way the legal profession is trained and operates must therefore count as unifying factors because lawyers thinking in national terms and working in a national context tend to prefer uniformity over diversity. But again, the concrete impact of these factors on legal unification is hard to measure.

Apart from the special case of the supranational law of the European Union, the significance of international law and international unification efforts is surprisingly limited *within* federal systems. Mostly, treaty or international model norms concern areas that are already governed by federal law and thus uniform; often, these norms have no direct (domestic) effect and can thus not themselves unify domestic law; and sometimes they even contribute to legal fragmentation by creating separate regimes for international cases.

In summary, when it comes to legal unification in federal systems, it seems that nothing beats the top-down exercise of central government power. All other means and methods are second best – less consistently employed, less reliable and, on the whole, less successful.[62] We will return to this point in order to see whether the respective strength of central legislative power is in fact correlated with the degree of uniformity in the federal systems here under consideration (infra Sect. 1.4.1.2).

1.3 Levels of Legal Unification

After reviewing and assessing the factors that drive legal unification in federal systems, it is time to ask how much these factors have actually accomplished. In short, how uniform *is* law in federal systems in the world today? The question is, of course, impossibly general. We will therefore attempt to answer it more specifically first with regard to particular areas of law and second with regard to the various systems covered in this study.[63]

The following findings have to be handled with circumspection because they derive from the (necessarily subjective) assessment of uniformity by insiders to the respective federal systems.[64] Thus, it would be foolish to place much, if any, confidence in the significance of small differences between the respective scores. At the same time, it is reasonable to assume that large discrepancies reflect real differences in uniformity. Accordingly, while the rankings we have performed should not be taken too seriously where small margins are involved, the big differences do matter and allow us to put legal areas and systems on a spectrum ranging from greater to lesser uniformity.

---

[62]Of course, one may respond that the challenge of legal unification in federal systems really begins where central government power ends, and where one must therefore resort to other means. In that case, the sum total of the national reports suggest that none of these other means is obviously superior to any other and that the best strategy will combine them as far as possible.

[63]Even on such a scale, gauging the respective degrees of uniformity demands rather broad generalizations.

[64]See Appendix 1.

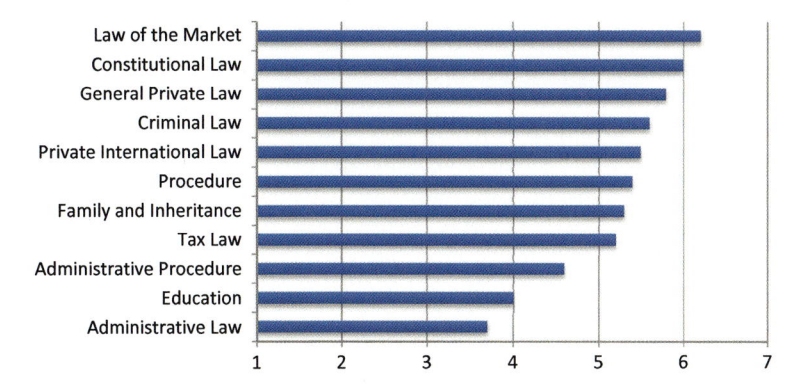

Fig. 1.1 Uniformity by area of law

1.3.1 Uniformity by Areas of Law

We can rank the major areas of law covered by our questionnaire (and across all systems involved) by their degree of average uniformity on a scale of 7 (completely uniform) to 1 (completely diverse) (Fig. 1.1).

Even with a heavy dose of distrust towards the precision of the uniformity scores, this ranking can be instructive. Most striking, we see that some areas of law tend to be more uniform than others. In addition, no major area of law is reported as always uniform or always diverse. Instead, most are clustered somewhere above or around the midpoint. If we imagine a reporter's score of 4.0 (the middle of our scale) to suggest the perception that a system's uniformity is as prominent as its diversity then this means that, on the whole in federal jurisdictions, law is perceived to be by and large more uniform than not; with only administrative law falling below that standard (i.e., below 4.0). Beyond these generalities, we offer four more specific observations.

First, the most unified area is "Law of the Market" (which includes corporate, securities, antitrust, labor and employment, intellectual property, banking, insurance, and bankruptcy law). This is true in virtually all systems. This may reflect the system-wide nature of the respective economies; at least according to standard wisdom, legal uniformity serves an integrated market by lowering transaction costs.

Second, constitutional law (understood as a generic reference to both central and component state constitutional norms) is not far behind (and the only other area with a score of 6.0 of higher). This reflects the fact that in most systems a single source (i.e., the central and thus uniform constitution) plays a dominant role in generating constitutional norms and that this source also has a unifying effect on member state constitutions (if any).[65] This also confirms the national reporters' emphasis on the strong unifying force of (central) constitutions (supra Sect. 1.2.1.1).

Third, certain major areas of law are somewhat less uniform than market and constitutional law but still considerably more uniform than diverse (all above 5.0). This group contains both general private law, i.e., contract, tort, and property, which (at 5.8) is almost as uniform as the more specific "Law of the Market", and family and inheritance law, which (at 5.3) is slightly more diverse, probably reflecting its closer ties to cultural differences among regions. The group also contains criminal, law, procedure, and private international law, which are all marked by about equal degrees of uniformity (5.6–5.4) and, somewhat below this, tax law (5.2).

Fourth, laws governing education, administrative law and procedure clearly rank at the bottom; this is also true in almost all jurisdictions covered here. At least with regard to the latter areas, i.e., administrative law and procedure, this is not surprising. After all, federations are, by definition, divided-power systems. Almost invariably, this means that component states have general authority over their own structure. At least some public power will therefore be exercised by the component states according to component state procedures. Also, administrative law and procedure often concern local affairs, such as zoning, building codes, and local public services, the regulation of which is thus often left to the subunits of the federation and sometimes even to the municipalities.[66] The relatively low degree of uniformity of the law governing education probably reflects the often intensely cultural and thus local concerns underlying this field.

1.3.2 The Uniformity by Federal System

If one averages the overall "uniformity scores" for each of the 20 federal systems covered by this study, they range from 6.7 (almost full uniformity) for Venezuela (and, close behind at 6.6, South Africa) to 1.1 for the Kingdom of the Netherlands. The Kingdom of the Netherlands is a clear outlier not only on unification, but also in its extremely loose federal architecture. Thus, we do not accord it much weight in the overall assessment and do not consider it further in this Chapter. The full results (minus the Netherlands) are displayed in Fig. 1.2.

---

[65]There are, of course, prominent exceptions, such as the European Union. The Spanish Constitution should be noted in this regard as well, as it is open-ended in the sense that it not only unifies, but also invites diversity. Indeed, the potential for diversity in the Spanish Constitution has not (yet) been exhausted.

[66]This idea of local autonomy as a means to enhance efficiency by encouraging sorting among (potential) residents of local jurisdictions has been championed since Charles M. Tiebout's classic article "A Pure Theory of Local Expenditures Export," 64 *The Journal of Political Economy* 416 (1956).

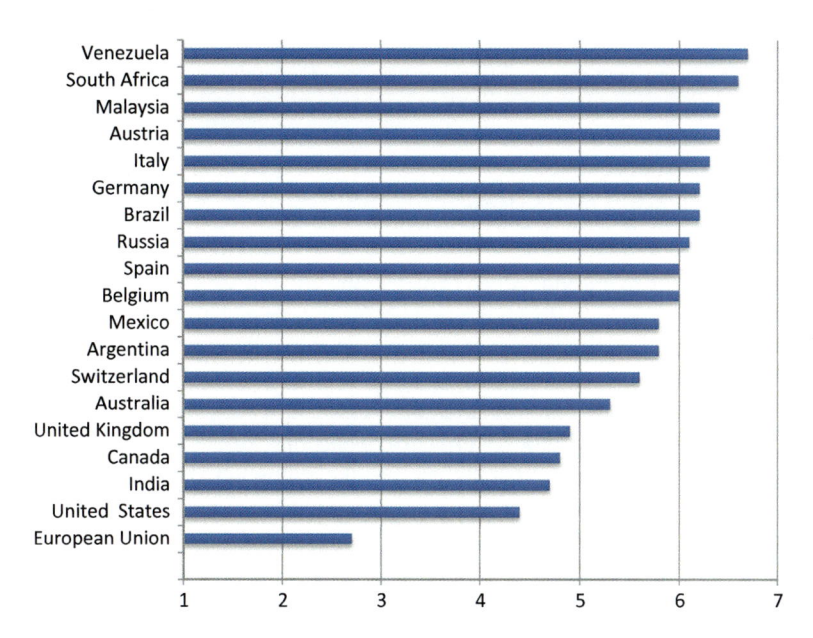

Fig. 1.2 Uniformity by federation

Even if we look at Fig. 1.2 with the appropriate amount of skepticism regarding the exact numbers and thus do not attribute much weight to small differences, four interesting observations emerge.

First, all national federal systems are located in the upper half of the Chart. With an average uniformity score of 4.0 or higher, their law has been assessed to be, on the whole, more uniform than not. In other words, in national federal systems, legal uniformity is perceived by insiders to be more the rule than the exception.

Second, the only system below the midpoint (4.0)[67] is also the only supranational federation, i.e., the European Union. Its uniformity score is so much lower than that of the rest (2.7 v. 4.4 for the least uniform national system) that it clearly stands out. One can almost say that in terms of legal uniformity, it is the European Union versus The Rest of the World, or, to put it differently, the supranational federation versus the various national orders.

Third, one can – roughly – put the national legal systems into two groups. The top group is larger and consists of Venezuela, South Africa, Austria, Malaysia, Italy, Brazil, Germany, Russia, Belgium, Spain, Argentina, Mexico, and Switzerland; while there is some distribution from the bottom to the top, their scores are roughly all within one point (6.7–5.8), with Switzerland falling slightly below that range (5.6). The bottom group is much smaller and consists of the United Kingdom, Canada, India, and the United States, all of which have significantly lower scores (all in the 4 s) than the top group. Australia sits somewhere in the middle between these two groups (at 5.3).

---

[67]Leaving aside the Kingdom of the Netherlands for the reasons explained above.

Of course, this picture raises more questions than it answers. In particular, what explains the differences we see? In other words, *why* is law apparently considerably much more uniform in some areas of law and in some federal systems than in others?

1.4 Explaining Unification

We do not claim to provide final explanations for the varying degrees of legal uniformity; however, we do generate what we deem to be plausible hypotheses related to the causes of the observed variance. This part takes first steps in exploring several structural, political, and cultural features that may contribute to the variation that we have seen. We emphasize at the outset, however, that our explanations are tentative. They point not to proven conclusions but to avenues for further empirical research. We shall briefly explore the following six factors: legislative power, structural centralization, civil v. common law, social cleavages, political parties, and age of a federation.[68]

1.4.1 The Legislative Power Hypothesis

As we have learned from the reporters' description of the means and methods of legal unification, the most important process for unification seems to be central legislation. If this is the case, we should see (all else being equal) a correlation between legal unification and central legislative powers. The first hypothesis that we shall investigate, then, is rather simple: *the more legislative authority resides with the central government, the more unified the law will be.* Call this the legislative power hypothesis.

To be sure, the effective use of allocated authority depends critically on a host of factors that enable the central government to exercise its authority. We intentionally leave these other factors aside for the moment, in the hope that there is sufficient variation among systems with regard to these other factors for a general correlation between the formal allocation of power and the level of unification to emerge.

To investigate our initial, and rather elementary, thesis about legislative power, then, we shall examine the formal[69] distribution of legislative authority in federal systems to see whether it correlates with the observed variation in legal unification. We shall do this, first, by looking at the variation across areas of law and, second, by looking at the variation across federal systems.

---

[68]Given the small number of observations and the difficulties that inhere in the underlying data, we are hesitant to pursue multivariate regression analysis at this point lest our explorations be given an improper air of scientific accuracy.

[69]In the following description we attend to the basic distribution of competences, not the more fine-grained interpretation of these power-allocating norms.

1.4.1.1 Legislative Centralization by Area of Legislation

To examine the variation in legal unification across different areas of the law, we shall examine three examples: (a) matters that are usually allocated to the center, (b) matters that are usually allocated to the component units, and (c) matters that are sometimes allocated to the center and sometimes allocated to the component units. We should find that matters in the first group correspond to those areas that are also the most unified, that matters in the second group correspond to those that are the least unified, and that matters in the third group lie somewhere in between on the overall level of unification. And, indeed, this is what we find.

1.4.1.1.1 Commerce

Of the areas covered by this study, the legislative power most consistently allocated to the central government is that over commerce[70]: the central government of every federation enjoys significant legislative jurisdiction over commercial matters.[71] In about half of these systems, the central government's legislative jurisdiction over commerce is exclusive, whereas in the other half it is concurrent. These powers range from the expansive concurrent powers of the U.S. Congress to regulate "Commerce... among the several States" to the more limited market harmonization powers of the European Union. Whether concurrent or exclusive, however, the grant of central legislative jurisdiction over market regulation is, as noted above, the single most consistent power allocation next to defense and nationality.

Most federations that enumerate central government powers over commerce will also, separately, allocate legislative jurisdiction to the center over intellectual property, banking and insurance, as well as labor and employment. Moreover, with the exception of the United States and the European Union, every federation provides express powers to the central level of government over significant portions of social security, pension, or welfare legislation. Given that the U.S. Commerce Clause has been interpreted expansively to allow direct regulation of this area, the European Union now stands alone as a federation that lacks direct central government power to regulate these areas.

---

[70]This study did not consider the law pertaining to defense or nationality. With the exception of the European Union, the central government of every single federation in our study enjoys broad powers over these areas. As these areas of governance do not correspond to any substantive area of legal unification that we asked about in our survey, the general allocation of these particular powers to the center does not help predict the legal unification we have studied here.

[71]The importance of some regulatory power over the market as a core characteristic of federations is indeed driven home by the Dutch exception. Here, where the center lacks power over the market, the center has *no* powers other than those in the realm of defense, international affairs, and nationality.

The general allocation of substantial legislative authority over commercial and economic matters, i.e., "The Law of the Market", thus correlates strongly with the general level of unification of this area of the law.

1.4.1.1.2 Education

If we turn to commonalities in the retention of legislative jurisdiction for the component units, we see, for example, that, with the exception of Malaysia, federations seem to leave education, along with language and cultural matters, overwhelmingly at the component state level.

Even federations with residual power allocation to the central government, such as Belgium, South Africa, and the United Kingdom, expressly allocate certain powers over language, culture, and education to the component states.[72] In systems with residual component government powers, these areas are frequently not mentioned at all or they are discussed only in ways that suggest highly limited powers at the central level. Accordingly, the central governments of the European Union, Germany (today), the Kingdom of the Netherlands, and the United States seem to have no direct regulatory powers over education. So, too, Canada places jurisdiction over education at the provincial level of governance. To be sure, central governments may exercise considerable power indirectly by conditioning the receipt of federal funds on state law reform in these (and other) areas. But the legislative power hypothesis would still suggest that, all other things being equal, areas of law that are subject to direct central regulation would be more uniform than areas of law subject only to central inducement through financial incentive.

To the extent that central governments are granted direct powers over education, culture, and language at all, these tend to be rather limited. In Argentina, for example, the central power over indigenous peoples and their bilingual and cultural education seems to be a kind of protective jurisdiction, not jurisdiction to impose dominant rules on a minority. In Argentina, Brazil, Germany (before its latest federalism reform), Russia, and Switzerland, the central government has power only over basic guidelines and coordination, and mostly in the area of higher education.

We see somewhat stronger central legislative jurisdiction over education in Italy, India, and South Africa, where the central government has concurrent power with the component states over education more generally. India and South Africa reserve the regulation of universities to the component states whereas Italy indicates a special exception for the autonomy of scholastic institutions.

Malaysia and Mexico stand out by granting the strongest powers over education to their central governments. In Malaysia, the federal government's jurisdiction over education is exclusive. In Mexico, the Federation has the exclusive power to

---

[72]This is true for India as well. With regard to education, disagreements over the center's regulatory powers led first to education being removed completely from the State to the Union List, and then to being transferred to its current location in the Concurrent List while leaving only certain regulatory powers over higher education on the Union List.

establish, organize, and sustain elementary, superior, secondary, and professional schools of scientific research, or fine arts and technical training, as well as practical schools of agriculture, mining, arts, and crafts. Moreover, the central level of government in Mexico has the power to make laws "seeking to unify and coordinate education in all the Republic." According to our survey, these are unusual powers for central governments to have in a federation.[73]

The general picture that emerges is that the bulk of authority over education is usually left to the component states. In several federations, the central government has no direct power over education at all, and in federations that empower the central government to act, specific delegations and exceptions preserve substantial power for the federal subunits. This finding also supports our legislative power hypothesis in that the area of education is also one of the least unified areas of the law.

1.4.1.1.3 Private Law, Criminal Law, and Procedure

The picture with regard to private law, civil procedure, criminal law, and criminal procedure is more mixed. Whereas most federations allocate substantial powers over these areas to the center, a significant minority of federations retains substantial, if not all, legislative authority over these areas for the component units.

Most civil law federations grant legislative jurisdiction over contracts, torts, property, family law, and succession to the center. This power is sometimes concurrent (as in Argentina, Germany, Spain, or Switzerland) and sometimes exclusive (Austria, Brazil, Russia, Italy, and Venezuela). Each of the countries mentioned so far also grants its central government power over criminal legislation and (with the exception of Argentina) civil and criminal procedure as well.

Three other systems fall into this first group of federations with strong central powers over substantive and procedural private and criminal law. India provides its central government with considerable jurisdiction over the substance and procedure of private law as well as criminal law, granting the center concurrent powers over these areas (with the apparent exception of torts and criminal procedure). Malaysia allocates substantive and procedural private and criminal law to the center, while placing only Islamic family and inheritance law and the limited jurisdiction over offences against Islam under the exclusive domain of the state sharia courts. And

---

[73]We are tempted to suggest that the strength of the central government's jurisdiction over education in federations is in large measure due to the degree of cultural diversity coupled with the distribution of financial resources. Thus, the strong central powers over education in Malaysia and Mexico may well be in large part a product of the existence of extreme poverty and a concomitant need for concerted action to lift the education level among the general population as well as of the absence of local resources on the part of the component states to do so on their own. This might also explain the general concurrent power over education in India and South Africa, and the joint power over education in Brazil or the power over the organization of education in Argentina. More systematic study would be needed, however, to confirm this intuition.

the mixed system of South Africa, in which federal powers are residual, leaves everything except for indigenous and customary law to the central government.

By contrast, Australia, the United Kingdom, and the United States, along with Mexico, the European Union and the Kingdom of the Netherlands, provide their central government few powers, if any, over general substantive or procedural private and criminal law.[74] Finally, in about half the systems, the power to determine administrative procedure is located at the component state level.[75]

We see that the mixed picture with regard to the allocation of powers over these areas corresponds to the intermediate level of unification of these areas of the law as compared to others. In contrast to the law of the market at the top end and the law of education towards the bottom, the allocation of legislative jurisdiction over private law, criminal law, and procedure does not follow any great regularity across all or even across an overwhelming majority of federal systems. In some federations, legislative power over these areas is allocated to the center, in others to the component states. At the same time, each of these areas of the law are, on the whole, also less unified than the law of the market and more unified than education. This, too, provides support for the legislative power hypothesis.

1.4.1.2 Legislative Centralization by Federation

A second way to examine our legislative power hypothesis is to consider the level of unification across federal systems. Put another way, we would expect that the more legislative authority the central government of any given federation has, the more unified the law in that federation is.

To investigate this second aspect of the legislative power thesis, we rated federations in terms of the centralization of legislative power and provided each with an index on a scale from 1 (decentralized) to 7 (centralized).[76] We then compared this "legislative centralization index" with the average unification score of the federation. The legislative power hypothesis would predict that the two scores would roughly track each other. More specifically, this would mean that the difference between our legislative centralization score and the average unification score would be reasonably small and reasonably constant across federations. Put

---

[74] Australia gives the central government legislative jurisdiction over marriage and divorce, and the UK's arrangement with Scotland leaves products liability with the central government. Canada stands out for having a different power allocation for general private law, on the one hand, and substantive criminal law, on the other. It reserves most private law ("property and civil rights") to the provinces while delegating marriage and divorce as well as substantive criminal law to the center.

[75] According to the National Report, Malaysia assigns "civil and criminal law and procedure and the administration of justice" to the federal government. We do not currently read this as assigning power over administrative procedure to the central government.

[76] The scoring is explained in further detail in Appendix 1.

1 Federalism and Legal Unification: Comparing Methods, Results...

Table 1.1 Uniformity and legislative centralization

	Average unification score	Legislative centralization	Difference between unification and legislative centralization
Venezuela	6.7	6	0.7
South Africa	6.6	6.5	0.1
Austria	6.4	5.5	0.9
Malaysia	6.4	5.5	0.9
Italy	6.3	6	0.3
Germany	6.2	5	1.2
Brazil	6.2	5.5	0.7
Russia	6.1	5.5	0.6
Belgium	6.0	5	1.0
Spain	6.0	5.5	0.5
Mexico	5.8	4	1.8
Argentina	5.8	5	0.8
Switzerland	5.6	5	0.6
Australia	5.3	4	1.3
United Kingdom	4.9	4.5	0.4
Canada	4.8	4	0.8
India	4.7	5	−0.3
United States	4.4	3	1.4
European Union	2.7	2	0.7

another way, the legislative centralization score of a given federation ought to predict that federation's average unification reasonably well and similarly well across federations.

This is, indeed, in general what we find. Table 1.1 shows the results organized by decreasing level of average unification. It shows that, by and large, the federations with high uniformity scores also enjoy high degrees of central legislative authority. This systematic correspondence is shown better in Fig. 1.3.

As both Table 1.1 and Fig. 1.3 show, the correlation between legislative centralization and average unification is strong and reasonably even[77]: for 15 out of 20 federations, the difference is 1.0 or below (averaging 0.6). Thus, as a general matter, this too supports our legislative power hypothesis. Yet, in some federations the average unification of law seems to reflect the legislative centralization score better than in others. In a few federations (at the top end), notably Mexico, the United States, Australia, and Germany, the law is considerably more unified than the

---

[77] We should emphasize that the empirically significant fact is the general regularity of the correlation between the legislative centralization score and the unification score across federations, not the correspondence of absolute scores for a particular federation taken in isolation. Although the measurement of legislative power and legal unification both use the same scale, the resulting score on each is an indication only of the relative achievement of any given federation with regard to either legislative power or legal unification. Thus, the absolute score that a federation receives on one measure need not correspond to the absolute score it receives on the other.

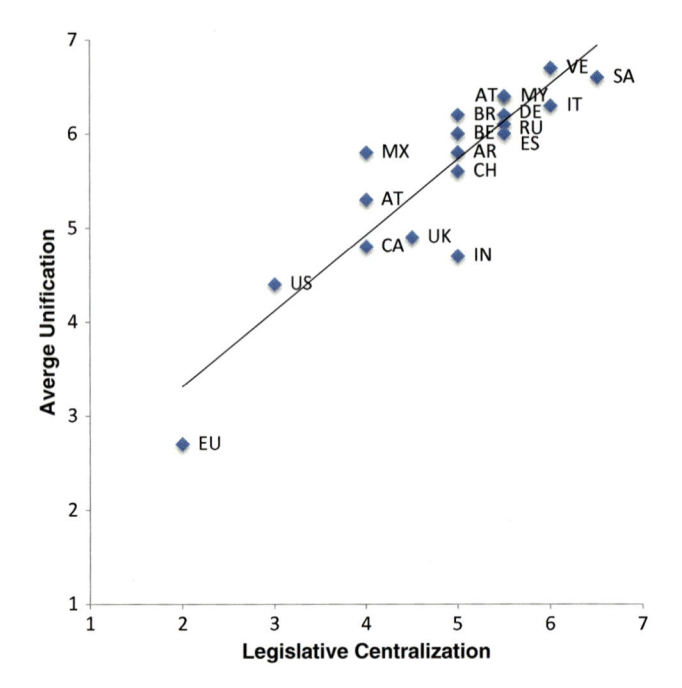

Fig. 1.3 Uniformity and legislative centralization

legislative centralization score would predict. And for India (at the bottom end), the average unification score is actually lower than the legislative centralization score would predict.

These differences in the correlation between the average unification score and legislative centralization score points to the existence of additional factors that may be at work in bringing about legal unification in federal systems. This, too, should come as no surprise. As we noted when introducing the legislative power hypothesis, the central government's *effective exercise* of legislative authority depends on more than the formal allocation of legislative jurisdiction. We shall consider some of these factors next.

1.4.2 Structural Centralization Hypothesis

The central government's ability to unify the law within a federation depends not only on the formal distribution of legislative authority but also on other aspects of constitutional architecture. These structures beyond the formal enumeration and limitations on powers (what Filippov, Ordeshook, and Shvetsova would call "Level

2" design features of a federation),[78] range from the federal distribution of executive and adjudicative powers to the component states' tax autonomy; they also depend on the strength of component state representation and participation in the central legislative process. The idea is still rather simple: strong central legislative powers combined with weak component state powers more generally should lead to more uniform law throughout the federation. Call this the structural centralization thesis.

The leading characteristic in this regard would be whether the system of government at the center is a parliamentary system or a presidential system with separation of powers. As the latter adds another "veto player"[79] to the central legislative process, one might expect separation of powers systems to produce less central legislation and, therefore, feature a lower degree of legal unification than parliamentary systems. The data, however, do not seem to bear this out – at least not in a straightforward manner. All Latin American federations are presidential systems and yet they fall toward the high end of the unification spectrum. And with the exception of the United States, all systems toward the low end of the unification spectrum are parliamentary systems. Although presidential systems may retard central government activity, other factors must clearly be at work to overwhelm the effect of the form of government on the unification of law.

Other structural characteristics similarly do not correlate independently with legal unification. Features such as the strength of the upper house of the legislature as a representative of component state interests, member state tax autonomy, component state judicial autonomy (i.e. central versus local power to interpret or apply component state law), central government power to execute central law, and central government power to adjudicate or apply central law, would all seem to affect the unification of law. And yet, taken individually, none seems correlated with the levels of unification that we find. We leave it to a further study to examine whether a combination of these factors can be combined sensibly into a structural centralization index that might be correlated with legal unification.

1.4.3 The Legal Traditions Hypothesis: Civil v. Common Law

In examining the level of legal unification across different federal systems (supra Table 1.1 and Fig. 1.3), we note that all civil law systems are located at the high end of the spectrum while all common law systems rank at the bottom. The only flaw in this picture is that the high group also contains two jurisdictions that are not civil law systems: Malaysia and South Africa. Yet, neither of them can be characterized

---

[78] Mikhail Filippov, Peter C. Ordeshook, and Olga Shvetsova, *Designing Federalism: A Theory of Self-Sustainable Federal Institutions* (New York: Cambridge University Press, 2004).

[79] George Tsebelis, *Veto Players: How Political Institutions Work* (Princeton: Princeton University Press, 2002).

	Civil Law Systems	Common Law Systems
High Unification	Venezuela (6.7) Austria (6.4) Brazil (6.2), Germany (6.2) Russia (6.1) Belgium (6.0), Spain (6.0) Argentina (5.8) Mexico (5.8) Switzerland (5.6)	
Low Unification		Australia (5.3) United Kingdom (4.9) Canada (4.8) India (4.7) United States (4.4)

Fig. 1.4 Uniformity by legal tradition

as a common law system either because they are hybrids.[80] Leaving them aside for a moment, the differences in the unification scores between the civil law and the common law jurisdictions are striking (Fig. 1.4).

The average score for the civil law group is 6.1 while it is 4.8 for the common law countries – a difference of more than one full point; this indicates that on average, law is significantly more unified in civil law systems than in common law jurisdictions. Note also that there is no overlap between these groups – the scores for the civil law countries range from 6.7 to 5.6 while scores for the common law group range from 5.3 to 4.4; in other words, even the most diverse civil law system (Switzerland) displays greater legal uniformity than the most unified common law jurisdiction (Australia). In short, the differences in degrees of legal uniformity seem linked to membership in the civil versus the common law group.

We are of course aware that the civil/common law dichotomy is time-worn and that has recently come under much attack in comparative law scholarship (although some use for the distinction still remains).[81] We recognize that from many perspectives, it makes little sense, and that especially in light of the ongoing interpenetration of legal systems, globalization of law, and the rise of the modern administrative state, most legal systems in the world are essentially hybrids. This

---

[80] South Africa is mixed civil/common law system, and Malaysia, with its colonial common law heritage now is *sui generis* due to the heavy, and increasing, influence of Islamic law. Another slight imperfection in the picture is the fact that some of the common law systems contain civil law elements, i.e., Canada (with Quebec), the United States (with Louisiana), and arguably even the United Kingdom (with Scotland as a mixed jurisdiction).

[81] See Mirjan Damaska, "The Common Law/Civil Law Divide: Residual Truth of a Misleading Distinction," 49 *Sup. Ct. L. Rev.* (Canada) 3 (2010).

reality signifies that civil law and common law systems are ideal types rather than empirical entities. Still, there is no gainsaying our data, which indicate that, with regard to legal uniformity, there is something to the distinction between these two families that cannot be ignored.

Yet, if membership in the civil law versus the common law group is linked to degrees of legal uniformity, this just leads to the question: why? Why does it matter for legal uniformity whether a federation belongs to one group rather than the other?

One reason might be that civil law systems are generally more centralized than common law jurisdictions. This, indeed, may be true. If we look back at the degree of legislative centralization, for example, civil law systems are located toward the higher end of the spectrum while common law systems are located toward the low end. This correlation, however, is far from perfect. With the exception of the United States, every common law system has one or more civil law system counterparts in which legislative powers are centralized to a similar degree.

It also does not appear that any one method of unification is more readily available in civil as compared to common law jurisdictions. We know that there is generally no greater unifying force of (federal) constitutions because these are tremendously strong in most common law countries as well. Nor is there greater uniformity in legal education and legal practice because based on the national reports, we have no reason to believe that in that regard, the common law jurisdictions lag behind the civil law world.

In the case of uniformity through legislation, the civil versus common law dichotomy may still have some purchase in that it reflects a combination of three highly specific and distinct features of a federal legal system that tends either toward unification or diversity of laws.

First, civil law legislatures tend to use the full extent of their constitutional powers to unify law as much as possible while common law countries tend not to. Where constitutions in civil law countries like Germany give concurrent jurisdiction to the center, this concurrent jurisdiction is almost exhaustively exercised by the center, resulting in a high degree of legal unification. This might express the civilian preference for hierarchical over coordinate structures of state authority as Mirjan Damaska famously described,[82] a preference which fosters the centralization. In any event, the tendency to exhaust central legislative powers is considerably weaker in common law countries. The United States Congress, for example, could surely rely on the Commerce Clause to legislate massively virtually all across commercial and private law – but it has used that power very selectively and, on the whole, sparingly. This may, in part, reflect certain citizen preferences that fetter the federal use of this clause.[83]

Second, and perhaps most important, where civil law country legislatures do use their lawmaking power in the traditional core areas of private, commercial, criminal,

---

[82]See Mirjan Damaska, *The Faces of Justice and State Authority* (New Haven: Yale University Press, 1986).

[83]Robert A. Mikos, "The Populist Safeguards of Federalism," 68 *Ohio St. L. J.* 1669 (2007).

and procedural law, they have tended to enact comprehensive codifications. This is an expression of the civil law tradition's habit to find law in a single authoritative text rather than in a multitude of individual decisions or scattered statutes. Codifications unify law with one stroke and on a massive scale – in fact, such unification has been among their primary purposes. To be sure, in less traditional areas, such as consumer protection, labor and employment relations or environmental law, codification projects lack the tailwind of history and often face significant political contestation. But even here, they often succeed and thus create legal uniformity across the board and for the whole nation in one fell swoop. Such massive national codification projects are almost unknown in common law jurisdictions. Again, while the US Congress could surely enact a national commercial or private law code (at least one covering contracts, torts, and moveable property), it has never made so much as a serious attempt to do so. Nor do Australia, Canada, India or the United Kingdom have national codifications on a civil law scale. Instead, these common law jurisdictions usually enact piecemeal statutes that do not aspire to unify the law to the same extent.

Central (especially concurrent) legislative power thus has different implications – indeed perhaps even different "meanings" – in civil and common law countries. In civil law systems, it is an implicit exhortation, perhaps even command, not only to legislate but to enact a comprehensive code in so far as possible. In common law systems, legislative power is essentially conceived of as a mere option that, if used at all, is exercised in a piecemeal fashion. Small wonder then, that the same amount of federal legislative jurisdiction results in much greater actual legal unification in civil law systems than in common law jurisdictions.

Third, and more speculatively, both these tendencies – to use the full extent of central power for the sake of legal unification and to codify broadly if possible – may ultimately express a fundamental property of the civil law mentality: the strong preference for legal uniformity and the concomitant dislike of legal diversity – which civil lawyers quickly associate with chaos. Civil lawyers prize clarity and predictability of legal rules more highly than their common law colleagues, and these values make them prefer uniformity over diversity. The civil lawyers' preferences are, like the common lawyers', likely the direct result of their legal education. In contrast to their Anglo-American colleagues, whose study of cases presents the law as a series of concrete decisions in particular instances and thus trains the students in the art of distinguishing one from the other, students in civil law faculties tend to encounter the law in the form of broad principles and systematically organized rules and are thus trained to generalize – and unify.

We emphasize the speculative nature of resorting, at this point, to the general preferences of civil lawyers as an explanation for legal uniformity. But it may help explain relatively high degrees of legal uniformity, especially in systems where the center does not have broad formal legislative powers over all the core areas of law. In Mexico, for example, where general private law is by and large left to the states, their respective codes frequently emulate, indeed often outright copy, the federal models. This may be attributable to a lack of resources at the state level. But it may also suggest that in a civil law country, legislative command from above is not necessarily required to establish significant uniformity because there is a strong tendency to create it voluntarily. In the civil law tradition, deviation from the common path is a serious matter. It is normally avoided unless the reasons for it are very strong.

The legal traditions hypothesis may be especially useful in understanding the European Union. The EU contains both civil and common law member states and, as such, cannot be assigned exclusively to one or the other legal family. One might think that the EU is predominantly a civil law organization, as it was originally founded by a group of civil law states and is overwhelmingly populated even today by lawyers with civil law training. Yet, at least for the first three decades of its existence, the EU functioned more like a common law system making law in a piecemeal fashion as far as necessary to reach a specific goal (a common market) and fixing potholes along the way. More recently, however, that has changed. As the subsequent treaties granted ever wider legislative powers to the EU, civil lawyers have pushed increasingly towards more uniformity on the European level. The latest manifestation of this trend is the effort to create a common private law of Europe, perhaps even in codified form. In this trend, the civilian penchant for uniformity through codification once against asserts itself. In certain areas, such as private international law and international civil procedure, it has already succeeded in codifying and thus unifying the law on a European scale unthinkable 20 years ago.

1.4.4 Political Parties

Political parties operate one step removed from the structural features just discussed. Filippov et al. usefully refer to these as "Level 3" design issues. As scholars from William Riker into the present have shown, political parties can bring together separated institutions as well as fragment a single parliament. In systems that have strong federation-wide political parties, the central level of governance can pass laws over regional objections more easily than in federations with strong regional parties. Put another way, a strong national party system can unify politics across regions and tends to dilute the representation of any distinct regional political will.

Our study does not presently consider political parties. Hence, we have not formulated a hypothesis in this regard. Still, it seems valuable to pursue this potential factor as a separate element of the analysis; in that regard, however, more research is required. If we were to formulate a thesis, it would be twofold: First, all else being equal, a federal system with strong regional parties would be lower on the legal unification index than a federal system with weak regional parties. Second, all else being equal, a federal system with strong national parties will be higher on the legal unification index than a federal system with weak national parties. These two can be independent of one another, as, for example, the United States has neither strong regional nor strong national parties. Any such future study should take care, however, to consider the extent to which political parties reflect or overlap with the presence of persistent, mobilized, social cleavages, to which we turn next.

1.4.5 Territorially Bounded Cleavages

Ethnic, cultural, linguistic, religious, historical, economic or other social differences that characterize the populations in some federal systems are likely to militate against legal unification. To be sure, such an effect is unlikely where the respective differences are evenly distributed throughout the federation, as in the United States; where the respective groups are not concentrated in particular regions, they will probably not insist on (geographic) legal diversity nor resist lawmaking at the national level (and thus legal uniformity). But an impact on legal uniformity is likely where such differences are "lumpy", i.e., associated with particular regions, as in the multinational federations of Belgium, Canada, Spain, and arguably the United Kingdom; here, these differences can amount to real "cleavages" that may be politically mobilized to split the federation. In such federations, states, provinces, and regions that consider themselves different from the rest have reason to resist federal lawmaking (and thus legal uniformity) for the sake of maintaining regional differences.[84]

If we examine the raw data on unification of laws, they do not bear out this effect. To be sure, India, the United Kingdom, and Canada are at the low end of the unification index. At the same time, however, Belgium and Spain figure toward the high end of legal unification. What would merit further study is the effect of social cleavages while holding structural centralization constant. That is, federations with strong territorially bounded cleavages may weaken the exercise of central power even where the center has been granted considerable authority. Put another way, all else being equal, systems in which territorially bounded cleavages run deep should feature less legal unification than systems in which cleavages are either scattered throughout the federation or do not figure prominently (i.e., are not politically mobilized) at all.

We would expect the importance of cleavages to be particularly great when the subunits with a special sense of identity are large in comparison to the whole federation. Belgium, Canada, and the United Kingdom are the most obvious cases in point. In Canada and the United Kingdom, the separate identity of the subunit even corresponds to adherence to a (partially) different legal tradition, as both Quebec and Scotland are civil law influenced jurisdictions in common law dominated federations. And in Belgium, there are only two subunits of roughly equal size so that no one is clearly superior to the other. Obviously, a large and powerful subunit can more easily obstruct federal legislation (and unification) than a small one: the federal legislature in Belgium cannot subdue an obstructionist Wallonia or Flanders; the Canadian parliament cannot commandeer Quebec; and the United Kingdom

---

[84]This does not necessarily mean that federations with social cleavages are *generally* less centralized or exhibit less legal uniformity than those without social cleavages. But it suggests that whatever potential for decentralization lies within a federation's constitutional architecture will be guarded more carefully in systems with lumpy social cleavages than in those without such a federal society. In systems without social cleavages or where social cleavages are randomly dispersed through the federation, we would expect system-wide left-right politics to take over and dilute the federation's structural potential for decentralization.

cannot ride roughshod over Scotland. By contrast, where the areas with a special identity are smaller (and less powerful) in relation to the whole, they can be more easily brought into line by the rest. Perhaps that helps to explain why Swiss law is surprisingly unified despite considerable cleavages – among the 26 cantons, none is so clearly dominant that it can be seriously obstructionist, not to mention make credible secessionist noise.

1.4.6 The Age of Federations

Finally, one might wonder whether the age of federal systems plays a role for the degree of legal uniformity. One problem with this question is that in many cases, such as Germany, Russia or the United Kingdom, age is a dubious measure because it is not clear at what point the federation was born, so to speak – when the federal system first came together or when the exact present form of federalism (i.e., the current constitution) was adopted.[85] But even if the age is determined, its relevance depends exactly on the aspect we focus on.

If one focuses just on whether law in federal systems grows more uniform over time, the answer is that there is no evidence for such any *general* trend. As a federation, Germany is much older than Italy, yet its law is no more uniform (and at least arguably, somewhat less so). In general, the overall correlation between age and uniformity of law is decidedly poor.

Beneath this general picture, however, the situation is more complex. In some federations, the uniformity of law has increased significantly over time. This is noteworthy in the United States, mainly because of the massive growth of federal law in the twentieth century which is likely to continue as the federal government is now determined to exercise much tighter control over larger parts of the economy; in Russia during the last decade because of President Putin's rigorous centralization program; in Switzerland where federal law has grown as well and even procedural uniformity (both civil and criminal) has now been accomplished; and also in the European Union where legal unification has skyrocketed during the last 20 years although it still remains at a level below all national systems.[86] But in many other systems, such as Austria, Germany or India, the situation has been largely stable over long periods of time. And in some countries, the trend has actually been in the opposite direction: where federalism is "devolutionary", i.e., embraced for the very reason of decentralizing power, uniformity of course tends to *decrease* as time goes on. This has recently been noticeable in Belgium, Italy, Spain, and the United

---

[85] In Germany, one would probably look to the unification under Bismarck in 1871 but could also argue for the adoption of the *Grundgesetz* in 1949. In Russia, one could go back to the early days of the Soviet Union (1922) or look at the current constitution (1993). In the United Kingdom, one could go back as far as the Act of Union with Scotland (1707) or consider only the devolution project of the last 20 years.

[86] Another, although special, case in point is Venezuela, where federalism has by and large been suffocated over the last decade by an authoritarian regime.

Kingdom. It should also be noted that the very categories of "integrative" versus "devolutionary" federations must be taken with a grain of salt, as some systems may well have different phases over time.[87]

One final observation is nonetheless noteworthy in this context: in all civil law systems in which federalism would be called "integrative" (i.e., where it brought the system together in the first place), legal uniformity has tended to rise over time. In some of these systems, like Austria and Germany, it rose quickly in an earlier period and has long since leveled off; in others, like Switzerland, it has continued to rise more gradually.[88] The European Union also belongs in this category. It is true that the uniformity level in the EU is still very low compared to national systems, but the EU is relatively young, and legal uniformity within it has risen rapidly especially over the last 20 years. Since the EU is largely shaped by the civil law tradition, one can expect this tendency to continue. A major retarding force in this process is the United Kingdom – not accidentally the European Union's largest common law member.

1.5 Conclusion

This investigation aims at filling a significant gap in the literature on comparative federalism by describing and analyzing the means, extent, and background of legal unification within federal systems. Its analysis of "unification" includes the "harmonization" of law as a lesser degree of likeness. It focuses on the unification of legal rules, not of actual outcomes in concrete disputes, and it is limited to official law, excluding non-state rules. Covering 20 federal systems from 6 continents, it cuts across a wide variety of national federal systems and also includes the supranational federation of the European Union. It is based on National Reports written by specialists, information provided by additional lawyers from each of the systems covered, and supplemented by our own research.

Among the manifold *means and methods* of legal unification, clearly the most powerful modes operate top-down. Federal constitutions perform two separate functions in this regard. First, through directly applicable norms they establish a common ground for the exercise of all public authority throughout the system. Second, constitutions allocate jurisdiction within the federation, usually, as we have found, granting significant lawmaking power to the center. The National Reports suggest that the exercise of this central lawmaking is the most common, important, and effective path to legal uniformity. Other means and methods of legal unification play a distinctly secondary role. Uniform interpretation by central courts is still fairly important in many systems, especially where the central judiciary has power not only over federal but also over member unit law. By contrast, unification on

---

[87] See Halberstam, *supra* note 2.

[88] It took Switzerland more than 60 years to unify its private law (1848–1907/1911) and until the present, i.e., about 160 years to unify its civil and criminal procedure

the horizontal level, i.e., through voluntary coordination among the member units' legislatures, judiciaries, or executives, plays a significant role only in a few systems. And legal unification through private actors, i.e., via restatements, principles or similar devices, is an important factor mostly in the United States and the European Union. Legal education and legal practice both have a system-wide orientation in virtually all federations (except for the European Union) and should count as unifying forces as well, although their concrete impact is almost impossible to measure. Finally, compliance with norms from outside the federation plays a crucial role only for the members of the European Union; in most other instances, the various federations' widespread participation in international unification projects contributes astoundingly little to *internal* legal unification (i.e. among their component states) – largely because the areas concerned are typically governed (internally) by federal law and thus already uniform within the respective countries.

The *degree of legal uniformity* in federal systems is, on the whole, higher than one might have expected. In every national federation, the author of the National Report as well as almost all the additional experts consulted judged their own system to be, on the whole, more uniform than diverse.[89] The European Union stands apart in this regard; as the only supranational regime, the reporters and other experts judged the law within the EU to be by and large more diverse than uniform. The degree of uniformity also differs substantially across subjects. The law of the market as well as constitutional law are the most uniform; general private, criminal, procedural, and private international law occupy a middle ground; and administrative law and procedure as well the law governing education, language and culture, are the most diverse.

The primary *explanation* for the different degrees of uniformity among subject matters as well as among the various federal systems is likely the different degree to which lawmaking power is allocated to the center rather than to the member units. Subject matter areas under central control are much more uniform than those left to the member states. And in federations with strong central lawmaking power, uniformity is almost consistently higher than in federations in which legislative jurisdiction is more widely distributed. In other words, where law can be made at the center, it usually will be, and if it is, legal uniformity will result. In a sense, this is only to be expected. At the same time, it should give one pause before embracing too quickly the argument[90] that a federation's benefits of experimentation and diversity can be reaped equally by decentralization within a unitary system.

---

[89]The only exception is the extremely loose federation of the Kingdom of the Netherlands, which is atypical in almost all regards and should therefore not distract from the conclusion in the text. The National Report for the United States describes US-American law as "not uniform...[but] largely harmonized", meaning that while there are "numerous inconsistencies in the law", they are mostly "matters of detail only" (which can, however, "be extremely important in individual cases"). We consider this evaluation consistent with our general conclusion.

[90]See, e.g., Malcolm M. Feeley and Edward Rubin, *Federalism: Political Identity and Tragic Compromise* (Ann Arbor: University of Michigan Press, 2008); Malcolm M. Feeley and Edward Rubin, "Federalism: Some Notes on a National Neurosis," 41 *UCLA L. Rev.* 903 (1994).

Yet, it is also clear that factors other than the allocation of legislative jurisdiction play a significant role as well. Further research is needed, for example, to investigate the extent to which the overall degree of structural centralization of power in a federation is related to legal uniformity. In this context, the difference between presidential and parliamentary systems and the strength of an upper house in the legislative process may be especially relevant.

One influential factor supported by our data is the importance of the civil law tradition. Civil law systems are clearly more uniform than common law federations. The main reasons are probably their more extensive use of central lawmaking power and the civilian penchant for comprehensive codification.

The make-up of the political party system can also have a significant unifying effect, e.g., where strong national parties can mute local interests, or a diversifying impact, e.g., where strong regional parties successfully push for local constituencies.

A retarding factor may be the existence of major ethnic, cultural, linguistic, religious, economic or other social differences within the population. Where such differences are "lumpy," that is, where distinct populations are concentrated in particular regions, these differences create relevant "cleavages" within a federation (as in Belgium, Canada, or the United Kingdom) which make legal unification harder to accomplish (and perhaps also less desirable).

Finally, the age of federations can play a role, although it may easily work in opposite directions. Where federalism is "integrative" (i.e., the coming together of previously separate units) legal uniformity typically grows over time, at least in civil law systems. By contrast, where federalism is "devolutionary" (i.e., the decentralization of a previously unitary system), uniformity tends to diminish as time goes on.

This study and our comparative overview answer some important questions, but they also raise many others. Much of the information gathered through the National Reports and from additional local experts needs to be confirmed in light of the conclusions that we have drawn. More data need to be collected, especially about aspects the relevance of which became clear only while working on this project. And several forces that we have identified as potentially influencing the degree, modalities, and background of legal unification within federal systems, currently lie beyond our National Reports, and will thus require additional research.

Appendices

Appendix 1: Methods

Collecting Data About Degrees of Uniformity

We began by asking each national reporter to rate 47 areas of the law in their country on a scale of uniformity from 1 to 7 by filling out a "scorecard". We encouraged each expert to consult others within his or her system to the extent the national reporter did not feel comfortable answering all the questions on his or her own. The national reporter's score is therefore merely one expert's (or a small coordinated group's) subjective judgments of the level of uniformity within that particular system. And yet, one strength of expert estimates is that they allow us to capture what country specialists have in mind when they talk and write about legal unification in the literature.[91]

This left us with two reliability concerns. The first was a straightforward concern about the reliability of our national reporter's view of his or her system as compared to what another (independent) expert's view of that same system might have been. We sought to address this problem by obtaining at least one additional score for each system from another expert whom we judged to be as qualified as the national reporter to assess the level of unification in his or her system across the spectrum of fields listed on the scorecard. If the second expert answered fewer than 75 % of the questions asked (or gave a "0" for more than 25 % of the answers), we eliminated him or her and engaged a third (and, if necessary, fourth) expert. This ensured that the "surviving" experts were as broadly confident about their perception of unification across all areas of the law within their own system as was the primary national reporter.

The second was a concern about comparability across systems, i.e., about intercoder reliability between the national reporters from different systems. This latter concern was that one national reporter's view of what constitutes uniformity (as a general matter) might be biased as compared to the views of a national reporter from a different system. Because this latter concern about intercoder reliability related specifically to the reliability of reporters across systems, we termed this the problem of intersystemic coding reliability.

We addressed this second concern by also giving the additional experts a separate set of eight control questions designed to identify a systematic bias in rating uniformity more generally. Each of these control questions presents a hypothetical scenario of laws in a hypothetical federation with regard to a particular area of the law and asks the coder to rate the level of uniformity for the hypothetical federation

---

[91]Cf. Kenneth Benoit and Michael Laver, "Estimating Party Policy Positions: Comparing Expert Surveys and Hand-Coded Content Analysis," 26 *Elect. Stud.* 90–107 (2007).

within that given area of law.[92] Each of these questions sought to elicit an answer that would reveal a different kind of bias. For example, in one scenario we present a federation in which all but one of twelve constituent jurisdictions have the same law. In another question, we present a federation in which every constituent jurisdiction has a speed limit, but the speed limits vary between 55 and 65 mph. The point with each of these questions was not to look for right or wrong answers, but simply to ensure intercoder reliability in the sense of checking that each coder took roughly the same general approach to coding uniformity and disuniformity when presented with the same scenario.

We disqualified experts whose average score on the control questions was more than one standard deviation from the average score that all the other additional experts gave to the control questions. This ensured that the surviving experts were what we termed "intersystemically reliable," because they had shown generally to rate uniformity in a manner roughly similar to the other experts. This helped us increase the reliability of comparing unification scores across different systems. Again, where we eliminated one expert as unreliable, we turned to a third and in some cases even a fourth. For logistical reasons of solicitation and timing, we occasionally wound up with more than one intersystemically reliable "second opinion" for a given system.[93]

In calculating a particular system's unification score for an individual area of the law, for sub-scores across several areas of the law, and for the overall average unification score across all areas of the law, we then took the average of the national reporter's and additional (surviving) experts' scores.

Legislative Centralization Index

The two principal authors of this study separately evaluated legislative centralization by taking into account (1) the breadth and number of areas assigned to the center under the text of the constitution, (2) the practical importance of the various fields (e.g., weighing "commercial law" more heavily than "water rights"), (3) where we had sufficient information, how grants of federal legislative power have been interpreted (e.g., the broad interpretation of the commerce clause under the U.S. Constitution), and 4) whether residual legislative power is assigned to the center

---

[92]This practice was developed to correct for instances when respondents use the ordinal response categories in questions in different ways, which may bias the validity of analyses based on the resulting data can be biased. Anchoring vignettes is a survey design technique intended to correct for these problems. See Gary King, Christopher J. L. Murray, Joshua A. Salomon, and Ajay Tandon, "Enhancing the Validity and Cross-Cultural Comparability of Measurement in Survey Research," 97 *Am. Polit. Sci. Rev.* 567–583 (2003).

[93]For four systems (Germany, Italy, Spain, United Kingdom) we wound up with two intersystemically reliable scores in addition to the score of the national reporter. For two systems (Canada and Argentina) we wound up with four intersystemically reliable scores in addition to the score of the national reporter.

or the member units. Each of us arrived at a composite score indicating, for each federation, the concentration of powers at the central level of government on a scale ranging from 1 (lowest) to 7 (highest). When we compared our individual scores, we found that we agreed in the overwhelming majority of cases. Where we did not, our disagreement was small (one point or less), and we arrived at an agreement or compromise after some discussion.

We did not consider how broadly, forcefully, or successfully the respective legislative powers at the central or member state level have been or are exercised. We also ignored both the broader institutional architecture and the social or political context in which the allocation of primary legislative jurisdiction was embedded. The legislative centralization index is therefore intended as an index solely of the formal allocation of legislative jurisdiction in any given federation.

Appendix 2: *National Reporter Questionnaire and Scorecard*

UNIFORM LAW AND ITS IMPACT ON NATIONAL LAWS
LIMITS AND POSSIBILITIES
Intermediary Congress of the International
Academy of Comparative Law
Mexico City, 13–15 November 2008
Questionnaire
on

Unification of Laws in Federal Systems

General Reporters
Daniel Halberstam
Mathias Reimann

Introduction

This study investigates the unification of laws in federal systems. We seek to ascertain the level of legal unification within each system, to understand the institutional, social, and legal background against which legal unification occurs, and to explore the means by which unification is achieved and by which diversity is sustained in each federal system.

The questionnaire consists of six parts. Part I invites you to write a brief overview of the federal system, in particular as it pertains to the issue of unification. Parts II–IV provide a series of broad questions about the distribution of power, means of unification, and institutional and social background. Most of the questions in Parts II–IV are divided into specific sub-questions. Please answer all sub-questions to the extent they are applicable. Part V is a "unification scorecard," which will ask you to score the level of uniformity and indicate the various causes and sources of uniformity and diversity in several specific areas of law. In Part VI, we ask for a brief essay reflecting your general assessment, conclusion, and/or prognosis on legal unification in the federal system on which you are reporting.

While some of the questions in Parts II–IV may be answered in a simple yes/no format, others invite reporters to respond in narrative fashion, to emphasize the points important in their own legal system. Your answers to these questions should provide, whenever possible, a historical and evolutionary perspective. Where appropriate, they should point out whether and how norms, facts, or circumstances have changed over time in a significant manner. They should also indicate future trends if such trends are sufficiently discernible.

Given that some of the questions may overlap with others, you should feel free to make cross-references where appropriate, as long as your answers cover all the points raised in the specific question to which you are responding. Where there are no meaningful answers in a given system please say so and briefly explain why. Of course, each reporter may wish to add information of particular significance in his or her federal system not covered by the questionnaire.

Throughout the questionnaire, we use the term "unification" (of law). The reports (both national and general) should encompass "harmonization" of law as well. For purposes of this questionnaire, we view unification and harmonization as different points on a spectrum of "likeness." In other words, we are interested not only in "sameness" of law throughout a federation but also in "similarity."

Finally, we use the phrases "central" government and "component" state or government to refer to the various levels of government in a federal system. To the extent that the constitution recognizes and protects other political subdivisions (e.g. language communities, regional communities, municipalities, or counties), please explain and please include these in your discussion of component powers whenever applicable. Note that in the unification scorecard (Part V), we specifically break out municipal (and other sub-component state) legislation as one potential factor causing diversity.

Overview

Please provide a very brief historical overview of the federal system and its development. You might do this in as little as 250 words and no more than 500 words (i.e., about ½–1 single-spaced page). Please highlight those factors that you deem most relevant in your system to the relation between central and component state power and the degree of uniformity of law.

The Federal Distribution and Exercise of Lawmaking Power

1. Which areas of law are subject to the (legislative) jurisdiction of the central authority?

    (a) Which areas of (legislative) jurisdiction do constitutional text and doctrine formally allocate to the central government?
    (b) Which of these powers are concurrent and which are exclusive?
    (c) Briefly name the most important/most frequently used constitutionally specified sources authorizing central government regulation (e.g., in the United States, the commerce clause)?
    (d) Briefly describe the most important areas of central government regulation in practice-based terms (e.g., labor law, consumer protection law, environmental law, civil procedure)?

2. Which areas of law remain within the (legislative) jurisdiction of the component states?

    (a) What areas of (legislative) jurisdiction do constitutional text and doctrine allocate to the component states?
    (b) Which of these are exclusively reserved to the states and which are concurrent powers?

(c) Does the exercise of central concurrent power constitutionally prevent the states from exercising their concurrent power?
(d) In practice, what are the most important areas of exclusive or predominant component state government regulation (e.g., education, family law, procedure)?
(e) In practice, what are the most important areas (if any) in which central and component state regulation coexist?

3. Does the constitution allocate residual powers to the central government, the component states, or (in case of specific residual powers) to both?
4. What is the constitutional principle according to which conflicts (if any) between central and component state law are resolved (e.g., supremacy of federal law)?
5. Do the municipalities – by virtue of the constitution or otherwise – have significant lawmaking power and if so, in what areas?

The Means and Methods of Legal Unification

1. To what extent is legal unification or harmonization accomplished by the exercise of central power (top down)?

   (a) via directly applicable *constitutional* norms? (e.g., the equal protection clause in the US requires specific features of family law; due process limits in personam jurisdiction)
   (b) via central legislation (or executive or administrative rules)?
      (i) creating directly applicable norms
      (ii) mandating that states pass conforming (implementing) legislation (e.g., *Rahmengesetze*, EC directives)
      (iii) inducing states to regulate by conditioning the allocation of central money on compliance with central standards
      (iv) indirectly forcing states to regulate by threatening to take over the field in case of state inaction or state action that does not conform to centrally specified standards
   (c) through the judicial creation of uniform norms by central supreme court(s) or central courts of appeal?
   (d) through other centrally controlled means, such as centrally managed coordination or information exchange among the component states (e.g., Europe's "Open Method of Coordination")?

2. To what extent is legal unification accomplished through formal or informal voluntary coordination among the component states? (somewhat bottom up, coordinate model)

   (a) by component state legislatures, e.g., through uniform or model laws?
   (b) by component state judiciaries, e.g., through the state courts' consideration of legislative or judicial practice of sister states?

(c) by the component state executive branches, e.g., component state governors' agreements?

3. To what extent is legal unification accomplished, or promoted, by non-state actors (e.g., in the US: American Law Institute, National Commissions on Uniform State Laws; in Europe: Principles of European Contract Law (Lando Principles, etc.))?
    (a) through restatements
    (b) through uniform or model laws
    (c) through standards and practices of industry, trade organizations or other or private entities?
    (d) To what extent do the activities listed in (a)–(c), above, provide input for unification or harmonization by central action (top down) or by the states (coordinate)?

4. What is the role of legal education and training in the unification of law?
    (a) Do law schools draw students from throughout the federal system?
    (b) Does legal education focus on (1) central or system-wide law or (2) component state law?
    (c) Is testing for bar admission system-wide or by component state?
    (d) Is the actual admission to the bar for the entire federal system or by component state?
    (e) Do graduates tend to set up their practice or take jobs anywhere in the federation?
    (f) Are there particular institutions of (primary, graduate or continuing) legal education and training that play a unifying role (e.g., internships by state court judges at central courts, national academies or training programs)?

5. To what extent do external factors, such as international law, influence legal unification?
    (a) Does compliance with international legal obligations play a role?
    (b) Does international voluntary coordination play a role (e.g., participation in international unification or harmonization projects, UNCITRAL, UNIDROIT, Hague Conference on Private International Law, etc.)?

Institutional and Social Background

1. The Judicial Branch
    (a) Is there a court at the central level with the power to police whether central legislation has exceeded the lawmaking powers allocated to the central government?

(b) If yes, do(es) the central court(s) regularly and effectively police the respective constitutional limitations? (Please explain and give examples.)
(c) Is there a court at the central level with power authoritatively to interpret component state law?
(d) Are there both central and state courts, and if so, are there trial and appellate courts on both levels?
(e) Are there other mechanisms for resolving differences in legal interpretation among central and/or component state courts? If yes, please describe their nature and the extent of their use.

2. Relations between the Central and Component State Governments

   (a) Does the central government have the power to force component states to legislate?
   (b) Who executes central government law? (the central government itself or the component states?) If it depends upon the areas involved, please explain.
   (c) Are component states or their governments, or other communities, represented at the central level, and if so, what is their role in the central legislative process?
   (d) How and by whom are component state representatives at the central level elected or appointed?
   (e) Who has the power to tax (what)? The central government, the component states or both?
   (f) Are there general principles governing or prohibiting multiple taxation?
   (g) Are there constitutional or legislative rules on revenue sharing among the component states or between the federation and the component states?

3. Other Formal or Informal Institutions for Resolving Intergovernmental Conflicts
    Are there other institutions (political, administrative, judicial, hybrid or sui generis) to help resolve conflicts between component states or between the central government and component states?

4. The Bureaucracy

   (a) Is the civil service of the central government separate from the civil services of the component states?
   (b) If there are separate civil service systems, to what extent is there lateral mobility (or career advancement) between them?

5. Social Factors

   (a) Are there important racial, ethnic, religious, linguistic or other social cleavages in the federation? If yes, please briefly describe these cleavages.
   (b) Are distinct groups evenly or randomly dispersed throughout the federation or are they concentrated in certain regions, territories, states or other political subdivisions? If they are concentrated in certain regions, etc., please explain how this concentration relates to the structure of the federal system.

(c) Is there significant asymmetry in natural resources, development, wealth, education or other regards between the component states? If yes, please explain how this relates to the structure of the federal system.

Unification Scorecard

The following unification scorecard asks you to assess the degree of legal uniformity across a host of areas on a very basic scale and to indicate the predominant means/causes of uniformity and diversity.

We have listed various substantive and procedural areas of the law. Please indicate for each area your assessment of the degree of legal uniformity across the federal system. You may wish to consult a practitioner or other expert for fields that lie outside your area of expertise.

Please score the degree of uniformity on a scale of 1–7, whereby:

1 = no or low degree of uniformity
4 = medium degree of uniformity
7 = high degree of uniformity

Note that 1 and 7 are not to be considered ideal points never achieved in practice. For example, a score of 1 would be compatible with the existence of some legal similarity, harmonization, or uniformity across a small subset of component states, as long as there is no or only minimal uniformity across the entire federal system. Conversely, a score of 7 would be compatible with a situation in which a single, centrally issued legal rule governs and yet there is some very minimal diversity in the process of adjudication.

Do not use a score of 4 in cases where you do not know and simply cannot ascertain the level of uniformity or in situations where a uniformity score, for whatever reason, is simply not applicable. If you remain unable to determine the level of uniformity for a given area even after consulting with another practitioner or expert or the question is simply inapplicable, please mark down a score of 0.

If, in any given area, we have omitted a significant specialized sub-area that would be scored differently from the general area, please explain and if possible, provide a score for that area in a separate note which you may attach in an appendix. (For example, in the area of torts, we have broken out the sub-field of "products liability;" in the area of criminal law, it might make sense in a particular system to break out "drug offenses".)

After scoring the degree of uniformity, please check off the applicable box(es) to indicate the principal means by which the degree of uniformity is achieved for that particular area. Please check off more than one box whenever applicable. Please use an X to mark the box.

Please also check off the applicable box(es) indicating the principal sources or reasons for diversity for that particular area.

Finally, we invite you to create a brief appendix with any comments you may have on individual scorecard entries.

Unification Scorecard
Uniformity Diversity
due to

	Uniformity score #, 1 (low) to 7 (high)	Directly applicable constitutional norm	Directly applicable central legislation	Central mandates that component states pass conforming laws	Central financial inducement to the component states	Central threat to displace nonconforming state legislation	Central judiciary's creation of uniform norms	Component state legislatures' horizontal coordination	Component judiciaries' horizontal coordination	Non-state actors' efforts to create restatements	Non-state actors' efforts to create model laws	Private industry standards and practices	International legal obligations	International voluntary coordination	Exclusive component state power	Concurrent component state power	Exclusive municipal or sub-state power	Concurrent municipal or sub-state power
1. PRIVATE LAW **A. Classic core** 1. Contracts																		
(a) *General*																		
(b) *Commercial*																		
(c) *Consumer*																		
2. Tort																		
(a) *General*																		
(b) *Products liability*																		
3. Property																		
(a) *Real*																		
(b) *Personal*																		
(c) *Secured transactions*																		

4. Family	
(a) *Marriage*	
(b) *Divorce*	
(c) *Parents and children (incl. custody)*	
(d) *Adoption*	
5. Succession	
(a) *Wills*	
(b) *Intestate succession*	
(c) *Trust arrangements (or the equivalent)*	
B. Commercial law and economic regulation	
1. Business organizations	
2. Securities regulation	
3. Antitrust/competition law	
4. Labor	
(a) *Collective bargaining*	
(b) *Employment*	
5. Negotiable instruments	
6. Intellectual property	
7. Banking	
8. Insurance	
9. Bankruptcy	
2. Criminal law	

(a) Definition of crimes (and defenses)														
(b) Sentences														
3. PUBLIC LAW														
A. Constitutional														
1. Fundamental rights														
2. Organizational structure of the state														
B. Administrative														
1. Police														
2. Zoning														
3. Water														
4. Environmental law														
5. Civil service														
6. Education														
7. Provision of social security														
8. Welfare														
4. TAX														
A. Personal income														
B. Corporate														
C. Sales/VAT														
D. Property														
E. Inheritance/ estate														

5. PROCEDURE													
A. Civil													
B. Criminal													
C. Administrative													
D. Private international law/conflicts law													
1. Domestic conflicts law (within the federation)													
2. International conflicts law (involving other countries)													
E. Arbitration													

Conclusion

We invite you to write a brief conclusion on the state of unification in your system more generally, e.g., discussing whether the predominant state of the law is full unification, mere harmonization, diversity of law with or without mutual recognition among the component states, and whether there is pressure to change the status quo. We have in mind an essay of between 250 and 500 words.

Appendix 3: Supplemental Expert Scorecard and Control Questions

Unification Scorecard

The following unification scorecard asks you to assess the degree of legal uniformity across a host of areas on a very basic scale and to indicate the predominant means/causes of uniformity and diversity.

We have listed various substantive and procedural areas of the law. Please indicate for each area your assessment of the degree of legal uniformity across the federal system. You may wish to consult a practitioner or other expert for fields that lie outside your area of expertise.

Please score the degree of uniformity on the following scale of 1–7:

1 = no or low degree of uniformity
4 = medium degree of uniformity
7 = high degree of uniformity

Note that 1 and 7 are not to be considered ideal points never achieved in practice. For example, a score of 1 would be compatible with the existence of some legal similarity, harmonization, or uniformity across a small subset of component states, as long as there is no or only minimal uniformity across the entire federal system. Conversely, a score of 7 would be compatible with a situation in which a single, centrally issued legal rule governs and yet there is some very minimal diversity in the process of adjudication.

Do not use a score of 4 in cases where you do not know and simply cannot ascertain the level of uniformity or in situations where a uniformity score, for whatever reason, is simply not applicable. If you remain unable to determine the level of uniformity for a given area even after consulting with another practitioner or expert or the question is simply inapplicable, please mark down a score of 0.

After completing Part A, please score the 8 generic scenarios in Part B.

Thank you very much for your effort and cooperation!

A. *Unification Scorecard for* _____

1. PRIVATE LAW **A. Classic core**	
1. Contracts	
(a) *General*	
(b) *Commercial*	
(c) *Consumer*	
2. Tort	
(a) *General*	
(b) *Products liability*	
3. Property	
(a) *Real*	
(b) *Personal*	
(c) *Secured transactions*	
4. Family	
(a) *Marriage*	
(b) *Divorce*	
(c) *Parents and children (incl. custody)*	
(d) *Adoption*	
5. Succession	
(a) *Wills*	
(b) *Intestate succession*	
(c) *Trust arrangements (or the equivalent)*	

B. Commercial law and economic regulation	
1. Business organizations	
2. Securities regulation	
3. Antitrust/competition law	
4. Labor	
(a) *Collective bargaining*	
(b) *Employment*	
5. Negotiable instruments	
6. Intellectual property	
7. Banking	
8. Insurance	
9. Bankruptcy	
2. CRIMINAL LAW	
A. Definition of crimes (and defenses)	
B. Sentences	
3. PUBLIC LAW	
A. Constitutional	
1. Fundamental rights	
2. Organizational structure of the state	
B. Administrative	
1. Police	
2. Zoning	
3. Water	
4. Environmental law	
5. Civil service	
6. Education	

7. Provision of social security	
8. Welfare	
4. TAX	
A. Personal income	
B. Corporate	
C. Sales/VAT	
D. Property	
E. Inheritance/estate	
5. PROCEDURE	
A. Civil	
B. Criminal	
C. Administrative	
D. Private international law/conflicts law	
1. Domestic conflicts law (within the federation)	
2. International conflicts law (involving other countries)	
E. Arbitration	

B. *Generic Scorecard*
On this page, we ask you to score 8 hypothetical legal scenarios. Please rate the uniformity of law in each of the following scenarios, using the same scale (1–7) that you used in the previous part. Each of the Federations in the following scenarios has 12 component states.

1. In the Federation of A, family law, including divorce, is a matter of component state law. All component states allow divorce on a no-fault basis (i.e., allowing divorce on demand), and all component states have the same marital property regime. In dividing marital property upon divorce, however, about half the component states penalize a party for marital fault, such as adultery, desertion, or physical violence against the spouse, while the other states do not consider such factors. *Please rate the uniformity of divorce law:* ____
2. In the Federation of B, speed limits are a matter of state law. Four component states set it at 55 mph, four at 60 mph, and four at 65 mph. *Please rate the uniformity of speed limits:* ____
3. In the Federation of C, there is a comprehensive statute (code) governing all aspects of criminal procedure in both the central and component state courts. There are differences in the lower courts' interpretation of various provisions of this statute, and there is a central supreme court which routinely resolves conflicts arising among the lower courts. *Please rate the uniformity of the law of criminal procedure:* ____
4. In the Federation of D, 11 are common law jurisdictions and thus recognize the institution of a trust while the twelfth is a civil law jurisdiction and does not. In that twelfth component state, there can be no division between legal and equitable title and hence no trust (only a contractual obligation to administer property in another's interest). *Please rate the uniformity of the law of trust:* ____
5. In the Federation of E, the law of commercial contracts is a matter of component state law and comprehensively codified on the component state level (i.e., each component state has its own statute comprehensively regulating commercial contracts). The text of these statutes is virtually identical. They are authoritatively interpreted by the component state supreme courts, which has created some differences in interpretation (e.g., states supreme courts draw the line between permissible liquidated damage clauses and impermissible penalty clauses differently). *Please rate the uniformity of the law of commercial contracts:* ____
6. In the Federation of F, the law of succession is exclusively a matter of component state law. Six component states recognize wills. The other six do not recognize wills, so that in these states all of a decedent's property is subject to the rules of intestate succession fixed by law. *Please rate the uniformity of the law of wills* ____

7. In the Federation of G, product liability is exclusively state law. About half of the component states impose strict liability for all defects. The remaining states impose strict liability only for manufacturing defects (defects affecting single items in a production line) but require the showing of negligence for design defects (defects affecting a whole production line) and instruction defects (insufficient warning). *Please rate the uniformity of the law of product liability*: ____
8. In the Federation of H, sales/VAT tax is exclusively a matter of component state law. Six component states impose a sales/VAT tax on all sales. The other six impose a sales/VAT tax only on luxury goods for personal consumption. (The tax rate is the same throughout the federation.) *Please rate the uniformity of the law of sales/VAT tax*: ____

Part II
National Reports

Chapter 2
The Argentine Federal Legislative System

Alfredo M. Vítolo

2.1 Overview

This essay analyzes the tensions existing in Argentina as a federal country, between federal and provincial (state) legislative power. When the Argentine Constitution was drafted more than a century and a half ago, the only federation then existing in the world was the United States, and our Founding Fathers looked to it as a model.[1] The result, however, was substantially different. Nowadays, and for different reasons, Argentina has a highly harmonized legal system, although the harmonization has been mostly obtained at the expense of federalism. Despite the Constitutional design, most legislation is federally enacted while only minor matters remain in fact within the powers of the provinces.

Section 2.1 of this essay will deal with the history of Argentina's federalism, trying to find a thread running through the development of its constitutional regime. In Sect. 2.2, I will describe the main features of Argentina's federalism, while Sect. 2.3 will be devoted to examining the division between federal, concurrent and provincial legislative powers, as well as the degree of harmonization existing at the different levels. Finally, in Sect. 2.4, I will try to reach some conclusions regarding the particular features of Argentina's federalism and legal system.

Alfredo M. Vítolo, Professor of Constitutional Law and Human Rights, University of Buenos Aires, Argentina. Board Member (2009–present), Argentine Association of Comparative Law.

[1] Our constitution is based on the Constitution of the United States, the sole model of federation existing in the world (see n. 10 infra).

A.M. Vítolo (✉)
Department of Public Law I Human Rights, University of Buenos Aires, Figueroa Alcorta 2263, C1425CKB Buenos Aires, Argentina

Argentine Association of Comparative Law, Buenos Aires, Argentina
e-mail: avitolo@derecho.uba.ar

2.2 A Brief History of Argentina's Federalism

There is no doubt that all federal regimes are transactional regimes[2]: they reflect a transaction between centrifugal, dispersive forces, which emphasizes government within small communities, and centripetal, centralizing, ones trying to make those communities mere administrative divisions subject to central power.[3] But sociological reality and historical development cause these forces to work differently in different nations. This consideration was clearly present in the minds of the Argentine Constitution's Founding Fathers. While they took the United States Constitution as their model, they turned this model into an original creation in its own right.[4] As Alexis de Tocqueville indicated in Democracy in America: "the growth of nations presents something analogous to this; they all bear some marks of their origin. The circumstances that accompanied their birth and contributed to their development affected the whole term of their being".[5]

After obtaining political independence from Spain (1810–1816), the people of the former *Virreynato del Río de la Plata*, located at the southernmost tip of the Americas, began a 40-year discussion (which on many occasions turned into military confrontations) about the best possible political structure for the new country. For the time being, this situation prevented the adoption of a sustainable constitutional regime. Under Spanish rule, the *Virreynato* had had a *de jure* centralized form of government. Yet, the distances between the different cities (as well as the distance between Spain and the colonies), and the poor means of communication created a need for local governments which, during colonial times, were represented by the institution of the *cabildos* (town councils), following the Spanish continental tradition.

In 1776, the Spanish king Carlos III ordered the creation of the *Virreynato del Rio de la Plata* by separating its territory from the *Virreynato del Perú*. The new viceroyalty (which comprised the territory of today's Argentina, Uruguay, Paraguay, the south of Brazil, the south of Bolivia and the north of Chile) was created as a consequence of the Portuguese menace at the River Plate. For that reason, Buenos

---

[2] See James Bryce, *The American Commonwealth*, Vol. I, p. 48. Spanish translation by Adolfo Posada and Adolfo Buylla, Madrid, Spain.

[3] Jorge Reinaldo Vanossi, *Situación Actual del Federalismo*, Depalma, 1964, p. 3. John Jay, "The Federalist Papers *no.* 2' shows this tension: "It is well worthy of consideration ... whether it would conduce more to the interest of the people of America that they should, to all general purposes, be one nation, under one federal Government, than that they should divide themselves into separate confederacies, and give to the head of each, the same kind of powers which they are advised to place in one national Government."

[4] See, among others, Dardo Pérez Guilhou, *Historia de la originalidad constitucional argentina*, Instituto Argentino de Estudios Constitucionales y Políticos, Mendoza, 1994.

[5] Alexis de Tocqueville, *Democracy in America*, First Part, Chapter II (1835).

Aires, then a small port city of merchants (and smugglers) located on the western margin of the river, was made capital in preference to the more important internal cities of Córdoba and Chuquisaca (now Bolivia).[6]

A few years later, the most important reform of the legal structure of Spain's American colonies was adopted, when Carlos III enacted the *Real Ordenanza de Intendentes*. Under this ordinance, the viceroyalty was divided into eight *intendencias* (provinces) and four *gobernaciones* (governorships), each with their local government with greater power than that held by the previous governors, though each still subject to the legal authority of the viceroy. This ordinance has been considered by some historians as the legal starting point of Argentina's federalism.[7]

In 1806 and 1807, British attempts to invade Buenos Aires were repelled. These attempts made viceroy Sobremonte flee inland to Cordoba, leaving Buenos Aires to its own devices, and creating in its people a strong sense and desire for self-government. This sense was strengthened by the fact that many of the city's leaders were influenced by the ideas of the French and American revolutions, and by the philosophies and political theories of Montesquieu, Rousseau, and Locke.

When the Spanish government fell under Napoleon's hands in May of 1810, the people of Buenos Aires, reflecting the new political ideas of the time regarding the source of political power, held a general assembly (*cabildo abierto*) and demanded the reversion of sovereignty to the people.

On that occasion, however, those in favor of the *status quo* stressed the point that the meeting was only a local one, and that the *cabildo* of Buenos Aires – a local municipal body – alone could not represent the whole of the *Virreynato* and depose the viceroy. In order to solve this problem, an interim *Junta* was established to replace the viceroy. In one of its initial actions, this *Junta* invited the other main cities of the viceroyalty to send their representatives in order to form the *Junta Grande* (Big Junta). In this manner, the federal nature of our national government was fixed from the very beginning of our nation's independent life.[8]

Yet, the discussion at the *cabildo abierto* of May 22, 1810 was in fact the beginning of a major struggle between *unitarios* (those in favor of a centralized government, based in Buenos Aires) and *federales* (favoring the federation); this conflict dominated the first half of the nineteenth century and led to petty civil wars and anarchy. During that era, two constitutional initiatives, one in 1819, and the other in 1826, led essentially by the Buenos Aires elites, tried unsuccessfully to organize the national government as a centralized and unified regime. In between

---

[6]For a more complete description on the rise of Buenos Aires, *see generally,* David Rock, *Argentina, 1516–1987,* University of California Press, 1987, chapter II.

[7]See, for example, María Laura Sanmartino de Dromi, *La Real Ordenanza de Intendencias de Carlos III y el origen del federalismo argentino*, Universidad Complutense de Madrid, 1989.

[8]As indicated by Juan Bautista Alberdi, the most influential constitutional scholar of the time and a key influence in the drafting of the Constitution (although he did not form part of the Constitutional Convention): "The May Revolution... created a state of things that over the course of the years has acquired legitimacy: it created the provincial regime" (Juan Bautista Alberdi, *Bases y puntos de partida para la organización política de la República Argentina*, El Ateneo, Madrid, 1913, p. 158).

those two failed attempts, the fall of the national government (Directoriate) in 1820 marked the beginning of a 30-year period without any national government. While some scholars considered this an anarchical period, others saw it as a period for the consolidation of the local (provincial) political structures, which years later would give birth to the Constitution.[9]

The final triumph of the *federales* in 1852 led to the adoption of the 1853–1860 Constitution,[10] modeled along the lines of the US Constitution, the "*sole federative model [then] existing in the world*", in the words of José B. Gorostiaga, one of the Founding Fathers and a key drafter of the Constitution.[11] This Constitution, which, though amended several times (most recently in 1994) remains in force, specifically provides that "the Argentine Nation adopts the federal, representative and republican form of government".[12]

2.3 The Main Features of Argentina's Federalism

Despite being drafted along the lines of the US constitutional model, Argentine federalism has its own unique features. As Juan Bautista Alberdi explained, the differences between the two countries were substantial: "... Different from what has happened in the North American [British] colonies, throughout its colonial history, the Argentine Republic has formed a single people, a sole and big consolidated state, a unitary colony... forbidding us to consider the Argentine Republic as something different than a single state, although federal and composed by many provinces, each with their own sovereignty and limited and subordinated liberties".[13]

The Constitution acknowledges the prior existence of the member states (provinces), even indicating that the constitutional convention delegates which adopted the Constitution as representatives of the people of the Argentine Nation, did so, "by will and election of the provinces comprising the same",[14] and allows

---

[9]Jorge Reinaldo Vanossi, indicates that "the reference included in the Preamble [to the Constitution] to the will of the provinces as the key factor in the establishment of the Constitutional Convention, serves no other purpose than recognizing the role played by the provinces in the entire process leading to it" (Jorge R. Vanossi, *Situación Actual del Federalismo*, Depalma, 1964, p. 22).

[10]While the Constitution was enacted in 1853, the largest province, Buenos Aires, did not participate in the Constitutional Convention, and *de facto* seceded from the federation, even enacting its own constitution in 1854, where it declares its sovereignty. When in 1859, it rejoined the federation, the 1853 federal constitution was subject to a broad reform the following year, giving rise to what is now known as the "1853/1860 Constitution".

[11]Emilio Ravignani, *Asambleas Constituyentes Argentinas, Instituto de Investigaciones Históricas de la Facultad de Filosofía y Letras de la Universidad de Buenos Aires*, vol. IV, p. 468.

[12]Constitución de la Nación Argentina, *hereinafter* Arg. Const., Sec. 1.

[13]Juan B. Alberdi, *cit.*, p. 88.

[14]Arg. Const. Preamble. See also n. 8, *supra*.

Congress to admit new provinces to the national territory[15] (a process which ended in 1984 with the creation of the province of Tierra del Fuego, a former national territory).

The Constitution guarantees the provinces the free enjoyment of their own provincial institutions without interference of the federal government,[16] requiring solely that each member state enact its own constitution under the republican representative form of government, that it guarantee at least those rights and guarantees recognized by the federal Constitution, and that it secure the administration of justice, the municipal regime and the primary education of its people.[17] Under this clause, the whole federal Bill of Rights (the first part of the Constitution, entitled *"Declaraciones, Derechos y Garantías"* ("Declarations, Rights and Guarantees") acts essentially as a minimum standard for provincial regulation as it is directly enforceable against the provinces. Yet, these federal standards do not mean, as Joaquín V. González explained, a requirement that the local constitutions be "an identical, word-for-word copy or an almost exact and equal copy of the national one. For the provincial constitution is the code that condenses, organizes and gives imperative force to the whole natural law that the local community has to govern itself, to all the inherent original sovereignty, which [sovereignty] has only been delegated [to the central government] for the ample and broad purpose of founding the Nation. Therefore, within the legal mold of the codes of rights and powers of a [provincial constitution,] there may be the broadest variety that can be found in the diversity of the physical, social, and historical characteristics of each region or province, or in their particular wishes or collective abilities".[18] As indicated by one of the current Supreme Court justices, "federalism involves the recognition and respect towards the identity of each province, which constitutes a source of vitality for the republic since it allows a plurality of experiments and the provincial search of their own ways to design, maintain and perfect the local republican systems".[19]

Nonetheless, the Constitution of 1853 included some unique features which placed strong limitations on provincial autonomy and federalism. Among other restrictions, it specifically required that the provincial constitutions be subject to prior approval by the federal Congress, and it subjected local governors to federal impeachment, among other restrictive clauses. The 1860 amendment, however,

---

[15] Arg. Const. Sec. 13.

[16] Arg. Const., Sec. 122. As indicated by the Supreme Court in one of its early cases: *"the Federal Constitution of the Republic was adopted for its governing as a Nation and not for the individual government of the Provinces, which according to Sec. 105 (now 122) have the right to be ruled by their own institutions... meaning that they preserve absolute sovereignty in all those matters relating to the non delegated powers"* (*D. Luis Resoagli v. Prov. de Corrientes s/cobro de pesos*, FALLOS 7–373 (1869)).

[17] Arg. Const., Secs. 5, and 123.

[18] Joaquín V. González, *Manual de la Constitución Argentina*, pp. 648–649.

[19] *Partido Justicialista de la Provincia de Santa Fe v. Provincia de Santa Fe s/acción declarativa*, Carlos S. Fayt, concurring opinion. FALLOS, 317:1195 (1994).

enacted when the province of Buenos Aires rejoined the federation,[20] eliminated most of these limitations, including the two features just mentioned, with the idea to bring the Argentine Constitution more in line with its American model and to improve federalism. As the Report prepared by the Examining Commission of the Federal Constitution indicated, the reason for the elimination "rested in the respect to the fundamental principle of provincial sovereignty in all matters that do not harm the Nation. As stated before, each province shall have the right to use that sovereignty to its own limits, giving itself those laws it considers most convenient to its own happiness, for which it is not for Congress to legislate in the name of a Province, substituting the representation of that sovereignty, since that action undermines the fundamental principles of the federative association according to which the political personality of the people cannot be eliminated".[21] As we shall see, however, some other limitations on federalism remained.

2.4 Legislative Powers

Being a federal country formed by 23 provinces and 1 autonomous city (the city of Buenos Aires), in Argentina legislative power is shared between the federal Congress and the provincial legislatures. Section 121 of the federal Constitution states that "Provinces retain for themselves all powers not delegated by this Constitution to the federal Government". Residual legislative power thus lies with the provinces. Therefore, the federal congressional power is theoretically limited, since Congress can only pass laws on matters either expressly or implicitly allowed by the federal Constitution.

2.4.1 Substantive Law

Notwithstanding this basic allocation of power, the power of the federal Congress to enact legislation is broad, since the Constitution grants Congress the power not only to enact federal law with regard to certain limited, subjects (customs, interstate matters – including interstate commerce–, foreign affairs – including approving treaties–, immigration and citizenship, trademarks, patents, etc.) and all required laws to accommodate the federal interest in federal areas within each province (such as national parks, military installations, etc.), the respective laws being enforced by the federal courts; but also gives legislative power over all substantive law to the federation (civil, criminal, commercial, labor and mining), a major departure from the US model. This substantive law, although federally enacted, is applied and enforced by local (provincial) authorities.

---

[20]See note 9.
[21]Emilio S. Ravignani, *Asambleas Constituyentes...*, vol. IV, pp. 773.

The reason for this departure – which was the subject of a vigorous debate in the 1853 Constitutional Convention – lies in the history of our country and, to a certain extent, in the political battles of the time. As to the first reason, the system reflects the already mentioned Spanish tradition where, contrary to the US development, the whole *Virreynato* was subject to a single set of laws (other than petty municipal matters entrusted to the local *cabildos*).[22] As to the underlying political reasons, although the Constitution was the result of the triumph of the *federales* (those in favor of the federation), the supporters of a centralized form of government remained strong. At the Constitutional Convention, the fear of a return to periods of anarchy as a consequence of multiple legislation on the same matters, and a lack of trust of the competence of the provincial legislatures to enact complex laws (both as a political and a technical matter),[23] decided the final outcome.

At the Constitutional Convention, Gorostiaga, the main drafter of the Constitution, replied to the objections raised by Zavalía, who considered that granting Congress the power to enact substantive law would imply the plain destruction of federalism, arguing that "if each province is left with this power, the country's laws would become a great maze from which unconceivable ills will result".[24] Juan Bautista Alberdi concurred with this position: "a country with as many civil or criminal codes as provinces, will neither be a federal or centralized state, it would be chaotic".[25]

In this sense, Section 75 of the Constitution, which describes the powers of Congress, is a broad grant of federal legislative power, with subsection 12 being the main source of central government regulation. In its current wording, this clause provides: "Congress is empowered... § 12. To enact the Civil, Commercial, Criminal, Mining, Labor and Social Security Codes, in unified or separate bodies, provided that such codes do not alter local jurisdictions; and their enforcement shall correspond to the federal or provincial courts depending on the respective jurisdictions for persons or things; and particularly, to enact general laws of naturalization and nationality for the whole nation, based on the principle of nationality by birth or by option for the benefit of Argentina; as well as laws on bankruptcy, counterfeiting of currency and public documents of the State, and those laws that may be required to establish trial by jury".

In addition, Subsection 32 of the same Section 75 increases such powers, by sealing any gaps that might exist in congressional power: "Congress is empowered... § 32. To make all appropriate laws and rules to put into effect the aforementioned powers, and all other powers granted by this Constitution to the Government of the Argentine Nation".

---

[22]For a detailed analysis, see Clodomiro Zavalía, *Derecho Federal*, Tercera Edición, Compañía Argentina de Editores, Buenos Aires, 1941, Chap. 1.

[23]*See* José Manuel Estrada, *Curso de Derecho Constitucional*, 2da. Edición, Tomo III, ECYLA, 1927, p. 25.

[24]Emilio Ravignani, *Asambleas constituyentes...*, Vol. *IV*, p. 528.

[25]Juan Bautista Alberdi, *Elementos de Derecho Público Provincial Argentino*, 1ra. Parte, Cap. 1, §I, El Ateneo, Madrid, 1913, p. 285. See also Joaquín V. González, *cit.*, p. 487.

Therefore, according to the Constitution, all civil (contracts, torts, property, obligations, family law and estates), criminal, commercial, mining as well as labor and social security laws are enacted by the federal Congress, although, as mentioned, their enforcement is entrusted to the provincial authorities, and any cases involving such matters are litigated before provincial judges.[26]

As a consequence of this broad delegation of authority, the provinces are expressly forbidden to enact legislation on these matters.[27] In this sense, the federal Supreme Court has interpreted the constitutional grant of authority in a manner highly deferential to the federal power, indicating that "all laws providing for the private relations of the inhabitants of the Republic ... are within the power to enact the fundamental codes that the Constitution grants exclusively to Congress",[28] and that *"our decisions have reiterated that this power is exclusive ... [, therefore], its exercise cannot be shared by the provincial autonomies, who may only consider the advantages or disadvantages of the [congressionally enacted] institutions, leaving them subsistent or promoting their reform"*.[29] Only if Congress fails to enact those codes, or in subjects not covered by them, do the provinces retain their lawmaking power as regards such matters.

2.4.2 Exclusive Provincial Legislative Power

The provinces may, therefore, enact laws only on subjects other than those delegated to Congress by the Constitution This includes all matters pertaining to the structure of their respective provincial governments, police and municipal matters, as well as the power to lay and collect direct taxes (most of which, however, through the usage of uniform laws, has been delegated to the federal government), as well as on concurrent matters (see infra. Sect. 2.4.3). Defining the areas of provincial authority is not easy, given the broad federal grant. However, as one prominent and oft-cited scholar on federalism has indicated, that provincial power extends to all matters required for "the satisfaction of the needs required by the civil government of each province, having as their limits the inherent competences of the central government for the direction of the foreign relations and the satisfaction of the general requirements of the Nation".[30]

---

[26] Arg. Const., Sec. 75 § 12.

[27] Arg. Const., Secs. 121 and 126.

[28] *Rossi y Roca,* FALLOS, 147:29 (1926). Id. *Juan F. Shary*, FALLOS, 103:373 (1905); *Etcheverry c/Pcia. De Mendoza*, FALLOS, 133:161 (1920), among others.

[29] *Arizu,* FALLOS, 156:20 (1929), En igual sentido: *Manuel de la Orden c/Ingenio San Isidro S.R.L.*, FALLOS, 235:304 (1956).

[30] Arturo N. Bas, *El derecho federal argentino. Nación y provincias*, t. I, Ed. Abeledo-Perrot, 1927, p. 70.

2.4.3 Concurrent Powers

The Constitution expressly maintains certain delegated matters as concurrent powers of both the federal government and the provinces. This includes matters concerning human and economic development; the protection of natural resources and of the environment; education, recognition and protection of native communities, as well as the laying and collection of indirect taxes; the promotion of new industries; and the development of means of transportation.[31] In all these matters, however, federal law wins over local law in the event of conflict.

The Supremacy Clause, Section 31 of the Argentine Constitution, which is worded almost identical to Article VI, Paragraph 2 of the US Constitution, is clear in stating the supremacy of federal law: "This Constitution, the laws of the Nation enacted by Congress in pursuance thereof, and treaties with foreign powers, shall be the supreme law of the Nation; and the authorities of each province shall be bound thereby, notwithstanding any provision to the contrary included in the provincial laws or constitutions...".

In practice, in most areas of concurrent powers, the federal Congress enacts the framework rules, while the provinces complete the details with their local legislation. This authority has been strengthened by the 1994 amendment to the Constitution. Section 41 of the Constitution for example, requires Congress to "regulate the minimum [environmental] protection standards, and [require] the provinces [to enact] those rules necessary to reinforce them, without altering their local jurisdictions". In the same sense, Section 75, §19, empowers Congress "to enact organization and framework laws (*"leyes de organización y de bases"*) referring to education, consolidating national unity and respecting provincial and local characteristics".

2.4.4 Federal Establishments

Another area of potential conflict between national and provincial legislative power is the enactment of legislation to be applied in those geographic areas which, although within the territory of a Province, are used for federal purposes. In this matter, the original Section 75 §27 of the Constitution, modeled along Section 1, Subs. 8, §17 of the US Constitution, empowered Congress "to exercise exclusive legislation over... those places acquired by purchase or cession in any of the provinces, for the purpose of establishing fortresses, arsenals, magazines or other establishments of national service". The federal government considered that, according to the plain reading of the clause, those territories were in fact federalized so that all provincial power over them were excluded.[32]

---

[31] Arg. Const., Sec. 75 §18 and 19.
[32] Joaquín V. González, *Manual...*, *cit.*, p. 493.

The provinces, however, never accepted this interpretation and attempted in numerous instances to exercise police and taxation power over these territories, which the provinces continued to consider to be provincial. The Supreme Court was then required to specify the scope of the constitutional clause. It indicated that "exclusive legislation by the federal Congress in those areas acquired in the provinces for establishments of national service is that which concerns the fulfillment of the purpose of the [federal] establishment; and provincial legislative and administrative powers in the area are not excluded, except as they interfere, directly or indirectly, with the fulfillment of the federal aim".[33] The Court considered that the national purpose of the establishment cannot "damage the constitutional foundations of provincial autonomy, which would happen if the acquisition of the property would transfer to the new owner, if that is the Nation, the political power over the same".[34]

The discussion was finally settled by the 1994 constitutional amendment, which amended the clause (now Section 75 §30) deleting the "exclusivity" provision, and clarifying its scope. The clause now reads, along the lines of case law precedents: "Congress shall have the power... to enact the legislation necessary for the achievement of the specific ends of premises of national interest in the territory of the Republic. Provincial and municipal authorities shall hold power to levy taxes and power of police over these premises, insofar as they do not interfere with the achievement of those ends".

2.4.5 Uniform Laws – Taxation

In addition, Congress has found other mechanisms to increase its lawmaking power at the expense of the provinces. The constant usage, since the mid-1930s, of "Uniform Laws" (*leyes convenio*), to be approved and adopted by the provinces, and the already mentioned precedence that federal law has over provincial law in concurrent matters (education, environmental, development, etc.), have greatly diminished the role of local legislatures.

Under these schemes, some provincial legislatures have entered into harmonization agreements with the federal government. These agreements were then put for other provinces to join (e.g. the Inter-Tribunal Communications Act, Law 22,172). In addition, the federal Constitution encourages the provinces to enter into inter-provincial treaties for purposes of their economic and social development.[35] Still, most of the harmonization process is federally-driven, especially as regards the imposition and collection of taxes.

---

[33] *Marconneti, Boglione y Cía.*, FALLOS 154:312 (1929); *Frigorífico Armour*, FALLOS 155:104 (1929); *Cardillo c/S.A. Marconetti Ltda.*, FALLOS 240:311 (1958).
[34] *Cardillo, cit.*
[35] Arg. Const., Sec. 125.

Congressional legislation usually "invites" the provinces to adhere to national standards. While such adherence is voluntary in theory, the political pressure from the central government is high, and the provinces usually either follow the national directive or suffer the consequences of not receiving federal funds.

In this context, the federal government is allowed to grant subsidies and other financial aids to those provinces whose own funds are insufficient. This mechanism has been customarily used by different administrations to align the provinces with the federal government's aims.

In addition, the Constitution, after the 1994 amendment, expressly allowed the federal creation and collection of certain taxes, as a concurrent power with the provinces a matter which had formerly been within the exclusive realm of the provinces (but a matter which the provinces had long ago surrendered). The new clause requires that these taxes should be shared between the federal government and the provinces by means of an agreed sharing regime (*coparticipación*), and that the transfer of funds to the provinces be automatic.[36] The underlying rationale for this mechanism was that it would help to reduce the development gap between rich and poor provinces, creating what has been called "concerted federalism" (*federalismo de concertación*).[37] Yet, even though almost twenty years have passed since the constitutional amendment was enacted, no sustainable agreement as regards the sharing of the funds has yet been reached. As a result, the system still operates under a rule established by the military government back in the 1970s, a time when federalism was *de facto* suspended.

This sharing regime has essentially proven a failure since the federal government maintains the highest portion of such funds, and the richest provinces are reluctant to reduce their share, arguing that they receive the highest portion of internal migration (roughly 40 % of the country's total population live in the Province of Buenos Aires alone – which does not even include the city of Buenos Aires).

A specific body, the *Comisión Federal de Impuestos* (Federal Tax Commission) formed by representatives of the federal and provincial governments, is entrusted with the task of overseeing the system and of resolving conflicts that may appear between local and federal claims to shared taxes. This body acts as a main source of harmonization as regards tax legislation at all levels.

2.4.6 Municipal Legislation

The Constitution, in its 1853/1860 wording, required the provinces and their constitutions to ensure the municipal regime.[38] That, however, was the beginning of a long discussion as to whether the municipalities were true autonomous bodies or

---

[36] Arg. Const. Sec. 75 §2.
[37] Pedro J. Frías, *Introducción al derecho público provincial*, 1980, p. 217.
[38] Arg. Const., Sec 5.

mere decentralized agencies of the provincial governments. The 1994 constitutional amendment, following the trend started by the Supreme Court in the *Rivademar* case,[39] added to the constitutional older provision the requirement that the municipalities be autonomous *vis-à-vis* the provincial (state) government.[40] Based on that, each municipality within the provinces is entitled to enact its own municipal charter, determine its own form of government (within the representative republican model), elect its own officers, enact local regulations and collect local taxes (generally, permits, sewage, lighting, and other local utilities' fees). Despite the autonomy granted by the federal constitution to provincial municipalities, it is important to note that municipal legislation is pretty similar throughout the country, although no specific harmonization rules exist.[41] In addition, since not all provinces have yet completed the system reform required by the 1994 constitutional amendment, in many provinces a unique and unified municipal system exists (e.g., in the province of Buenos Aires). Finally, big municipalities within the greater Buenos Aires area, whose low income population exceeds that of many small provinces, are also usually hostages to political pressures from the federal government: either they agree with national directives (sometimes contrary to the political orientation of the provincial government) or they find themselves excluded from large grants of federal funds. This system allows the local officers to stay in power, and it *de facto* contributes to legal harmonization.

Another source of legal harmonization is that it has been customary for provincial governments to enter into agreements with sister provinces of their same region on common matters – practice that is encouraged by the Constitution after the 1994 amendment.[42] In this context, the provinces have established a number of inter-provincial agencies to help them in reaching common grounds vis-à-vis the federal government (for example, the *Consejo Federal de Inversiones* – Federal Investment Council).

2.4.7 Regionalization

One of the key aims proclaimed by the 1994 constitutional amendment was to improve federalism. In order to improve the situation of the provinces, the Constitution expressly authorized them to create regions for their social and economic development.[43] This new feature of the Argentine Constitution will help the provinces to adopt harmonized policies and legislation to solve their common needs. It is therefore a key instrument towards harmonization of the law in the country.

---

[39] FALLOS 312:326 (1989).

[40] Arg. Const., Sec. 123.

[41] See, María Gabriela Abalos, *Autonomía Municipal: ¿Realidad o utopía?*, Mendoza, 2007.

[42] Arg. Const., Secs 124 and 125.

[43] Arg. Const., Sec. 124.

2.4.8 Case Law as a Source of Harmonization – Court Reports – Legal Education and Admission to the Bar

The legislative system in Argentina must be considered highly harmonized because, as mentioned above[44], all substantive legislation is federally enacted (though locally applied), and for the other reasons explained in this essay.

Still, as also mentioned, according to the federal Constitution, the judicial jurisdiction over federally-enacted substantive law remains with the provinces (save for those limited cases of federal *in personam* jurisdiction).[45] Thus, each province enacts its own procedural rules and sets up its own provincial courts whose decisions are final and not appealable to the federal courts, save for special situations in which the supremacy of the Constitution or of federal law is at stake. To the extent that the provinces are autonomous bodies, there is no court with the power to unify the interpretation given by provincial judges of substantive federally-enacted law (unlike the situation, e.g., in France with the *Cour de Cassation*). Even in those limited cases where a provincial high court decision involving substantive law can be taken to the Supreme Court by means of a special discretionary proceeding (*Recurso Extraordinario*), the Supreme Court does not have the power to extend its ruling beyond the particular case at hand since there is no constitutionally-mandated *stare decisis* principle.

Yet, although the absence of a final authority regarding the interpretation of (federal) substantive law may lead to substantially different legal constructions, this has not occurred. Many factors have contributed to maintaining a highly harmonized system.

To begin with, until very recently, law reviews and case reports (managed by private commercial companies were focused mainly on cases from the main jurisdictions (essentially the city of Buenos Aires) even though they had a nationwide circulation. Therefore, lawyers and judges in the provinces have as their main source of reference the same set of cases. This is also the case with law treatises and other reference materials.

In addition, courts at all levels are increasingly trying to interact, searching for common grounds to resolve cases. In 1994, provincial supreme courts established a body called JUFEJUS, the *Junta Federal de Cortes y Superiores Tribunales de Justicia*, which unites all members of the highest judicial bodies in each province. Its aims are, among others, to foster the independence of the judiciary and to contribute to the training of provincial judges and magistrates. Since 2006, on the initiative of the Supreme Court, an annual judicial conference has been held which involves both provincial and federal judges. These bodies actually help judges to share their experience and to reach common grounds, thus serving as a major source of harmonization of judicial practice and interpretation. We must

---

[44] See Sec. 2.4.1 supra
[45] Arg. Const. Sec. 75 §12.

also mention that, at the request of the Second National Judicial Conference, the Supreme Court established an internet portal, the *Centro de Información Judicial* (Judicial Information Center, www.cij.gov.ar), to act as a resource-sharing tool for judges of all jurisdictions. Finally, there are other internet sites both official and private, which provide access to judicial decisions and academic publications.

While the influence of non-state actors in the harmonization process is limited, one major source is legal education. Most law schools in the country are federally accredited, which means that they follow national standards and that their degrees are recognized countrywide. While the law school curricula in the provinces (even in national universities) include courses on "provincial laws and institutions", most of their curricula are heavily loaded with courses on substantive (uniform) law and on federal laws and regulations. Additionally, provincial law schools do not attract as many students as the national ones (Buenos Aires and Córdoba being the most important), which draw their pool of students from throughout the country.

Law degrees allow law school graduates to practice law in the whole country without having to pass any additional exam or admission test. The only requirement for admission to legal practice is the (formal) registration before the local (provincial) bar. Thus graduates can set up their practices anywhere within the country, which has also helped the creation of a unified view of the law.

Local bar and lawyers' associations throughout the country usually organize continuing legal education courses, and such courses or seminars rarely relate to local laws and practices. Their pool of professors and instructors is generally drawn from bar associations of large cities. While the courses are not mandatory, they contribute to form a common vision of the law countrywide.

2.4.9 *International and Community Law*

The influence of international law and community law (*Mercosur*) on the practice of law in the provinces is limited, essentially due to lack of knowledge and training of local judges and practitioners.

The 1994 constitutional amendment, however, has granted international law a key position in the Argentine hierarchy of rules. The 1853 Constitution, with a wording similar to the US Constitution, established that international treaties, together with the Constitution and federal laws were the "supreme law of the land", taking precedence over provincial laws.[46] Still, the possibility that a local court had to deal with a matter involving an international treaty was very limited. This situation has recently changed due to the proliferation of Human Rights' treaties which establish obligations of countries as regards all people within their jurisdiction and which

---

[46] Arg. Const. Sec. 31.

require federal countries "to adopt appropriate provisions for the fulfillment" of the obligations by the constituent units of the federation.[47]

Endorsing a 1992 Supreme Court decision[48] holding that international treaties have precedence over internal legislation, the constitutional amendment of 1994 ratified this principle and even gave "constitutional hierarchy"[49] to a series of enumerated international documents. All these treaties are self-executing and thus constitute binding domestic law, enforceable in both federal and state courts. The same is true for the rules enacted by the *Mercosur* and other international bodies, which the Argentine Constitution also grants precedence over federal and state laws.[50] Moreover, recent Supreme Court's decisions have required that judges take international laws and international rulings (such as those of the Inter-American Court of Human Rights) into consideration. In their exercise of judicial review, judges should thus subject internal laws and regulations to scrutiny under international conventions; this entails the power to declare such laws "unconventional".[51]

This situation is surely a major step towards legal harmonization, not only at the national, but also at the international level.

2.5 Conclusion

The analysis shows why the constitutional design of Argentina can – and has been – defined as a "Unified Federation" (*Unidad Federativa*): although the underlying regime is a federal system, the Constitution allocates numerous and crucial powers to the central (federal) government. In reality, the federation has shifted to a highly centralized government. The main reasons for that development are the limited practice of democratic government (during most of the period 1930–1983, the country was under military rule which mostly disregarded provincial autonomy), and the recurrent economic crises, which have made the provinces highly dependent on federal funds., Recent trends, however, which have started with the constitutional amendment of 1994, can bring new strength to federalism, at least in the form originally envisaged by our Founding Fathers. Harmonization of laws at both the national and international levels is an important goal, but it should not be pursued at the expense of the autonomy of the constituent entities of the country or the sovereignty of nations.

---

[47] *See*, for example, American Convention on Human Rights, Sec. 28§2.
[48] *Ekmekdjián c. Sofovich*, FALLOS 315:1492 (1992).
[49] Arg. Const., Sec. 75 §22.
[50] Arg. Const. Sec. 75 §24.
[51] *Mazzeo*, FALLOS 330:3248 (2007).

Chapter 3
The Australian Federation: A Story of the Centralization of Power

Cheryl Saunders and Michelle Foster

3.1 Overview

The Australian federation comprises a national or Commonwealth government and six States. Australia also has three self-governing territories and several dependent territories. The self-governing territories are often treated in the same way as the States for practical purposes but they do not have the same measure of constitutional autonomy as the States and will not be dealt with further in this chapter. The Commonwealth Constitution enumerates 40 legislative powers that are assigned to the Commonwealth, primarily in section 51. One, in section 51(xxxix), authorizes legislation "incidental to the exercise of any power vested by this Constitution ... in the Government," thus also bringing the executive power into play. Unless a Commonwealth power is exclusive, expressly or by necessary implication,[1] the States retain concurrent power in these areas. In the event of inconsistency between Commonwealth and State law, the former prevails, under section 109 of the Constitution.

The High Court of Australia sits at the apex of the Australian judiciary as the final appellate court in both federal and State jurisdiction. The Court also interprets and applies the Commonwealth Constitution, both in its original jurisdiction and on appeal from other courts. The High Court's interpretative method has changed significantly over time, with implications for the federal division of power. For two decades from the time of federation in 1901, two interpretative techniques tended to favour State over Commonwealth power. The doctrine of implied immunity of

---

[1] Australian Constitution, ss 52, 90, 114.

C. Saunders (✉) • M. Foster
Melbourne Law School, University of Melbourne, University Square,
185 Pelham St., Carlton 3035, VIC, Australia
e-mail: c.saunders@unimelb.edu.au; m.foster@unimelb.edu.au

instrumentalities proceeded on the assumption that the Commonwealth and States generally were immune from each other's laws.[2] In resolving ambiguities in the meaning and scope of Commonwealth powers, the doctrine of reserved State powers drew on an assumption that the Constitution reserved to the States all powers not expressly conferred on the Commonwealth.[3]

The *Engineers' Case*[4] marked the end of this phase of judicial federalism. The High Court overturned previous authority and held that the Constitution should be interpreted literally, without preconceived notions about federalism or reserved State powers. In conjunction with an interpretive principle associated with Justice O'Connor in *Jumbunna*,[5] that the words of a Constitution should be interpreted broadly, this literal and generous approach to constitutional interpretation has produced a progressive expansion of Commonwealth legislative power. The High Court now gives full effect to the literal terms of the enumerated heads of Commonwealth power. Attempts to limit their scope in the interests of federal "balance" typically are rejected – with rhetorical flourish – as invoking the discredited reserved powers doctrine.[6]

Despite this prevalent trend, conceptions of federalism retain some influence at the margin. Although the *Engineers' Case* repudiated reliance on implications drawn from federalism, by 1947 earlier hints[7] that there might after all be implied limitations on Commonwealth powers crystallized. In *Melbourne Corporation*,[8] the Court held that the Commonwealth cannot use its power to discriminate against a State or States or to threaten the continued existence of the States or their capacity to function. The principle has occasionally been applied to invalidate Commonwealth law, most recently in 2009.[9] Federalism also has played a role in two recent, significant decisions concerning the scope of the executive power in section 61.[10] It now is clear that the inherent executive power of the government

---

[2] The most cited case for this is *D'Emden v Pedder* (1904) 1 CLR 91.

[3] See, e.g., *R. v. Barger* (1908) 6 CLR 41; *Huddart Parker & Co Pty Ltd v. Moorehead* (1909) 8 CLR 330.

[4] *Amalgamated Society of Engineers v. Adelaide Steamship Co Ltd* (1920) 28 CLR 129 ('*Engineers' Case*').

[5] *Jumbunna Coal Mine NL v. Victorian Coal Miners' Association* (1908) 6 CLR 309.

[6] See, e.g., *Commonwealth v. Tasmania* (1983) 158 CLR 1. The most recent example of the High Court's categorical rejection of federalism arguments as a potential restriction on Commonwealth power is the 'Workchoices' decision: see *NSW v. the Commonwealth* (2006) 229 CLR 1.

[7] *West v. Commissioner of Taxation (NSW)* (1937) 56 CLR 657; *Federal Commissioner of Taxation v. Official Liquidator of EO Farley Ltd* (1940) 63 CLR 278.

[8] *Melbourne Corporation v. Commonwealth* (1947) 74 CLR 31.

[9] *Queensland Electricity Commission v. Commonwealth* (1985) 159 CLR 192; *Re Australian Education Union; Ex parte Victoria* (1995) 184 CLR 188; *Victoria v. Commonwealth* (1996) 187 CLR 416 ('*Industrial Relations Act Case*'); *Austin v. Commonwealth* (2003) 215 CLR 185; *Clarke v Commissioner of Taxation* (2009) 240 CLR 272.

[10] *Pape v Federal Commissioner of Taxation* (2009) 238 CLR 1; *Williams v Commonwealth* [2012] HCA 23; (2012) 288 ALR 410.

to act without authorization from Parliament is limited by considerations drawn from both federalism and representative democracy. In the more recent of these cases, the Court relied in part on considerations of federalism in finding that the Commonwealth required legislative authority to enter into at least some contracts and expenditure programs. Any such legislation must, of course, be supported by a source of federal legislative power.

3.2 The Federal Distribution and Exercise of Lawmaking Power

3.2.1 *Central Legislative Jurisdiction*

Section 51 of the Australian Constitution confers the following, largely concurrent powers on the Commonwealth:

- (i) trade and commerce with other countries, and among the States
- (ii) taxation
- (iii) bounties
- (iv) borrowing money on the public credit of the Commonwealth
- (v) postal, telegraphic, telephonic and other like services, including telecommunications
- (vi) defence
- (vii) lighthouses
- (viii) astronomy and meteorology
- (ix) quarantine
- (x) fisheries beyond territorial limits
- (xi) census and statistics
- (xii) currency
- (xiii) banking other than State banking
- (xiv) insurance other than State insurance
- (xv) weights and measures
- (xvi) bills of exchange and promissory notes
- (xvii) bankruptcy and insolvency
- (xviii) intellectual property
- (xix) naturalisation and aliens
- (xx) foreign corporations and trading or financial corporations formed within the limits of the Commonwealth (It has been held that this power does not enable the Commonwealth to form corporations.)
- (xxi) marriage
- (xxii) divorce
- (xxiii) invalid and old-age pensions
- (xxiiiA) various social security allowances and benefits

- (xxiv) service and execution of process
- (xxv) recognition of laws throughout Australia
- (xxvi) the people of any race for whom it is deemed necessary to make special laws
- (xxvii) immigration and emigration
- (xxviii) influx of criminals
- (xxix) external affairs
- (xxx) relations with Pacific islands
- (xxxi) acquisition of property on just terms for any purpose in respect of which the Parliament has power to make laws
- (xxxii) railways for military purpose
- (xxxiii) acquisition of railways, with State consent
- (xxxiv) railway construction, with State consent
- (xxxv) conciliation and arbitration for the prevention and settlement of industrial disputes extending beyond the limit of any one State
- (xxxvi) matters where the Constitution states "until the Parliament otherwise provides", for example, in respect of the electoral system and the qualifications of Members of Parliament.
- (xxxvii) matters referred by the Parliaments of the States
- (xxxviii) exercise of power that the United Kingdom could have exercised in 1901, on the request of the States
- (xxxix) matters incidental to the execution of any power vested by the Constitution in the Parliament, the government or the judiciary.

Section 52 confers exclusive power on the Commonwealth over:

- (i) choosing the seat of government
- (ii) matters relating to the public service
- (iii) other matters declared to be within the exclusive power of the Parliament. This includes imposition of customs and excise duties and bounties[11] and the raising of military forces.

In addition, the Commonwealth has a spending power, the scope of which is limited, although its precise boundaries require further clarification by the High Court.[12] The Commonwealth also has an express power to make grants to States "on such terms and conditions as the Parliament thinks fit",[13] which has been interpreted broadly to include grants in State areas of legislative competence.[14]

---

[11] Australian Constitution s 90.

[12] *Williams v the Commonwealth* [2012] HCA 23; (2012) 288 ALR 410. See also *Pape v Federal Commissioner of Taxation* (2009) 238 CLR 1.

[13] Australian Constitution s 96.

[14] *First Uniform Tax Case* (1942) 65 CLR 373; *Second Uniform Tax case* (1957) 99 CLR 575.

The powers in section 52 are expressed to be exclusive to the Commonwealth, as is the power to impose customs and excise duties and bounties.[15] Most of the powers specified in section 51 are concurrent, but some are exclusive to the central government in practice. Section 114 precludes the States from raising or maintaining a military force and thus effectively makes the defence power exclusive. Section 115 does the same for the power over currency, by prohibiting the States from coining money. Other powers are inherently available only to the Commonwealth. Borrowing on the public credit of the Commonwealth is an example.

The most important and frequently used constitutionally-specified sources authorizing central government regulation are taxation (section 51(ii)), corporations power (section 51(xx)), and external affairs (section 51(xxix)).

In practice, anything falling within the specified heads of power in section 51 is an important area of central government regulation. Of particular importance are the areas of competition law, consumer protection, corporations and securities regulation, intellectual property, most aspects of social security, immigration, maritime law, broadcasting and telecommunications, aviation, bankruptcy, banking, marriage, superannuation, the postal service, and indigenous affairs.

3.2.2 State Legislative Jurisdiction

The Constitution does not expressly allocate any legislative jurisdiction to the States, but provides that their pre-federation legislative powers continue subject to the provisions of the Commonwealth Constitution.[16] Thus the States have any power that is not expressly withdrawn from them, exclusively vested in the Commonwealth, or which the Commonwealth does not validly exercise (in a manner that excludes State power under section 109). In general, most areas of power allocated to the Commonwealth are concurrent powers. Notably, however, the areas of "state banking" and "state insurance" are reserved to the States as explicit exceptions from the powers conferred on the Commonwealth.

In the event of inconsistency between the two laws, the exercise of central concurrent power renders the State law invalid. Conflicts between central and component state laws are resolved under the principle of supremacy of federal law.[17] A broad approach to the meaning of inconsistency by the High Court means that Commonwealth legislation is deemed to be supreme not only where it is directly or indirectly inconsistent with State law, but where it merely evinces an intention to "cover the field" of regulation.[18] This interpretative trend further facilitates the centralization of Commonwealth power in Australia.

---

[15] Australian Constitution s 90.
[16] Australian Constitution s 107.
[17] Australian Constitution s 109.
[18] *Ansett Transport Industries (Operations) Pty Ltd v Wardley* (1980) 142 CLR 237.

In practice, the most important areas of predominant State regulation are in education, health, housing, transport, workplace accidents, civil (e.g., tort, contract, property) and criminal law, agriculture, municipal law, and water law. The most important areas in which central and component State regulation co-exist are consumer protection, industrial relations, anti-discrimination, human rights, and the environment.

The municipalities do not have significant law-making power. Their principal powers are garbage collection, some local planning, parks, gardens, and roads.

3.3 The Means and Methods of Legal Unification

3.3.1 Unification and Harmonization Through the Exercise of Central Power (Top Down)

There are a few constitutional norms, which in varying degrees apply to both Commonwealth and State legislation, and which may have a harmonizing effect. An implied freedom of political communication has led to some harmonization of laws, particularly with respect to defamation.[19] Limitations derived from Chapter III of the Constitution regarding the separation of powers require States to have a Supreme Court with supervisory jurisdiction in the State sphere,[20] and preclude the States from enacting legislation that would impair the integrity of the State court systems.[21] Section 92 of the Constitution also requires the freedom of interstate trade and commerce and precludes both spheres of government from enacting legislation that infringes that express freedom, as interpreted by the courts.[22]

Commonwealth legislation typically involves unification, as it generally applies equally to all States and renders inconsistent State law invalid. While the Commonwealth has never mandated that the States pass conforming implementing legislation and could not constitutionally do so, it may induce the States to regulate by conditioning central funding on compliance with central standards. This is an important means of legal unification or harmonization, since the Commonwealth has very substantial capacity to induce states to regulate pursuant to the grants power,[23] in a federation with a high degree of fiscal imbalance. Using the power in section 96 to grant financial assistance to any State on such conditions as it sees fit, the Commonwealth effectively took over tertiary education and has achieved a degree

---

[19] *Lange v Australian Broadcasting Commission* (1997) 189 CLR 520. All six states enacted uniform defamation laws which commenced on 1 January 2006.
[20] *Kirk v Industrial Relations Commission of New South Wales* (2010) 239 CLR 531.
[21] *Kable v Director of Public Prosecutions (NSW)* (1996) 189 CLR 51.
[22] See for example, *Betfair Pty Ltd v Western Australia* (2008) 234 CLR 418.
[23] Australian Constitution s 96.

of harmonization of school curricula. It should be noted that in some instances the imposition of conditions on financial grants from the Commonwealth is related to a set of agreed principles or criteria developed in consultation with the states, although the bargaining position of the two spheres of government is by no means equal. Since 2008, the regulatory framework for the making and implementation of grants arrangements is provided by the Intergovernmental Agreement on Federal Financial Relations,[24] and is given effect through the COAG Council System (of which more below).[25]

Occasionally, the Commonwealth will indirectly force the States to regulate by threatening to take over the field in the face of state inaction or state action that does not conform to the Commonwealth's standards. This happened, for example, in the field of environmental protection. Another example is in the field of defamation, where, following a number of unsuccessful attempts at establishing uniform law, the then federal Attorney-General threatened in 2004 to introduce a national defamation law if the states were unable to agree on a set of uniform laws. Ultimately, in 2005 each state enacted uniform defamation legislation effective from 1 January 2006.

The judicial branch plays a substantial role in creating unified norms. The High Court is the final appellate court for all Australian jurisdictions, and since High Court rulings bind all state judiciaries, there is only one common law in Australia. For example, in a case on appeal from the New South Wales Supreme Court, the High Court abandoned the "proximity" test for determining a duty of care in the tort of negligence, adopting a "salient features" approach.[26] As a result, all jurisdictions in Australia have followed suit.

3.3.2 Unification Through Voluntary Coordination Among the States (Bottom Up)

A considerable amount of uniformity and harmonization occurs in the Australian federation through voluntary co-ordination between States. For example, in 1993 the six states and two territories entered into the Australian Uniform Credit Laws Agreement, in which they acknowledged that it is in the interests of the public for laws regulating the provision of consumer credit to be uniform. Accordingly, they agreed to establish and implement a co-operative scheme, the objects of which are to ensure that "the legislation relating to the Scheme is, and continues to be, either uniform throughout Australia; or in any State or Territory where it is not uniform, consistent with the uniform laws".[27] Accordingly, "template" legislation was passed in Queensland in 1995,[28] and all other states and territories have passed

---

[24] http://www.coag.gov.au/the_federal_financial_relations_framework
[25] http://www.coag.gov.au/about_coag
[26] *Caltex Oil (Australia) Pty Ltd v Dredge "Willemstad"* (1976) 136 CLR 529.
[27] Australian Uniform Credit Laws Agreement 1993, Recital B(a)(i) and (ii).
[28] *Consumer Credit (Queensland) Act* 1994.

enabling legislation which adopts the template legislation and applies it in the State or Territory "as in force from time to time." It should be noted, however, that more often than not the Commonwealth also is involved in such co-operative models of regulation. There are presently almost 90 uniform legislative schemes, a list of which is maintained on the website of the Australasian Parliamentary Counsels' Committee.[29]

It may be noted that the Commonwealth Constitution also provides a "reference" power,[30] which gives the Commonwealth Parliament power to legislate on any matter referred to it by a State or States. References are voluntary; the Commonwealth cannot compel States to refer issues. The reference power has been used not merely for harmonization but also to ensure reciprocal recognition of standards through the enactment of the mutual recognition legislation. In 1992, the Heads of Government at the Commonwealth, State and Territory levels agreed "to establish a scheme for implementation of mutual recognition principles for goods and occupations for the purpose of promoting the goal of freedom of movement of goods and service providers in a national market in Australia."[31] In accordance with this agreement, the States referred legislative power to the Commonwealth to enable the enactment of the *Mutual Recognition Act 1992* (Cth).

Depending on whether the issue in the particular case involves the common law or statute, a State court may contribute to the harmonization of laws through consideration of prior decisions of courts in a sister State. Where a case involves the determination of principles of the common law, the interpretation or application of uniform national legislation, or even the interpretation of an "identical or substantially similar" statute to that of another state, the reasoning of an earlier court in another State will likely be followed on the basis of comity, unless the previous decision is clearly wrong or if particular considerations of justice apply in the instant case.[32]

Australia has a network of intergovernmental ministerial (or "COAG") councils with the central government as a key player. The COAG councils coordinate action across a range of government fields with varying degrees of effectiveness. The most important body is the Council for Australian Governments (COAG itself), which is the peak intergovernmental forum in Australia, comprising the Prime Minister, State Premiers, Territory Chief Ministers and the President of the Australian Local Government Association (ALGA). Another COAG Council of particular relevance to law reform is the Standing Council on Law and Justice (SCLJ) which is composed of the federal Attorney-General as well as the state and territory Attorneys-General and the New Zealand Attorney-General. This is sometimes the forum through which uniform or model laws are developed.

---

[29] http://www.pcc.gov.au/uniform/National%20Uniform%20Legislation%20table.pdf

[30] Australian Constitution s 51 (xxxvii).

[31] Agreement Relating to Mutual Recognition, 1992, Recital A.

[32] *Farah Constructions Pty Ltd v Say-Dee Pty Ltd* (2007) 230 CLR 89.

3.3.3 Legal Unification Through Non-state Actors

While non-State actors do play a role in legal unification, this does not occur in the same way or to the same extent as in the United States. There are very few non-state actors that contribute to legal unification. Two examples are the Law Council of Australia and Standards Australia. There are some groups dedicated to a very particular issue: for example, the Property Law Reform Alliance is a coalition of legal and industry associations "committed to bring about uniformity and the reform of property law and procedures in Australia."[33] Certain State actors should be noted also, including the Australian Law Reform Commission and the equivalent State Commissions. These bodies are established within the public sector, but they are largely independent of the government. They prepare reports proposing reform of various areas of law which may lead to unification, although this is not a necessary consequence.

Non-State actors also do not systematically propose uniform or model laws, although again, the Law Reform Commissions may propose uniform law from time to time. The *Australian Law Reform Commission Act* 1996 (Cth), for example, provides that its functions include the consideration of proposals for "uniformity between State and Territory laws" in relation to matters referred to it by the Attorney-General,[34] and "for complementary Commonwealth, State and Territory laws about those matters".[35] An example of the ALRC's role in producing harmonization of laws is in respect of the laws of evidence. In a 1987 report, the ALRC recommended that there should be a uniform law of evidence throughout Australia and appended draft legislation to its report. In 1995, the Commonwealth and NSW parliaments each enacted legislation substantially based on the ALRC's draft legislation.[36] In 2001, Tasmania passed broadly similar legislation and Victoria followed suit in 2008.[37] Concrete steps gradually are being taken in other jurisdictions towards the harmonization of evidence laws in line with the uniform model.

There is some unification through industry standards and practices. Many industries have a common code of practice, such as the insurance industry code of practice. Standards Australia is a non-State body which develops industry standards. It is recognized as the peak standard setting body in Australia by the Commonwealth government.

Although few non-state actors contribute to legal unification, the work of the Law Reform Commissions provide a significant amount of input, albeit in a small range of areas due to the need for referrals and the time needed to prepare reports. The extent to which the reports are adopted varies.

---

[33] Submission to the Standing Committee on Legal and Constitutional Affairs, House of Representatives, 31st March 2005.

[34] *Australian Law Reform Commission Act* 1996 (Cth), s 21(1)(d).

[35] *Ibid*, s 21(1)(e).

[36] See the *Evidence Act 1995* (Cth) and *Evidence Act 1995* (NSW). The Acts are in most respects identical.

[37] *Evidence Act 2001* (Tas); *Evidence Act 2008* (Vic).

3.3.4 The Role of Legal Education in Unification of Law

Australian law schools draw students from throughout the federation, although the vast majority still attend university in their home state. The focus of legal education will depend first on whether the particular area of law studied is regulated by the common law or by statute, and if the latter, then under which statutory scheme. If the common law is predominant in a given area, legal education will focus on pronouncements of the common law by the High Court, in the context of developments throughout the common law world, and will also look at relevant judgments of other States. By contrast, if Commonwealth legislation is primary in the area, legal education will focus on this. And if State legislation is primary in the area, legal education will focus on the State statute with some reference to the legislation of other States. Very little legal education focuses on the intergovernmental schemes that now so dominate government in Australia; this is a problem that requires urgent attention.[38]

Testing for and admission to the bar is by component state, with mutual recognition of qualifications between the States. It is a fairly simple process for barristers to be cross-admitted to other States. When admitted to practice in a component state, it is then possible upon registration to practice in the federal courts wherever they sit in Australia at the time.

Graduates will often practice within the State of their education for a variety of personal reasons. For instance, having studied in that State, their network of friends and contacts would likely be similarly based in that state. One additional factor is that graduates will have been taught the legislation of that particular state, which might to some degree influence them to practice within the State of their education. However, there is no organized system whereby graduates must practice in the State of their education.

Some institutions of legal education also play a unifying role in the country. Central courts will take clerks from potentially anywhere in Australia. There also exists the College of Law, which runs continuing legal education courses and traineeships after university. This College only operates in Queensland, New South Wales and Victoria (thus, covering the most populated eastern states) as well as Western Australia. While this may not unify the substance of the law, it is likely to unify practice.

3.3.5 External Influences on Legal Unification

International law does not have immediate effect on Australian domestic law, which requires legislation first to be passed giving effect to both treaty and custom.

---

[38]A subject on the Law of Intergovernmental Relations is, however, offered at Masters level in at least one Law School.

3 The Australian Federation: A Story of the Centralization of Power

However, the Commonwealth has broad power to implement treaties through domestic legislation, as bona fide international obligations trigger central power, through the "external affairs" head of power.[39] An example is the *International Criminal Court Act 2002* (Cth) which was enacted in order to facilitate compliance with Australia's obligations following ratification of the Statute of the International Criminal Court.[40] States also may pass laws giving effect to international law, relying on the broad plenary power enjoyed by State parliaments.[41] One recent example is the Victorian Charter of Human Rights and Responsibilities Act 2006, which gives effect to the International Covenant on Civil and Political Rights. International law may also indirectly influence domestic law, through interpretation of statutes to comply with international norms. A prominent example of the impact of international law is the *Mabo* case, in which indigenous native title to land was recognized at common law on the basis of reasoning that took into account international human rights principles.[42]

Voluntary participation in international harmonization projects plays a role in legal unification. Australia's participation in the Hague Conference on Private International Law, the International Institute for the Unification of Private Law (UNIDROIT) and the United Nations Commission for International Trade Law (UNICITRAL) has supported federal legislation in a range of areas (which necessarily has a harmonizing effect), including civil aspects of international child abduction.[43] It has also had a role in the area of Intellectual Property through the Berne Convention, the Paris Convention, and WIPO.

3.4 Institutional and Social Background

3.4.1 The Judicial Branch

The High Court of Australia has the power to determine whether central legislation exceeds the lawmaking powers allocated to the Commonwealth. The High Court also has the power authoritatively to interpret component State law, and to resolve differences in legal interpretation among central and component state courts.

The High Court regularly polices constitutional limitations, although its interpretative method favours central power. A relatively prominent and recent example

---

[39] Australian Constitution s 51(xx).

[40] See also the *International Criminal Court (Consequential Amendments) Act 2002*, which amended the Criminal Code Act 1995 and other legislation as a consequence of the *International Criminal Court Act 2002*.

[41] See e.g., Section 16 of the Victorian Constitution.

[42] *Mabo v. Queensland [No 2]* (1992) 175 CLR 1.

[43] See R.G. Mortensen, *Private International Law in Australia* (Butterworths, 2006) at 23.

is *Workchoices*,[44] in which the Court held that the corporations power (s 51(xx)) supported extensive regulation of industrial relations in Australia. There are examples where central power was checked: for example, the *Incorporation Case*,[45] where the Commonwealth was held not to have the power to regulate incorporation of corporations, and *Austin*,[46] which invalidated a federal tax in its application to members of State judiciaries. The effectiveness of these limitations in restraining central power varies between each restriction.

There are both central and state courts, which are organized as follows: The central court system is made up of the High Court, Federal Court, Family Court, and Federal Magistrates Court. All have trial and appellate divisions except for the Federal Magistrates Court. Each State has a local and district court, as well as a Supreme Court and Court of Appeal. Each Territory has a local court, and a Supreme Court and Court of Appeal.

3.4.2 Relationship Between the Central and Component State Governments

The central government has no power to force component states to legislate. However, by use of the grants power,[47] the central government may offer a monetary incentive to legislate. The central government is responsible for executing central government law.

The States are represented in the Upper House (the Senate) of the bicameral legislature by Senators directly elected in each State. The States are equally represented, although in practice Senators vote along party lines. The system of proportional representation that is used for Senate elections enables independent candidates and minor parties to gain greater representation than is possible in the House of Representatives. As a result, the Senate has developed a role as a "house of review". The Senate has equal powers with the House of Representatives except with respect to bills appropriating money or imposing taxation, which cannot originate in the Senate, and most of which cannot be amended by the Senate, although such bills may be rejected.[48]

The Senate is directly elected by the people, in a manner which differs from elections for the House of Representatives in the following ways: (1) The Senate is elected on the basis of proportional representation, whereas elections for the

---

[44] *New South Wales v. Commonwealth* (2006) 229 CLR 1.
[45] *New South Wales v. Commonwealth* (1990) 169 CLR 482.
[46] *Austin v. Commonwealth* (2003) 215 CLR 185.
[47] Australian Constitution s 96.
[48] Australian Constitution s 53.

House of Representatives use preferential voting, a modification of the first past the post system; (2) Senators are elected for 6 years, with half retiring every 3 years. Members of the House of Representatives are elected for a maximum of 3 years; (3) Senators are chosen from the State as a single electorate.

Both the central government and the component states have a general taxing power. In practice, it is impossible for the States to impose income tax following the *Uniform Tax Cases*.[49] The power to impose customs and excise duties is exclusively vested in the central government and therefore cannot be exercised by the States.[50] Due to the High Court's broad interpretation of "excise duties",[51] the Commonwealth effectively has exclusive authority over the taxation of commodities.

There is no prohibition against multiple taxation in the Constitution. Nevertheless, multiple taxation is politically highly unpopular and tends not to occur.

The Constitution provides that any surplus is to be distributed as the Parliament "deems fair" amongst the States.[52] This provision is a dead letter as the Commonwealth parliament can validly appropriate any surplus revenue into trust funds, leaving nothing to distribute to the States.[53] However, the States and Commonwealth agreed, following the introduction of the Commonwealth Goods and Services Tax (GST) in 2000, that all GST revenue would be distributed to the States (Intergovernmental Agreement on the Reform of Commonwealth-State Financial Relations 1999). This agreement is scheduled to the legislation which carries it into effect.[54] The *Grants Commission Act* provides for the allocation of such moneys between the States on fiscal equalization principles.

3.4.3 *Other Formal or Informal Institutions for Resolving Intergovernmental Conflicts*

Ministerial Councils are the main alternative to the judiciary in resolving conflicts between component States or between the central government and component States. The party system may also play a role. Australia has a strong two-party system, and so political homogeneity between the governments of the States and of the Central federation may play a role in avoiding confrontation in some circumstances.

---

[49] *First Uniform Tax Case* (1942) 65 CLR 373; *Second Uniform Tax case* (1957) 99 CLR 575.
[50] Australian Constitution s 90.
[51] *Ha v NSW* (1997) 189 CLR 465.
[52] Australian Constitution s 94.
[53] *New South Wales v. Commonwealth* (1908) 7 CLR 179.
[54] *A New Tax System (Commonwealth-State Financial Arrangements) Act* 1999 (Cth), Schedule 2.

3.4.4 The Bureaucracy

The civil service of the central government is separate from the civil services of the component states.

There is a small but not major degree of movement between systems. It is not systematic or organized. Any movement between systems would be the result of any one or a combination of several factors: (a) general competition between systems for good staff; and (b) some public sector employees might move jurisdictions to follow political party preferences. For example, a Liberal party supporter might wish to work for a Liberal State government. Procedures exist to allow accrued employment entitlements to be recognized.

3.4.5 Social Factors

Australia has a diverse population with differences in origin, religion and socio-economic conditions. Yet diversity does not correlate to State boundaries except with regards to the Northern Territory, where 28 % of the population of the Northern Territory are indigenous, a feature that has an impact on policy making. The indigenous population is largely in the Northern Territory, Western Australia and northern Queensland, although groups can be found in all regions; this does not have an impact on the structure of the federal system.

The vast majority of the Australian population lives in the eastern States, and in particular New South Wales and Victoria, whose capital cities have traditionally been the centres of commerce in Australia. The difference in size between the States led to each State having equal representatives in the Upper House (the Senate) of the Federal legislature. Without this stipulation, the smaller colonies (which became the States upon federation) may not have federated from fear of the power of New South Wales and Victoria.

There is also significant resource asymmetry both in terms of the type of resources and the value of them. Tasmania and the Northern Territory receive the most fiscal equalization funds, followed by South Australia.

3.5 Recent Developments in Uniformity

We note that until recently there was quite a high degree of diversity and inconsistency in the law and practice relating to security interests in personal property, due to the fact that it is an area that is regulated by each individual state and territory. However, there has been a move in recent years towards a national or harmonized scheme, which has largely been driven by the work of the Standing Council on Law and Justice (discussed above). A new national system commenced in 2011 relying on Commonwealth legislation based upon both explicit Commonwealth legislative power and a reference from the States.[55]

The law of succession has traditionally been an area of state responsibility, with the result that each State and territory has its own, not necessarily consistent, scheme. However the SCLJ has initiated a project on Uniform Succession Laws, which is being coordinated by the Queensland Law Reform Commission and overseen by a national committee. In 1997 a report by the national committee on the Law of Wills was finalized which included model legislation. This has now been largely adopted in the Northern Territory, New South Wales, Victoria and Queensland. More recently, in April 2007, the NSW Law Reform Commission (the body given responsibility for the intestacy aspect of the project) released Report 116 (2007) – Uniform Succession Laws: Intestacy, which includes a model Bill. The final report by the Queensland Law Reform Commission was completed in April 2009, however as yet no uniform scheme is in place.

The Australian Constitution contains very few express fundamental rights which limit Commonwealth power and even fewer that expressly limit the power of state parliaments. However, as mentioned above in Sect. 3.3.1, the High Court has implied some limited rights from the text and structure of the Constitution that apply also to state parliaments, for example, freedom of political communication,[56] and some limitations derived from Ch III concerned with the separation of powers.[57] To the extent that these norms apply to the states, they have a harmonizing effect. On the other hand, in recent years a move away from harmonization in this area has occurred as a result of two jurisdictions, namely, the Australian Capital Territory and Victoria, adopting a Bill of Rights (see Human Rights Act 2004 (ACT) and Charter of Human Rights and Responsibilities Act 2006 (Vic)).

3.6 Conclusion

The history of Australian federation has been one of a gradual but definite move towards centralization of power. This has been achieved, as explained above, primarily by the High Court's wide and expansive interpretation of Commonwealth legislative power, especially regarding the corporations and external affairs powers. In addition, decisions of the High Court have permitted the Commonwealth to take over the field of income taxation, and have removed other important revenue-raising opportunities from the States. Combined with a wide view of the "grants power", this has produced an extremely strong Commonwealth government. In terms of

---

[55] See *Personal Property Securities Act (2009)* (Cth).

[56] See for example, *Coleman v Power* (2004) 220 CLR 1.

[57] This has been relied upon frequently in recent years: see most recently *Wainohu v New South Wales* (2011) 243 CLR 181.

the specific topic of this study, it has also produced a relatively high degree of unification of law, either because the Commonwealth is able to regulate an area directly (and thus impose uniformity throughout the federation) or to induce the states to conform to Commonwealth (uniform) policy in return for grants. In addition, in recent decades there has been increasing recognition that inconsistencies in laws between states on a range of topics leads to inefficiencies, unnecessary complexity and unfairness. This has led to calls for harmonization from a variety of constituents including industry bodies, law reform commissions and in some instances, the general public. For example, the relationship between the states and the Commonwealth, and the impact of our federal system on the ability of the nation to respond to many important contemporary issues was a significant feature of the 2007 federal election campaign. Thus, our conclusion is that the trend of the last century towards harmonization and unification will no doubt continue into the twenty-first century, ensuring that Australia will continue to be one of the most centralized federations in the world.

Chapter 4
Federalism and Legal Unification in Austria

Anna M. Gamper and Bernhard A. Koch

4.1 Overview

The Republic of (then: German-)Austria was founded in the aftermath of the First World War by a unilateral declaration made by representatives from the German-speaking component states (*Länder*) of the former Austro-Hungarian Empire in Vienna. Following this declaration of 21 October 1918, the constituent *Länder* themselves also gave their explicit approval to join the new Republic. It took two more years, however, to adopt the new Federal Constitution (*Bundes-Verfassungsgesetz*, hereafter *B-VG*),[1] which was negotiated between the political parties as well as between the central government and the *Länder*. Federalism has for many years been a crucial issue of constitutional discussion, but despite several single-issue reforms, no large-scale reform of the federal system has been realized yet.

Although it is one of the leading constitutional principles, Austrian federalism has always been described as "weak" due to a high degree of centralism within

---

[1] Strictly speaking, the Austrian Federal Constitution does not only consist of the B-VG, but also of a large number of additional federal constitutional acts, single federal constitutional provisions within ordinary federal laws and several laws dating back to the former Austro-Hungarian monarchy (until 1918), which, as well as certain state treaties, were given the status of federal constitutional law. An English translation of a selection of important federal constitutional laws can be found at http://www.ris.bka.gv.at/Englische-Rv/

A.M. Gamper (✉)
Department of Public Law, State and Administrative Theory, University of Innsbruck,
Innrain 52d, 6020 Innsbruck, Austria
e-mail: anna.gamper@uibk.ac.at

B.A. Koch
Department of Civil Law, University of Innsbruck, Innrain 52,
6020 Innsbruck, Austria
e-mail: b.a.koch@uibk.ac.at

the federal system. Centralism becomes most manifest in the weakness of the second chamber at the federal parliamentary level, which is composed of *Länder* representatives, as well as in the distribution of competences. Moreover, the federation has the power to enact the Fiscal Adjustment Act, even though the *Länder* and municipalities take part in the political negotiations preceding its enactment. The *Länder* do not have a broad sphere of constitutional autonomy either: Since the Federal Constitution determines most institutional aspects of the *Länder* (such as the *Land* Parliaments, *Land* Governments and the relations between them), they can add little more than details, even though they may be more creative with regard to additional constitutional elements that do not contradict the Federal Constitution (e.g. in the arena of state aims) according to the rather restrictive understanding of the Constitutional Court, or certain individual issues which they may regulate according to an explicit authorization of the Federal Constitution. On the other hand, however, the *Länder* are responsible for the execution of many federal affairs that, even though they remain a matter of the federal competence, are executed by the *Land* Governors and, as of 1 January 2014, Administrative Courts in the *Länder* (indirect federal administration). Moreover, a number of instruments of co-operation and co-ordination serve *Länder* interests: The *Länder* cannot only conclude treaties with each other and with the federation respectively under Article 15a B-VG, they may also participate to a considerable degree in the national decision-making in EU matters. Apart from these formal instruments, the *Länder* also co-operate informally through joint conferences (the most important of which is the Conference of *Land* Governors), and their own liaison office. Austrian federalism can therefore be described as co-operative as well as rather symmetric, since the *Länder*, with few exceptions, all have the same constitutional status.

Since Austria is a civil law jurisdiction, court decisions do not have any binding effect beyond the case in which they are rendered. In practice they nevertheless shape the law as persuasive to practitioners. This is particularly true for rulings by the three supreme courts, the Austrian Supreme Court (*Oberster Gerichtshof*, reviewing cases in civil, commercial and criminal matters), the Constitutional Court (*Verfassungsgerichtshof*, dealing with constitutional matters), and the Administrative High Court (*Verwaltungsgerichtshof*, hearing certain appeals in administrative matters).

4.2 The Federal Distribution and Exercise of Lawmaking Power

1. The allocation of powers is entrenched mainly in Articles 10 through 15 of the B-VG. The federation is responsible for the legislation and execution of an impressive number of tasks (Art 10 B-VG). A much shorter list of matters (Art 11 B-VG) includes those that are shared between the federation (as regards legislation) and the *Länder* (as regards execution). Another rather short list comprises areas in

which the federation is responsible for framework laws while the *Länder* are called to implement them (through their own legislation) and to execute the resulting laws (Art 12 B-VG). As is usual in most federal systems, the *Länder* also hold a residual competence (Art 15 para 1 B-VG), being thus responsible for all matters that have not been enumerated explicitly in favor of the federation. Since most (important) matters are explicitly enumerated, however, not very much remains in the residual *Länder* sphere. Yet, apart from these main distribution models, there are a large number of more specific power-sharing regimes, within and without the B-VG, which are neglected in the following.

The catalogue of Articles 10–12 B-VG includes the following specific competences:

(i) Exclusive federal powers under Article 10 B-VG

1. The Federal Constitution, in particular elections to the National Council, and referenda as provided by the Federal Constitution; the constitutional judiciary; the administrative judiciary (as of 1 January 2014, excluding the organization of the administrative courts of the *Länder*); elections to the European Parliament; European citizens' initiatives;
2. External affairs including political and economic representation with regard to other countries, in particular the conclusion of international treaties, notwithstanding *Länder* competences in accordance with Article 16 para 1; demarcation of frontiers; trade in goods and livestock with other countries; customs;
3. Regulation and control of entry into and exit from the Federal territory; immigration and emigration; including the right of residence in case of significant reasons; passports; residence ban, expulsion and turning back at the frontier; asylum: extradition;
4. Federal finances, in particular taxes to be collected exclusively or in part on behalf of the Federation; monopolies;
5. The monetary, credit, stock exchange and banking system; the weights and measures, standards and hallmark system;
6. Civil law affairs, including the rules relating to economic association but excluding regulations which render real property transactions, legal acquisition on death by individuals outside the circle of legal heirs not excepted, with aliens and transactions in built-up real property or such as is earmarked for development subject to restrictions by the administrative authorities; private endowment affairs; criminal law, excluding administrative penal law and administrative penal procedure in matters which fall within the autonomous sphere of competence of the *Länder*; administration of justice; establishments for the protection of society against criminal or otherwise dangerous persons; copyright; press affairs; expropriation in so far as it does not concern matters falling within the autonomous sphere of competence of the *Länder*; matters pertaining to notaries, lawyers, and related professions;

7. The maintenance of peace, order and security including the extension of primary assistance in general, but excluding local public safety matters; the right of association and assembly; matters pertaining to personal status, including the registration of births, marriages and deaths, and change of name; aliens police and residence registration; matters pertaining to weapons, ammunition and explosives, and the use of fire-arms;
8. Matters pertaining to trade and industry; public advertising and commercial brokerage; restraint of unfair competition; antitrust law; patent matters and the protection of designs, trademarks, and other commodity descriptions; matters pertaining to patent agents; matters pertaining to civil engineering; chambers of commerce, trade, and industry; establishment of professional associations in so far as they extend to the Federal territory as a whole, but with the exception of those in the field of agriculture and forestry;
9. The traffic system relating to the railways, aviation and shipping in so far as the last of these does not fall under Article 11; motor traffic; matters, with exception of the highway police, which concern roads declared by Federal law as Federal highways on account of their importance for transit traffic; river and navigation police in so far as these do not fall under Article 11; the postal and telecommunications system; environmental compatibility examination for projects relating to these matters where material effects on the environment are to be anticipated and for which the administrative regulations prescribe an alignment definition by way of ordinance;
10. Mining; forestry, including timber flotage; water rights; control and conservation of waters for the safe diversion of floods or for shipping and raft transport; regulation of rivers; construction and maintenance of waterways; regulation and standardization of electrical plants and establishments as well as safety measures in this field; provisions pertaining to electric power transmission in so far as the transmission extends over two or more *Länder* matters pertaining to steam and other power-driven engines; surveying;
11. Labour legislation in so far as it does not fall under Article 12; social and contractual insurance; attendance allowances; chambers for workers and salaried employees with the exception of those relating to agriculture and forestry;
12. Public health with the exception of burial and disposal of the dead and municipal sanitation and first aid services, but only sanitary supervision with respect to hospitals, nursing homes, health resorts and natural curative resources; measures to counter factors hazardous to the environment by exceeding input limits; clear air maintenance notwithstanding the competence of the *Länder* for heating installations; refuse disposal in respect of dangerous refuse, but in respect of other refuse only in so far as a need for the issue of uniform regulations exists; veterinary affairs; nutrition affairs, including foodstuffs inspection; regulation of commercial

transactions in seed and plant commodities, in fodder and fertilizer as well as plant preservatives, and in plant safety appliances including their admission and, in the case of seed and plant commodities, likewise their acceptance;
13. Archive and library services for the sciences and specialist purposes; matters pertaining to Federal collections and establishments serving the arts and sciences; matters pertaining to the Federal theatres with the exception of building affairs; the preservation of monuments; religious affairs; census as well as – allowing for the rights of the *Länder* to engage within their own territory in every kind of statistical activity – other statistics in so far as they do not serve the interests of one *Land* only; endowments and foundations when their purposes extend beyond a single *Land*'s sphere of interests and they have hitherto not been autonomously administered by the *Länder*;
14. Organization and command of the Federal police; settlement of the conditions pertaining to the establishment and organization of other protective forces with the exception of the municipal constabularies; settlement of the conditions pertaining to the armament of the protective forces and their right to make use of their weapons.
15. Military affairs; matters pertaining to war damage and welfare measures for combatants and their surviving dependants; care of war graves; whatever measures seem necessary by reason or in consequence of war to ensure the uniform conduct of economic affairs, in particular with regard to the population's supply with essentials;
16. The establishment of Federal authorities and other Federal agencies; service code for and staff representation rights of Federal employees;
17. Population policy in so far as it concerns the grant of children's allowances and the creation of burden equalization on behalf of families;

(ii) Concurrent federal powers under Article 11 B-VG

1. Nationality;
2. Professional associations in so far as they do not fall under Article 10, but with the exception of those in the field of agriculture and forestry as well as in the field of alpine guidance and skiing instruction and in that of sport instruction falling within *Länder* autonomous competence;
3. Social housing affairs except for the promotion of domestic dwelling construction and domestic rehabilitation;
4. Highway police;
5. Redevelopment;
6. Inland shipping as regards shipping licences, shipping facilities and compulsory measures pertaining to such facilities in so far as it does not apply to the Danube, Lake Constance, Lake Neusiedl, and boundary stretches of other frontier waters; river and navigation police on inland waters with the exception of the Danube, Lake Constance, Lake Neusiedl, and boundary stretches of other frontier waters;

7. Environmental impact assessment for projects relating to these matters where material effects on the environment are to be anticipated; in so far as a need for the issue of uniform regulations is considered to exist, the approval of such projects;
8. Animal welfare (unless federal matter due to other provisions), but excluding the exercise of hunting and fishing.

(iii) Concurrent federal powers under Article 12 B-VG

1. Social welfare; population policy in so far as it does not fall under Article 10; public social and welfare establishments; maternity, infant and adolescent welfare; hospitals and nursing homes; requirements to be imposed for health reasons on health resorts, sanatoria, and health establishments; natural curative resources;
2. Public institutions for the adjustment of disputes out of court;
3. Land reform, in particular land consolidation measures and resettlement;
4. The protection of plants against diseases and pests;
5. Matters pertaining to electric power in so far as they do not fall under Article 10;
6. Labour legislation and the protection of workers and employees in so far as it is a matter of workers and employees engaged in agriculture and forestry.

Federal powers are always established by enumerating them explicitly (no residual competence of the federation). Several powers are granted to the federation on the condition that "there is need for uniform federal law" (objective parameter) or if "the federation considers uniform federal law necessary" (subjective parameter with discretionary power for the federal government).

Another important example which manifests the distinctive character of the Austrian distribution of competences is the federation's competence to enact certain pieces of subsidiary legislation if the *Länder* fail to do so in time (Art 15 para 6, 16 para 4, 23d para 5 B-VG). This concerns cases where the *Länder* are responsible for the implementation of international treaties, federal framework laws and EU law. The *Länder* remain competent, however, which means that if they enact legislation at a later date, the federation's subsidiary measures cease to be in force.

While it is hard to assess which of the competences allocated to the federation are most important, key matters include foreign affairs, civil law, commercial law, criminal law, defence, labour law, civil, criminal and administrative procedure, fiscal equalisation, trade and industry, immigration, the maintenance of peace and security, and many matters pertaining to schools and education, to environmental law, to land-use planning, to health and social welfare etc. There are, however, reservations and exceptions to nearly all of the subject matters.

2. Regarding the areas of the law remaining within the jurisdiction of the *Länder*, it is important to note that the *Länder* have residual competence under Article 15 para 1 B-VG which means that all subject-matters not enumerated as federal are *Länder* powers. Although this clause seems to be *Länder*-friendly, there is, in fact, little that is left to them.

Some of their powers are enumerated insofar as they are concurrent (see Art 11 and 12 B-VG) or in special cases such as Art 115 para 2 B-VG (local government). According to constitutional doctrine and case law, enumerated subject-matters have to be interpreted in light of their historic meaning (including more modern matters, if there is a close and systematic connection between the historic meaning and the new matter). If there remains any doubt, whether a subject-matter is a federal or a *Land* power, it is regarded as the latter. Again, this method of interpretation is not applied very often, since most subject-matters clearly fall under a federal power.

Exclusive powers under the residual competence are not enumerated explicitly, but comprise those "remaining" competences that are not listed as federal. One could mention building law, fishery, hunting, fire police, tourism, sport, transfer of real estate, agriculture, youth protection, protection of nature, general aspects of zoning etc.

In principle, the Austrian allocation of powers is characterized by the principle of exclusivity of (either federal or *Land*) powers. Even in case of Articles 11 and 12 of the B-VG, where competences are shared, powers are not really concurrent as the entities have different spheres of competence: only the federation is competent to enact (framework-) legislation while the *Länder* have the power to enact implementing legislation and to execute the law. Nevertheless, there are several exceptions to this rule: As mentioned, some powers are granted to the federation on the condition that "there is need for a uniform federal law" (objective parameter) or if "the federation considers uniform federal law as necessary" (subjective parameter with discretionary power for the federal government). In this case, uniform federal laws may be adopted, and the *Länder* may only deviate from these uniform federal laws if this is "indispensable".

In a few cases, ordinary federal laws may entitle the *Land* legislatures to adopt specific legislation on a single-issue-basis (e.g., in water law). If, however, the federal law-maker wants to retain the competence for these issues, the *Länder* receive no power over them. Another problem is the interpretation of subject-matters, since an extensive interpretation of federal powers reduces the matters that fall under the residual competence.

While it is difficult to assess what the most important areas of exclusive or predominant component state government regulation are, one could mention the *Land* competence on general aspects of zoning, building law, nature protection, local government and the transfer of real property as examples.

A legislative competence of particular quality and scope is the constitutional autonomy of the *Länder* (Art 99 B-VG). They are entitled to adopt their own *Land* constitutional law as long as it complies with the Federal Constitution (which, however, constrains the *Land* constitutions to a high degree).

Since powers are usually exercised exclusively, there are hardly any cases where the federation and the *Länder* enact rules in exactly the same field or under the same power. One of the few examples occurs under Article 15 para 9 of the B-VG, according to which the *Länder* may adopt ancillary legislation in the fields of civil and criminal law (which are classic federal powers) if this is "indispensable" for the effectiveness of their own competences. Another case of co-existence occurs in those rare cases where both a federal and a *Land* law are required to put a certain measure into effect (e.g., if federal and *Land* borders are rearranged). Under the aegis of co-operative federalism, the federation and the *Länder* may also conclude formal agreements (called concordats) in complex matters which require harmonised legislation. This concerns areas within both entity's sphere of power, but involve separate, yet intersecting, competences.

3. Residual power is allocated to the *Länder* under Article 15 para 1 of the B-VG. As regards schools and education (Art 14 B-VG), *Länder* powers are enumerated, whilst the federation holds the residual power (and vice versa in case of agri- or silvicultural schools and education, according to Art 14a B-VG), but this is only a "microcosm" within the "macrocosmic" allocation of powers.

4. Since Austria is a highly centralistic federal state, it is perhaps surprising to find that no principle such as the "supremacy of federal law" exists. There is only the supremacy of federal constitutional law that has to be observed under all circumstances. This means that ordinary federal laws on the one hand and constitutional or ordinary *Land* laws on the other hand are on an equal level. There may be particular instances, however, where ordinary federal laws also enjoy "supremacy", e.g. federal framework laws under Article 12 B-VG.

According to the Constitutional Court, both the federation and the *Länder* may regulate the same subject matter if they address different aspects. Since complex subject matters involving a variety of aspects may – in the long run – lead to a plethora of different norms with contradictory effects, the Constitutional Court assumes that Austrian federalism is based on a "principle of mutual consideration" (not explicitly mentioned in the Federal Constitution) that obliges both the federation and the *Länder* to consider the legislative interests of the other entity in order to avoid undermining them excessively. *In abstracto*, the principle treats both tiers equally, although it has hitherto been applied more often in favor of the federation.

5. The municipalities, though they form the "third tier" of territorial entities in Austria, have no legislative powers and are not considered as constituent states of the federal system. All their "competences", including those that are exercised within their "autonomous" sphere (which, being broadly defined in the Federal Constitution, nevertheless require explicit transferral to the municipal level by ordinary laws of the federation or *Länder*), derive from either federal or *Land* competences. These municipal "competences" are always of an administrative rather than legislative nature, which corresponds to a municipal organisation that provides for elected councils rather than parliaments. The highest, i.e. most abstract, type of norm that may be issued by a municipality is that of a "decree" or "ordinance".

4.3 The Means and Methods of Legal Unification

1. One way to accomplish legal unification is via directly (and explicitly) applicable constitutional norms addressing the exercise of central power. For example, Article 21 para 4 B-VG provides: In order for the service code, the staff representation

regulations, and the employee protection scheme of the federation, the *Länder,* and the municipalities to develop along equal lines, the federation and the *Länder* have to inform each other about their plans in these matters.

According to Article 4 B-VG, the federal territory is a uniform currency, economic and customs area, and intermediate customs barriers or other traffic restrictions may not be established within the federal territory.

Another example is the so-called "principle of homogeneity" regarding the electoral system, where the B-VG explicitly stipulates (Art 95, 117 B-VG) that the *Länder* must not adopt electoral laws (with regard to *Land* or municipal elections) which would narrow the (active and passive) suffrage in comparison to elections at the federal level.

Apart from these explicit provisions, all other parts of the Federal Constitution, insofar as they do not refer to the federal level only, also have a unifying effect. This is true not only for the leading constitutional principles (democracy, republicanism, federalism, rule of law, separation of powers, human rights), but also for other principles or constitutional provisions of a more general character. With regard to the principle of democracy, the Constitutional Court has struck down *Land* legislation, including *Land* constitutional legislation, if it did not observe the absolute predominance of representative democracy, even though provisions on the relation between representative and direct democracy at *Länder* level were not explicitly provided in the Federal Constitution.

In the cases in which the federation may enact uniform laws if it "deems" them necessary or if they "are" necessary, uniform laws were enacted at the earliest date.

Where the *Länder* fail to implement EU law, international treaties or federal framework laws, the federation may enact subsidiary measures, but the *Länder* do not thereby lose their competence to enact measures at a later date.

In matters falling under Article 12 B-VG, the federation may enact framework laws which the *Länder* have to implement through their own legislation, and to execute.

The federation is responsible for fiscal equalisation, and although Fiscal Equalisation Acts are usually negotiated between representatives of the three tiers for political reasons, the federation is clearly predominant in these negotiations. One example how the federal government forces the *Länder* to restrict their budgets is a provision of the Fiscal Equalisation Act that threatens the *Länder* with heavy reductions of their financial resources unless they enter into a "voluntary" agreement under Article 15a B-VG binding themselves to stabilize their budgetary deficits (which shall help to keep Austria within the EU convergence criteria).

The *Länder* prefer to enter into agreements with each other in order to achieve uniform standards throughout Austria rather than face the threat of a federal constitutional amendment, which would transfer one of their powers to the federal level (although the Federal Council would have an absolute veto in that case, it has never exercised such a veto because it represents party politics rather than *Länder* interests).

Where the *Länder* are obliged to implement EU law (as far as it is not directly applicable) when it falls into their sphere of powers, the federal government is obliged to inform the *Länder* without undue delay about all plans at the European level that may concern them. The Federal Council, moreover, holds several powers in accordance with the Lisbon Treaty which may be exercised in order to protect *Länder* competences (subsidiarity monitoring, subsidiarity action). Since EU law often affects several aspects and competences from the perspective of the Austrian allocation of powers, both the federal government and the *Länder* may be called on to implement it. In this case, the federal government has a particularly strong position insofar as it receives and distributes most information from the EU and works as a clearing house or interface between the EU and the *Länder* so that the federal government appears almost as a supervisory authority of the sub-units.

The Austrian Constitutional Court does not really "create" uniform norms, since courts in Austria cannot positively "create" norms inasmuch as their decisions are not binding in any general normative sense. The Constitutional Court has nevertheless developed what could be called a "homogeneity judicature" in several fields. Note also that the Austrian *Länder,* as of 1 January 2014, only have administrative courts, but no further judiciary of their own, particularly not in civil or criminal matters. The difficulty is that the Federal Constitution consists of a variety of different principles that are phrased in a rather vague manner. Occasions may arise for the Court to interpret these principles in a way that cannot always be predicted. One example is the Court's judgment on a *Land* constitutional provision that provided more instruments of direct democracy at the *Land* level than the Federal Constitution did at the federal level. Although the Federal Constitution does not contain any explicit provision that refers to direct democracy at the *Land* level, the Court held that the explicit provisions for the federal level contained implicit restrictions also with regard to direct democracy within the *Länder*.

The Constitutional Court may also review cases on the need to enact uniform federal laws (except the cases in which it is up to the federal government's discretion to "deem" uniform federal laws necessary) or where the *Länder* thought it indispensable to deviate from these laws.

2. The Federal Constitution provides for a specific formal instrument that allows the *Länder* to co-ordinate their law-making where necessary. Under Article 15a B-VG, they may conclude formal agreements (concordats), either with each other or with the federal government. This is particularly useful in complex fields where more than one tier is concerned, where harmonized laws are necessary, and where such a voluntary agreement is to be preferred to a federal constitutional amendment that re-allocates powers. Such agreements are concluded very frequently, e.g., in the fields of environmental protection, development planning, health and social welfare.

The governors of the Austrian *Länder* meet several times a year in the so-called "*Landeshauptmännerkonferenz*" which is an informal and voluntary body. Being a stronghold of *Länder* power that is much better able to defend *Länder* interests than the Federal Council, the *Landeshauptmännerkonferenz* has been called a "power in the shadow". There are also other joint bodies where the *Land* executives co-operate, such as the conference of certain senior public servants at the *Land* level or conferences where certain members of the *Land* governments meet. The *Länder* have also informally established their own "liaison office", which facilitates cooperation and co-ordination between them and is particularly valuable with regard to the exchange of information.

3. In light of the limited range of subject matters remaining within the legislative powers of the *Länder*, there is little room for internal unification of originally diverse laws to begin with. While academic writing occasionally proposes changes to specific solutions found in the laws of one *Land* by pointing at the corresponding rules in other *Länder*, or by suggesting (mostly in descriptive rather than legislative terms) a new general model for a specific subject matter, there is no established initiative promoting harmonization by way of restatements or by model laws in any of the areas left to the *Länder*.

There are some "semi-state" actors which play a certain role in the legislative process not only on the federal, but also on the state level. The principal economic interest groups, including the federal chambers of commerce, agriculture and labor, for example, all have corresponding institutions on the level of the *Länder*. There is compulsory membership in these public entities, which are regulated by federal law. Among other tasks and responsibilities, they are called upon to comment on legislation that affects the interests of their constituent groups, and they are invited to nominate members to certain committees and advisory bodies. To the extent legislation on the level of the component states concerns the agenda of these interest groups, it is highly likely in practice that their representatives will pursue a uniform strategy throughout the country, which may play a certain limited role in supporting harmonization. However, this impact depends more on their political weight on a day-to-day basis than on any pre-determined degree of importance.

Other institutions that may support legal harmonization include the Austrian Standards Institute (*Österreichisches Normungsinstitut*), a non-profit organization accredited by federal law, which prepares the Austrian Standards (*ÖNORMEN*) for industry. Furthermore, there are true non-state interest groups which are more or less active in promoting uniformity in all component state laws for the subject matters affecting their constituency. For example, the Austrian Alpine Club (*Österreichischer Alpenverein*) is interested in matters of the environment and regional planning. However, these activities can best be described as lobbying, and their influence on the actual legislative process does not exceed the impact of equivalent activities in other countries.

4. Law is currently taught at six Austrian universities (including the Vienna University of Economics and Business, which offers a special business law degree program), each attracting students from the entire country, even though for practical reasons, faculties tend to draw their student bodies from the regions geographically closer to them.

Legal education focuses primarily on system-wide law, not only because this indeed accounts for the majority of laws in force. Regulations do not restrict law faculties' curricula to any specific component state law but invariably speak of "Austrian" law without any separation between federal and component state law. However, certain aspects of administrative law falling under the competence of the *Länder* may be selectively referred to in class, with a natural tendency of each faculty member to draw such examples from the *Land* where the university is seated or from adjacent *Länder*. However, textbooks for students are invariably aimed at the entire country, and exams in theory are not limited to one or more specific *Länder* (even though the range of subjects on a particular exam may in practice be reduced to the laws of a specific *Land* by announcement of the examiner in advance).

Bar admission is governed by federal law, the Attorneys Act (*Rechtsanwaltsordnung*, RAO) and the Bar Examination Act (*Rechtsanwaltsprüfungsgesetz*, RAPG). Admission to the bar is overseen by the Chamber of Attorneys (*Rechtsanwaltskammer*) in the *Land* where the candidate is registered as a trainee (*Konzipient*). The RAO institutes Chambers of Attorneys to represent the interests of attorneys in each *Land*, and provides each Chamber with disciplinary powers and jurisdiction over all attorneys having their office (geographically) in that *Land*. All nine Chambers are united in the Austrian Conference of Chambers of Attorneys (*Rechtsanwaltskammertag*).

Bar exams are administered by panels instituted at the seat of each *Oberlandesgericht* (Court of Appeals) for all *Länder* within its respective jurisdiction. Just as at the universities, the subjects tested are primarily system-wide law. Section 20 of the RAPG, which lists the subjects of the oral part of the bar examination, speaks of "Austrian" law exclusively without differentiating between or referring to the laws of the *Länder*. However, to the extent the laws of the *Länder* fall under the range of subjects of the exam, the focus will primarily be on the *Land* of the candidate in practice (though not necessarily so).

Admission to the bar is invariably for the entire federal system and to all courts irrespective of the place where the exam was taken or where the attorney is registered (§ 8 RAO). Attorneys are free to establish offices throughout the country.

In theory, graduates could set up their practice anywhere in the federation. More than 40 % of all attorneys work in Vienna, where 20 % of the Austrian population lives. Larger law firms (again primarily seated in Vienna) draw their staff from the entire country. Still, for pragmatic reasons, graduates tend to remain either within the vicinity of their original domicile or of their place of study.

Institutions of legal education do not play a major role in unifying the law of Austria, although they do not interfere with unification either. The Academy of Austrian Attorneys (*Anwaltsakademie*), for example, which administers training for future attorneys as well as continuing legal education, does not offer courses tailored to any specific component state law.

5. The *Länder* are obliged to implement international treaties as far as their powers are affected by them. If they fail to do so in time, the federal government will take over the responsibility and be entitled to adopt subsidiary measures, even though the *Länder* still remain competent. If they implement these treaties at a later date, the federal government's measures cease to be in force. A similar procedure takes place with regard to the implementation of EU law, if the European Court of Justice declares that the *Länder* failed to implement EU law in due time.

While international voluntary coordination does play a certain role on the federal level in an international context, it has almost no impact on the harmonization of laws internally. There may be very limited ad hoc influences on the legislation of the *Länder* by way of their factual representation in international initiatives such as the Alpine Convention, but this impact remains at a fairly low level. In 2011, however, the Land Tyrol co-founded the European Grouping of Territorial Cooperation together with the Italian Autonomous Provinces of South Tyrol-Alto Adige and Trentino. Within the context of this new legal person, the three partner-regions want to cooperate as much as possible, including also the "voluntary" harmonization of their respective legislation in areas that fall into their competence.

4.4 Institutional and Social Background

1. The Constitutional Court (*Verfassungsgerichtshof*) can be petitioned to intervene when federal legislation has exceeded the law-making power allocated to the federal government. The Court may, among numerous other functions, review and strike down both federal and *Land* laws (both constitutional and ordinary laws, as well as decrees and administrative rulings), on an abstract or concrete basis, if they are unconstitutional. The Court's adjudication is perhaps rather more centralistic than *Länder*-friendly, but this is also due to the rather centralistic concept of the Austrian Federal Constitution and on the whole a rather casuistic field of jurisdiction.

All courts, in particular the ordinary courts, the Constitutional Court, and the administrative courts, may have to interpret *Land* law provided that they have to apply it in a given case. On the appeal of the federal government or the *Länder* governments, moreover, the Constitutional Court decides whether draft laws or decrees, if enacted, would be in compliance with the allocation of powers. The statement in which the Court expresses its opinion ("*Rechtssatz*") is regarded as an "authentic interpretation" of the Federal Constitution and the Court itself considers it to be binding. No other kind of *ex ante*-review is allowed by the Court, and there is no formal obligation to consider precedents otherwise, even though it is highly advisable as well as routine for state authorities to follow the opinion expressed by one of the three Austrian Supreme Courts (*Oberster Gerichtshof, Verwaltungsgerichtshof, Verfassungsgerichtshof*).

In civil and criminal matters there are no state courts since the "ordinary" (i.e. civil and criminal) judiciary constitutes a sole federal power (Art 82 para 1 B-VG). Nevertheless, the ordinary courts are geographically located in the *Länder* and certain ordinary courts and courts of appeal are misleadingly called "*Landesgericht*" or "*Oberlandesgericht*" respectively.

As of 1 January 2014, the *Länder* will for the first time partake in the judicial power as *Länder* administrative courts will be established that will hear appeals in most administrative matters, while two federal administrative courts will be mainly responsible for procurement, asylum and financial issues. Appeals against their decisions go to the Administrative High Court or to the Constitutional Court, but in both cases certain restrictions apply.

2. In principle, the central government does not have the power to force component states to legislate. In case of delayed implementation of international or EU law (in the latter case, if the delay is ascertained as a fact by the European Court of Justice), the federal government may take subsidiary measures unless the *Länder* legislate themselves. Moreover, the *Länder* may be held responsible to bear the costs arising from the Republic's liability for delayed implementation.

The execution of federal law depends on the allocation of powers since there are some instances (Art 11, 12 B-VG) where the *Länder* are responsible for executing matters that are regulated by federal law. Most subject-matters, however, are exclusive federal matters (Art 10 B-VG), which means that the federation is responsible both for the legislation and the execution. Even if Article 102 B-VG provides that the *Länder* are charged to execute most of these matters on behalf of the federation, the federation is and remains formally competent. There is thus no need for an expensive double structure of administration: the *Länder* administrative authorities, including, as of 1 January 2014, the *Länder* administrative courts, normally take care of federal administration. There are numerous exceptions to this rule, though.

The *Länder* are represented in the Federal Council (*Bundesrat*), which is the second chamber of the Federal Parliament. Normally, however, the Federal Council may only exercise a suspensive veto. Even in those rare cases where it is entitled to an absolute veto, it never makes use of it for political reasons. De facto, the Federal Council is a chamber of political representatives who follow the policies of the coalition governments with a constitutional majority in the National Council rather than represent the interests of the *Länder*.

In a few cases in the legislative process, the *Länder* (represented by the *Land* Governments) have direct rights of approval (in addition to whatever the Federal Council decides) so that each *Land* could prevent certain draft laws from coming into effect.

Every time a *Land* parliament is re-elected, it itself re-elects its delegates to the Federal Council. This means that the Federal Council is a permanent body that is not elected or re-elected as a whole, but whose members change from time to time, according to the election dates of each *Land* parliament. The number of delegates varies between a minimum of 3 and a maximum of 12 delegates according to the proportions between the *Länder* and their respective numbers of citizens.

The power to tax is arranged by the Fiscal Equalisation Act, which is an ordinary federal statute. In legal terms, the federation may decide "who gets what" (although there is a political tradition to negotiate the Fiscal Equalisation Act anew every 4 years between the federation, the *Länder,* and the municipalities). Section 4 of the Fiscal Constitutional Act, however, obliges the federation to take care of the administrative tasks imposed by the federal legislation on the various tiers and of their abilities so that a Fiscal Equalisation Act would be unconstitutional if it excessively neglected these criteria. According to the present Fiscal Equalisation Act, some taxes are exclusive federal taxes, some exclusive *Länder* taxes, some exclusive municipal taxes, but a considerable part of the revenue is shared between these tiers, regardless which level levies the tax. All taxes that are not mentioned in the Fiscal Equalisation Act (most of them are) are left to the *Länder*. This allows them to invent their own subjects of taxation, which they are, however, highly reluctant to do for fear of becoming unpopular with their citizens.

Section 6 of the Fiscal Constitutional Act explicitly allows that identical taxes are levied regarding the same objects. It is up to the Fiscal Equalisation Act to decide whether – if at all – and which – if any – taxes are ultimately being distributed among the *Länder*.

Within the limits of the Fiscal Constitutional Act mentioned earlier, revenue sharing is provided by the Fiscal Equalisation Act. The most important taxes are shared taxes, levied by the federation. The revenue is shared between the federation, the *Länder*, and the municipalities.

3. Most relevant institutions resolving intergovernmental conflicts have already been mentioned, namely the Constitutional Court and, more informally, the *Länder* conferences, and the liaison office of the *Länder*. The Federal Council should rather not be mentioned in this context since it does not really represent *Länder* interests in practice. In the context of European integration, there are several intergovernmental working groups where the tiers closely co-operate and exchange information.

An important new body was founded in 1999 when the federation, the *Länder* and (after the necessary express constitutional authorisation) the municipalities concluded a formal agreement on a so-called "consultation mechanism": Every time one of these tiers plans a draft law or decree that would impose financial burdens on the other tiers, this plan has to be discussed in a consultation committee that consists of equal numbers of representatives of all three tiers. If no consensus is reached, the tier that proposes the plan has to bear the financial burden. Although the consultation mechanism is not applied very frequently, its very existence seems to advise the tiers to negotiate certain laws informally at an earlier date. Another such agreement ("Austrian Stability Pact 2012") was concluded in 2012 in order to enable the Republic to keep within the limits set by the EU convergence criteria: According to this agreement, the federation, the *Länder* and the municipalities have to stabilize their budgets in order to restrict the overall national deficit.

4. The civil service of the federation is separate from the civil services of the *Länder*. According to Article 21 B-VG, each is responsible for the laws regulating their own civil servants and public employees, including those of the municipalities and municipal associations for whom *Land* legislation is mainly responsible. While a rigid "principle of homogeneity" applicable to the pertinent law of the federation and the *Länder* was repealed in 1999, a "lighter version" of this principle still exists.

According to Article 21 para 4 B-VG, public employees are guaranteed at all times the possibility of alternating service among the federation, the *Länder*, the municipalities and the municipal associations. Legal provisions that vary the weight accorded to terms of service depending on whether they were served with the federation, a *Land*, a municipality or a municipal association are inadmissible. In order to enable each tier's service code, staff representation regulations and employee protection scheme to develop along equal lines, the federation and the *Länder* have to inform each other about their plans in these matters.

5. Apart from the "modern minorities" (including mostly migrant workers from Turkey, the Balkan States and Northern Africa), there are six indigenous national minorities (Croatian, Slovenian, Hungarian, Czech, Slovakian and Roma) that enjoy a specific status of legal recognition (primarily certain language rights) due to their ethnic and linguistic distinctiveness. There are, however, neither racial nor religious nor any other social cleavages in the federation that would be of importance in the present context.

The national minorities just mentioned live in the South and East of Austria, but, apart from having lived there for a long time, they do not have a particular relationship to the legal status of a *Land* and certainly are not concentrated in a political subdivision of their own.

Austria is a rather symmetric federal state, and there are no extreme disparities between the *Länder*, although each of them has a distinctive geography. Small as the country is, there are no significant natural resources such as oil and gas, but water (of an excellent quality) is available in enormous quantities and also used for producing hydroelectric power. Education is mainly the same across the country, since most matters pertaining to schools and education fall under the federal competence; not all *Länder*, however, have a university of their own. The small Western *Länder* are richer and more developed than at least some of the regions in the East and South of Austria, with the exception of Vienna which is the capital and a *Land* at the same time, and which enjoys a privileged status also with regard to fiscal equalisation.

4.5 Conclusion

Due to the highly centralistic nature of Austrian federalism, full unification surely is the predominant feature since the federation is exclusively competent for an extremely ample catalogue of matters in which thus no harmonization is needed. Since the allocation of powers, yet unreformed as it is, is highly fragmented and complex, there nevertheless remain many fields where harmonized legislation (to be adopted by the federation and the *Länder*, each with regard to different aspects of the same matter) is useful, and the co-operative way of concluding voluntary agreements under Article 15a B-VG is a particularly commendable tradition. Still, the question of a reform of the federal system and of the allocation of powers in particular has been on the table for many years. The problem was aggravated by Austria's EU membership, which revealed all the weaknesses of the system of allocation of power when "harmonic" implementation of EU law is necessary. The Constitutional Court helps to overcome some of these difficulties, e.g., through the development of the "principle of mutual consideration" or through various shapes of the "principle of homogeneity". At the same time, however, application of these principles is based on a narrow understanding of *Länder* autonomy. Even though this does not lead to outright centralization, it leads to uniformity of legislation.

Given this situation, why have a federal system with an inherent allocation of powers at all? Why have an allocation of powers if it is uniformity that is wanted in so many fields? Legally speaking, as long as the principle of federalism remains one of the leading principles of the Austrian Federal Constitution, it could not be abolished without a qualified constitutional amendment, including a referendum. The historical identity of the *Länder* which is still strongly felt by their citizens, especially in the Western part of Austria, as well as the geographic and economic differences between them seem to plead for the continuance of the federal system, even though a reform is needed. The proposals made during the Austrian Constitutional Convention (2003–2005) as well as the ideas suggested by the members of the Special Parliamentary Committee and the small expert group that were established afterwards were highly controversial and it is unlikely that the deep gap between the political parties and between the federation and the *Länder* as to a reform of federalism will be bridged in the near future.[2] The reform of Austrian federalism thus seems to follow a path of rather small steps-as to which the very latest, namely the establishment of genuine administrative courts of the *Länder* will surely be of greater impact.

---

[2] The aforementioned expert group presented a draft for the reform of the federal state on 11 March 2008, which was opposed by the *Länder* and thus failed to be realized.

Chapter 5
Belgium: A Broken Marriage?

Alain-Laurent Verbeke

5.1 Overview

5.1.1 A Francophone Centralized State

The territory of present-day Belgium has no history as a single unit before 1830. With the French Revolution, the territory was fully absorbed by France. After the fall of Napoleon in 1814, at the Vienna Congress, it became part of the newly created United Kingdom of the Netherlands, under King William I of the House of Orange. This was a Dutch speaking Protestant State, deeply resented in the Catholic South with its Francophone elite. Already in 1830, the South broke away and the Kingdom of Belgium was born. In 1831, the Belgian Federal Congress wrote a liberal constitution that created a unitary parliamentary state with a constitutional monarch. There was no shared sense of "Belgian" identity and no sense of a single

---

Alain-Laurent Verbeke, Full Professor of Law at the Universities of Leuven & Tilburg and Visiting Professor of Law Harvard Law School, Attorney in Brussels. The author wishes to thank Prof. Dr. André Baron Alen (Leuven), Judge in the Constitutional Court and Prof. Dr. Kurt Deketelaere (Leuven/Dundee), Chief of Cabinet of the Flemish Minster of Public Works, Environment and Nature Conservation, for their valuable comments and suggestions.

A.-L. Verbeke (✉)
Full Professor of Law at the Law Faculty of the University of Leuven, Department of Private Law, Leuven, Belgium

Full Professor of Law at the Law Faculty of Tilburg University, Department of Private Law, Tilburg, The Netherlands

Visiting Professor of Law Harvard Law School, Harvard University, Cambridge, MA, USA

Attorney, member of the Bar of Brussels, Brussels, Belgium
e-mail: alain.verbeke@law.kuleuven.be

people seeking nationhood. The line dividing Europe into a Germanic North and Latin South cuts across Belgium – dividing it in a Flemish North (Dutch speaking, 60 %) and a Walloon South (French speaking, 40 %).[1]

During the nineteenth century, a strong centralized government made French the single official language, imposed also on Flanders. From the outset, the Walloon industrialized region was economically dominant, with Flanders relying on subsistence agriculture. Within Belgium, there was rampant social and economic discrimination against those who spoke Dutch. Towards the end of the nineteenth century a Flemish movement emerged, with a major focus on language rights. The 1898 "Law of Equality" nominally recognized the validity of both languages in official documents.

5.1.2 Constitutional Revisions

A critical change occurred in 1932 and 1935, when for purposes of governmental activities, two monolingual regions were created on the basis of a territorial line dividing the country into two parts. The use of language in administrative matters, primary and secondary education, as well as in judicial matters was to be based exclusively on location – not the mother tongue of the individual citizen. In Flanders, Dutch became the only official language, and in Wallonia, the official language was exclusively French. Brussels and certain border areas were said to be bi-lingual.

By the mid-1960s, the Flemish gross regional product per capita surpassed that of Wallonia.[2] Today, the Flemish Region of the country is substantially richer than the Walloon Region. Since 1970, contemporaneous with economic rise of the Flemish Region,[3] five sets of constitutional revisions (and a pending sixth reform of state) have transformed Belgium's governmental structure from a strong unitary federal system into a federal structure of mind-boggling complexity, in which substantial power has devolved to sub-federal governmental units. Two major principles have dominated these reforms.[4] The first is the devolution of more powers and autonomy to the component states. The second one is minority protection: of the Francophone people (40 %) in the country at large, and of the Flemish people (20 %) in Brussels (see infra Sect. 5.2.4).

---

[1] Total population of ca 11,000,000.

[2] L. Hooghe, Belgium: Hollowing the Center, in *Federalism and Territorial Cleavages*, Eds. Ugo M. Amoretti and Nancy Bermeo, Johns Hopkins University Press: Baltimore. 2004, pp. 56–57.

[3] The Flemish demand for reform in 1970 aimed at cultural and language rights (reflected in Communities) and the Walloons at economic autonomy (reflected in Regions), in order to improve the bad economic situation in the South.

[4] A. Alen & K. Muylle, *Handboek van het Belgisch Staatsrecht*, Kluwer, Antwerp. 2011, n. 253–256.

5.1.3 A Federal State

Article 1 of the Constitution declares Belgium to be a Federal State, constituted by Communities and Regions. Power and responsibility is allocated to governments for each of three Communities (French, Flemish, and the small German part) (article 2) and for three Regions (Wallonia, Flanders, and the bilingual Brussels Capital Region) (article 3). According to article 4 of the Constitution, Belgium comprises four language areas (Dutch, French, bi-lingual Brussels and German).[5] Every municipality in the country belongs to one of them. In these areas, all public affairs, between the government and citizens, in administrative, judicial and all other public matters, must absolutely be conducted in the language of the territory, i.e., Dutch, French or German in the monolingual areas, and Dutch and French in Brussels.[6] This is said to consecrate the territoriality principle, with several legal consequences, most importantly the territorial competence of Communities and Regions (see infra Sect. 5.2.4).

The Flemish Region comprises the Dutch language area, the Walloon Region the French and German language area, and the Brussels Capital Region the bilingual language area. The Flemish Region also comprises the Provinces of Antwerp, Limburg, East-Flanders, Flemish Brabant and West-Flanders. The Walloon Region consists of Hainaut, Liège, Luxemburg, Namur and Walloon Brabant.

The Flemish Community not only includes the Flemish language area but is also competent for the Flemish institutions in the Brussels Capital Region. The same goes for the French Community, including the French language area, and the French institutions in the Brussels Capital Region (articles 127 § 2 and 128 § 2 of the Constitution). The German-speaking Community consists of the German language area.

The Communities and Regions have separate, directly elected, parliamentary-style legislatures, a legislatively accountable executive body, and broad and exclusive policy responsibility and authority in specified areas. Although the Flemish Community and Region remain separate legal entities, their powers are executed in Flanders by one single Parliament and Government. Belgium therefore has six in lieu of seven parliaments and governments: one federal, and five on the component state level (Flanders, Brussels, Walloon Region, French Community, and German Community). Belgian federalism is said to be of an asymmetrical nature: although the distinction between Community and Region is fundamental, their

---

[5]This is a small German-speaking area along the eastern border with a population of about 75,000.

[6]With a mitigation through 'language facilities' in 27 municipalities in a monolingual Region, where it is allowed to use the language of a protected minority in public matters. There are six border municipalities in Flanders with facilities for Francophone people, four border municipalities in Wallonia with facilities for Dutch speakers, six municipalities in Flanders on the border with Brussels, with facilities for Francophone people, nine municipalities in the German language area with facilities for Francophone people and two municipalities in Wallonia with facilities for German speaking people.

functioning is not identical in all parts of the country.[7] In Flanders, the powers of the Region are executed by Community institutions, while on the Francophone side, some Community powers are executed by Regional institutions. Also, the Brussels institutions have at several points a different status than in the other Regions.

5.1.4 Towards a Confederate State[8]

The evolution is one of reverse federalism: not from separate entities towards a federation, but from a very centralized government to an unraveling of the federal power towards Communities and Regions. This evolution has not yet come to an end. The Flemish demand more devolution, towards a confederate model. This was the big issue for the June 10, 2007 and the June 13, 2010 federal elections. In the 2007 federal elections a Flemish cartel between the Christian-Democrats and a (at the time) small nationalist party N-VA won the elections with an overwhelming victory for their leader Leterme. Since that date, at least until Fall 2011, the country has been in a deep institutional crisis. Flemish parties demand a substantial state reform, Francophone parties refuse.

Since mid 2007, the political scenario has been worse than a bad Hollywood B movie. More than 6 months of negotiations in the second half of 2007 led nowhere. In despair, on Christmas 2007, the King asked the Former Prime Minister Verhofstadt to form a provisional government until Easter. At the end of March 2008, with an agreement on a first round of minor issues for devolution[9] and the hope for a more substantial reform by mid July, Leterme took over as new Prime Minister with a government held hostage by the magical date of July 15. On July 14, 2008, no further progress was made in the negotiations for a state reform, and on that evening, the Prime Minister offered his resignation to the King. After a short cool-off period, the King refused this resignation and appointed three Mediators who had time until mid-September 2008 gathering the parties around an agenda for state reform. The financial crisis of the fall 2008 shifted the attention towards even more urgent matters. However, in the aftermath of the government intervention to save Fortis bank, Prime Minister Leterme had to resign around Christmas of 2008.

Herman Van Rompuy, the current President of the EU Council, became the new Prime Minister. Being called to Europe, he left the job in November 2009

---

[7] A. Alen & K. Muylle, 2011, n. 263–264.

[8] In the Belgian context, this concept does not necessarily refer to a cooperative model between independent states, but also to the extreme devolution of powers to the component states within the framework of one single independent State, in which, however, the powers of the Central Government have become extremely limited.

[9] Involving several transfers of power on minor issues, not discussed in this Report because not yet approved. See Proposal for a Special Act on Institutional Measures, *Belgian Senate* 2007–2008, n. 4-602/1, 5 March 2008.

and Leterme took over again. This Leterme II government was broken up at the end of April 2010 when the Flemish liberals resigned. New federal elections were unavoidable in June 2010. The result was a revolutionary landslide victory for Flemish nationalists N-VA in Flanders, led by the charismatic Bart De Wever who brought the party to the number one position as the largest political party in the country. In the South there was a clear victory for francophone socialists PS, led by Elio Di Rupo.

For more than a year, until the Summer of 2011, these two were trying to broker a deal for a new Belgian institutional design and attempt to form a government, without any success however. In the meantime Leterme II continued as a "resigning" government taking care of day to day current affairs. It was only after the largest Belgian party, N-VA, left the negotiation table in July 2011, that DiRupo as "formateur" (and Prime Minister to be) was finally able, after a record setting 541 days, and without any majority on the Flemish side of the Federal Parliament, to form a government on 6 December 2011, between the Socialists, Christian-Democrats and Liberals.

In the meantime while trying to form a government coalition, Di Rupo reached in the fall 2011 a political consensus about the state reform. Since the constitution requires a complex majority in Parliament for state reform, a political agreement (the so called Butterfly agreement) between no less than eight parties (the socialists, Christian-Democrats, Liberals and green parties on both sides of the country) was finalized. This agreement includes a complex package of state reforms on diverse matters (infra). The implementation of this sixth state reform will take place in several steps. The first part of the reform laws has been signed on July, 19 2012. The next part of the implementation is still a work in progress.

The opinions about this agreement are very divergent. Proponents and opponents of this agreement take into account that this is not a terminus. The big discussion about Federalism versus Confederalism has already started. Since new federal elections will take place in June 2014 at the latest and these federal elections will probably take place at the same time of the Regional and the Community (and the European) elections, a new institutional crisis is not an unrealistic scenario.

5.2 The Federal Distribution and Exercise of Lawmaking Power

Questions: *(1) Which areas of law are subject to the (legislative) jurisdiction of the central authority?; (2) Which areas of law remain within the (legislative) jurisdiction of the component states?; (3) Does the constitution allocate residual powers to the central government, the component states, or (in case of specific residual powers) to both?; (4) What is the constitutional principle according to which conflicts (if any) between central and component state law are resolved (e.g., supremacy of federal law)?; (5) Do the municipalities – by virtue of the constitution or otherwise – have significant law making power and if so, in what areas?*

From the concept of reverse federalism, it follows that there is a devolution of powers from the central, i.e., federal level to the Component States, Communities and Regions. The fundamental basis for this transfer of powers is the Special State Reform Act of 8 August 1980 (SSRA), as amended.

The Federal authority is being dismantled in a dual fashion: by transferring powers upwards to the European Union (and to the European Court of Human Rights) (see article 34 of the Constitution), and downwards to the Communities and Regions. The latter is the process of federalization. In the context of the present Report, we only deal with this phenomenon.

5.2.1 The System of Distribution of Powers

5.2.1.1 Enumerated Powers

Articles 127–130 of the Constitution enumerate powers for the Communities. Article 134 gives legislative powers to the Regions, through a special majority Act. Communities and Regions are competent to enact legislative norms, called Decrees (and Ordinances in Brussels),[10] in areas explicitly allocated to them by the Constitution or by Special Acts. They also have the implied power to make rules as far as necessary for the execution of an enumerated power (article 10 SSRA). Constant case law of the Constitutional Court teaches an exhaustive interpretation of these enumerated powers. Given the autonomy of the Communities and the Regions, and the exclusivity of their powers (see infra), enumerated powers are presumed to be total and exceptions must be interpreted restrictively.[11] This reduces the need for implied powers, and it explains the Constitutional Court's rather restrictive stance toward the use of implied powers.[12]

Accessory or complementary powers are functional or instrumental competences enabling an efficient execution of the powers transferred. Examples are the power to establish decentralized services and institutions (article 9 SSRA) and the power to create an autonomous administration (article 87 SSRA).[13]

Article 19, § 1, first section SSRA, provides that the Communities and the Regions execute their powers, without any prejudice to the powers that have been reserved after October 1, 1980,[14] by the Constitution to the Federal Acts of Parliament. Since there was no distribution of powers before the State Reform of 1980, the term "Act of Parliament" in the Constitution, dating from before

---

[10] With a slightly different legal status.

[11] There are, however, many exceptions, keeping several aspects of such powers with the central Federal authority (see infra).

[12] A. Alen & K. Muylle, 2011, n. 360–362.

[13] A. Alen & K. Muylle, 2011, n. 411–414.

[14] This is the date the SSRA entered into force.

October 1, 1980, refers to any legislative norm.[15] It can be a Federal Act, a Community or Regional Decree or a Brussels Ordinance. This depends on the area, i.e., on whether it is one in which the power has been allocated to Communities or Regions, or an accessory power thereof. In matters referred to by the Constitution, after October 1, 1980, as to be regulated by an Act of Parliament, it is clear that such Act of Parliament is a Federal Act, and thus constitutes a reserved power for the Federal authority, in the sense of article 19 § 1, first section SSRA. This prohibition for Communities and Regions to legislate in areas reserved for the Federation, does not follow from the Constitution itself, but from this Special State Reform Act. The Constitutional Court has therefore ruled that it is possible for a Community or Region to legislate in matters reserved for the Federal authority, if a special and explicit permission to do so is given by a Special State Reform Act, or if such legislation may be based on implied powers as provided in article 10 SSRA.

5.2.1.2 Residual Powers

The central federal authority is involved in a constant process of devolving its powers. All areas not allocated to the Communities or Regions remain under the competence of the federal authority, i.e., the federal authority keeps all residual powers.

Yet, that principle is subject to change: article 35 of the Constitution, introduced by the 1993 State Reform, states that the federal authority has competence only in matters that have been explicitly allocated to it; according to this provision, therefore, residual powers rest with the Communities and Regions. This article, however, has not yet entered into force. It remains a dead letter until a new article in the Constitution enumerates the exclusive powers of the Federal authority and a special majority Act of Parliament has determined how the residual powers will be executed by the Communities and Regions.[16] In spite of the sixth state reform negotiated in Fall 2011, it does not seem very likely that this article 35 will soon become effective, although some people very recently mentioned this matter as a part of the coming seventh reform of state.

5.2.1.3 Exclusive Powers and the Principle of Verticality

The distribution of powers is based on the principle of exclusivity. The idea is that one legal issue should in principle be addressed exclusively by only one legislator. This relates to the autonomy of Communities and Regions, and the equal position of Federal Acts of Parliament and Decrees. This principle also serves to eliminate conflicts of competence. Yet, since there are many exceptions to the principle of exclusivity of powers, conflicts are not lacking in practice (see infra).

---

[15]A. Alen & K. Muylle, 2011, n. 372–374.
[16]A. Alen & K. Muylle, 2011, n. 58.

The principle of verticality implies that the government that is competent for the regulation of an area also is competent for the execution of its own norms. An exception to this principle are the limited concurrent powers, with the federal authority establishing the norms and the Communities or Regions executing them (see infra).

5.2.1.4 Shared, Parallel and Concurrent Powers[17]

First of all, there are situations of partial exclusivity. Some aspects of a certain matter are exclusively awarded to one authority, and other aspects to another. These are shared powers. This is a consequence of the numerous exceptions made to the power transfers to Communities or Regions, reserving some powers for the federal authority. There are numerous examples, illustrating the famous Belgian competence chaos: e.g., the power of youth protection is allocated to the Communities but several aspects are reserved for the federal authority (article 5, § 1, II, 6° SSRA); the power of policing dangerous and unsafe enterprises belongs to the subunits but labor protection remains a federal competence (article 6, § 1, II, 3° SSRA); the same is true for agriculture and offshore fishing (article 6, § 1, V SSRA). Many other examples could be added.

Second, in case of parallel competences, there is a cumulative and parallel execution of powers on several levels concerning the same area or topic. Several authorities are then competent, each for their own territory and with their own means and institutions. E.g., the power for the public industrial initiative was qualified by the Constitutional Court as a parallel power shared by the federal authority and the Regions. In the SSRA we can find other examples: e.g., scientific research, a parallel power for the Federal authority, the Regions and the Communities (article 6bis, § 1 and § 2 1°); establishing and governing public credit institutions, is a parallel power for the Federal authority and the Regions (article 6, § 1, VI, first section, 2° and fifth section, 2°). The same goes for fundamental rights such as equal rights for men and women (article 11bis of the Constitution), the right to privacy and family life (article 22 of the Constitution), the right of a child to respect for its moral, physical, psychological and sexual integrity (article 22bis of the Constitution), the right to have a dignified human life (article 23 of the Constitution), and the right to consult and receive a copy of any official government document (article 32 of the Constitution).

Third, there are situations in which the principle of exclusivity is not applied but rather replaced by concurrent powers. In the case of total concurrent powers, the Communities or Regions are allowed to regulate only as long as the Federal authority has not enacted, and any subunit regulation is abolished as soon as there is a federal regulation. There is only one example of this form of jurisdiction: the tax power of Communities and Regions based on article 170, § 2 of the Constitution

---

[17]A. Alen & K. Muylle, 2011, n. 364.

(see infra Sect. 5.4.2.1). This power is limited to areas where no federal tax exists, and a later federal tax abolishes the communal or regional tax, if this appears necessary. This criterion of necessity is subject to the control of the Constitutional Court.

More frequent are limited concurrent powers. Here, the federal authority determines the basic rules while the Communities or Regions usually complement and apply these rules (sometimes they must apply them unchanged). In doing so, the Communities or Regions may only make the rules stricter but cannot relax them. As indicated above, this is an exception to the principle of verticality. Examples are the mere application by the Regions of federal norms on employment of foreigners (article 6, § 1, IX, 3 SSRA), and the power for the Regions to complement and apply federal norms on government works and assignments (article 6, § 1, VI, fourth section, 1 SSRA). The Constitutional Court has given such power of complementing and applying to the Communities and Regions also in matters of fire security, the duty to motivate particular acts of government, and regarding restrictions on the right of privacy and family life. In all of these cases, the federal norms are a minimum that may be complemented by the Communities and Regions, without prejudice to the federal norms.

5.2.1.5 Solving Conflicts

A distinction is made between conflicts of powers and conflicts of interests.[18] While the former is a legal conflict, the latter is supposed to be of a political nature. The job to prevent conflicts of power is handled by the Legislation Department of the Council of State, whose opinions are not binding but command high moral authority (article 141 of the Constitution). The job to resolve conflicts of power is handled by the Constitutional Court (article 142 of the Constitution). Awaiting a Special Act for the prevention and resolution of conflicts of interests (article 143 of the Constitution), this remains in the hands of the existing Committee of Consultation (article 31 of the Ordinary State Reform Act (OSRA) 9 August 1980), with 12 members, and with a double parity, between Flemish and Francophone, and between members of the Federal Government and of the Regional and Community Governments. When exceeding a certain power forms the basis of a conflict, then the legal procedure applicable to power conflicts is followed.

Article 143 § 1 of the Constitution imposes on the Communities and the Regions the principle of Federal Loyalty (*Bundestreue*) in the execution of their powers, in order to prevent conflicts of interest in the Federal State. It is clear, however, that the principle of Federal Loyalty also plays a dominant role in the prevention and solution of conflicts of power. The principle of proportionality (see infra) applied by the Constitutional Court is in fact an application of this Federal Loyalty. The political agreement on the sixth reform of state of 2011 puts the controlling power upon this Federal Loyalty in the hands of the Constitutional Court.

---

[18] A. Alen & K. Muylle, 2011, n. 418–419.

Conflicts of powers are decided according to the nature of the powers involved. In case of concurrent jurisdiction, the federal norm prevails over the Community or Regional norm. In the case of shared and parallel jurisdiction, both norms are equal to each other. Even with both instances remaining within the limits of their powers, it is possible that there is an overlap or a conflict. Both the Legislation Department of the Council of State and the Constitutional Court resolve these conflicts according to the proportionality principle. No government may, even within the limits of its competences, take measures that would make it disproportionately difficult for another government authority to execute its powers in an efficient manner. The Constitutional Court applies the same principle to the exclusive powers, both of the Federation, and of the Communities or Regions, and both to their material powers and to their territorial powers. The proportionality principle is thus inherent in any execution of power.[19]

5.2.2 Territorial Powers[20]

Obviously, federal powers can be applied in the whole country of Belgium. This is not the case for the Communities and Regions. The four language areas laid down in article 4 of the Constitution (see supra Sect. 5.1) delimit their territorial jurisdiction. As indicated, this coincides with their territory for the three Regions and for the German Community. This is however not the case for the Flemish and the French Community who execute their powers, except in case of language matters, not only in their own area, but also in those institutions in the Brussels Capital Region that must be considered exclusively part of their Community (see supra Sect. 5.1).

This has led to different interpretations of the concept of a Community. The French Community favors the personality principle: a Community is related to a group of individual citizens that are united by a same language and culture. This approach would allow the French Community to claim competence over all Francophone citizens, wherever they live, even in Flanders. The Flemish Community vehemently opposes such interpretation which ignores the constitutional territorial distribution of competences. The Constitutional Court firmly upholds the territoriality principle.[21] The Constitution establishes an exclusive distribution of territorial powers. All legislation of a Community must be limited to the territory under the competence of such Community. Indeed, the exclusive powers doctrine requires that each concrete relation or situation is regulated by only one legislator (see supra). The Constitutional Court must ensure that Communities do not exceed their territorial or material jurisdiction.

---

[19] A. Alen & K. Muylle, 2011, n. 365.

[20] A. Alen & K. Muylle, 2011, n. 299–303.

[21] Constitutional Court, n. 9 and 10, 30 January 1986; n. 17, 26 March 1986; n.29, 18 November 1986; n.51, 19 April 2006.

The Court has, however, softened its stance in matters of culture.[22] Here, a limited deviation from the territoriality principle seems to be accepted. Given the specific nature of promotion of culture, it is possible that the execution of Community powers in this area may have some consequences outside the territory of the respective Community. Such extraterritorial consequences of measures for the promotion of culture are accepted if they respect the proportionality principle. In particular, they must not infringe the cultural policies of the other Community. Another restriction imposed by the Court is that a Community cannot protect its minority situated in another language area.

5.2.3 Material Powers

5.2.3.1 Communities

The powers of the Communities include cultural matters, education, personalized matters (see infra.) use of language, cooperation between the Communities and international cooperation in the areas mentioned (articles 127–130 of the Constitution). Within the limits of their powers, Communities (and also the Regions) may sanction non-compliance with their legislative norms, which means that the component states have important criminal law power.[23] The political agreement on the sixth reform of state provides the Communities and the Regions with a positive injunction power concerning these federal powers and an increasing say in the prosecution and the criminal policy of the Public Prosecution.

Cultural matters are described exhaustively in article 4 SSRA. Among them are the libraries and museums, radio and television, written press, youth policy, sport, and tourism. Personalized matters are intrinsically linked to the life of a citizen in his Community. They are described in article 5 SSRA and include two categories: health policy and aid to individuals. The social security system, however, is excluded from communal power and reserved to the federal government, although the political agreement of 2011 changes in a complex way some small parts of powers. Health policy includes health care in and outside of hospitals (with important exceptions concerning the basic rules for hospital policy and sickness and invalidity insurance), health education and preventive health care. General health policy is a residual power of the Federation. Aid to individuals includes various measures of social welfare to families, immigrants, disabled persons, senior citizens, juveniles, detainees, etc. However, an important exception, again reserved for the Federation, is the regulation of the minimum standards of subsistence.[24]

---

[22]Constitutional Court, n. 54/96, 3 October 1996; Comments of A. Alen & P. Peeters, in *European Public Law* 1997, 165–173.

[23]A. Alen & K. Muylle, 2011, n. 379–380bis.

[24]A. Alen & K. Muylle, 2011, n. 385.

Education is the most important Community power. Since the 1988 reform, this competence is quasi total. Limited exceptions are the determination of the beginning and end of the mandatory education age, the minimum conditions for awarding a diploma, and pension regulation.

The political agreement of 2011 on the sixth reform of state provides an enlargement of power on a number of very specific matters which already belonged to the Communities.

5.2.3.2 Regions

The regional powers are, in execution of article 39 of the Constitution, specified in article 6 SSRA. Although some of them are very broad, there are always exceptions, reserving some aspects to the federal government. The Regions also have the authority to enter into international treaties with respect to matters within their Jurisdiction.

Since 2002, the Regions have power over the subordinate authorities such as municipalities and provinces (see infra Sect. 5.2, question 5). Exceptions are civil registry, police and fire departments, and pension regulation of personnel. Article 6, § 1, VI SSRA combines a very large allocation of powers on economic policy and development to the Regions (section 1) with important exceptions reserving powers to the federal authority, justified by the functioning of an economic and monetary union (sections 3–5).[25] Tax law will be discussed infra Sect. 5.4.2.6; there have been important transfers to the Regions, although the Federation remains mainly in charge of taxation.

Other competences include environmental and urban planning, environmental policy, water policy, land and nature regulation and conservation, housing (except Federal powers regarding leases), agricultural policy (again, except important Federal powers), offshore fishing, energy, some aspects of labor policy, public works and transportation. In spite of the exhaustive interpretation of the latter powers by the Constitutional Court, large exceptions reserve important aspects to the federal government, such as railroads, air traffic, general police and regulation on traffic and transport, technical regulations, etc. Infrastructures exceeding the territorial limits of a Region require a cooperation agreement (see infra Sect. 5.4.3).

The political agreement of 2011 on the sixth reform provides an enlargement of power on a number of very specific matters.

5.2.3.3 Federal Government

In the areas of public law, social law, economic law, criminal law, and tax law, numerous powers have been transferred from the federal to the state component

---

[25] A. Alen & K. Muylle, 2011, n. 408–410.

level. Still, the federal authorities clearly have vast material powers (see, e.g., those enumerated in article 6, § 1, VI, in fine SSRA). As we have seen, many of the transferred powers are qualified by plenty and sometimes large exceptions, reserving substantial powers for the Federal government. Several areas of law completely remain with the Federation. Its competence includes e.g. private law, commercial law, corporate law, banking and finance, competition law, industrial and intellectual property law, labor and social security law, the bulk of tax law and of the justice system. One should of course keep in mind that the Federation's impact in these areas is decreasing because of transfers upwards to the European Union.

5.2.4 Minority Protection[26]

At the federal level, there are a variety of mechanisms to ensure that neither the Flemish nor the Francophone parties, acting on their own, can impose decisions on the other language group. A governing majority in Parliament always requires a coalition and the Belgian constitution prescribes that the cabinet must have an equal number of ministers from each language group, apart from the Prime Minister. This means that the coalition's necessarily cut across language lines and typically include at least four of the six major parties.[27] Because of what is known as the "cordon sanitaire," all parties have agreed with each other never to include the Flemish Federalists (the Vlaams Belang) in the governing coalition. The reason for this is not so much this party's persistent calls for Flemish independence but what is regarded as its racist hostility to immigrants and its fascist antecedents.

Each Member of Parliament in the Federal House of Representatives is elected for a 4 year term in geographically defined districts from party lists on the basis of proportional representation and is assigned either to the French or the Dutch language group, depending on the language area.[28] Certain "special laws" require concurrent majorities from each language group as well as a two-thirds overall majority (article 4 final section of the Constitution). The "Alarm Bell Procedure" (article 54 of the Constitution), although rarely invoked, enables a three-quarter majority of either language group to suspend the enactment of any proposed legislation[29] that is thought to adversely affect that group. If invoked, the legislative process is suspended and the matter is referred to the Council of Ministers for further consideration and negotiation. Unless an acceptable compromise is reported out in 30 days, the government would most likely fall.

---

[26] A. Alen & K. Muylle, 2011, n. 306–323.

[27] See also L. Hooghe, "A Leap in the Dark: Federalist Conflict and Federal Reform in Belgium." Occasional Paper #27, Western Societies Program. Cornell University: Ithaca. 1991. Nevertheless for the first time in three decades a Francophone holds the top position since 2011.

[28] Except for the Brussels Capital Region and some surrounding suburbs, all of the electoral districts are monolingual.

[29] Except for budget matters and for special majority laws.

Analogous mechanisms and procedures are available in the Brussels Capital Region to protect the Flemish minority there.

Question 5. Do the municipalities – by virtue of the constitution or otherwise – have significant law making power and if so, in what areas?

As indicated, subordinate authorities like the Provinces and Municipalities are under the control of the Regions. Over the years the law making power of these subordinate authorities has been drastically limited and effectively reduced to an implementing or advisory role to the powers of the higher authorities.[30] Being lower authorities, they are under the judicial control of administrative action and under the administrative supervision of the higher authorities, in particular the Regions.

Especially the Provinces have become mere coordinators between these higher authorities and the Municipalities. An important power for the Municipalities is the civil registry (article 164 of the Constitution) and the police (article 184 of the Constitution), which are both, however, subject to the ultimate control of the federal government.

5.3 The Means and Methods of Legal Unification

5.3.1 To What Extent Is Legal Unification or Harmonization Accomplished by the Exercise of Central Power (Top Down)?

5.3.1.1 Via Directly Applicable Constitutional Norms? (e.g., The Equal Protection Clause in the US Requires Specific Features of Family Law; Due Process Limits in Personam Jurisdiction)

The traditional individual civil and political rights and liberties in the Constitution, such as right to privacy and family life, have a direct effect. The same goes for the fundamental rights and liberties guaranteed in the ECHR as well as those in the UN Covenant on Civil and Political Rights. Obviously, the EU-Treaty has direct effect as well. The traditional rights and liberties enjoyed in Belgium also have a horizontal effect or *Drittwirkung*, i.e., on the relationship between individual citizens. Since only states can be brought before the European Court of Human Rights, this has introduced an indirect horizontal effect, imposing a positive duty on the Member States to take all measures needed to guarantee the effective protection of the rights and liberties also on the horizontal relationship between individual citizens.

Socio-economical rights and liberties such as the right to labor or housing have no direct effect. In some cases, however (e.g., access to free education, social assistance), there is a mitigated form of direct effect through a duty of standstill: it

---

[30] Some autonomy remains, protected by the Constitutional Court against infringements of, e.g., the Regions and Communities (A. Alen & K. Muylle, 2011, n. 191 bis).

is then forbidden for the government to take measures that would lower the level of protection substantially below the one existing at the time of the entering into force of such a fundamental right. The Constitutional Court has accepted such standstill obligation also for the right of protection of a safe environment.[31]

Since the famous Franco-Suisse Le Ski judgment of the Cour de Cassation (Supreme Court, to be distinguished from the Constitutional Court) of 27 May 1971, it is accepted as a general principle of law that an international treaty with direct effect (self-executing), prevails over all legislation, both previous and future laws of all kinds. There is no discussion also that EU-law prevails even over the Belgian Constitution (see article 34 of the Constitution). However, as to the relationship between other international treaties and the Belgian Constitution, there is a difference of opinion between the Supreme Court and the Constitutional Court. The former has decided that the ECHR prevails over the Constitution, unless the latter provides greater protection.[32] This is not the opinion of the Constitutional Court which has ruled that the Treaty must respect the Constitution in the internal legal order: it is not allowed for the legislator to do indirectly by approving a Treaty what it cannot do directly, namely infringe upon the Constitution.[33]

5.3.1.2 Via Central Legislation (or Executive or Administrative Rules)?

5.3.1.2.1 Creating Directly Applicable Norms

This is the manner in which federal legislation operates in the whole country in the many areas that are still federal (see supra Sect. 5.2.3, in fine).

5.3.1.2.2 Mandating that States Pass Conforming (Implementing) Legislation (e.g., Rahmengesetze, EC Directives)

In the framework of limited concurrent powers, it is possible, but not required, for Communities and Regions to complement federal legislation without infringing on the basic framework (see supra Sect. 5.2.1).

5.3.1.2.3 Inducing States to Regulate by Conditioning the Allocation of Central Money on Compliance with Central Standards

The Federal government cannot unilaterally impose obligations on the Communities and Regions. Moreover, authorities may only spend money on projects within their

---

[31]Constitutional Court, n. 135/2006, 14 September 2006; n. 137/2006, 14 September 2006; n. 87/2007, 20 June 2007.
[32]Cour de Cassation 16 November 2004, *Rechtskundig Weekblad* 2005–2006, 387.
[33]Constitutional Court, n. 26/91, 16 October 1991; n. 12/94, 3 February 1994.

competence (*Die Ausgaben folgen den Aufgaben*), except when allowed by the Special Financing Act (see infra Sect. 5.4.2.5).[34] Therefore, to condition the use of central money on compliance with central standards, either a special majority Act or a cooperation agreement approved by Parliaments concerned would be needed.

5.3.1.2.4 Indirectly Forcing States to Regulate by Threatening to Take Over the Field in Case of State Inaction or State Action That Does not Conform to Centrally Specified Standards

This would not be possible, given the fundamental principle of autonomy of the Communities and the Regions. There is no principle or right of substitution, except a rather symbolic one in article 16 § 3 SSRA: if Belgium is condemned by an international or supranational court for non-compliance by a Community or a Region with an international or supranational obligation, then the Federal authority can, under some circumstances, substitute for the Community or Region concerned in order to execute such judgment.

5.3.1.3 Through the Judicial Creation of Uniform Norms by Central Supreme Court(s) or Central Courts of Appeal?

There is no doctrine of stare decisis. However the judgments of the Cour de Cassation (Supreme Court) have a strong unifying power (see infra Sect. 5.4.1.4).[35] The same goes for the Council of State in administrative matters and for the Constitutional Court.

These highest courts play an important role in the formulation of general principles. For example, the principle of the proportionality of sanctions,[36] or of compliance with the equality principle, are applied by all three tribunals, using the same criteria and applying the same tests – the Supreme Court to lower court judgments, the Council of State to administrative actions, and the Constitutional Court to legislative norms.

---

[34] A. Alen & K. Muylle, 2011, n. 513.

[35] The unifying power of the judgments of the Courts of Appeal is limited to the jurisdiction area of such Court. It is not unusual to see a split of opinion between different Appellate Courts, not only but often following the linguistic lines (Antwerp, Ghent, Brussels Flemish Chambers vs. Liège, Mons and Brussels French Chambers).

[36] Constitutional Court, n. 81/2007, 7 June 2007.

5.3.1.4 Through Other Centrally Controlled Means, Such as Centrally Managed Coordination or Information Exchange Among the Component States (e.g., Europe's "Open Method of Coordination")?

In light of the phenomenon of reverse federalism, and of the basic principle of the autonomy of the Communities and the Regions, the evolution of Belgian law is not towards more unification or harmonization, but towards devolution and regionalization.

5.3.2 To What Extent Is Legal Unification Accomplished Through Formal or Informal Voluntary Coordination Among the Component States? (Somewhat Bottom Up, Coordinate Model)

There are several mechanisms and committees for consultation, cooperation and coordination between the different Communities, Regions and the Federation (see infra Sect. 5.4.3). Their goal, however, is not to strive for unification or harmonization but try to coordinate the different component state regulations and federal regulations in a way that makes them operational.

There certainly is some influence between the component states, where one will follow the other to some extent. Again, this is not in a spirit of unification, but more of competition. For example, in the area of gift and estate tax, all Regions have followed the Flemish example to introduce special reductions and exemptions with numerous conditions. But these requirements, although similar to a large extent, may vary substantially in their specific and concrete technicalities, sometimes adding to the chaos rather than to harmonization.

5.3.3 To What Extent Is Legal Unification Accomplished, or Promoted, by Non-state Actors (e.g., In the US: American Law Institute, Federal Commissions on Uniform State Laws; in Europe: Principles of European Contract Law (Lando Principles, etc.))?

5.3.3.1 Through Restatements

There are no such unification projects in Belgium.

5.3.3.2 Through Uniform or Model Laws

There are no such unification projects in Belgium.

5.3.3.3 Through Standards and Practices of Industry, Trade Organizations or Other or Private Entities?

Given the cleavage between Flemish and Francophone people, such initiatives remain regional, even when these matters are within the federal powers.

5.3.3.4 To What Extent Do the Activities Listed in Sects. 5.3.3.1, 5.3.3.2 and 5.3.3.3, Above, Provide Input for Unification or Harmonization by Central Action (Top Down) or by the States (Coordinate)?

Again, this does not apply to Belgium.

5.3.4 What Is the Role of Legal Education and Training in the Unification of Law?

5.3.4.1 Do Law Schools Draw Students from Throughout the Federal System?

Given the linguistic cleavage, 99 % of the Belgian students at Flemish law schools are Flemish and vice versa for Wallonia. In some Flemish law schools such as the University of Leuven, there are a large number of international students, from all over Europe in the framework of the EU Erasmus Program, but also from outside of Europe, in the framework of LLM Programs. Thus, ironically, there are more students from abroad than from the other parts of Belgium.

5.3.4.2 Does Legal Education Focus on (i) Central or System-Wide Law or (ii) Component State Law?

Since vast areas of law remain federal, legal education focuses on the federal law. Quite often the approach is different, from one's own particular Flemish or Francophone perspective, e.g., in constitutional law. Also in matters of e.g., private law or commercial law, case law of the Flemish tribunals and courts and Flemish scholarship tends to be ignored in Francophone legal education, because of the linguistic barrier.

In areas in which the law has been regionalized, the legal education will typically, only or primarily focus at the legislation of the respective Region or Community, e.g., law of education, environmental law, gift and estate tax.

5.3.4.3 Is Testing for Bar Admission System-Wide or by Component State?

The same cleavage applies to the Bar admission. Flemish lawyers will have to pass Flemish Bar Admission tests, and Francophone lawyers the Francophone Bar. The legal knowledge tested there is the same as under 5.3.4.2.

5.3.4.4 Is the Actual Admission to the Bar for the Entire Federal System or by Component State?

Admission is for the entire federal system.

5.3.4.5 Do Graduates Tend to Set Up Their Practice or Take Jobs Anywhere in the Federation?

Graduates tend to remain in their own Region, except for those taking jobs in Brussels, where there is a more profound mix between Flemish and Francophone professionals, both in law firms and in companies, mostly in a larger international context (see infra Sect. 5.4.5).

5.3.4.6 Are There Particular Institutions of (Primary, Graduate or Continuing) Legal Education and Training That Play a Unifying Role (e.g., Internships by State Court Judges at Central Courts, Federal Academies or Training Programs)?

There are virtually no such institutions except for a few private initiatives. I am, e.g., member of the Organizing Board and Visiting Professor in a Postgraduate Program on Estate Planning, offering half of the courses in Dutch and half in French, co-organized by the Flemish and the Francophone Free Universities of Brussels, VUB and ULB.

5.3.5 *To What Extent Do External Factors, Such as International law, Influence Legal Unification?*

International law, and certainly EU law, has an influence in that it takes away power to legislate, mostly on the level of the federation. EU Directives have a unifying effect, in particular regarding individual rights and liberties. The Antidiscrimination Directives, e.g., force both federal and regional as well as communal legislation to comply with them.

5.4 Institutional and Social Background

5.4.1 The Judicial Branch

5.4.1.1 Is There a Court at the Central Level with the Power to Police Whether Central Legislation Has Exceeded the Lawmaking Powers Allocated to the Central Government?

The Constitutional Court controls the constitutional distribution of powers between the Federation, the Communities, and the Regions.

5.4.1.2 If Yes, Do(es) the Central Court(s) Regularly and Effectively Police the Respective Constitutional Limitations? (Please Explain and Give Examples)

There is a vast case law on these issues. Since there is no precise list of rules on the distribution of powers, but a rather complicated set of provisions embodied in the Constitution and in State Reform Acts, the Court has a large margin of interpretation with regard to these rules and its own competence. The Court has considered itself competent to decide whether an issue must be regulated by Ordinary Act of Parliament of by Special Majority Act.[37] The Court also ruled that the complementary or accessory powers for Communities and Regions are rules of distribution of powers.[38] The same goes for rules in Acts of State Reform imposing a procedure of consultation between the Federal State, the Communities or the Regions.[39] Other examples are the case law on the principle of territoriality (see supra, Sect. 5.2.2) and the principle of the exclusivity of the distribution of powers (see supra, Sect. 5.2.1).

The Constitutional Court is also competent for judicial review of the constitutionality of a federal act of Parliament, a decree or ordinance regarding the fundamental rights and liberties, in particular the principle of equality and non-discrimination. It is safe to say that such review has become the primary task of the Constitutional Court.[40]

---

[37]Constitutional Court, n. 18/90, 23 May 1990.
[38]Constitutional Court, n. 24/86, 26 June 1986.
[39]Constitutional Court, n. 2/92, 15 January 1992; n. 68/96, 28 November 1996; n. 74/96, 11 December 1996; n. 49/99, 29 April 1999.
[40]A. Alen & K. Muylle, 2011, n. 455–458.

5.4.1.3 Is There a Court at the Central Level with Power Authoritatively to Interpret Component State Law?

Article 84 of the Constitution states that only an act of parliament can give an authentic interpretation of acts of parliament, i.e., an interpretation that is generally binding for everyone (subject to control of the Constitutional Court). Given the principle of mutual autonomy of the federal and component state authorities, article 133 of the Constitution teaches that only a decree can give an authentic interpretation of decrees. Strictly speaking, it follows from the Constitution that this only applies to decrees of the Communities, and that neither decrees of the Regions nor Brussels ordinances have such power of authentic interpretation. Quite logically, however, for the regional decrees, such power has been implicitly accepted by the Constitutional Court.[41]

5.4.1.4 Are There Both Central and State Courts, and if so, Are There Trial and Appellate Courts on Both Levels?

The entire judiciary system is Federal (articles 147, 150–151, 156–157 of the Constitution),[42] with civil tribunals and courts, criminal tribunals and courts, labor tribunals and courts, commercial tribunals and courts, and in wartime military courts. There is a level of first instance, and an appellate level (mostly the Courts of Appeal), and for legal (but not factual issues) ensuring the unity of law, a third level with the Supreme Court (Cour de Cassation). For administrative law, there are administrative tribunals, and the Council of State. At the apex, there is of course the Constitutional Court.

5.4.1.5 Are There Other Mechanisms for Resolving Differences in Legal Interpretation Among Central and/or Component State Courts? If Yes, Please Describe Their Nature and the Extent of Their Use

There are no such mechanisms in Belgium.

5.4.2 Relations Between the Central and Component State Governments

5.4.2.1 Does the Central Government Have the Power to Force Component States to Legislate?

The central government has no such power. The Communities and Regions are autonomous. See supra Sects. 5.2.1.3 and 5.3.1.2.4.

---

[41] Constitutional Court, n. 193/2004, 24 November 2004; n. 25/2005, 2 February 2005.
[42] A. Alen & K. Muylle, 2011, n. 530–590.

5.4.2.2 Who Executes Central Government Law? (The Central Government Itself or the Component States?) If It Depends upon the Areas Involved, Please Explain

The principle of verticality implies that the authority responsible for a regulation also carries this out. An exception are the limited concurrent powers (see supra Sect. 5.2.1).

5.4.2.3 Are Component States or Their Governments, or Other Communities, Represented at the Central Level, and if so, What Is Their Role in the Central Legislative Process?

See infra Sect. 5.4.2.4.

5.4.2.4 How and by Whom Are Component State Representatives at the Central Level Elected or Appointed?

Political life in Belgium is conducted along linguistic lines. There is no longer any major political party that operates on both sides of the linguistic frontier. By reason of internal conflicts relating to language and cultural autonomy, all three of the major parties – the Christian Democrats, the Liberals, and the Socialists – have, for four decades by now, split into separate French-speaking and Flemish parties.[43] In the Federal elections, citizens must vote in geographically defined areas – choosing exclusively from party lists of their own language group. Thus, a person who lives in Flanders must vote for a Dutch-speaking party. Similarly, a person voting in the Walloon Region must choose a French-speaking party. With the limited exception of the Brussels area and some surrounding suburbs, these six parties do not compete in the Federal Parliamentary elections.[44] Nor do political parties compete across the language line in the Community and Regional elections, with the exception of the Brussels Capital Region.[45]

---

[43] By the 1930s, the Catholic party became divided into two linguistic "wings" – one Flemish and one French-speaking – over the issue of Flemish cultural autonomy, and later in 1968, the Christian Democrats formally split into two separate Parties, as part of the conflict surrounding the Catholic University of Leuven/Louvain. Similarly, in the 1960s and 1970s, as Walloon economic conditions declined, Walloon Federalist Parties sprouted up, with federalist-socialist agendas, which threatened the larger Socialist Party and led to its division in 1978. The Federal Liberal Party also broke up along Flemish and Francophone lines in 1971.

[44] K. Deschouwer. "The Changing Nature of Belgian Consociationalism: 1961–2001," *Acta Politica*, Section 4.

[45] Kris Deschouwer, "Kingdom of Belgium," in *Constitutional Origins, Structure, and Change in Federal Countries*, ed. John Kincaid, et al., *A Global Dialogue on Federalism* (Montreal: Published for Forum of Federations and InterFederal Association of Centers for Federal Studies by McGill-Queens's University Press, 2005), p. 60.

This means that any politician at the central level is, though not formally, in some informal way a representative of his or her Community or Region. This situation has been identified as a major democratic problem since federal politicians are essentially unaccountable to half of the population.

Formally, there are no component state representatives in the House of Representatives (150 members), which is the most important legislative body. In the Senate, 40 of the 71[46] members are directly elected, 25 by Flemish and 15 by Francophone voters, reflecting the demographic proportions in the country. Then there are 21 Community Senators, ten of them appointed by and from the Flemish Parliament, ten by and from the Parliament of the French Community and one by and from the Parliament of the German Community. They are clearly the representatives of the respective Communities in the Federal Senate. They have no other role or powers than those of an ordinary Senator. Finally there are ten additional Senators appointed by cooptation by the 61 Senators mentioned, 6 of them on the Flemish side and 4 on the Francophone side.

The political agreement of 2011 on the sixth reform of state has changed and limited the role of the Senate. After the next Community and Regional elections of 2014, it will become a non-permanent "Senate of the state components" with 50 Community Senators and 10 appointed by the Community parliaments.[47]

5.4.2.5 Who Has the Power to Tax (What)? The Central Government, the Component States or Both?

See infra Sect. 5.4.2.6.

5.4.2.6 Are There General Principles Governing or Prohibiting Multiple Taxation? Are There Constitutional or Legislative Rules on Revenue Sharing Among the Component States or Between the Federation and the Component States?

In execution of articles 175 and 177 of the Constitution, the Special Financing Act (SFA) of 16 January 1989, as amended 13 July 2001, introduces the principle of financial federalism: financial means can only be spent by an entity on projects within its powers (see supra Sect. 5.3.1.2.3).[48] The Communities and Regions have large financial means to execute their powers in an autonomous way. Their fiscal autonomy to levy taxes is, however, rather limited for the Regions and virtually non-existent for the Communities. The sources of financing of the Communities

---

[46]One must add the Senators by virtue of Law, being the sons and daughters of the King, from the age of 18, with voting rights from the age of 21.
[47]A. Alen & K. Muylle, 2011, n. 161bis and n. 241bis.
[48]A. Alen & K. Muylle, 2011, n. 508–513bis.

and Regions are mainly four: (1) a direct constitutional taxing power (article 170, § 2); (2) a constitutional power to charge fees for specific services rendered (article 173); (3) loans (article 49 SFA); and most importantly (4), their allocated shares in the federal tax revenues.

The first source appears strong in theory, but it is weak in practice. It is the general power to levy taxes, awarded directly by the Constitution to the Communities and the Regions (article 170 § 2). This is an autonomous power aimed at acquiring financial means and not constrained by the material powers of the Communities or Regions. However, the proportionality test will limit such power if the non-fiscal side effect of a tax appears to be its primary goal and would be a disproportionate infringement on the distribution of material powers. An important restriction is that the fiscal Decrees or Ordinances must respect the limits of their territorial powers. This makes Community taxation virtually impossible for the Flemish and the French Communities, since it is not possible, in the Brussels area, to determine how and to whom such taxation would be applied.

As has been noted (supra Sect. 5.2.1), this general taxation power is the only total concurrent power between the Federation and the state components, with a hierarchy of norms and superiority of the fiscal Federal Act of Parliament over a fiscal decree or ordinance. A federal act of parliament may determine the exceptions to this state component power, as they seem necessary (article 170 § 2, section 2 of the Constitution). It is therefore in the power of the Federation to determine a priori what taxation remains within and outside of the jurisdiction of the Communities and Regions, as well as to limit or abolish existing Community or Regional taxes ex post, under the condition that the necessity for such a measure can be shown. Based on these limitations, large areas of tax law remain federal, such as personal income tax, VAT, and company tax.

Taxes on water and garbage are in the exclusive power of the Regions. In addition, article 3 SFA transfers the revenues and the regulation of 12 specific taxes exclusively to the Regions, e.g., gift and estate tax, real estate transfer tax, real estate ownership tax, traffic tax, radio and TV tax, tax on games and gambling.

The fourth source mentioned is the most important one. The federal authority determines, claims and receives personal income tax and VAT, but transfers parts of the revenue to the Communities and the Regions. Personal income tax is transferred based on its localization, with an 80 % Francophone and a 20 % Flemish share for taxes levied in Brussels. The VAT revenues allocated to the financing of education is determined on the basis of the number of students (article 39, § 2 SFA). There are two techniques. The first is a system of shared taxes. Parts of personal income tax and VAT are received by the federal authority in a uniform way throughout the whole country and then allocated to the Communities, without any possibility for these Communities to apply tax cuts or tax surplus (article 6, § 1 SFA). Part of the personal income tax revenue is allocated to the Regions in a system of joint taxes. Here, the Regions are allowed, within some limits, to levy a tax surplus or allow tax cuts.

The political agreement of 2011 on the sixth reform of state contains a considerable reform of the Special Financing Act (SFA) with 12 specific goals. In general the fiscal autonomy of the Regions increases, the Communities and the Regions are expected to take on more fiscal responsibility, while the solidarity continues within limited acceptable boundaries and the financial stability of the state components is assured. The implementation of these points is still a work in progress and is not in effect as of today (Feb. 2013).

5.4.3 Other Formal or Informal Institutions for Resolving Intergovernmental Conflicts. Are There Other Institutions (Political, Administrative, Judicial, Hybrid or Sui Generis) to Help Resolve Conflicts Between Component States or Between the Central Government and Component States?

Belgium is evolving from a dual form to a more cooperative version of federalism.[49] The principles of equality of federal acts and decrees, and of exclusivity of the distribution of powers, as conditions for the autonomy of the Communities and the Regions, were not able to realize an effective dualist system. The sharing of responsibilities at different levels, federal, regional, and communal, and the many links and sometimes overlaps between their powers, gave rise in the 1980s to all kinds of informal cooperation (in addition to the formal procedures and the Committee of Consultation, supra, Sect. 5.2.1) and political agreements not based on written law, such as policy protocols for health care. However, the strict principle of autonomy of the different authorities often proved to be an obstacle for more far-reaching cooperation.

Therefore, the State Reforms of 1988 and 1993 have attempted to remove obstacles and have expanded the possibilities for cooperation between the federal and the communal and regional levels. Cooperation agreements may deal with the joint establishment and management of services and institutions, joint execution of autonomous powers, common development of initiatives (article 92bis, § 1 SSRA). Besides this possibility to conclude cooperation agreements, there are situations where such an agreement is imposed (article 92bis, § 2-4quater SSRA). In most cases the agreement must be approved by federal act, decree or ordinance. Article 77, first section, 10 of the Constitution makes the Chamber and the Senate equally competent for legislation approving cooperation agreements between the Federal State, the Communities and the Regions.

Article 6, §§ 12–7 SSRA imposes several consultation procedures, in particular between the Federal Government and the Governments of the Regions. It also provides that the Committee of Consultation can create Inter-ministerial Conferences (article 31bis, first section OSRA), and must create one for Foreign Policy (article 31bis, second section OSRA).

---

[49] A. Alen & K. Muylle, 2011 n. 501.

5.4.4 The Bureaucracy

5.4.4.1 Is the Civil Service of the Central Government Separate from the Civil Services of the Component States?

The Federal State, the Communities and the Regions have each established their own administration (see supra Sect. 5.2).

5.4.4.2 If There Are Separate Civil Service Systems, to What Extent Is There Lateral Mobility (or Career Advancement) Between Them?

The administrations are separate and autonomous, and there is no formal system of lateral mobility or career advancement.

Since the Communities and Regions enjoy more power on several matters, a discussion is going on about the possible consequences towards the civil servants who now work for the Federal administration but might be relocated to the administration of the state components.

5.4.5 Social Factors

5.4.5.1 Are There Important Racial, Ethnic, Religious, Linguistic or Other Social Cleavages in the Federation? If Yes, Please Briefly Describe These Cleavages

It is quite obvious that Belgium today is a country with two peoples living in a divided society.[50] Early in the twentieth century, King Albert I was told by a Walloon political leader: "Sire, You reign over two peoples. In Belgium there are Walloons and Flemish; there are no Belgians".[51] This is an overstatement if it is meant to suggest that a Belgian identity counts for *nothing*.[52] There seem to be some common attitudes on both sides of the language divide, including a pragmatic willingness to compromise and skepticism of government. Belgians take pride in the restaurant culture in their country (which is said to have more Michelin stars per

---

[50] The following text under 5.4.5.1 is a quotation, taken literally from Robert Mnookin & Alain Verbeke, "Persistent Nonviolent Conflict with No Reconciliation: The Flemish and Walloons in Belgium", 72 *Law and Contemporary Problems* 2009, Spring (151), 164–166.

[51] This quote comes from a published letter to the Belgian King written by J. Destree, a Walloon Socialist leader. See A. Alen, "Nationalism – Federalism – Democracy. The example of Belgium," *Revue européenne de droit public* 1993, Vol. 5, n. 1, p. 47.

[52] Some even suggest that the younger Flemish are more willing to identify with Belgium, possibly because they lack first-hand experience with linguistic discrimination W. Swenden & M.T. Jans, "Will it Stay or will it Go? Federalism and the Sustainability of Belgium," *West European Politics* 2006, Vol. 29(5), p. 889.

capita than France) and share a love for outstanding food and drink. Nevertheless, survey evidence suggests that for most citizens, their Belgian identity is thin, at least in comparison to their local or Regional identity.[53] No one knows the words of the national anthem, and Belgium is one of the least nationalistic countries in the world. Belgians are quick to suggest that there are real cultural differences between the Walloons and the Flemish. The conventional wisdom is that the Flemish are more disciplined and harder working, like the Northern European, Germanic cultures, while the Walloons take after the more fun-loving Latin's in Southern Europe.[54] Politically and ideologically, there are some conspicuous differences: the socialist tradition is much stronger in the Walloon Region, and the Flemish are much more committed to a market economy.[55] While nearly everyone throughout the country is nominally Catholic, the Walloon Region is more secular, and in Flanders the proportion of observant Catholics is higher.

It seems uncontestable today that within Belgium, the language cleavage has been embedded in a governmental structure that reinforces the sense that there are "two peoples" who are likely to drift further apart and not closer together in the foreseeable future.[56] Ordinary citizens may participate in the political process only among their own language group, except for a small political elite who must interact and negotiate in the federal government. There are no mass media – i.e., federal newspapers, television stations, or radio stations – that are aimed at both the French- and Dutch-speaking Communities.[57] The daily newspapers are exclusively Dutch, French, or German.[58] Television and radio stations have been separate in Flanders and Wallonia since 1960,[59] and each Community has its own public broadcasting organization regulated by its language Community rather than by the federal government.[60]

---

[53] Liesbet Hooghe, 2004, p. 65.

[54] Against "clichés", see Rudy Aernoudt, *Vlaanderen Wallonië. Je t'aime moi non plus*, Roularta Books: Roeselare. 2006, pp. 17–35.

[55] Research indicates that the partisan control over the administration in Wallonia impacts on the French-speaking governments' resistance against organizational and HR management reforms, while Flanders has been a modernizer in administrative reform (M. Brans, C. De Visscher & D. Vancoppenolle. "Administrative Reform in Belgium: Maintenance or Modernisation?", *WEP* 29(5), 2006, pp. 979–998).

[56] See also Martin Euwema & Alain Verbeke, "Negative and Positive Roles of Media in the Belgian Conflict : A Model for De-escalation", 93 *Marquette Law Review* Fall (139), 2009, pp. 140–150.

[57] Martin Euwema & Alain Verbeke, 93 *Marquette Law Review* 2009, Fall, 2009, pp. 150–158.

[58] Els De Bens, "European Media Landscape: Belgium," European Journalism Centre. 2000. http://www.ejc.nl/jr/emland/belgium.html

[59] Kris Deschouwer, "Kingdom of Belgium," in *Constitutional Origins, Structure, and Change in Federal Countries*, ed. John Kincaid, et al., *A Global Dialogue on Federalism* (Montreal: Published for Forum of Federations and InterFederal Association of Centers for Federal Studies by McGill-Queen's University Press, 2005), p. 50.

[60] Belgian newspapers, however, are self-regulated by a single association, the Federation of Editors. "Country Profile: Belgium," BBC News. 14 May 2006. http://news.bbc.co.uk/2/hi/europe/country_profiles/999709.stm

The degree of residential and workplace segregation in the Flemish and Walloon Regions is stunning. Belgians sometimes describe themselves as "living separately together." Within Wallonia, very few Dutch-speaking people reside or work, and very few Flemish live in or commute to Wallonia. Flemish businessmen in prosperous southwest Flanders complain that because even unemployed Walloons are unwilling to commute to Flanders, they often hire workers from neighboring France. Within Brussels (where about 80 % of the population speaks French at home) there is a modest degree of residential integration. The Brussels workplace tends to be more integrated because many Flemish people who live in Flanders commute to Brussels for work. The Flemish who work or live in Brussels are typically reasonably fluent in French.

While Belgium is a small country, there is surprisingly little social interaction between Flemish and Walloons. Millions of Belgians are literally unable to communicate because they cannot speak each other's language. The degree of linguistic segregation in the schools – from the elementary level through the universities – is striking. At all levels the curriculum of any particular school is typically taught exclusively either in French or Dutch. While some families intentionally cross-enroll their children so that they might better learn the other language, this is the exception. Nor is there a shared Federal commitment to make Belgians bi-lingual. While on both sides of the language divide, elementary schools beginning in the fourth grade do offer a few hours a week of language instruction in the other language, few Walloons ever learn to speak Dutch with any degree of fluency. In the year 2000, researchers found that in Wallonia 17 % know Dutch in addition to French. The proportion of bilingual Flemish people is much higher: 57 % know French and Dutch, and 40 % know English as well. In Wallonia, only 7 % are trilingual.[61]

5.4.5.2 Are Distinct Groups Evenly or Randomly Dispersed Throughout the Federation or Are They Concentrated in Certain Regions, Territories, States or Other Political Subdivisions? If They Are Concentrated in Certain Regions, etc., Please Explain How This Concentration Relates to the Structure of the Federal System

The linguistic cleavage between Flemish, Francophone and German speaking people coincides largely with territorial separation. Most Flemish live in Flanders, most Francophone citizens in Wallonia, and most German speaking in the East Cantons. This affects the structure of the federal system in a substantial way, since the concept of language areas, which is the basis for the principle of territoriality, is based on it (see supra, Sect. 5.1). There is of course the notable exception of

---

[61] Victor Ginsburgh & Shlomo Weber, "La dynamique des langues en Belgique," *Regards Economiques*, Institut de Recherches Economiques et Sociales de l'Université Catholique de Louvain, June 2006, n. 42, 4.

Brussels where a large majority of the people speak French, living mixed with a Dutch speaking minority. Note that Brussels is becoming more and more an international melting pot with languages such as English, Spanish, and even Arabic spoken. The specific Brussels situation certainly has a strong impact on the structure of the federal system, with the creation of the Brussels Capital Region and all its complicated and delicate consequences (e.g. how the Communities relate to that Region; supra, Sect. 5.2.2).

An extremely sensitive issue are the "border" municipalities, i.e., suburbs of Brussels that are situated on Flemish regional territory, but in which the vast majority of the inhabitants are Francophone. This phenomenon is known as the 'Frenchification' of Brussels and its surroundings. This has affected the federal system (e.g. language facilities, supra Sect. 5.1) and has had a huge impact on the political situation and the relationship between the two groups. These substantially Francophone municipalities on Flemish soil have become a symbolic catalyst for the conflict that has put the country in an institutional crisis, with passionate reactions, such as the refusal by the Flemish Government to appoint Francophone Mayors who refuse to conduct all official meetings solely in Dutch, and with the enormous discussion on the electoral district of Brussels-Halle-Vilvoorde and its alleged unconstitutionality. This discussion about the electoral and judicial district Brussels-Halle-Vilvoorde has finally come to an end since the electoral B-H-V-district has been divided according to the first chapter of the sixth reform of state which has been implemented on July 19 2012. The judicial district Brussels will be reformed as well.

5.4.5.3 Is There Significant Asymmetry in Natural Resources, Development, Wealth, Education or Other Regards Between the Component States? If Yes, Please Explain How This Relates to the Structure of the Federal System

Wallonia used to have vast natural resources, especially in the form of coal mines. This made it the rich part of the country; one of the first regions in Europe to become industrialized as early as the nineteenth century (see supra, Sect. 5.1). Development, wealth, education were all at higher levels in the Francophone parts, and situated in Brussels and Wallonia. As mentioned before, this has drastically changed over the twentieth century, especially after World War II. The traditional industries declined and foreign investment shifted dramatically to Flanders. Since the end of the 1960s, Flanders has been the more prosperous Region, and it has constantly been moving upwards while Wallonia has declined, creating an ever-widening gap. Today, Flanders is one of the richest Regions in Europe, Wallonia among the poorest. Flemish education is among the top in the world, Wallonia is far below.

This relates to the structure of the federal system in that solidarity mechanisms ensure vast transfers of money from Flanders to Wallonia, especially in the social security system. Another example is the 2000 reform transferring revenues from

VAT to the Communities, using a formula that enabled the Francophone Community to pay for its education deficit. The reform of the Special Financing Act (supra Sect. 5.4.2.6) maintains this principle and reassures the state components that they will win nor lose any financial help due to this reform. This is guaranteed by a so called fixed 'equalizing amount' for the next 10 years and will be reduced the 10 years after.[62]

These disparities also matter for the future structure of the federal system in that the Walloons fear any form of devolution and see it as a signal that Flanders wants to let them down and break solidarity. Despite the Walloon Marshall plan and some signs of economic recovery in the South, the gap remains huge. Flanders argues that Wallonia must take responsibility for itself and that money transfers must be conditioned on economic performance. This argument finds support in the fact that some Regions in Wallonia which have received enormous subsidies from the European Union, such as Hainaut, have shown not to be able to use them for the better.

5.5 Conclusion

There was enormous Flemish pressure to change the status quo. Since the last two federal elections, in June of 2007 and June of 2010, the Flemish negotiators have not stopped to press further for substantial state reform. The Francophone "No" that stood firmly for many years, at some point seemed to come to a more realistic position of readiness to cooperate with a state reform of sorts. After N-VA left the negotiations, Di Rupo managed to broker a state reform deal and a six-party coalition government in the Fall of 2011. This sixth state reform (1) settles the historical problem of Brussels-Halle-Vilvoorde (BHV) by splitting this electoral and judicial district, (2) comprises a limited reorganization of the Brussels government; (3) adapts the Financing Law; and (4) organizes further devolution to the communities and regions. Critics claim it to be too little too late. Some powers to regulate labor markets are devolved to the regions, but the federal government retains control of the collective bargaining process. To a limited degree the regions will now have the power to raise or lower income taxes. But corporate taxes remain a national prerogative. Moreover, to protect Wallonia, there is a "solidarity mechanism" that will insure that a regions' share of income taxes will be no less than its share of the total Belgian population. The social security system remains mainly at the federal level.[63]

Hence, this state reform confirms both the inevitable tendency of further devolution towards a more confederate model and the typical Belgian pattern of complicated technical compromises lacking all coherence. Its implementation is

---

[62]A. Alen & K. Muylle, 2011, n. 513bis.

[63]Robert Mnookin & Alain Verbeke, 72 *Law and Contemporary Problems* 2009, Spring, p. 186.

now on the table of the government. It will, however, not correct the fundamental defects of a dysfunctional political system.[64] The challenge for Belgians is not to make their peace with national integration, but to re-invent a genuine relationship between Flemish and Francophone, and to organize their living separately together in a collaborative way. This calls for more open communication, trust, respect, and empathy.

All of these virtues seem to have been lost during the intense game of chicken of the last half decade. All actors, even the media, are caught in a war of positional bargaining full of Emotions, Ego and Escalation. In spite of the temporary peace the sixth state reform has brought, Belgium remains in desperate need for moral and political leadership that can break this vicious cycle of the three "E"s.[65]

---

[64] Ibid.

[65] Martin Euwema & Alain Verbeke, Negative and Positive Roles of Media in the Belgian Conflict: A Model for De-escalation, 93 Marquette Law Review 2009, Fall, 163–171.

Chapter 6
Federalism and Legal Unification in Brazil

Jacob Dolinger and Luís Roberto Barroso

6.1 Overview

The lands now corresponding to Brazil were discovered on 22 April 1500 by the Kingdom of Portugal, one of the maritime superpowers at that time. In 1822, after an almost pacific transition, Brazil became independent and assumed the form of a unitary State governed by a constitutional monarchy. The monarchic regime was superseded in 1889 through a military coup that did not encounter any substantial resistance from the Crown or social sectors. Throughout its 67 years of existence, the monarchy fought small revolts in different spots of the large national territory, many of which were inspired by the wish to implement a Federation. Not by chance, the Proclamation of the Republic launched the shift to the federal form of state, which was one of the foundational principles of the first Republican Constitution of 1891.

The 1891 Charter drew its inspiration directly from the United States' federal shape: it attributed express powers to the central authority (the Federal Union), while reserving the remaining powers to states, which held purportedly great autonomy. In reality, however, the Union has always exercised strong control over states, sometimes by means of federal interventions. This centralizing tonic has not changed significantly over time. After the 1891 Constitution, five other Constitutions came into force, all of which maintained the Federation with different degrees of formal autonomy for states. At any rate, Brazil has always observed the

---

J. Dolinger (✉)
University of Sao Paulo, São Paulo, Brazil

Hague Academy of International Law, The Hague, Netherlands
e-mail: dolinger@unisys.com.br

L.R. Barroso
Rio de Janeiro State University (UERJ), Rio de Janeiro, Brazil
e-mail: lrbarroso@uol.com.br

centralizing tendency in practical terms, particularly because many Brazilian states are financially dependent on the central power.

Generally speaking, this picture remains valid as to the Constitution presently in force, which was promulgated on October 5, 1988. As we shall see in this report, the central authority retains a large share of regulatory authority on nearly all the most important subject matters. Nevertheless, three introductory remarks should be made. The first concerns the entities which make up the Brazilian Federation. In addition to the central authority and the states (there are now 26), the Brazilian Federation has also a second local level, represented by municipalities (numbering more than 5,000). The municipalities' autonomy is even more limited, as they are subject to both the Federal Constitution and to the constitution of the state where they are located. Furthermore, the vast majority suffer financial difficulties, and rely largely on resources distributed by the Union and the states. Finally, to complete the review of federal entities, there is the Federal District: the City of Brasília. This is the capital of the Republic and the location of the federal branches of government. It is a *sui generic* federal entity halfway between state and municipality, holding prerogatives of both inasmuch as it cannot be subdivided into municipalities (Federal Constitution, art. 32, *caput* and 1st §).

The second remark concerns the manner in which the Federal Constitution gives autonomy to the federal entities and organizes the central authority framework. States are entitled to organize themselves through state constitutions. The municipalities and the Federal District achieve their organization through Organic Laws (*Leis Orgânicas*). In effect, however, the Federal Constitution is very detailed and exercises a strong influence, so that states, the Federal District, and the municipalities do not have too much ground to innovate as far as their political structures are concerned.

Each of the entities has its own legislative and executive branches, whose members are elected by direct vote in the sphere of each jurisdiction (*circunscrição*). The Union, the states, and the Federal District also have their own judicial branches, which are mostly formed by judges selected through public contests. In the Courts of Appeal, judges are appointed by the chief executive of the Union or the respective state. In the federal superior courts, the President submits his nominations for approval to the Federal Senate. Self-administration is a recognized prerogative of the federal entities, which organize their own bureaucratic structures in addition to performing acts and executing contracts in their interest.

The third introductory remark is related to the system of allocating powers among the federative entities. The 1988 Constitution distanced itself from the federation model of the United States and became more similar to the German model by setting forth the so-called cooperative federalism. It follows that beyond the subjects that are in an entity's exclusive jurisdiction, the Constitution also establishes areas of joint action in both legislative and political-administrative matters. In the area of concurrent legislative jurisdiction, the Union shall enact norms of general content and states shall deal with more specific aspects. Municipalities may legislate on matters of local interest. In cases of substantive concurrent jurisdiction, the Union, states, and municipalities shall observe the logic of the predominant interest (national, regional or local; respectively). The Constitution also provides for the tax jurisdiction of the three federal spheres. Here, there is no joint action, but part of the revenue collected by the Union shall be delivered to the states, the Federal District, and municipalities in accordance with constitutional standards.

After the many ups and downs that it has experienced, Brazilian federalism is now at a special moment of its history. The (small) decentralization promoted in 1988 has presently – 20 years after the Constitution's approval – created a suitable scenario for new discussions on old ideas, as well as for bills designed to establish a more important role for states and municipalities.

6.2 The Federal Distribution and Exercise of Law Making Power

As mentioned, the legislative jurisdiction of the Union is exclusive in some cases and concurrent in others. The exclusive jurisdiction is provided in article 22 of the Constitution, which includes the following subjects:

(i) Civil,[1] commercial, criminal, procedure, electoral, agrarian, maritime, aeronautic, space and labor law;
(ii) condemnation (*desapropriação*);
(iii) civil and military requisitions, in case of imminent danger and in war;
(iv) waters, energy, information technology, telecommunications and radio;
(v) postal service;
(vi) the monetary and measures system, titles and metals guarantees;
(vii) credit policy, exchange, insurance and value transferences;
(viii) international and interstate commerce;
(ix) national transport policy guidelines;
(x) regime of ports, lake, river, maritime, air and aerospace navigation;
(xi) traffic and transport;
(xii) mines, other mineral resources and metallurgy;
(xiii) nationality, citizenship and naturalization;
(xiv) indigenous peoples;
(xv) emigration and immigration, entrance, extradition and expulsion of foreigners;

---

[1]"Civil" here does not refer to the classic division between the *common law*, of Anglo-Saxon origin, and the *civil law*, whose origin was based on the slow development and systematization of Roman legal principles, and which developed initially in continental Europe. In Brazilian Law, as in other countries of the Germanic-Roman family, the expression *civil law* also refers to the rules concerning most of the legal relations among private parties, including contracts, liability, family law and succession law. The word *civil* is used in the Constitution and in statutory law in general with this second meaning.

(xvi) organization of the national employment system and conditions precedent to the exercise of professions;
(xvii) organization of the Judiciary, the Public Prosecutors Office (*Ministério Público*), and the public
(xviii) attorney's office of the Federal District and the territories, as well as their administrative organization;
(xix) statistics, cartographical and geological national systems;
(xx) savings accounts system, drawing and guarantee of popular savings;
(xxi) consortium and lotteries;
(xxii) general rules of organization, staff, war material, guarantees, mobilization of the military policemen and military fire departments;
(xxiii) competence of the federal police and federal traffic police;
(xxiv) social security;
(xxv) guidelines and basis of national education;
(xxvi) public registries;
(xxvii) nuclear activities of any kind;
(xxviii) general rules for bidding and contracting, in all modalities, for the government itself, government entities (*autarquias*) and government foundations of the Union, states, Federal District, and municipalities and for public corporations and government-controlled companies;
(xxix) territorial defense, aerospace defense, maritime defense, civil defense, and national mobilization;
(xxx) commercial publicity.

The Federal Constitution authorizes the Union to delegate to the states legislative jurisdiction to rule on specific aspects concerning the subjects above, in accordance with federal complementary laws (*leis complementares*) to be enacted (for example, Complementary Law number 103/2000 authorizes the states to establish minimum wage for certain professions).

The subjects on which the Union, States, and Federal District may legislate jointly are provided for in article 24 of the Federal Constitution, which includes the following:

(i) tax, finance, prison, economic, and urban law;
(ii) budget;
(iii) commercial registries;
(iv) legal fees (*custas*);
(v) production and consumption;
    forests, hunting, fishing, fauna, nature conservancy, defense of the land and natural resources; environment protection and control of pollution;
(vi) protection of the historical, cultural, artistic, tourist and landscape heritage;
    responsibility for damages to the environment, to the consumer, to assets and rights of artistic, esthetic, historical, touristic, and landscape interest;
(vii) education; culture, teaching and sports;
(viii) creation, functioning and procedure in minor issues courts (*juizado de pequenas causas*);

(ix) procedural matters
  (x) social security, protection and healthcare;
  (xi) juridical assistance and public attorneys;
  (xii) protection and social integration of disabled persons;
  (xiii) protection of children and youths;
  (xiv) organization, guarantees, rights and duties of the civil police forces.

In such matters, the Constitution sets forth that the Union shall enact general rules, and leaves to the states the undertaking of complementing federal law by enacting specific rules. In case the Union does not exercise its competence, states are authorized to rule entirely. This is to avoid that the central authority's inertia leaves important matters unregulated which would prevent the states from performing their functions. As soon as the Union finally acts, the occasional general rules enacted by states will go out of force.

It must be stressed that the central authority does not have a preference to rule upon the joint matters listed under Article 24. For those matters, the Constitution sets up a division of work, assigning to the Union the task of enacting general rules. The expression 'general rules' is subject to a broad interpretation, and is understood to include guiding principles and also rulings on issues that by their very nature demand a uniform national regulation. States, in turn, develop the law from the point of those general rules. Article 24 thus reduces state autonomy, but it also limits the federal jurisdiction by preventing the Union from ruling completely on such matters. Nonetheless, in practice, it is very difficult to distinguish general from specific rules. Cases of doubt have been interpreted by the courts in favor of the Union.

As a result of the extensive legislative jurisdiction of the Union, little room is left for the states to legislate. Besides the subjects on which states legislate in cooperation with the Union (article 24), few important issues are within their jurisdiction. Even though article 25 of the Constitution attributes to the state governments the residual powers,[2] nearly all areas that matter most in practice are reserved to central government regulation, as seen above. In addition, the municipalities have their own exclusive area of legislative jurisdiction that concerns matters of local interest. The Constitution also admits that municipal legislation complements state legislation as to issues of predominantly local interest. These two circumstances further reduce the states' legislative autonomy. The most important areas concerning state law are those related to state organization (of the judicial, executive and legislative branches), state taxation, and administrative law (governing public servants and public services).[3]

The previous remarks lead to the conclusion that the Brazilian Constitution does not establish the supremacy of federal law. If the central authority oversteps the

---

[2] Except to create new taxes – this residual power is allocated to the Union (Federal Constitution, article 154).

[3] The legislative jurisdiction over taxes is concurrent. Nonetheless, the Federal Constitution substantially distributes such jurisdiction among the federal entities. Article 155, for example, specifically enumerates those taxes constitutionally attributed to states.

limits of its legislative competence, the resulting law will be unconstitutional and, as a consequence, void. As explained above, in areas of concurrent jurisdiction, the Union shall only enact general rules. The enactment of specific rules – invading the states' jurisdiction – violates the allocation of legislative jurisdiction set forth in the Constitution. Obviously, the specific rules enacted by states shall be compatible with the general rules made by the central authority.

Aside from the concurrent legislative jurisdiction, legal doctrine points out standards based on constitutional prerogatives to resolve conflicts between laws of the different federal entities. Accordingly, a federal statute on mining or transportation (areas within the central authority's exclusive jurisdiction) may conflict with state or municipal statutes on the environment. The basic standard for resolving this kind of conflict is to identify the predominant interest (national, regional or local). In addition, specific prerogatives (e.g., regulating transportation) prevail over more generic ones (e.g., the environment). For example, states shall not exercise their authority regarding environmental issues by limiting the emission of pollutants from automobiles in a manner that conflicts with the limit set forth by the central government. Furthermore, the exercise of legislative or substantive prerogatives by an entity shall not totally prevent other entities from exercising their own prerogatives (e.g., the states' environmental legislation shall not infringe the federal legislation on mining).

As stated before, the Constitution expressly confers jurisdiction on municipalities: (i) to legislate in matters of local interest; and (ii) to supplement federal and state law (again, to protect the local interest) (Article 30). The local interest concept is also somewhat vague, but the prevalent understanding is that the interest shall be predominantly local, without affecting other municipalities, states or the country as a whole. For example, the Brazilian constitutional court (*Supremo Tribunal Federal*, *STF*) has consolidated its jurisprudence in the sense that municipalities – and only they – have jurisdiction to set the working hours for commercial enterprises, like drugstores (STF, *DJU 21* Sept. 2001, AgRg no RE 252.344/SP, Rel. Min. Carlos Velloso). By contrast, municipalities may not regulate the working hours of banks because that would have an impact on the national system for payment of checks (STF, *DJU 3* July. 1981, RE 80.365/PR, Rel. Min. Antonio Neder).

6.3 The Means and Methods of Legal Unification

The Constitution itself largely contributes to legal unification in Brazil. Many of its articles are directly applicable to states and municipalities, including articles concerning the essential organization of such entities (i.e., the composition and functioning of their branches of government), as well as a long catalog of fundamental rights (individual, political and social) and a wide set of rules on the organization and work of the Public Administration.

Moreover, the STF acknowledges the existence of the so-called *principle of symmetry*, according to which states, the Federal District, and municipalities shall comply with many rules defined by the Federal Constitution to govern the activities of the central authority. This includes those provisions related to the separation of powers (e.g., states and municipalities shall not create new mechanisms of checks and balances) and also provisions related to the legislative process (e.g., states and municipalities are prevented from making procedural rules differing from those established for the Union by the Federal Constitution) (STF, *DJU* 9 Nov. 2007, ADIn 2873/PI, Rel.ª Min.ª Ellen Gracie).

The greatest driver of unification, however, is the wide area reserved to the Union's exclusive legislative jurisdiction (Article 22). As mentioned above, not only does the Constitution reserve certain matters – e.g., public transportation and telecommunications – to the central government, it also reserves vast fields of law, such as civil, criminal, corporate, procedural, and labor law. That is why federal legislative activity is so important in terms of directly applicable rules.

By contrast, the Federal Constitution restricts the Union from coercing states, the Federal District or municipalities to enact laws. Although the Constitution provides for some mechanisms of redirecting resources from the Union to the states, the Federal District, and municipalities (*e.g.*, part of the revenue obtained from federal income tax), it does not authorize the central authority to condition the allocation of such resources on the submission or transfer of any legislative prerogatives. Nor does it empower the central authority to withdraw from states, the Federal District, or municipalities those prerogatives on either a permanent or a temporary basis.

In general, the Federal Constitution does not allow the courts to create rules except those regarding their internal organization. Nevertheless, judicial interpretation of broad constitutional provisions has played an important role in the distribution of jurisdiction between the Union and states, usually to favor the Union or simply to reduce state autonomy (especially with the principle of symmetry). In constitutional interpretation, the STF plays a leading role. In Brazil, as in the United States of America, all judges may apply the Constitution directly, as well as refrain from applying legal rules they deem not to be in accordance with the Constitution. The STF has the last word on such issues and may act through a variety of mechanisms, including by means of an appeal named *recurso extraordinário* (*extraordinary appeal*). In 2004, the Constitution was amended to give the STF the power to decline hearing *recursos extraordinários* in cases that do not deal with matters of general interest; that is, in which the issue at stake has no relevance to the constitutional system as a whole. This was an attempt to give the Court some control over its docket by reducing the enormous amount of appeals adjudicated every year. The mechanism is in some way similar to the *writ of certiorari* of the United States Supreme Court and the power not to accept constitutional complaints (*Verfassungsbeschwerden*) of the German Federal Constitutional Court.

Yet concerning the creation of rules by courts, there is a particular situation which deserves special comment. In some cases, the Constitution establishes a right but leaves the exact content or form of that right for the legislative branch to establish by statute. . Where the legislature fails to enact such a statute, thereby making the exercise of the constitutional right impracticable, the Constitution provides for a specific remedy: the writ of injunction (*mandado de injunção*) (Articles 5, LXXI,

102, I, *q*, and 105, I, *h*). Originally, the STF assumed that a decision in a writ of injunction should not create the missing rule, but should limit itself to declaring the legislature's failure to act unconstitutional. In 2007, the Court changed its view, deciding that it should create the applicable rule itself, albeit on a temporary basis, until the legislature acts. The Court did exactly that in the following scenario: the Constitution recognizes workers' general right to strike (Article 9). Another provision sets forth the same right for public servants but determines that the exercise of such right be regulated by a federal statute (Article 37, VII). As that statute had not yet been enacted, the prevailing opinion was that public servants were not authorized to strike. In its decision, the STF determined that while a specific statute had not been enacted, public servants were in fact allowed to strike in accordance with the provisions of the law governing the workers' general right to strike. (STF, *DJU* 6 Nov. 2007, MI 670/ES, Rel. Min. Maurício Corrêa).

Legal unification also occurs through the cooperation or coordination of the various federal entities' legislatures or courts. For those matters in which all entities have to act jointly (e.g., environmental protection), the Constitution sets forth that the central authority shall enact legislation to regulate the cooperation between the various legislatures (Federal Constitution, art. 23, sole paragraph). Such law has not been enacted yet. In some areas, however, the federal legislature has created national systems to coordinate joint action of the three federal spheres; these systems also provide for information exchange. An example is the Environment National System (*Sistema Nacional do Meio Ambiente – SISNAMA*) (Federal Statute n. 6.938/81). Similarly, in the field of health, the Federal Constitution itself integrated public services into a single network, the Unified Health System, which is regionalized and hierarchically organized (*Sistema Único de Saúde* – SUS) (Article 198). Usually, those systems are tasked with the creation of normative acts to implement statutes related to the field in which they develop their activities. Consequently, they play an important role in the unification of Brazilian law.

Coordination between state legislatures is rarer. There is only one case of formal coordination between states provided for by the Federal Constitution. The States will coordinate with regard to the states' value-added tax on distribution of goods and services (*imposto estadual sobre a circulação de mercadorias e a prestação dos serviços de comunicação e de transporte interestadual e intermunicipal*), especially concerning exemptions and other tax benefits. This is to avoid a "tax war" that would harm all parties. The coordination is obtained through formal agreements (*convênios*) on the subject executed by states (Federal Constitution, art. 155, II e § 2º, XII, *g*). In other fields, there is spontaneous (informal) coordination. One state or municipality's legislation may inspire enactment of similar legislation by others, assuming the former is worth emulating. For example, there is a great deal of similarity across state laws on Public-Private Partnerships (PPP), a type of contract that has been practiced in other countries for a long time. Brazil's central government formally introduced this type of contract in 2004 by law providing general rules on the subject.

State judiciaries sometimes analyze jurisprudence from the courts of other states although they are not bound to do so. Generally, the parties themselves inform courts about decisions favorable to their interests as a means of argumentation. This can influence legal unification where the court of one state is persuaded by the reasoning of a court from another state. More important, however, is the existence of certain appeals with the purpose of unifying jurisprudence on the national level. When two or more courts interpret a federal statutory provision differently, the Constitution allows the losing party to file an appeal (*recurso especial*) to the Superior Court of Justice (*Superior Tribunal de Justiça – STJ*), which has the function of harmonizing the interpretation of federal law.

The role of non-state actors in legal unification is insignificant. For instance, there are no mechanisms such as the Restatements compiled in the United States of America. Books by legal authorities contain comments on the codes (such as the civil code, the code of civil procedure, and the penal code), with references to the most important judicial decisions regarding each issue. Such works – some of them well-known and frequently consulted – play an informative role, transmitting knowledge and helping courts to decide in accordance with dominant legal interpretation. It would not be correct, however, to say that they play a significant role in legal unification.

In certain matters, Brazil became a party to internationally uniform laws. This is the case with the Convention providing a Uniform Law for Bills of Exchange and Promissory Notes –Geneva 1930– and the Convention providing a Uniform Law for Checks –Geneva 1931– which were both incorporated into Brazilian Law in 1966. Such initiatives do not have a unifying effect within the Federation, however, as they concern matters in which the Union already has exclusive jurisdiction; the unification effect is thus merely international. Thus, although compliance with international legal obligations is arguably relevant as a matter of Brazilian law, its influence in internal legal unification is practically nonexistent since the vast majority of international norms concern subjects which the Brazilian Constitution reserved to the central authority. The same is true regarding international voluntary coordination. As the vast majority of such projects is related to areas regulated by the central authority, conventions, model statutes, or any other instrument adopted under the auspices of UNCITRAL, UNIDROIT or the Hague Conference on Private International Law play virtually no role in unifying the law in Brazil.

Standards and practices of industry associations and other private entities also are of little importance to unification. Such sources have not significantly influenced lawmaking, and even less legal unification, within the Federation. Despite their general influence, which varies in significance by sector, private entities play but a small role in the political process in general. Again, the large concentration of prerogatives in the central authority naturally reduces the role of unification mechanisms. This also reduces the private sector's interest in promoting unity.

Finally, legal education plays a role in unification. Law schools in Brazil accept students based on their performance on entrance exams, and may accept candidates from anywhere in the country. Although schools usually attract students from the surrounding regions – i.e., from inside the state in which they are located – one does find some students moving to different places to study law. Legal education concentrates on the Constitution and federal law. That is because the federal legislative jurisdiction includes the main issues and legal branches, be it through exclusive jurisdiction (*e.g.*, civil, criminal, procedure, corporate and labor law) or through the enactment of general rules (*e.g.*, tax, financial and largely administrative law).

To practice law in Brazil, one ought to be a member of the Brazilian Bar Association (*Ordem dos Advogados do Brasil – OAB*), a national entity with a branch in each state. Membership is established through admittance to the branch of the state in which the candidate wishes to establish his professional domicile, after being approved by passing a written exam.

The lawyer registered in a certain state branch of the OAB may exercise his or her profession in other states on an occasional basis (up to five lawsuits per year). Beyond this limit, he or she will need a supplementary membership in the branch of those states in which he or she wishes to act regularly. Federal Statute number 8.906/94 regulates the matter. However, professionals usually stay where they studied or return to their original state if they attended school somewhere else. Some state capitals are known for attracting students from elsewhere, due to their greater economic development. Rio de Janeiro and especially São Paulo are the main examples. Brasília, which is the federal capital, attracts law firms and professionals because it is the home to the two highest Brazilian Courts, the *Superior Tribunal de Justiça* (STJ) and the *Supremo Tribunal Federal* (STF).

6.4 Institutional and Social Background

The aim of this subchapter is to describe briefly the institutional organization of the federal entities and point out important social aspects that may interfere with legal unification.

Let us begin with the judicial branch. As mentioned before, any judge may refrain from applying statutes he or she deems unconstitutional, so this control is exercised by the entire judicial branch. Nonetheless, the final decision whether a statute is unconstitutional is reserved for the STF, which may make its decision in a number of ways. The Constitution allows the Court to examine in abstract the constitutionality of a specific statute in an action proposed by any of a certain group of authorities or institutions. The Court may also review ordinary judicial decisions finding a statute unconstitutional via the *recurso extraordinário* (extraordinary appeal) as explained above.

Therefore, courts – especially the STF – are regularly called upon to verify that federal legislation is within constitutional limits. For example, the Federal Constitution provides the central authority with jurisdiction to establish general rules on public procurement and administrative contracts (Article 22, XXVII). Assuming these directives are otherwise respected, states and municipalities may enact specific rules that apply to their own administrative bodies. The STF has decided that some provisions of the Federal Statute on Public Biddings and Administrative Contracts (Federal Statute n. 8.666/93) only apply to the central authority, once they go beyond the general rules and invade the jurisdiction of the other federal entities. Such provisions concerned specific limits to the donation of goods by the public sector (STF, *DJU* 11 Nov. 1994, ADInMC 927/RS, Rel. Min. Carlos Velloso).

Beyond constitutional review, however, there is no central court with power to authoritatively interpret component state law. The STF may declare unconstitutional a statute enacted by the Union or the states in a direct action of unconstitutionality (*ação direta de inconstitucionalidade*). It may also undertake, with regards to any statute – federal, state, or municipal – the so-called "interpretation in conformity with the Constitution" (*interpretação conforme a Constituição*), first developed by the German Federal Constitutional Court. By this technique the Court does not declare in the abstract that a rule of law is unconstitutional – the text remains in force – but it forbids certain interpretations of the provision, inasmuch as such interpretations are not in accordance with the Constitution. By thus prescribing a certain interpretation, the Court causes a unifying effect. It is to be stressed, however, that the Court's purpose is not unification. Instead, the Court's judgment represents its understanding that other interpretations violate the constitutional order and therefore must be avoided.

Besides the judicial structure of the central authority, each state has its own judiciary. In all cases – in the state as well as in the federal sphere – there is an appellate court. Also, there are two courts with national general jurisdiction: the STF has the final word on constitutional interpretation, while the STJ has the final word on interpretation of federal law. There are also specific higher courts for the labor, military, and electoral law. It is important to note also that whereas there are courts organized by the Union and by the states, the judicial branch – like the Public Prosecutors Office (*Ministério Público*) – is treated as an institution of national character. The Union and the state branches just represent a division of labor among these entities with regard to the administrative organization of the courts. This has important consequences: all judicial institutions are subject to common principles defined by the Federal Constitution, and there shall be no arbitrary distinction between federal and state civil servants, especially as to their wages (STF, *DJU* 17 Mar. 2006, ADI 3367/DF, Rel. Min. Cezar Peluso; STJ, *DJU* 20 May. 2002, EREsp 114908/SP, Rel.ª Min.ª Eliana Calmon).

To avoid divergence regarding the interpretation of federal law, the Constitution provides for the *recurso especial* appeal to be filed before the STJ (Article 105, III, c). Thus, if a party shows that a state or federal appellate court interpreted a federal statute in a manner different from another appellate court, it may make use of such appeal. The STJ then decides which interpretation shall prevail. In Brazil, there is no *stare decisis* principle. Consequently nothing prevents a court from applying a different understanding than the one endorsed by the STJ. Nevertheless, procedural law has been going through alterations in order to stimulate the observance of previous judgments, and also to simplify unification through appeals.

Lawsuits and conflicts between the Union, the states, and the Federal District are adjudicated by the STF (Article 102, I, *f*).

As to the executive branch, each federative entity has its own structure. As a general rule, the central authority has its own administrative body that is in charge of applying statutes enacted by the Union. In many cases, however, the Union has legislative jurisdiction – exclusive or concurrent – over matters in which states and municipalities have executive authority. In these cases, local entities apply federal law, exclusively or together with their own legislation, in accordance with the coordination standards previously mentioned. In the field of criminal law, for example, the Union has exclusive legislative jurisdiction (Art. 22, I), but in the majority of cases, states have authority to investigate crimes and judge the accused. Public registries (*e.g.*, the real estate owners' registry) are regulated by federal law (Art. 22, I and XXV), but such registries are almost always run by agents which act under the supervision of the states and are subject to the states' appellate courts' control (Article 236).

The National Congress, which is bicameral, constitutes the legislative branch of the central authority. It consists of the House of Representatives (*Câmara dos Deputados*) – an organ of popular representation – and the Federal Senate. The Federal Senate's main purpose is to represent the states and the Federal District, in isonomic conditions: each elects three senators (Article 46). As a rule, the Senate takes part in all federal lawmaking and additionally has important exclusive prerogatives, many of which are related to the Federation – *e.g.*, establishing limits and conditions on domestic and international credit transactions of the Union, states, Federal District and municipalities (Art. 52, VII). The people of each state elect the three senators through direct voting for a term of 8 years (Federal Constitution, art. 46). The elections occur every 4 years, so that at every election the Senate is partially renewed (elections are for 1/3 and 2/3 of the vacancies, alternately). In practice, since senators are not chosen by the authorities of the states and the Federal District, they are usually more bound to their political parties than to the interests of the entities they are supposed to represent. For that reason, the Senate plays more the role of an Upper House than that of a House of the states.

The three levels of the Federation have their own tax prerogatives (the Federal District has both state and municipal prerogatives). There are different tax species and such classification is important in establishing the proper jurisdictional apportionment. The *taxas* are fees paid in consideration for administrative activities that directly benefit taxpayers, and may be collected by the entity which renders the activity (Article 145, II). Electrical supply, for example, is a public service of the Union usually executed by delegation to private enterprises. The remuneration for this service is obtained through the *taxa*. All entities may also impose "improvement contributions" (*contribuições de melhoria*) when a public work causes a significant rise in the value of certain private real estate properties; the entity which performs the work will have jurisdiction to levy the contribution. All entities may also require their public servants to make social security contributions (*contribuições previdenciárias*) to finance social security systems for their benefit (Article 149, 1st §).

The main tax species is the *imposto*. The Constitution indicates the situations that justify charging *impostos* (*e.g.*, income, real estate, or rendering a service to third parties), and divides the power to tax among the various entities. The Union may establish and charge taxes over: (a) imports; (b) exports; (c) income and profits; (d) industrial goods; (e) credit, exchange and insurance transactions, or transactions related to securities; (f) rural properties; and (g) large fortunes (Art. 153). States may establish and charge taxes over: (a) *mortis causa* succession and donations of any assets; (b) distribution of goods and services (equivalent to sales tax) and transportation services between states and between municipalities; and (c) automobile ownership (Art. 155). Municipalities may tax: (a) urban properties; (b) *inter vivos* conveyance of real estate or of rights over real estate (except for guarantees, as well as assignment of rights to purchase); and (c) services of any nature not within the states' jurisdiction, as defined in a complementary federal law (Article 156). Only the Union may (a) create new taxes (Article 154, I), and (b) establish extraordinary taxes to finance a war effort (Article 154, II).

There are two more tax species provided for in the Constitution that are within the Union's exclusive jurisdiction: (a) the "mandatory loans" (*empréstimos compulsórios*), which are unusual and are generally charged for regulatory purposes, to discourage a certain activity, or to reduce the quantity of circulating cash. The resources so obtained must be returned within a reasonable period (Article 148). Next, the Union may charge (b) "other contributions" (Article 149): (i) *social contributions*, assessed on employers and employees, which are designed to finance the general social security system (education, health, pensions and social assistance); (ii) *contributions for the intervention in the economic field*, imposed upon private agents acting in strategic economic sectors, such as fuels and lubricants, and which are designed to finance state activities in these areas; (iii) *contributions in the interest of social or economic categories*, assessed on individuals acting in areas or professions particularly regulated, and designed to finance a supervision system. Lawyers, for example, shall pay a yearly contribution to finance the activities of OAB (Brazilian Bar Association).

Finally, municipalities may impose a "contribution" to finance public lighting (*contribuição para o custeio da iluminação pública* – Article 149-A).

It is easy to notice, then, that the Brazilian tax system is rigidly defined in the Constitution; double taxation is not possible. Frequently many different taxes are levied on the same production chain, each of them related to a specific aspect. On a hypothetical production chain, for example, the following taxes could be assessed: value-added tax on distribution of goods and services (assessed by the state), the social contribution on profits (assessed by Union), and income tax (also assessed by the Union). The large quantity of taxes and their rates, which are often implemented on a very progressive scale, make the overall Brazilian burden very high.

Besides establishing the tax prerogatives for each entity, the Constitution provides for mechanisms for transferring resources from the Union to the states, the Federal District, and municipalities; and also from states to municipalities. For example, part of the income tax assessed by the central authority shall be delivered to the other entities. This system is established in Articles 157 and 158 of the Constitution and the resources may not be withheld due to political disagreements. The Union may only refrain from remitting resources to entities which are debtors and are not performing their duties or which have not made the minimum investments in health, as required by the Constitution (Article 160). There is also an indirect form of sharing revenues. The Constitution sets forth that resources obtained from certain Union taxes will be partially allocated to Participation Funds (*Fundos de Participação*), and these resources shall be shared among the states, the Federal District, and municipalities or invested in less-favored regions (Article 159). The standards of sharing are set forth in federal legislation and aim to promote a social-economic balance among states and municipalities (Article 161, II).

Finally, significant social factors are worth mentioning briefly. Brazilian society is very diverse both ethnically and religiously. Nonetheless, such differences do not engender any kind of sectarian political movements. In the past, in the southern region of the country (the states of Rio Grande do Sul, Paraná and Santa Catarina), which has received many waves of immigrants from European countries (Italians, Germans, Azoreans and others), there were a few separatist movements, mainly during the nineteenth century. Nowadays, however, such movements are no longer significant.

The different ethnic and religious groups are fairly uniformly distributed throughout the national territory without any particular concentration, especially as far as political factors are concerned. The Northeast Region of the country concentrates a higher percentage of African-Brazilians. In some states, like Bahia, this group is the majority of the population. In the south, conversely, European immigrants prevail. Yet, while such concentrations result in large cultural diversity, they do not have a significant political impact.

With regards to natural resources, Brazil is a vast and diverse country. Each of the five regions of the country – northern, northeastern, center-western, southern and southeastern – has its particular advantages. Some areas concentrate strategic resources, such as oil in the continental shelf of the southeast (although there are smaller deposits in other areas). The existence of areas of large biological diversity, specially the Amazon Forest – whose greater part is located in the north, within the Brazilian borders – and the *Pantanal*, situated in the center-west – should be noted. A great part of the northeastern region, however, suffers from arid conditions with land not naturally suitable for agriculture, forcing people in the region to migrate to the shore and to the southeastern capitals in search of jobs. Indeed, the economic and social development of the different states has been very unequal, being higher in the south and southeast of the country. Such differences result in the demographic concentration in these areas due to domestic migration.

The Constitution states that the reduction of regional inequalities is a fundamental objective of the Federative Republic of Brazil (Article 3, III). There are not, however, relevant institutional mechanisms to force the Public Administration to implement such task. A noteworthy exception is the previously mentioned Participation Funds (*Fundos de Participação*), which consist of certain percentages of the central authority's revenue obtained from taxes. Federal law sets forth the standards for apportionment, and determines that 85 % of the resources are to be invested in the less-favored regions of the country (northern, northeastern and center-western) while the remaining 15 % shall go to the richer states (those situated in the south and the southeast).

6.5 Conclusion

There is a high degree of uniformity of legal rules within the Brazilian federal system. The main reasons for that are: (i) the area reserved to the Union's exclusive legislative jurisdiction (Article 22) is remarkably large and includes nearly all the main branches of law (civil, criminal, corporate, procedure, labor law, etc); and (ii) there are many constitutional provisions which are directly applicable to the Union, the states and the municipalities, including a long list of fundamental rights as well as a wide set of rules on the organization and functioning of the Public Administration, which bind all federative spheres.

Acknowledgement The authors thank Gabriel Valente dos Reis, Vanessa Constantino Macharette, Eduardo Bastos Furtado de Mendonça and Thiago Magalhães Pires for their most valuable assistance in all stages of the preparation and drafting of the present report.

Chapter 7
Unification of Laws in Federal Systems: The Canadian Model

Aline Grenon

7.1 Introduction

Canada is a complex country that could perhaps best be described as an accident of colonial history. In order to understand its legal structure and the forces for and against unification that coexist within the country, an overview of Canada's historical, political and social situation is required.

Beginning in 1534, France colonized the eastern and all of the central parts of the territory that now form part of Canada, then populated by various indigenous peoples. Civil law, the law of the colonial power, thus applied in this territory as a matter of course. In the Treaty of Paris, 1763, the colony was ceded to Great Britain and following this transfer of power, Great Britain attempted to impose English common law on the territory. However, this change of legal regime gave rise to numerous grievances and Great Britain finally agreed to restore, with certain exceptions, the French civil law tradition, insofar as it related to the "Property and Civil Rights" of the population.[1]

Aline Grenon, Full professor (retired), Faculty of Law, University of Ottawa, Ottawa, Canada; also member of the bars of Ontario and Quebec. A version of this report has been published in Nathalie Vézina, dir., *Le droit uniforme: limites et possibilités, Cowansville (Québec), Yvon Blais,* 2009, 33–61.

[1] Section VIII of the *Quebec Act, 1774* (U.K.), 14 George III, c. 83, reprinted in R.S.C. 1985, App. II, No. 2. For more detailed descriptions of the legal upheavals during this period, see Henri Brun, "Le territoire du Québec: à la jonction de l'histoire et du droit constitutionnel" (1992) 33 C. de. D. 927; Michel Morin, "Les changements de régimes juridiques consécutifs à la Conquête de 1760"

A. Grenon (✉)
Faculty of Law, Common Law Section, French Common Law Program, University of Ottawa, Ottawa, ON, Canada
e-mail: Aline.Grenon@bell.net

Less than 30 years later, the *Constitution Act, 1791*[2] divided the territory into two provinces, predominantly English-speaking Upper Canada and predominantly French-speaking Lower Canada, separated by the present boundary between the provinces of Ontario and Quebec. The Legislature of Upper Canada immediately abandoned the civil law in favor of the common law.[3] As for Lower Canada, not only did it retain the civil law but it also, in due course, codified it.[4]

A year after the codification of Quebec civil law, the *Constitution Act, 1867*[5] created the Dominion of Canada, composed of the provinces of Nova Scotia, New Brunswick, Ontario (formerly Upper Canada) and Quebec (formerly Lower Canada). Legislative powers were distributed between the federal Parliament on the one hand and the four new provincial Legislatures on the other, and it was expressly provided that the provinces could legislate with respect to property and civil rights, thereby ensuring that Quebec retained the French civil law tradition in the sphere of private law. Ontario, Nova Scotia and New Brunswick retained the English common law tradition. The other six provinces that subsequently joined the federation (Prince Edward Island, Manitoba, British-Columbia, Saskatchewan, Alberta, and Newfoundland) also received or opted for the common law.

In addition to these ten provinces, present-day Canada also includes three territories, Yukon, Northwest Territories and Nunavut.

Based on its 2006 Census, Canada has a population of over 31,000,000. Of that number, the mother tongue of approximately 18,000,000 is English; the mother tongue of approximately 7,000,000 is French and approximately 6,000,000 have a mother tongue other than English or French. There are approximately 1,200,000 aboriginal people in Canada – Inuit, Métis and First Nations people.

Francophones constitute the majority in Quebec. Elsewhere in Canada, the majority is anglophone although there are also important francophone minorities in Ontario and New Brunswick and an important anglophone minority in Quebec, primarily in the City of Montreal. In the territory of Nunavut, the majority of the population is Inuit and there are important aboriginal populations in the other two Territories together with smaller aboriginal populations elsewhere in Canada.[6]

These ethnic and linguistic differences give rise to cleavages in the federation. No doubt the most important is the cleavage between francophones and anglophones, the two main linguistic groups in the country. Between 1980 and 1995, two unsuccessful referenda were held in the Province of Quebec with a view to obtaining

---

(1997) 57 R. du B. 689; see also Peter W. Hogg, *Constitutional Law of Canada*, looseleaf, 5th ed. (Toronto: Carswell, 2007) at 2.1–2.10 [Hogg].

[2](U.K.), 31 George III, c. 31, reprinted in R.S.C. 1985, App. II, No. 3.

[3]Upper Canada Statutes, 1792, 32 Geo. III, c. I, s. III.

[4]The civil law of Quebec was first codified in 1866; see *An Act respecting the Civil Code of Lower Canada*, S. Prov. C. 1865 (29 Vict.), c. 41.

[5](U.K.), 30 & 31 Vict., c. 3, reprinted in R.S.C. 1985, App. II, No. 5 ["*Constitution Act, 1867*"].

[6]Statistics Canada, online: www.statcan.ca

the secession of the province from the federation.[7] In addition, since the early 1990s, the Bloc Québécois, a sovereignist party at the federal level, has received substantial support from the Québec population. For example, in the federal election on October 14, 2008, the Bloc secured 49 of 75 seats from Quebec (there are 308 seats in the House of Commons). The advent of this strong regional political party had the effect of reducing the importance of the Liberal and Conservative parties nationally since it became very difficult for these two parties to obtain coast to coast mandates. Following the last federal election, the country was essentially divided between the Conservative party representing the West and the Liberals representing the Center and the East, subject of course to the strong presence of the Bloc in Quebec. The election on May 2, 2011 took everyone off-guard. The Liberal and the Bloc parties were decimated and the Conservative party, a right-of-center party, obtained a majority. However, Quebec maintained its tendency to surprise and muddy the waters by voting massively in favour of the New Democratic Party, a left-of-center party. As a result, the NDP became the official opposition party for the first time in its history and the majority of the NDP members of Parliament now come from Quebec. The NDP, a federalist party, will now have to give serious consideration to Quebec interests. How the francophone-anglophone cleavage plays out within the NDP caucus and within Canada in the next few years remains to be seen.

A cleavage also exists between white and aboriginal communities. The latter must deal with substantial issues relating to health and welfare, education, unemployment and prison incarceration.[8] Despite efforts by aboriginal leaders, the issues are very complex and political will at both the federal and provincial levels leaves something to be desired. As a result, progress in dealing with these issues has been slow.

Finally, there has also been considerable asymmetry arising from the advanced economic development of central provinces (Ontario and Quebec) and the relative under-development of western and especially eastern provinces. Recently, however, the manufacturing base of central Canada has weakened, while the resource-based economies of the east and especially the west have begun to strengthen rapidly and to diversify. In addition, equalization payments to less well-off provinces have enabled them to maintain reasonable levels of education, health and social services.

Such is, very briefly, the historical, political and social background against which Canada's unique approach to harmonization and unification of laws has developed.

---

[7]See *Reference re Secession of Quebec,* [1998] 2 S.C.R. 217.

[8]For a detailed analysis of these issues, see Canada, Royal Commission on Aboriginal Peoples, *Report of the Royal Commission on Aboriginal Peoples* (Ottawa: The Commission, 1996); see also *People to People, Nation to Nation. Highlights from the Report of the Royal Commission on Aboriginal Peoples,* online: Indian and Northern Affairs Canada (http://www.ainc-inac.gc.ca/ch/rcap/rpt/index_e.html)

7.2 The Distribution and Exercise of Lawmaking Power

7.2.1 Exclusive Powers

As is the case with all federations, law-making power is distributed between the central or federal government and the state or provincial governments that form part of the federation. In Canada, these powers are essentially distributed pursuant to sections 91 and 92 of the *Constitution Act, 1867*.[9]

On the basis of section 91 of the *Constitution Act, 1867*, the exclusive legislative authority of the Parliament of Canada extends to the following subjects:

1. Repealed.
1A. The Public Debt and Property.
2. The Regulation of Trade and Commerce.
2A. Unemployment insurance.
3. The raising of Money by any Mode or System of Taxation.
4. The borrowing of Money on the Public Credit.
5. Postal Service.
6. The Census and Statistics.
7. Militia, Military and Naval Service, and Defence.
8. The fixing of and providing for the Salaries and Allowances of Civil and other Officers of the Government of Canada.
9. Beacons, Buoys, Lighthouses, and Sable Island.
10. Navigation and Shipping.
11. Quarantine and the Establishment and Maintenance of Marine Hospitals.
12. Sea Coast and Inland Fisheries.
13. Ferries between a Province and any British or Foreign Country or between Two Provinces.
14. Currency and Coinage.
15. Banking, Incorporation of Banks, and the Issue of Paper Money.
16. Savings Banks.
17. Weights and Measures.
18. Bills of Exchange and Promissory Notes.
19. Interest.
20. Legal Tender.
21. Bankruptcy and Insolvency.
22. Patents of Invention and Discovery.
23. Copyrights.
24. Indians, and Lands reserved for the Indians.
25. Naturalization and Aliens.
26. Marriage and Divorce.

---

[9]For more information relating to the distribution of legislative power in Canada, see Hogg, *supra* note 1 and Patrick J. Monahan, *Constitutional Law*, 3rd ed. (Toronto: Irwin Law, 2006).

27. The Criminal Law, except the Constitution of Courts of Criminal Jurisdiction, but including the Procedure in Criminal Matters.
28. The Establishment, Maintenance, and Management of Penitentiaries.
29. Such Classes of Subjects as are expressly excepted in the Enumeration of the Classes of Subjects by this Act assigned exclusively to the Legislatures of the Provinces.

Among the 30 subjects, the most important and frequently used are trade and commerce, employment insurance, taxation, defence, currency and banking, bankruptcy and insolvency, patents, copyrights, Indian affairs, citizenship, marriage, divorce and criminal law. In addition, the opening words of section 91 of the *Constitution Act, 1867* allocate residual power to the central government. It is there stated that the Parliament of Canada can "make Laws for the Peace, Order, and good Government of Canada, in relation to all Matters not coming within the Classes of Subjects by this Act assigned exclusively to the Legislatures of the Provinces".

Pursuant to section 92 of the *Constitution Act, 1867,* each province may exclusively make laws in relation to the matters enumerated in that section. Specifically, the exclusive legislative authority of the provinces extends to the following subjects:

1. Repealed.
2. Direct Taxation within the Province in order to the raising of a Revenue for Provincial Purposes.
3. The borrowing of Money on the sole Credit of the Province
4. The Establishment and Tenure of Provincial Offices and the Appointment and Payment of Provincial Officers.
5. The Management and Sale of the Public Lands belonging to the Province and of the Timber and Wood thereon.
6. The Establishment, Maintenance, and Management of Public and Reformatory Prisons in and for the Province.
7. The Establishment, Maintenance, and Management of Hospitals, Asylums, Charities, and Eleemosynary Institutions in and for the Province, other than Marine Hospitals.
8. Municipal Institutions in the Province.
9. Shop, Saloon, Tavern, Auctioneer, and other Licences in order to the raising of a Revenue for Provincial, Local, or Municipal Purposes.
10. Local Works and Undertakings other than such as are of the following Classes:
    (a) Lines of Steam or other Ships, Railways, Canals, Telegraphs, and other Works and Undertakings connecting the Province with any other or others of the Provinces, or extending beyond the Limits of the Province.
    (b) Lines of Steam Ships between the Province and any British or Foreign Country.
    (c) Such Works as, although wholly situate within the Province, are before or after their Execution declared by the Parliament of Canada to be for the general Advantage of Canada or for the Advantage of Two or more of the Provinces.

11. The Incorporation of Companies with Provincial Objects.
12. The Solemnization of Marriage in the Province.
13. Property and Civil Rights in the Province.
14. The Administration of Justice in the Province, including the Constitution, Maintenance, and Organization of Provincial Courts, both of Civil and of Criminal Jurisdiction, and including Procedure in Civil Matters in those Courts.
15. The Imposition of Punishment by Fine, Penalty, or Imprisonment for enforcing any Law of the Province made in relation to any Matter coming within any of the Classes of Subjects enumerated in this Section.
16. Generally all Matters of a merely local or private Nature in the Province.

In addition to these exclusive powers, section 92A, added to the *Constitution Act, 1867* in 1982,[10] grants the provinces exclusive legislative power over non-renewable natural resources, forestry resources and electrical energy within a province. Finally, pursuant to section 93 of the *Constitution Act, 1867*, the provinces "may exclusively make Laws in relation to Education".

It must be noted that it is only the provinces that receive their legislative authority from the *Constitution Act, 1867*. The three territories, by contrast, merely have the powers that the Parliament of Canada has chosen to delegate to them, since Parliament has plenary legislative powers over the territories.[11]

In practice, the most important areas of exclusive or predominant provincial government regulation are those relating to : (1) property and civil rights (in essence, rights relating to private law, thereby allowing the provinces to enact legislation in relation to property law, commercial law, labour law, wills and estates and family law, for example); (2) education; (3) health and welfare; and (4) the administration of justice in the province (including civil procedure and the constitution, along with maintenance and organization of courts having both civil and criminal jurisdiction).

In addition, based on the provinces' ability to make laws pursuant to section 92(13) (property and civil rights) and section 92(16) (matters of a merely local or private nature), it can be argued that there exists a provincial residuary power comparable to the federal power.[12]

As stated earlier, the enumerated powers granted pursuant to section 91 are "exclusive" to the Parliament of Canada and the same is true of the powers granted to the provinces pursuant to section 92. Yet some of the provincial powers, of which the most important is the power to legislate in relation to property and civil rights, come into conflict with the exclusive powers granted to the Parliament of Canada. Since

---

[10]*Constitution Act, 1982,* being Schedule B to the *Canada Act 1982* (U.K.), 1982, c.11, reprinted in R.S.C. 1985, App. II, No. 44.

[11]*Constitution Act, 1871* (U.K.), 34 & 35 Vict., c.28, reprinted in R.S.C. 1985, App. II, No. 11.

[12]See Peter W. Hogg, Q.C. & Wade K. Wright "Canadian Federalism, the Privy Council and the Supreme Court: Reflections on the Debate About Canadian Federalism" (2005) 38 U.B.C. L. Rev. 329 at para. 22; see also Lord Watson in *Ontario (A.-G.) v. Canada (A.-G.),* [1896] A.C. 348 at 365 (often described as the *Local Prohibitions Case*).

1867, this has been the subject of numerous decisions by the Judicial Committee of the Privy Council in England, and by the Supreme Court of Canada when it became the court of last resort in 1949.

Although there is clear historical evidence to demonstrate that the *Constitution Act, 1867* was intended to create a strong federal government, judicial interpretation of sections 91 and 92 has had the opposite effect. In particular, the provincial power over property and civil rights in section 92(13) has been very broadly interpreted and federal powers that might potentially overlap with section 92(13) have been given a more limited interpretation. For example, the Judicial Committee of the Privy Council held that anything relating to property and civil rights within a province was excluded from the federal power over the regulation of trade and commerce granted pursuant to section 91(2).[13] This obviously had the effect of dramatically reducing the ambit of federal power in this field.

It must be noted, however, that where validly anchored federal legislation and validly anchored provincial legislation contradict each other, courts will recognize federal legislation as paramount. This will be discussed in more detail below.

Because of the judicial interpretation of sections 91 and 92 of the *Constitution Act, 1867*, there is today considerable overlap between federal and provincial laws, with the result that federal and provincial legislation coexists in many areas (for example, corporate law, securities regulation, highways and ports). According to an article published in 2000, "[t]he only exclusively federal areas are military defence, veterans' affairs, postal service, and monetary policy"; as for the provinces, the only exclusive areas are "municipal institutions, lands and forests, roads, liquor licensing, and elementary and secondary education".[14]

7.2.2 Concurrent Powers

Section 92A, added to the *Constitution Act, 1867* in 1982, grants to the provinces the non-exclusive or concurrent power to enact laws relating to the export of non-renewable natural resources, forestry resources and electrical energy from a province to another part of Canada.

In 1951, section 94A was added to the *Constitution Act, 1867*, granting Parliament concurrent power to enact laws in relation to old-age pensions and

---

[13]The leading case is *Citizens Insurance Co. v. Parsons* (1881), 8 App. Cas. 406.

[14]Garth Stevenson, "Federalism and Intergovernmental Relations" in Michael Whittington & Glen Williams, eds., *Canadian Politics in the 21st Century* (Scarborough: Nelson, 2000) 79 at 88. However, this statement is now less accurate with respect to municipal institutions; for example, the 2004 federal budget provided municipalities with a goods and services tax rebate worth $7 billion over 10 years for their areas of greatest need and the 2005 budget provided $5 billion over 5 years in gas tax funds, together with a commitment of up to $800 million for transit funding (see http://www.infc.gc.ca/media/news-nouvelles/gtf-fte/2005/20050823saskatoon-eng.html)

supplementary benefits.[15] Federal legislation enacted pursuant to this section is, however, subject to provincial laws, which take precedence in case of conflict. To date, only Quebec has enacted such a law.[16]

Finally, section 95 of the *Constitution Act, 1867* grants Parliament and the provinces concurrent power over agriculture and immigration but provides that, in the event of a conflict between a federal and a provincial law, federal law takes precedence.

Since the environment is not, as such, a subject matter of legislation under the *Constitution Act, 1867*, the Supreme Court of Canada has held that it is an area of concurrent jurisdiction. Specifically, the jurisdiction of the Parliament of Canada in this area can be inferred from various powers, including its criminal law power and its general power to legislate for peace, order and good government in situations of national concern; provincial jurisdiction, by contrast, can be inferred from various subsections in section 92 of the *Constitution Act, 1867*.[17]

Administrative procedure is clearly an area of concurrent jurisdiction, although this is not explicitly stated in the *Constitution Act, 1867*.[18] The expression "administrative procedure" is very broad and necessarily includes the numerous regulations and safeguards put in place by the Parliament of Canada or by the provinces in the exercise of their respective jurisdictions. For example, section 91(2) of the *Constitution Act, 1867* (regulation of trade and commerce) clearly allows the Parliament of Canada to establish procedures of an administrative nature in the exercise of this jurisdiction. The same is true for the provinces: section 92(4) of the *Constitution Act, 1867* (establishment and tenure of provincial offices and the appointment and payment of provincial officers) is one of many possible areas of provincial jurisdiction which obviously create a need for procedures of an administrative nature. It should also be noted that although a number of provinces have enacted legislation relating to administrative procedure, to date, federal administrative agencies are not subject to any such legislation.[19]

---

[15] See the *British North America Act, 1951* (U.K.), 14 & 15 Geo. VI, c. 32 and the *Constitution Act, 1964* (U.K.), 1964, c. 73.

[16] *Quebec Pension Plan*, S.Q. 1965, c. 24.

[17] The leading case is *Friends of the Oldman River Society v. Canada (Minister of Transport)*, [1992] 1 S.C.R. 3. See also *A.G. Canada v. Hydro Quebec*, [1997] 3 S.C.R. 213; *114957 Canada Ltée (Spraytech, Société d'arrosage) v. Hudson (Town)*, 2001 SCC 40, [2001] 2 S.C.R. 241 at para. 33.

[18] It must, however, be noted that the *Constitution Act, 1867* refers specifically to criminal and civil procedure. Section 92(14) of [the Constitution] gives jurisdiction to the provinces with respect to the "Administration of Justice in the Province, including the Constitution, Maintenance, and Organization of Provincial Courts, both of Civil and of Criminal Jurisdiction, *and including Procedure in Civil Matters in those Courts*" [emphasis added]. Section 91(27) gives jurisdiction to the Parliament of Canada with respect to "[...] Procedure in Criminal Matters".

[19] With regard to the absence of federal legislation in this area, see Robert W. Macaulay & James L.H. Sprague, *Practice and Procedure Before Administrative Tribunals*, looseleaf (Scarborough, Ont.: Carswell, 2004) at 9–20. With regard to provincial legislation, see for example, *Statutory Powers Procedure Act*, R.S.O. 1990, c. S-22; see also the model administrative procedure code

Finally, matters relating to culture are also areas of concurrent jurisdiction. The Supreme Court of Canada has stated:

> The Constitution of Canada does not include an express grant of power with respect to "culture" as such. Most constitutional litigation on cultural issues has arisen in the context of language and education rights. However, provinces are also concerned with broader and more diverse cultural problems and interests. In addition, the federal government affects cultural activity in this country through the exercise of its broad powers over communications and through the establishment of federally funded cultural institutions. Consequently, particular cultural issues must be analyzed in their context, in relation to the relevant sources of legislative power.[20]

7.2.3 Taxing Powers

Both the federal and provincial governments have the power to tax. Pursuant to subsection 91(3) of the *Constitution Act, 1867*, the Parliament of Canada has the power to raise money "by any Mode or System of Taxation". As for the provinces, subsection 92(2) grants them a power of direct taxation in order to raise revenue for provincial purposes. Section 92A also allows the provinces to indirectly tax non-renewable natural resources, forestry resources, and electric energy.

The constitutional rules just mentioned ensure that there is no multiple, indirect taxation. Yet, federal and provincial powers overlap in the area of direct taxation. This has not been the subject of major conflict, because Parliament and the provinces have entered into agreements relating to the definition, collection and sharing of such taxes.

In addition, there are constitutional and legislative rules on revenue sharing between the federal government and the provinces. Specifically, section 36 of the Constitution commits Canada to providing "equalization payments" in order to ensure that all provinces have sufficient revenues to provide comparable levels of public services at comparable levels of provincial taxation. Yet attempts by the federal and provincial governments to establish acceptable revenue sharing criteria has led to lengthy, complex, ongoing, and sometimes acrimonious debate.[21]

---

proposed by the Uniform Law Conference of Canada at http://www.ulcc.ca/en/us/index.cfm?sec=1&sub=1m3

[20] *Kitkatla Band v. British Columbia (Minister of Small Business, Tourism and Culture)*, 2002 SCC 31, [2002] 2 S.C.R. 146 at para. 51.

[21] On December 5, 2003, the Council of the Federation was created. The Premiers of Canada's ten provinces and three territories are members of the Council. As stated on its website (www.councilofthefederation.ca), the objectives of the Council are to: "promote interprovincial-territorial cooperation and closer ties between members of the Council, to ultimately strengthen Canada; foster meaningful relations between governments based on respect for the Constitution and recognition of the diversity within the federation; [and] show leadership on issues important to all Canadians". Such an institution will, it is hoped, prove useful in resolving the many conflicts that arise between the provinces or between the federal and provincial governments.

7.2.4 Resolution of Conflicts Between Federal and Provincial Legislation

The constitutional principle according to which conflicts between federal and provincial laws relating to the same matter are resolved is that of federal paramountcy – in cases of conflict, federal law prevails. This principle is not contained in the *Constitution Act, 1867* but once again is the result of judicial decisions. As a rule, however, it is only when there is express contradiction between federal and provincial legislation, or contradiction with the purpose of federal legislation, that the courts will rely on the principle of paramountcy.[22]

7.3 The Means and Methods of Legal Unification

7.3.1 At the Federal Level

7.3.1.1 Unification of Provincial Legislation

Certain sections of the *Constitution Act, 1867* were initially enacted with a view to ensuring federal oversight relating to provincial legislation[23] and could have been used to ensure its unification; however, there is now a clear understanding to the effect that Parliament will never resort to these sections.

Although the federal government is not in a position to force the provinces to legislate, it can certainly attempt to persuade the provinces to do so by various means, including ratification of treaties to be implemented by the provinces and use of its spending power.

The latter is of major importance since the federal government has in fact induced the provinces to adopt uniform legislation by this means.[24] The *Canada*

---

[22]*Multiple Access Ltd. v. McCutcheon*, [1982] 2 S.C.R. 161; *Bank of Montreal v. Hall*, [1990] 1 S.C.R. 121.

[23]Sections 55–58 & 90 allow the Parliament of Canada to (1) disallow or nullify any law passed by a province within 2 years of its enactment; (2) disallow provincial laws relating to education and even enact remedial legislation; (3) instruct the lieutenant governors of the provinces to withhold consent to provincial bills or to reserve them for the consideration of Parliament. In addition, section 94 of the *Constitution Act, 1867* granted to Parliament the power to enact laws providing for the uniformity of laws dealing with property and civil rights in Ontario, New Brunswick and Nova Scotia (Quebec was excluded). However, such a federal law could only take effect if the provinces in question adopted and enacted it and no such law has ever been enacted.

[24]Since the Constitution is silent in this regard, the federal spending power is inferred from other powers (to levy taxes, to legislate in relation to "public property" and to appropriate federal funds). See *Reference re Canada Assistance Plan (B.C.)*, [1991] 2 S.C.R. 525 at 567; Hogg, *supra* note 1 at 6.8 "Spending Power".

*Health Act*²⁵ is an example of federal legislation conditioning the allocation of central money to the provinces in compliance with central standards; it requires provinces to satisfy certain federal conditions, such as universal access to required medical treatment, in order to receive health care funding from the federal government.

The spending power thus provides the federal government with considerable influence in numerous areas of provincial jurisdiction, including post-secondary education. In addition, huge federal budget surpluses during a portion of the last decade provided the federal government with the funding required to engage in this exercise, despite protests from provincial governments, particularly Quebec.²⁶

Apart from the ratification of treaties and the use of the spending power, there are also occasional threats by the federal government to take over certain fields in order to establish a uniform system in certain areas, but so far, the government has been reluctant to act on its threats. For example, to date, corporate securities have been regulated primarily at the provincial level. The possibility has been raised of the federal government creating a single securities regulator, replacing the existing checkerboard system. This led to skirmishes between the federal government and the provinces in the past and became full-scale conflict once the federal government signalled its intention to push ahead with such a proposal.²⁷

7.3.1.2 Harmonization of Bijural Federal Legislation

The limited power of the federal government to promote unification of provincial law must be contrasted with its much more tangible power to harmonize its "bijural" legislation, that is, federal enactments relying on underlying provincial law for

---

²⁵R.S.C. 1985, c. C-6.

²⁶See *A new division of Canada's financial resources: report* (Quebec, Commission sur le déséquilibre fiscal, 2002), online: Commission sur le déséquilibre fiscal (http://www.desequilibrefiscal.gouv.qc.ca/en/document/rapport_final.htm); see also Alain Noël, Nicolas Marceau, Andrée Lajoie, Luc Godbout, "Déséquilibre fiscal – Le problème demeure entier" *Le Devoir* (17 June 2008) A7.

²⁷The Supreme Court of Canada held in 2011 that the proposal of the federal government was not valid under section 91(2) of the *Constitution Act, 1867*; see *Reference Re Securities Act*, 2011 SCC 66, [2011] 3 S.C.R. 837. The federal government has now begun a process of cooperative negotiations with the provinces with a view to creating the Cooperative Capital Markets Regulators (CCMR), to be based in Toronto and to be responsible for overseeing common national rules. This involves the passing of matching provincial legislation allowing the provinces to retain ultimate legislative authority over the subject; see Barrie McKenna et al., "Ottawa renews push for national securities regulator", *The Globe and Mail* (19 September 2013) online: http://www.theglobeandmail.com; see also Gorden Isfeld & Barbara Shecter, "Jim Flaherty: Ottawa, B.C. and Ontario agree to establish co-operative securities regulator". *Financial Post* (19 September 2013) online: http://business.financialpost.com.

their meaning and effect.[28] In this regard, on June 1, 2001, sections 8.1 and 8.2 of the *Interpretation Act* of Canada came into force.[29] These sections, set out below, contain the principles which underlie the interpretation of bijural federal legislation.

8.1 Both the common law and the civil law are equally authoritative and recognized sources of the law of property and civil rights in Canada and, unless otherwise provided by law, if in interpreting an enactment it is necessary to refer to a province's rules, principles or concepts forming part of the law of property and civil rights, reference must be made to the rules, principles and concepts in force in the province at the time the enactment is being applied.	8.1 Le droit civil et la common law font pareillement autorité et sont tous deux sources de droit en matière de propriété et de droits civils au Canada et, s'il est nécessaire de recourir à des règles, principes ou notions appartenant au domaine de la propriété et des droits civils en vue d'assurer l'application d'un texte dans une province, il faut, sauf règle de droit s'y opposant, avoir recours aux règles, principes et notions en vigueur dans cette province au moment de l'application du texte.
8.2 Unless otherwise provided by law, when an enactment contains both civil law and common law terminology, or terminology that has a different meaning in the civil law and the common law, the civil law terminology or meaning is to be adopted in the Province of Quebec and the common law terminology or meaning is to be adopted in the other provinces.	8.2 Sauf règle de droit s'y opposant, est entendu dans un sens compatible avec le système juridique de la province d'application le texte qui emploie à la fois des termes propres au droit civil de la province de Québec et des termes propres à la common law des autres provinces, ou qui emploie des termes qui ont un sens différent dans l'un ou l'autre de ces systèmes.

Section 8.1 first recognizes the authority of both the common law and the civil law, by confirming that they are both sources of the law of property and civil rights. It clearly states that if "in interpreting an enactment it is necessary to refer to a province's rules, principles or concepts forming part of the law of property and civil rights", then "unless otherwise provided by law" the rules, principles and concepts

---

[28] The terms "bijural" and "bijuralism" are Canadian neologisms coined to reflect the co-existence of civil law in Quebec and the common law elsewhere in Canada with respect to matters of private law ("property and civil rights"). Given the growing importance of aboriginal law in Canada and the existence of variations in the law from one province to the other (not only between Quebec and the other provinces, but also among the common law provinces), Canada is occasionally referred to as being multijural or plurijural. In that particular context, use of the terms "multijural" and "plurijural" is accurate. Although it can be argued that there are three legal traditions in Canada (aboriginal, civil law, and common law) and perhaps more than three if the aboriginal tradition is subdivided into different components, only two legal traditions have primary relevance in the context of property and civil rights, which fall within the jurisdiction of the Canadian provinces. These matters are regulated by the civil law applicable in Quebec, and by the common law applicable elsewhere in Canada. In these circumstances, the term "bijural" and its companion term "bijuralism" are appropriate, since they refer to the two legal traditions that form the basis of provincial jurisdiction in matters relating to property and civil rights.

[29] R.S.C. 1985, c. I-21; ss. 8.1 and 8.2 were added to the *Interpretation Act* by the *Federal Law—Civil Law Harmonization Act, No. 1*, S.C. 2001, c. 4, s. 8.

in force in the province at the time the enactment is being applied provide the backdrop for the federal legislation.

Section 8.2 deals with the terminology used in a federal enactment to describe a private law rule. That terminology must be understood to have a meaning that is compatible with the legal system of the province in which the enactment is applied, unless "otherwise provided by law". For example, depending on the province or territory in question, as a general rule, if a federal enactment uses the expression "trust", it refers either to the trust developed by Equity, in the common law provinces and territories of Canada, or to the trust described in articles 1260–1298 of the *Civil Code of Québec*. By thus confirming that the common law and the civil law are equally authoritative, the federal government recognizes the importance of both traditions: both are clearly placed on an equal footing for the purpose of interpreting bijural federal legislation.

The federal government is in the process of reviewing its legislation in order to ensure that bijural federal legislation uses the concepts and terminology that are true to both the common law and civil law traditions. It is in this sense that federal legislation is said to be "harmonized".[30]

As a result, in Canada, the terms "harmonization" and "unification" are used differently in the federal and provincial contexts.

Federal Conception of Harmonization: federal legislation that relies, for its meaning and effect, on underlying provincial law in relation to property and civil rights is described as "bijural". Since provincial law in relation to property and civil rights is based on civil law in Quebec and on the common law elsewhere in Canada, bijural federal legislation is said to be "harmonized" when it has been drafted, reviewed or modified to ensure that it takes both legal traditions into consideration.

Provincial Conception of Harmonization and Unification: as will be seen below, in the provincial context, the terms "unification" and "harmonization", or their variants, appear to be viewed as synonymous: they refer to proposals that seek to ensure that provincial laws dealing with similar subject matter are similar or identical. There may, however, be a slight difference in degree between the two terms: "unification" is perhaps more likely to describe identical legislation whereas "harmonization" describes legislation that is similar but not identical. As a result, in the provincial context, the meaning of the word "harmonization" is very different from its meaning in the federal context

Accordingly, in this report, the term "harmonization" refers only to federal efforts relating to bijural federal legislation, whereas the term "unification" refers to proposals seeking to ensure that provincial laws dealing with similar subject matter are similar or identical.

---

[30]For more information relating to bijural federal legislation and the harmonization process, see *Canadian Legislative Bijuralism Site*, online: Department of Justice Canada (http://www.bijurilex.gc.ca); see also, Aline Grenon, "*The Interpretation of Bijural or Harmonized Federal Legislation: Schreiber v. Canada (A.G.)*", Case Comment, (2005) 84 Can. Bar. Rev. 131 at 134–149.

As will be illustrated in Sect. 7.4 below, bijural federal legislation can be interpreted differently in Quebec and in the common law parts of Canada as a result of sections 8.1 and 8.2, and this can be said to fly in the face of unification. Yet, in the particular context of the Canadian federation, these sections, whose primary purpose is to set out the principles for interpreting bijural federal legislation, also seek to respect legal diversity by recognizing the authority in Canada of both the common law and the civil law in matters relating to property and civil rights. Although these sections will inevitably give rise to variations in the application of bijural federal legislation, they will also foster, in this writer's opinion, a heightened awareness of the strengths and weaknesses inherent in both legal traditions and may in certain circumstances produce a measure of uniformity. This will be discussed in more detail in Sect. 7.4.

With respect to unification (rather than harmonization) initiatives, the Law Reform Commission of Canada (1971–1993) and its successor, the relatively short-lived Law Commission of Canada (1997–2006), did play a role.. With the unfortunate demise of the latter, due to lack of funding from the federal government, representatives of the federal government now remain involved in unification initiatives primarily through the work of the Uniform Law Conference of Canada, discussed below.

7.3.2 At the Provincial Level

Representatives of the provincial governments are primarily involved in unification initiatives via the work carried out by the Uniform Law Conference of Canada, whose role is discussed in more detail below. In addition, provincial premiers meet often, and these meetings can result in agreements, among some or all of the premiers, relating to uniform legislation.

7.3.3 The Role of the Courts

The Supreme Court of Canada was created pursuant to section 101 of the *Constitution Act, 1867,* which authorized Parliament to establish "a General Court of Appeal for Canada". This section also gave rise to the creation of the Federal Court of Canada, composed of trial and appellate courts (final appeals are to the Supreme Court). Finally, each province has trial and appellate courts, pursuant to section 92(14) of the *Constitution Act, 1867.*

The Supreme Court of Canada plays a role with respect to both harmonization and unification of law. When the Court was initially established, it was viewed as a means of developing a unified legal system. Although this is now less often the case, at least insofar as bijural federal legislation is concerned, the Court can and does create uniform norms when called upon to interpret other federal legislation. In addition, since it is the "General Court of Appeal for Canada", it hears appeals from provincial courts and can also establish uniform norms in respect of provincial law.[31]

It has been held that section 92(14) gives full jurisdiction to provincial courts over federal, provincial or constitutional matters.[32] This is, however, subject to the following caveats:

1. appeals from all provincial courts of appeal are to the Supreme Court of Canada, thereby ensuring a measure of uniformity at the national level;
2. with respect to matters under federal jurisdiction, if federal law is silent with respect to the forum of adjudication, provincial courts will have jurisdiction unless Parliament has stipulated the forum; in some cases (for example, criminal law, divorce, bankruptcy and insolvency) Parliament has specifically granted jurisdiction to provincial courts;
3. certain federal matters must be brought before the Federal Court of Canada;
4. pursuant to section 96 of the Constitution, the federal government appoints the judges "of the Superior, District, and County Courts in each Province, except those of the Courts of Probate in Nova Scotia and New Brunswick", thereby granting the federal government a certain degree of control over these courts.

Courts in the common law provinces and territories of Canada will almost invariably consider legislative or judicial practice of other common law provinces and will occasionally consider those of Quebec. As for Quebec courts, they will consider legislative or judicial practice of common law provinces if the issues involve federal legislation or provincial legislation similar to that found in the other provinces (for example, insurance law or company law). Decisions by these courts can give rise to uniform interpretation of similar provincial enactments. Yet, the reverse can also occur and in these circumstances, the Supreme Court of Canada may be called upon to resolve conflicting decisions rendered by provincial court of appeals, thereby contributing to uniform interpretation of provincial law.[33]

Finally, although the Supreme Court of Canada will normally resolve differences in legal interpretation among courts, legislation will occasionally be adopted at the federal, provincial or territorial levels with a view to resolving such differences. For example, the Supreme Court of Canada recently missed a rare opportunity to unify, in conformity with civil law concepts, Quebec personal property security rules with similar rules applicable elsewhere in Canada[34] but a degree of unification could still be achieved if the Quebec or the federal government were to modify existing federal or provincial legislation.[35]

---

[31] But see *infra* notes 33 & 34 and accompanying text.

[32] *Valin v. Langlois* (1879), [1880] 3 S.C.R. 1 at 19; *Ontario (A.G.) v. Pembina Exploration Canada Ltd.,* [1989] 1 S.C.R. 206 at 217.

[33] See e.g. *Re Giffen,* [1998] 1 S.C.R. 91, where the Supreme Court resolved conflicting approaches of the Ontario and Saskatchewan court of appeals, relating to personal property security.

[34] See *Lefebvre (Trustee of); Tremblay (Trustee of)*, 2004 SCC 63, [2004] 3 S.C.R. 326; *Ouellet (Trustee of)*, 2004 SCC 64, [2004] 3 S.C.R. 348.

[35] In this regard, see Aline Grenon, La problématique entourant les « sûretés-propriétés » au Québec: *Lefebvre (Syndic de); Tremblay (Syndic de)* et *Ouellet (Syndic de)*" (2005) 35 R.G.D. 285.

7.3.4 Other Means of Achieving Unification

7.3.4.1 Uniform Law Conference of Canada

The Uniform Law Conference of Canada (ULCC) was "founded in 1918 to harmonize the laws of the provinces and territories of Canada, and where appropriate the federal laws as well".[36] It is composed of two sections: the Criminal Section and the Civil Section. Its work is carried out by delegates appointed by the member governments.

Criminal Section: although criminal laws fall mainly under federal jurisdiction in Canada (section 91(27) of the *Constitution Act, 1867*), the administration of criminal justice is largely provincial, pursuant to section 92(14). The Criminal Section accordingly allows representatives from both levels of government, together with other interested parties such as defence counsel and judges, to meet and discuss proposals to improve the criminal justice system.

Civil Section: as stated on the ULCC website, the Civil Section "assembles government policy lawyers and analysts, private lawyers and law reformers to consider areas in which provincial and territorial laws would benefit from harmonization. Sometimes the federal government has related responsibilities, and it participates in the appropriate discussions in such cases. The main work of the Civil Section is reflected in 'uniform statutes', which the Section adopts and recommends for enactment by all relevant governments in Canada. On occasion the Section adopts a 'model statute', on which it expresses no opinion as a matter of policy, but which it offers as a method of harmonization where member governments want to use it". Since 1990, all uniform statutes are drafted in both English and French.

In an article published in 1997, it was stated that as of 1995, the ULCC "had adopted 93 uniform acts, of which 77 were still current".[37] It was also pointed out that this record compared favourably with that of the National Conference of Commissioners on Uniform State Laws (NCCUSL): as of 1989, the NCCUSL had approved 135 uniform acts which remained current.[38]

Overly modest funding and the lack of a strong commitment on the part of governments have constituted major problems for the ULCC in the past. However, following consultations with many stakeholders, including government representatives, the ULCC adopted an ambitious project, i.e., the Commercial Law Strategy,

---

[36] See online: Uniform Law Conference of Canada (http://www.ulcc.ca); for a recent article relating to the ULCC, see Arthur Close, "The Uniform Law Conference and the Harmonization of Law in Canada" (2007) 40 U.B.C. L. Rev. 535 [Close].

[37] Jacob S. Ziegel, "Harmonization of Private Laws in Federal Systems of Government: Canada, the USA, and Australia" in Ross Cranston, ed., *Making Commercial Law: Essays in Honour of Roy Goode* (Oxford: Clarendon Press, 1997) 131 at 145.

[38] *Ibid.* at 154–155.

in order to modernize and harmonize commercial law in Canada. The Strategy was approved by all Ministers of Justice in December 1999 with a commitment to provide funding to permit it to move forward.

The Strategy encompasses areas such as sale of goods, international sale of goods, secured transactions, federal secured transactions, commercial liens, documents of title, the holding and transfer of investment securities, electronic commerce, leases, licensing of intellectual property, negotiable instruments and cost of credit disclosure. Of these elements, priority has been given to promoting the speedy enactment of uniform acts pertaining to e-commerce, commercial liens and cost of credit disclosure (including uniform regulations relating to the latter), and to actively press forward with other important initiatives relating to e-commerce and federal secured transactions.

According to the ULCC website, much of the work of the Commercial Law Strategy is now complete.[39] Current versions of the relevant statutes are available on the website.[40]

7.3.4.2 The Legal Profession and Law Schools

The role of the legal profession, including law schools, in promoting unification is difficult to evaluate. Although the conservatism of the legal profession constitutes an obstacle to unification, there exist committed jurists willing to push forward with such initiatives. As for Canadian law schools, although they draw students from throughout the federal system, the tendency is for students who have been raised in common law provinces to attend one of the law schools in those provinces. In a similar vein, students raised in Quebec attend law school there.

Legal education invariably focuses on both federal and provincial law. Insofar as the latter is concerned, however, most law schools in the common law parts of Canada focus on the common law and on statute law that is relevant to the province in which they are located. Quebec law schools, by contrast, focus on the *Civil Code of Québec,* provincial statutes and Quebec doctrine and court decisions. As a result, apart from federal law, most law graduates are knowledgeable in only common law or civil law.

Still, a limited number of graduates acquire knowledge of both systems, since the law schools of the University of Ottawa, McGill University, *Université de Montréal* and *Université de Sherbrooke* provide students with the opportunity to acquire a bijural legal education.[41] Although such knowledge cannot be said to

---

[39]See e.g. the *Status of Uniform Acts Recommended by the Commercial Law Strategy,* online: Uniform Law Conference of Canada (http://www.ulcc.ca/en/civil-section/27-civil-section-commercial-law-strategy)

[40]*Ibid.*

[41]See the websites of these law schools for further information relating to these programs. Law students elsewhere in Canada who wish to acquire such an education have to transfer to another law school.

promote unification of law, it does allow a small group of jurists to acquire a better understanding of the strengths and weaknesses inherent in both systems. In conjunction with the possible effects of sections 8.1 and 8.2 of the *Interpretation Act* of Canada, discussed in more detail in Sect. 7.4 below, this could generate positive results in years to come.

Students who have obtained their degree from a Canadian law school and who wish to practice must first be admitted to the bar of a specific province, since admission to the bar is not system-wide. As a rule, those admitted to one bar will set up their practice or take employment in the province or territory in which they have been admitted. But once a lawyer has been admitted to the bar of one province or territory, mobility between provinces and territories is now facilitated as a result of the efforts of the Federation of Law Societies of Canada.[42] Increased mobility may lead to increased awareness of unnecessary divergences in the laws of the various provinces and thereby promote unification.

Certain other legal institutions also play a unifying role. In addition to the law schools that provide students with the opportunity to acquire a bijural legal education (in this regard, it must be noted that many judges of the Federal and Supreme courts of Canada make a point of hiring law clerks with a bijural legal background), the National Judicial Institute, which develops and delivers educational programs for all federal, provincial and territorial judges, perhaps plays such a role, despite the fact that one of its stated objectives is to reflect Canada's diversity.[43]

7.3.4.3 Restatements

In Canada, there are no restatements similar to those published by the American Law Institute. Instead, reliance is placed on compilations or digests such as *Halsbury's Laws of Canada* or the *Canadian Abridgment,* produced by commercial publishers. These compilations are less relevant in Quebec private law matters, because of the codification of civil law principles and the existence in Quebec of important works of doctrine, primarily published in French. As a result, the impetus toward unification provided by publications equivalent to the American restatements is not available in Canada.

7.3.4.4 Industry, Trade and Other Entities

Industry, trade or other organizations can promote legal unification, either through lobbying or by establishing standards and practices that are subsequently reflected in uniform or harmonized legislation. Two such groups are the Canadian Council

---

[42] See www.flsc.ca

[43] See www.nji.ca

of Insurance Regulators[44] and the Canadian Securities Administrators,[45] although the role played by the latter is ambiguous. As stated on the website of the Canadian Securities Administrators, the group is "a voluntary umbrella organization of Canada's provincial and territorial securities regulators". Although its stated objective is "to improve, coordinate and harmonize regulation of the Canadian capital markets", it is clear that this is to be carried out by the provinces and territories, rather than by the federal government. The harmonization sought by this group appears to fall short of the full unification that would result if the federal government were to proceed with a single securities regulator.[46]

7.3.4.5 International Factors

Compliance with international legal obligations no doubt has an influence on legal unification, although the extent of the influence cannot be verified.

In addition, Canadian representatives are involved in various international unification projects, including those put forward by UNCITRAL, UNIDROIT and the Hague Conference on Private International Law. For example, the Canadian government and, with the help and encouragement of the ULCC, all the provincial and territorial governments, have adopted legislation based on the Model Law on International Commercial Arbitration, adopted by UNCITRAL on June 21, 1985.[47] Canada is also a party to the Hague Conference *Convention on the Law Applicable to Trusts and on their Recognition*,[48] the UNCITRAL *United Nations Convention on Contracts for the International Sale of Goods*[49] and the UNIDROIT *Convention Providing a Uniform Law on the Form of an International Will*.[50]

Involvement in such international unification projects could eventually give rise to domestic unification initiatives.

7.4 The State of Unification in Canada

Because federal and provincial objectives with respect to unification are not the same, the state of unification in Canada has to be discussed separately, at both the federal and provincial levels.

---

[44] See www.ccir-ccrra.org

[45] See www.csa-acvm.ca

[46] See *supra* note 26 and accompanying text.

[47] See *Selected Uniform Statutes in alphabetical order*, online: Uniform Law Conference of Canada (http://www.ulcc.ca/en/us/index.cfm?sec=1&sub=1i6); see also Close, *supra* note 36 at 553, n. 44.

[48] 1 July 1985, Can. T.S. 1993 No. 2, (entered into force in Canada 1 January 1993).

[49] 11 April 1980, Can. T.S. 1992 No. 2, (Also known as the Vienna Convention of 1980, entered into force in Canada 1 May 1992).

[50] 26 October 1973, Can. T.S. 1978 No. 34, (entered into force in Canada 9 February 1978).

7.4.1 Unification and Harmonization at the Federal Level[51]

At the federal level, *with the exception of bijural legislation*, the predominant state is full unification: that is, legislation is applied uniformly throughout the country. *Insofar as bijural federal legislation is concerned*, however, the predominant state appears to be diversity of law. As discussed previously, pursuant to sections 8.1 and 8.2 of the *Interpretation Act,* bijural federal legislation relies on underlying provincial law for its meaning and effect. Since this law can vary from one province to the other, bijural legislation can vary in its application.[52]

Since the coming into force of sections 8.1 and 8.2 of the *Interpretation Act*, the Supreme Court of Canada and the Federal Court of Appeal have not hesitated to refer to these sections when called upon to interpret bijural federal legislation. *D.I.M.S. Construction Inc. (Trustee of) v. Quebec (A.G.)*[53] is an excellent illustration of the effects of these sections.

One of the issues in that case was the application of section 97(3) of the *Bankruptcy and Insolvency Act*,[54] ("BIA"), to the effect that the law of set-off applies to all claims against the estate of the bankrupt. Depending on how broad the rules of set-off are (in Quebec civil law, the equivalent term is "compensation"), they can have a significant effect in a bankruptcy context. With respect to set-off, Quebec civil law and Canadian common law take two very different approaches. On the one hand, Canadian common law, via the principle of equity, permits set-off even where it might be prejudicial to the interests of third parties, including creditors.[55] On the other hand, Quebec civil law places great importance on the acquired rights of third parties and the law of compensation reflects that concern.[56]

The BIA does not specify what law applies to set-off in the bankruptcy and insolvency context. The Supreme Court of Canada was therefore of the opinion that section 97(3) was based on underlying provincial law. Since *D.I.M.S.* arose in Quebec, the Court refused to apply the equitable concept of set-off and applied the Civil Code provisions instead. As a result, the law in Quebec and the law elsewhere in Canada relating to set-off in the context of bankruptcy law are now different, the law in the rest of Canada having a broader effect than the civil law rules.

A decision such as *D.I.M.S.* places Parliament in a difficult situation. Given the imperative wording of sections 8.1 and 8.2, it can be expected that Parliament will

---

[51] Much of the information in this section is contained in the preliminary chapter of the following book: Aline Grenon & Louise Bélanger-Hardy, eds., *Elements of Quebec Civil Law – A Comparison with the Common Law of Canada* (Toronto: Thomson Carswell, 2008) at 10–21.

[52] In this regard, it must be noted that provincial law can vary not only between Quebec and the common law provinces, but also among the common law provinces.

[53] 2005 SCC 52, [2005]2 S.C.R. 564 [*D.I.M.S.*].

[54] R.C.S. 1985, c. B-3.

[55] See John A.M. Judge & Margaret E. Grottenthaler, "Legal and Equitable Set-Offs" (1991) 70 Can. Bar Rev. 91 at 117.

[56] See arts. 1672–1682, 2644 C.C.Q.

as a rule accept the absence of a uniform result in the application of its bijural legislation in order to preserve the integrity of both legal systems underlying this legislation. Yet, if Parliament believes that a uniform result is desirable or perhaps even essential, the legislation will have to be amended. If, for example, Parliament decides to amend the BIA with respect to set-off, what rule would it adopt? Most likely, the rule would be chosen after a through comparative study, in the process of which Parliament would have to answer the following policy question: in the context of the BIA, should set-off be subject to the rule that preserves the principle of equality among the creditors, or the rule that allows the court to exercise discretion so as to exempt a creditor from that principle?

Parliament may never have to deal with that question, however, since the Supreme Court of Canada has not yet had the opportunity to examine the issue of common law set-off in the context of section 97(3) of the *Bankruptcy and Insolvency Act*. If or when the Court is given this opportunity, it might decide to overturn existing common law cases and opt for an approach similar to the one in Quebec, thereby re-establishing uniformity in this area.

Before sections 8.1 and 8.2 were enacted, it often happened when interpreting bijural federal legislation that courts opted for a construction derived from the common law, and the result was applied to the country as a whole. Little if any thought was given to the inherent strength or weakness of the underlying common law or to the impact of the legislation on the civil law of Quebec. That approach no longer applies and comparison between Quebec civil law and Canadian common law has now taken on real practical importance: in cases with national ramifications (for example, the bankruptcy of a corporation having places of business in Quebec and elsewhere in Canada), it becomes necessary to take those differences into consideration in applying federal law. At the same time, as illustrated in *D.I.M.S.*, this comparison highlights the strengths and weaknesses of the private law on which federal legislation is based. This can be expected to contribute not only to the development of Canadian comparative law but ultimately, to better uniform federal law achieved either by means of legislative amendment or judicial interpretation.[57]

7.4.2 Unification at the Provincial Level

At the provincial level, unification of law is, on the whole, viewed as a desirable objective and the ULCC is actively involved in the process. The level of unification found in the common law provinces and territories is probably at least on par with

---

[57]For a recent article pertaining to article 8.1 of the *Interpretation Act* and its role at the Supreme Court of Canada, see Aline Grenon, "Le bijuridisme canadien à la croisée des chemins? Réflexions sur l'incidence de l'article 8.1 de la *Loi d'interprétation*", (2011) 56 McGill L. J. A slightly modified and up-dated English version of this article will be published in 2014 in the Osgoode Hall Law Journal.

the level found in American states. It may even be superior, particularly since the Supreme Court of Canada is in a position to ensure uniform interpretation of provincial law.

The civil law jurisdiction of Quebec is also involved in the ULCC initiatives. A paper presented at an annual meeting of the ULCC reveals that Quebec, either in the Civil Code or in various statutes, has in fact adopted provisions that track many ULCC model laws adopted (more or less faithfully) in the common law provinces.[58]

7.5 Conclusion

In Canada, forces for and against unification coexist. On the one hand, commercial expediency and the need to simplify law help to promote unification. On the other hand, the country's relatively small population, its bijural nature and the fact that private law is under provincial jurisdiction are part of the numerous forces that hinder unification. As a result, full unification is impossible. Partial unification in some areas is the most that can be expected and even in areas such as securities regulation, where legal uniformity would be both logical and cost-effective, unification initiatives are fraught with difficulty.

---

[58]Frédérique Sabourin, "Les lois de la CHLC et le Code civil du Québec" (Paper presented to the annual meeting of the Uniform Law Conference of Canada, St. John's, Newfoundland and Labrador, 21–25 August 2005) [original French version available at http://ulcc.ca/fr/poam2/ULCC_Acts_Quebec_Civil_Code_Fr.pdf; English translation available at http://ulcc.ca/en/poam2/ULCC_Acts_Quebec_Civil_Code_En[1].pdf]

Chapter 8
The European Union: A Federation in All but Name

Jan Wouters, Hanne Cuyckens, and Thomas Ramopoulos

8.1 Overview

The EU has often been referred to as a *sui generis* entity situated somewhere between an international organization and a nation state, which displays both intergovernmental and supranational features. The European integration process is one of continuous pulses and it is therefore important to briefly give an overview of the developments which have progressively led to the establishment of the European Union ('EU', 'Union') as it exists today.

Jan Wouters, Jean Monnet Chair, Full Professor of International Law and International Organizations, Director of the Leuven Centre for Global Governance Studies and Institute for International Law, Leuven University; Visiting Professor, College of Europe (Bruges) and Sciences Po (Paris).

Hanne Cuyckens, Assistant, Institute for International Law, Research Fellow, Institute for International Law / Leuven Centre for Global Governance Studies, Leuven University.

Thomas Ramopoulos, Research Fellow, Institute for International Law / Leuven Centre for Global Governance, Leuven University.

J. Wouters (✉)
Jean Monnet Chair ad personam EU and Global Governance, Full Professor of International Law and International Organizations and Director, Leuven Centre for Global Governance Studies – Institute for International Law, KU Leuven, Belgium

House de Dorlodot, Deberiotstraat 34, 3000 Leuven, Belgium

College of Europe, Brugge, Belgium

Sciences Po, Paris Cedex 07, France
e-mail: jan.wouters@ggs.kuleuven.be

H. Cuyckens • T. Ramopoulos
Institute for International Law/Leuven Centre for Global Governance Studies,
KU, Leuven, Belgium
e-mail: hanne.cuyckens@law.kuleuven.be; thomas.ramopoulos@ggs.kuleuven.be

The early stages of European integration began after the end of the Second World War with the establishment of the Council of Europe in 1949. But it was not until the six founding Member States decided to establish the European Coal and Steal Community ('ECSC') by a treaty signed in Paris on 18 April 1951 that the process of 'deeper' integration, involving stronger supranational features, was initiated.[1] The initiative of establishing such a community revolving around the production of coal and steel was launched by French Foreign Minister Robert Schuman. He believed that by pooling production of coal and steel under the ECSC, war between France and Germany would become practically impossible and he proposed to place the whole Franco-German coal and steel production under one joint High Authority, in an organisation open to the participation of other countries of Europe.[2] Belgium, Italy, Luxembourg and the Netherlands decided to join France and Germany in this organisation. The distinguishing character of the ECSC at that time was that it was much more than a traditional intergovernmental organisation: it operated in a supranational manner, with policies conducted independently from the Member States by the High Authority.

The supranational formula proved to be a success and the Benelux countries in 1955 proposed to their partners in the ECSC to extend this formula towards other sectors and more precisely to move towards the setting-up of a common market and cooperation in the area of atomic energy.[3] This proposal was further discussed at a meeting in Messina the same year and Paul-Henri Spaak, Belgian Foreign Minister at that time, was asked to report on the feasibility of such extension. This was judged to be feasible and the six Member States, gathered in Rome, signed on 25 March 1957 the Treaty establishing the European Economic Community ('EEC') and the Treaty establishing the European Atomic Energy Community ('EAEC'). The three Communities each had their own institutions at the beginning but later on these were progressively merged (the European Parliament and the Court of Justice in 1957 and the Council of Ministers and the Commission in 1967 with the Merger Treaty).

In the early 1960s Member States started to discuss the need to balance the growing importance of the EEC in international economic relations with a common foreign policy.[4] This issue was very contentious and at the beginning it was decided to establish a system of foreign policy cooperation on a purely intergovernmental basis, situated entirely outside the framework of the Communities.[5] Even though the European Political Cooperation ('EPC') and the Communities were kept formally separated, a lot of issues were overlapping and gradually a link grew between the EPC meetings of the Foreign Ministers and the meetings of the Council of the

---

[1] A. Rosas and L. Armati, *EU Constitutional Law: An Introduction* (Hart Publishing, 2010), 2.

[2] Statement by Robert Schuman, Minister of Foreign Affairs of France, 9 May 1950, in S. Patijn (ed.), *Landmarks in European Unity: 22 Texts on European Integration* (Sijthoff, 1970), 47.

[3] P.S.R.F Mathijsen, *A Guide to European Union Law as Amended by the Treaty of Lisbon* (Sweet & Maxwell, 2010), 15.

[4] C. Bretherton and J. Vogler, *The EU as a Global Actor* (Routledge, 2006), 164.

[5] C. Bretherton and J. Vogler, (op. cit.), 164.

European Communities. Co-operation in the sphere of foreign policy was referred to formally for the first time in the European Single Act adopted in 1986.[6] In 1992, the Treaty on European Union ('TEU', 'EU Treaty' or 'Maastricht Treaty') converted the EPC into the second pillar of the Union, the Common Foreign and Security Policy ('CFSP'). Other areas in which Member States gradually started coordinating their policies outside the sphere of competence of the Communities were the trans-border aspects of justice, crime and home affairs. Until the entry into force of the Maastricht Treaty on 1 November 1993, these areas were purely intergovernmental and outside the framework of the institutions.[7] With the Maastricht Treaty, intergovernmental cooperation between the Member States in the fields of Justice and Home Affairs ('JHA') was henceforth to be conducted on the basis of Title VI of the EU Treaty, the so-called 'third pillar'. Furthermore, upon the entry into force on 1 May 1999 of the Treaty of Amsterdam the judicial cooperation in civil matters, immigration and asylum policy was transferred from the third to the first pillar, thus narrowing the third pillar to Police and Judicial Cooperation in Criminal Matters. It is important to recall here that even though the CFSP and JHA were transferred into the area of Union law by the Maastricht Treaty, the decision-making remained largely intergovernmental in opposition to the supranational method applied to the areas within the ambit of the Communities (first pillar).

Apart from its introduction of a pillar structure for the EU the Maastricht Treaty considerably extended the sphere of action of the Community pillar, which was no longer confined to the economic sphere. In order to take this extension of competences into account the EEC was renamed the European Community ('EC').[8] The most important change was the decision to gradually establish an economic and monetary union ('EMU') with the ultimate objective to adopt a common currency.[9]

In the meantime, the number of EU Member States was increased on six different occasions.[10] Currently, there are 28 Member States and negotiations have started with other States on their accession to the Union.[11]

---

[6]The Single Act was signed by the Member States on February 17 and 28, 1986. It conferred new competences on the Community but did not alter the latter's general objectives of the Community: see K. Lenaerts and P. Van Nuffel, *European Union Law* (Sweet & Maxwell, 2011), 36.

[7]S. Peers, EU Justice and Home Affairs Law (non-civil), in P. Craig and G. De Burca (eds.), *The Evolution of EU Law* (Oxford University Press, 2011), 269.

[8]C.W.A. Timmermans, The Genesis and Development of the European Communities and the European Union, in P.J.G. Kapteyn and V. Van Themaat (eds.), *The Law of the European Union and the European Communities* (Kluwer Law International, 2008), 33.

[9]F. Snyder, EMU – Integration and Differentiation: Metaphor for European Union, in P. Craig and G. De Burca (eds.), (op. cit.), 693.

[10]1951: France, Germany, Italy, Belgium, the Netherlands and Luxemburg; 1973: Denmark, Ireland and the United Kingdom; 1981: Greece; 1986: Portugal and Spain; 1995: Austria, Finland and Sweden; 2004: Cyprus, the Czech Republic, Estonia, Hungary, Latvia, Lithuania, Malta, Poland, Slovenia and the Slovak Republic; 2007: Bulgaria and Romania.

[11]Accession negotiations are also being considered or being conducted with the following countries: the former Yugoslav Republic of Macedonia; Iceland; Montenegro; Serbia and Turkey.

On 29 October 2004, the heads of state or government of the Member States assembled in Rome signed the Treaty establishing a Constitution for Europe. However, the process of ratification was blocked after negative referenda in France and the Netherlands, and the idea of establishing a 'European Constitution' was abandoned. In its place came a 'Reform Treaty', the Treaty of Lisbon signed on 13 December 2007,[12] which amended the TEU and the EC Treaty. After a long and difficult ratification process it entered into force on 1 December 2009. While the TEU kept its name, the EC Treaty was renamed 'Treaty on the Functioning of the European Union' ('TFEU').

The Lisbon Treaty made a number of fundamental changes to the EU's institutional architecture. Among other changes, the EC was replaced and succeeded by the EU, which was also given legal personality explicitly.[13] Moreover, the pillar structure was formally abolished, although the CFSP retains a special place and remains "subject to specific rules and procedures".[14] Of the original three European Communities – the ECSC had lapsed after 50 years in 2002 – only the EAEC remains in place as a distinct organisation.

8.2 The Federal Distribution and Exercise of Lawmaking Power

8.2.1 Which Areas of Law Are Subject to the (Legislative) Jurisdiction of the Central Authority?

According to article 5(2) TEU, "the Union shall act only within the limits of the competences conferred upon it by the Member States in the Treaties to attain the objectives set out therein". This is the so-called principle of conferral. The competences that have not been conferred upon the EU remain with the Member States.[15] Along the same line, article 13(2) TEU establishes the twin principle of conferred powers of the institutions. It provides that "each institution shall act within the limits of the powers conferred on it in the Treaties, and in conformity with the procedures, conditions, and objectives set out in them".

Next to these candidate countries, there is also a list of potential candidates, namely Albania, Bosnia and Herzegovina; and Kosovo.

[12]Treaty of Lisbon amending the Treaty on European Union and the Treaty establishing the European Community, signed at Lisbon, 13 December 2007.

[13]Respectively Art. 1, third para., TEU and Art. 47 TEU.

[14]Art. 24(1), second para., TEU.

[15]Art. 5(2) in fine TEU; see also Art. 4(1) TEU and Declaration No 18 in relation to the delimitation of competences attached to the Lisbon Treaty.

The exercise of these competences is further governed by the principles of subsidiarity and proportionality. The principle of subsidiarity, as laid down in article 5(3) TEU, stipulates that "in areas which do not fall within its exclusive competence, the Union shall act only if and in so far as the objectives of the proposed action cannot be sufficiently achieved by the Member States (...) but rather, by reason of the scale or effects of the proposed action, be better achieved at Union level". The principle of proportionality, laid down in article 5(4) TEU, requires EU action not to exceed what is necessary to achieve the objectives contained in the Treaties. The application of these two principles is further governed by Protocol No. 2 on the application of the principles of subsidiarity and proportionality.[16] The most important innovation introduced by the Lisbon Treaty with regard to the principle of subsidiarity is the enhanced role accorded to national parliaments.[17] According to article 6 of Protocol No. 2 they indeed have the right to send to the Presidents of the European Parliament, the Council and the Commission, a reasoned opinion stating why they consider that the draft in question does not comply with the principle of subsidiarity. Regrettably, while the Protocol imposes obligations on the Commission to ensure compliance with both the principle of subsidiarity and the principle of proportionality, national parliaments are given a role only in relation to the first principle and not the latter.[18]

It follows from the principle of conferral that every legally binding EU act must be based on a grant of power.[19] In other words every act of the EU must be based on a specific or general treaty provision. The determination of the correct legal basis is crucial since it is the legal basis that determines the extent of the competence and the way the EU exercises it, i.e. the procedure to be followed in order to adopt the act in question, and often also the type of instrument that is to be adopted.[20] In other words, to paraphrase the Court of Justice of the European Union ('CJEU' or 'Court'), "[t]he choice of the appropriate legal basis has constitutional significance".[21] Failing to respect the prescribed procedure results in a violation of the balance of power between EU institutions and/or between the Union and its Members States, and failing to respect the limits of a competence derived from the legal basis in question infringes upon the principle of conferral.[22] Given the importance of a proper legal basis, it follows that "the choice of the legal basis for a measure may not depend

---

[16]Protocol No. 2 annexed to the TEU and TFEU on the application of the principles of subsidiarity and proportionality [2012] O.J. C 326/206.

[17]P. Craig, Institutions, Power, and Institutional Balance, in P. Craig and G. De Burca (eds.), (op. cit.), 76.

[18]P. Craig, Institutions, Power, and Institutional Balance, in P. Craig and G. De Burca (eds.), (op. cit.), 77.

[19]K.S.C. Bradley, Power and Procedures in the EU Constitution: Legal Bases and the Court, in P. Craig and G. De Burca (eds.), (op. cit.), 86.

[20]K. Lenaerts and P. Van Nuffel, (op. cit.), 113–114.

[21]Opinion 2/00 *Cartagena Protocol* [2001] ECR I-9713, para. 5.

[22]K.S.C. Bradley, Power and Procedures in the EU Constitution: Legal Bases and the Court, in P. Craig and G. De Burca (eds.), (op. cit.), 86.

simply on an [EU] institution's conviction as to the objective pursued but must be based on objective factors which are amenable to judicial review".[23] With regard to supervision of the choice of the correct legal basis, the CJEU plays an important role. Indeed, "[i]n its legal basis case law, the Court performs two of the principal functions of a Constitutional Court in a federal-type polity, defining the division of powers between the centre and the component states, and regulating the balance of powers between the institutions or branches of government".[24] It is important to note, however, that it is not necessary for a competence to have been *explicitly* established by a treaty provision. Indeed, the CJEU has developed a theory of *implied* competences. This theory is especially important in the area of external relations where it has been used to such an extent that it has become a fundamental part of the EU's external relations constitutional framework.[25] It is not within the ambit of this report to trace back the entire evolution of the CJEU's case law on this matter, but some important elements will be pointed to. In its 1971 *ERTA* judgment, the CJEU established the doctrine of implied external powers of the EU based on the link between these implied external powers and the existence of internal measures in the field in question.[26] The CJEU held that "the Community enjoys the capacity to establish contractual links with third countries over the whole field of objectives defined by the Treaty. This authority arises not only from an express conferment by the Treaty, but may equally flow from other provisions of the Treaty and from measures adopted, within the framework of those provisions by the Community institutions".[27] The theory of implied external powers is now well-established in the CJEU's case law[28] and has by now made it to the text of the Treaties.[29] Two rationales for implied powers have been progressively established: the existence of EU rules in the field in question (cf. *ERTA*) and the existence of a Union objective for the attainment of which internal competences need to be complemented by external ones (cf. later case law, such as opinion 2/91).[30]

---

[23]Case 45/86 *Commission v Council* [1987] ECR 1493, para. 11.

[24]K.S.C. Bradley, Power and Procedures in the EU Constitution: Legal Bases and the Court, in P. Craig and G. De Burca (eds.), (op. cit.), 104.

[25]G. De Baere, *Constitutional Principles of EU External Relations* (Oxford University Press, 2008), 16.

[26]M. Cremona, External Relations and External Competence of the European Union: The Emergence of an Integrated Policy, in P. Craig and G. De Burca (eds.), (op. cit.), 220.

[27]Case 22/70 *Commission v Council* [1971] ECR 263, para. 16.

[28]E.g. Opinion 1/76 *Draft Agreement establishing a European laying-up fund for inland waterway vessels* [1977] ECR 741, paras. 1–7; Opinion 2/91 *Convention No 170 of the International Labour Organization concerning safety and the use of chemicals at work* [1993] ECR I-1061, para. 7; Opinion 2/94 *Accession by the Communities to the Convention for the Protection of Human Rights and Fundamental Freedoms* [1996] ECR I-1759, para. 26; Opinion 1/03 *Competence of the Community to conclude the new Lugano Convention on jurisdiction and the recognition and enforcement of judgments in civil and commercial matters* [2006] ECR I-1145, para. 114.

[29]See articles 3(2) and 216 TFEU.

[30]M. Cremona, External Relations and External Competence of the European Union: The Emergence of an Integrated Policy, in P. Craig and G. De Burca (eds.), (op. cit.), 221.

There are two types of treaty provisions on which EU action can be based: sectoral provisions being the enabling provisions for action in a specific policy field or functional provisions allowing for action in different fields in order to pursue specified objectives.[31] The EU institutions most frequently rely on the specific treaty articles which provide for a competence in a particular matter. In the absence of such specific (sectoral) provisions, they may resort to the second category of treaty provisions: the functional provisions. Examples of such provisions are Article 352 TFEU and article Articles 114 and 115 TFEU (*see infra*). Article 352 TFEU, often referred to as the 'flexibility clause', confers upon the Union a supplementary tool to achieve the EU's objectives "[i]f action by the Union should prove necessary, within the framework of the policies defined in the Treaties, to attain one of the objectives set out in the Treaties, and the Treaties have not provided the necessary powers". The objectives pursued by the EU are listed in article 3 TEU. It has been argued by some authors that the reach of the flexibility clause after Lisbon has been broadened compared to the same provision before Lisbon (former article 308 TEC).[32] Indeed, previously, article 308 TEC referred to the situation in which action should prove necessary to obtain, in the course of the operation of the common market, one of the objectives of the EC, whereas now article 352 TFEU refers to action in the framework of the policies of the treaties in general, that is both the TEU and the TFEU.[33] However, it had already been the practice of EU institutions to interpret and apply article 308 TEC as broadly as possible. This had led the Court to try to circumscribe this apparent 'competence creep.'[34] Thus, contrary to the view of some commentators, as delineated above, it can be submitted that the new broader but also more detailed wording of article 352 TFEU actually brings the text of the Treaties in line with practice, partly making irrelevant the 'competence creep' debate. This, however, is not the case with article 114 TFEU, which has remained virtually unchanged and gives rise to the same concerns.[35]

Apart from the EU's fundamental principles regarding the existence of competences, it is important to look at the rules with regard to the nature of the competences. Before the entry into force of the Lisbon Treaty, there was no real catalogue listing the competences of the Union. Nowadays, not only is there such a catalogue of competences (see articles 3–6 TFEU) in place, but the Lisbon Treaty also stipulates the nature of these different competences.

---

[31] K.S.C. Bradley, Power and Procedures in the EU Constitution: Legal Bases and the Court, in P. Craig and G. De Burca (eds.), (op. cit.), 86.

[32] A. Rosas and L. Armati, (op. cit.), 20.

[33] A. Rosas and L. Armati, (op. cit.), 21. However, see Declaration No 41 on Article 352 of the Treaty on the Functioning of the European Union, which states that Art. 352 refers to the objectives as set out in Art. 3(2), (3) and (5), and not solely for the objectives stated in 3(1). Remarkably, no mention is made of Art. 3(4) TEU. See also Declaration No 42 on Article 352 of the Treaty on the Functioning of the European Union.

[34] Opinion 2/94 *Accession by the Communities to the Convention for the Protection of Human Rights and Fundamental Freedoms* [1996] ECR I-1759, paras. 27–35.

[35] A. Dashwood, M. Dougan, B. Rodger, E. Spaventa and D. Wyatt, *Wyatt and Dashwood's European Union Law* (Hart Publishing, 2011), 105–111.

The areas in which the EU has exclusive competence are listed in article 3(1) TFEU: customs union; the establishing of the competition rules necessary for the functioning of the internal market; monetary policy for the Member States whose currency is the euro; the conservation of marine biological resources under the common fisheries policy and the common commercial policy. Article 3(2) TFEU further stipulates that "[t]he Union shall also have exclusive competence for the conclusion of an international agreement when its conclusion is provided for in a legislative act of the Union or is necessary to enable the Union to exercise its internal competences, or in so far as its conclusion may affect common rules or alter their scope." Article 3(2) seems to be a codification of the CJEU's case law with regard to the EU's competence to conclude international agreements, as developed since the 1971 *ERTA* case (*supra*).[36] When the EU has exclusive competence in a specific area, this means that only the EU is competent to legislate and adopt legally binding acts with regard to this specific area. Consequently, the Member States are only allowed to act in these fields if they are empowered by the Union to do so or in order to implement Union acts.[37]

The second category of Union competences, i.e. the areas in which the Union and the Member States have shared competences, is covered by article 4 TFEU. These areas are: internal market; social policy; economic, social and territorial cohesion; agriculture and fisheries (except for the conservation of marine biological resources, which is an exclusive EU competence); environment; consumer protection; transport; trans-European networks; energy; area of freedom, security and justice and common safety concerns in public health matters. It is important to note that this is a non-exhaustive list since pursuant to article 4(1) TFEU "[t]he Union shall share competence with the Member States where the Treaties confer on it a competence which does not relate to the areas referred to in article 3 TFEU [exclusive competence] and 6 TFEU [areas in which the EU supports, coordinates or supplements the actions of the Member States]." Shared competences of the EU are thus in the first place defined negatively: every area conferred upon the EU by the TFEU that does not fall under its exclusive competence or under its competence of support, coordination or supplementing is to be considered a shared competence. Article 4(2) TFEU supports this by stating that "[s]hared competence between the Union and the Member States applies in the following *principal* areas" (emphasis added). The fact that shared competence is defined negatively and non-exhaustively seems to suggest that shared competence is the norm with regard to EU competences, even if this could perhaps have been stated more clearly. Article 2(2) TFEU specifies that in areas where the EU and the Member States share competence both the EU and the Member States may legislate and adopt legally binding acts. However, based on the so-called 'principle of pre-emption', Member States can only

---

[36] A. Rosas and L. Armati, (op. cit.), 206.
[37] Art. 2(1) TEU.

exercise their competence to the extent that the EU has not exercised its competence and vice versa. Interestingly, it is added that the Member States "shall again exercise their competence to the extent that the Union has decided to cease exercising its competence."

Article 2(4) TFEU creates a special CFSP competence: "The Union shall have competence, in accordance with the provisions of the Treaty on European Union, to define and implement a common foreign and security policy, including the progressive framing of a common defence policy." At first glance, CFSP does not seem to fall within either of the two main categories outlined above: exclusive or shared competences. This also seems to be the case for economic and employment policies (article 2(3) TFEU), which are also dealt with separately. However, as seen above, the category of shared competences is defined negatively and non-exhaustively. It has therefore been deduced from this that "the two non-categorised areas mentioned in articles 2(3) and (4) must constitute a form of shared competence: it appears in any case that the intention was to indicate that the coordination prescribed in those fields is something more than the classic supporting system".[38]

A third category of competences is laid down in article 6 TFEU: the competence to carry out, in certain areas, actions to support, coordinate or supplement the actions of the Member States. The areas where such action can be undertaken are listed in article 6 TFEU: protection and improvement of human health; industry; culture; tourism; education, vocational training, youth and sport; civil protection and administrative cooperation. Article 2(5) TFEU stipulates that when exercising this kind of competence, the EU may not supersede the Member States' competence in these areas and that "[l]egally binding acts adopted on the basis of the provisions of the Treaties relating to these areas shall not entail harmonization of Member States' laws or regulations".

Lastly, the areas of research, technological development and space (article 4(3) TFEU) as well as those of development cooperation and humanitarian aid (article 4(4) TFEU) defy a simple categorisation based on the aforementioned description. Rather, they find themselves somewhere between the shared and supporting competences functioning as 'complementary' competences of the Union next to the national ones; for this reason, they are sometimes referred to as 'parallel competences'.[39] Thus, this highly complex system of allocation of Union competences has been formed in order to serve the needs of this European polity of States. As has been observed, the "Union as a 'constitutional order of states" has a unique character[40]; it constantly endeavours to strike a delicate balance between the centre and its constituent units while pursuing an integration path.

---

[38] A. Rosas and L. Armati, (op. cit.), 19–20.

[39] J.C. Piris, *The Lisbon Treaty: A Legal and Political Analysis* (Cambridge University Press, 2010), 77.

[40] A. Dashwood et al., (op. cit.), 131.

8.2.2 Which Areas of Law Remain Within the (Legislative) Jurisdiction of the Component States?

The EU has only those powers which it has received from the Treaties and the Member States hold all residual powers.[41] Consequently, competences not conferred upon the Union by its constitutive treaties remain with the Member States.[42] Thus, the governments of Member States may exercise exclusive or predominant national competence in all those areas in which the Union does not have any competence or in which the Union has only supporting or complementary competence. For example, Member State governments have almost full competence in the areas of education and family law. More generally, in other than commercial and economic and monetary areas, the Union's decision-making is often limited to measures meant to preserve the EU's basic principles, such as the prohibition of discrimination on the basis of nationality.

In areas where there are shared powers between the Union and the Member States (see *supra*, article 4 TFEU), Member States may exercise that competence as long as the Union does not step in. The power of Member States to act with a view to attaining the objectives of the Treaty ceases to exist once the EU actually exercises its own competence. This is the so-called principle of pre-emption as has already been briefly discussed above. Pre-emption means that when the EU has acted the Member States' power to do so ceases and the existing national rules must give way to the new EU provisions in so far as there is a conflict between them, in accordance with the principle of the supremacy of EU law.[43]

8.2.3 What Is the Constitutional Principle According to Which Conflicts (if any) Between Central and Component State Law Are Resolved (e.g., Supremacy of Federal Law)?

Conflicts between EU law and national law of the Member States are solved in accordance with the principle of supremacy or primacy of EU law.[44] This principle did not make it to the text of the Lisbon Treaty although it had been included in Article I-6 of the Constitutional Treaty as one of the fundamental principles

---

[41] K. Lenaerts, Constitutionalism and the Many Faces of Federalism, *American Journal of Comparative Law*, vol. 38, 1990, 213.

[42] P. Craig, Institutions, Power, and Institutional Balance, in P. Craig and G. De Burca (eds.), (op. cit.), 17.

[43] W. van Gerven, Federalism in the US and Europe, *Vienna Journal on International Constitutional Law*, vol. 1, 2007, 29.

[44] W. van Gerven, 2007, (op. cit.), 29.

of the Union. However, the 2007 Intergovernmental Conference decided to adopt Declaration No. 17 concerning primacy, which recalled that

> in accordance with well settled case law of the Court of Justice of the European Union, the Treaties and the law adopted by the Union on the basis of the Treaties have primacy over the law of the Member States, under conditions laid down by the said case law.[45]

It was further decided to append an opinion on primacy prepared by the Council's Legal Service which suggested that "[i]t results from the case law of the Court of Justice that primacy of EC law is a cornerstone principle of Community law."[46] According to this principle, laws adopted by the Union within the scope of its powers shall have primacy over the laws of the Member States. It entails duties for legislatures, courts, executives and any public authorities at national, subnational or local level. A national legislature must refrain from adopting laws that are inconsistent with binding rules of EU law and has a duty to modify national laws that are inconsistent with obligations under EU law.[47] With regard to the duties imposed upon the national courts, the CJEU has consistently held that

> a national court which is called upon, within the limits of its jurisdiction, to apply provisions of Community law is under a duty to give full effect to those provisions, if necessary by refusing of its own motion to apply any conflicting provision of national legislation, and it is not necessary for the court to request or await the prior setting aside of such provision by legislative or other constitutional means.[48]

Article 4(3) TEU, referring to the principle of sincere cooperation between the Member States and the Union, is also relevant in this context.[49] This principle obliges "the Union and its Member States [to] assist each other, in full mutual respect, in carrying out the tasks which flow from the Treaties."[50] It also more specifically obliges Member States to take any appropriate measures, general or particular, to ensure fulfilment of the obligations arising out of the Treaties or resulting from the acts of the institutions of the Union, to facilitate the achievement of the Union's tasks and to refrain from any measure which could jeopardize the

---

[45] Declaration No. 17 concerning primacy annexed to the Final Act of the Intergovernmental Conference which adopted the Treaty of Lisbon [2012] O.J. C 326/346. As aptly stated by Piris, the question in this regard revolves around the possible change this declaration may trigger in the attitude of some supreme courts of Member States that have been traditionally negative to this principle. J.C. Piris, (op. cit.), 79, footnote 15.

[46] Opinion of the Council Legal Service of 22 June 2007 in Declaration No. 17 (op. cit.).

[47] Bruno De Witte, Direct Effect, Primacy and the Nature of the Legal Order, in P. Craig and G. De Burca (eds.), (op. cit.), 340–341.

[48] Case C-184/89 *Nimz v City of Hamburg* [1991] ECR 297, para. 19. See also Case 6/64 *Flaminio Costa v ENEL* [1964] ECR 585; Case 106/77 *Amministrazione delle Finanze delle Stato v Simmenthal* [1978] ECR 629, para. 24; Opinion of AG Mazák in Case C-375/09 *Prezes Urzędu Ochrony Konkurencji i Konsumentów v Tele2 Polska sp. z o.o., devenue Netia SA* [2011] ECR 0000, para. 56.

[49] See also W. van Gerven, 2007, (op. cit.) 25.

[50] Article 4(3), first paragraph, TEU.

attainment of the Union's objectives.[51] To sum up, the article expresses the duty of Member States to cooperate in good faith in their dealings with the EU and between themselves.[52] This duty rests on all authorities of Member States, at every level.[53] It is also incumbent upon "the Union", consistently with the longstanding case law of the CJEU that the duty of sincere cooperation "imposes on Member States *and the Community institutions* mutual duties to cooperate in good faith" (emphasis added).[54] The EU institutions are thus also bound by the principle of sincere cooperation, both in their relations with the Member States and in their relations with each other.[55] Such a conclusion is only logical given the fact that, as the Court has mentioned, "the duty to cooperate in good faith is, by its very nature, reciprocal".[56] Since the entry into force of the Lisbon Treaty, this duty of mutual cooperation of the EU institutions can be found explicitly in the Treaties. Indeed, article 13(2) TEU states that "[t]he institutions shall practice mutual sincere cooperation."

Finally, it is important to also take into account the principle of consistent interpretation. It has been observed that this principle "applies as a corollary of the principle of primacy to facilitate the application of national law in a manner consistent with Union law".[57] This principle has been derived from the principle of sincere cooperation laid down in article 4(3) TEU and the obligation of result contained in article 288 TFEU as far as directives are concerned. It requires a national court, in cases where the application of a provision of its national law is likely to result in a conflict with a rule of EU law, to determine first whether the national rule can be interpreted and applied in such a way as to avoid a conflict – in other words whether it can be interpreted in such a way that it conforms with EU law.[58] There is an important caveat to this principle: in applying it national authorities should not infringe on general principles of national and EU law, and

---

[51] Article 4(3), second and third paragraphs, TEU.

[52] K. Lenaerts and P. Van Nuffel, (op. cit.), 147.

[53] W. Van Gerven, 2007, (op. cit.), 25.

[54] Case T-284/08 People's Mojahedin Organization of Iran v Council [2008] ECR II-3487, para. 52; Case T-341/07 *Jose Maria Sison v Council of the European Union et al.* [2009] ECR II-3625, para. 94; Case C-339/00 *Ireland v Commission* [2003] ECR I-11757, para. 71. See also case 230/81 *Luxembourg v European Parliament* [1983] ECR 255, para. 37; order in Case C-2/88 *Imm. Zwart and others* [1990] ECR I-03365, para. 17 and Case C-275/00 *First and Franex* [2002] ECR I-10943, para. 49.

[55] G. Chalmers, G. Davies and G. Monti, *European Union Law* (Cambridge University Press, 2010), 223–227.

[56] Case C-339/00 *Ireland v Commission* [2003] ECR para. 72.

[57] A. Rosas and L. Armati, (op. cit.), 59.

[58] See Case C-14/83 *Von Colson and Kamann v Land Nordrhein-Westfalen* [1984] ECR 1891, para. 26; Joined Cases C 397/01 to C 403/01 *Pfeiffer and Others* [2004] ECR I 8835, para. 113; Case C-406/08 *Uniplex (UK) Ltd v NHS Business Services Authority* [2010] ECR I-817, para. 45; Case C-555/07 *Seda Kücükdeveci v Swedex GmbH & Co. KG* [2010] ECR I-365, para. 48; Opinion of AG Sharpston in Case C-115/09 *Bund für Umwelt und Naturschutz Deutschland, Landesverband Nordrhein-Westfalen eV v Bezirksregierung Arnsberg* [2011] ECR 0000, paras. 81–84.

in particular on the principles of legal certainty and non-retroactivity. Thus, an interpretation *contra legem* of national law is excluded.[59] Rather the national court is required to interpret its national laws "*as far as possible* in the light of the wording and purpose of [EU legislation] [emphasis added]".[60]

8.3 The Means and Methods of Legal Unification

8.3.1 To What Extent Is Legal Unification or Harmonization Accomplished by the Exercise of Central Power (Top Down)?

8.3.1.1 Via Directly Applicable Constitutional Norms?

This question touches on the issue of the nature of the EU legal order as a constitutional order. This has been established by the CJEU in an incremental manner through the development of its case law.[61] After having established first the principles of direct effect and primacy since the 1960s, the Court only took the further step of pronouncing the constitutional character of the founding Treaties in 1986 in its *Les Verts* judgment.[62] It held that "the European Economic Community is a Community based on the rule of law, inasmuch as neither its Member States nor its institutions can avoid a review of the question whether the measures adopted by them are in conformity with the basic constitutional charter, the Treaty."[63]

---

[59]Case 80/86 *Kolpinghuis Nijmegen* [1987] ECR 3986, paras. 13–14; Case C-12/08 *Mono Car Styling SA, in liquidation v Dervis Odemis and Others* [2009] ECR I-06653, para. 61 and case law referred to therein; Case C-168/95 *Criminal Proceedings against Luciano Arcaro* [1996] ECR I-4705, para. 42; Joined Cases C-189/02 P, C-202/02 P, C-205/02 P to C-208/02 P and C-213/02 P *Dansk Rørindustri A/S et. al. v. Commission of the European Communities* [2005] ECR I- 05425, para. 221.

[60]Case C- 106/89 *Marleasing* [1990] ECR I-4135, para. 8; Case C-555/07 *Seda Kücükdeveci v Swedex GmbH & Co. KG* [2010] ECR I-365, para. 48 and case law referred to therein; Case C-109/09 *Deutsche Lufthansa AG v Gertraud Kumpan* [2011] ECR I-1309, para. 52.

[61]In this regard Ulrich Haltern has suggested that the case-law of the Court can be generally divided in two periods. During the first period the Court established and solidified the principles that constitute the building blocks of a constitutional order, such as the principles of primacy, direct effect and pre-emption, whereas in the latter period it has been placing its emphasis on constitutionalism. See U. Haltern, Integration Through Law, in A. Wiener and T. Diez (eds.) *European Integration Theory* (Oxford University Press, 2004), 179.

[62]J. Wouters, L. Verhey and P. Kiiver (eds.) European Constitutionalism Beyond Lisbon: Introductory Remarks, in *European Constitutionalism beyond Lisbon* (Intersentia, 2009), 4–5.

[63]Case 294/83 *Parti écologiste "Les Verts" v European Parliament* [1986] ECR 1339, para. 23; See also: Opinion 1/91 *EEA Agreement* [1991] ECR 6102, para. 21; Case C-15/00 *Commission v. European Investment Bank* [2003] ECR I-7281, para. 75.

Consequently, the constitutional norms within the EU system are those contained in the provisions of the Treaties, in other words, the norms of primary EU law.[64] After a brief overview of the development of the case law on direct effect – since the principle of primacy has already been analysed above – the issue of constitutionalism will be revisited, concluding with the post-Lisbon reality as illustrated in recent judgments of the CJEU.

The principle of direct effect is of cardinal important in understanding the manner in which norms of EU law affect national law. In the landmark *Van Gend en Loos*[65] case the CJEU ruled that

> the Community constitutes a new legal order of international law for the benefit of which the States have limited their sovereign rights, albeit within limited fields, and the subjects of which comprise not only Member States, but also their nationals. Independently of the legislation of the Member States, Community law therefore not only imposes obligations on individuals, but is also intended to confer upon them rights which become part of their legal heritage.[66]

In the same judgment, the Court set out the criteria under which a Treaty provision should be given direct effect:

> The wording of Article 12 contains a clear and unconditional prohibition which is not a positive, but a negative obligation. This obligation, moreover, is not qualified by any reservations on the part of states which would make its implementation conditional upon a positive legislative measure enacted under national law.[67]

These criteria were later relaxed by the CJEU. It is clear nowadays that Treaty provisions containing positive obligations can also have direct effect.[68] The CJEU summarized the criteria for granting direct effect as follows in *Hurd*:

> According to a consistent line of decisions of the Court, a provision produces direct effect in relations between the Member States and their subjects only if it is clear and unconditional and not contingent on any discretionary implementing measure.[69]

In his opinion in *Banks* Advocate General *Van Gerven* pointed to

> the eminently practical nature of the "direct effect" test: provided and in so far as a provision of Community law is sufficiently operational in itself to be applied by a court, it has direct effect. The clarity, precision, unconditional nature, completeness or perfection of the rule and its lack of dependence on discretionary implementing measures are in that respect

---

[64]The EU Charter of Fundamental Rights also contains constitutional EU norms since it has the same legal status as the Treaties (article 6(1) TEU).

[65]Case 26/62 *NV Algemene Transporten Expeditie Onderneming Van Gend en Loos v. Nederlandse Administratie der Belastingen* [1963] ECR 1.

[66]Ibid., 12.

[67]Ibid., 13.

[68]See already Case 57/65 *Lütticke II* [1966] ECR, 210.

[69]Case 44/84 *Hurd v. Jones* [1986] ECR 29, para. 47.

merely aspects of one and the same characteristic feature which that rule must exhibit, namely it must be capable of being applied by a court to a specific case.[70]

Having established the above principles, the CJEU declared the constitutional nature of the EU legal order in *Les Verts* and has ever since been expanding on the dictum of that case, making sure that both EU secondary and national legislation conform to EU primary law.[71] The insistence of the CJEU on the constitutional character of the EU legal order is best illustrated in the Kadi saga. There the Court reviewed the legality of international obligations undertaken by EU Member States within the framework of the UN in light of the constitutional legal order of the Union.[72] Thus, "the Kadi judgment seems to have been chosen by the CJEU as the dramatic moment in which to emphatically 'make whole on its promise of an autonomous legal order by clarifying the external dimension of European constitutionalism'".[73] Despite the criticism that the Kadi judgment has received over the approach adopted by the Court in its examination of the relation between the EU and international legal orders, the constitutional status of the EU legal order has not been disputed. Thus, it is safe to conclude that the EU legal order is a constitutional order playing an eminent role in the process of unification or harmonisation of national legal provisions.

8.3.1.2 Via Central Legislation (or Executive or Administrative Rules)?

8.3.1.2.1 Union Institutions Creating Directly Applicable Norms

EU institutions create directly applicable norms through regulations and decisions, as provided for in article 288 TFEU.[74] The current analytical effort proceeds in discussing the issues of binding effect, general and direct applicability and direct

---

[70]Opinion of AG van Gerven in Case C-128/92 *H.J. Banks v. British Coal Corporation* [1994] ECR I-1209, point 27. Cf. Bruno De Witte, Direct effect, primacy and the nature of the legal order, in P. Craig and G. De Burca (eds.), (op. cit.), 324.

[71]See: Opinion of AG Kokott in Case C-236/09 *Association Belge des Consommateurs Test-Achats ASBL and Others v Conseil des ministers* [2011] ECR I-773, para. 26; Case T-299/05 *Shanghai Excell M&E Enterprise Co. Ltd and Shanghai Adeptech Precision Co. Ltd v Council of the European Union* [2009] ECR II-00573 para. 57.

[72]Joined Cases C-402/05 P and C-415/05 P *Yassin Abdullah Kadi and Al Barakaat International Foundation v Council of the European Union and Commission of the European Communities* [2008] ECR I-06351, para. 281–282, 305–309, 316–317.

[73]G. De Burca, The European Court of Justice and the International Legal Order After *Kadi*, *Harvard International Law Journal*, vol. 51(1), 2010, 44 (quoting Daniel Halberstam, Local, Global, and Plural Constitutionalism: Europe Meets the World, 26, available at http://ssrn.com/abstract=1521016).

[74]Although also binding legislative acts, directives are examined immediately below since they rather constitute a means for EU institutions to commandeer Member States to pass conforming implementing legislation.

effect of these instruments. Lastly, this section includes a brief discussion of the effect of international agreements of the EU with third states and/or international organisations (article 216(2) TFEU) on the unification or harmonisation of domestic legislation.

According to the second paragraph of article 288 TFEU, regulations are generally applicable, binding in their entirety and directly applicable in all Member States. A regulation is first of all generally applicable, which means that it is applicable "to objectively determined situations and involves legal consequences for categories of persons viewed in a general and abstract manner."[75] In other words, the scope of application of a regulation is not restricted to specific individuals or situations, but extends to a number of undefined cases.[76] A regulation is further binding in its entirety as "it is intended to subject a situation to rules which are all-embracing and, where necessary, precise."[77]

They are also directly applicable in all the Member States. Indeed, "[b]y virtue of the very nature of regulations and of their function in the system of sources of Community law, the provisions of those regulations generally have immediate effect in the national legal systems without it being necessary for the national authorities to adopt measures of application."[78] This however does not entirely exclude the possibility for the Member States to take implementation measures.[79] In some cases, the Member States will even be required to do so or risk being in breach of EU law[80] and some provisions of regulations may "necessitate, for their implementation, the adoption of measures of application by the Member States."[81] In any case, "Member States are under a duty not to obstruct the direct applicability inherent in regulations"[82] and "are precluded from taking steps for the purpose of applying the regulation which are intended to alter its scope or supplement its provisions".[83]

---

[75]Case 6/68 Zuckerfabrik [1968] ECR 409, 415; Joined Cases 789/79 and 790/79 Calpak v. Commission [1980] ECR 1949, para. 9; Case 307/81 Alusuisse Italia v Council and Commission [1982] ECR 3463, para. 9; Case C-221/09 AJD Tuna Ltd v Direttur tal-Agrikoltura u s-Sajd and Avukat Generali [2011] ECR I-1655, para. 51.

[76]K. Lenaerts and P. Van Nuffel, (op. cit.), 894.

[77]Ibid., 894.

[78]Case C-278/02 Handlbauer [2004] ECR I-6171, para. 25. See also: Opinion of AG Mazák in Case C-434/08 Arnold und Johann Harms als Gesellschaft bürgerlichen Rechts v Freerk Heidinga [2010] ECR I-4431, para. 26.

[79]Case 230/78 *Eridiana* [1979] ECR 2749, para. 35; Opinion of AG Mazák in Case C-434/08 *Arnold und Johann Harms als Gesellschaft bürgerlichen Rechts v Freerk Heidinga* [2010] ECR I-4431, para. 26.

[80]Case 128/78 *Commission v. United Kingdom* [1978] ECR 2429.

[81]Case C-278/02 *Handlbauer* [2004] ECR I-6171, para. 26. See also Case C-403/98 *Azienda Agricola Monte Arcosu* [2001] ECR I-103, para. 26.

[82]Case 34/73 *Variola* [1973] ECR 981, para. 10; Opinion of AG Kokott in Case C-161/06 *Skoma-Lux sro v Celní ředitelství Olomouc* [2007] ECR I-10841, para. 54.

[83]Case 40/69 *Bollman* [1970] ECR 60, para. 4.

Finally, "by reason of their nature and their function in the system of sources of Community law, regulations have direct effect and are as such, capable of creating individual rights which national courts must protect".[84] It is important to note however that not all regulations will have direct effect. For a regulation to have direct effect the same conditions as for the direct effect of Treaty provisions need to be fulfilled[85]: it needs to be "clear and precise" and "not leave any margin of discretion to the authorities by whom it is to be applied" in order to have direct effect, and thereby entitle individuals to invoke its provisions in front of national courts.[86]

Just like regulations, 'decisions' referred to in article 288 TFEU are binding in their entirety (art. 288, fourth para. TFEU). Depending on their individual or general scope, they are respectively binding on their addressees or the Member States. The CJEU clarified their effects as follows:

> Decisions are to be binding in their entirety upon those to whom they are addressed. In the case of decisions addressed to the Member States, they are binding on all organs of the State to which they are addressed, including the courts of that State. It follows that, by virtue of the principle of precedence of Community law (...) the national courts must refrain from applying any national provisions (...) the implementation of which would be likely to hinder the implementation of a Community decision.[87]

Further, unlike regulations, decisions have not been expressly declared to be directly applicable.[88] This is probably a consequence of the fact that a decision can take various forms, since the term 'decision' is for example also used in the context of the CFSP (see Articles 26(1) and (2) and 31(1) TEU). However, according to article 31(1) TEU decisions taken in the context of CFSP are not legislative acts.[89] All other decisions are directly applicable.[90]

As to the direct effect of decisions a distinction needs to be made between decisions addressed to specific legal or natural persons and those addressed to the Member States. The former produce direct effect.[91] As to the latter, the response is not as straightforward but some guidance can be drawn from the case law of the CJEU. Thus, "in certain circumstances, a decision addressed to all Member States

---

[84]Case 43/71 *Politi* [1971] ECR 1039, para. 9. See also Case 93/72 *Leonesio* [1972] ECR 287, para. 5.

[85]K. Lenaerts and P. Van Nuffel, (op. cit.), 895.

[86]Case 9/73 *Carl Schlüter v Hauptzollamt Lörrach* [1973] ECR 1135, para. 32.

[87]Case 249/85 *Albako* [1987] ECR 2345, para. 17; Case C-262/97 *Rijksdienst voor Pensioenen v. Robert Engelbrecht* [2000] ECR I-07321, para. 40.

[88]A. Rosas and L. Armati, (op. cit.), 65.

[89]J.C. Piris, (op. cit.), 94, footnote 36.

[90]A, Kaczorowska, *European Union Law* (Routledge-Cavendish, 2009), 296.

[91]Ibid., 325.

could [also] produce direct effect in the sense that an individual could rely on it in a dispute with a public authority".[92] The CJEU explained the rationale for this as follows:

> Particularly in case where, for example, the Community Authorities by means of a decision have imposed an obligation on a Member State or all the Member States to act in a certain way, the effectiveness ('l'effet utile') of such a measure would be weakened if the national of that State could not invoke it in the courts and the national courts could not take it into consideration as part of Community law.[93]

The CJEU has further specified that

> [a]lthough the effects of a decision may not be identical with those of a provision contained in a regulation, this difference does not exclude the possibility that the end result, namely the right of the individual to invoke the measure before the courts, may be the same as that of a directly applicable provision of a regulation.[94]

In some cases, decisions will thus create directly applicable norms which, given the conditions are fulfilled, could also produce direct effect. The same conditions apply here as for the direct effect of directives (see below): "provisions of a decision may have direct effect only if they are precise and unconditional and the period, if any, within which a Member State had to comply with it has expired".[95]

International agreements between the EU and third states and/or international organisations also form a significant corpus of legal instruments that lead to the unification or harmonisation of domestic legislations in the EU Member States. Since the entry into force of the Lisbon Treaty the procedure to conclude international agreements has been streamlined and there is now a single provision governing the procedure for the conclusion of such agreements: article 218 TFEU.[96] According to Article 216(1) TFEU,

> [t]he Union may conclude an agreement with one or more third countries or international organisations where the Treaties so provide or where the conclusion of an agreement is necessary in order to achieve, within the framework of the Union's policies, one of the objectives referred to in the Treaties, or is provided for in a legally binding Union act or is likely to affect common rules or alter their scope.

It is important to point out that such agreements concluded by the Union are binding both upon the EU institutions and on its Member States (art. 216(2)

---

[92]Case 249/85 *Albako* [1987] ECR 2345, para. 10.

[93]Case 9/70 *Grad* [1970] ECR 825, para. 5; Case 23/70 *Haselhorst* [1970] ECR 881, para. 5; Case 187/87 *Saarland and Others* [1988] ECR 5013, para. 19; and Case C-223/98 *Adidas* [1999] ECR I-7081, para. 24.

[94]Case 9/70 *Grad* [1970] ECR 825, para. 5; Case 20/70 *Lesage* [1970] ECR 861, para. 5; and Case 23/70 *Haselhorst* [1970] ECR 881, para. 5.

[95]K. Lenaerts and P. Van Nuffel, (op. cit.), 918. See also, Case 156/91*Hansa Fleisch Ernst Mund* [1992] ECR I-05567, para. 15.

[96]A. Rosas and L. Armati, (op. cit.), 201. Before the entry into force of the Lisbon Treaty, article 24 TEU used to contain a special procedure for CFSP matters.

TFEU). Consequently, "it is incumbent upon the Community institutions, as well as upon the Member States, to ensure compliance with the obligations arising from such agreements".[97] International agreements form an integral part of the EU legal order.[98] Further, it falls within the jurisdiction of the CJEU to interpret these agreements even when completed as mixed agreements (completed between both the EU and its Member States on the one side and their counterparty on the other) when the provisions under review at least fall "in large measure within [Union] competence".[99] With regard to the hierarchy of norms, international agreements rank between the Treaties and secondary law. International agreements thus have primacy over secondary law.[100] Despite the occasional interchangeable use of direct applicability and direct effect by the Court of Justice, some conclusions based on its established case law can be drawn. Thus, international agreements have direct effect

> when, regard being had to its wording and to the purpose and nature of the agreement itself, the provision contains a clear and precise obligation which is not subject, in its implementation or effects, to the adoption of any subsequent measure[101]

In implementing these criteria, the Court found that the United Nations Convention on the Law of the Sea does not have direct effect.[102] Further, it has successively adjudicated that the GATT[103] and, subsequently, WTO law also lack direct effect.[104] However, regarding WTO law, the CJEU has accepted two exceptions to the impossibility to review EU law on the basis of GATT/WTO law. These are the

---

[97]Case 104/81 *Kupferberg* [1982] ECR 3641, para. 11.

[98]Case 181-73 *Haegeman* [1974] ECR 449, para. 5; Case 104/81 *Kupferberg* [1982] ECR 3641, para. 13.

[99]Case C-240/09 *Lesoochranárske zoskupenie VLK v Ministerstvo životného prostredia Slovenskej republiky* [2011] ECR I-1255, paras. 31–36; Case C-239/03 *Etang de Berre* [2004] ECR I-9325, paras. 13–31. See also Case 12/86 *Demirel v. Stadt Schwäbisch Gmünd* [1987] ECR 3719, para. 7–12.

[100]Case C-308/06 *Intertanko* [2008] ECR I-4057, para. 42.

[101]Case 12/86 *Demirel v. Stadt Schwäbisch Gmünd* [1987] ECR 3719, para. 14; *Case C-18/90 Kziber* [1991] ECR I-199, para. 15; Case C-162/96 *Racke v. Hauptzollamt Mainz* [1998] ECR I-3655, para. 31; Case C-262/96 *Sürül v Bundesanstalt für Arbeit* [1999] ECR I-2685, para. 60; Case C-300/98 Christian Dior [2000] ECR I-11307, para. 42; Case C-485/07 *Raad van bestuur van het Uitvoeringsinstituut werknemersverzekeringen v H. Akdas and Others* [2011] ECR 0000, para. 67.

[102]Case C-308/06 *Intertanko* [2008] ECR I-4057, paras. 54–65.

[103]See Joined Cases 21-24/72 *International Fruit Company* [1972] ECR-1219, paras. 19–28; Case C-280/93 *Germany v Council* [1994] ECR I-4973, paras. 108–110.

[104]Case C-149/96 *Portugal v. Council* [1999] ECR I-8395, para. 47; Case C-377/98 *Netherlands v. Parliament and Council ('Biotechnology Directive')* [2001] ECR I-7079, para. 52; Case C-76/00 P *Petrotub and Republica v. Council* [2004] ECR I-79, para. 53; Case C-93/02 P *Biret International v. Council* [2003] ECR I-10497, para. 61; Case C-377/02 *Léon Van Parys* [2005] ECR I-1465, para. 39.

Fediol[105] and *Nakajima*[106] exceptions that have been succinctly summarized as follows:

> where the Community intended to implement a particular obligation assumed in the context of the WTO, or where the Community measure refers expressly to the precise provisions of the WTO agreements, [...] it is for the Court to review the legality of the Community measure in question in the light of the WTO rules.[107]

Still, the CJEU has adopted a restrictive interpretation of these exceptions.[108] On the contrary the Court found in *IATA* that

> Articles 19, 22 and 29 of the Montreal Convention are among the rules in the light of which the Court reviews the legality of acts of the Community institutions since, first, neither the nature nor the broad logic of the Convention precludes this and, second, those three articles appear, as regards their content, to be unconditional and sufficiently precise.[109]

However this may be, according to well-established case law international agreements to which the EU is a party "are part of the Community legal order and [...] EU law should be interpreted in the light of their provisions."[110] Consequently, and given the primacy of international agreements over secondary EU law and national law, both EU and national legal instruments must be interpreted as far as possible in conformity with the provisions contained in international agreements.[111]

8.3.1.2.2 Union Institutions Commandeering Member States (Through e.g., Directives) to Pass Conforming Implementing Legislation[112]

EU institutions can also adopt directives in order to exercise their competences. This instrument allows them to command Member States to pass conforming

---

[105] Case 70/87 *Fediol* v *Commission* [1989] ECR 1781, para. 19.

[106] Case C-69/89 *Nakajima* v *Council* [1991] ECR I-2069, para. 31.

[107] Case C-149/96 *Portugal v. Council* [1999] ECR I-8395, para. 49; Case C-76/00 P *Petrotub and Republica v. Council* [2004] ECR I-79, para. 54; Case C-93/02 P *Biret International v. Council* [2003] ECR I-10497, para. 63.

[108] Case C-377/02 *Léon Van Parys* [2005] ECR I-1465, para. 40; Case C-351/04 *Ikea Wholesale Ltd* [2007] ECR I-7723, paras. 30–35.

[109] Case C-344/04 *IATA and ELFAA* [2006] ECR I-403, para. 39.

[110] A. Rosas, in J. Wouters, A. Nollkaemper and E. De Wet (eds.), *The Europeanisation of International Law: The Status of International Law in the EU and Its Member States* (TMC Asser Press, 2008), 76.

[111] See Case C-245/02 *Anheuser-Busch Inc. v BudÄĴjovický Budvar, národní podnik* [2004] ECR I-10989, para. 42; Case C-431/05 *Merck Genéricos* [2007] ECR I-7001, para. 35.

[112] The EU level commandeering the Member State level is inherent in EU law as opposed to the 'anticommandeering principle' applicable in the U.S. See W. van Gerven, *The European Union: A polity of States and Peoples* (Hart Publishing, 2005), 21–22. On this issue see also D. Halberstam, Comparative Federalism and the Issue of Commandeering, in K. Nicolaidis and R. Howse (eds.), *The Federal Vision: Legitimacy and Levels of Governance in the United States and the European Union* (Oxford University Press, 2001), 213–251.

legislation. A directive is binding as to the result to be achieved upon each Member State to which it is addressed, but leaves national authorities the choice of forms and methods (art. 288, third para. TFEU). However, the "area of choice left to the Member States regarding 'form and methods'" varies greatly and may even disappear, blurring the distinction between directives and regulations in this respect.[113] Directives can be addressed to one or more Member States. Directives addressed to all Member States "enter into force on the date specified in them or, in the absence thereof, on the 20th day following that of their publication [in the Official Journal of the European Union] (article 297(2) para. 2 TFEU)." Directives "which specify to whom they are addressed, shall be notified to those to whom they are addressed and shall take effect upon such notification (article 297(2) para. 3 TFEU)." Generally, directives will not only specify on which date they enter into force but will also specify the timeframe within which Member States have to transpose them, i.e. arrive to the prescribed result.[114] Thus, as a rule and contrary to regulations, directives are not directly applicable since Member States' authorities have the obligation to implement the directive within the period of time prescribed by it. Rather, given its result-based nature the directive becomes fully applicable only when the period prescribed for transposition has come to an end.[115] However, the CJEU has found that directives have binding legal consequences even before the expiry of the transposition period in that by virtue of articles 4(3) TEU and 288 TFEU Member States "must refrain from taking any measures liable seriously to compromise the result prescribed [by the directive]."[116]

Once the transposition period has expired, any Member State failing to fulfil this obligation of result correctly and in time, will face the possibility to be brought by the Commission (or other Member States) before the CJEU. It may also be held liable before a national court in a procedure initiated by a private individual who has suffered damage as a result of that Member State's failure to implement the directive correctly and/or on time.[117] This last point already leads to the controversial question of the direct effect of directives after the expiry of the transposition period. In this regard the CJEU has accepted that this cannot be excluded *a priori* based on the need to guarantee the effectiveness (*effet utile*) of directives.[118] However,

---

[113]T.C. Hartley, *The Foundations of European Union Law* (Oxford University Press, 2010), 223.

[114]K. Lenaerts and P. Van Nuffel, (op. cit.), 895.

[115]A. Rosas and L. Armati, (op. cit.), 64.

[116]Case C-129/96 *Inter-Environnement Wallonie* [1997] ECR I-7411, para. 45; Case C-157/02 *Rieser Internationale Transporte* [2004] ECR I-1477, para. 66; Case C-316/04 *Stichtung Zuid-Hollandse Milieufederatie* [2005] ECR I-09759, para. 42; Case C-138/05 *Stichtung Zuid-Hollandse Milieufederatie* [2006] ECR I-8339, para. 42.

[117]W. van Gerven, 2005, (op. cit.), 21. See Joined Cases C-6/90 and C-9/90 *Francovich and Others* [1991] ECR I-5357.

[118]Case 41/74 *Van Duyn v. Home Office* [1974] ECR 1337, para. 12; Case 8/81 *Becker v. Finanzamt Münster-Innenstadt* [1982] ECR 53, para. 49.

directives can only have vertical direct effect.[119] Also, directives or provisions thereof have direct effect in the relations between individuals and Member State authorities after the end of the transposition period if the relevant obligations imposed by them are "unconditional and sufficiently precise."[120] This "must be ascertained on a case by case basis, taking into account their nature, background and wording."[121] Lastly, it should be underlined that Member States cannot rely on their lack of or incorrect transposition of a directive against an individual.[122]

8.3.1.2.3 Inducing Member States to Regulate Through the Allocation of Central Money in Compliance with Centrally Established Standards

Economic, social and territorial cohesion constitutes one of the objectives of the EU (Article 3 TEU). According to article 174 TFEU, "the EU shall aim at reducing disparities between the levels of development of the various European regions and the backwardness of the least-favoured regions." These goals shall be taken into account when formulating and implementing the Union's policies and actions as well as when implementing the internal market. Article 175 TFEU further states that "[t]he Union shall also support the achievement of these objectives by the action it takes through the Structural Fund (European Agricultural Guidance and Guarantee Fund, Guidance Section, European Social Fund, European Regional Development Fund), the European Investment Bank and the other existing Financial Instruments". There is also the Cohesion Fund which provides financial contributions to projects in the field of the environment and trans-European networks in the area of transport infrastructure (Article 177 TFEU). This financial contribution will only be given to Member States which fulfil the criteria set out in Protocol No. 28 on economic and social cohesion, annexed to the Treaties.[123] These different funds induce Member States to regulate in compliance with centrally established standards with regard to the areas concerned.

---

[119]Case 152/84 *Marshall I* [1986] ECR 723, para. 48; Case C-91/92 *Faccini Dori* [1994] ECR I-3325, para. 24; Joined Cases 372-374/85 *Traen* [1987] ECR 2141, para. 24; Case C-224/09 *Nussbaumer* [2010] ECR I-9295, para.30.

[120]Case 148/78 *Pubblico Ministero v. Tullio Ratti* [1979] ECR 1629, para. 23; Joined Cases C-6/90 and C-9/90 *Francovich and Others* [1991] ECR I-5357, para. 11; Case C-62/00 *Marks & Spencer* [2002] ECR I-6325, para. 25; Joined Cases C-152/07, C-153/07 and 154/07 *Arcor E.A.* [2008] ECR I-5959, para. 40; Case C-184/10 *Mathilde Grasser v Freistaat Bayern* [2011] ECR 0000, para. 19.

[121]P.S.R.F. Mathijsen, (op. cit.), 32.

[122]See *inter alia* Case 148/78 *Pubblico Ministero v. Tullio Ratti* [1979] ECR 1629, para. 22; Case 80/86 *Kolpinghuis Nijmegen* [1987] ECR 3986, para. 8.

[123]Protocol No. 28 annexed to the TEU and TFEU on economic, social and territorial cohesion [2012] O.J. C 326/310.

8.3.1.2.4 Indirectly Compelling Member States to Regulate by Threatening to Take Over the Field in Case of State Inaction or State Action That Does Not Conform to Centrally Specified Standards

In cases of shared competence where Member States refuse to adopt certain provisions in their national legislation, the Union sometimes uses a pre-emptive threat of harmonization. In such cases, the Union makes an ultimatum to the relevant Member State: if the Member State does not legislate accordingly, the Union will adopt harmonization measures in this field. From that moment on, the Member State will lose the possibility to adopt national legislation in these areas (cf. *supra*: pre-emption).

8.3.1.3 Through the Judicial Creation of Uniform Norms by Central Supreme Court(s) or Central Courts of Appeal?

In the EU legal order, the case law of the Court of Justice, the General Court and the specialised courts forms an important source of law.[124] Based on article 19(1) TEU, their task is to "ensure that in the interpretation and application of the treaties the law is observed". While, in theory, their task is formally limited to ensuring that EU law is observed in its interpretation and application, it is practically uncontested that the European Courts do play an important role in developing the law.[125] The CJEU has, on numerous occasions, held that

> [t]he interpretation which the Court gives to a rule of [Union] law clarifies and defines where necessary the meaning and the scope of that rule as it must be or ought have been understood and applied from the time of its coming into force. It follows that the rule as thus interpreted may, and must, be applied by the Courts even to legal relationship arising and established before the judgment ruling or the request for interpretation provided that in other respects the conditions enabling an action relation to the application of that rule to be brought before the Courts having jurisdiction are satisfied.[126]

The interpretation given by the EU courts to rules of EU law is thus not merely declaratory, but also contributes to the further development of EU law.[127] Such practices often lead to complaints of judicial activism from Member States that are

---

[124]K. Lenaerts and P. Van Nuffel, (op. cit.), 932.

[125]Ibid., 932; G. Chalmers, G. Davies and G. Monti, (op. cit.), 157–158; T.C. Hartley, (op. cit.), 70.

[126]Case 24/86 *Blaizot* [1988] ECR 379, para. 27. See also Joined Cases C-367/93 to C-377/93 *Roders and others* [1995] ECR I-2229, para. 42; Case 269/96 *Sürül* [1999] ECR I-2685, para. 107; Case 347/00 *Angel Barreira Pérez* [2002] ECR I-8191, para. 44; Joined Cases C-453/02 and C-462/02 *Linneweber and Akritidis* [2005] ECR I-1131, para. 41; Case C-292/04 *Wienand Meilicke and Others* [2007] ECR I-01835, para. 34.

[127]K. Lenaerts and P. Van Nuffel, (op. cit.), 933.

unhappy with rulings of the EU courts.[128] To meet such criticism, the CJEU will, in exceptional cases, decide to limit the *ex tunc* effect of its judgments on the ground of legal certainty.[129]

8.3.1.4 Through Other Centrally Controlled Means, such as Centrally Managed Coordination or Information Exchange Among the Component States?

An example of coordination between the Member States and the EU is in the area of employment. According to article 145 TFEU, the Member States and the EU have to work towards a coordinated strategy for employment and particularly for promoting a skilled, trained and adaptable workforce and labour markets responsive to economic change. Member States shall regard promoting employment as a matter of common concern, having regard to national practices related to the responsibilities of management and labour.[130] To this end, Member States shall coordinate their action within the Council, which will set out social guidelines on an annual basis. On the basis of annual reports delivered by the Member States, the Council examines the implementation of these guidelines in the Member States' employment policies.[131] According to article 147 TFEU, the EU, in order to contribute to a high level of employment, will encourage cooperation between Member States and support and, if necessary, complement their action. The employment policy of the EU thus primarily aims to complement national policies and to encourage cooperation.

At the Lisbon European Council of 23 March 2000 the Heads of State or Government decided to improve the existing processes by introducing a new instrument: the open method of coordination. This policy approach was first adopted under the Maastricht Treaty with regard to the coordination of national macroeconomic policies and was further applied, even if in a somewhat different matter, to employment policy by the Treaty of Amsterdam.[132] The Lisbon Treaty extends this so-called open method for coordination towards social policy (article 156(2) TFEU), public health (article 168(2) TFEU), industrial policy (article 173(2) and research and technological development (article 181(2) TFEU). The open method

---

[128] W. van Gerven, 2005, (op. cit.), 150; But see T. Tridimas, The Court of Justice and Judicial Activism, *European Law Review*, vol. 21(3), 199–210 where it is being argued that the predominantly teleological method of interpretation of EU law by the CJEU has helped in the development of EU law without the Court exceeding its judicial function.

[129] K. Lenaerts and P. Van Nuffel, (op. cit.), 932.

[130] Cf. article 146(2)TFEU.

[131] Cf. Article 148 TFEU.

[132] G. De Burca, The constitutional challenge of new governance in the European Union, *European Law Review*, vol. 28(6), 2003, 824.

of coordination leaves a great amount of policy autonomy to the Member States and is based on a system which combines the elaboration of action plans or strategy reports by the Member States and the setting of guidelines or objectives at EU level. The evaluation of these action plans or strategy reports against the guidelines and/or objectives set at EU level creates an interactive process intended to lead to greater coordination and mutual learning in the concerned policy fields.[133]

As to economic policies of EU Member States, according to articles 121 and 126 TFEU these have been coordinated by means of multilateral surveillance of the economic developments in the Member States and the EU, and of the consistency of these policies with broad economic guidelines set out by the Council. However, the recent European sovereign debt crisis has proven that this decentralised and rather loose method of coordination is insufficient to sustain EMU. In light of this, there has been an overhaul of the economic governance architecture within the EU in the direction of centralising economic policies and giving teeth to economic and budgetary surveillance.[134] Where consensus could not be reached within the EU framework, a large majority of EU Member States adopted an international agreement,[135] the Treaty on Stability, Coordination and Governance in the Economic and Monetary Union, whose purpose is

> to strengthen the economic pillar of the economic and monetary union by adopting a set of rules intended to foster budgetary discipline through a fiscal compact, to strengthen the coordination of their economic policies and to improve the governance of the euro area, thereby supporting the achievement of the European Union's objectives for sustainable growth, employment, competitiveness and social cohesion.[136]

In addition further changes are underway, which will eventually transform the institutional setup of EMU into a full banking, economic, fiscal and political union.[137] Thus, legal unification in the field of economic policy is quickly moving from centrally managed coordination to centrally adopted and imposed 'hard' law.

---

[133] See for a more detailed analysis P. Craig, *EU Administrative Law* (Oxford University Press, 2006), 190–233.

[134] For an overview of the changes see J. Wouters and T. Ramopoulos, The G20 and Global Economic Governance: Lessons from Multi-level European Governance?, *Journal of International Economic Law*, vol. 15(3), 2012, 760–762.

[135] Only the United Kingdom and the Czech Republic decided not to become parties to this Treaty.

[136] Treaty on Stability, Coordination and Governance in the Economic and Monetary Union (TSCG), 2 March 2012, http://www.consilium.europa.eu/media/1478399/07_-_tscg.en12.pdf (consulted 22/01/2013).

[137] See European Commission, Communication from the Commission: A blueprint for a deep and genuine economic and monetary union. Launching a European Debate, COM(2012) 777 final/2, 30 November 2012, http://ec.europa.eu/commission_2010-2014/president/news/archives/2012/11/pdf/blueprint_en.pdf (consulted 22/01/13).

8.3.2 To What Extent Is Legal Unification Accomplished Through Formal or Informal Voluntary Coordination Among the Component States? (Somewhat Bottom Up, Coordinate Model)

As seen above, unification of laws in the EU can be realized through the adoption of regulations or directives (institutionalised legislative process) or can be the result of case law (institutionalised judicial process). Next to these institutionalised processes there is also a more informal process of unification (or approximation), which can be seen as "a growing together of rules through voluntary acts".[138]

The first process worth analysing here is the so-called 'spill-over' process. In the words of Walter van Gerven: "[w]ithin the EU Member States, [this process] refers to the impact which EC law has *indirectly* on the laws of Member States, as a result of legislative, regulatory, or judicial action of national authorities in areas which do not fall within the sphere of EC law – and which therefore remain outside of the framework of the EC's official harmonization process and are not directly affected by it".[139] Indeed, parts of national law affected by EU law often have an impact on other similar areas of national law which are not strictly affected by EU law but apply to similar situations or transactions.[140] Given the fact that the EU has only been conferred limited competences, it happens that parts or branches of national law, which were coherent before harmonisation, fall, as a result of this harmonisation, into different sets of rules within the same State and within the same area.[141] In other words, different rules will be applied to the trans-border transactions falling under EU law and to the local transactions falling purely under national law, even though both types of transactions fall within the same wider field. In such cases, it seems only normal that Member States, in order to restore

---

[138] W. van Gerven, Bringing (Private) Laws Closer to Each Other at the European Level, in F. Cafaggi (ed.), *The Institutional Framework of European Private Law* (Oxford University Press, 2006), 65.

[139] W. van Gerven, Bringing (Private) Laws Closer to Each Other at the European Level, in F. Cafaggi (ed.), (op. cit.), 65–66. See further A. Johnston, Spillovers from EU Law into National Law: (Un)Intended Consequences for Private Law Relationships, in D. Leczykiewicz and S. Weatherill (eds.), *The Involvement of EU Law in Private Law Relationships* (Hart Publishing, forthcoming).

[140] A good example is corporate law, where the scope of application of EU harmonization directives is typically restricted to one or several types of companies, whereas Member States have sometimes extended their implementation measures to other types of companies as well: see J. Wouters, European Company Law: Quo Vadis?, *Common Market Law Review* 2000, 257–307; Id., Towards a European Private Company? A Belgian Perspective, in H.J. De Kluiver and W. van Gerven (eds.), *The European Private Company?, Ius Commune Europaeum Series No 9*, (Antwerp, Maklu-Nomos, 1995), 161–186.

[141] W. van Gerven, Bringing (Private) Laws Closer to Each Other at the European Level, in F. Cafaggi (ed.), (op. cit.), 66.

the coherence within their national legal orders, tend to make both sets of rules converge; and this *not* because they are obliged to under EU law but in order to, for instance, improve legal certainty or establish equal treatment.[142] Convergence by way of spill-over from one part of the law into another within the same Member State, as described above, can also be the result of judicial action.[143] This occurs most frequently through general principles of law which are applied by the judiciary in every legal system in many different branches of the law. The development of common principles of law within the EU legal order and the Member States' legal orders leads to cross-fertilization and consequently to even more convergence between the different legal orders.[144] This process plays an important role in the area of administrative law, where, for example, the principle of proportionality has clearly been developing into a common principle within the different administrative law orders of the EU Member States.[145] It is also interesting to note that, while for private law, a spill-over effect resulted from the necessities of trans-border personal or commercial relations, according to Jürgen Schwarze, two very different factors have led to convergence of the administrative legal orders. These factors were the similar living conditions and administrative tasks in the Member States and the existing ties between the Member States and the necessity to safeguard the supremacy of Community law, as well as the need for as uniform Community law as possible.[146]

A second process worth mentioning here is the interplay between the CJEU and the European Court of Human Rights ('ECtHR') and more precisely the mutual learning process between both Courts. Since all EU Member States are also a member of the Council of Europe, an interplay between both Courts is only natural. The Member States are all bound by the provisions of the European Convention on Human Rights and Fundamental Freedoms ('ECHR') and subject to the jurisdiction of the ECtHR. However, the ECtHR has no competence (yet) to examine the compatibility of EU acts with ECHR provisions. This is bound to change in the near future since the Lisbon Treaty expressly foresees the possibility for the EU to accede to the ECHR (cf. art. 6(2) TEU) and relevant negotiations between the Council of Europe and the EU are at the final stages. Since this is not yet the case, the competence to examine the compatibility of EU acts with human rights provisions

---

[142] Ibid., 66.

[143] W. van Gerven, Bringing (Private) Laws Closer to Each Other at the European Level, in F. Cafaggi (ed.), (op. cit.), 66.

[144] Ibid., 67.

[145] J. Schwarze, The Convergence of the Administrative Laws of the EU Member States, *European Public Law*, vol. 4(2), 1998, 196.

[146] Ibid., 209.

remains with the CJEU as has been established by the Court itself since 1969.[147] Nevertheless, the ECtHR has competence over the conduct of the individual EU Member States, also when they take part in the preparation of EU legislation as members of the EU Council. Individuals increasingly bring proceedings before the ECtHR against EU Member States when they feel that their rights have been infringed upon by way of action attributable to the EU.[148] There is thus clearly room for concurrent jurisdiction and consequently there is a risk of conflicting decisions. Both Courts are very much aware of this risk and are therefore keen to engage in a mutual learning process and ensure as much convergence as possible when interpreting the ECHR provisions within their respective jurisdictions.[149] In this line article 52(3) of the Charter of Fundamental Rights of the European Union, which according to article 6(1) TEU has the same legal value as primary law in the EU, provides that "[i]n so far as this Charter contains rights which correspond to rights guaranteed by the Convention for the Protection of Human Rights and Fundamental Freedoms, the meaning and scope of those rights shall be the same as those laid down by the said Convention. This provision shall not prevent Union law providing more extensive protection." Thus, an effort by the two legal regimes can be observed to harmonize the level of human rights protection in their respective fields of competence.

Finally, the process of convergence between judicial decisions through mutual learning can also be found at the level of the national courts.[150] Indeed, the supreme courts of the Member States sometimes use comparative research when deciding on controversial issues.[151] In others words, it happens that a supreme court of a Member State, in order to find a solution for a particular question posed before it, examines whether supreme courts of other Member States have already dealt with a comparable case in the past and, if so, which answer was given.[152] However, this occurs quite rarely since legal cultures among Member States often diverge significantly whereas the different languages used within the EU Member States judicial systems render comparative research difficult.

---

[147]See *inter alia* 29/69 *Stauder v. City of Ulm* [1969] ECR 419; 11/70 *Internationale Handelsgesellschaft v. Einfuhr-und Vorratsstelle für Getreide und Futtermittel* [1970] ECR 1125; 4/73 *Nold v. Commission* [1974] ECR 491; 44/79 *Hauer v. Land Rheinland-Pfalz* [1979] ECR 3727; 265/87 *Schräder HS Kraftfutter GmbH* [1989] ECR 2237.

[148]W. van Gerven, Bringing (Private) Laws Closer to Each Other at the European Level, in F. Cafaggi (ed.), (op. cit.), 68.

[149]Ibid., 69. With regard to the interaction between both Courts, see also S. Douglas-Scott, A tale of two Courts: Luxembourg, Strasbourg and the Growing European Human Rights Acquis, *Common Market Law Review*, vol. 43, 2006, 629–665.

[150]W. van Gerven, Bringing (Private) Laws Closer to Each Other at the European Level, in F. Cafaggi (ed.), (op. cit.), 68.

[151]Ibid., 71.

[152]Ibid., 71.

8.3.3 To What Extent Is Legal Unification Accomplished, or Promoted, by Non-state Actors?

8.3.3.1 Through Restatements[153]

Direct norm generation by private actors in the EU is more recent but has grown substantially over the last 20 years. It has arisen in the context of pursuing a common private law of Europe. Its origins lie in the *Commission on European Contract Law* set up in the early 1980s and led by Professor Lando. This commission, a private initiative constituted of a body of lawyers drawn from all the Member States of the EU, has developed the *Principles of European Contract Law* (PECL), also called the Lando Principles.[154] The idea behind this project was to produce a statement of the principles which according to the group were underlying the private law of all the individual EU Member States.[155] The principles were compiled in a period of over 20 years in a restatement-like fashion.[156] Article 1:101 of the principles, which concerns their application, specifies that "the principles are intended to be applied as general rules of contract law in the European Union".[157] This project was followed by many other similar initiatives, such as, for example, *The Study Group on a European Civil Code* set up by Professor von Bar, a member of the Lando Group, whose aim was to take the example of what the PECL had done for general contract law and apply the same methodology to the rest of private law.[158] Recently the Lando group and the von Bar group have merged into a larger study group taking care of a variety of issues, such as specific contracts, moveable property, torts, trusts, etc.[159] There are also many other groups working in the vast area of private law on restatements of the common principles of European law: from *the Academy of European Private Lawyers* (the Gandolfi Group), which has produced a code of general contract law, to *the EC Group on Tort and Insurance Law* (the Spier Group)

---

[153]For an interesting comparison between restatements in Europe and the US see: H. Schulte-Nölke, Restatement in Europe and in the US: Some Comparative Lessons, in R. Brownsword, H.-W Micklitz, L. Niglia and S. Weatherill (eds.), *The Foundations of European Private Law* (Hart Publishing, 2011), 11–30.

[154]O. Lando and H. Beale (eds.), *Principles of European Contract law, Parts I and II* (The Hague, 2000); O. Lando, E. Clive, A. Prüm and R. Zimmermann (eds.), *Principles of European Contract law, Part III* (The Hague, 2003).

[155]H. Beale, The Development of European Private Law and the European Commission's Action Plan on Contract Law, *Juridica International*, 2005, 5.

[156]O. Lando, Principles of European Contract Law: An Alternative to or a Precursor of European Legislation, *American Journal of Comparative Law*, vol. 40, 1992, 579.

[157]For an overview of the principles as well as the recent developments, see the Lando's group website: http://frontpage.cbs.dk/law/commission_on_european_contract_law/index.html (consulted 21/01/13).

[158]H. Beale, (op. cit.), 5.

[159]Ibid., 5.

and the *Common Core of European Private Law* (Trento Project), which looks at how typical cases would be resolved in the various national systems, to name a few.[160]

A different approach was taken by Walter van Gerven, who initiated a collection of casebooks each covering a different field of law, the so-called *Ius Commune Casebooks for the Common Law of Europe*. This project applies a bottom-up approach and its purpose is "to uncover common solutions to legal problems in the various legal systems functioning within the territory of the EU Member States (...)".[161] These solutions are to be found in a variety of legal sources (statutory rules, judicial decisions and legal writings) which, when analysed in detail, demonstrate the existence of principles, rules and concepts which different legal systems, even if not all of them, have in common.[162]

In this context, it is also important to point to the work of the European Law Institute (ELI). Founded in June 2011 as an independent organisation, this institute seeks to improve the quality of European law.[163] More specifically, it aims "to initiate, conduct and facilitate research, to make recommendations, and to provide practical guidance in the field of European legal development".[164] It is too early to assess whether the work of the Institute effectively contributes to the legal unification of European law but its activities are worth following. Indeed, the Institute has high ambitions, pursuing a "quest for better law-making in Europe and the enhancement of European legal integration".[165] To this end, its core tasks include, amongst others, "to evaluate and stimulate the development of EU law, legal policy, and practice, and in particular make proposals for the development of the *acquis* and for the enhancement of EU law implementation by the Member States" and "to conduct and facilitate pan-European research, in particular to draft, evaluate and improve principles and rules which are common to the European legal systems".[166]

In addition to these different private initiatives, there are also three "official" projects that should be mentioned: *the EC Consumer Law Compendium, the Common Frame of Reference* (CFR) and *the proposal for a Common European Sales Law* (CESL). With regard to the first, the Commission established an international research group with the view of starting a research project called the EC Consumer Law Compendium. This Compendium was placed under the leadership of Prof. Hans Schulte-Nölkefor and was to comparatively analyze the implementation of eight consumer law directives into the national legal systems of the then 28 Member

---

[160] Ibid., 5–6.

[161] W. van Gerven, A Common Framework of Reference and Teaching, *European Journal of Legal Education*, 2004, 8.

[162] Ibid., 8.

[163] See their Manifesto available at https://www.europeanlawinstitute.eu/fileadmin/user_upload/p_eli/ELI_Manifesto_final_11-04-16.pdf (consulted 30/01/13).

[164] Ibid.

[165] Ibid.

[166] Ibid.

States, including the gathering of information about case law and administrative practice.[167] This study is part of the research the Commission has undertaken in the process of preparing the review of the consumer *acquis*.[168] It has resulted in the establishment of an EU Consumer Law Acquis Database.[169] Secondly, the European Commission also finances a research group to prepare a Common Frame of Reference (CFR) the stated aim of which is to provide non-binding fundamental principles, definitions and model rules in the area of contract law. These could serve as a model for legislators, judges and arbitrators working in the EU institutions and the Member States on legislation or adjudication in view of finding common solutions and bringing contract law closer to each other.[170] In this process the Outline Edition of the final academic Draft Common Frame of Reference (DCFR) was published in 2009.[171] This document was drafted by the Study Group on a European Civil Code and the Research Group on existing EC Private Law and contains Principles, Definitions and Model Rules of European Private Law.[172] As stated in the DCFR itself, this document "is (amongst other things) a possible model for an actual or 'political' Common Frame of Reference (CFR)".[173] Transforming the DCFR from an academic product into a binding legal document through the establishment of a 'political' CFR would most likely increase its harmonising effect, which however does not mean that the current document does not already contribute to a certain extent to the Europeanisation of Member States' private law.[174] Thirdly, on 11 October 2011, the European Commission proposed a draft Regulation for

---

[167]See http://ec.europa.eu/consumers/rights/cons_acquis_en.htm (consulted 21/01/13).

[168]Prof. Dr. Hans Schulte-Nölkefor, EC Consumer Law Compendium: Comparative analysis; February 2008, 30, http://ec.europa.eu/consumers/rights/docs/consumer_law_compendium_comparative_analysis_en_final.pdf (consulted 21/01/13).

[169]To consult the database go to: http://www.eu-consumer-law.org (consulted 21/01/13).

[170]See Action Plan on a more Coherent European Contract Law, COM(2003) 68 final, 12 February 2002, http://eur-lex.europa.eu/LexUriServ/LexUriServ.do?uri=COM:2003:0068:FIN:EN:PDF (consulted 22/01/13), in which the CFR was proposed and the Commission Communication on European Contract Law and the Revision of the Acquis: the Way Forward, COM(2004) 651 final, 11 October 2004, http://eur-lex.europa.eu/LexUriServ/LexUriServ.do?uri=COM:2004:0651:FIN:EN:PDF (consulted 21/1/13), which sets out the Commission's follow up to the 2003 Action Plan.

[171]C. Von Bar, E. Clive, H. Schule-Nôlke et al. (eds.), *Principles, Definitions and Model Rules of European Private Law, Draft Common Frame of Reference (DFCR)* (Sellier, 2009), http://ec.europa.eu/justice/policies/civil/docs/dcfr_outline_edition_en.pdf (consulted 21/01/13).

[172]Ibid., 3.

[173]Ibid., 8; For a critical analysis of this process see for example: M.W. Hesselink, If You Don't Like Our Principles We Have Others. On Core Values and Underlying Principles in European Private Law: A Critical Discussion of the New 'Principles' Section in the Draft Common Frame of Reference, in R. Brownsword, H.-W Micklitz, L. Niglia and S. Weatherill (eds.), *The Foundations of European Private Law* (Hart Publishing, 2011), 59–71 and I. Tzankova and M. Gramatikov, A Crtitical Note on Two EU Principles: Proceduralist View on the Draft Common Frame of Reference, in R. Brownsword, H.-W Micklitz, L. Niglia and S. Weatherill (eds.), *The Foundations of European Private Law* (Hart Publishing, 2011), 421–435.

[174]J. Lindholm, 'DCFR, Please Meet National Procedure': Enforcing the Frame of Reference using National Procedural Law, in R. Brownsword, H.-W Micklitz, L. Niglia and S. Weatherill (eds.), *The Foundations of European Private Law* (Hart Publishing, 2011), 485.

a Common European Sales Law (CESL).[175] This proposal is currently in the process of being negotiated within the EU having already gained the support of the European Parliament's Economic Affairs Committee.[176] This initiative should be put in the same context as the other initiatives of the Commission to improve the quality and coherence of European contract law.[177] According to the proposal "differences in contract law between Member States hinder traders and consumers who want to engage in cross-border trade within the internal market".[178] Its overall objective is "to improve the establishment and the functioning of the internal market by facilitating the expansion of cross-border trade for business and cross-border purchases for consumers".[179] This objective can be achieved "by making available a self-standing uniform set of contract law rules including provisions to protect consumers, the Common European Sales Law, which is to be considered as a second contract law regime within the national law of each Member State".[180] The initiative concerns the creation of an *optional* instrument; the proposal does "not aim to replace existing national laws, but would act as an alternative optional regime to the existing contract law regimes in each Member State".[181] The optional character of the proposed regime has raised a number of questions. For some this is one of the principal reasons why they are in favour of such a system, since the optional character of it means that it 'could do no harm'.[182] Others however wonder whether such an optional instrument can effectively provide for more harmonisation since

---

[175] See Proposal for a Regulation of the European Parliament and of the Council on a Common European Sales Law, COM(2011) 635 final, 11 October 2011,http://eur-lex.europa.eu/LexUriServ/LexUriServ.do?uri=COM:2011:0635:FIN:en:PDF (consulted 30/01/13).

[176] Opinion of the Committee on Economic and Monetary Affairs for the Committee on Legal Affairs on the proposal for a regulation of the European Parliament and of the Council on a Common European Sales Law, (COM(2011)0635 – C7–0329/2011 – 2011/0284(COD)), 11 October 2012, http://www.europarl.europa.eu/sides/getDoc.do?pubRef=-%2f%2fEP%2f%2fNONSGML%2bCOMPARL%2bPE-491.011%2b02%2bDOC%2bPDF%2bV0%2f%2fEN (consulted 30/01/13).

[177] E. Van Schagen, The proposal for a Common European Sales Law: How its Drafting Process Might Affect the Optional Instruments Added Value for Contract Parties, in A.L.M. Keirse and M.B.M. Loos (eds.), *Alternative Ways to Ius Commune: The Europeanisation of Private Law* (Intersentia, 2012), 86.

[178] Proposal for a Regulation of the European Parliament and of the Council on a Common European Sales Law, COM(2011) 635 final, 11 October 2011, 2, http://eur-lex.europa.eu/LexUriServ/LexUriServ.do?uri=COM:2011:0635:FIN:en:PDF (consulted 30/01/13).

[179] Ibid., 4.

[180] Proposal for a Regulation of the European Parliament and of the Council on a Common European Sales Law, COM(2011) 635 final, 11 October 2011, p. 2, http://eur-lex.europa.eu/LexUriServ/LexUriServ.do?uri=COM:2011:0635:FIN:en:PDF (consulted 30/01/13).

[181] UK Ministry of Justice, A common European Sales Law for the European Union – A proposal for a Regulation from the European Commission. The Government response, 34, available at https://consult.justice.gov.uk/digital-communications/common-european-sales-law (consulted 30/01/13).

[182] Ibid., 14. More in general, the study of the UK Ministry of Justice provides for a good critical analysis of the initiative.

its implementation "depends on the voluntary adoption of the harmonised rules by private parties".[183] Even though none of the aforementioned initiatives has, to date, led to the creation of legally binding instruments, they constitute steps towards a future common private law of Europe.

8.3.3.2 Through Standards and Practices of Industry, Trade Organizations or Other or Private Entities?

European integration has made it possible for trade unions and employer organizations to engage in collective bargaining and collective agreements at the European level, where these were formerly situated only at a national level. From the outset the social partners have been given a role within the European decision-making: they have from the beginning had an advisory role in decision-making as members of the European Economic and Social Committee (EC/EAEC) and of the ECSC Consultative Committee. According to articles 150 and 160 TFEU management and labour also have to be consulted by the Employment Committee as well as the Social Protection Committee. The Union shall further promote and recognise the role of the social partners at its level, taking into account the diversity of national systems (art. 152 TFEU). Even more relevant is the fact that the dialogue between management and labour at the EU level can lead to contractual relations, including agreements (art. 155(1) TFEU). Such agreements are usually referred to as European collective agreements. Such agreements have been concluded on parental leave, part-time work and fixed-term work. According to article 155(2) TFEU, agreements concluded at EU level can be implemented by a Council decision if the signatory parties jointly request it and provided that it concerns matters covered by article 152 TFEU, i.e. areas in which the EU is competent to provide support and complement the activities of the Member States. The first agreements concluded by management and labour where implemented at the EU level via directives.[184] Social partners thus now have the possibility to bargain and set standards for employment relations at the EU level, beyond the national borders.

Next to trade unions and employers' associations, private actors, and more specifically corporations, are also playing an important role in EU policy-making, more precisely in regulatory policy making. Private regulation is increasingly seen as an important complement to public regulation and new regulatory models coordinating public and private regulation have progressively emerged.[185] To this

---

[183]E. Van Schagen, The Proposal for a Common European Sales Law: How its Drafting Process Might Affect the Optional Instruments Added Value for Contract Parties, in A.L.M. Keirse and M.B.M. Loos (eds.), *Alternative Ways to Ius Commune: The Europeanisation of Private Law* (Intersentia, 2012), 107.

[184]K. Lenaerts and P. Van Nuffel, (op. cit.), 680–681.

[185]F. Cafaggi, Rethinking private regulation in the European regulatory space, *EUI Working Paper LAW*, n° 2006/13, 2–3.

extent, Fabrizio Cafaggi recognises five models of regulation: public regulation, co-regulation, delegated private regulation, ex post recognized private regulation and private regulation.[186] In some areas, especially in the area of human and labour rights, environmental protection and anti-corruption, private self-regulation is becoming a standard practice.[187]

8.3.4 What Is the Role of Legal Education and Training in the Unification of Law?

According to article 6(e) TFEU, the Union shall have competence to carry out actions to support, coordinate or supplement the actions of the Member States in the area of education, vocational training, youth and support. Article 165(1) TFEU states that the EU "shall contribute to the development of quality education by encouraging cooperation between Member States and, if necessary, by supporting and supplementing their action, while fully respecting the responsibility of the Member States for the content of teaching and the organization of education systems and their cultural and linguistic diversity". It is in this context that several programmes have been adopted since 1986, such as ERASMUS, LINGUA, TEMPUS and SOCRATES.[188] These different programmes aim at enhancing co-operation between institutions of higher education in the EU by promoting links between educational institutions and encourage the mobility of teachers and students. TEMPUS furthermore encourages such exchanges with the EU's neighbouring countries.[189]

Legal education in the EU Member States mainly focuses on component state law. Nevertheless, EU law is also dealt with but not with the same intensity by all universities. In most universities EU law is taught as a separate course, in other universities parts of EU law are taught in combination with related parts of component state law, whereas still other universities in their introductory courses combine EU and international law. Comparative law classes are present in most universities as well. In addition, there are some important post-graduate institutions focusing more specifically on the teaching of EU law. To illustrate this point a few institutions are worth mentioning. Firstly, there is the College of Europe.[190] The College has a campus in Bruges and one in Natolin (Warsaw) and is a centre of academic excellence, which focuses on postgraduate European studies in legal, economic, political, international relations and interdisciplinary domains.

---

[186]Ibid.

[187]Ibid.

[188]K. Lenaerts and P. Van Nuffel, (op. cit.), 405–406.

[189]For more information on these different programs see http://ec.europa.eu/education/index_en.htm (consulted 22/01/13).

[190]See http://www.coleurope.eu/ (consulted 22/01/13).

The College also offers training courses for executives and public sector officials. Secondly, there is the European University Institute (EUI) in Florence founded in 1972 by the six founding EEC Member States.[191] The goal of the Institute is to provide advanced academic training to PhD students and promote high level research in a European perspective in history, law, economics, political and social sciences. Thirdly, the Academy of European Law (ERA), which provides training for lawyers, judges and other legal practitioners and provides for a forum for debate in order to keep up with the developments of EU law, is also worth mentioning.[192] Finally, the Joint Research Centre of the European Commission offers temporary jobs to work in one of the EU institutions and offers training courses to new Member States (including their judges) in order to help them with the implementation of EU policies.[193]

With regard to student mobility within the EU, it still remains quite marginal, even though, as seen above, the EU has developed programmes, the most important of which is the ERASMUS programme, to encourage student mobility within Europe.[194] The latest Eurobarometer survey shows that only one in seven (14 %) young Europeans said they have been or were abroad at the time of the survey for education or training.[195] This can partly be explained by the high degree of heterogeneity which characterises the European academic landscape.[196] Indeed, universities are primarily organised at national and regional levels and display great differences in terms of their organisation, governance and operating conditions.[197] This heterogeneity also concerns differences in the number of places available, the length of studies, the quality of education, the language and the level of fees; and thus directly affects the students' decision to study abroad.[198] It is not surprising that the UK is by far the most important 'student-importer' and Greece the biggest 'student-exporter'.[199] Students are also often reluctant to spend time abroad given the linguistic and cultural differences as well as the legislative differences and

---

[191] See http://www.eui.eu/Home.aspx (consulted 22/01/13).

[192] See its official site http://www.era.int (consulted 22/01/13).

[193] See http://ec.europa.eu/dgs/jrc (consulted 22/01/13).

[194] I. Katsirea and A. Ruff, Free Movement of Law Students and Lawyers in the EU: A Comparison of English, German and Greek Legislation, *International Journal of the Legal Profession*, vol. 12(3), 368.

[195] MEMO/11/292, Flash Eurobarometer on Youth on the Move, 13/05/2011, http://europa.eu/rapid/press-release_MEMO-11-292_en.htm?locale=EN (consulted 22/11/13).

[196] Irina Katsirea and Anne Ruff, Free Movement of Law Students and Lawyers in the EU: A Comparison of English, German and Greek Legislation, *International Journal of the Legal Profession*, vol. 12(3), 368.

[197] Commission of the European Communities, Communication on the role of the universities in the Europe of knowledge, COM(2003) 58 final, 5 February 2003, 5, http://eur-lex.europa.eu/LexUriServ/LexUriServ.do?uri=COM:2003:0058:FIN:en:pdf (consulted 22/01/13).

[198] I. Katsirea and A. Ruff, (op. cit.), 368.

[199] A.P. Van der Mei, *Free Movement of Persons within the European Community: Cross-border Access to Public Benefits* (Hart Publishing, 2003), 392.

problems of recognition.[200] These problems seem to be even amplified in the area of legal studies given the great diversity of legal cultures and traditions.[201] In any case, the latest Eurobarometer survey seems to indicate that the greatest obstacle to the mobility of students is financial, and more specifically, the lack of funding.[202] The EU institutions have always stressed the importance of student mobility and have taken measures to tackle the potential obstacles to such movement (adoption of common or similar teaching programmes, establishment of programmes of financial aid/grants, harmonisation of duration of studies –cf. the Bologna process, etc.) but it seems that additional efforts need to be undertaken in order to convince more students to study abroad.

With regard more specifically to the testing for the bar exam, this is a competence of the Member States. In theory, admission to the bar is only granted for the Member State in which the bar exam was taken. However, the Council has adopted a certain number of directives in order to stimulate free movement of lawyers, both in terms of freedom to provide services and freedom of establishment. Before analysing these two specific directives it is important to briefly look at Directive 2005/36/EC on the recognition of professional qualifications.[203] This directive is especially relevant with regard to the free movement of lawyers since it applies to "all nationals of a Member State wishing to pursue a regulated profession in a Member State, including those belonging to the liberal professions, other than that in which they obtained their professional qualifications, on either a self-employed or employed basis".[204] With regard to the effects of the recognition the Directive stipulates that "[t]he recognition of professional qualifications by the host Member State allows the beneficiary to gain access in that Member State to the same profession as that for which he is qualified in the home Member State and to pursue it in the host Member State under the same conditions as its nationals".[205] This directive does not affect the application of the specific directives concerning provision of services by and establishment of lawyers since these two directives do not concern recognition of professional qualification but the recognition of the right to practice.[206] Directive 2005/36/EC applies to the specific situation of the recognition of professional qualifications for lawyers wishing *immediate* establishment *under* the professional title of the host Member State.[207] The two specific directives concerning provision of services by and establishment of lawyers are Directive 77/249/EEC facilitating the effective exercise by lawyers of the freedom to provide services and Directive

---

[200] I. Katsirea and A. Ruff, (op. cit.), 368.

[201] Ibid., 368.

[202] Press release, Half of young Europeans ready to work abroad, IP/11/567, Brussels, 13 May 2011, http://europa.eu/rapid/press-release_IP-11-567_en.htm?locale=EN (consulted 22/01/13).

[203] Directive 2005/36/EC of the European Parliament and of the Council of 7 September 2005 on the recognition of professional qualifications, O.J.L 255, 30/09/2005, 22–142;

[204] Ibid., art. 2(1).

[205] Ibid., art. 4(1).

[206] K. Lenaerts and P. Van Nuffel, (op. cit.), 265.

[207] Ibid., 265–266.

98/5/EC facilitating practice of the profession of lawyer on a permanent basis in a Member State other than that in which the qualification was obtained.[208] These two directives complement the possibilities of cross-border legal practice contained in the recognition of diploma's regime, allowing lawyers to exercise their freedom to provide services in another Member State and allowing them to establish themselves in another Member State, in other words, to practice their profession on a permanent basis in another Member State.

Next to the mobility of lawyers in the EU, it is also interesting to look at the mobility of graduates in general. It is interesting to note in this regard that, according to the latest Eurobarometer survey, 53 % of young people in Europe are willing or would like to work in another European country.[209] However, the survey also highlights "a huge gap between the widespread desire of young people to work abroad and actual workforce mobility: less than 3 % of Europe's working population currently lives outside their home country".[210] EU nationals wishing to work in other Member States benefit from the freedoms granted by the Treaties and EU legislation, more precisely they benefit from the rules regarding the free movement of workers, and its counterpart for self-employed persons, the freedom of establishment.[211] According to these rules, Member States are, in essence, prohibited from restricting nationals of other Member States to take up an employment on their territory. Just as it is the case for the free movement of students, the EU thus also stimulates the free movement of workers, but the number of workers engaging in such mobility is also quite low.

8.3.5 *To What Extent Do External Factors, such as International Law, Influence Legal Unification?*

The impact of international agreements between the EU and third States and/or international organisations on legal unification within the EU was given attention above. The present section is confined to the effect of general international law, in particular customary international law, on the same process. The CJEU has held on numerous occasions that the EU "must respect international law in the exercise

---

[208]Council Directive 77/249/EEC of 22 March 1977 to facilitate the effective exercise by lawyers of freedom to provide services, O.J. L 078, 26/03/1977, 17–18 and Directive 98/5/EC of the European Parliament and of the Council of 16 February 1998 to facilitate practice of the profession of lawyer on a permanent basis in a Member State other than that in which the qualification was obtained, O.J. L 077, 14/03/1998, 36–43.

[209]MEMO/11/292, Flash Eurobarometer on Youth on the Move, 13/05/2011, http://europa.eu/rapid/press-release_MEMO-11-292_en.htm?locale=EN (consulted 22/11/13).

[210]Press release, Half of young Europeans ready to work abroad, IP/11/567, Brussels, 13 May 2011, http://europa.eu/rapid/press-release_IP-11-567_en.htm?locale=EN (consulted 22/01/13).

[211]Irina Katsirea and Anne Ruff, Free Movement of Law Students and Lawyers in the EU: A Comparison of English, German and Greek Legislation, *International Journal of the Legal Profession*, vol. 12(3), 368.

of its powers and that [EU law] must be interpreted, and its scope limited, in the light of the relevant rules of [...] international law".[212] The Court has also declared itself competent to examine whether the validity of EU acts "may be affected by reason of the fact that they are contrary to a rule of international law".[213] Thus, at first sight it seems to take into account general international law when interpreting EU law.[214] This is in line with the Treaty provisions in force since the Lisbon Treaty that refer to international law. Thus, article 3(5) TEU states that the Union "shall contribute [...] to the strict observance and the development of international law." Furthermore, article 21(1), first paragraph; TEU adds that "the Union's action on the international scene shall be guided by the (...) respect for the principles of the United Nations Charter and international law". Finally, the EU must also take into account the undertakings of the United Nations and other international organisations when exercising its powers.[215] However, although it is outside the scope of this chapter to delve into an exhaustive analysis of the attitude of the CJEU and the other EU institutions toward international law, one should not lose sight of the fact that the CJEU has been in practice rather more ambivalent – if not guarded – vis-à-vis the effects of international law within the EU legal order.[216] Besides, international voluntary coordination also plays a role with regard to legal unification and harmonisation in the EU. The EU is, for example, a member of the Hague Conference on Private International law.[217] According to article 1 of its Statute, the purpose of the Hague Conference on Private International law is "to work for the progressive unification of the rules of private international law".[218] Thus, international law as well as voluntary international coordination consolidate the legal unification process within the EU legal order.

---

[212] Case C-286/90 *Poulsen and Diva Navigation* [1992] ECR I-6019, para. 9. See also Case C-162/96 *Racke* [1998] ECR I-03655, para. 45; Joined Cases C-402/05 P and C-415/05 P *Kadi and Al Barakaat International Foundation* [2008] ECR. I-6351, para. 291; Case C-386/08 *Brita* [2010] ECR I-1289, paras. 39–41; Case C-366/10, Air Transport Association of America and Others v. Secretary of State for Energy and Climate Change [2011] ECR 0000, para. 101.

[213] Joined Cases 21–24/72 *International Fruit Company* [1972] ECR 1219, para. 6.

[214] See among others: Case C-286/90 *Poulsen and Diva Navigation* [1992] ECR I-6019, para. 10; Case C-162/96 *Racke v. Hauptzollamt Mainz* [1998] ECR I-3655, paras. 37–60; Case C-308/06 *Intertanko* [2008] ECR I-4057, para. 52; Case C-203/07 P *Greece v. Commission* [2008] ECR I-8161, para.64; Case C-135/08 *Rottmann* [2010] ECR, para. 53.

[215] K. Lenaerts and P. Van Nuffel, (op. cit.), 879. See also Joined Cases C-402/05 P and C-415/05 P *Kadi and Al Barakaat International Foundation* [2008] ECR. I-6351, para. 293.

[216] See further J. Wouters, J. Odermatt and T. Ramopoulos, Interactions Between the CJEU and the EU Legislature in the Application of International Law, in M. Cremona and A. Thies (eds.), *The European Court of Justice and External Relations Law – Constitutional Challenges* (Hart Publishing, forthcoming).

[217] *The European Community became a Member of the Hague Conference on 3 April 2007. With the entry into force of the Treaty of Lisbon on 1 December 2009, the European Union replaces and succeeds the European Community as from that date.* http://www.hcch.net/index_en.php?act=states.details&sid=220 (consulted 22/01/13).

[218] Statute of the Hague Conference on Private International Law (entered into force on 15 July 1955), http://www.hcch.net/upload/conventions/txt01en.pdf (consulted 22/01/13).

8.4 Institutional and Social Background

8.4.1 The Judicial Branch

The powerful and successful role played by the CJEU in the process of legal unification within the EU has by now become clear. This section goes into the procedural rules surrounding the function of the Court situated at the central level with the power to police whether the central legislator has exceeded the powers attributed to it. The Member States can, indeed, bring an action for annulment against an act of the European Parliament, the Council, the European Commission and the European Central Bank (article 263 TFEU). In such cases, the CJEU shall review the legality of these acts and has the power to declare the act void if the action is well founded (article 264 TFEU). Member States can also bring an action before the Court if the institutions fail to act (article 265 TFEU). Even individuals can bring an action for annulment before the General Court (before the Lisbon Treaty: the European Court of First Instance), with appeal possible before the CJEU, against binding acts of the aforementioned institutions which are addressed or are of direct and individual concern to them in order to review the legality of EU actions (Article 263 TFEU). There are different possible grounds for annulment, lack of competence being one of them. Indeed, an EU act which falls outside of the EU's competence can be annulled.[219] In most cases, however, the dispute will turn around the legal basis of the contested act.[220] In such cases, the act is annulled either for lack of legal basis or for use of the wrong legal basis.[221] If the Treaty provision used as legal basis for the concerned act is insufficient to support its content, then the act will be annulled for lack of legal basis.[222]

Another important question is whether there is a court at the central level with the power to interpret component state law. In theory, such a court does not exist at the European level. It is for the Member State judges to interpret their laws in conformity with EU law.[223] However, according to article 267 TFEU, Member

---

[219] See for example Case 294/83, *Les Verts* [1986] ECR 1339, para. 25.

[220] K. Lenaerts and P. Van Nuffel, (op. cit.), 115–116.

[221] A. Rosas and L. Armati, (op. cit.), 226. For examples see: Case C-94/03 *Commission v Council* [2006] ECR I-1; Case C-178/03 *Commission v Parliament and Council* [2006] ECR I-107; Joined Cases C-313/04 and C-318/04 *Parliament v Council and Commission* [2006] ECR I-4721; Case C-413/04 *Parliament v Council* [2006] ECR I-11221; Case C-414/04 *Parliament v Council* [2006] ECR I-11279; Case C-403/05 *Parliament v Commission* [2007] ECR I-9045; Case C-133/06 *Parliament v Council* [2008] ECR I-3189; Case C-155/07 *Parliament v Council* [2008] ECR I-8103; Case C-166/07 *Parliament v Council* [2009] ECR I-7135.

[222] See for example Case C-376/98 *Germany v European Parliament and Council* [2000] ECR I-8419; Case C-211/01 *Commission v Council* [2003] ECR I-8913.

[223] On the limits of the duty of Union-conform interpretation of domestic legal provisions see: Case C-106/89 *Marleasing v. La Commercial* [1990] ECR I-4135, paras. 7–8; Case C-111/97 *EvoBus Austria GmbH v. Novog* [1998] ECR I-5411, para. 21.

States courts can (and in certain circumstances must) refer a question for preliminary ruling to the CJEU with regard to the interpretation of a rule of primary or secondary EU law.

Article 267 TFEU furthermore states that when a question regarding the interpretation of primary or secondary EU law or the validity of secondary law is raised before a Member State court, this court *may*, if it considers that a decision on the question is necessary to enable it to give judgment, request the CJEU to give a ruling thereon. In the case where such a question is pending before a Member State court against whose decisions there is no judicial remedy, the court in question *must* bring the matter before the CJEU. This rule has been interpreted by the CJEU. Two points are worth mentioning here. First of all, in line with the text of article 267 TFEU, the 'lower' Member State courts have the choice between referring a question regarding the *interpretation* of rules of EU law to the CJEU or interpreting, though subject to appeal, these rules themselves. Based on a strict reading of the text of article 267 TFEU, this should also be the case with regard to the validity of secondary law in front of 'lower' courts. The CJEU, however, has decided, that when a Member State court, regardless of its level, is faced with a question regarding the *validity* of (secondary) EU law, then it *must* address a request for preliminary ruling to the CJEU.[224] Indeed, "where the validity of an act is challenged before a national court the power to declare the act invalid must (...) be reserved for the Court of Justice".[225] Consequently, a lower court does not have the power to declare an EU act invalid. Secondly, the CJEU has held that the duty to request a preliminary ruling that lies on the highest Member States courts based on article 267 TFEU is not absolute. Indeed, the CJEU has established four cases in which the higher courts are not obliged to do so: (1) the question is irrelevant for the outcome of the case; (2) the question is materially identical to that of a previous preliminary ruling in a similar case; (3) the question is decided by previous judgement of the CJEU but the proceedings and question were not strictly identical; and (4) the correct application of the EU rule is so obvious as to leave no scope for any reasonable doubt as to the manner in which the question raised is to be resolved.[226] It should be noted here that the significance of the preliminary procedure cannot be overestimated. In having become "the principal vehicle for imposition of judiciary driven Community discipline",[227] it guarantees in practice the harmonisation of national rules.

---

[224] Case 314/85 *Foto-Frost* [1987] ECR 4199.

[225] Ibid., para. 17.

[226] Case 283/81 *CILFIT* [1982] ECR 3415, para. 21. See also K. Lenaerts, D. Arts and I. Maselis, *Procedural Law of the European Union* (Sweet & Maxwell, 2006), 72–76.

[227] J.H.H. Weiler, Journey to an Unknown Destination: A Retrospective and Prospective of the European Court of Justice in the Arena of Political Integration, *Journal of Common Market Studies*, vol. 31(4), 421.

8.4.2 Relations Between the Central and Component State Governments

The EU is governed according to the principle of indirect administration, which itself stems from the principle of subsidiarity (article 4(3), second para. TEU and article 291(1) TFEU; see also article 197(2) TFEU). This has also been referred to as 'executive federalism', a concept drawn from the German Constitution, in which the Länder (the component states) are responsible for the implementation of federal legislation. In the same manner the implementation of the central law within the EU lies primarily on the shoulders of its Member States.[228] However, there are some significant exceptions to this principle in the fields of competition law (articles 105–106 TFEU) and of the control of aid granted by Member States (article 108 TFEU) as well as the adoption of measures implementing legislative acts, which are directly handled by the European Commission.[229] A strong illustration of 'executive federalism' in the EU is the implementation of the EU directives.[230] Indeed, as seen above, an obligation rests upon the Member States to transpose the directive into their legal order within a certain period of time or they risk being sanctioned (see *supra*).

This leads to another point, that of the control exerted by the central government on the execution by the component states of their obligations under central state law. If the European Commission considers that a Member State has failed to fulfil an obligation under the Treaties, it may bring the matter before the Court of Justice (article 258 TFEU). If the Court finds that the Member State in question has failed to fulfil its obligations under the Treaties, the State shall be required to take the necessary measures to comply with the judgment of the Court (article 260(1) TFEU). If the State in question fails to comply with the judgment of the Court, the latter may impose penalties (article 260(2) TFEU).

It is also important to mention that EU Member States are strongly represented within the EU institutions. First of all, there is the European Council comprising the Heads of State or Government of the EU Member States, and the Council, which consists of "a representative of each Member State at ministerial level, who may commit the government of the Member State in question (...)" (Article 16(2) TEU). Member States themselves determine the person of ministerial rank who will represent them.[231] According to Article 16(1) TEU, the Council exercises legislative and budgetary powers and carries out policy-making and coordination functions. Depending on the subject matter the Council shall meet in different configurations (Article 16(6) TEU). Then there is also COREPER (the Committee of Permanent Representatives), which, according to Article 16(7) TEU "shall be

---

[228] See further: J.C. Piris, (op. cit.), 97–98.
[229] Ibid.
[230] W. van Gerven, 2005, (op. cit.), 20.
[231] K. Lenaerts and P. Van Nuffel, (op. cit.), 486.

responsible for preparing the work of the Council". Each Member State delegates a Permanent Representative to COREPER, who has the status of ambassador based in Brussels and is accompanied by a Deputy Permanent Representative. Even though COREPER does not have formal decision-making power, it nonetheless has an important task, since it is responsible for ensuring consistency of the EU's policies and actions, and make sure that the fundamental principles of legality, subsidiarity, proportionality and correct legal basis are respected as well as the rules concerning competences, budget, transparency and the quality of drafting.[232] COREPER is assisted by a large number of working groups, which are partly composed of civil servants of the 28 Member States. Finally, there is the Committee of the Regions, which, according to Article 300(3) TFEU consists of "representatives of regional and local bodies who either hold a regional or local authority electoral mandate or are politically accountable to an elected assembly". These members, who shall not exceed 350, are appointed by the Council acting unanimously on a proposal from the Commission (Article 305 TFEU). It has an advisory task in the areas determined by the Treaties (transport, employment, social policy, etc.), in particular those which concern trans-border cooperation (Article 307 TFEU).

Taxation is not a competence that has been transferred to the EU and it therefore remains with the Member States. Taxation is traditionally an area important for national sovereignty and this explains why it remains exclusively within the competence of Member States. Taxes are thus levied by the Member States. However, the EU has three sources of revenue with regard to its own resources: (1) levies, premiums, additional or compensatory amounts, additional amounts or factors, Common Customs Tariff duties and other duties established or to be established by the EU institutions in respect of trade with non-member countries, customs duties on products under the expired ECSC Treaty as well as contributions and other duties provided for within the framework of the common organisation of the markets in sugar; (2) the application of a uniform rate valid for all Member States to the harmonised VAT assessment base and (3) the application of a uniform rate to the sum of all the Member States' Gross National Income's (GNI).[233] Member States shall retain, by way of collection costs, 25 % of the amounts referred to with regard to the first source of own revenue.[234] The EU can also impose fines or penalties on undertakings for violation of EU competition rules (article 103(2)(a) TFEU). As the EU has only very limited taxation powers, there is no need to establish general rules governing double taxation between the EU on the one side and the Member States on the other side. Most rules in this field consist of double taxation agreements concluded amongst the Member States. There are, however, a few directives such as, for example, Council Directive 2003/49/EC on a common system of taxation

---

[232] See for the various dimensions of COREPER including its relation to the other institutions, *Le Coreper dans tous ses Etats* (Presses Universitaires de Strasbourg, 2000).

[233] Council Decision 2007/436/EC, Euratom of 7 June 2007 on the system of the European Communities' own resources, O.J. L 163/17, 23/06/2007, article 2(1).

[234] Ibid., article 2(3).

applicable to interest and royalty payments made between associated companies of different Member States[235] and Council Directive 69/335/EEC on indirect taxes on the raising of capital.[236] In the words of Giandomenica Majone, the EU remains a "regulatory polity" – a polity with administrative instruments but little fiscal capacity.[237]

8.4.3 The Bureaucracy

The civil service of the Member States is completely separate from the EU civil service.[238] The institutions and the bodies of the Union are currently employing more than 38,000 officials.[239] They are all subject to the Staff Regulations of officials of the European Communities and the Conditions of Employment of other servants of the European Communities.[240] These rules are based on article 336 TFEU. The EU distinguishes two categories of employees: staff officials and the other servants. Staff officials refers to "any person who has been appointed, as provided for in these Staff Regulations, to an established post on the staff of one of the institutions of the Communities by an instrument issued by the Appointing Authority of that institution",[241] whereas temporary staff, auxiliary staff, contract staff, local staff and special advisers fall under the category 'other servants'.[242] The rules applied to both categories are different. There is some mobility ('detachment') between the national civil service and the EU civil service, but this is quite marginal.

---

[235] Council Directive 2003/49/EC of 3 June 2003 on a common system of taxation applicable to interest and royalty payments made between associated companies of different Member States, O.J.L 157, 26/06/2003, 49.

[236] Council Directive 69/335/EEC of 17 July 1969 concerning indirect taxes on the raising of capital, O.J. L 249, 3/10/1969, 25.

[237] Cited in A. Moravcsik, Federalism in the European Union: Rhetoric or Reality, in K. Nicolaidis and R. Howse (eds.), (op. cit.), 170.

[238] The only exception is the post-Lisbon European External Action Service where up to forty percent of the personnel consists of Member States' diplomats serving there on a temporary basis.

[239] K. Lenaerts and P. Van Nuffel, (op. cit.), 590.

[240] Règlement (CEE, Euratom, CECA) n 259/68 du Conseil, du 29 février 1968, fixant le statut des fonctionnaires des Communautés européennes ainsi que le régime applicable aux autres agents de ces Communautés, et instituant des mesures particulières temporairement applicables aux fonctionnaires de la Commission, O.J.L 56, 04/03/1968, 1–7.

[241] Staff Regulations of Officials of the European Communities and Conditions of Employment of other Servants of the European Communities, I-4, http://ec.europa.eu/civil_service/docs/toc100_en.pdf (consulted 21/01/13).

[242] Ibid., II-3.

8.4.4 Social Factors

The EU is far from being homogeneous and there are large differences in mentalities and perceptions of European values.[243] It is home to 450 million Europeans from diverse ethnic, cultural and linguistic backgrounds.[244] The question whether one can speak of a common European identity has been a popular subject of discourse amongst scholars and politicians alike. In this regard, it has been argued that there is no *demos* in Europe.[245] Rather, "[c]itizens in the Member States of the EU share little underlying sense of distinct 'European' national identity, derived from a common history, culture or philosophy."[246] This line of argumentation seems at first glance to be further consolidated in light of recent enlargements. The EU now counts 28 Member States, making it all the more heterogeneous. However, this view does not go uncontested. On the contrary, it has been suggested that an approach of "country first, but Europe, too is the dominant outlook in most EU Member States."[247] It is submitted that the latter view is the better one since it seems to capture more accurately the complex European identity formation landscape. It would be epistemologically short-sighted to refuse the existence or significance of a European identity based on the parallel existence of national identities. Besides, the European project has never been about forging a common European identity at the expense of national ones.

It is also important to note that there are a number of minorities in Europe, especially linguistic minorities, like the Roma. The EU attaches great importance to minority protection. Minority protection is for example one of the key criteria for accession to the Union.[248]

Finally, there is also a large asymmetry of natural resources within the EU. It is here that the European Social Fund (ESF) steps in. This is one of the EU's Structural Funds, set up to reduce differences in prosperity and living standards across EU Member States and regions, and therefore promoting economic and

---

[243] W. van Gerven, 2005, (op. cit.), 47.

[244] Communication from the Commission to the Council, the European Parliament, the Economic and Social Committee and the Committee of the Regions – Promoting Language Learning and Linguistic Diversity: an Action Plan 2004–2006, COM(2003) 449 final, Brussels, 24/07/2003, 24, http://eur-lex.europa.eu/LexUriServ/LexUriServ.do?uri=COM:2003:0449:FIN:EN:PDF (consulted 22/01/13).

[245] J.H.H. Weiler, Does Europe Need a Constitution? Reflections on Demos, Telos and the German Maastricht Decision, *European Law Journal*, 1/2, 219–258.

[246] A. Moravcsik, Federalism in the European Union: Rhetoric or Reality, in K. Nicolaidis and R. Howse (eds.), (op. cit.), 178.

[247] T. Risse, Social Constructivism and European Integration, in A. Wiener and T. Diez (eds.), (op. cit.), 166–167.

[248] For more information on the subject see G. Kinga, *Minority Governance in Europe* (Open Society Institute, 2002) 378p and G. Toggenburg, *Minority Protection and the Enlarged European Union* (Open Society Institute, 2004), 181p.

social cohesion.[249] Most money goes to those Member States and regions where economic development is less advanced. The other main Structural Fund is the European Regional Development Fund. The Fund aims to promote economic and social cohesion by correcting the main regional imbalances and participating in the development and conversion of regions.[250]

8.5 Concluding Remarks

The question of unification of laws in federal systems is an inherently complex question. The difficulties in the effort to present in a coherent and consistent manner developments within federal entities are only magnified when the EU becomes the entity under investigation. It has been an intentional choice to leave aside the partly theoretical discussion surrounding the nature of the EU as a federal post-Westphalian political creature. On the contrary the focus was on the actual features of the EU. The latter is a constantly evolving political organism with a declared goal to bring together and integrate the states and peoples of Europe but whose *finalité politique* cannot really be said in public. The EU has a clear-cut, two-level structure of governance: central institutions and national governments. The distribution of competences between these two levels is based on the principles of subsidiarity, proportionality and pre-emption whereas the principle of primacy of EU law applies in cases of conflict between central and national laws. Central EU authorities enjoy a variety of legal and political instruments with which they steer the process of legal unification and harmonization. At the same time Member States often find it opportune to harmonize their legislations with EU legislation even in areas for which this is not mandatory. This legal construct has proven, nonetheless, highly successful and functional primarily thanks to the integrative role of the Court of Justice. Throughout its existence the Court has had a specific policy orientation when giving its judgments and opinions: "the promotion of European integration."[251] Often confronted with accusations of judicial activism, the Court has been tireless in keeping the European project on track. However, the significance of not strictly legal factors in the process of legal harmonization should not be underrated. Non-state actors within the EU, dense relations and cooperation among legal practitioners and scholars, and in general the constantly deepening interaction among Europeans have profound effects in this process.

---

[249] http://ec.europa.eu/esf/main.jsp?catId=35&langId=en (consulted 22/01/13).

[250] http://europa.eu/legislation_summaries/employment_and_social_policy/job_creation_measures/l60015_en.htm (consulted 22/01/13).

[251] T.C. Hartley, (op. cit.), 72.

Chapter 9
Unification of Laws in the Federal System of Germany

Jürgen Adam and Christoph Möllers

9.1 Overview

The German Constitution – the *Grundgesetz* – is a federal constitution. Three levels of government may be distinguished: At the federal level, the *Bund*; at component state level, the 16 *Länder*; and at local level, the *Gemeinden* (municipalities), which are part of the *Länder* administration. The *Länder* are very different in size and population: Size ranges from around 400 km^2 (Bremen) to over 70,000 km^2 (Bayern), and population from around 660,000 (Bremen) to nearly 18 million (Nordrhein-Westfalen). In the "city-states" of Berlin, Bremen and Hamburg, local and state levels are identical.

Historically, federalism is a well-known concept in Germany: The constitution of the German Reich of 1871 created a federal state as well as the – albeit less federal – *Weimar* constitution of 1919. Then, the totalitarian national-socialist German state abolished virtually all federal elements, concentrating powers of government at the central level. Thus, when the Parliamentary Council met to deliberate over a new constitution in 1948, historical precedence was not the only reason to opt for a federal system; there was also a strong feeling that history had painfully proven centralism a dangerous concept. This view was certainly shared by the Western Allies who constantly pushed towards a more decentralised structure, although not always with success.

When analysing the actual state of federalism in Germany, it is helpful to keep in mind that the *Grundgesetz* was created under very peculiar historical circumstances,

---

J. Adam (✉)
Justizministerium Baden-Württemberg, Schillerplatz 4, 70173 Stuttgart, Germany
e-mail: adamjuer@web.de

C. Möllers
Juristische Fakultät, Humboldt-Universität zu Berlin, Unter den Linden 9, D-10099 Berlin, Germany
e-mail: christoph.moellers@rewi.hu-berlin.de

and that today's circumstances are very much different. During the 60 years of the *Grundgesetz* as the German constitution, German society and politics have experienced great changes; Germany has become reunited; and – maybe most important for the way in which the concept of federalism is working in German constitutional law and politics today – Germany has become part of a European Union, which has a federal structure of its own.

In general, there has been a centralization of federal legislative powers through numerous constitutional amendments between 1949 and the 1990s. Since then, two reforms in 1994 and 2006 gave some legislative powers back to the states. The problem remains that not all states are actually interested in legislating on their own and/or are too small and too understaffed to organize a professional legislative process. Legislative autonomy is mainly a project of the larger states.

9.2 The Federal Distribution and Exercise of Lawmaking Power

Within the general framework of the German constitution, distribution of powers between the federal, state, and local government levels is often described as a system of "vertical separation of powers" (Konrad Hesse). Somewhat contrary to this picture, the *Grundgesetz* strongly concentrated legislative powers at the federal level where they have been widely used. Whereas in theory, legislative powers are generally vested in the *Länder* and the *Bund* must rely on a specific catalogue of enumerated competences, in practice the *Bund* enjoys broad liberty as to the subject of its legislation and the remaining areas of *Länder* powers are quite narrow.

9.2.1 Areas of Law Subject to the Legislative Jurisdiction of the Central Authority

The *Grundgesetz* expressly provides for two types of federal legislative competences: exclusive and concurrent. The Federal Constitutional Court (*Bundesverfassungsgericht*; hereinafter "FCC") has also recognized certain forms of unwritten – or implied – powers.

9.2.1.1 Exclusive Powers

Exclusive powers are enumerated in Article 73 *Grundgesetz* (GG). Article 73 GG lists 17 main areas of federal competence, including foreign affairs and defence, citizenship in the Federation, the operation of federal railways, postal and telecommunication services, the legal relations of persons employed by the Federation, intellectual property and copyright, the prevention of international terrorism, laws on weapons and explosives, and production and use of nuclear power for peaceful means. It should be noted that some areas of legislative competences listed here – for example, "currency, money, and coinage" and the "unity of the customs and trading area" – have in fact been transferred to the European Union to a significant degree.

Other areas of exclusive federal powers of legislation may be found throughout the *Grundgesetz*. To a large extent, they are concerned with the internal organization of the federal government. Examples for this kind of competence are (i) the regulation of the election of the *Bundestag* and of electoral review (Art. 38 sec. 3, Art. 41 sec. 3); (ii) the federal budget, borrowing of funds, and the assumption of pledges, guarantees, and similar commitments (Art. 110 sec. 2, 112, 115 sec. 1); and (iii) the organisation and jurisdiction of the FCC and the other federal courts, as well as the status of their judges (Art. 93 sec. 3, 94 sec. 2, 95 sec. 3, 98 sec. 1, 96 sec. 2).

The foreign affairs and defence power of Article 73 Number 1 is supplemented by provisions assigning to the *Bund* the general task to maintain relations with foreign states (Art. 32 sec. 1), to conclude treaties (Art. 59), to determine a state of defence in cases in which the federal territory is under attack by armed forces (Art. 115a sec. 1) or to declare such a state of defence terminated and conclude peace (Art. 115l sec. 2, 3), and to transfer sovereign rights to international organisations (Art. 24), with special provisions governing the transfer of powers to the European Union (Art. 23).

An important competence, finally, is located in Article 79 sec. 2 GG: It is the power to amend the constitution itself. A majority of two thirds in the *Bundestag* and in the *Bundesrat* is needed, which ensures that besides consent of the parliamentary opposition (at least in "normal" political times), a broad majority of the *Länder* is needed. However, the hurdle proved not to have been set too high, as the *Grundgesetz* has been amended well over 50 times since 1949.

9.2.1.2 Concurrent Powers

Concurrent powers of the Federation are listed in Article 74 GG. They include:

- No. 1: The complete fields of civil law/private law, criminal law, civil and criminal procedure including the court system, and regulation of the legal professions;
- No. 7: Public welfare;
- No. 11: Economic affairs, namely mining, industry, supply of power, crafts, trades, commerce, banking, stock exchanges, private insurance, with certain exceptions;
- No. 12: Labor law, including the organizations of enterprises, occupational safety and health, and employment agencies, as well as social security including unemployment insurance;

- No 19: Large areas of public health, namely measures against dangerous and communicable human and animal diseases, admission to the medical professions, regulation of pharmacies, drugs, medical and health products, narcotics, and poisons;
- No. 20: The law on food products including animals used in their production, the law on alcohol and tobacco, essential commodities and feedstuffs, as well as protective measures in connection with the marketing of agricultural and forest seeds and seedlings, the protection of plants against diseases and pests, as well as the protection of animals;
- No. 22: Road traffic, motor transport, construction and maintenance of long distance highways;
- No. 25: State liability;
- No. 27: Rights and duties regarding the status of civil servants, including judges, of the *Länder*.

With regard to a certain number of concurrent competences – for example, the economic affairs power mentioned above – Article 72 sec. 2 states that the Federation will have the right to legislate on matters falling within Article 72's scope if and to the extent that establishing equivalent living conditions throughout the federal territory, or the maintenance of legal or economic unity, renders federal regulation necessary for the national interest. Before 1994, this requirement had been weaker, and the FCC had all but refused to enforce it, holding that assessment of necessity was a prerogative of the federal political process. The constitutional reform of 1994 then limited the exercise of central concurrent power in general by a new necessity clause. After the reform, the Court felt compelled to apply the new formula strictly and struck down several federal laws because of lack of necessity for a federal rule. This led to today's compromise: With regard to the concurrent powers not mentioned in Article 72 sec. 2, the *Bund* is now at complete liberty as to whether and to what extent the powers are used. Within the scope of Article 72 sec. 2, federal laws may provide that federal legislation that is no longer "necessary" may be superseded by *Länder* law (Art. 72 sec. 4).

As in the case of exclusive competences, it must be kept in mind that to a certain – and growing – extent, concurrent powers of the *Bund* have been transferred to the European Union. For example, the federal power to pass laws preventing the abuse of economic power (Art. 74 sec. 1 no. 16) is currently relevant only to the extent to which EU antitrust law (Art. 101, 102 of the Treaty on the Functioning of the EU and secondary legislation) leaves room for member state legislation.

9.2.1.3 Unwritten Powers (Implied Powers)

Unwritten or implied powers acknowledged by the FCC and constitutional doctrine are usually divided in three groups: "Natural" competences, "contextual" competences and "annex competences". "Natural" competences (*Kompetenzen kraft Natur der Sache*) apply if it is evident that a matter can only be regulated by the central authority, e.g. the seat of the federal government or the federal flag. "Contextual" and "annex" competences (*Kompetenzen kraft Sachzusammenhang/Annexkompetenzen*) encompass matters bearing a close relationship to matters explicitly referred to in federal legislation. For example, court fees are viewed as standing in a context with court procedure, and with regard to federal highways, highway patrol is characterized as an annex matter.

9.2.1.4 Use of Federal Powers

The *Bund* has made extensive use of virtually all applicable sources of legislative power. For example, the complete field of classical private law – contracts, torts, property, family law and the law of successions – is covered by the (federal) civil code (*Bürgerliches Gesetzbuch*); criminal law is governed by the (federal) penal code (*Strafgesetzbuch*). The organization of civil, criminal, administrative, tax, and social security courts is governed by the (federal) court organisation statute (*Gerichtsverfassungsgesetz*), and there are also (federal) codifications of civil as well as criminal procedure (code of civil procedure – *Zivilprozessordnung*; code of criminal procedure – *Strafprozessordnung*). All these matters are covered by Article 74 sec. 1 number 1, and they are not subject to the "necessity" clause of Art. 72 sec. 2 described above. This may serve as an example of the extent of legal unification that is obtained through federal legislation. Notably, the codifications mentioned here were passed already under the constitution of 1871; however, they have been widely amended under the *Grundgesetz*. "Introductory statutes" (*Einführungsgesetze*) passed with the civil code and the penal code regulate the (small) extent to which *Länder* powers remain in these areas.

9.2.2 Areas of Law Remaining Within the Legislative Jurisdiction of the Component States

Turning to the powers left to the *Länder*, it is helpful to start with a look at the principles governing the relations of state and federal powers of legislation.

9.2.2.1 Constitutional Principles

Article 30 and Article 70 sec. 1 GG formulate as a general principle that all residual powers not mentioned in the federal constitution are vested exclusively in the component states. On matters within the exclusive legislative power of the Federation, the *Länder* have power to legislate only when and to the extent that they are expressly authorized to do so by federal law (Art. 71 GG). On matters within the concurrent legislative power, the *Länder* have power to legislate so long as and to the extent that the Federation has not exercised its legislative power by enacting a law (Art. 72 sec. 1). Therefore, use of the concurrent legislative power has an effect of preemption. As a consequence, true conflicts of federal and *Länder* law arise rarely. If they do, federal law prevails according to the supremacy clause of Article 31 GG.

An exception providing for a complicated scheme of interacting state and federal powers is stated in Article 72 sec. 3, which was passed as an amendment only in 2006. According to this provision, in certain fields like hunting, protection of nature, and distribution of land the *Länder* may enact laws at variance with federal legislation. Federal laws on these matters enter into force no earlier than 6 months following their promulgation unless otherwise provided with the consent of the *Bundesrat*. As for the relationship between federal law and law of the *Länder*, the supremacy principle is not applied. Instead, the latest law enacted will take precedence. This could create a certain ping-pong effect between the levels.

9.2.2.2 Powers of the *Länder*

There is no positive catalogue of legislative powers reserved to the *Länder*. Given the great number of federal competences and the degree to which the *Bund* has made use of them, not too many areas remain untouched areas of competence for the *Länder*. Nevertheless, there are several worth mentioning:

- Police law: Organisation, procedure and substantive powers of the police are still to a large degree subject to *Länder* legislation. Federal police power is basically limited to national and international cooperation in the field of major crimes prevention and to national infrastructures like federal highways, airports, and trains. Yet, where police are investigating crimes that have already taken place (rather than working to prevent future dangers to the public), they are subject to the federal code of criminal procedure, which also regulates the powers of public prosecutors.
- Culture: School and university education, state and church relations. This field used to be quite untouched by federal influence, and it is customary to talk of *Kulturhoheit* (cultural sovereignty) of the *Länder*.
- Procedure in and organization of the respective states themselves: The *Länder* have each their own constitutions, and may freely regulate matters like election of their state parliaments, their budget, their administrative organisation and procedure including that of local governments, as long as Article 28 GG is observed (see below Sects. 9.2.3 and 9.3.1.1). Nonetheless, some important areas are partly subject to federal legislation, especially civil service (Art. 74 sec. 1 no. 27), state liability (Art. 74 sec. 1 no. 25), and public procurement (heavily regulated by the EU and the federal act against restraints on competition).

In these fields, all *Länder* have passed extensive legislation.

9.2.2.3 Coexistence of Central and Component State Regulation

Federal and *Länder* regulation coexist in fields in which federal power is legally limited or has factually been limited to certain aspects of law, e.g. in the field of public service law of the *Länder*, or as far as "regulatory competition" is introduced by Article 72 section 3 GG (see above).

Joint tasks (*Gemeinschaftsaufgaben*) are defined by Articles 91a and 91b GG as matters of co-financing in the area of infrastructure and university planning. This legal instrument, which adds to the powers of the Federation, has been severely restricted by the constitutional reform of 2006.

9.2.3 Lawmaking Power of Municipalities

Municipalities are subject to *Länder* legislation. However, Article 28 section 1 GG guarantees a right to self-administration. Therefore, the *Länder* cannot strip local governments from certain core competences. Most local government codes distinguish between original powers of local governments and state powers delegated to municipalities; autonomy of municipalities is more limited with regard to the latter. The most important case of municipal rule-making is probably the power to pass zoning ordinances. Within the hierarchy of norms, these rules enjoy a lower rank than *Länder* legislation; they are a special form of administrative law-making.

9.3 The Means and Methods of Legal Unification

9.3.1 Legal Unification or Harmonization Through the Exercise of Central Power

By and large, legal unification has been accomplished through federal legislation and its interpretation by federal and state courts to such a high degree that other centrally controlled means, such as centrally managed coordination or information exchange among the component states, do not play a role.

9.3.1.1 Directly Applicable Constitutional Norms

The basic human rights conferred on citizens by the *Grundgesetz* (Arts. 1 to 19) are directly applicable with regard to every act of government in Germany, be it federal or state (Art. 1 section 3 GG). This has led to a certain degree of unification in many fields in which the states have legislative powers, as these areas encompass several basic rights: Article 5 section 3, guaranteeing the freedom of academic teaching and research, corresponds to the *Länder* powers regarding university education; Article 6, guaranteeing parental freedom of education, and Article 7, providing for the government's general responsibility for schooling, bear relevance for matters of primary and high school education. Another example from the school sector in recent times is the influence of Article 4 section 1 – freedom of religion – on *Länder* regulation of teachers and students wearing headscarves for religious reasons. The FCC and the Federal Court of Administrative Law have, in several landmark cases during recent years, ruled on limits of the *Länder's* discretion to ban especially wearing of headscarves by teachers.

Another source of unification is Article 28 GG. According to section 1 of the Article, the constitutional order of the *Länder* must conform to the principles of republican, democratic, and social government, as well as to the rule of law as it is shaped by the *Grundgesetz*. In each of the *Länder*, counties, and municipalities, the people must be represented by a body chosen in general, direct, free, equal, and secret elections. Section 2, guaranteeing autonomy for municipalities, has already been discussed (Sect. 9.2.3).

9.3.1.2 Federal Legislation

As already described (Sect. 9.2.1.4), federal legislation has unified many important areas of law in Germany. It might be added that the unifying effect of federal law is further strengthened by the federal cabinet's power to pass administrative guidelines for the execution of federal statutes by the *Länder* (Art. 84 sec. 2, 85 sec. 2 GG).

Federal statutes mandating state legislation exist today mainly in the form of parliamentary acts by the *Bundestag* empowering the *Länder* administrations to issue regulations (*Rechtsverordnungen*). The power to issue regulations must always be limited by parliamentary statute under the *Grundgesetz* (Art. 80 section 1 GG). *Rahmengesetze*, federal laws defining a legal framework within which the *Länder* could regulate details by their own legislative means, were abolished in the course of constitutional reform in 2006; Article 72 section 3 (see above Sect. 9.2.2.1) was inserted as a replacement.

Federal instruments inducing states to regulate by conditioning the allocation of central money on compliance with central standards or indirectly forcing states to regulate by threatening to take over the field in case of state inaction or state action that does not conform to centrally specified standards are currently not known; due to the prominent role of directly applicable federal legislation there is hardly any need for such means.

9.3.1.3 Judicial Creation of Uniform Norms by Federal Courts

The influence of the judiciary will be discussed below after an overview on the judicial system in Germany (Sect. 9.4.1).

9.3.1.4 Legal Unification Through Formal or Informal Voluntary Coordination Among the Component States

In many areas, there is close cooperation of the *Länder* in matters of legislation. This is mainly a domain of the executive branch. There are committees on all levels from the prime ministers to much more inferior sub-heads of divisions of special ministries. Some co-ordination structures like the conference of ministers of culture even have administrative staff of their own.

Legislative bodies come into play as soon as formal treaties between the *Länder* are involved. For example, this is the case in the field of radio and TV, and also with regard to university admission: The *Länder*, running public universities in Germany, have installed a central (but not federal) agency handling admissions for subjects like medicine in which demand regularly exceeds capacities. This example illustrates at the same time the unifying influence of the basic rights as interpreted by the FCC: The central admissions agency was founded in the first place because the FCC required the states to handle admissions efficiently in order to comply with the constitutional freedom to choose a profession guaranteed by Article 12 GG.

Model Codes have played a certain role in the legislation of the *Länder*, especially in the 1970s, e.g., with regard to municipal law and police law. In the field of administrative agency procedure, the federal statute that regulates federal agency procedure serves as model code. Virtually all *Länder* have passed statutes basically identical to the federal model. Administrative *court* procedure, on the other hand, is regulated uniformly by the federal code of administrative courts procedure – *Verwaltungsgerichtsordnung* – under the "procedure" clause of Article 74 section 1 Number 1 (see above Sect. 9.2.1.4).

The role of component state judiciaries is discussed separately (Sect. 9.4.1).

9.3.2 *Legal Unification Accomplished by Non-state Actors*

As an example of non-state actors accomplishing legal unification to a certain degree, the German Standards Institute (*Deutsches Institut für Normung* – DIN) may be mentioned. It is a private organisation in the field of – mostly technical – standardisation and may be compared with the ISO on the international level. The DIN, for example, plays an important role with regard to certain fields of contract law and public procurement law. Traditionally, the DIN has issued so-called "*Verdingungsordnungen*" consisting of model terms for construction and services contracts and for tender procedures preceding the conclusion of these contracts. The *Bund* and the *Länder* used to prescribe application of these model terms by public authorities through executive orders. These executive orders were usually regarded as binding authorities and used only internally. Thus, (potential) contractors could enforce the model terms only insofar as they were formally integrated into a contract. As contractual terms, however, they were subject to interpretation not only by trial and state courts, but also by the federal courts, as the federal courts are authorized to interpret contractual terms as soon as they are standardly used in an area overlapping the jurisdictions of the state courts of appeal.

The procurement rules were hardly enforceable at all. Even there, however, an indirect unifying effect resulted from the civil case law on pre-contractual liability, which could in certain cases arise from a breach of the DIN model terms. Meanwhile, the model terms of procurement have been transferred into statutory law for procurement projects exceeding the thresholds of the EU directives on public procurement.

In the field of commercial law, commercial custom is recognized as a source of law by section 346 of the federal commercial code (*Handelsgesetzbuch*). Via this clause, model regulations like the INCOTERMS may be used by the courts to define contractual obligations if an individual contract does not regulate certain questions.

9.3.3 The Role of Legal Education and Training in the Unification of Law

Legal education in Germany consists of two phases, a phase of university education (about 4 years) and a phase of practical training (2 years). A state examination organised (mainly) by state ministries of justice takes place after each phase. Law schools draw students from throughout the federal system. Legal education focuses mostly on federal law with the exception of administrative law, which covers police law and municipal law. In general, mobility of graduates is high, starting with the possibility to switch to another state for practical training after the first state exam. After the second state exam, graduates tend to set up their practice or take jobs anywhere in the Federation. Testing for bar admission is state-wide; however, the actual admission to the bar is for the entire federal system except when applying for the bar of the *Bundesgerichtshof* (federal Supreme Court) in civil matters.

9.3.4 External Factors Influencing Legal Unification

As repeatedly mentioned before, European law is an important external factor in unifying the legal order in Germany. The EU has legislative powers in many fields subject to *Länder* jurisdiction and may regulate matters either directly (via regulations) or indirectly via directives which the *Länder* then have to implement. Currently, for example, the *Länder* have long realised the influence exerted upon their sphere of competence from Brussels and are actively involved in the European legislative process through the Committee of the Regions. They also have own representations in Brussels. A staged system of *Länder* participation in the decision-making process of the European Union depending on the grade of involvement of state interests is prescribed by Article 23 GG.

To a lesser degree, the European Convention of Human Rights and the case law of the European Court of Human Rights may lead to unified rules in certain fields. Decisions of the Court are not directly applicable in Germany, but according to the FCC, they have to be taken into account to a degree that for practical purposes comes close to direct applicability after all.

International voluntary coordination has been an increasing factor since the 1990s, especially in the field of education through the Organisation for Economic Co-operation and Development OECD. The *Länder* participate in the PISA studies, a comparative study between member states on the state of school education with the conference of ministers of culture playing a central role. The PISA results have been subject to an intense public discussion, and may have increased competitive elements in German federalism, as the *Länder* aim at good results especially for their own educational systems. Another example is the Bologna process aiming to unify academic credit systems and grades and to foster Europe-wide mobility of students. It has been implemented to a large degree by the *Länder*. Nevertheless, critical voices are still to be heard, especially in the field of legal education which so far has remained quite untouched by the Bologna process (see also above).

9.4 Institutional and Social Background

9.4.1 The Judicial Branch

9.4.1.1 Overview

State and federal courts form parts of an integrated judicial system in Germany. The judiciary as a whole is heavily regulated by federal law. It is divided into five branches: There are ordinary courts (with civil and criminal sections), labor courts, administrative courts, tax courts, and social security courts. In each of these branches (with the exception of tax courts), there are trial courts and appellate courts on state level and a supreme appellate court at the federal level. Appeals to the federal courts are in general limited to cases of a certain importance. At the trial courts, suits are in most cases decided by mixed panels of one to three professional judges and two lay judges. In civil matters, no lay judges are involved. The courts of appeal and the federal courts in labor and social security matters also have lay judges drawn from competing social groups (such as employers and employees as lay judges in labor courts).

There is in general no formal principle of *stare decisis*; theoretically, a court may disregard all kinds of precedents as long as it is convinced that its own interpretation of the law is correct. However, in practice, courts are taking case law from courts throughout the Federation into account. The chance that a judgment may be appealed, however, will often lead to special attention being paid to the case law of the courts that would decide on an appeal.

Limited *stare decisis* is provided for by federal law with regard to the state courts of appeal and the federal courts. If one of these courts intends to decide a question of federal law in a way differing from existing decisions of courts at the same level, it has to refer the question to the court of next higher instance. In the case of the federal courts, this means that the question will have to be decided by a joint senate of the five federal supreme courts.

9.4.1.2 Judicial Creation of Uniform Norms

As precedents are not formally binding under German law, with the sole exception of certain decisions by the FCC (sec. 31 of the FCC statute), courts cannot in a technical sense create norms. However, decisions by the higher courts – especially the federal supreme courts – will usually be followed. *Rechtsfortbildung*, i. e. the development of the law, is named explicitly as a task for the federal courts in several federal statutes. The influence of courts upon the law as it is applied is traditionally strong, especially in the field of civil law. For decades, rules of pre-contractual liability (*culpa in contrahendo*) have been applied by the civil courts according to landmark decisions going back to around 1900, although there were no statutory norms providing for such liability to be found within the civil code. State liability is another interesting case: Although some basic provisions exist (partly in the civil code and partly in the *Grundgesetz*), important legal doctrines have been developed entirely by the (federal) judiciary. Interestingly enough, an attempt of the *Bund* to pass a statute on state liability failed in 1982; the statute was declared void by the FCC for lack of federal competence. In 1994, a federal legislative competence for state liability was inserted into the *Grundgesetz*, but so far it has not been used.

Thus, the federal courts' "case law" does have a strong unifying effect. Technically, however, what the federal courts do is interpretation of federal statutory law. As a rule, they are not entitled to interpret state law. Certain exceptions apply in the field of administrative law to the extent it is textually identical with federal law; also, the *Länder* may delegate the power to decide appeals on questions of state law to the federal courts (Art. 99 GG). But for the most part, there is no court at the central level with power authoritatively to interpret component state law.

When looking at the role of the *Länder* judiciaries, one must keep in mind that the law that most state courts enforce most of the time is federal law. This is especially true with regard to civil and criminal courts. Only administrative courts have to deal with state law to a significant degree. As far as interpretation of federal law goes, courts will usually take into account decisions of courts throughout the republic, regardless of the *Land* they belong to. The same is probably true with regard to state law to the extent that the *Länder* norms concerned are similar.

9.4.1.3 Constitutional Courts

Constitutional courts play a special role within the judiciary. Citizens may invoke the FCC's jurisdiction, for example, only after the ordinary course of remedies against an act of government has been exhausted. The Court may then decide only questions of federal constitutional law, while state constitutional courts may review decisions of state courts and agencies with regard to state constitutional law. The *Grundgesetz* allows a *Land* to delegate jurisdiction over state constitutional matters to the FCC (Art. 99 GG). Until a few years ago, the *Land* of Schleswig-Holstein had made use of this possibility. Nowadays, constitutional courts exist in all states; their practical impact, however, should not be overestimated.

The FCC is explicitly appointed to resolve conflicts between the Federation and the *Länder* (*Bund-Länder-Streit*), or among the *Länder* in the case of alleged breaches of constitutional obligations (Art. 93 section 1 no. 3, 4). The FCC also has competence to decide upon the compatibility of state law with federal law or the constitution, as well as the compatibility of federal law with the constitution (see explicitly Article 93 section 1 number 2 GG; this power can become relevant in other kinds of procedures as well). The latter competence includes the power to police whether federal legislation has exceeded the lawmaking power allocated to the federal government. A "compatibility" decision of the FCC can be requested by state governments, by one third of the *Bundestag*, or by the federal government. There is also a special procedure of federal character affecting the compatibility of federal statutes with Article 72 section 2 GG. Municipalities have the possibility of lodging a constitutional complaint alleging that their guaranteed autonomy rights under Article 28 GG have been infringed by the legislature (Art. 93 section 1 no. 4b GG). In the past, the FCC has repeatedly struck down federal statutes as well as *Länder* statutes for lack of competence.

9.4.2 Relations Between the Central and Component States Governments

9.4.2.1 Power of the Central Government to Force Component States to Legislate

While one can argue that the legislative "framework" power formerly stated in Article 75 included the Federation's power to make the *Länder* pass legislation, no such power is to be found in current constitutional law after the repeal of that Article. It is not clear how the FCC would react if the *Bund* tried to "commandeer" legislation by the states. This has not been attempted in practice.

Therefore, the question whether the *Bund* could enforce such obligations is largely theoretical as well. Procedurally, the *Bund* could file a *Bund-Länder-Streit* at the FCC. Reasons for such a lawsuit could arise in the context of implementation of EU directives. The *Bund* might be interested in forcing a *Land* to implement a directive on matters within the *Länder* competences, since the Commission could sue Germany – that is, the Federation – for breach of the EU Treaty due to a lack of correct implementation (Art. 258 TFEU). In the case of a verdict for penalty payments against Germany (Art. 260 sec.2 subsec. 2 TFEU), the *Bund* could also try to sue for damages against the *Land* or the *Länder* responsible for the delayed implementation. However, there have not been any such suits so far.

9.4.2.2 Execution of Federal Law

The basic rule of the *Grundgesetz* is that the *Länder* execute federal laws in their own right (Art. 83 GG). "In their own right" means, first, that there is no direct hierarchical control exerted by the federal government. While the Federal Government may, with the consent of the *Bundesrat*, issue general administrative rules (Art. 84 sec. 2) and exercise oversight to ensure that the *Länder* execute federal laws properly (Art. 84 sec. 3), it cannot order the *Land* to act in a certain way. Its only method of enforcement is to ask the *Bundesrat* for a determination whether that *Land* has violated the law, and if the *Bundesrat* refuses, to file a suit with the FCC (Art. 84 sec. 4).

Second, administration in the *Länder's* "own right" allows the *Länder* to establish the requisite authorities and regulate their administrative procedures themselves. If federal laws provide otherwise, the *Länder* may enact deviating regulations (see Art. 84 sec. 1 for further details).

In certain – rare – cases, the *Länder* execute federal laws not in their own right, but on federal commission (Art. 85); this is the case, for example, in the field of production and utilization of nuclear energy (Art. 87c). Most important, this means that the *Land* authorities have to follow instructions from the competent highest federal authorities (Art. 85 sec. 3).

Third and finally, in some areas federal law is executed by federal agencies. Article 87 states that foreign service, federal financial administration, and administration of federal waterways and shipping shall be conducted by federal administrative authorities with their own administrative substructures, and that a federal law may establish Federal Police authorities. There is also a federal defence administration (Art. 87b). Another example of federal administration is the federal bank, whose competences have – in accordance with Article 88 GG – been transferred to the European Central Bank to a significant degree.

Financial administration is, as an exceptional case, to a certain degree "mixed". Most taxes are administered by the financial authorities of the *Länder*; federal tax authorities administer customs duties and some other taxes. The organization of the *Länder* authorities and the uniform training of their civil servants may be regulated by a federal law requiring the consent of the *Bundesrat*. Inasmuch as intermediate authorities have been established, their heads are appointed in agreement with the Federal Government (Art. 108 sec. 2). The Federation, on the other hand, has to consult *Land* governments when appointing heads of federal intermediate authorities (Art. 108 sec. 1). A federal law requiring the consent of the *Bundesrat* may provide for collaboration between federal and *Land* revenue authorities in certain matters of tax administration (Art. 108 sec. 4).

In general, however, "mixed" administration is not tolerated by the *Grundgesetz*. In 2003, the Federation passed a law establishing "mixed" agencies in the field of social security. The idea was that the federal employment agency and the municipalities should form joint ventures in order to provide a "one-stop system" for welfare benefits for the unemployed. After some municipalities and counties had sued against the reform, the FCC struck down the provisions about the joint ventures in December 2007, arguing that because such a form of mixed administration was not provided for in the *Grundgesetz*, it infringed the guarantee of local autonomy in Article 28 sec. 2 GG. The Court set a deadline for the federal legislature to reform the law by December 2010. This resulted in a new Art. 91e GG being inserted into the constitution, providing for cooperation of federal and state/municipal authorities in respect of basic support for persons seeking employment.

9.4.2.3 Representation of Component States at the Central Level, and Their Role in the Central Legislative Process

The *Länder* participate in the legislation and administration of the Federation and in matters concerning the European Union through the *Bundesrat* (Art. 50). The *Bundesrat* consists of members of the *Land* governments appointed (and recallable) by these governments (see Art. 51). A *Land's* number of votes depends on its population and ranges from three to six. Depending on the subject matter of a bill adopted by the *Bundestag*, the *Bundesrat* either has to consent to it or only has the possibility to object. While the *Bundestag* may overrule an objection by the *Bundesrat*, there is no comparable possibility when consent of the *Bundesrat* is necessary. A Joint Committee made up of members of both the *Bundestag* and the *Bundesrat* will attempt to find solutions in cases of differences between the two chambers of parliament (Art. 53a GG). Reduction of the number of cases in which consent of the *Bundesrat* is needed was a main purpose of the constitutional reform 2006, because the permanent need for consent among the *Länder* governments made it very difficult for the parliamentary majority at the *Bundestag* to pass laws on controversial subjects. Since the late 1970s, the political majority in the *Bundestag* has often differed from the majority in the *Bundesrat*. This made it necessary in many cases to organise all-party coalitions in order to pass legislation.

According to Article 76 sec. 1 GG, the *Bundesrat* (i.e. its majority) may introduce bills in the House of Representatives (*Bundestag*). The *Bundesrat* is entitled to state its position on bills of the Government before they are submitted to the *Bundestag*.

9.4.3 Taxation and Revenue Sharing

9.4.3.1 The Power to Tax

Article 105 sec. 1 of the Basic Law empowers the Federation to legislate on customs duties and fiscal monopolies and allocates to the Federation the concurrent power to legislate on all other taxes the revenue from which accrues to it wholly or in part or where the conditions provided for in Article 72 sec. 2 apply. The Federation has partly transferred its competences to Brussels – customs duties are regulated as well as collected by the EU – and has exhausted its concurrent powers. For practical purposes, the component states' legislative powers are limited to the ones explicitly named in Article 105 sec. 2a, i.e. the power to legislate on local excise taxes (which, however, has mostly been delegated to the municipalities) and, since 2006, the power to set the rate for the tax on real estate sales.

Identical taxes are prohibited. Taxes are identical when the facts justifying the taxation coincide and the same source of economical capability is charged. This is especially the case when the object and criteria of taxation coincide. This prohibition is explicitly mentioned in Article 105 IIa to restrict the exclusive power of the *Länder*.

9.4.3.2 General Constitutional and Legislative Rules on Revenue Sharing

A highly complicated system governs revenue sharing in Germany.

In a first step, Article 106 GG distributes the yield of different taxes between the Federation, the *Länder*, and the municipalities ("primary vertical financial balancing"). While the yield of certain taxes is given exclusively to either the Federation or the *Länder* (Art. 106 sec. 1, 2), the most lucrative tax revenues accrue to the *Länder* and the Federation jointly: Article 106 sec. 3 names the income taxes, corporation taxes and turnover taxes. The revenues of income taxes and corporation taxes accrue to the Federation and the component states in equal shares. The sharing of the revenue of the turnover taxes is determined by federal statute (requiring the consent of the *Bundesrat*) following certain constitutional principles.

In a second step, tax yields accruing to the *Länder* are attributed to the single states by Article 107 ("primary horizontal financial balancing"). In a third step, Article 107 provides for the so-called secondary horizontal financial balancing process: In order to ensure a reasonable equalization of the disparate financial capacities of the *Länder*, with due regard for the financial capacities and needs of municipalities, the Federation is required to pass a law governing claims of "poorer" *Länder* against "richer" ones for equalization payments, as well as the criteria for determining the amounts of such payments. Finally, as a fourth step, financially weak Länder may receive – and in extreme cases be entitled to – supplementary allocation of funds from the Federation ("secondary vertical financial balancing").

The whole process does not aim at total equality of financial resources but at a compensation for structural disadvantages of certain states. As one can easily imagine, it leads to a lot of disputes between the Federation and the *Länder*, and also (or even more) between "rich" and "poor" states.

9.4.4 The Bureaucracy

The Federation and the *Länder* each have their own civil service. So far, the cultures and legal frameworks are very similar for several reasons. First, Article 33 section 5 states that the law governing the public service shall be regulated and developed "with due regard to the traditional principles of the professional civil service". These principles, including life-long employment, due financial compensation, and eligibility of any citizen for public office according to his or her aptitude, qualifications and professional achievements (Art. 33 section 2), are strictly enforced by the FCC; they are binding on the Federation and the *Länder* as well. Second, until 2006, the Federation had a "framework" legislative competence for matters of the civil service, leaving very limited freedom for regulation by the *Länder*. But since the reform of 2006, the states have the power to define careers and salary of their civil service as they like. This will probably lead to greater differences between the states in the future.

Lateral mobility between civil services of different states is theoretically possible but – apart from the case of university professors – difficult and rare in practice. Mobility from state civil services to federal civil services is much higher. Many holders of federal offices have started their careers within the civil services of the states. This is especially true with respect to federal judges and prosecutors; virtually all of them (with the FCC being an exception) are drawn from state judiciaries.

9.4.5 Social Factors

Racial, ethnic, religious, linguistic or other social cleavages within the Federal Republic of Germany should not be overestimated. However, some aspects may be highlighted.

There is probably still a certain cultural cleavage between traditionally Protestant regions – e.g., the very north of Germany or Württemberg (a region in the southwest of Germany around Stuttgart) – and Catholic areas such as the Rhineland (Bonn, Cologne, and their surroundings) or Bavaria.

Then, due to obvious historical reasons, differences exist between the "old" *Länder* in the west and the eastern *Länder* forming the GDR before 1990. There is still a considerable amount of special federal legal regulations directed at the situation of the "new" states, e.g. special taxation rules. However, different states perform differently beyond these group identities. To give but one example, former East German states are to be found among the groups of most and least indebted states in the Federation as well.

Since the 1980s there has been a social asymmetry between southern states (Bavaria, Baden-Württemberg, Saxonia, Thuringia) and northern states in which the south performs better in many regards and is socially and politically more conservative than the north. The most important legal effect is the distribution of taxes and its consequences for the financial balancing process mentioned above. In historical perspective, natural resources have played a certain role in this context: Nordrhein-Westfalen, for example, was a financially strong state as long as its coal deposits were an important economic factor. Today, coal mining in Germany is economically possible only with large sums of state subsidies, and Nordrhein-Westfalen has become one of the receiving states in the financial balancing process.

Distinct ethnic groups play a role on a state level rather than on a federal level. In Schleswig-Holstein there is a Danish minority with special provisions guaranteeing their representation in Parliament. Parts of the population of Brandenburg and Sachsen belong to the Slavic people of the *Sorben*; they enjoy certain privileges such as speaking their language in court.

9.5 Conclusion

In Germany, the central instrument for unification of the legal order has always been the federal power to regulate matters directly. This starts with the great codifications of German private, commercial, and penal law under the constitutional monarchy in the nineteenth century. On the whole, this has led to a highly uniform legal order within Germany. Legislative powers of the states remain mostly in the realm of administrative and somewhat technical law. Most matters subject to intense public discussion, such as penal law, family law, or labor law, are federalized. In this situation, other ways and means of legal harmonisation are rarely used.

German federalism can be characterized as an "executive federalism" (*Böckenförde*), meaning that the political meaning of federalism lies in the power of the states to implement federal laws and in the political influences of the *Länder* executives on the federal level, above all through the *Bundesrat*.

Chapter 10
India: From Political Federalism and Fiscal Centralization to Greater Subnational Autonomy

Sunita Parikh

10.1 Overview

The historical foundations of Indian federalism derive from a disparate range of factors. First, during British colonial rule, control was divided between direct rule of British provinces and indirect rule of Indian Princely States. The British provinces retained considerable political and economic autonomy, and although the Princely States were in practice subject to British authority, they were politically quite diverse. The creation of Pakistan and the departure of the Muslim League from Indian politics removed the most powerful voice for a weak central government and autonomous sub-national units, and the dominant Indian National Congress strongly preferred a centralized institutional structure. But the integration of the Princely States into independent India, the legacy of provincial discretion, and the adoption of the framework of the Government of India Act of 1935 all contributed to the development of constitutional provisions for a federal system.

Within the federal framework, however, there were historical precedents and institutional mechanisms that provided opportunities for centralizing power in the national government, especially in the judicial and legislative arenas. Despite the lack of an indigenous apex court until 1937 – appeals from the provincial High Courts were heard by the Privy Council in London – the judiciary had been integrated for nearly a century. After the establishment of India as a Crown Colony of the British Empire in 1858, the East India Company courts and the British Crown courts were unified into a single hierarchy in each British province. The Government of India Act introduced an apex court, the Federal Court of India,

---

S. Parikh (✉)
Department of Political Science, Washington University in St. Louis, St. Louis, MO, USA
e-mail: saparikh@wustl.edu

to hear disputes among provinces and the Princely States, and the new Constitution of India essentially transformed this court into the Supreme Court of India, retaining its justices, its conditions of judicial appointment, and its jurisdictions.

Just as unification of the judiciary was achieved by wholesale adoption of the colonial judicial structure, the harmonization of Indian law has been aided by the continuation of British common law and the Penal and Civil Codes introduced in the nineteenth and early twentieth centuries, as well as by the constitutional primacy of national legislation. Yet, an important exception to this centralization of judicial and legislative authority can be found in policies that recognize ethnic diversity. For example, although most religious communities are subject to secular common law, Indian Muslims are still governed by Islamic Law (*sharia*) in areas of personal law. In addition, several Indian states have established their own policies for low-caste groups known as Other Backward Classes (OBCs), and these policies can diverge widely because they reflect historical and contextual characteristics. Nevertheless, despite the religious, linguistic, and economic diversity that characterizes Indian society, the overall tenor of Indian law and legislation reflects a centralized authority that allows sub-national units autonomy in a highly circumscribed set of policy areas.

10.2 The Federal Distribution and Exercise of Lawmaking Power

The general framework of the constitution recognizes a division of power among the national, state, and municipal levels. For the first four decades after independence was achieved, the vast majority of power was allocated between the center and the state governments, with municipalities having restricted areas of influence. The 1992 passage of the 73rd Amendment to the Constitution empowered municipal governments, known as panchayats, with great powers to raise revenue, pursue social justice policies, and direct economic development.

Articles 245 and 246 of the Constitution stipulate the distribution of legislative powers between the central government and the states. These powers are enumerated in Lists 1, 2 and 3 of the 7th Schedule of the Constitution.

List 1 specifies those matters over which the Union Parliament has full and exclusive power to legislate. It comprises 99 items, including defense, military forces, defense industries, international affairs, major ports, communication (posts, telegraphs, and broadcasting), interstate commerce, regulation of trading corporations and multi-state companies, insurance, trademarks and patents, acquisition of property, industries "in the public interest," mines and oilfields, interstate rivers, higher education standards, major monuments and archaeological sites, union and state elections, taxes on non-agricultural income, customs and excise taxes, corporate taxes, and estate taxes.

The most important and most frequently used sources of central power are trade and commerce, taxes, acquisition of property, defense, Article 356 (President's Rule), preventive detention, Scheduled Caste/Schedule Tribe affairs, patents, trademark and copyright, mining and oil, customs and excise, income tax.

List 2 of the 7th Schedule enumerates 61 items that are within the states' exclusive powers to legislate. They include maintenance of public order, police, judicial administration below the High Court level, prisons, public health and sanitation, regulation of alcohol production, sales, and consumption, land reform, water, intrastate trade and commerce, universities, betting and gambling, agricultural income taxes, property taxes, *octroi*, sales taxes, and luxury taxes. The most important areas of exclusive component state regulation are the areas of public order, police, sales and *octroi* taxes, land reform, agricultural regulation, administration of justice, and universities.

List 3 of the 7th Schedule enumerates 52 items over which the central and state governments have concurrent powers. They include criminal law, preventive detention at the state level, marriage and other personal law, bankruptcy, revenue and special courts, civil procedure, regulation and maintenance of forests, trade union and industrial disputes, charitable institutions, workplace regulation, education, and contracts. The exercise of central concurrent power does not prevent the states from exercising their concurrent power. Nevertheless, with a very limited exception, state laws must be in harmony with central legislation. Article 248 stipulates that residual power resides with the Union Parliament.

Article 254(1) states that with regard to List 3, where the Union and State Legislatures have concurrent powers, if a State law relating to a concurrent subject is "repugnant" to a Union Law relating to the same subject, then, whether the Union law is prior or later in time, the Union law will prevail and the State law shall, to the extent of such repugnancy, be void. The one exception to this doctrine can be found when the President of India has assented to the state law: the State Act will prevail in the state and overrule the provisions of the Central Act in the applicability to that State only.

The Doctrine of Severability further stipulates that if a portion of a statute is found to be invalid, the remainder of that statute may be retained as long as it is independent of the invalid portion. If the statute can no longer be implemented without recourse to the invalid portion, then the entire statute becomes invalid.

There are three levels of municipal government in India: *panchayats* at the village level, municipal councils for small towns, and municipal corporations for cities. The increased powers accorded them since the implementation of the 73rd and 74th Amendments have led to greater local responsibilities for the development and implementation of economic policies, as well as more local governance over health and education. While the bulk of revenue is still raised by the center and the states, the local units have acquired greater discretion over spending.

10.3 The Means and Methods of Legal Unification

10.3.1 Legal Unification Through the Exercise of Central Power (Top Down) via Directly Applicable Constitutional Norms

The Constitution of India is the only constitutional document; there are no state-level constitutions, and citizenship inheres only at the national level rather than coexisting at the state and national levels. The allocation of residual power to the center, the greater allocation of exclusive powers of legislation to the center, and the doctrines of repugnancy and severability all serve to harmonize legislation and statutes according to the preferences of the central government. Articles 249 and 250 specify the conditions under which the Union Parliament is empowered to pass legislation that is ordinarily allocated exclusively to the states in List 2 of the 7th Schedule. Responsibilities for the protection and implementation of the Fundamental Rights and Directive Principles of State Policy, enumerated in Parts I, II, and IV of the Constitution (Articles 12 through 51) lie with the central government, as does the ultimate responsibility for the protection of minority groups.

While the states and the center have concurrent powers over criminal and civil procedure, the Codes of Civil and Criminal Procedure, the Indian Penal Code, and other administrative and legal statutes derived from the colonial Anglo-Indian codes are all promulgated and revised at the central government level.

The Supreme Court's appellate jurisdiction requires it to consider and reconcile contradictory decisions that are issued by the High Courts, which are the equivalent of State Supreme Courts. In India's integrated judicial system, there is no appellate judiciary separate from the High Courts.

10.3.2 Unification Through Formal or Informal Voluntary Coordination Among the Component States (Bottom Up)

There are no formal mechanisms for coordination among the states. High Court justices of a component state will regularly refer to the decisions of their counterparts in their opinions; the decisions of the older and more prestigious High Courts, e.g. Bombay, Calcutta, Madras and Allahabad, will frequently appear as influences on decisions in other courts In addition, there are informal and formal personnel appointments that increase coordination. Registrars and Secretaries of the

High and Supreme Courts are regularly appointed as justices to High Courts, and Supreme Court justices frequently join High Court benches during the Supreme Court's recess periods.

10.3.3 Unification Through Non-state Actors

By far the most important non-state institution contributing to legal unification is the Law Commission. The Law Commission of India was established in 1955 and given responsibility to recommend revisions of laws inherited from the colonial period. Since that Commission concluded its 3-year term in 1958, 16 Commissions have succeeded it, issuing over 200 reports with recommendations for revisions that include harmonization and unification of existing laws. The Commission considers, among other issues, disparities among High Court decisions: for example, Report #136 examined "Conflicts in High Court Decisions on Central Laws – How to foreclose and how to resolve."

In addition to the Law Commission, there is also the Indian Law Institute, which is a quasi-independent research and training institute with university-level status. It trains LLM and PhD students, holds workshops and seminars, and publishes a law journal.

10.3.4 The Role of Legal Education and Training in Unification

Legal training in India contributes to the unification of law. There are two forms of legal training in higher education, the traditional 3-year law curriculum and the more recently established specialized law institutes. The curricula of both types of institutions are regulated and supervised by the Bar Council of India. Legal education focuses almost exclusively on system-wide law.

As with other institutions of higher education, law colleges tend to attract students from the states in which they are located. The specialized law universities draw students from throughout the federal system.

The Bar Council of India supervises and regulates admission to the bar, which is system-wide. Once an applicant has finished the legal training requirements and successfully passed the Bar Council examination, he is eligible to practice throughout India. Practically speaking, the vast majority of advocates practice in their home states and localities.

The Indian Law Institute and the specialized universities have taken a leading role in providing LLM and PhD training which are more closely comparable to North American law schools. Supreme Court Justices usually select their clerks from the specialized law universities. Justices of High Courts may sit as Acting or Additional Justices on other state High Courts (Article 224A).

10.3.5 External Influences on Unification

Indian Courts are frequently aware of and sensitive to international legal obligations when issuing rulings, but the overall impact is difficult to quantify. Indian legal professionals regularly participate in international projects, through the UN agencies and other organizations.

10.4 Institutional and Social Background

10.4.1 The Judicial Branch

The Constitution of India grants the Supreme Court original and appellate jurisdiction in reviewing the constitutionality of legislation, as well as disputes between the Union Government and the states or between states. It is the final appellate court for all cases arising from the states. There are subordinate courts at the state level, and each state has a High Court, which has both original and appellate jurisdiction. There are no central trial courts apart from the Supreme Court, which has original jurisdiction over a number of issues and functions as a trial court.

The Supreme Court currently comprises 31 justices including the Chief Justice. The Court is divided into benches of two, three, or four justices to hear ordinary cases and five or more justices to hear cases with constitutional ramifications. If the Court reconsiders a case that was previously decided by a constitution bench, the new bench must be larger than the previous one. Thus, the Court sat in an *en banc* panel of 13 justices to decide the *Keshavananda Bharati v. State of Kerala* (1973) case, which reconsidered the decision in *Golak Nath and others v. State of Punjab* (1967), which had been decided by a previous *en banc* panel of 11).

Below the High Court level, state governments convene District Courts at the level of the administrative districts, and subordinate courts for civil and criminal jurisdiction. There are also special courts established by statute that hear cases related to the specific subjects, e.g. the Anti-Hijacking Act (1982), The Immoral Traffic (Prevention) Act (1987), the Narcotic Drugs and Psychotropic Substances (Amendment) Act (1988), the Prevention and Corruption Act (1988), and the Terrorist Affected Areas (Special Courts) Act (1984). Finally, the recognition of Muslim personal law, or *sharia*, has led to the establishment of *sharia* personal law courts.

The large backlog of cases that has accumulated at every level of the judiciary has led to the establishment of Fast Track courts and *Lok Adalats*. The latter courts are designed as an alternative dispute resolution mechanism and are intended to reach compromises rather than adjudicate between adversarial positions. There are also dispute resolution systems that provide an alternative to the governmental *sharia* courts, including *dal ul qaza* courts.

The Supreme Court has asserted its authority over constitutional issues from the year of its inception, when it struck down all or part of central and state laws regarding acquisition of property and preventive detention on the grounds that they violated the Fundamental Rights provisions of the Constitution. The Court battled the executive branch throughout the 1950s and 1960s on the issue of compensation for acquired property and asserted its primacy over constitutional issues in *Golak Nath and others v. State of Punjab* (1967). In that decision, the Court asserted that there was a "basic structure" to the Constitution and that Parliament's amending power did not encompass the abridging of the Fundamental Rights provisions. In 1971, after a landslide victory, Indira Gandhi's Congress-dominated Parliament responded by passing three constitutional amendments that specifically granted Parliament the rights that *Golak Nath* had curtailed. Two years later, in *Keshavananda Bharati v. State of Kerala* (1973), the Court overruled many of the holdings of *Golak Nath* but retained its insistence on the basic structure argument, of which the most important components were the Fundamental Rights. The Parliament retaliated by ignoring the norms by which Chief Justices were selected and by passing amendments which explicitly revoked the Court's power of judicial review. The authority that the Court lost in these amendments was restored by the post-Emergency Janata Government in 1977, and in the 1980 *Minerva Mills v. Union of India* case, the Court and the recently reelected Congress government compromised by accepting the basic structure argument for Fundamental Rights while removing the right to property from that list.

While the above cases have been crucial in limiting the potentially unchecked power of the Union Government, the Supreme Court has been less aggressive in challenging another arena in which the center has dominated the states. Article 356 provides for the dissolution of state governments by the President of India in the event of a "breakdown of the constitutional machinery." This Article, which was carried over from the colonial Government of India Act, was hotly debated in the Constituent Assembly amid fears that it would be used for political purposes rather than as a power of last resort. These fears have been realized, as President's Rule has been invoked to dissolve elected state governments more than 100 times; an expert observer estimates that over half of these uses have been political rather than necessary according to the stipulated constitutional conditions. Nevertheless, while the Supreme Court has occasionally challenged the imposition of President's Rule, it has done so with great caution at best and great timidity at worst.

The imposition of President's Rule and the use of this instrument for political gain was greatest in the era of majority Congress Party government, especially during periods when the Party was trying to shore up its electoral support or recoup losses. Since 1992, the constraints of coalition governments at the center and the strength of regional parties in the states have resulted in a decrease in the use of President's Rule.

10.4.2 Relations Between the Central and Component State Governments

In addition to its constitutional authority to legislate on state issues, the central government has authority to legislate on issues from List 2 of the 7th Schedule that pertain to two or more states. Parliament does not have the power to compel a single state to legislate on issues relevant only to that state. Historically, the dominance of the Congress party at the central and state levels has led to uniformity between the two, but with the advent of coalition governments and strong state-centric parties, the formal boundaries may be more frequently tested.

Central government law is executed by central agencies as well as by the component states. For example, certain taxes are levied by the central government but collected and remitted back to the center by state agencies. The Finance Commission and the Planning Commission require states to execute aspects of the Five Year Plans, which are centrally devised. Analogously, criminal and civil procedures are concurrent list subjects, and the laws are promulgated by the center, but the judicial administration below the High Courts is the responsibility of the component states.

The *Rajya Sabha*, or Council of States, which is the upper house of the bicameral Union Parliament, represents the states in the central government. It is elected by members of the state legislative assemblies. The number of members per state is determined by a method of proportional representation.

Both the central and component state governments have the power to tax, but the majority of taxing authority lies with the central government. The specific areas of taxation are stipulated in the Lists of the 7th Schedule. To date, the central government's dominance in taxation has meant that multiple taxation across state levels has not been an issue. With the economic reforms and political decentralization of the last decade, however, this relationship may change.

Articles 268 through 293 specify the distribution of revenues between the central government and the states. The Finance Commission, which is a constitutionally mandated ministry, is responsible for distributing financial resources according to the mandates of the Directive Principles and other provisions in the constitution. Of historically greater importance is the Planning Commission, an extra-constitutional organization responsible for formulating and implementing the economic Five Year Plans. From the 1950s through the 1990s, the bulk of national revenues were allocated according to Plan directives. While state leaders are frequently members of the Planning Commission and wield influence in the Plan process, there are no formal channels through which all states' interests are expressed.

The economic reforms initiated in the late 1980s and early 1990s have eased restrictions on economic policy making by the states, but the extent to which states have been able to take advantage of increased economic power has varied considerably. The vast majority of taxing power continues to lie with the center, but more prosperous states, as well as those which have been able to attract outside investment, have grown at a greater rate than poorer states and those with inferior infrastructure.

In addition, although states' ability to borrow are formally constrained by the requirement for central government approval, state borrowing and debt loads increased dramatically under decentralization. Politicians engaged in competitive electoral races frequently resort to inefficient economic subsidies in order to attract votes, and given the fragile nature of coalitions at the center, their political influence reinforces the cycle of borrowing and makes it difficult for the center to impose hard budget constraints.

10.4.3 The Bureaucracy

There are national Civil Services (e.g., Indian Administrative Service, Indian Police Service, Indian Forest Service) and analogous state-level bureaucracies. Members of the national civil services may be assigned either to the central government or to state-level "cadres." Admission to all services is obtained through a highly competitive exam system. There is a single central-level exam, and the applicant's performance on the exam determines the specific cadre to which s/he will be invited. The IAS cadre is the most prestigious and most competitive. Some cadres, such as the Indian Statistical Service, admit new members according to specialized skills.

There is very little mobility between the two civil service systems. The exams are separate and the status of the all-India services is much higher than that of the state services. Since exams are taken by applicants in their 20s, it is difficult to shift from one to the other.

10.4.4 Social Factors

India is an extremely heterogeneous nation, and its heterogeneity is one of the factors behind the founding elites' choice of a federal system. The partition of British India into the independent nations of India and Pakistan drew attention away from another difficult task: integrating the hundreds of nominally sovereign Princely States into these newly independent polities. The vast majority of States were incorporated into the sovereignties that surrounded them, but a handful were either resistant to join or were ambivalent about which nation to choose. For example, the sovereign of the Princely State of Hyderabad expressed a wish either to stay independent or to join Pakistan, despite Hyderabad's geographical location in southern India, hundreds of miles from either Pakistani territory. Hyderabad was eventually incorporated into India after a show of force by the Indian military.

The Maharajah of Jammu and Kashmir's sudden decision to sign the instruments of accession in 1948, after a threat of insurgency, has created not only an enduring, open-ended conflict between India and Pakistan, but it led to the creation of autonomous provisions that give Kashmir a special status within the Indian federal system. Article 370 of the Constitution limits the power of the national parliament to make laws for the State only in the areas of defense, foreign affairs and communications.

The 8th Schedule of the constitution lists 18 official languages, not including English, and this linguistic heterogeneity reflects regionally specific ethnic identities. The Census of India enumerates six distinct religious affiliations, of which Muslims and Sikhs comprise the largest proportions. The Constitution recognizes and categorizes the lowest categories of the Hindu caste system and the aboriginal population as Scheduled Castes and Scheduled Tribes respectively; these groups are granted reserved seats in parliament as well as affirmative action in national institutions of higher education and public employment. Reservations are roughly according to their percentage of the population, which is 14 and 7 % respectively. In addition, the Supreme Court, the Union Parliament, and several State Assemblies have recognized other low-caste groups, termed Other Backward Classes (OBCs) and provided affirmative action in higher education and employment at the national levels and within analogous state institutions in some (but not all) states.

The provision of reservations to SC/ST groups was expanded at the national and state levels without much opposition, but the extension to OBC groups, especially in states outside southern India and at the national level, was met with considerable opposition and at times led to sustained, deadly violence between social groups and between members of competing political parties. The Supreme Court's decision in *Indira Sawhney v. Union of India and others* (1992) upheld the constitutionality of OBC reservations to national institutions of education and employment, including the prestigious Indian Administrative Service and the Indian Institutes of Technology. It emphasized in its ruling, however, that the government was responsible for identifying and excluding the "creamy layer" of OBC groups, i.e., those members who were the best off social and economically, and who therefore did not need the compensatory benefits of reservations.

Some groups are relatively evenly dispersed throughout the federation, although they are more numerous in some states than others; Muslims, Christians, Scheduled Castes and Scheduled Tribes fall into this category, since they are found in every state. Other groups are more concentrated; Sikhs, for example, are overwhelmingly found in Punjab state and more recently in Delhi state. The northeast states are disproportionately composed of Scheduled Tribes. OBC populations vary by state, and both the historical experiences and the extent of the population affect the likelihood that state-level affirmative action policies will be promulgated.

The linguistic/regional distinctions were a major impetus behind the Linguistic Reorganization of the States Act of 1956, which redrew subnational boundaries to reflect linguistic patterns of settlement. Other new states have been created in response to demands by ethnic groups, whether linguistic, tribal, or religious, most prominently the creation of the states of Punjab and Haryana and the creation of new states in northeast India. Despite the regular creation of additional states to satisfy regional demands, these demands have continued to increase. For example, the demand for a new state of Telengana, which has been a political issue since the 1950s, has reemerged as a major focus of collective action. Although the government agreed to its creation in 2009, implementation has been delayed due to resistance from the states from which it would be created.

Despite repeated statements by the central government since the 1950s to the effect that Plan expenditures are designed to ameliorate asymmetries between states, rich states have remained rich and poor states have tended to remain poor. While some poorer states have become more prosperous, the overall divisions have stayed relatively stable since independence. The central government recognizes this distinction and categorizes certain particularly disadvantaged states, as "special states" in economic statistics; this designation is correlated with greater central government support. The decentralization and economic reforms that began in the 1990s have exacerbated these differences at the same time that Plan expenditures are becoming proportionately less important and states are able to exercise more financial entrepreneurship.

10.5 Conclusion

Indian federalism could be characterized as one of centralized power, especially in the first four decades of the nation's independence and the coinciding era of the dominance of the Congress Party. Since 1989, however, the center has been governed primarily through multi-party coalitions, and the decentralization that accompanied economic reforms has resulted in a shift in power from New Delhi to the state capitals. The states' abilities to raise revenue independently are still somewhat hampered, but the growth in state discretion over economic decision-making has given states with greater resource and capital endowments the ability to surge ahead of poorer, less well governed states.

Chapter 11
Emergence of the Italian Unitary Constitutional System, Modified by Supranational Norms and Italian Regionalism

Louis Del Duca and Patrick Del Duca

11.1 Historical Perspectives

Italy emerged in the 1860s as a unitary state by joining, under the king of *Piemonte*, what had been the territories of Modena, Parma, Tuscany, Austrian-occupied Lombardy-Veneto, the Papal States and the Kingdom of the Two Sicilies. The governmental structures in these territories collapsed at the moment of unification, thereby reinforcing centralization of government in the Piemontese-created State.[1] The *Piemontesi* imported French administrative law, not to assure individual rights, but rather to assure effective administration of State power. Italy's first constitution,

---

Louis F. Del Duca, Edward N. Polisher Distinguished Faculty Scholar, Penn State Dickinson School of Law; B.A. Temple University; JD Harvard Law School; *laurea in giurisprudenza*, Università di Roma. Patrick Del Duca, Professor of Law from Practice, UCLA Law School; Partner, Zuber Lawler & Del Duca LLP; B.A. Harvard College; DEA Université de Lyon II, Faculté de Sciences Économiques; JD Harvard Law School; *laurea in giurisprudenza*, Università di Bologna; Ph.D. European University Institute.

[1] Louis F. Del Duca and Patrick Del Duca, *An Italian Federalism?—The State, Its Institutions and National Culture as Rule of Law Guarantor*, AMERICAN JOURNAL OF COMPARATIVE LAW 54: 799 (2006) (publishing parts of the present work); Daniel Ziblatt, STRUCTURING THE STATE: THE FORMATION OF ITALY AND GERMANY AND THE PUZZLE OF FEDERALISM (2006).

L. Del Duca (✉)
Penn State Dickinson School of Law, Pennsylvania State University, Lewis Katz Building, 333 West South Street, 17013-2899 Carlisle, PA, USA
e-mail: lfd2@psu.edu

P. Del Duca
UCLA Law School, University of California, Los Angeles, CA, USA

Zuber Lawler & Del Duca LLP, Los Angeles, CA, USA
e-mail: pdelduca@zuberlaw.com

the *statuto Albertino*, was that of a ruling monarch according the populace limited rights. The monarch's ability to change its constitution at will exemplified the State's brittle quality.

This weakness facilitated emergence of the fascist State in the 1920s, with popular ratification, and increased centralization. Its constituent administrative units were Italy's 103 provinces, each under an appointed prefect. Establishment of national management, labor and professional "corporativist" associations worked to overcome regional and other heterogeneity of Italian society, and facilitated centralization of power.

Italy's first post-World War II referendum established itself as a Republic, eliminating the monarchy tainted by association with fascism. In reaction to the previous regime's disregard of rights and its centralization of authority at the State, *i.e.*, central, level, the subsequent 1948 Constitution proclaimed fundamental principles and rights, provided for Regions, and established a Constitutional Court to protect its principles and rights and its Regions' sphere of activity. In contemporary Italy, the term "State" can be understood as referring to the national, central power, and the Regions can be understood as the constituent member units of the State.

The Constitution provides for 20 Regions, divided into provinces and municipalities. Five outlying Regions (Friuli-Venezia-Giulia, Sardegna, Sicily, Trentino-Alto Adige/Südtirol, and Valle d'Aosta) were accorded so-called Special Statutes by the Constitution's Article 116, that afforded them recognition of some immediate autonomy upon the Constitution's adoption, reflective of comparative geographic isolation, prior legislative and administrative self-sufficiency, and linguistic minorities.[2] Trentino-Alto Adige/Südtirol and its provinces Trento and Bolzano also benefit from treaty guarantee of autonomy.[3]

National political considerations regulated the labored pace of establishing the Regions as meaningful entities within the State. The Christian Democrats, recognizing that they would maintain national predominance with coalition partners, delayed implementing the constitutional provisions for developing the Regions, while the Communists, excluded from national power, advocated empowering them.[4] The end of the Cold War changed the Italian political landscape, allowing Italy to define itself as a state comprised of Regions with the beginnings of meaningful political autonomy. The divide between Christian Democrats and other parties of the center left who held power on the national level throughout the post war period on the one hand, and the communists who achieved power only in certain regions on the other hand, became mooted by the end of the cold war. This allowed development of

---

[2]On the legal status of linguistic minorities in Italy, see Patrick Del Duca, CHOOSING THE LANGUAGE OF TRANSNATIONAL DEALS: PRACTICALITIES, POLICY AND LAW REFORM 105–106, 156–159 (American Bar Association, 2010).

[3]*See* Lorenzo Dellai, *Ai confini dell'Italia e al centro dell'Europa/At the Frontier of Italy and at the Centre of Europe*, in NATION, FEDERALISM AND DEMOCRACY: THE EU, ITALY AND THE AMERICAN FEDERAL EXPERIENCE 19–24 (Fabbrini, Sergio, ed., 2001).

[4]*See* Yves Mény, *The Political Dynamics of Regionalism: Italy, France, Spain*, in REGIONALISM IN EUROPEAN POLITICS 1–28 (Roger Morgan, ed., 1986).

the consensus required to implement the constitutional provisions that contemplated Regions. National legislative measures gave substance to the Regions,[5] consolidated by a constitutional amendment in 2001, and accompanied throughout by decisions of the Constitutional Court supportive of development of the Regions.

Nonetheless, the Italian State retains elements of national control typical of a unitary state. Its courts are national, as are its legal professions and training. Its civil, commercial, corporate, criminal and family laws remain uniform national bodies of law. Its Parliament retains the power to establish essential principles to contain exercise by the Regions of their powers. Italy's Constitutional Court, a national institution, is at the forefront of defining the relationships between Italy's Regions and its central State authorities.

11.2 Distribution of Legislative Powers Among the State, Regions and Local Governments

11.2.1 2001 Constitutional Amendment

The 2001 amendment of Italy's Constitution created a new Title V, titled "Regions, Provinces, Municipalities." The new Title V conceives Regions and other local governments as having, within their defined spheres of activity, equal dignity with the State. The pre-2001 amendment text considered Regions and other local government entities the base of a pyramid, hierarchically-presided by the State.

The Constitution's new Article 117, first paragraph, initially affirms that the legislative power is to be exercised by the State and the Regions in respect of the Constitution, "as well as the restrictions derived from the community [European Union] order and international obligations."[6] Article 117 then proceeds to:

1. reserve to the State exclusive legislative power in 17 enumerated matters (Art. 117, second paragraph);
2. enumerate 20 matters of concurrent State and Regional legislative power, subject to State legislative determination of "fundamental principles," (Art. 117, third paragraph); and,
3. reserves to the Regions legislative power in every other matter (Art. 117, fourth paragraph).

---

[5]DPR no. 616 of July 24, 1977, GAZZ. UFF. no. 234 of Aug. 29, 1977; Law no. 59 of March 15, 1997, GAZZ. UFF. no. 63 of March 17, 1997; D.L. no. 112 of March 31, 1998, GAZZ. UFF. no. 92 of April 21, 1998, ord. supp. no. 77, rectification GAZZ. UFF. no. 116 of May 2, 1997; D.L. no. 115 of March 31, 1998, GAZZ. UFF. no. 96 of April 27, 1998.

[6]Although some translations of the Italian constitution add article sub-numbering, the present work closely tracks the actual numbering conventions of the Italian text.

11.2.2 Seventeen Exclusive State Powers

The 17 categories as to which Article 117, second paragraph, grants exclusive legislative power to the State are:

(a) foreign policy and international relations of the State; relations of the State with the European Union; right of asylum and legal condition of citizens of States not belonging to the European Union;
(b) immigration;
(c) relations between the Republic and religious confessions;
(d) defense and Armed Forces; security of the State; arms, munitions and explosives;
(e) money, protection of savings and financial markets; protection of competition; exchange system; tax and accounting system of the State; equalization of financial resources;
(f) bodies of the State and relative electoral laws; state referenda; election of the European Parliament;
(g) order and administrative organization of the State and of the national public entities;
(h) public order and safety, other than local administrative police;
(i) citizenship, civil status and registry; [the Italian alphabet omits the letters j and k]
(l) jurisdiction and procedural norms; civil and criminal order; administrative justice;
(m) determination of the essential levels of performances concerning civil and social rights that must be guaranteed throughout the national territory;
(n) general norms on instruction;
(o) social security;
(p) electoral legislation, bodies of government and fundamental functions of Municipalities, Provinces and Metropolitan Cities;
(q) customs, protection of national borders and international prophylaxis;
(r) weights, measures and determination of time; informational, statistical and computer coordination of local, Regional and State public administration data; intellectual property; and
(s) protection of the environment, the ecosystem and cultural goods.

In a practical sense, Italy's continued reliance on civil (Italy's civil code addresses commercial, family and tort law, among other topics), criminal, civil procedure and criminal procedure codes, all adopted as national legislation, provides national uniformity on a core of matters that promotes maintenance of a national identity. Even following the 2001 amendments to increase Regional autonomy, the national Constitution through its Article 117(l), as noted above, makes express provision to continue to reserve to State legislation "jurisdiction and procedural norms, civil and criminal legal framework, and administrative justice."

11.2.3 Twenty Concurrent State and Regional Powers

Article 117, third paragraph, designates 20 matters as within the concurrent jurisdiction of the State and the Regions. It provides that "in the matters of concurrent legislation, the legislative power belongs to the Regions, except for the determination of the fundamental principles, reserved to legislation of the State." The concurrent legislative powers of the Regions can be understood as a form of subordinate powers, in that Article 117, third paragraph, reserves to the State the determination of the fundamental principles for their exercise. This constraint maintains continuity with the constitutional provision prior to the 2001 amendment that Regions could issue "legislative norms" within a specified list of subject matters "in the limits of the fundamental principles established by laws of the State," provided that such norms were not "in contrast with the national interest and those of other Regions." The 20 concurrent subject matters now identified by Article 117, third paragraph, are:

1. relations of the Regions, international and with the European Union;
2. foreign trade;
3. protection and safety of work;
4. instruction, excepting autonomy of scholastic institutions and with exclusion of professional instruction and formation;
5. professions;
6. scientific and technological research and support for innovation for the productive sectors;
7. protection of health;
8. nutrition;
9. sport regulation;
10. civil protection;
11. governance of territory,
12. civil ports and airports;
13. major transportation and navigation networks;
14. regulation of communication;
15. production, transport and national distribution of energy;
16. supplementary social security;
17. harmonization of public accounts and coordination of public finance and tax system;
18. giving value to cultural and environmental goods and promotion and organization of cultural activities;
19. savings institutions, rural savings institutions, credit enterprises of regional character; and,
20. entities of land and agricultural credit of regional character.

11.2.4 Reserved Regional Powers

Article 117, fourth paragraph, is a "reserved powers" clause. Powers not exclusively reserved to the State's legislative power or designated as concurrent powers are reserved to the Regions. Article 117, fourth paragraph, provides that the Regions hold "the legislative power in reference to every matter not expressly reserved to the legislation of the State." The significance of the reservation of un-enumerated legislative powers to the Regions will be defined only in time, but will remain constrained by (i) the exclusive reservation of the 17 broad subject matters to State legislative power and (ii) the limitation that as to the 20 matters made the object of concurrent State and Regional legislative power, the Regions may legislate only in conformity with the fundamental principles legislatively established by the State.

11.2.5 Additional Constitutional Mechanisms Facilitating National Unity

11.2.5.1 Free Circulation; National Government Substitution; Court of Accounts Audits

The Constitution (Article 120) offers additional mechanisms to assure national unity, notwithstanding the other constitutional provisions that favor Regional autonomy. It prohibits Regions from impeding free circulation of persons and goods, or limiting the right to work. Moreover, it allows the national government to substitute itself for Regions and other local governments:

1. to assure respect of international and European obligations;
2. in cases of grave danger for health and public welfare; and,
3. to protect legal or economic unity, particularly essential levels of services concerning civil and social rights.

As part of the constitutional glue bonding State and local governments, Article 120 provides that the procedures relative to such substitution are to be defined by law in accord with principles of "subsidiarity" and "loyal collaboration."

In addition to the State power to substitute itself for Regional and other local governments, the President of the Republic, having heard a Parliamentary Commission's opinion, can dissolve a Regional Council and remove the President of a Regional *Giunta* in the event that either acts "contrary to the Constitution or in grave violation of the law," as well as for reasons of "national security."[7] Regions and other local governmental entities also remain subject to audit by the national Court of Accounts (*Corte dei Conti*).

---

[7] CONST. art. 126.

Reflective of the increasing Regional autonomy, the 2001 constitutional amendment eliminated the State commissar assigned to each Region to "oversee" coordination of State and Regional administrative functions.[8]

11.2.5.2 Constitutional Court as Arbiter Between State and the Regions

The Constitutional Court adjudicates "controversies relative to the constitutional legitimacy of the laws and of the acts, having force of law, of the State and of the Regions," and "on conflicts of attribution between powers of the State and on those between the State and the Regions, and among the Regions" (Constitution Article 134). Most of the Constitutional Court's case law arises from referral of questions concerning the constitutionality of a law by ordinary judges who determine that such a question is pertinent to a pending proceeding. However, the Constitutional Court has original jurisdiction over disputes in which the State or a Region challenges an act as exceeding the "sphere of competence" accorded respectively to the Region or the State (Constitution Article 127).

Throughout its rulings, the Constitutional Court devotes particular attention to "fundamental" and "supreme" principles. The 1948 Constitution labels its opening articles "fundamental principles." Among them are: popular sovereignty "exercised in the forms and limits of the Constitution;" promotion of local autonomies; and, advancement of linguistic minorities. In particular, Article 5 of the Constitution provides as part of the "fundamental principles":

> The Republic, one and indivisible, recognizes and promotes local autonomies, implements in the services that depend on the State the most broad administrative decentralization, adapts the principles and methods of its legislation to the needs of autonomy and decentralization.

However, the Constitutional Court itself has defined the notion of fundamental principles even more broadly than those expressly listed as such in the opening articles of the Constitution. Faced in 1988 with the constitutionality of a Bolzano Provincial Council member's immunity from prosecution for having disparaged the Italian flag, the Court procedurally dodged the question, but declared, with a *Marbury v. Madison* bravura:

> The Italian Constitution contains some supreme principles that cannot be subverted or modified in their essential content either by laws of constitutional amendment or other constitutional laws. Such are principles that the Constitution itself explicitly contemplates as absolute limits to the power of constitutional revision, such as the republican form [of government] (Const. art. 139), as well as principles that, although not expressly mentioned among those not subject to the principle of constitutional revision, are part of the supreme values on which the Italian Constitution is based.[9]

---

[8]CONST. art. 124, abrogated by Constitutional Law no. 3 of Oct. 18, 2001, GAZZ. UFF. no. 248 of Oct. 24, 2001.

[9]Corte cost. judgment no. 1146 of Dec. 15, 1988, considerations in law, ¶2.1, GAZZ. UFF. of Jan. 11, 1989, *prima serie speciale* no. 2.

As an example of the Constitutional Court's action as arbiter of allocation of governmental powers, its decision no. 70 of 2004 addressed a challenge by the State to Tuscany Region legislation.[10] With the challenged legislation, the Region claimed ability to act in place of municipalities and provinces failing to approve hazardous waste remediation plans in a timely fashion.

The Constitutional Court acknowledged that Constitution article 117(2)(p), as amended 2001, reserves definition of "fundamental functions" of municipalities, provinces and metropolitan cities exclusively to State legislation, while Constitution article 118(1) delegates all administrative functions to municipalities unless legislation justified on criteria of "subsidiarity, differentiation, and adequacy" allocates power to a different governmental level. The Court reasoned that because the State power of substitution established by Constitution article 120 derives from the need for State substitution to protect essential State interests as articulated by article 120, such power of State substitution is "extraordinary and additive." The Court accordingly concluded that the State power of substitution is not exclusive and upheld the Regional law. The Court further noted that its pre-2001 amendment jurisprudence on criteria for State substitution of Regions remained valid. The Court concluded that the criteria for a Region to substitute itself for its municipalities and provinces include that the criteria for substitution, both as to substance and procedure, be well defined and that the principle of "loyal collaboration" among governmental levels mandated procedural guarantees to assure that undue exercise of a power of substitution be avoided.

11.2.5.3 Practical Predominance of Central Government Legislation

For now, the abundant legislative production by Italy's national Parliament and Government, including its basic codes and ample normative material outside the code framework, substantially outweighs its Regions' legislative production. Regions began significant legislation only recently, and the heavy preponderance of national law predates them. However, even as Regional legislation grows in importance, a confluence of factors will work to preserve influence of national law on key points. They include Italy's Constitution and the Constitutional definition of the State's ongoing role, the national judiciary working predominantly in the civil law tradition, and continued reliance on national codes for core legal topics of civil, commercial and criminal law.

Italian Regions perform significant roles in respect of administration of health care, implementation of public works, environmental regulation, land use and planning, agriculture, public instruction, cultural activities, and tourism promotion. These activities occur within nationally determined constraints, including national

---

[10]Corte cost. judgment no. 70 of March 2, 2004 (*Pres. Cons. v. Toscana*), GAZZ. UFF. of March 10, 2004, *prima serie speciale* no. 10.

constitutional principles, fundamental principles established by State legislation, and the predominant role of national revenue collection and establishment of expenditure budgets.

Collaboration in funding and direction of the health care system is certainly the largest budget category for collaboration between Regions and the State. Health care, as to which Regions function essentially as conduits for transfer of State funds to local health units and hospitals, constitutes over 60 % of their total outlays.

Under Constitution Article 117, paragraph 4, as amended 2001, the Regions have residual legislative powers. But, the State retains ultimate responsibility for assuring the rule of law in respect of the Constitution.

11.2.6 Financial Autonomy of Regions and Local Governments

The Constitution (Article 119) provides that Municipalities, Provinces, Metropolitan Cities and Regions are to have financial autonomy relative to revenue and expenditures. It further provides that they are to have "autonomous resources". They are to establish and apply their own taxes and income, "in harmony with the Constitution and according to principles of coordination of the public finance and of the tax system." They are to benefit from shares of the property taxes referable to their territory. State law is to establish an "equalization fund", "without strictures of use" for territories with lesser "tax capacity" per inhabitant.

The resources mentioned in the previous paragraph are to be sufficient to allow the Municipalities, Provinces, Metropolitan Cities and the Regions to finance entirely the public functions attributed to them.

The concluding paragraph of Article 119 affirms that the Municipalities, Provinces, Metropolitan Cities and the Regions have their own patrimony. It allows them to make recourse to indebtedness "only to finance expenses of investment." Any State guarantee of their debts is excluded.

11.2.7 Administrative Powers of Municipalities

Municipalities have no formal law-making power. However, they do have administrative powers. Their exercise of these powers includes the articulation of norms that *de facto* constitutes the exercise of law-making power.[11]

---

[11]*See* CITTÁ A CONFRONTO: LE INSTITUZIONI METROPOLITANE NEI PAESI OCCIDENTALI (Giuseppe Franco Ferrari and Pierciro Galeone, eds.) (Societá editrice il Mulino, Collana dell'Associazione Nazionale Comuni Italiani, 2011) (an anthology of contributions on local financial autonomy prepared in view of pending reforms in Italy, including an essay at p. 35 by Patrick Del Duca, *Governo e forme di finanziamento delle aree metropolitane negli Stati Uniti. Una guida per la navigazione*, highlighting the importance of market discipline on local government finance through borrowing via issuance of bonds).

The Constitution attributes "administrative functions" to Municipalities (Article 118, first paragraph). The exception to this general attribution is the attribution of administrative functions to Provinces, Metropolitan Cities, Regions and the State in order to assure their "unitary exercise". Such attribution is to be on the basis of the principles of "subsidiarity, differentiation and adequacy". Municipalities, Provinces and Metropolitan Cities are constitutionally defined as holders of their "inherent administrative functions" and "of those conferred by state or regional law" (Article 118, second paragraph). It further provides that State law is to regulate coordination between State and Regions in the subject matters of immigration and of public order and safety, as well as the forms of "understanding and coordination" in the subject matter of protection of cultural goods.

11.3 Means and Methods of Legal Unification

11.3.1 Unification by Exercise of Central Government Power

National law, comprised of the Constitution, national legislation and the civil law tradition, predominates in Italy in both formal and practical ways.

In a formal sense, the Civil Code, adopted 1942, reinforces national uniformity by defining a hierarchy of sources of Italian law, comprised of national legislation, followed by regulations and then usages.[12] The 1948 Constitution placed Constitutional law at the head of this list, and added Regional law, which within the spheres of concurrent legislative power established in Title V of the Constitution may displace national statutory and regulatory law other than such law which constitutes the determination of fundamental principles by the State within the meaning of Article 117, paragraph 3. In addition, it may not displace constitutional law.[13] European Union law trumps the sources of law identified in Italy's Civil Code by virtue, and on the terms, of its acceptance in Italy through the Constitution's article 11.

11.3.1.1 Constitutional Court Definition of Limits of State Direction of Regional Expenditures

The Constitutional Court addressed the Constitution article 117(3) reservation to State legislation of definition of fundamental principles of public finance

---

[12] CIV. CODE, art. 1, Provisions of the Law in General, Sources of Law, amended by Law no. 218 of May 31, 1995, GAZZ. UFF. ord. supp. no. 128 of June 3, 1995.
[13] CONST. art. 138.

coordination in a 2005 ruling.[14] The ruling resolved an original jurisdiction case in which Campania, Marche, Tuscany, and Val d'Aosta challenged the constitutionality of 2004 State legislation addressing the national deficit, insofar as such legislation undertook to restrict Regional and local budgetary autonomy.

The Court at the outset of its analysis addressed a standing issue as to whether Regions could challenge restrictions on municipal and other local government expenditures. In determining that the Regions did have the necessary standing, the Court relied on reasoning that the connection between Regional and local governmental attributions is so tight that inappropriate invasion of local government attributions is "potentially susceptible" of harming Regional powers as well.

To contain costs, the challenged law purported to limit Regions and local governments to accomplishing procurement either through contracts established by the national treasury ministry, or otherwise within nationally established price and quality parameters. The Court reaffirmed the principle "constantly affirmed by the jurisprudence of this Court" by which

> norms that establish specific limitations relative to individual headings of expense in budgets of the regions and the local entities do not constitute fundamental principles of coordination of public finance, in the senses of article 117(3) of the Constitution, and they therefore harm the financial autonomy of expenditure guaranteed by Constitution article 119.

Further, the Court cited several of its recent decisions for the proposition that the State may impose budgetary policy limitations on Regions and local government entities, but only with "discipline of principle," "for reasons of financial coordination connected to national objectives, conditioned also by community [European Union] obligations."[15] For such limitations to respect Regional and local government autonomy, the Court observed, they must be focused on either "the amount of the current deficit" or in a transitory manner "the growth of current

---

[14]Corte cost. judgment no. 417 of Nov. 14, 2005, GAZZ. UFF. of Nov. 16, 2005, *prima serie speciale* no. 46. For similar reasoning, *see* Corte cost. judgment no. 88 of March 10, 2006, GAZZ. UFF. of March 15, 2006, *prima serie speciale* no. 11 (Court voided 2005 State budget law limitation on Friuli-Venezia Giulia Region's future ability to hire at-will employees, as violating Region's Special Statute-guaranteed autonomy, citing in ¶5 considerations in law, among others, judgment no. 417 of Nov. 14, 2005, here discussed.). *See also* Corte cost. judgment no. 118 of March 24, 2006, GAZZ. UFF. of March 29, 2006, *prima serie speciale* no. 13 (upholding Friuli-Venezia Giulia challenge to 2005 State budget law provision for State funds to promote first family home purchase, on ground that social funds in areas outside State legislative power "must be assigned generically for social purposes without the above-indicated constraint of specific destination." ¶9.1 considerations in law, *id.*).

[15]*Id.*, citing Corte cost. judgment no. 36 of Jan. 26, 2004, GAZZ. UFF. of Feb. 4, 2004, *prima serie speciale* no. 5; and referencing Corte cost. judgments nos. 376 of Dec. 30, 2003, GAZZ. UFF. Jan. 7, 2004, *prima serie speciale* no. 1; 4 of Jan. 13, 2004, GAZZ. UFF. of Jan. 21, 2004, *prima serie speciale* no. 3; and, 390 of Dec. 17, 2004, GAZZ. UFF. of Dec. 22, 2004, *prima serie speciale* no. 49.

expenditure of the autonomous entities," but the State can establish only "an overall limit, that leaves the entities themselves broad liberty of allocation of the resources."[16]

11.3.1.2 Constitutional Court Jurisprudence on National Power

Constitutional Court jurisprudence has extensively developed the ramifications of Regional government. Indeed, one of the Court's first decisions invalidated, as incompatible with the Constitution article 120 prohibition on limiting right to work, legislation of the autonomous Province of Bolzano. In the challenged legislation, the Province, relying on the Special Statute of Trentino-Alto Adige, sought to create a system to regulate artisans that *de facto* excluded participation of artisans from outside the Region.[17]

The State may within 60 days of publication challenge a Regional law before the Constitutional Court as exceeding Regional power.[18] Likewise, a Region can challenge a law or act having the force of a law, either of the State or another Region.[19] This mechanism, established by the 2001 amendment, superseded the previous mechanism that treated Region and State less equally. Formerly the State could also challenge the Regional Council to re-adopt the challenged Regional measure, as well as then ask Parliament to reconsider the measure as substantively inappropriate.[20]

The Constitutional Court has issued a continuing stream of rulings addressing spheres of State and Regional action. Such rulings increased following the 2001 Constitutional amendment that redefined the status of the Regions. Common issues in this litigation are environmental protection, often concerning waste disposal,[21]

---

[16]Corte cost. judgment no. 417 of Nov. 14, 2005, citing Corte cost. judgment no. 36 of Jan. 20, 2004, at ¶6 findings in law. In judgment no. 417 of Nov. 14, 2005, the Court went on to conclude:

> In the instant case, the provisions challenged do not fix general limits to deficit or to current expenditure, but they establish limits to expenditures for studies and consultancy assignments conferred to parties outside the administration, to expenses for missions abroad, representation, public relations and conventions, as well as to expenses for acquisition of goods and services; limitations that, regarding individual headings of expense, do not constitute fundamental principles of coordination of public finance, but do comport an inadmissible invasion into autonomy of the entities for expenditure management. *Id*

[17]Corte cost. judgment no. 6 of June 15, 1956 (*Pres. Cons. v. Bolzano*), available at www.cortecostituzionale.it
[18]CONST. art. 127.
[19]*Id.*
[20]CONST. art. 127, in force from 1948 to 2001.
[21]Under CONST. art. 117(2)(s). *E.g.,* Corte cost. judgment no. 505 of Dec. 4, 2002 (*Soc. Ecograf s.p.a. v. Prov. Treviso*), GAZZ. UFF. of Dec. 11, 2002, *prima serie speciale* no. 49 (voiding Veneto Region's limitation on disposal in Veneto landfills of other Regions' hazardous waste).

interplay of national taxation and equalization of Regional financial resources,[22] allocation of powers between Regions and State regarding social security,[23] powers of municipalities, provinces and metropolitan cities,[24] and health care.[25] The Constitutional Court's president in early 2008 noted a drop in the number of such cases brought to the court, falling from 111 in 2006 to 52 in 2007. He attributes the drop to the Court's growing jurisprudence in interpretation of the 2001 Constitutional amendment, and consequently the ability of the parties concerned to resolve their disputes politically, in application of the principle of "loyal collaboration" as articulated by the Court.[26]

11.3.2 Standing Regional Conferences

The Conference of the Regions and the Autonomous Provinces was created among the Regions in 1981.[27] It considers itself equivalent to the Conference of State Governors in the United States. It seeks improvement of relationships with the State by virtue of elaborating common positions among Regional governments and establishment of a permanent inter-regional framework to diffuse "best practices", to advocate the system of Regional governments, and to underline the role of

---

[22]Under CONST. art. 117(2)(e). *E.g.,* Corte cost. judgment no. 296 of Sept. 26, 2003 (*Pres. Cons. v. Piemonte*), GAZZ. UFF. of Oct. 1, 2003, *prima serie speciale* no. 39 (voiding Regional legislation providing tax exemption for Olympic organizing entity and alternative energy vehicles); Corte cost. judgment no. 94 of March 28, 2003 (*Pres. Cons. v. Lazio*), GAZZ. UFF. of April 2, 2003, *prima serie speciale* no. 13 (upholding Regional law subsidy scheme for "historic business places").

[23]Under CONST. art. 117(2)(o). Corte cost. ord. no. 526 of Dec. 9, 2002, GAZZ. UFF. of Dec. 11, 2002, *prima serie speciale* no. 49 (declaring inadmissible as inadequately posed a first instance judge question concerning compatibility, of a Regional law regulating publically-subsidized rents, with constitutional reservation to State of assuring national civil and social rights minimum standards).

[24]Under CONST. art. 117(2)(p). *See, e.g.*, Corte cost. judgment no. 201 of June 11, 2003, GAZZ. UFF. of June 18, 2003, *prima serie speciale* no. 24 (Lombardia Region legislation limiting State-mandated incompatibility of simultaneous holding of Regional and municipal councilor positions to larger municipalities, unconstitutional); Corte cost. judgment no. 376 of July 23, 2002, GAZZ. UFF. of July 31, 2002, *prima serie speciale* no. 30 (as Court denies, under the pre-2001 Constitution Title V, Emilia-Romagna and Liguria challenges to State administrative procedure reform measures, it invites renewed challenges under amended Title V (at ¶5 considerations in law)).

[25]Under CONST. art. 117(3). *See, e.g.*, Corte cost. judgment no. 88 of March 27, 2003, GAZZ. UFF. of April 2, 2003, *prima serie speciale* no. 13 (voids State effort to regulate provision of addiction treatments); Corte cost. judgment no. 282 of June 26, 2002, GAZZ. UFF. of July 3, 2002, *prima serie speciale* no. 26 (voiding Regional law purporting to suspend electroshock and lobotomy therapy).

[26]Annual Press Conference of the President of the Constitutional Court, February 14, 2008, *available at* www.cortecostituzionale.it

[27]*See* www.regioni.it

the Region in the construction of the European Union. It maintains a permanent secretariat and study center in Rome–*Centro interregionale di studi e documentazione* (Cinsedo).

The "Conference State-Regions" exists by virtue of statute and decree adopted in the period from 1983 through 2000.[28] The Constitutional Court has recognized it and its functioning as part of the necessary implementation of the principle of "loyal collaboration" among levels of government.[29] The Conference offers opinions on proposals of the State for legislation and regulation, and is the venue for the State and the Regions to reach agreements for coordinated action among them. There is a similar "Conference State-Cities", and a "Unified Conference" that includes the Conference State-Regions and the Conference State-Cities".[30]

11.3.3 Regional Government

A Region's constitution is its *Statuto* (Statute), which "in harmony with the Constitution," determines its form of government, organization and operation.[31] A Region is governed by a popularly-elected Regional Council.[32] To promote distinction between Regions and State, a Regional Council member may not also serve in Parliament.[33] The *Giunta* is the Region's executive body, appointed by its popularly elected President.[34] If the President fails a Regional Council confidence vote by an absolute majority of the Council members, called by at least a fifth of the Council, the Council is dissolved for new elections, and the *Giunta*'s mandate revoked; resignation of three-fifths of the Council achieves the same result.[35]

Relevant industry, trade and other organizations are typically of national scope. As an example, labor negotiations are handled nationally between labor and management groups.

---

[28]*See* statutory and regulatory materials cited at http://www.governo.it/Conferenze/c_stato_regioni/norme.html

[29]*E.g. Corte Costituzionale* Decision no. 116 of March 23, 1994, GAZZ. UFF. of April 13, 1994.

[30]*See* www.regioni.it

[31]CONST. art. 123. The Regional Council may modify a Regional Statute by absolute Council majority in two votes at least 2 months apart, which the State has 30 days to challenge before the Constitutional Court. Constitutional Law no. 1 of Nov. 22, 1999, art. 3. If a 50th of the Region's voters or a fifth of the Regional Council triggers a referendum, the modification is valid only if approved by a majority of votes cast. *Id.* How Regions will recraft their charters remains to be seen.

[32]CONST. art. 121, 122.

[33]CONST. art. 122.

[34]*Id.*

[35]CONST. art. 126.

11.3.4 Role of Legal Education

Italy's legal professions are national and contribute to assuring a national legal culture. Their national quality corresponds to the national governance of its law faculties, and the national system to select and promote law professors. Moreover, the law faculties' influence in imparting a national legal culture extends beyond the formal legal professions because they train such a broad slice of Italian university students, even as only a fraction of such students pursue formal careers in law.

The nationally-defined careers available to university graduates in law include lawyer, State attorney, notary, magistrate (which includes civil and criminal judges and prosecutors), administrative judge, and law professor. A further legal profession, open to university graduates in economics and business, is that of *commercialista*, a business-oriented advisor intermediate between a lawyer and an accountant. Specialized training, apprenticeship, and examination are required for each category. Mid-career changes from one profession to another are rare.

Italian law faculties, with limited exceptions, are State schools. They offer open enrollment to students with a secondary school diploma, the *maturità* earned by passing the secondary school exit examination, typically at age 19. A full 5-year degree course of study allows access to the apprenticeships and examinations prerequisite to lawyer, magistrate, and notary careers. Although recently universities have some latitude to determine courses of study, law curricula remain substantially uniform, and their degrees nominally equivalent.

To become a professor, a law graduate undertakes a further graduate degree in law and sits for a State examination to become a university researcher. With one or more established professors' tutelage, the aspiring academic can hope to win a university academic post in national competitions based principally on evaluation of publications.

National legislation regulates the bar,[36] and an *avvocato* (lawyer) may practice throughout Italy. Until recent legislation abrogated the setting of legal and other professional fees,[37] the *Consiglio Nazionale Forense* (National Bar Council) fixed allowable fees at a national level for *avvocati*, although a client could consensually pay more.

The centralization of legal services for substantial business activities in Milan and Rome contributes to the national character not only of the formal legal system, but also of its practical application. Recent evidence suggests that the larger Italian firms, frequently with a foreign law firm affiliation and typically based in Milan and

---

[36]R.D.L. no. 1578 of Nov. 27, 1933, GAZZ. UFF. no. 281 of Dec. 5, 1933, converted into law and amended by Law no. 36 of Jan. 22, 1934, GAZZ. UFF. no. 24 of Jan. 30, 1934, amended by Law no. 406 of July 24, 1985, art. 2, GAZZ. UFF. no. 190 of Aug. 13, 1985.

[37]D.L. no. 223 of July 4, 2006, art. 2(a), GAZZ. UFF. no. 153 of July 4, 2006, rectified GAZZ. UFF. no. 159 of July 11, 2006, converted into law by Law no. 248 of August 4, 2006, GAZZ. UFF. no. 186 of August 11, 2006, ord. supp., coordinated text GAZZ. UFF. no. 186 August 11, 2006 ord. supp.

Rome, are among the most profitable anywhere.[38] Such large, organized law firms focus on securities, financial and other business matters, and relative to the bulk of other lawyers practicing in smaller firms or as individual practitioners, collect a share of legal fees disproportionate to their number.[39]

Italian notaries draft and authenticate legal instruments including contracts, wills, corporate charters, and real property and other conveyances.[40] In particular, the system for tracking corporate charters and real property ownership is nationally uniform. To become a notary, a law graduate attends one of a limited number of a 2-year notary schools, apprentices with a notary for 2 years and then takes a challenging national examination to earn the assignment to provide notarial services in a specific territory.[41]

11.3.5 Role of International Law and Other External Factors

Annual delegation to the Government of responsibility to issue the necessary measures was the practical expedient to resolve the legislative impasse that created a chronic deficiency in legislation to implement European Union norms.[42]

The Constitutional Court's resolution of the practicalities of Italian courts' application of European law is a resounding declaration of the supremacy of constitutional values. Just as the Court has positioned itself as the arbiter of the bounds of Region and State spheres of action, it has also in respect of European law established itself as the guardian of Italian constitutional "fundamental principles."

In the 1960s the Italian Constitutional Court and the European Court of Justice took conflicting positions on the relation between European Community law and Italian law.[43] The European Court asserted a monist view under which Community law took supremacy over national law. Specifically, it considered the Treaty of Rome to have instituted a new legal system to which national law was subject. As an implication of this view, the Court of Justice asserted that any Italian court must apply relevant European Community law to disputes before such a court. Initially,

---

[38]Cobianchi, Marco, and Seghetti, Roberto, *Legalrisiko: Guerra tra i re della parcella*, PANORAMA 113 (Feb. 23, 2006), reporting average annual partner revenue in the 43 largest Italian firms over €1.3 million.

[39]*Id.*, reporting such firms billing €1 billion of the €8.5 billion annually collected by all practicing Italian lawyers.

[40]There are about 5,000 notaries. Federazione Italiana delle Associazioni Sindacali Notarili, *available at* www.federnotai.it

[41]*See Consiglio Nazionale del Notariato* (National Notary Council) web site: www.notariato.it

[42]Law no. 86 of March 9, 1989, GAZZ. UFF. no. 58 of March 10, 1989. *See* Mengozzi, Paolo, EUROPEAN COMMUNITY LAW: FROM THE TREATY OF ROME TO THE TREATY OF AMSTERDAM 144–46 (2nd ed., 1999).

[43]*See* Antonio La Pergola and Patrick Del Duca, *Community Law, International Law, and the Italian Constitution*, AMERICAN JOURNAL OF INTERNATIONAL LAW 79: 598 (1985).

the Italian Constitutional Court took the dualist view that European Community law and Italian law constituted two separate legal systems. In the initial formulation of its position, the Constitutional Court expressed the view that European Community law would be applied by Italian courts only through a procedure of constitutional judicial review as established by Italy's Constitution. In practice this meant that an Italian court would be able to apply European law only following reference of a question to the Constitutional Court and a consequent Constitutional Court decision directing the referring court to apply the European law.

A critical turning point in the Constitutional Court's view was its 1985 *Granital* decision. There the Court concluded that the dualist view, *i.e.* the view that the Italian and Community legal systems were separate legal systems, was nonetheless compatible with the routine, direct application of Community law by all Italian courts. Although the Constitutional Court has made clear that what Italy's Constitution establishes regarding "fundamental principles of the constitutional order and inalienable rights of the human person" prevails in any event, it has determined that Italy's Constitution, based on its Article 11 provision for acceptance of international organizations, otherwise allows supremacy of European law over Italian law.[44] It reached this conclusion by reasoning that the Constitution Article 11 acceptance of Italy's participation in international organizations and Italy's ratification of the European treaties implied a broad opening to the second legal system, *i.e.* what is now the European Union legal system. The Constitutional Court, however, maintained the sovereignty of the Italian legal system and the Constitutional Court's own role as the guarantor of the integrity of the Italian Constitution, by providing that any question involving "fundamental principles of the constitutional order and inalienable rights of the human person" continue to be referred to the Constitutional Court.[45]

The 2001 constitutional amendment that redefined the Regions' role acknowledges the European law view that such law directly applies to Regions. It provides that Regions, within their subject matter, "participate in decisions directed to the formation of community normative acts and provide for the implementation and execution of international agreements and of European Union acts," albeit "in respect of the norms of procedure established by law of the State," that are to "regulate the means of exercise of power of substitution [by the State] in case of noncompliance."[46] Of the two parts of this Constitutional acknowledgement, *i.e.*, that Regions have a voice in the formulation of European norms and that they may directly apply such norms, the latter appears of greater import. Indeed, the Treaty

---

[44]Corte cost. judgment no. 170 of June 8, 1984 (*Granital*), GAZZ. UFF. no. 169 of June 20, 1984, at point 7 of the considerations of law. *See* La Pergola and Del Duca, *supra* note 43, and *Bundesverfassungsgericht* (German Federal Constitutional Court), BVERFGE 73, 339 (*Solange II*), at 376, referencing La Pergola and Del Duca, *supra* note 43, as it reached a conceptually analogous result for Germany.

[45]*Id.*

[46]CONST. art. 117.

on European Union contemplates at best a consultative role on European legislative activity for the Committee of the Regions that it constitutes.[47] Further, even as to the Regions' actions to implement European norms directly, the Constitution expressly preserves the State's various tools to constrain Regional action beyond the bounds of what the Constitution contemplates.

Italy is a member of the Hague Conference on Private International Law. Of 39 Conventions that the Hague Conference tracks on its web site, Italy has ratified or at least signed 20. Although this is less than the 30 ratified or signed by the Netherlands, it is nonetheless sufficient to put Italy in the upper echelon of Hague Conference members defined by ratifications and signatures.

Italy is one of the 60 elected members of UNCITRAL, with its current term expiring in 2016.

Italy is a member of UNIDROIT. Italy hosts the UNIDROIT headquarters in Rome, and pursuant to the UNIDROIT charter, names its president.

11.4 Effect of Institutional and Social Background

11.4.1 The Judicial Branch

The State institution most prominently responsible for initial application of the constitutional rule of law in post-War Italy is its *Corte Costituzionale*, the only court in Italy with the power of constitutional review of laws, principally following referral of questions from other courts, but also through original jurisdiction of disputes among key governmental authorities, such as the State and the Regions. Conceived by Italy's 1948 Constitution, it commenced operation in 1956. Fifteen judges serving 9-year terms comprise the Constitutional Court. Consistent with Italian jurists' view that the Court's power to invalidate laws is a combined quasi-legislative and judicial function, the Court is selected one-third jointly by the two Houses of Parliament, one-third by the President, and one-third by the highest ordinary and administrative courts (Court of Cassation, Council of State and *Corte dei Conti*).

In addition to the pivotal constitutional role of Italy's Constitutional Court, the national organization of its ordinary and administrative courts reinforces the national quality of its justice system. Although ordinary and administrative judicial districts are organized by Region and province, all courts are part of the State.

A national magistracy, constitutionally guaranteed autonomy from Parliament and Government, staffs the ordinary courts and public prosecutor positions.[48] Public prosecutors, known as *Procuratori della Repubblica*, are career magistrates.

---

[47]Treaty on European Union, Part 5, Title I, Chapter 4, OJ C 325 (Dec. 24, 2002).
[48]CONST. art. 101–105.

The *Consiglio Superiore della Magistratura* (Superior Council of the Magistracy, "CSM") is the national body that governs the magistracy. The CSM's composition is designed to provide national assurance of judicial and prosecutorial autonomy. It is presided by the President of the Republic and composed of the President of the Court of Cassation's First Section, and the Court of Cassation's *Procuratore Generale* (public prosecutor), with the balance of its members magistrates elected two thirds by all ordinary judges, and one third by Parliament from law professors or lawyers practicing more than 15 years.[49] Entrance to the magistracy occurs through a national competitive examination, open to candidates trained in law.[50] The CSM is responsible for promoting magistrates.[51]

The judges who serve on administrative courts are not part of the magistracy; they are part of the executive, rather than the judicial, branch of government. Although not within the CSM's scope, their selection and promotion, on a uniform national basis, is intended to afford them similar impartiality, as well as to assure uniform national application of the law that they apply.[52] Selection of administrative judges, like ordinary judges, is based on educational qualifications and competitive examination pursuant to national legislation governing the Regional administrative courts and the Council of State.[53] All administrative judges must be graduates of an Italian law faculty, with new judges required to have completed the 5-year university study in law; however, they need not be members of the bar.

The ordinary courts exercise jurisdiction over general civil, commercial, labor, and criminal matters. Since 1993 they are structured, in ascending order, as Justices of the Peace, Tribunals, Courts of Appeal, and the Court of Cassation.[54]

Pursuant to Constitution Article 125, the State provides an administrative court headquartered in each of the Regions (*Tribunale Amministrativo Regionale*, a Regional Administrative Tribunal—"TAR") with jurisdiction over administrative actions in that Region. The *Consiglio di Stato* (Council of State), part of which provides substantive advice on administrative matters, is the supreme administrative court. Three of its six sections provide opinions, some binding, to the public administration. The other three hear appeals from TARs. The public administration

---

[49]CONST. art. 104–106; Law no. 44 of March 28, 2002, GAZZ. UFF. no. 75 of March 29, 2002.

[50]Law no. 150 of July 25, 2005, art. 2(1)(b); Law no. 262 of Nov. 5, 2004, GAZZ. UFF. no. 261 of Nov. 6, 2004; CONST. art. 106(1).

[51]CONST. art. 105. Magistrates were promoted principally on seniority rather than merit. Law no. 570 of July 25, 1966, GAZZ. UFF. no. 186 of July 28, 1966; Law no. 831 of Dec. 20, 1973, GAZZ. UFF. no. 333 of Dec. 29, 1973. Recent reform allows more rapid promotion based on evaluation of merit. Law no. 150 of July 25, 2005.

[52]Law no. 1034 of Dec. 6, 1971, art. 13, 14, 15 and 16, GAZZ. UFF. no. 314 of Dec. 13, 1971.

[53]DPR no. 214 of April 21, 1973, art. 14–20, GAZZ. UFF. no. 131 of May 22, 1973. Regio Editto no. 2417 of Aug. 18, 1831, three decades before Italy's unification, created the Council of State to address substantive public administration questions. It commenced as an administrative court pursuant to Law no. 2248 of March 20, 1865 (All. E), GAZZ. UFF. of April 27, 1865. Law no. 1034 of Dec. 6, 1971, establishes the TARs.

[54]Law no. 374 of Nov. 21, 1991, art. 49, 50.

is understood to include all levels of government. Pursuant to Constitution Article 113, recourse to the courts is to be available to protect "rights and legitimate interests" against the public administration, while national law is to determine when courts can annul acts of the public administration.

Several special administrative courts exist, of which the most important in shaping the State's constitutional role is the *Corte dei Conti* (Court of Accounts), whose primary functions are review of public finances, auditing, and prosecution of misconduct regarding public assets, extending to all governmental bodies, including Regions, provinces and municipalities.[55] Its review as a national government entity of local finances is further national assurance of the constitutional rule of law and of the correct conduct of Regional, provincial and municipal governments, particularly in respect of their finances.

11.4.2 National Electoral System

The Italian parliament is comprised of a Chamber of Deputies and the Senate of the Republic. Seats of deputies are distributed among electoral districts in proportion to population. Senators are elected by Regional popular votes, with the number of Senators per Region distributed according to population, but with the constraints pursuant to Constitution Article 57 that no Region may have less than seven senators, except that Molise has two, and the Valle d'Aoste has one. The total number of elected Senators is 315, and the total number of deputies is 630. Twelve deputies and six senators are elected by Italians residing outside Italy. Article 59 makes any past President of the Republic a senator for life, until such time as such a person renounces the office, and empowers the President of the Republic to name as senators for life "five citizens that have illustrated the Country for highest merits in social, scientific, artistic and literary field".

From the 1948 Constitution's adoption, Italy employed proportional representation to impede any one political party dominating national life.[56] Accordingly, Parliament closely reflected the various parties' electoral strength through the post-war period. Nationally, proportional representation fragmented electoral representation among parties, making government practical only by broad coalition. In contrast, individual party or narrow coalition governance of Regions and municipalities was common.

---

[55]CONST. art. 100(2).

[56]*See* Alberto Pasolini Zanelli, *The Electoral Reform in Italy: Towards a Majority System,* in ITALY IN TRANSITION: THE LONG ROAD FROM THE FIRST TO THE SECOND REPUBLIC: THE 1997 EDMUND D. PELLEGRINO LECTURES ON CONTEMPORARY ITALIAN POLITICS (Paolo Janni, ed., 1998).

Starting in the 1990s, Italy wrestled with ways to render its electoral mechanisms more decisive. In 1993 it determined to elect its Parliament on a predominantly first-past-the-post system. Another 1993 reform provided direct popular mayoral election in larger municipalities (with a run-off between the two leading candidates absent a first round majority), thereby allowing new talent entry into Italian politics.

In 2005, Italy returned to the proportionality model for national elections, but on national results for the Chamber of Deputies and Regional results for the Senate.[57] To address conflicting objectives of promoting electoral coalitions, assuring Parliamentary majorities able to govern, and protecting linguistic minorities and smaller parties, the proportionality is subject to thresholds to receive seats as well as premiums for receiving the most votes.[58]

A June 2006 referendum rejected an amendment of Italy's Constitution.[59] The amendment under heading of "devolution" (nominally greater health, education and public safety powers to Regions) would have encouraged parties to campaign through coalitions whose leader would become Prime Minister, as well as redefined Parliamentary roles.[60] Under the amendment only the Chamber of Deputies would ordinarily have considered legislative matters constitutionally reserved to the State, and undertaken confidence votes to unseat the Prime Minister and the Government. The renamed "Federal Senate of the Republic" would have considered only legislation within concurrent State and Regional power, plus budget legislation. In each case, the other House could propose modification, but the initial House would retain the definitive vote. In limited matters, concerning national maintenance of "civil and social rights" and "electoral legislation, governmental entities and fundamental functions of Municipalities, Provinces and Metropolitan Cities," both Houses would vote.

---

[57]Law no. 270 of Dec. 21, 2005, GAZZ. UFF. no. 303 of Dec. 30, 2005, ord. supp. no. 213.

[58]*Id.* In April 2006 Italians resident abroad first elected members of Parliament, an idea raised with the 1993 electoral reforms. Law no. 459 of Dec. 27, 2001, GAZZ. UFF. no. 4 of Jan. 5, 2002; Constitutional Law no. 1 of Jan. 17, 2000, GAZZ. UFF. no. 15 of Jan. 20, 2000; Constitutional Law no. 1 of Jan. 23, 2001, GAZZ. UFF. no. 19 of Jan. 24, 2001; DPR no. 104 of April 2, 2003, GAZZ. UFF. no. 109 of May 13, 2003; Law no. 270 of Dec. 21, 2005. Ballots in the four "in the world" districts may be cast by candidate name, unlike for domestic candidates elected by position on party list. *Id.* The close election lent significance to the 12 Deputies and 6 Senators so chosen. *La Cassazione conferma la vittoria dell'Unione*, LA REPUBBLICA (April 19, 2006).

[59]*Referendum, il trionfo del No*, LA REPUBBLICA (June 26, 2006). Of the 53.6 % of eligible voters participating, 61.7 % rejected the amendment. *Id.* Parliament, when adopting the amendment as Constitutional Law, failed to reach the majorities to obviate a referendum, GAZZ. UFF. no. 269 of Nov. 18, 2005. The Court of Cassation then for the first time found all three referendum triggers satisfied. *Referendum contro devolution: quorum ampiamente superato*, LA REPUBBLICA (March 14, 2006).

[60]Constitutional Law, GAZZ. UFF. no. 269 of Nov. 18, 2005.

11.4.3 Taxation Powers and Revenue Sharing

Until the 2001 Constitutional amendment discussed below, the Regions had no power to impose taxes; they depended solely on State revenue sharing. In large measure they continue to do so. The 2001 reform clarifies that Regions and other local governments set their own budgets and have their own resources, including to impose taxes, albeit "in harmony with the Constitution and according to the principles of coordination of public finance and tax system."[61] They are to participate proportionately in State taxes concerning their territory,[62] while State law is to establish an equalization fund for distribution to entities with lesser tax capacity per inhabitant (Regions limiting exercise of their taxing authority risk less ability to tap the fund),[63] and the State may selectively direct further resources.[64] Regions and other local governments may incur debt "only to finance expenses of investment," and no State guarantee is allowed.[65]

The available statistics suggest that Regions are exploring use of their augmented powers of taxation to build revenue bases,[66] albeit from a rickety foundation. Regional revenue bases include taxes on business activity, which Regions may adjust upward or downward by about 30 % from the nationally set base and differentiate in application by taxpayer category,[67] personal income taxes collected through a Regionally adjustable surcharge on income declared for State income

---

[61]CONST. art. 119.

[62]*Id.* On the particular, but analogous, rights of special statute Regions, *see* Emanuele Barone Ricciardelli, *Il rapporto tra finanza statale e finanza regionale: analisi di una recente sentenza della Corte Costituzionale*, TRIBUTI ON LINE: RIVISTA DEL MINISTERO DELL'ECONOMIA E DELLE FINANZE (June 2006).

[63]D.L. no. 56 of Feb. 18, 2000, art. 7, GAZZ. UFF. no. 62 of March 15, 2000.

[64]CONST. art. 119. On the Constitutional Court's role in determining limits on State control of Regional "equalization funds" spending, *see* Corte cost. judgment no. 49 of Jan. 29, 2004, GAZZ. UFF. of Feb. 4, 2004, *prima serie speciale* no. 5 (validating Emilia-Romagna Region challenge to State targeting of infrastructure funding).

[65]*Id.* Local government bond finance is emerging, to support capital investment and to securitize tax and other receivables. *See, e.g.*, reports of Dexia Crediop, an investment bank, *available at* www.dexia-crediop.it

[66]One set shows Regions' tax receipts as percent of total receipts climbing: 33.8 % in 1999, 37.8 % in 2000, 38.9 % in 2001, 39.1 % in 2002, and 39.8 % in 2003, with the balance substantially State transfers. Table 25.6, Istituto Nazionale di Statistica, ANNUARIO STATISTICO ITALIANO 2005 (Nov. 2005). Another set shows Regions in 2001 deriving 49.9 % of revenues from their own taxation, growing to 58.9 % in 2002, Fig. 3.1 at p. 129, Istituto Nazionale di Statistica, *Statistiche delle Amministrazioni pubbliche, Anni 2001–2002*, ANNUARIO (3) (2005), with the balance State transfers. *Id.* at Table 3.1 at p. 140 *et seq.*

[67]*Imposta Regionale sulle Attività Produttive* ("IRAP"), introduced by D.L. no. 446 of Dec. 15, 1997, art. 16, GAZZ. UFF. no. 298 of Dec. 23, 1997, upheld by European Court of Justice, Case C-475/03 (Oct. 3, 2006), as not reached by European limits on value added tax.

tax,[68] and dedicated shares set by State law in national value added tax[69] and gasoline excise tax revenues,[70] as well as miscellaneous Regionally set taxes including vehicle registration taxes and hazardous waste disposal surcharges.[71]

11.4.4 Non-judicial Resolution of Intergovernmental Conflicts

11.4.4.1 National Referenda

From its 1948 inception Italy's Constitution has contemplated two national referendum types: national law abrogation and reconsideration of constitutional amendment.[72] Each allows a disgruntled political minority of sufficient relevance direct recourse to the national electorate.

An abrogative referendum, on petition by 500,000 voters or five Regional Councils, achieves total or partial repeal of a law or an act having force of law if a majority of the electorate votes and a majority of valid votes cast supports the repeal.[73] Tax, budget, and treaty ratification laws, plus amnesties and pardons, are not subject to abrogative referenda.[74]

Constitutional amendments are by Constitutional laws, approved by each house of Parliament twice, at least 3 months apart, by absolute majority of each house the second time.[75] Should the second vote be a lesser majority, the amendment is subject to popular referendum triggered within 3 months of its publication by one fifth of the members of a house, 500,000 voters, or five Regional Councils.[76] Once the referendum is triggered, the measure is valid only if approved by a majority of those voting.[77]

---

[68]D.L. no. 446 of Dec. 15, 1997, art. 50, as amended by D.L. no. 56 of Feb. 18, 2000.

[69]Instituted for ordinary statute Regions by D.L. no. 56 of Feb. 18, 2000, art. 2.

[70]Instituted for ordinary statute Regions by Law no. 549 of Dec. 28, 1995, art. 3(12), GAZZ. UFF. no. 302 of Dec. 29, 1995, ord. supp., as amended by D.L. no. 56 of Feb. 18, 2000, art. 4, 12.

[71]See, e.g., Marco Annunziata and István Székely, *The Evolving Role of Regions in Italy: The Financing and Management of Health Care Services*, in International Monetary Fund, ITALY: SELECTED ISSUES, IMF Staff Country Report No. 00/82, (July 2000) at 95–96.

[72]Respectively, CONST. art. 75, CONST. art. 138. Regional territory and statute modification may also involve referenda of those directly concerned. Respectively, CONST. art. 132, CONST. art. 123.

[73]CONST. art. 75.

[74]Id. The Constitutional Court resolves disputes over such issues. Constitutional Law no. 1 of March 11, 1953, GAZZ. UFF. no. 62 of March 14, 1953.

[75]CONST. art 75.

[76]Id.

[77]Id.

Italy began as a Republic by a June 2, 1946 referendum on Republic vs. Monarchy (the Republic prevailed with 54 %).[78] The next referendum was not until 1974 (a failed referendum to revoke a law allowing divorce), followed by 1978 referenda on antiterrorism measures and political party finance, 1981 referenda on terrorism, life imprisonment, right to bear arms and abortion, and a 1985 referendum on pensions, and from then through 2003, Italians were called 12 times to vote on 41 referenda.[79]

Increased recourse to referenda coincides with the breakdown of uninterrupted center-left coalition governments and intensification of hollowing out the State's role in the 1990s, from below by Regionalization and from above by implementation of Italy's European obligations. The referenda reaffirm the national electorate's voice while affording a decisive mechanism to address political questions.

11.4.4.2 New Deal Institutions

In the 1990s Italy focused on invigoration of the State by implementing antitrust, energy, securities, telecom, and privacy authorities on the US New Deal model of independent regulatory commission with technical expertise. European Union directives motivated reform of national law in the relevant subject matters together with creation of the new authorities, a kind of State institution not previously present in Italy, divorced from the State's existing bureaucracy.[80]

CONSOB (*Commissione Nazionale per le Società e le Operazioni di Borsa*—National Commission for Companies and Securities Exchange Operations), Italy's first independent regulatory authority, created by 1974 legislation, addresses Italy's securities markets. Other independent authorities established in the 1990s are: the Communication Regulatory Authority (Agcom), Regulatory Authority for Electricity and Gas, which has overseen introduction of competition into Italian electricity markets; Authority for protection of personal data; Antitrust Authority; Authority for Oversight of Public Works; and National Commission of Guaranty of Implementation of the Law on Strike in Essential Public Services. Each is created by national legislation and run by an independent commission whose members are chosen in ways intended to assure independence.

---

[78]Ministero dell'Interno, http://referendum.interno.it/ind_ref.htm

[79]*Id.*

[80]*See* Patrick Del Duca and Duccio Mortillaro, *The Maturation of Italy's Response to European Community Law: Electric and Telecommunications Sector Institutional Innovations*, FORDHAM INTERNATIONAL LAW JOURNAL 23: 536 (2000); Lucia Musselli, *Direttive comunitarie e creazione amministrativa di un mercato nei servizi pubblici*, DIRITTO AMMINISTRATIVO 79 (1998).

11.4.5 Public Administration

Hiring and funding of the State and Regional public administrations are separate, but subject to common constitutional principles. Pursuant to Constitution Article 97(3), employment in the public administration, of the State, Regions, provinces and municipalities, is by public competition unless otherwise specified by law. Regions may not make unfounded exceptions, as the Constitutional Court emphasized in finding unconstitutional a Regional law that would have given priority to job candidates previously employed by the Region.[81] A significant portion of public administration employees are now subject to civil, rather than public law, *i.e.* employment disputes are resolved by ordinary courts applying the Civil Code rather than administrative courts applying public administrative law. Such employees are subject to collective bargaining between representative unions and a State agency.[82]

Italy's national bureaucracy will continue to dwarf that available to the Regions for the foreseeable future. By one count, the State employs about two million people, while as of 2002 Regions employed 90,000; provinces 58,000, municipalities, the traditional local government unit, 480,000; and local health and hospital authorities 700,000.[83] Although Regional autonomy and responsibilities are increasing, the weight and simple numerical preponderance of the State public administration challenges Regions in their efforts to develop their fields of action. Further, turnover in the public administration is slow. Even through the 1970s much of the public administration began employment with the State well prior to the 1948 Constitution.[84] The numerical weight of the State public administration and the continuing political battles as to direction of the State suggest that, the process of Regionalization and Italy's adoption of New Deal-style authorities notwithstanding, the longstanding, broadly-perceived issues of effectiveness of many parts of Italy's public administration will remain challenges.

---

[81] Corte cost. judgment no. 81 of March 3, 2006, GAZZ. UFF. of March 8, 2006, *prima serie speciale* no.10 (invalidates 2005 Abruzzo Region budget law provision for employment and career advantages to Regional employees, finding no basis for exception to "assuring access to public employment of the most competent and meritorious." ¶4.1.1 holdings in fact, *id.*).

[82] *Agenzia per la rappresentanza negoziale delle pubbliche amministrazioni* (Agency for negotiating representation of public administrations). D.L. no. 29 of Feb. 3, 1993, GAZZ. UFF. no. 30 of Feb. 6, 1993; D.L. no. 80 of March 31, 1998, GAZZ. UFF. no. 82 of April 8, 1998; D.L. no. 165 of March 30, 2001, GAZZ. UFF. no. 106 of May 9, 2001.

[83] Table 1.1 at p. 30, Istituto Nazionale di Statistica, *Statistiche delle Amministrazioni pubbliche, Anni 2001–2002. See* Cassese, Sabino, *Lo stato dell'amministrazione pubblica a vent'anni dal rapporto Giannini*, Giornale di diritto amministrativo (1) 99 (2000); Stefano Nespor, and Federico Boezio, *Quanti sono gli impiegati pubblici?*, RIP LA RIVISTA DELL'IMPIEGO E DELLA DIRIGENZA PUBBLICA no. 3 (2005); Pietro Virga, L'AMMINISTRAZIONE LOCALE (2nd ed., 2003).

[84] *See* Rodolfo "Rudy" Lewanski, *Executive Civil Servants and Politicians in Italian Administration: Some Empirical Evidence from Large Municipalities*, Paper presented at NISPAcee 9th Annual Conference on "Government, Market and the Civic Sector: The Search for a Productive Partnership," Riga, Latvia (May 10–12, 2001).

11.4.6 Asymmetries

The immediate special autonomy granted upon the Constitution's initial adoption to five outlying regions reflecting their prior legislative and administrative self-sufficiency and linguistic minorities has already been addressed.[85]

Although Italy's predominant language is now Italian, its first parliamentary debates when it emerged as a unified country in the 1860s were conducted in French, as the fraction of the population that spoke the variant of Tuscan that emerged as modern Italian was extremely limited. At Italy's unification, 10–12 % of the population is estimated to have been Italian-speaking, with 75 % illiteracy, accentuated in the south.[86] Through World War II, an important dimension of construction of the Italian state was the promotion and diffusion of standard Italian. The Italian constitution of 1948, adopted in reaction to the debacle of fascism, introduces a different emphasis, by providing that the Italian Republic is to protect linguistic minorities.[87] The charters of the special statute regions created in conjunction with the 1948 constitution provide specific rights in respect of language, *e.g.*, for German speakers in Trentino-Alto Adige/Südtirol and for French in Valle d'Aosta. Relatively recent national legislation in implementation of the constitutional provision for protection of linguistic minorities focuses on education and interactions with the public administration. It provides for protection of the language and culture of members of Italy's linguistic minorities who speak Albanian, *Catalán*, Croatian, French, Friulian, German, Greek, Ladino, Occitan, *Provençal*, Sardinian, and Slovenian.[88] Southern Italy's economic lag behind northern Italy remains a concern. Through the 1990s it was addressed principally by direct State subsidies and economic development initiatives outside the framework of the Regions.[89]

The continuing invention of an Italian federalism under the 1948 Constitution is not fundamentally the accommodation of territorial cleavages, *i.e.* a self-aware minority's concentration in a specific territorial area,[90] but rather redefinition of the State to accommodate national political impasse through invention of governmental levels other than the State itself, accompanied by devolution and delegation of

---

[85]See *supra* note 2 and accompanying text.

[86]Lucy Riall, GARIBALDI: INVENTION OF A HERO 135–36 (2007).

[87]Italian Constitution, art. 6. See Louis Del Duca and Patrick Del Duca, *An Italian Federalism?— the State, its Institutions and National Culture as Rule of Law Guarantor*, AMERICAN JOURNAL OF COMPARATIVE LAW 54: 799 (2006).

[88]Law no. 482 of Dec. 15, 1999, GAZZ. UFF. no. 297 of Dec. 20, 1999.

[89]*See* Carlo Trigilia, SVILUPPO SENZA AUTONOMIA. EFFETTI PERVERSI DELLE POLITICHE NEL MEZZOGIORNO (1994).

[90]*See* Ugo M. Amoretti, *Federalism and Territorial Cleavages*, in FEDERALISM AND TERRITORIAL CLEAVAGES 1–23, 2 (Ugo M. Amoretti and Nancy Bermeo, eds., 2004) (essays on federalism and territorial cleavage in Belgium, Canada, France, India, Mexico, Nigeria, Russia, Spain, Switzerland, Turkey, and United Kingdom, plus Italy).

responsibilities.[91] Italy's Christian Democrat-led coalition governments could not conceive national leadership by a Communist party that might turn away from Western Europe and the United States, but the energy of the left-wing opposition excluded from national power found expression in development of Regional and municipal autonomy. More recently, the *Lega Nord* and voices of the political right crafted a national role from Regional and municipal foundations.

11.5 Conclusion

Regionalization and Supranationalism in Italy have proceeded concurrently as means of working around political impasses in politics at the national level. Their progress has redefined the State's essence, paradoxically reinforcing its role as guarantor of the constitutional rule of law. Both Regionalization and Supranationalism with time appear to be contributing to distill the State's premier purpose to the highest level, namely, assuring the constitutional rule of law. In legal matters, the Italian system is likely to remain highly unified. Its constitutional court and national government work effectively to assure that Italy's European Union and other international obligations are implemented uniformly. Its Regional governments focus almost entirely on land use, health care and other matters that do not challenge the pre-eminence of national institutions, including the national codes and statutory law, the importance of the state budget and public administration, and the exclusively national system of courts.

The national political process, although frequently manifesting sustained impasse, has in actuality been creative in affirming the State and its institutions through their deconstruction by Regionalization and Supranationalism. The State in the expression of national politics instigates the nascent federalism, and the State's institutional mechanisms of control assure it's unfolding within the parameters of the constitutional rule of law. These mechanisms range from the Constitutional Court's role as arbiter of the bounds of State and Regional responsibilities, to the veto effects of national referenda, the budgetary controls under the continuing dominance of State revenue-sharing, and the *Corte dei Conti* audit of all governmental bodies. The uniformity of national legal culture further affirms the State's continuing role as guarantor of the constitutional rule of law. Within this framework, the Italian electorate has begun to vote in ways that alternate State governance among political groupings, while simultaneously supporting increasingly vibrant Regional and municipal polities.

---

[91] Ugo M. Amoretti, *Italy: Political Institutions and the Mobilization of Territorial Differences*, in FEDERALISM AND TERRITORIAL CLEAVAGES 181–200 (Ugo M. Amoretti and Nancy Bermeo, eds., 2004), although focusing on the last decade's "political mobilization of the territorial cleavage between north and south," recounts Italian politics and governmental structures consistently with the present State reconstruction and constitutional rule of law analysis.

The Italian State arose as a unitary State because the territorial entities that Piemonte incorporated into the new State of Italy lacked effective political institutions to sustain any federal system.[92] Moreover, the Piemonte regime's elitist character, with its flexible constitution, paved the way for degeneration into the fascist debacle. In view of this history, that Italy's present flourishing as a State under the constitutional rule of law is so tied to the development of its Regions, accompanied by its participation in the supranational European Union, is a happy irony, which builds upon Italy's diverse histories of its regions, yet also their common history with the rule of law. Although slow in developing, recourse to regionalization under the 1948 Constitution to work around political impasses, is building political capacity for Regional government, ranging through public administration, taxation, and regional politics distinct from national politics. The story of the Italian State's Regionalization and Supranationalism is a story of continuous procedural adjustments to work through and around national-level political impasses by newly invented institutions and practices.

The tools for State control of the Regions, including the Constitutional Court's protection and promotion of Regional spheres of activity, together confirm classification of Italian Regionalism as a system of Regional autonomy guaranteed by a national constitution, certainly not the joining of sovereign states in a federal or supranational union. Conversely, the Regions' legislative and budgetary autonomy confirm Italian Regionalism as more than the mere decentralization of administrative functions evidenced in unitary states.

---

[92] *See* Ziblatt, *supra* note 1.

Chapter 12
Federalism and Legal Unification in Malaysia

Hean Leng Ang and Amanda Whiting

12.1 Overview

The current Federation of Malaysia is now comprised of the former British colonies of Penang and Malacca (the Straits Settlements), nine former British protectorates previously ruled by Malay sultans (the Federated and Unfederated Malay States of Selangor, Negri Sembilan, Pahang, Perak, Johor, Kedah, Kelantan, Perlis and Terengganu) and the two Borneo states of Sabah and Sarawak (also former British possessions). The Borneo States are referred to as East Malaysia, and the rest as Peninsular (or, sometimes, West) Malaysia. The Federation also includes three Federal Territories: the wealthy capital city of Kuala Lumpur, the new purpose-built administrative capital of Putrajaya, and the small island of Labuan located near the coast of Sabah.[1]

ANG Hean Leng, LLB (Malaya); LLM (Melbourne); Advocate and Solicitor, High Court of Malaya; Sessional Lecturer, School of Arts and Sciences, Monash University (Sunway Campus), Selangor, Malaysia.

Amanda WHITING, Doctor, BA(Hons); Dip Ed; Grad Dip Modern Languages (Indonesian); LLB (Hons); PHD (History) (Melbourne), Associate Director, Malaysia, Asian Law Centre, The University of Melbourne, Australia.

[1] For a standard history, see Virginia Matheson Hooker, *A Short History of Malaysia*: *Linking East and West* (Sydney: Allen & Unwin, 2003).

H.L. Ang (✉)
Level 17 Menara Tokio Marine Life, Lee Hishamnuddin Allen & Gledhill,
189 Jalan Tun Razak, 50400 Kuala Lumpur, Malaysia

School of Arts and Sciences, Monash University (Sunway Campus), Selangor, Malaysia
e-mail: ahl@lh-ag.com

A. Whiting
University of Melbourne Law School, Asian Law Centre, Melbourne 3010, Victoria, Australia
e-mail: a.whiting@unimelb.edu.au

English law was introduced gradually from 1807 via direct colonization of the Straits Settlements and the more indirect method of "advice" offered to the Malay sultans by British "Residents" or "Advisors". It was imposed over the top of Malay *adat* (customary laws) – a mixture of local and mostly unwritten customs strongly inflected by Islamic law – and Islamic law (*syariah*) which had been introduced gradually from the fifteenth century and became associated with Malay princely rule. Older accretions of Buddhist and Hindu law and ritual continued, but in a minor way, and were mostly incorporated into *adat*.[2] During the era of British tutelage, immigration – from India and China, in particular – was encouraged to supply labor for colonial economic projects. Populations of Indians and Chinese had been resident in the Malay archipelago prior to the arrival of the British, but their numbers clearly increased because of colonial policy.

By 1895, four of the Malay princely states formed a Federation (the Federated Malay States, FMS) and agreed that their affairs would be coordinated by a Resident-General appointed by the British. In retrospect, this process can be seen as preparing the way for the larger post-independence Federation.[3] After World War II and the defeat of the occupying Japanese forces, the returning British authorities recognized the eventuality of independence for Malaya. The first step was a proposal for a unitary state, the Malayan Union, but this was opposed passionately by the newly formed Malay nationalist party, the United Malays National Organization (UMNO) because, amongst other things, it ceded too much of the former sovereignty of the Malay states and their traditional rulers. Another basis for opposing the Union was its equal conferral of citizenship upon migrants from India and China. Leaders of the newly emerging Indian and Chinese political parties also opposed the Union, in part because it was profoundly undemocratic. Hence the British abandoned the plan after a year, and instead set about establishing the Federation of Malaya, which lasted from 1948 until full independence (Merdeka) in 1957.

The constitutional arrangements for Merdeka and the Federal Constitution were drafted in London by a commission (the Reid Commission) which had consulted widely amongst the political elite in Malaya. It was particularly guided by the wishes of the Alliance, a coalition of UMNO, the Malayan Indian Congress (MIC) and the Malaysian Chinese Association (MCA) which had struck a multi-cultural political bargain for power-sharing after independence.[4] The Malay rulers (Sultans) in each state were also consulted and separately represented at the Commission's

---

[2] Andrew Harding, "Global Doctrine and Local Knowledge: Law in Southeast Asia" (2002) 51(1) *International and Comparative Law Quarterly* 35.

[3] Andrew Harding, *Law, Government and the Constitution in Malaysia* (Leiden: Brill, 1996), 17–18.

[4] See the lengthy treatment in *id*. passim, but esp 24–40, and Joseph M Fernando, *The Making of the Malayan Constitution* (Kuala Lumpur: Malaysian Branch of the Royal Asiatic Society, 2002). The Reid Commission report is appended to Kevin Tan and Thio Li-ann (eds.) *Constitutional Law in Malaysia and Singapore* (Singapore: Butterworths, 1997) and J.C. Fong, *Constitutional Federalism in Malaysia* (Kuala Lumpur: Thompson/Sweet & Maxwell Asia, 2008).

hearings. A significant aspect of that elite consociational bargain was the grant of full citizenship for ethnic minorities in return for the recognition of the "special place" of the Malays in the Federation and continuation of pre-federation special protective measures for them, such as land reservations and preferential access to the civil service, as well as recognition of Malay (Bahasa Malaysia or Bahasa Melayu) as the national language. Some of the "traditional" privileges of the Malay sultans in the states were also recognized and preserved in this arrangement, as was the place of Islam as the "religion of the federation".[5]

The Federation was extended by the admission of the Crown Colony of Singapore and of the British protectorates of Sabah and Sarawak in 1963, thus forming the Federation of Malaysia (previously Malaya).[6] Singapore was expelled in 1965. Sabah and Sarawak negotiated special treatment as the price of their admission, and so they are in a relatively more powerful position *vis à vis* the central government than are the other states.[7]

It is impossible to understand the dynamics and complexity of federal-state relations in Malaysia without appreciation of the political control exerted by UMNO since independence. UMNO has dominated the coalition National Front (Barisan Nasional, BN, the successor to the Alliance from 1974) since 1957, and it has retained power by being returned with strong majorities at each federal election between 1957 and 2013. Furthermore, most of the component states have been governed by UMNO-led coalitions for most of the period since 1957. Kelantan, which was ruled by the Islamic party, Parti Islam se-Malaysia (PAS), between 1959–1977, and 1990 to the present, is the notable exception.[8] The UMNO party-political machine has been able to use party discipline – and financial incentives – to align state and national political and legislative priorities.[9] The picture in the Borneo states of Sabah and Sarawak is more complex, as both states have been able

---

[5]There is much written about this, but see especially Harding, *Law, Government and the Constitution*, supra note 3, at pp. 24–40; and Joseph M Fernando, "The Position of Islam in the Constitution of Malaysia" (2006) 37(2) *Journal of Southeast Asian Studies* 249.

[6]There is an extensive literature; two useful recent treatments are Tan Tai Yong, *Creating "Greater Malaysia:" Decolonization and the Political Merger* (Singapore: ISEAS, 2007) and Regina Lim, *Federal-State Relations in Sabah, Malaysia: The Berjaya Administration, 1976–85* (Singapore: ISEAS, 2008). Despite the more limited scope promised in the title, the latter in fact provides a useful coverage of the 1963 merger.

[7]B.H. Shafruddin, *The Federal Factor in Government and Politics of Peninsular Malaysia* (1987), 38 characterizes the federation as a "two-tier federation system: the Federation of Malaya which federated the original eleven States and the Federation of Malaysia which federated these States with the three new States".

[8]The neighboring state of Terengganu was briefly governed by PAS from 1999 to 2004, and Penang, on the opposite side of the peninsula, was briefly governed by the opposition liberal party Gerakan following the 1969 elections; however Gerakan subsequently joined the UMNO-led coalition in 1973.

[9]Mohammad Agus Yusoff, *Malaysian Federalism: Conflict of Consensus* (Bangi: Penerbit Universiti Kebangasaan Malaysia, 2006), 27, 323–347, especially pp. 325, 335, 340; and Lim, *Federal-State Relations*, supra note 6, p. 53.

to assert greater *de jure* and *de facto* autonomy from the centre; nonetheless, the influence of UMNO is apparent.[10] Malaysian political scientist Mohammad Agus Yusoff concludes "Thus, it seems clear that a fundamental dimension of centre-state relations is the basically political nature of the constitutional framework within which they operate in the Malaysian context; the federal government has always actively sought to ensure that the governments in the states are formed from the same party or from a member of the coalition of parties ruling at the centre".[11]

However, at the most recent general election in March 2008, while the ruling BN coalition retained power, it suffered massive losses (including the loss of several component state governments). At the time of writing, the BN coalition no longer retains the two-thirds majority needed to push through constitutional amendments.[12] The political effect of this is that federal-state relations, particularly on the peninsula, are now more fractious and unpredictable than they have been for most of Malaysia's history. Some of the states have begun to use their legislative power to enact laws, such as the Freedom of Information enactments of Selangor and Penang, which markedly depart from national policies.[13]

Race and religion are constant factors in Malaysian political life; indeed, one well known public intellectual refers to his country as "multi-racist" rather than "multi-racial".[14] The race riots that occurred in Peninsular Malaysia in the context of a federal election in May 1969 are a kind of national trauma. The episode is not well understood and indeed public discussion is discouraged.[15] A state of emergency was declared and parliamentary rule was suspended for 2 years. The episode, which

---

[10]See, generally, Mohammad Agus Yusoff, *Malaysian Federalism*, *supra* note 9, chapters 5 and 6; Lim, *Federal-State Relations*, *supra* note 6, chapters 3–6.

[11]Mohammad Agus Yusoff, *supra* note 9, at p. 330.

[12]The PAS government was returned in Kelantan, and in addition component parties of the newly formed opposition coalition Pakatan Rakyat (composed of the Democratic Action Party (DAP), PAS and the National Justice Party (Keadilan Rakyat)) gained control of the states of Penang, Selangor, Perak and Kedah. Political developments and by-elections since 2008 have resulted in a shift of power away from the opposition in several parliamentary and state constituencies. The most dramatic instance is Perak, where several Pakatan Rakyat members defected to the Barisan Nasional, triggering a constitutional crisis: see Audrey Quay (ed.) *Perak: A State of Crisis: Rants, Reviews and Reflections on the Overthrow of Democracy and the Rule of Law in Malaysia* (Petaling Jaya: LoyarBurok Publications, 2010). Despite these electoral shifts, BN has not regained the crucial two-thirds majority: as of May 2013, BN held 133 out of 222 federal constituencies.

[13]*The Freedom of Information (State of Selangor) Enactment 2010* received bipartisan support in the Selangor Legislative Assembly and was enacted in early 2011: R. Nadeswaran, "A Step Forward for Transparency" *The Sun* 6 April 2011; tabling of Penang's Freedom of Information bill has been postponed to allow for further community consultation, "Tabling of Info Bill put off" *The New Straits Times*, 4 May 2011.

[14]Farish Noor, "Malaysia and the Myth of Tanah Melayu" Part 1, 22 August 2007; Part 2, 29 August 2007 www.othermalaysia.org.

[15]In a recent book, human rights activist and historian Kua Kia Soong challenges the official version of May 13. *See* Kua Kia Soong, *May 13: Declassified Documents on the Malaysian Riots of 1969* (Petaling Jaya, Selangor: Suaram, 2007).

was represented by politicians such as future Prime Minister Mahathir Mohamad[16] as being justifiably caused by the anger of the Malays at their poverty relative to the more prosperous immigrant Chinese community, was answered by the New Economic Policy (NEP), a government plan for radical social engineering based on affirmative action for the Malay ethnic majority. This state planning instrument has formally come to an end. Nevertheless, similar policies continue, although they are also not given legal form. They are not evident from the architecture of the constitution or the formal laws, which only express the bare bones of the consociational bargain of 1957, with its recognition of the place of Islam and the special position of the Malay rulers in the federation, and recognition in article 153 of Malay land reservations and Malay quotas in business licences, educational institutions, scholarship places and public service appointments. Racial preference for ethnic Malays in education and business (including government-linked business and tendering) is thus achieved more by policy than law. Nevertheless, the social and political reality of race-based politics must be understood to appreciate the Malaysian legal system.

The Federation that was established in 1957 was already strongly central. Nothing has changed over the years to make it less so, and Malaysia's peculiar cocktail of race, religion and politics contributes, in complex ways, to maintain the strength of the center and the weakness of the states. Southeast Asian constitutional law expert Andrew Harding concludes that Malaysia is "not a true federation but rather a quasi-federation" because of the strong centripetal forces at work.[17]

12.2 The Federal Distribution and Exercise of Lawmaking Power

12.2.1 Central Legislative Jurisdiction

The legislative domain of the Federal Parliament in Malaysia (the central authority) is expressly set out in the Ninth Schedule of the Federal Constitution in two lists. The Federal List (List I), enumerates matters with respect to which the Parliament may make laws, and the Concurrent List (List III), itemizes matters within the legislative competence of both the Federal Parliament and State Legislative Assemblies. The Federal List is extensive. It includes all major aspects of government and public functions. In comparison, the matters in the Concurrent List are relatively less

---

[16]Mahathir bin Mohamad, *The Malay Dilemma* (Singapore: D. Moore for the Asia Pacific Press, 1970).

[17]Harding, *Law, Government and the Constitution, supra* note 3, at p. 182. See also the view of Malaysian political scientist Mohammad Agus Yusoff, *supra* note 9, at p. 325, that "the Malaysian federal constitution was established on a basis favouring a distinct gravitational pull of power towards the centre, providing the states with only a circumscribed autonomy".

significant. List II of the Ninth Schedule enumerates those matters which fall within the jurisdiction of the component States. By virtue of article 77, residual legislative power resides with the component states, i.e., if a matter is not enumerated in any of the Ninth Schedule Lists, then it falls within the competence of a State Legislature. Below is a table setting out the constitutional distribution of legislative jurisdiction.

Distribution of legislative jurisdiction (ninth schedule, federal constitution)		
Federal list (List I)	State list (List II)	Concurrent list (List III)
1. External affairs	1. Malay custom and the religion of Islam	1. Social welfare
2. Defence	2. Land	2. Scholarships
3. Internal security	3. Agriculture and forestry	3. Protection of wild animals and wild birds
4. Civil and criminal law and procedure and the administration of justice	4. Local government	4. Animal husbandry, prevention of animal cruelty
5. Federal citizenship, naturalization and aliens	5. Services of a local character	5. Town and country planning
6. Federal government machinery; and elections to Federal Parliament and State the Legislative Assemblies	6. State public works and water	6. Vagrancy and itinerant hawkers
7. Finance (including currency, banking and tax)	7. State government machinery	7. Public health, sanitation and the prevention of diseases
8. Trade, commerce and industry (including insurance, intellectual property)	8. State holidays	8. Drainage and irrigation
9. Shipping, navigation and fisheries	9. Creation of offences related to state matters	9. Rehabilitation of mining land and soil eroded land
10. Communication and transport	10. Inquiries for state purposes	9A. Fire safety measures
11. Federal works and power; water supplies except those wholly within one state	11. Indemnity related to state matters	9B. Culture and sports
12. Surveys, inquiries and research	12. Turtles and riverine fishing	9C. Housing and provisions for housing accommodation
13. Education	12A. Libraries, museums and historical sites other than those declared federal	9D. Water supplies and services
	Supplementary matters for Sabah and Sarawak (List IIA)	
14. Medicine and health	13. Native law and custom	9E. Preservation of heritage
15. Labour and social security	14. Incorporation of state authorities and bodies	*Supplementary matters for Sabah and Sarawak* (List IIIA)

(continued)

(continued)

Distribution of legislative jurisdiction (ninth schedule, federal constitution)		
Federal list (List I)	State list (List II)	Concurrent list (List III)
16. Welfare of the aborigines	15. Ports and harbours other than those declared federal	10. Personal law
17. Professional occupations	16. Cadastral land surveys	11. Adulteration of foodstuffs and other goods
18. Federal holidays	17 (repealed)	12. Shipping under 15 tons
19. Unincorporated societies	18. In Sabah, the Sabah Railway	13. Water power
20. Control of agricultural pests	19 (repealed)	14. Agricultural and forestry research
21. Newspapers, publications, publishers, printing and printing presses	20 water supplies and services (subject to federal list)	15. Charities and charitable trusts operating wholly within the State
22. Censorship		16. Theatres, cinemas and places of amusement
23. Theatres and cinemas and places of public amusement		17. Elections to the State Assembly during the period of indirect elections
25. Co-operative societies		18. In Sabah, until 1970, medicine and health
25A. Tourism		
26. Prevention and extinguishment of fire		
27. Matters relating to Federal Territories		

Matters in the State List (List II) may also be legislatively exercised by the Parliament for purposes of implementing an international obligation, or promoting uniformity of the laws of two or more component States, or upon the request of a component State's Legislative Assembly.[18] Federal laws made to meet an international obligation may only be introduced into Parliament after consultation with the government of any State concerned, yet it seems that the States do not have a constitutional capacity to veto such laws.[19] However, a Federal law made for purposes of uniformity or upon a State's request must be legislatively adopted by a particular State before coming into operation in that State. According to article 76(3) such a law will be considered as State, rather than Federal law, and as such may be amended or repealed by a subsequent State law. Additional exceptions apply in relation to certain subject matter. In implementing the Federation's international obligations, the Parliament may not legislate in relation to Islamic law matters, Malay custom, or the native law and customs of Sabah and Sarawak: thus "sensitive

---

[18]Federal Constitution, art 76 (1) (a), (b), (c).
[19]Federal Constitution, art 76(2).

issues" are immune from amendment in this manner.[20] With regard to the matters of land and local government (concerning which there are also constitutionally established consultative bodies), express adoption and incorporation of the Federal laws into State enactments by the State Legislative Assemblies is not required if the Federal law is made for the purpose only of ensuring uniformity of law and policy.[21] This allows the central government much more legislative power to harmonize the laws in these two areas.

Constitutional provision for the proclamation of a state of emergency can also profoundly affect the Federal-State distribution of legislative (and executive) power. Once a state of emergency has been proclaimed under article 150 – where the executive "is satisfied that a grave emergency exists whereby the security, or the economic life, or public order of the Federation or any part thereof is threatened"[22] – then the Federal Parliament may make laws on any matter, regardless of the Ninth Schedule division of legislative competence, and indeed "notwithstanding anything in this constitution".[23] While a state of emergency is in force, no Ordinance issued by the executive and no Parliamentary statute can be declared invalid for inconsistency with *any* provision of the Constitution.[24] Furthermore, during a declared state of emergency, Federal executive authority extends "to any matter within the legislative authority of a State and to the giving of directions to the Government of a State".[25] The only constitutional limit on this "breathtakingly wide power"[26] is provided by clause 6A which provides that Parliament's legislative power under article 150 does not extend to matters of Islam or Malay custom or the native laws and customs of Sabah and Sarawak, nor may it be used to pass laws inconsistent with existing constitutional provisions regarding religion, citizenship or language. Of the four states of emergency proclaimed since Merdeka in 1957,[27] two were directed to resolving political disputes *within* a State. On both occasions the Federal government intervened directly in the States of Sabah[28] and Kelantan[29] to ensure that the political outcome favored the central government. Malaysian

---

[20]Federal Constitution, art 76(2).

[21]Federal Constitution, art 76(4).

[22]Federal Constitution, art 150(1).

[23]Federal Constitution, art 150(5). This means that the constitutional requirement to consult with the Conference of Rulers (the council of hereditary Malay sultans accompanied by and acting on the advice of their elected advisors) before certain kinds of laws are presented to parliament does not apply.

[24]Federal Constitution, art 150(6).

[25]Federal Constitution, art 150(4).

[26]Harding, *Law, Government and the Constitution*, supra note 3, at p. 155.

[27]In 1964, 1966, 1969 and 1977: *see generally*, Harding, *Law, Government and the Constitution*, supra note 3, at pp. 159–163; Wu Min Aun, *The Malaysian Legal System* (3rd edition) (Kuala Lumpur: Longmans, 2005), 307–324.

[28]*Emergency (Federal Constitution and the Constitution of Sarawak) Act* 1966; *see* Harding, *Law, Government and the Constitution*, supra note 3, at pp. 160–161.

[29]*Emergency Powers (Kelantan) Act* 1977; *see* Harding, *Law, Government and the Constitution*, supra note 3, at pp. 162–163.

constitutional expert Professor Andrew Harding concludes that these powers are "alarming from the point of view of the States" since they indicate that "there are no legal or political limitations, during the currency of an emergency proclamation, on the power of the Federation to interfere with the division of legislative and executive powers between the Federation and the States, or even to violate a State constitution."[30] The fact that such intervention has not occurred more often perhaps owes more to political self-restraint on the part of the ruling coalition government (the Barisan Nasional) than to legal impediment.

Articles 73 and 74 of the Federal Constitution permit the Federal Parliament to make laws for the whole or any part of the Federation, and to legislate extra-territorially. Furthermore, the Federal Parliament may legislate for the States for the purposes set out in article 76: to implement an international obligation; to promote uniformity between two or more States; when requested to do so by a State Legislative Assembly; and, for the purpose of ensuring uniformity of law and policy, in relation to land and local government. Examples of Federal legislation enacted pursuant to article 76 include the *National Land Code* 1966, the *Local Government Act* 1976, the *Land Conservation Act* 1960, and the *National Forestry Act* 1984.

Amendments to the Federal Constitution are made by federal law.[31] As such, the Federal Parliament is empowered to amend the Federal Constitution. Apart from the threshold requirement of an affirmative vote of two-thirds majority in both houses of Parliament, there is no requirement of consent from each component state to amend the constitution even on matters such as admitting new state or territory into the federation.[32] Special safeguards are provided, however, for Sabah and Sarawak in relation to specific matters such as citizenship, appointment of judges in Sabah and Sarawak,[33] religion, language and the special treatment of natives of Sabah and Sarawak.[34] Otherwise, component states have an indirect safeguard over amendment of the Federal Constitution through the Conference of Rulers, whose consent is required in respect of certain matters such as the special privileges of the Malays, the National Language, and the natives of Sabah and Sarawak. The consent of the Conference of Rulers is also required for any constitutional amendment touching restrictions on freedom of expression, citizenship, the privileges of Federal Parliament and the State Legislative Assemblies, federal guarantees regarding the state constitutions, and the Rulers themselves.[35]

---

[30]Harding, *Law, Government and the Constitution*, *supra* note 3, at p. 161. *See also* B.H. Shafruddin, *supra* note 7, at pp. 30–33.

[31]Federal Constitution, art 159(1).

[32]*The Government of the State of Kelantan v. The Government of the Federation of Malaya and Tunku Abdul Rahman Putra Al-Haj* [1963] MLJ 355; Johan Shamsuddin Sabaruddin, "The Kelantan Challenge" in Andrew Harding and H.P. Lee (eds.) *Constitutional Landmarks in Malaysia: The First 50 years 1957–2007* (Kuala Lumpur: LexisNexis, 2007).

[33]*Robert Linggi v. The Government of Malaysia* Kota Kinabalu High Court Suit No. K21-07-2009 (unreported).

[34]Federal Constitution, article 161E.

[35]Federal Constitution, article 159 (5).

Of the items in the Federal List, the most significant in terms of impact upon the nation are internal security (including police and preventive detention); civil and criminal law and procedure (which involves the entire administration of justice with the exception of state-based Islamic law (*syariah*), courts of limited jurisdiction, and the native courts of the East Malaysia States of Sabah and Sarawak (discussed below)); finance (including banking and taxation)[36]; trade, commerce and industry; communications and transport; education; health; labor and social security; the press and censorship. Considering the importance of tourism to the Malaysian economy, that subject of legislative power may be deemed significant also.[37] Finally, while land is itemized as a State matter in List II of the 9th Schedule, the Federal Parliament has used its powers under article 76(4) to enact a *National Land Code* (1966), which applies to all of Peninsular Malaysia (but not East Malaysia[38]).

In light of the extensive matters with respect to which the Parliament may make laws, which include almost all significant aspects of private and public laws (and see also the overview to this part, above), most of these areas are significant in practice-based terms, and very few areas are less significant than the others. Federal law is disproportionately more significant than State law. As noted in the Overview, international and Malaysian commentators consider that Malaysia may best be classified as a quasi-federation rather than a true federation, or at least that the centralizing forces are remarkably strong.[39] Indeed, the former Chief Minister of the state of Melaka complained in 1979 that "in many other federations municipal councils have much more powers than State Governments in Malaysia."[40]

12.2.2 State Legislative Jurisdiction

Peninsular Malaysian States have a limited legislative jurisdiction expressly conferred by Federal Constitution Articles 73 and 72 and enumerated in List II of the 9th Schedule (discussed above): Islamic law and personal law (these are narrowly

---

[36]Note that taxation as a federal matter is also authorized by Federal Constitution, article 96.

[37]In relation to tourism, it should be noted that prior to 1994, this was a residual matter and hence the subject of state laws and policies. In that year the Federal Parliament amended the federal legislative list to include Tourism as a federal matter – a step that plainly still rankles with the former Attorney General of Sarawak, who tartly observes that the states were not consulted even though the amendment plainly affected them in significant ways: Fong, *Constitutional Federalism*, supra note 4, at p. 56.

[38]Federal Constitution, article 95D expressly precludes the extension to Sabah and Sarawak of uniform federal legislation with respect to land or local government which might otherwise be made pursuant to article 76(4).

[39]Harding. *Law, Government and the Constitution*, supra note 3, at p. 182. For a contrasting, but much earlier view, see Salleh Abas, "Federalism in Malaysia: Changes in the First Twenty Years" in Tun Mohamad Hashim, H.P. Lee and F.A. Trindade (eds.) *The Constitution of Malaysia: Its Development 1957–1977* (Kuala Lumpur: Oxford University Press, 1978), chapter 8.

[40]Adib Hj Mohd Adam, as reported in the *New Straits Times*, 22 July 1979, cited in Fong, *Constitutional Federalism*, supra note 4, at p. 65, note 46.

defined, see below); land; agriculture; local government; services of a local character (for example, burial grounds, markets and fairs); public works for a state purpose, state roads, water and riparian rights (but not water supply); the machinery of state government; state holidays; creation of offences in respect of State List matters; inquiries for State purposes; indemnity in respect of State List matters; turtles and riverine fishing; libraries, museums and historical monuments and archives (Of course, the Federal Parliament may legislate on these matters with respect to the Federal Territories of Kuala Lumpur, Labuan and Putrajaya.) Two of these State items, land and local government, may be subjected to central control by laws made "for the purpose only of ensuring uniformity of law and policy"[41] and this has been achieved through the enactment by the Federal Parliament of *National Land Code* 1966 and the *Local Government Act* 1976. Furthermore, the National Land Council and the National Council for Local Government (established under articles 91 and 95A respectively, and discussed briefly below) coordinate national policy in these two areas.

As part of the political bargain exacted at the time of their accession to the Federation in 1963,[42] the East Malaysia states of Sabah and Sarawak enjoy comparatively more autonomy than the original States: the national codes governing land and local government do not apply to them,[43] and they have control over immigration, which is elsewhere a federal matter.[44] Their enlarged jurisdiction includes the basic State List and is supplemented by List IIA, which itemizes: native law and custom (more broadly defined than in the original State List); incorporation of authorities and bodies set up under State law; ports and harbours (other than those declared to be federal); cadastral land surveys; the railway (only for Sabah); and, subject to the Federal List, water supplies and services. Apart from the supplementary legislative list, Sabah and Sarawak are granted additional legislative powers by other provisions of the Federal Constitution in relation to: sales tax (Article 95B(3))[45]; borrowing powers (Article 112B); export duty on minerals produced in Sabah and Sarawak (Article 112C(3)); royalties on minerals produced in Sabah and Sarawak (Article 112C(4)); and the right to practice before courts in Sabah and Sarawak (Article 161B).

---

[41] Federal Constitution, art 76(4).

[42] *See* Harding, *Law, Government and the Constitution, supra* note 3, at pp. 40, 173–176; Wu Min Aun, *supra* note 27, at p. 47.

[43] Federal Constitution, art 95D.

[44] *Immigration Act 1959/63* (Revised 1974) (Act 155)), Part VII Special Provisions for East Malaysia. This is actually a conferral of federal *executive* power upon the East Malaysian state governments. The power includes the right to refuse entry of West Malaysians into East Malaysia, and to require West Malaysians to obtain a work permit in order to obtain gainful employment in East Malaysia. Originally intended to protect the natives of East Malaysia from being outnumbered by internal migration from the comparatively more developed peninsular states, these provisions have been used also to prevent scrutiny of East Malaysian governance and the conduct of elections, see 'Denied Entry, Bersih Chief Sues Sarawak Government' *The Malaysian Insider* June 14, 2011.

[45] Although it was inserted in the constitution when the East Malaysian states joined in 1963, it has not been enlivened until recently, with the *State Sales Tax Enactment* 1998 (Sabah).

While these supplementary powers grant more legislative authority and independence to Sabah and Sarawak than to the other component States, the additional powers are relatively less significant as most important areas of legislation remain with the Federal Parliament.

The Federal Constitution permits federal legislative power to be conferred upon the States by a valid Federal Statute: article 76A. Thus the States' legislative powers can be extended by the Federal Parliament to include any of the matters in the Federal legislative list (List I). One instance of this is the *Incorporation (State Legislatures Competency) Act* 1962 (Revised 1989) (Act 380) which allows State Legislative Assemblies to pass enactments relating to the incorporation of State bodies corporate, a subject which otherwise falls under the legislative jurisdiction of the Federal Parliament. Sabah and Sarawak also enjoy greater legislative power indirectly.

Component States may continue to exercise any concurrent legislative power, but any state law inconsistent with a federal law shall be void to the extent of the inconsistency.[46] Procedurally, the Federal Constitution mandates a 4 week period between the publication of a bill dealing with a concurrent matter and further legislative action, apparently to allow time for federal-state consultation to avoid possible conflict.[47] An exception is where there is ground of urgency.[48] It is questionable whether 4 weeks is sufficient time to enable meaningful consultation.[49]

Federal laws are much more significant than State laws, but the most important areas of component States' regulation in practice are land, Islamic law, Sabah and Sarawak's native law and custom, and local government-related matters.

State jurisdiction over Islamic law (*syariah*) is increasingly important and the topic of *syariah* jurisdiction is increasingly contentious, as rival religious and political forces tussle over the jurisdictional boundary between the two systems, a line which is imperfectly demarcated by Federal Constitution Article 121(1A) and the tangled mess of case law interpreting and applying it.[50] In Malaysia, the *syariah* jurisdiction of the States is enumerated – and thereby confined – in item 1 of List II of the 9th Schedule, where it is defined as Islamic law relating to family law (betrothal, marriage, divorce, maintenance, adoption, legitimacy and guardianship), inheritance and gifts, charitable and religious trusts; Malay

---

[46]Federal Constitution, art 74(4).

[47]Federal Constitution, art 79(2); Fong, *supra* note 4, at pp. 75–76.

[48]Federal Constitution, art 79(2).

[49]Fong, *supra* note 4, at p. 75.

[50]See further Thio Li-ann, "Jurisdictional Imbroglio: Civil and Religious Courts, Turf Wars and Article 121(1A) of the Federal Constitution" in Andrew Harding and H.P. Lee (eds.) *Constitutional Landmarks in Malaysia: The First 50 Years 1957–2007* (Kuala Lumpur: LexisNexis, 2007) and Amanda Whiting, "Desecularizing Malaysian Law?" in Sarah Biddulph and Pip Nicholson (eds.) *Examining Practice, Interrogating Theory: Comparative Law in Asia* (Leiden: Martinus Nijhoff, 2008).

customs; Islamic religious revenue, the regulation of mosques; and the "creation and punishment of offences by persons professing the religion of Islam against the precepts of that religion"; the organization of *syariah* courts; and the determination of matters of Islamic law and doctrine and Malay custom. Because this item includes the family law and personal faith of more than half the population of Malaysia, it is of great importance. Since Islamic law is a matter for the States (but of course for the Federal Parliament in relation to Federal Territories) whereas law, justice and the courts are matters for the Federation, the growing tensions between the secular, common-law based legal system and Islamic law are also a manifestation of dissonance between the secular Federal Constitution and State and Federal Territory *syariah* statutes and subordinate rules, as well as the rival jurisdictions of the secular national court system and the state-based *syariah* courts.[51]

With respect to the peninsular States, land and local government are the most important areas where central and component State regulation coexist. In essence, the federal laws – *National Land Code* 1966 and *Local Government Act* 1976 – set out the operational framework and general principles, and the State and State agencies make the detailed enactments, rules and regulations.

Control over water is emerging as an area of great importance because of the trend to privatization of water resources as well as concern about water quality and security.[52] The constitutional provisions are complex and overlapping. The Federal Parliament has responsibility for water supplies, rivers and canals except those wholly within one State, and the production, distribution and supply of water power.[53] The States have responsibility for water, including rivers and canals but excluding water supplies and services, and for riparian rights,[54] as well as over turtles and riverine fishing.[55] Drainage and irrigation are concurrently shared, and, confusingly, item 9D of the Concurrent List also specifies concurrent responsibility for water supplies and services "subject to the Federal list". In addition, the East Malaysian States share concurrent power with the Federal Parliament over production, distribution and supply of water power and hydro-electricity.[56] The States appear to have the larger share in this distribution of power and responsibility over water. Nevertheless, the recent establishment of a Water Services Commission[57]

---

[51] See further Whiting, "Desecularising Malaysian Law?," *supra*, at pp. 223–266; Amanda Whiting, "Secularism, The Islamic State and the Malaysian Legal Profession," *Asian Journal of Comparative Law* 5.1 (2010): Article 10, 21–23. http://www.bepress.com/asjcl/vol5/iss1/art10

[52] See Sharifah Zubaidah Bt. Abdul Kader Al Junid, "Towards Good Water Governance in Malaysia: Establishing an Enabling Legal Environment" [2004] *Malayan Law Journal* civ 3.

[53] Federal Constitution, 9th Schedule, List I, item 11(b).

[54] Federal Constitution, 9th Schedule, List II, item 6(c).

[55] Federal Constitution, 9th Schedule, List II, item 12.

[56] Federal Constitution, 9th Schedule, List IIIA, item 13.

[57] Through enactment of the Federal *Suruhanjaya Perkhidmatan Air Negara Act* [National Water Services Commission Act] 2006.

and the passage of the federal *Water Services Industry Act* 2006 point to increased federal regulation.[58] Additionally, various federal laws have an indirect impact upon water management.[59]

Similarly, practical enforcement of environmental standards involves the coexistence of Federal and State laws.[60] The various federal laws on environment including the framework *Environmental Quality Act* 1974 (Act 127) and the subsidiary rules made thereunder have to be read in conjunction with various State laws and local ordinances dealing with such environmental matters as land, planning, local government, water (including water supplies), forestry and mining. The system is complex and confusing and of little obvious benefit to the environment.[61]

12.2.3 Residual Powers

The constitution, in Article 77, expressly allocates residual legislative power to the component States. However, in view of the comprehensiveness of the Ninth Schedule Lists, there is in reality little residual power.[62] The Federal Parliament can further reduce the extent of the residual power by amending the legislative lists to expressly bring certain items not previously provided for (and therefore arguably residual in nature) under the Federal List. There is also a perceived reluctance on the part of the courts to consider a matter which is not enumerated in any of the legislative lists as a residual matter.[63] This was certainly the approach adopted by the Court of Appeal in the *Bakun Dam case*, which concerned a conflict between the Federal *Environmental Quality Act* and a state development plan.[64]

---

[58]The *Water Services Industry Act 2006* recites that it was enacted to "ensure uniformity of law and policy" throughout Peninsular Malaysia.

[59]Such laws include *Street, Drainage and Building Act 1974*; *Irrigation Areas Act 1953*; *Fisheries Act 1985*; *Food Act 1983*; *Environmental Quality Act 1974*; *Sewerage Services Act, 1993*; *Road Transport Act 1987*; *Exclusive Economic Zone Act, 1984*; *Land Conservation Act 1960*; *Land Acquisition Act 1960*; *National Forestry Act 1984*. See the discussion in Sharifah Zubaidah bt. Abdul Kader Al Junid, *supra* note 52, at notes 17–29.

[60]*See generally* Azmi Sharom, "Malaysian Environmental Law: Ten Years After Rio" (2002) *Singapore Journal of International & Comparative Law* 6: 855–890.

[61]Alan Tan, *Preliminary Assessment of Malaysia's Environmental Law* (Asia Pacific Centre for Environmental Law, National University of Singapore) *available at* http://www.law.nus.edu.sg/apcel/dbase/malaysia/reportma.html#sec3

[62]Tan Poh Ling, "Malaysia" in Tan Poh Ling, *Asian Legal Systems: Law, Society and Pluralism in East Asia* (1997) 263, 271.

[63]Fong, *supra* note 4, at p. 56 and 57.

[64]*Ketua Pengarah Jabatan Alam Sekitar & Anor v. Kajing Tubek & Ors* [1997] 3 MLJ 23; [1997] 4 CLJ 253 ("The Bakun Dam case").

12.2.4 Conflicts Between Central and State Law

Federal law takes precedence over State law in areas where component States may also legislate. Article 75 of the Federal Constitution invalidates any State law inconsistent with a Federal law to the extent of the inconsistency.[65]

However, such a situation of conflict arises only in relation to matters falling within the Concurrent List, or laws made by the Parliament relating to matters under the State List for purposes of implementing Malaysia's international obligations or of promoting uniformity of the laws of two or more component states pursuant to Federal Constitution article 76. If either the Federal Parliament or a State Legislative Assembly made "conflicting" laws pertaining to matters for which it lacked jurisdiction pursuant to the Ninth Schedule Lists or any other constitutional provisions, such a "conflict" would be a question of jurisdiction rather than of conflict.

12.2.5 Municipal Law-Making Power

The municipalities – city councils, municipal councils and district councils – do not have any significant law-making power, but do make subsidiary laws in relation to the administration of local authority areas and services rendered locally.[66] However, these subsidiary laws must be approved by the component State legislature.

At independence in 1957, local government bodies were democratically elected; however local government elections were suspended in 1965 (at the time of confrontation with Indonesia)[67] and elected local authorities were finally and totally abolished by federal law in 1974.[68] Municipalities and local bodies are now appointed by State governments and hence their political orientation tends to coincide with that of the appointing State.[69]

12.3 The Means and Methods of Legal Unification

12.3.1 Exercise of Central Power (Top Down)

The exercise of central power (top down) has been the most effective method in creating uniform law with respect to matters under the State and Concurrent Lists.

---

[65]For example, *City Council of Georgetown & Anor v. The Government of the State of Penang & Anor* [1967] 1 MLJ 169, invalidating the *Municipal (Amendment) (Penang) Enactment* 1966 (Penang); and see the discussion in Wu Min Aun, *supra* note 27, at p. 51.

[66]*See, e.g.*, sections 73, 78 and Part XIII of the *Local Government Act 1976* (Act 171)).

[67]Emergency (Suspension of Local Government Elections) Regulations 1965.

[68]Through the Local Government (Temporary Provisions) Act 1973.

[69]*See generally* Harding, *Law, Government and the Constitution*, *supra* note 3, at p. 122.

Most uniform laws are made in accordance with the Federal Constitution. And occasionally, where the Parliament is not expressly granted legislative jurisdiction to enact uniform laws, it adopts the direct route of amending the Federal Constitution to have its legislative jurisdiction enabled.

The Federal Constitution as the supreme law of the land has a direct impact on State laws. All laws, including State laws, must be consistent with the Federal Constitution, and any inconsistent laws are to the extent of the inconsistency void.[70] In that regard, the provisions of the Federal Constitution such as those in Part II concerning fundamental liberties[71] contribute towards legal unification and harmonization of State laws, or at least towards preventing inconsistent State laws. For instance, the constitutional guarantee of freedom of association was invoked to invalidate a State law disqualifying a member of the State legislative assembly purely on the basis that he ceased to be part of a political party after he was elected.[72] On the other hand, there has been litigation impugning State Islamic laws on the basis that they have violated constitutional guarantees of freedom of religion and equality of the sexes. So far, these court cases have been unsuccessful, as the Federal civil courts have become increasingly reluctant to assert the supremacy of the secular constitution and its rights and guarantees or to claim federal jurisdiction when faced with rival claims from state *syariah* courts.[73]

A method of creating unified law, not expressly provided for but constitutionally viable, is to amend the legislative lists in the Federal Constitution in order to widen the Federal Parliament's legislative jurisdiction and narrow that of the States. Except in relation to certain more heavily entrenched topics, provisions of the Federal Constitution can be amended by a Federal law passed by a two-thirds majority of the members present in each house of the Federal Parliament.[74] As the same political coalition has held power by a significant majority at federal level (and in most of the States) from independence in 1957 until March 2008, the government of the day has always had the requisite votes and there have been many constitutional amendments.[75] If the legislative lists are amended in this way, the process could bypass the need for component State legislatures' separate and express consent,

---

[70]Federal Constitution, article 4.

[71]*Faridah Begum Bte Abdullah v. Sultan Haji Ahmad Shah Al Mustain Billah Ibni Almarhum Sultan Abu Bakar Ri'ayatuddin Al Mu'adzam Shah* [1996] 1 MLJ 617, [1996] 2 MLJ 159 is an instance where the Federal Court remarked that even if the Parliament were to enact a law conferring a right on a foreign Commonwealth citizen to sue the Ruler, it would be void for illegality and unconstitutionality because the Federal Constitution, art 155(1) requires such a right to be reciprocally effective in both countries.

[72]*Dewan Undangan Negeri Kelantan & Anor v Nordin Salleh & Anor* [1992] 1 CLJ 72 (Rep).

[73]See above, part II, section 2 and more generally: Thio Li-ann, "Jurisdictional Imbroglio" *supra* n 52 discussing leading cases, and Whiting, "Desecularizing Malaysian Law?," *supra* note 50, examining three recent cases in detail.

[74]Federal Constitution, article 159.

[75]*See generally*, Harding, *Law, Government and the Constitution, supra* note 3; *see, e.g., id.*, at p. 54.

as would be otherwise required under article 76 of the Federal Constitution. Yet consultation with the States did precede the 2005 amendment to the legislative lists, removing "water supplies and services" from the State List and inserting it in the Concurrent List.[76] Following the amendment, the Parliament duly enacted the *Water Services Industry Act 2006* (Act 655), an act to provide for and regulate water supply services throughout peninsular states and federal territories.

Apart from the written provisions of the Federal Constitution, there are in Malaysia not really any recognized constitutional norms that relate to legal unification or harmonization. There are two primary and practical reasons for this. The first is the extensive legislative power granted to the Federal Parliament. The second is the low level of litigation involving the constitutionality of State laws.

Nonetheless, the constitutional principle that a Federal legislature is presumed not to intend to make laws that conflict with the basic fabric of the constitution (including its federal nature) is recognized in Malaysia. That presumption entails a further principle of interpretation for courts to follow: when construing constitutionally valid but potentially conflicting State and Federal laws, "a harmonious result should, as far as possible, be aimed at."[77] These principles of harmonious construction were applied in a landmark environmental law case (*Bakun Dam case*) concerning the development of a huge hydro-electric dam in Sabah. In that case, the Court of Appeal's harmonious interpretation of the Federal and State laws favored the State development proposal over the national environmental regime. While the approach of the Court of Appeal in construing the Federal environmental law is considered controversial and has been challenged in subsequent litigation,[78] nevertheless the principle of constitutional law it applied is considered well settled.[79]

Central legislation is the most often used, and most effective, means to unify and harmonize State laws, particularly with respect to the peninsular States.

The Parliament may also make laws for other matters in the State List for the purpose of promoting uniformity of the laws of two or more component States, or if so requested by the State legislatures, but the component States would have the final say as such federal laws would not come into operation in the States concerned

---

[76]Consultation with the state governments was apparently undertaken: Fong, *Constitutional Federalism, supra* note 4, at p. 86.

[77]*The Bakun Dam case*, supra note 64, at p. 274.

[78]For example: See *PP v Ta Hsin Enterprise Sdn Bhd* [1998] 4 CLJ Supp 241; *Malaysian Vermicelli Manufacturers (Melaka) Sdn Bhd v PP* [2001] 7 CLJ 74.

[79]This constitutional principle of harmonious construction is not to be confused with the "basic structure" doctrine enunciated by the Indian Supreme Court, which acts as an implied restriction upon parliament's legislative power to enact constitutional amendments that alter the framework and foundational principles of the constitution: *Kesavananda v. State of Kerala ARI 1973 SC 1461*. This principle has been considered, but rejected, by Malaysian courts in a succession of cases. See Fong, *Constitutional Federalism supra* note 4, at p. 200–202, discussing *Phang Chin Hock v. Public Prosecutor* [1980] MLJ 70, *Mark Koding v. Public Prosecutor* [1982] 2 MLJ 120, *Loh Kooi Choon v Government of Malaysia* [1977] 2 MLJ 187.

until they have been adopted by a law made by the State legislatures.[80] Unlike federal laws concerning land and local government made under cognate provisions, the applicable law made by this process would be State law, not Federal law, and accordingly could be amended or repealed by the respective State legislatures. An example is the *National Forestry Act* 1984 (Act 313), a Federal law which was adopted by peninsular States passing separate State Enactments to the same effect.[81]

There is no general scheme by which the central government could use legislation to require the component States to pass conforming or implementing legislation in relation to any matter. However there are *constitutional* requirements for a certain level of uniformity across the State constitutions. Article 71 of the Federal Constitution requires that the component State constitutions have certain common and essential provisions (contained in the Eighth Schedule of the Federal Constitution), such as that the hereditary ruler (or appointed Yang di-Pertua Negri) must act on advice, failing which the Parliament may by law make provisions for the same or for removing inconsistent provisions. Additionally, article 3(3) requires the states of Malacca, Penang, Sabah and Sarawak (i.e., those States without hereditary Malay rulers) to provide in the State constitutions that the Yang di-Pertuan Agong is the head of the religion of Islam in the respective State.

Both the Federal Government and the component peninsular State governments (but not Sabah and Sarawak) are required to follow policy formulated by the National Land Council (NLC), a consultative body created by article 91 of the Federal Constitution to formulate national policies relating to land utilization in agriculture, forestry and mining.[82] By contrast, the provision relating to consultation between the components of the Federation and the NLC in relation to proposed legislation is directory or discretionary rather than mandatory.[83]

The other national council established under the Federal Constitution with similar provisions, is the National Council for Local Government,[84] empowered to formulate national policies relating to local government. It operates in a similar fashion to the NLC.

---

[80] Federal Constitution, article 76 (1) (b), (c).

[81] Another example is the *Wood-Based Industries (State Legislatures Competency) Act* 1984. *See generally* Rozanah Abd Rahman "Deforestation in Malaysia: A Legal Framework for Ecosystem Protection" [1996] 4 CLJ (Articles).

[82] Federal Constitution, article 91(5).

[83] Federal Constitution, article 91(6). There is an interesting discussion in Choo Chin Thye and Lucy Chang Ngee Weng, "Constitutional Procedure of Consultation in Malaysia's Federal System" [2005] 4 MLJ xiii. The National Land Council, in turn, established the National Forestry Council in 1971. That body focuses on forestry matters leading to the issuance of the National Forest Policy and consequently, the National Forestry Act 1984 (Act 313). The Act has been adopted by all peninsular states by way of laws enacted by the respective state legislatures resulting in uniformity throughout these states. The governments of Sabah and Sarawak continue to maintain their own forestry policies and laws.

[84] Federal Constitution article 95A.

Though the central government may impose terms and conditions when making specific-purpose grants to any component States (such as grants for the maintenance of local authorities[85]) we have not been able to discover whether such conditions in practice relate to the state *enacting* laws that comply with central standards, and if so, in what areas of law. There is otherwise no known State inducement hinging upon compliance with central standards. Grants from the central (and much wealthier) government to the component States are otherwise constitutionally guaranteed and awarded pursuant to formulae provided for in article 109 and detailed in the 10th Schedule of the Federal Constitution.

The central government has stepped in and taken over in situations where it feels that the matter could best be governed by the centre as opposed to the States.[86] For instance, the Parliament amended the Legislative Lists in the Federal Constitution to remove water supplies from the State List (excluding Sabah and Sarawak) and to insert the same in the Concurrent List, and proceeded to enact the *Water Services Industry Act* 2006 (Act 655). Water supply services throughout peninsular States and Federal Territories may now be federally regulated. Through the *Sewerage Services Act* 1993 (Act 508) the Federal Government has similarly curtailed component States' legislative and executive powers in relation to sewerage services, a subject matter that falls within the Concurrent List.[87] Pursuant to the statute, sewerage services responsibilities which had previously been provided by local and state authorities other than a few States and one local authority[88] have been transferred to the Federal Government and subsequently privatized.[89] The success of the Federal Government in persuading most State and local authorities to transfer these responsibilities is attributable to the political control by the Federal Government over most State Governments.[90]

It is unclear exactly what role the central courts play in unification of norms. Malaysia has a plural legal system of English-introduced common law (called "civil law" when it is contrasted with Islamic law), *adat* (Malay and indigenous customary laws) and Islamic law.

---

[85] *State Grants (Maintenance of Local Authorities) Act* 1981, section 3.

[86] These situations should be distinguished from Barisan Nasional's political interference in the government of a component state, as occurred in the constitutional crises in Sarawak (1966), Kelantan (1977) and Perak (2008–2009), referred to above.

[87] Sewerage Services Act 1993, Preamble and Section 3.

[88] Kelantan, Sabah, Sarawak and the local authority of Johor Bahru city.

[89] See Abdul-Rashid Abdul Aziz, "Unraveling of BOT Scheme: Malaysia's Indah Water Konsortium" (2001) *Journal of Construction Engineering and Management* November/December 457–460; "Up to IWK to Expand its Services, says Deputy Minister" *BERNAMA Malaysian National News Agency* 7 September 1998; Mimi Syed Yusof, "Nod by Kelantan to IWK takeover" *The New Straits Times* (Malaysia) 23 June 1997; Ho Wah Foon, "Sewerage Services is Trying to Keep its Head Above Water" *The Straits Times* (Singapore) 30 June 1996; Ho Wah Foon, "Indah Water Finalises New Sewerage Rates" *The Straits Times* (Singapore) 26 June 2006.

[90] In relation to the East Malaysian State of Sabah, see further Regina Lim, *Federal-State Relations*, *supra* note 6, at p. 70.

The civil law courts come under Federal, not State, jurisdiction and so there is a single, national and uniform court system throughout Malaysia in relation to matters arising under general law: public law (constitutional and administrative law), private law (contracts, property, tort) and commercial matters (including Islamic banking), most criminal law and procedure (except for offences against the precepts of Islam), and family law (except for the family law of Muslims). The apex court – the Federal Court – is thus able to create uniform general (or civil) law norms, via precedent, for the whole nation.

In relation to customary law or *adat*, there are significant differences between the peninsular States and East Malaysia. There are no longer separate *adat* courts in the peninsula, and *adat* has mostly been incorporated into the administration of Islamic law (discussed below), a process made inevitable by the juridical identification of Malay ethnicity with Islam in the constitution.[91] For the natives of East Malaysia, there are separate courts to handle matters arising under Malay customary law and the customary laws applicable to non-Malay indigenous peoples (who may not be Muslims). These are State courts, not Federal courts, and there is no appeal from the native system to the Federal courts. They exercise a limited jurisdiction over matters conferred by State enactments (typically land and succession, family law, sexual relations, and offences against customary law).[92]

Islamic law and the *syariah* courts are matters for the 13 component States, and the Federal Parliament only has jurisdiction over Islamic law in relation to the Federal Territories (most significantly, the capital city of Kuala Lumpur). This means that there are 14 separate *syariah* jurisdictions, each drawing upon separate enabling laws and diverse *syariah* statutes (covering areas such as *syariah* criminal law, *syariah* criminal procedure, *syariah* evidence, *syariah* family law, and administration of *syariah* law) but no national and apex *syariah* court of appeal to provide unification or harmonization of doctrine. Furthermore, since 1988 there can no longer be any appeal from a State *syariah* court to the apex, secular Federal Court. There is thus no possibility of that national court exerting any judicial pressure for uniformity within *syariah* jurisprudence or for harmony with the secular, general law.[93]

---

[91] Federal Constitution, art 160 " 'Malay' means a person who professes the religion of Islam, habitually speaks the Malay language, conforms to Malay custom..."

[92] See Wu Min Aun, *supra* note 27, at pp. 227–258.

[93] This is because of the insertion of article 121(1A) into the Federal Constitution in 1988 – its subsequent history is examined in Thio Li-ann, "Jurisdictional Imbroglio" *supra* note 50. Recent suggestions that the general law ought to be Islamized or brought more into harmony with Islam have generated heated debate – discussed in Whiting, "Desecularising Malaysian Law?" *supra* note 50 – yet there is little prospect of this happening, at least in the short term, despite the fact that it is the expressed aim of one of the units of the Federal Attorney-General's Chambers: see www.agc.gov.my/agc/agc/adv/adv.htm for the mission statement: "conduct studies on the federal laws to determine whether the implementation of the laws would be in conflict with Islamic laws and to propose any amendment or reform to the laws to bring it in line with Islamic laws".

While there are great similarities across all *syariah* jurisdictions, there are significant differences as well – for example discrepancies in the provisions enabling or discouraging a husband from entering into a polygamous union, or the (unenforceable[94]) enactment in the State of Kelantan of full *hudud* offences and punishments, such as amputation for theft, and the death penalty for apostasy[95] – and modernizing Islamic groups have pointed to these divergences as evidence of the need for a uniform, national (and progressive) *syariah* system.[96] The use of model laws and advice from the Federal religious affairs bureaucracy to encourage uniformity in the *syariah* system is also briefly examined immediately below.

Well-funded and resourced Islamic Federal bureaucracies, such as JAKIM (the Islamic Development Department) and the Department of Syariah Judiciary (JKSM) exert a powerful central influence upon local, State-based *syariah* institutions and practices, and JAKIM drafts model *syariah* laws for the States to adopt.[97] While this may seem to exemplify central and top-down influence rather than a coordinated approach initiated by the component States, it is clear that the States do have the capacity to resist or mitigate central pressure and that unification of *syariah* proceeds in a consultative manner. In part this is because the division of legislative competence in the federation requires that the model law must be expressly adopted by each of the State legislatures. It is during this process that States may and

---

[94]The Kelantan *hudud* laws are unenforceable because the punishments mandated by the state enactment are in direct conflict with a federal law, *Federal Syariah Courts* (*Criminal Jurisdiction*) *Act* 1965 (rev 1988), section 2, which limits punishments for offences against Islam. As criminal law is a federal matter, and state legislative competency over Islam is narrowly circumscribed in 9th Schedule, List II, item 1, the federal law prevails over the inconsistent state enactment by virtue of Federal Constitution article 75. See further M.B. Hooker, "Submission to Allah: The Kelantan Syariah Criminal Code (II) 1993" in Virginia Hooker and Norani Othman (ed.) *Malaysia*: *Islam, Society and Politics* (Singapore: ISEAS, 2003), 80–100.

[95]*See generally* Jaclyn Ling-chien Neo, "'Anti-God, anti-Islam and Anti-Qur'an': Expanding the Range of Participants and Parameters in Discourse over Women's Rights and Islam in Malaysia" (2003) 21 *UCLA Pacific Basin Law Review* 29; Shad Saleem Faruqi "The Malaysian Constitution, The Islamic State and Hudud Laws" in K.S. Nathan and Mohamad Hashim Kamali (eds.) *Islam in Southeast Asia*: *Political, Social and Strategic Challenges for the 21st Century* (Singapore: Institute of Southeast Asian Studies, 2005); and Virginia Hooker and Norani Othman (eds.) *Malaysian Islam, Society and Politics*: *Essays in Honour of Clive Kessler* (Singapore: Institute of Southeast Asian Studies).

[96]Examined in Amanda Whiting "In the Shadow of Developmentalism: The Human Rights Commission of Malaysia at the Intersection of State and Civil Society Priorities" in C. Raj Kumar and D.K. Srivastava (ed.) *Human Rights and Development*: *Law, Policy and Governance* (Hong Kong: LexisNexis, 2006). *See further* Norani Othman, "Grounding Human Rights Arguments in Non-Western Culture: Shari'a and Citizenship Rights of Women in a Modern Islamic State" in Joanne Bauer and Daniel Bell (eds.) *The East Asian Challenge for Human Rights* (Cambridge: CUP, 1999).

[97]Kikue Hamayotsu, "Politics of Syariah Reform: The Making of the State Religio-Legal Apparatus" in Virginia Hooker and Norani Othman (eds.) *Malaysia*: *Islam, Society and Politics* (Singapore: ISEAS, 2003), 55–79. A detailed evaluation of the modernization of *syariah* is in Donald Horowitz, "The Qur'an and the Common Law: Islamic Law Reform and the Theory of Legal Change" (1994) 42 *American Journal of Comparative Law* 233 (Part 1) and 543 (Part 2).

do amend and vary the model law.[98] Although a greater extent of uniformity in *syariah* law has been achieved recently (especially with regard to procedure), there remain significant differences amongst component State laws, occasionally resulting in different outcomes of similar fact-situations in different component States.[99] The differences also reflect the different level of tolerance in each State's population towards specific provisions of *syariah*, such as polygamy or female-initiated divorce.

Back in the secular realm, the constitutionally mandated national consultative councils for land and local government, discussed above, also perform the role of disseminating information between the components of the federation and fostering uniformity of law.

A federal bureaucracy, the Law Revision and Reform Division of the Attorney-General's Chambers, contributes to legal modification and unification through the following functions: translation of laws from English into Bahasa Malaysia, the national language; investigation of the need to revise (consolidate and modernize) older State and Federal laws and preparation of revised texts[100]; extension of peninsular Malaysian laws to East Malaysia or to the Federal Territories (after consultation and approval with the relevant state and federal authorities, as the case may be). Since 2002, this division of the AG's chambers has also conducted law reform activities. Its mandate includes overcoming obsolete laws, removing overlapping and anomalous laws, achieving uniformity in the law, and modernizing Malaysian laws in tandem with globalization.[101] Such law reform activities are to be conducted through consultation with government departments, the legal profession, academics, non-government organizations and industry (as appropriate) in relation to law reform proposals. The revision work has been conducted consistently since the late 1960s, with considerable success. From 2003, 11 State law revision divisions have been established for the peninsular Malaysian States, and the two East Malaysian States have also established their own law revision and law reform units with their respective State bureaucracies. The State enactments under which

---

[98] See generally Neo, "Anti-God" *supra* note 95.

[99] These diverse and conflicting outcomes are frequently reported critically in the mass media and are also the subject of a modernizing *syariah* law reform campaign by the women's advocacy group Sisters In Islam. For typical news commentary, see: "In dire need of uniformity" *New Sunday Times* 12 January 2003; "States asked to gazette Islamic Family Law Immediately" *Bernama Daily Malaysian News* 14 January 2003; "Malaysian Gov't Mulls Standardisation Of Syariah Laws" *Bernama Daily Malaysian News* 11 January 2003; "Amended Islamic Family Law Can Be Model For All States" *Bernama Daily Malaysian News* 14 January 2006; "PM to chair special meeting on Syariah Law" *Bernama Daily Malaysian News* 13 January 2003; "Perlis's Move On Polygamy Is In The Interest Of Children, Says Shahidan" *Bernama Daily Malaysian News* 6 January 2003; "Cabinet Approves Six Draft Bills To Streamline Islamic Laws" *Bernama Daily Malaysian News* 11 February 2000; "Sarawak State Assembly Passes Six Syariah Bills" *Bernama Daily Malaysian News* 6 November 2001.

[100] This must be done in accordance with *Revision of Laws Act* 1968, s 6(1).

[101] Law reform was added to the Law Revision Division's functions in 2002: see the website of the Attorney General's Chambers at www.agc.gov.my/agc/agc/rev/act1.htm

they conduct their revision work are themselves instances of legal uniformity, as they are based upon a model Federal law, drafted by the federal Attorney-General. These State agencies are supported and guided by the central bureaucracy.[102] Moreover the extension project has also proceeded apace: since 1963, according the Attorney-General's chambers, 281 Federal laws have been extended (sometimes with modification) to East Malaysia or the federal territories, and it is proposed to extend a further 117 laws.[103] It is, however, too soon to give an accurate assessment of the new law reform program.[104]

The federal Attorney-General's Chambers has recently established a division to further the harmonization of civil law (common law) with *syariah*, with the apparent assumption that the former ought to be brought into line with the latter. So far it has sponsored conferences and seminars but not achieved any legislative changes.[105]

12.3.2 Formal or Informal Voluntary Coordination Among the States (Bottom Up)

Model laws have been used to achieve a high degree of uniformity in Islamic law, as discussed above. However, this process is generally initiated by the central body rather than the component States.

All Federal and State matters are within the jurisdiction of a single hierarchy of civil courts, centrally governed at the Federal level. There is no component State judiciary with similar jurisdiction. In relation to the State based Islamic courts, there is only a very limited cross-vesting scheme and published reports of *syariah* decisions are still not plentiful.[106] However the powerful and well-funded federal

---

[102] Attorney-General's Chambers Malaysia Annual Report 2005/2006, "Law Revision and Reform Division", pp. 170–171.

[103] See the website of the Law Revision and Reform Division at www.agc.gov.my/agc/agc/rev/rev.htm and the Attorney-General's Chambers Malaysia Annual Report 2005/2006, "Law Revision and Reform Division", p. 158.

[104] The Attorney-General's Chambers Malaysia Annual Report 2005/2006, "Law Revision and Reform Division" pp. 159–160 itemises 9 law reform references for 2005 and 10 for 2006, on the topics of: private agencies; copyright; the secular family law; community service as a sentencing alternative; compensation for victims of crime; limitation of actions; the revision of laws scheme; human trafficking; no fault liability insurance for motor vehicles; regulation of the legal profession; banking; child care; investment; road transport; offshore companies; cooperative societies; care centres; financial services in the federal territories; and Malaysian standards.

[105] The harmonization project (Projek Harmonisasi) was officially launched in December 2007, but has apparently been longer in the making. See the Attorney-General's Chambers website: www.agc.gov.my/agc/agc/adv/adv.htm.

[106] The Federal Department of Syariah Judiciary has begun to publish case reports prospectively, but there does not seem to be much effort to publish older decisions.

Department of Syariah Judiciary (Jabatan Kehakiman Syariah Malaysia, JKSM) attempts to coordinate State *syariah* institutions and practices.[107]

Other than through the National Land Council and the National Local Government Council and other similar initiatives organised by the central government, there seems to be little coordination among the component State executive branches.

Nonetheless, the traditional State rulers – the hereditary Malay rulers and the appointed Yang di-Pertua Negri in those States without Malay rulers – do meet regularly in the Conference of Rulers to deliberate on national policy from the perspective of their own privileges as well as the interests of their States. In conference they are accompanied by the elected political executive of their respective States. Since the Conference of Rulers must be consulted before any changes can be made to certain constitutional provisions affecting the "sensitive issues" as well as certain provisions affecting the States, it acts as a form of safeguard for the federal nature of the Constitution.[108] However, as already mentioned, the BN coalition has governed the nation and most states since independence, so it is unlikely that the political advice given to the Rulers at the Conference will depart far from central government policies.

12.3.3 The Role of Other State and Non-state Actors

Most legislation, whether involving unification or not, is initiated by the governments and there is minimal contribution from or consultation with non-state actors. There is no independent Law Commission, for example, and such law reform or legal revision work as takes place is initiated from within government bureaucracies.

Yet Malaysian civil society organizations, the statutory National Human Rights Commission and the Bar Council (the executive arm of the peninsular Malaysian Bar) regularly comment on law reform issues, including the desirability of legal uniformity or harmonization within the federation or with international legal standards.[109] The women's advocacy organization Sisters in Islam has been persistent in campaigning for uniformity of *syariah* law across the Federation, using the comparatively more progressive Federal Islamic law statutes as models for the States to follow. Since 1988 it has pushed for further reforms, and through its

---

[107] See the official website of the JKSM: www.jksm.gov.my, where the official mission statement includes standardizing the Islamic legal system in the nation and streamlining Islamic legal processes throughout the country.

[108] See further Harding, *Law, Government and the Constitution*, *supra* note 3, at p. 72 ff.

[109] See Amanda Whiting, "Situating Suhakam: Human Rights Debates and Malaysia's National Human Rights Commission" (2003) 39(1) *Stanford Journal of International Law* 59; Andrew Harding and Amanda Whiting, "'Custodians of Civil Liberties and Justice in Malaysia': The Malaysian Bar and the Moderate State" in Terence C. Halliday, Lucien Karpik and Malcolm M. Feeley (eds.) *Fates of Political Freedom: The Legal Complex in the British Post-Colony* (Cambridge: Cambridge University Press, 2012), chapter 7.

popular publications, legal clinics and campaigns it draws public and government attention to the shortcomings of the current *syariah* system and the need for uniformity throughout Malaysia and conformity with human rights standards.[110] Coalitions of women's rights groups can claim responsibility for persuading the federal government to include gender in the equal rights clause of the Constitution (article 8), as part of its campaign to bring Malaysian laws into harmony with international human rights standards.[111] They can also claim responsibility for the *Domestic Violence Act* 1994,[112] which took a decade to negotiate because, although criminal law is a Federal matter, State *syariah* authorities had to be persuaded that the law contained nothing inimical to Islamic law. Civil society influence for legal change or unification of law in the areas of environmental law or the rights of indigenous peoples have been markedly less successful.

12.3.4 The Role of Legal Education and Training in the Unification of Law

Generally, law schools in Malaysia at the undergraduate level focus on Federal laws and do not have enough materials and demand to teach courses on State laws. Furthermore, there is a peninsula-centric attitude towards legal education and the legal systems of Sabah and Sarawak receive minimal attention. This is probably explained by the fact that civil courts are federal courts, that most of the laws are federal laws, and the highly centralized nature of public governance and administration in Malaysia. Legal education and training, therefore, have very little impact in the unification of the general law in Malaysia, although it does acknowledge and thereby reinforce the centralizing tendency in the Federation. Awareness of State laws is mostly attained after graduation, in the workplace or through ad-hoc training conducted by State bar committees (in the case of Sabah and Sarawak, the State Law Associations).

Furthermore, the compulsory legal education subjects dealing with Islamic law in both the general law universities and the International Islamic University of Malaysia do not venture deeply into the specific differences between the peninsular States, but focus more on questions of underlying principle and common doctrine. In this they would seem to contribute to a general movement towards harmonization

---

[110] The official website is http://www.sistersinislam.org.my/

[111] Malaysia is a state party to the International Convention to Eliminate All Forms of Discrimination Against Women, and has submitted its first and second periodic reports – Malaysia, *Combined Initial and Second Periodic Report to the Committee on the Elimination of Discrimination against Women* (UN Doc CEDAW/C/MYS/1-2, 12 April 2004).

[112] Information about the campaign is at http://www.awam.org.my/networks/jag_vaw_activities.htm; see further Cecilia Ng, Maznah Mohamad and Tan beng hui, *Feminism and the Women's Movement in Malaysia: An Unsung (R)evolution* (Abingdon: Routledge, 2006), 41–62.

of Islamic legal doctrine within the Federation, but this is perhaps achieved through under-emphasizing the small but significant differences in substance and procedure mentioned above, although particular courses on Islamic Family law may address these issues.[113]

There are several law schools in Malaysia, all situated in peninsular Malaysia.[114] Because of ethnic Malay students having long received preferential access to tertiary educational institutions in Malaysia under the NEP and successor plans, many Malaysian students of non-Malay ethnicity are obliged – if they can afford it – to obtain legal qualifications from overseas law schools, typically in Singapore, the United Kingdom, Ireland, Australia and New Zealand. This differential experience must affect law graduates' exposure to legal training and law reform ideas, although the authors are not aware of any recent qualitative or quantitative study of this issue.

Testing for bar admission is uniform nationwide for Malaysian nationals who have completed legal education in Malaysia or Singapore. Admission to practice in Peninsular Malaysia is controlled by the *Legal Profession Act* 1976, which deems all admitted advocates and solicitors to be members of the Malaysian Bar.[115] Yet admission to practice in the East Malaysia states is regulated by the *Advocates Ordinance* (*Sabah*) and *Advocates Ordinance* (*Sarawak*). These are protectionist measures, restricting the right to practice in the East Malaysian States to lawyers who can demonstrate a "connection" with the state by birth or residence, unless an ad hoc admission licence has been approved.[116] Such ad hoc applications may be, and apparently frequently are, challenged by the State guilds, the Sabah Law Association and the Advocates' Association of Sarawak.[117] This restriction has been judicially extended to apply to arbitration proceedings, and any other forum of dispute resolution in Sabah and Sarawak.[118]

Malaysian nationals who have obtained their legal qualifications outside of Malaysia (unless at one of the English Inns of Court) must also pass the Certificate of Legal Practice (CLP) examination administered by the Qualifying Board established by the *Legal Profession Act* 1976 under Part II of the Act. Pass rates are not high and the exam itself has been the subject of scandal and criticism in the recent

---

[113]We are indebted to Dr. Maizatun Mustafa of the law faculty at the International Islamic University of Malaysia for this information.

[114]University of Malaya; National University of Malaysia (Universiti Kebangasaan Malaysia); the International Islamic University Malaysia; University of Technology MARA (Universiti Teknologi MARA), University of Northern Malaysia (Universiti Utara Malaysia); Multimedia University; the Islamic University College Malaysia. Overseas universities also offer legal education in Malaysia and several private colleges offer the University of London External LLB.

[115]*Legal Profession Act* 1976, s 43.

[116]For example, under s 10(c) of the Sabah *Ordinance*.

[117]Note further that even with an ad hoc practicing licence, a peninsular Malaysia lawyer must also apply for and receive a work permit from the Immigration Department of the relevant East Malaysian State.

[118]*In Re Mohamed Azahari Matiasin (Applicant)* [2011] 2 CLJ 630.

past.[119] Due to widespread concern at the falling standard of new entrants to the profession, the Malaysian Bar is currently devising a Common Bar Course, based upon vocational education courses in the United Kingdom and other common law jurisdictions, as a single point of entry to the profession for both private practitioners and public sector lawyers.[120]

In relation to the State *Syariah* Courts, the admission of *syarie* lawyers is subject to each component state's law, the rules of which are not uniform.[121] Lawyers admitted to practice according the provisions of the *Legal Profession Act* 1976 may practice in *syariah* courts if they also fulfil the requirements to be *peguam syarie* (*syariah* lawyers), typically a requirement to demonstrate to the state Majlis (religious affairs council) a "sufficient knowledge of Islamic Law".[122] With the professionalization of *syariah* instruction via the Faculty of Law at the well-regarded International Islamic University of Malaysia, and now also the Islamic University College Malaysia, a degree in *syariah* is likely to be accepted as evidence of sufficient knowledge. There is a further requirement in Rules made pursuant to the Federal Territories and some of the state *syariah* statutes, but not present in the governing statutes themselves, that a *peguam syarie* must profess the religion of Islam, as well as demonstrate knowledge of Islamic law. This faith requirement is currently being tested in the courts.[123] Hence Muslim members of the Malaysian Bar who also demonstrate knowledge of Islam, for example by obtaining a *syariah* diploma or passing sufficient *syariah* subjects in their LLB studies at other universities, may qualify to practice is *syariah* courts, subject to any additional requirements set by the state Majlis. However a *peguam syarie* will not necessarily meet the requirements of admission to practice set out in the Legal

---

[119] A typical example of hostile media commentary is Julian Puvenaswaran, "Purpose of CLP exam – you tell me", letter to the editor, Malaysiakini, 20 October 2006 www.malaysiakini.com

[120] Malaysian Bar, Ad Hoc Committee on the Common Bar Course, Report 2010–2011, available at http://www.malaysianbar.org.my/ad_hoc_committee_on_the_common_bar_course/ad_hoc_committee_on_the_common_bar_course.html; see further Roger Tan, "High Time for a New Bar" *Sunday Star*, 6 February 2011, and posted to Malaysian Bar at http://www.malaysianbar.org.my/members_opinions_and_comments/high_time_for_a_new_bar.html

[121] Sharifah Zubaidah bt. Syed Abdul Kader, "How To Become A Syarie Lawyer" (1995) 1 CLJ cxlix.

[122] As provided for in *Administration of Islamic Law (Federal Territories) Act* 1993, s59 (1).

[123] Victoria Martin, for several decades a practicing member of the Malaysian Bar, subsequently obtained a Diploma of Syariah Law and Practice from the International Islamic University and sought admission to practice as a *peguam syarie* from the Federal Territories Islamic Affairs Council. Her application was refused because she is not a Muslim. Her High Court challenge to the validity of the faith stipulation in the Rules argued that the parent act was *ultra vires* and in violation of Federal Constitutional guarantees of equality before the law and freedom of association. The judicial review in the High Court was unsuccessful, but succeeded in the Court of Appeal: see further Whiting "Secularism", *supra* note 51, pp 21–23; Hafiz Yatim, "Non-Muslim loses bid to practice in Syariah Courts" *Malaysiakini* 17 March 2011; "Appeals Court rules non-Muslim lawyers eligible to practise as syariah lawyers in Federal Territories" *Bernama* 21 June 2013.

Practice Act 1976 for admission to practice in the secular system. The result is that some members of the Malaysian Bar are also practitioners in *syariah* courts, and the Malaysian Bar also has a subcommittee for *syariah* law. In addition there is a professional association for *Peguam Syarie*, the *Peguam Syarie* Association of Malaysia (*Persatuan Peguam Syarie Malaysia*, PGSM).[124]

Graduates with appropriate LLB qualifications may set up practice in any of the states of peninsular Malaysia, as advocates and solicitors are admitted to the High Court of Malaya for the peninsula, not to only a particular state within the federation. As stated above, however, admission to practice in either of the Borneo States of Sabah and Sarawak requires a demonstrated "connection" to that state by birth or residence, although ad hoc admissions of peninsular lawyers can be arranged.

As at the end of 2009, official Bar statistics show that there were 13,196 registered practitioners. Of these, 72.15 % were "junior lawyers", i.e. of less than 7 years standing. Based on these figures, majority of lawyers were sole practitioners (51.12 %), a further 43.01 % practiced in small (2–5 person) firms, and only 0.3 % practiced in firms with over 31 members.[125] The overwhelming majority of lawyers practice in the larger cities. Slightly more recent statistics for 2010 show that more than half of all practicing lawyers are concentrated in Kuala Lumpur, the capital city, and the surrounding (and wealthiest) state of Selangor, whereas the smaller states have less than 400 lawyers each.[126] There are currently 1,157 lawyers on the Bar roll of Sarawak, although these figures may include non-practicing lawyers. There are also approximately 260 firms.[127] The Sabah Law Association records the presence of 209 firms in that state (including branch offices), but does not presently list the total number of practitioners.[128]

Currently 2,114 *peguam syarie* are recorded as practising throughout the federation by federal Department of Syariah Judiciary, although note that they must be separately accredited and registered in each of the 14 jurisdictions of the Federation

---

[124]See further Amanda Whiting, "The Training and Practice of 'Islamic Lawyers' in the Federal Territories of Malaysia" in R. Michael Feener, Mark E. Cammack and Clark B. Lombardi (eds.) *Islamic Legal Professionals in Contemporary Southeast Asia* (forthcoming).

[125]*See* http://www.malaysianbar.org.my/general_notices/bc_general_statistics_2009.html

[126]As at the end of 2010, there were 13358 lawyers, and 6008 legal firms in peninsular Malaysia and the distribution by state or territory is as follows: Federal Territory of Kuala Lumpur, 5459 lawyers, 1724 firms; Selangor, 2863 lawyers, 1522 firms; Johor, 1028 lawyers, 584 firms; Penang, 1057 lawyers, 531 firms; Perak, 655 lawyers, 391 firms; Kedah, 373 lawyers, 229 firms; Negri Sembilan, 362 lawyers, 230 firms; Pahang, 330 lawyers, 190 firms; Melaka, 328 lawyers, 173 firms; Kelantan, 314 lawyers, 185 firms; Perlis, 32 lawyers, 221 firms; Federal Territory of Labuan, 12 lawyers and 7 firms; "others" (presumably including the new federal administrative capital of Putrajaya), 105 lawyers, but no firm statistics available. Source: http://www.malaysianbar.org.my/legal_directory_statistics.html. This total does not include those admitted to practice in Sabah or Sarawak. There are around 1575 *syariah* lawyers.

[127]Advocates' Association of Sarawak, http://sarawak-advocates.org.my/index.php/rolls-a-directories/rolls (list of lawyers) and http://sarawak-advocates.org.my/index.php/rolls-a-directories/legal-firms (list of firms).

[128]Sabah Law Association: http://www.sabahbar.org.my/firms.aspx

(i.e., the 13 states and the Federal Territories) where they wish to practice. Because some *peguam syarie* are certified to practice in several jurisdictions, the total number for Malaysia will be less than the combined totals for each separate jurisdiction. Currently, there are approximately 263 accredited *peguam syarie* in the Federal Territories (Kuala Lumpur, Putrajaya and Labuan), and 205 registered *peguam syarie* in the surrounding state of Selangor. Other states with more than 200 peguam syarie are Kelantan (258), Penang (249) and Terengganu (226). Pahang had 174 Islamic lawyers, but all the other states had fewer than 150.[129]

It seems that the percentage of graduates setting up their own practice immediately following admission to practice is relatively low, but we have no hard data. A recent proposal mooted in the media by the *de facto* Law Minister to prevent inexperienced lawyers from setting up their own firms seem to imply that some are doing so and this is perceived as a problem,[130] but such comments by the government should be treated with caution as government politicians routinely criticize standards and ethics of the Bar in retaliation for Bar condemnation of state breaches of human rights.[131]

There are no institutions of legal education and training that play such a unifying role. However, in respect of specific areas of law, there are institutions that push for unification of laws of those specific areas. For instance, the Institute of Islamic Understanding (Institut Kefahaman Islam Malaysia, IKIM) – which is in fact a semi-autonomous government department[132] – has been advocating a uniform and harmonised Islamic law in the component states. The federal department of *syariah* judiciary (Jabatan Kehakiman Syariah Malaysia, JKSM) organizes the rotation of state *syariah* judges throughout the federation so that they can gain wider experience, and this practice can be assumed to contribute in some as yet unmeasured way towards uniformity of decision making in the *syariah* system.[133] Furthermore, as noted above, an express mission of JKSM is to promote uniformity of Islamic law in the nation.

---

[129] All figures are taken from the official list on the Federal Department of Syariah Judiciary website www.jksm.gov.my, carian peguam syarie (syariah lawyer search) http://www.jksm.gov.my/jksmv2/index.php?option=com_wrapper&view=wrapper&Itemid=187&lang=bm. For completeness, the remaining figures are as follows: Johor, 128; Kedah, 86; Melaka, 145; Negri Sembilan, 139; Perak, 56; Perlis, 49, Sabah, 61, Sarawak, 75. Analysis of gender breakdown, based on different statistics, is made in Amanda Whiting, "The Training and Practice of 'Islamic Lawyers,'" *supra* note 124.

[130] "Peguam kurang pengalaman tidak dibenar buka firma sendiri" *Utusan Malaysia* 23 July 2008 http://www.malaysianbar.org.my/berita/komen_undang_undang/peguam_kurang_pengalaman_tidak_dibenar_buka_firma_sendiri.html

[131] See Harding and Whiting, *supra* note 109.

[132] For this reason it was not mentioned in the discussion non-state actors, above. Its website, clearly showing close connections with the government, is http://www.ikim.gov.my/v5/index.php

[133] Kikue Hamayotsu, *supra* note 97, at p. 61.

To the extent that the Malaysian Bar is a national body,[134] it can be assumed to play such a unifying role in a practical sense. It conducts many continuing legal education seminars and workshops, and all new graduates are required to attend, and pass, the Bar's Legal Ethics course as a precondition for admission to practice. However continuing legal education is not (yet) compulsory in Malaysia. Additionally, State Bar Committees conduct regular seminars and workshops for members, and sometimes interested members of the public.

12.3.5 External Influences on Legal Unification

As noted above, although it is expressly provided in the Federal Constitution that the Federal Parliament may make laws for the component states for purposes of implementing an international obligation (Article 76(1)(a)), to the best of our knowledge, no such laws have been made under this mechanism. The statutory National Human Rights Commission (SUHAKAM) has a mandate to advise the government regarding accession to international human rights treaties and in relation to the formulation of legislation.[135] It has interpreted this mandate broadly, and uses the occasion of its annual reports to Parliament to recommend that Malaysia participate in the principal international human rights covenants and, on a more modest scale, that it amend security and censorship laws to bring them closer to international human rights standards. These recommendations have so far been ignored, and the annual reports are never given serious consideration by the Federal Parliament or Executive.[136] Nevertheless the central government has made some efforts to bring Malaysian law into conformity with Malaysia's state party obligations under the *Convention on the Elimination of All Forms of Discrimination Against Women*. In 2001, the equality clause of the Federal Constitution was amended to prohibit discrimination on the basis of gender, and some other laws have been amended, too (see above, Sect. 12.3.3). In March 2011, Malaysia announced that it would become a state party to the Rome Statute establishing the International Criminal Court. Yet it is not clear what, if any, changes to domestic law will flow from this, as the Law Minister stated that membership in the International Criminal Court would not require Malaysia to abolish detention without trial under the *Internal Security Act*.[137]

---

[134] As noted above, the Malaysian Bar technically covers West Malaysia only; the two East Malaysian States each have a separate bar association: the Advocates' Association of Sarawak and Sabah Law Association.

[135] *Human Rights Commission of Malaysia Act 1999*, sections 4(1) (b), (c).

[136] *See generally* Amanda Whiting, "Situating Suhakam: Human Rights Debates and Malaysia's National Human Rights Commission" (2003) 39 *Stanford Journal of International Law* 59–98; and "In the Shadow of Developmentalism" *supra* note 96, at p. 550.

[137] "Nazri: Malaysia to join ICC" *The Star Online*, 22 March 2011.

12.4 Institutional and Social Background

12.4.1 The Judicial Branch

The apex court, the Federal Court is conferred with exclusive jurisdiction to determine whether central legislation has exceeded lawmaking powers allocated to the central government. This is expressly set out in the Federal Constitution, in Article 128(1) (a). Generally speaking, the apex court in Malaysia has been reluctant to interpret the constitution robustly so as to invalidate Acts of Parliament, or subordinate instruments made under them; instead, judges have tended to defer to the government of the day.[138]

Legal determinations of the validity of Federal or State law on the basis that the respective legislature exceeded its lawmaking powers are rare. There is nonetheless a constitutionally prescribed mechanism to have such determinations judicially made.[139] The jurisdiction to make such determinations lies exclusively with the Federal Court, and may be invoked particularly in proceedings between the Federation and any component States. In other proceedings, however, permission of the Federal Court must be sought before it will hear any determination for a declaration of invalidity on the basis of legislative incompetency. The threshold is reasonably low, so as to allow most challenges to commence, i.e., the applicant must show an arguable case.

To date, there is only one reported case in which a Federal Law was successfully challenged on the basis that it exceeded the Parliament's lawmaking powers by trespassing into the States' legislative domain. In that case,[140] the law at issue was a federal provision making it a penal offence for any person to cause disharmony, disunity or feelings of enmity, hatred or ill-will, on grounds of religion, between persons or groups of persons professing the same or different religions. In a 3–2 majority decision, the Supreme Court (then the apex court) found the penal provision to be "in pith and substance" a law on the subject of the religion of Islam, a legislative item under the State List, with respect to which only the component States have power to legislate, and not a law for public security, as the federal government had contended. Hence the impugned section of the Federal penal code was declared constitutionally invalid. There have also been only a few cases where state laws have been declared invalid for trespass into the federal legislative list. One example

---

[138]Malaysian constitutional scholar Shad Saleem Faruqi proposes that this is because Malaysian judges are still "steeped in the British tradition of parliamentary supremacy", *Document of Destiny: The Constitution of the Federation of Malaysia* (Malaysia: Star Publications, 2008), 83; see further *Sheridan and Groves, The Constitution of Malaysia* 5th edition, edited by Dato' V.C. Vorah, Philip T.N. Koh and Peter S.W. Ling (Kuala Lumpur: Malayan Law Journal, 2004), 38.

[139]Federal Constitution, article 4(3), (4).

[140]*Daud bin Mamat & Ors v. Government of Malaysia* [1988] 1 MLJ 119.

of a successful challenge is *City Council of Georgetown v. Government of Penang* [1967] 1 MLJ 169, which invalidated state laws for inconsistency with the federal *Local Government Elections Act 1960*.

On the other hand, Malaysian courts are more willing to entertain challenges to the lawfulness of executive and administrative action based on the well-accepted principles of judicial review: illegality, irrationality, procedural impropriety and proportionality. Judicial review of the executive is available under section 25(2) of the *Courts of Judicature Act 1964* and Order 53 of the *Rules of the High Court 1980*, and there are hundreds of reported decisions.[141]

The superior courts (the High Court, the Court of Appeal and the Federal Court) are empowered to construe all laws including State constitutions and laws and rule on their constitutionality. However, with regard to a challenge to the validity of a State law on the ground that it exceeded the lawmaking powers of the State legislature, the same mechanism applies as set out above in relation to challenges to Federal law. Leave before the Federal Court must be sought before specific declarations on invalidity can commence.

It is widely accepted that the Federation's judicial power vests with the two High Courts co-ordinate jurisdiction (the High Court of Malaya and the High Court of Sabah and Sarawak), the appellate Court of Appeal and the Federal Court as the apex court. These (three-tiered) courts are centrally governed at the federal level, having jurisdiction over both the Federal and State Lists matters. There is no component State judiciary with similar jurisdiction.

A separate *syariah* court system exists within each component state, having jurisdiction only in that state over matters specified in Item 1 of the State List, i.e., matters of Islamic personal and family law, and only over persons professing the religion of Islam. There are also Federal *syariah* courts, but their jurisdiction is confined to the Federal territories of Kuala Lumpur, Putrajaya and Labuan. Like the civil courts, the *syariah* courts have both trial and appellate courts (in certain states, two-tiered, others three-tiered). Each State's (and the federal territories') *syariah* appellate procedure terminates within the State's (or the federal territories') hierarchical court system, as there is no national court of appeals for Islamic Law. Appeals from the *syariah* system to the apex court in the civil system (i.e., to the Federal Court) were terminated in 1988 through constitutional amendment (the insertion of article 121(1A) into the Federal Constitution). The effect of this amendment is that *syariah* courts have exclusive jurisdiction over Islamic law matters bestowed upon them by constitutionally valid state (or federal territories) *syariah* enactments.

Hence a frequent area of conflict is between Federal law, especially the civil and political rights guaranteed in the Federal Constitution, and provisions in State or Federal Islamic statutes. These are construed as jurisdictional conflicts, and most

---

[141] Kamal Halili Hassan, "Development of Judicial Review in Malaysian Industrial Law" (2006) 8(1) *Australian Journal of Asian Law* 25–67; Shad Saleem Faruqi, *Document of Destiny*, *supra* note 138, at pp. 75–76.

often arise in the context of conversion into or out of Islam (including instances where Muslims have voluntarily renounced Islam and may thereby become liable for the offence of apostasy under Islamic law). Generally speaking, the civil courts have deferred to the *syariah* courts and declined to exercise federal jurisdiction. The effect has been in most cases that the non-Muslim applicant (or the person claiming to have left Islam, as the case may be) is not able to obtain redress in the secular system, because that system has refused to seize jurisdiction; yet the applicant may have no access to the *syariah* courts (which only have personal jurisdiction over Muslims) or may not wish to recognize the jurisdiction of the *syariah* courts (because the applicant contests being, or any longer being, a Muslim). These cases have been extremely controversial and divisive in Malaysian society, and are the subject of much academic and civil society commentary.[142]

In addition to the civil (national) and *syariah* (State and Federal territories) systems just examined, there are separate native court systems in the two States of East Malaysia, exercising both trial and appellate jurisdiction in each instance. They are of very limited jurisdiction, and may not hear and determine matters already governed by state *syariah* laws, the laws of the States and most Federal Laws. In Sarawak there is a six-tier hierarchy, from Headman's Court through Chief's Court, Chief's Superior Court, District Native Court, Resident's Native Court to the apex Native Court of Appeal. The system is established under the *Native Courts Ordinance 1992* (Sarawak) (replacing the *Native Courts Ordinance 1955*).[143] The native courts in Sabah have a less complex hierarchy of only three tiers: Native Court, District Native Court, and Native Court of Appeal. Sabah native courts exercise jurisdiction bestowed by the *Native Courts Enactment 1992* (Sabah).[144] Native courts exercise exclusive jurisdiction over matters conferred by their respective enabling statutes, and there is no appeal to the civil High Court of Sabah and Sarawak (one of the two national High Courts of co-ordinate jurisdiction).

12.4.2 The Relationship Between the Central and State Governments

There is no direct method by which the central government can force component States to legislate, although there is a constitutional provision mandating essential

---

[142]For some academic commentary, see: Thio Li-ann, "Jurisdictional Imbroglio" *supra* note 50; Salbiah Ahmad, "The Freedom of Religion Impasse and Powers of the High Court" (2003) XXII (no 3) INSAF (The Journal of the Malaysian Bar) 60; Whiting, "Desecularizing Malaysian Law?," *supra* note 50; Thio Li-ann "Apostasy and Religious Freedom: Constitutional Issues Arising from the Lina Joy Litigation" [2006] 2 MLJ 1; Whiting, "Secularism," *supra* note 51.
[143]See the description in Wu Min Aun, *supra* note 27, at pp. 244–249.
[144]See Ibid., 249–258.

common elements in the State constitutions (contained in the 8th schedule to the Federal Constitution), failing which the Parliament may by law make provisions for the same or for removing inconsistent provisions.

Instances where the Federal parliament may legislate on State List matters, pursuant to Federal Constitution article 76, have been discussed above in Part II, as have instances where the central government and Federal Parliament may, in times of a declared state of emergency, make laws for a State or even suspend the State constitution,[145] or advise the ruler of a State to pass regulations.[146]

The central government executes central government law. The police and public service are central government matters.[147] Of course component States have smaller public service bodies to execute their own functions. If the central government does require the assistance of the State government to execute central government law, then it must provide the necessary funding for this purpose.[148]

Each component State is allowed two representatives in the upper chamber of the bicameral Federal Parliament (the Dewan Negara, or Senate).[149] These State senators are chosen by their respective State legislative assemblies, not directly elected by popular vote, and so the political complexion of the upper house is a direct mirror of state politics. There are also a total of four senators representing the three Federal Territories.[150] Additional senators are appointed by the Yang di-Pertuan Agong because of their distinguished public record or achievements in the professions, commerce, industry, agriculture, culture or social service, or because they are representatives of racial minorities or are capable or representing the interests of aborigines.[151] (The term "aborigine" means an indigenous person of the Peninsula, not one of the more numerous native peoples of Sabah or Sarawak).[152] Pursuant to this provision, two senators each representing the aborigines and the Siamese community in Malaysia (mostly in northern parts bordering Thailand) have been appointed.

The senators representative of the States and the minority communities do not have a very influential role in the legislative process, as they are always in the minority in the Senate, since 26 are elected, but 44 appointed. Although article 45(4) of the Federal Constitution allows the Parliament by federal law to increase

---

[145]Federal Constitution, articles 148, 158; and see *Stephen Kalong Ningkan v. Government of Malaysia* [1968] 1 MLJ 119.

[146]See the discussion of the 1977 Kelantan Emergency and the *Emergency Powers (Kelantan) Act 1977 (Act 192)*), above, Part II, section 1, overview.

[147]Federal Constitution, 9th Schedule, List I, item 3 (a) (police) and item 6 (machinery of government).

[148]Federal Constitution, art 80(4) (6). See, for instance: *Printing of Qur'anic Texts Act 1986* (Act 326)).

[149]Federal Constitution, article 45 (1) (a).

[150]Federal Constitution, art 45 (1) (aa).

[151]Federal Constitution art 45(1) (b), 45 (2).

[152]Federal Constitution, art 160.

the number of members to be elected for each component state to three from two and to provide for the state senators to be elected by the direct vote, and to decrease the number of appointed members, there has not been any political will for the same. Likewise, no political will exists to realize the constitutional drafters' recommendations that the centre-nominated senators be reduced or abolished completely.[153] It is very rare for the senators to engage in a meaningful debate of bills approved by the House of Representatives, and even rarer to have bills rejected.[154]

Malaysia practices fiscal centralization. While both central and component State governments have the power to tax, the Federal Constitution in Part III of the 10th Schedule limits what the States may collect. The central government is empowered to impose and collect a wide-range of taxes including such important taxes as individual income and corporate taxes, sales tax and taxes arising from exports and imports.

State governments have comparatively less capacity to collect taxes, and rely upon sources such as fees and receipts in respect of specific services rendered by departments of the State governments, licenses, assessment rates, and revenue from lands, mines and forests. The East Malaysia States of Sabah and Sarawak are allowed more sources of revenue.[155] For instance, these states are allowed to collect state sales taxes and import duty and excise duty on petroleum products.

Generally, as the States are allowed to tax items enumerated in Part III, Tenth Schedule (and also Part V for Sabah and Sarawak), and a few items representing minor revenues, the issue of multiple taxation is not as relevant as in other federations.

The component States have taxing power only over minor items, the largest sources being receipts from land sales, revenue from lands, mines and forests, entertainment duty and Islamic religious revenue. For Sabah and Sarawak, additional sources of revenue include import and excise duties on petroleum products and export duty on timber and other forest produce.

Revenues collected by the Federal Government are shared with the component State governments through capitation grants that are calculated by reference to State population. The formula is constitutionally mandated.[156] The Federal Government also issues special grants for development projects in component States on an ad hoc basis.[157]

---

[153] See Shafruddin, *Federal Factor supra* note 7, at p. 18.
[154] See further Harding, *Law, Government and the Constitution*, *supra* note 3, at pp. 30–31, 79, 96.
[155] Federal Constitution, article 112 C and Tenth Schedule, Part V.
[156] Federal Constitution, art 109 and schedule 10.
[157] *See generally* Harding, *Law, Government and the Constitution*, *supra* note 3, at p, 176ff.

12.4.3 Other Formal and Informal Institutions for Resolving Intergovernmental Conflicts

All constitutional disputes can be resolved through the jurisdiction of the ordinary courts. Yet, the constitution assigns the Federal Court as the proper forum to determine whether a law is valid or whether a lawmaking body was competent to enact a law.[158]

The Federal Constitution further provides for resolution of specific cases of disputes between governments by way of a tribunal. This involves disputes of three types. The first concerns disputes about the value of land transacted between the central and State governments. The tribunal set up is called the Land Tribunal.[159] The second relates to disputes with regard to the monetary valuation of payments due to the State government by reason of its rendering executive duties at the request of the central government that are otherwise the responsibility of the central government.[160] The third relates to contribution over use of lands and buildings owned by either governments in lieu of local rates which would otherwise be payable.[161]

The institution of the Conference of Rulers[162] can be seen as another forum to resolve intergovernmental disputes. It has the constitutional function of deliberating on national policy, and when it performs this function the Rulers are accompanied by the political heads of their respective governments and must act on their advice.[163] Although the hereditary royalty have lost most of their former personal political power and now seem to enjoy a purely iconic function as symbols of traditional Malay culture and modern Malay national pride, nevertheless when convened in the Conference of Rulers along with the political executive, they can provide a less politicized (and more discrete) forum for the discussion of central-state matters.[164] The Conference of Rulers is also a consultative body: The federal constitution requires consultation with it on appointments to the Public Service Commission, the Education Service Commission, the Election Commission and the Auditor General.[165] Judicial appointments are made in this way too, but since 2009, a statutory Judicial Appointments Commission makes recommendations regarding

---

[158]*See supra* section 1.

[159]Federal Constitution, art 87.

[160]Federal Constitution, art 80(6).

[161]Federal Constitution art 156.

[162]Federal Constitution, art 38 and 5th Schedule.

[163]Federal Constitution, art 38 (3).

[164]See in this regard the comments of Harding, *Law, Government and the Constitution, supra* note 3, at p. 72.

[165]Fong, *supra* note 4, at pp. 236–241.

appointment and promotion of judges to the Prime Minister, who then consults with the Conference of Rulers before making his recommendation to the Agong.[166]

There are other constitutionally established consultative bodies. When making financial decisions affecting the States, the federal government must consult the National Finance Council, composed of representatives of each of the states[167]; according the former Sarawak Attorney General J.C. Fong, consultation in this manner "ensures that the financial or economic affairs of the Federal Government and those of the States are discussed within the Council and both Federal and State Governments have a forum to consult each other, on all financial issues affecting them".[168] The National Council for Local Government was established by constitutional amendment to coordinate the overlap of local government functions which straddle federal and state responsibilities.[169] It formulates national policy, and the federal and state governments must consult it in respect of proposed legislation affecting local government matters.[170] The National Land Council, established by article 91, has similar powers and functions.

12.4.4 The Bureaucracy

For the most part, the civil service of the central government is separate from the civil services of the component States. The civil service of the central government is administered by the Public Services Commission Malaysia, while the majority of the States have their separate public service commissions. Yet the civil service of four States (Malacca, Penang, Negeri Sembilan and Perlis) comes under the jurisdiction of the federal Public Services Commission.[171]

Joint services, common to the central government and one or more of the component States (or at the request of the States concerned, to two or more States), may be established by federal law.[172] Pursuant to this, *Joint Service (Islamic Affairs Officers) Act* 1997 (Act 573) has been enacted to establish a joint service

---

[166]Established by *Judicial Appointments Commission Act 2009* (Act 695); appointment provisions in sections 22–28, read with Federal Constitution article 122B.

[167]The National Finance Council is established by article 108 of the Federal Constitution.

[168]Fong, *supra* note 4, at p. 243.

[169]Fong, *supra* note 4, at pp. 243–244. Sabah and Sarawak participate in the Council but are not voting members.

[170]Federal Constitution, article 95A (5), (6), (7).

[171]*See* Article 139 of the Federal Constitution for Penang and Malacca; for Perlis and Negeri Sembilan: *Public Services Commission (Extension of Jurisdiction) Enactment*, 1958 (Perlis), *Public Services Commission (Extended Jurisdiction) Order*, 1960 (Perlis), *Public Services Commission (Extension of Jurisdiction) Enactment*, 1959 (Negeri Sembilan) and *Public Services Commission (Extension of Jurisdiction) Order*, 1959 (Negeri Sembilan). See further Shafruddin, *The Federal Factor supra* note 7, chapter 4.

[172]Federal Constitution, art 133.

for Islamic Affairs Officers in the Federal Territories, and the states of Malacca, Negeri Sembilan, Penang, Selangor, Perlis and Terengganu. The power to appoint, confirm, emplace on the permanent or pensionable establishment, promote, transfer and exercise disciplinary control over these joint services officers are vested in the federal Public Services Commission.[173]

In four States where public service is governed by the Federal Public Service Commission – Malacca, Penang, Negeri Sembilan and Perlis – lateral mobility exists between these States' civil system and the central government's civil system.[174] For instance, the post of Perlis Secretary of State was recently filled by a former deputy secretary-general of a federal ministry who has served at both the State and Federal level.[175] Mobility is also provided under joint services such as the Joint Service for Islamic Affairs Officers.[176] Although component States may have their separate civil service, the States may yet turn to the central Public Services Commission and other central commissions for appointments. State constitutions may provide, as the Perak Constitution does, that the appointments of the State Secretary, State Legal Adviser and State Financial Officer be made by the appropriate service commissions,[177] which appears to be the commissions at the central level, namely the Public Services Commission and the Judicial and Legal Service Commission provided under the Federal Constitution. If so, it may be the case that once appointed, the State government through its Menteri Besar (Chief Minister) may not be able to unilaterally suspend or fire these officers.[178] There is clearly potential for political interference and centre-state conflict if the federal appointee takes a different view of matters from that adopted by the state, as recently occurred in constitutional crisis in Perak, when the UMNO appointed State Secretary frustrated the decisions of the Pakatan Rakyat members of the State Legislative Assembly.[179]

12.4.5 Social Factors

The question of whether there are important social cleavages in the federation is at once a very straightforward and an extremely complex question to ask about Malaysia. Politics and law are saturated with both religion and race, and it is impossible to explain the course of post-colonial history without reference to them.

---

[173] *Joint Service (Islamic Affairs Officers) Act* 1997 (Act 573), s 4.

[174] See Public Service Commission Circular No. 1 of 2005 http://www.spa.gov.my/pls/portal/docs/PAGE/SPA_CONTENT/MAKLUMAT_KORPORAT/MK_PROFIL/MK_PEKELILING/MKP_PANDUAN_TUKAR/PEK105.PDF.

[175] "Perlis gets new State Secretary", New Straits Times, http://www.nst.com.my/Current_News/NST/Wednesday/NewsBreak/20080326150355/Article/index_html.

[176] *Joint Service (Islamic Affairs Officers) Act* 1997 (Act 573), section 5.

[177] *Constitution of the State of Perak*, article 36C.

[178] "Suspensions not valid, says Chief Secretary to Govt", *New Straits Times*, 13 May 2009.

[179] See Quay, *Perak: A State of Crisis*, supra note 12.

Malaysia is a multicultural polity – a government census records a population of 66.1 % Malay (including other indigenous peoples, many of whom are not Muslims), 25.3 % Chinese, 7.4 % Indian and 1.2 % "other".[180] Ethnic Malays enjoy constitutionally entrenched privileges in relation to land, licenses and public office,[181] as well as politically entrenched policy objectives (under the New Economic Policy (NEP) and its successors), that deliver to them preferential access to social and economic benefits, particularly government contracts, housing and places in higher education.[182] Openly questioning these privileges and policies is discouraged, and indeed might be viewed as sedition[183] according to the logic that challenging Malay hegemony ("Ketuanan Melayu") will provoke communal violence on the scale of "May 13", the post-election "race riots" in 1969. Politicians frequently conjure the memory of the May 13 riots to justify preferential treatment for ethnic Malays as a solution to the social and economic "backwardness" of the Malays and the "dominance" of the Chinese.[184] Electoral politics is conducted by race-based political parties[185] continuing the "consociational bargain" of the Merdeka constitutional negotiations in 1957, when communal political leaders agreed amongst themselves to grant citizenship to non-Malays as long as Malay-Muslim privileges were retained and entrenched.[186] An aspect of this bargain is the special position of Islam in the Federation, which is declared in article 3 of the constitution to be the religion of the Federation. Nevertheless, the Supreme Court has ruled that this provision did not establish a state religion or a theocracy,[187] and religious freedom for other faiths is constitutionally guaranteed in articles 3 and 11.

---

[180]Economic and Planning Unit, *Third Outline Perspective Plan 2001–2010* (Putrajaya: Economic and Planning Unit, Prime Minister's Office, 2001), table 6.1, "Population Structure 1990–2010".

[181]Federal Constitution articles 89 (Reservation of Land for Malays), 152 (National Language) and 153 (Reservation of quotas in respect of services, permits, etc. for Malays and Natives of any of the States of Sabah and Sarawak).

[182]There is a huge literature on this topic. Key recent studies include: Lee Hock Guan, "Affirmative Action in Malaysia" *Southeast Asian Affairs 2005* (Singapore: ISEAS, 2005), 211–228 and Edmund Terence Gomez, "Governance, Affirmative Action and Enterprise Development: Ownership and Control of Corporate Malaysia" in Gomez, *The State of Malaysia: Ethnicity, Equity and Reform* (London: RoutledgeCurzon, 2004), chapter 6.

[183]*Sedition Act 1948* (Act 15), s 3(1)(f) criminalizes advocating change to the constitutionally expressed Malay privileges; and the Malay-controlled government periodically threatens its critics with punishment under s 3(1)(e).

[184]This is the infamous analysis of former Prime Minister Mahathir bin Mohamad in *The Malay Dilemma, supra* note 16. For a different view of the May 13 riots, see Kua Kia Soong, *May 13, supra* note 15.

[185]Mavis Puthucheary and Norani Othman (eds.) *Elections and Democracy in Malaysia* (Kuala Lumpur: Universiti Kebangsaan Malaysia, 2005), chapter 1.

[186]Fernando, "The Position of Islam" *supra* note 5; and more generally *The Making of the Malayan Constitution, supra* note 4.

[187]That is, according to the Supreme Court in *Che Omar bin Che Soh v. Public Prosecutor* [1988] 2 MLJ 55. The meaning of article 3 and the place of religion in the federation are now important political and legal questions: see Whiting, "Secularism," *supra* note 51.

Generally, all major ethnic groups (Malay, Indian and Chinese) are found in every state in significant numbers, although some more than the others. As a leading Malaysian federalism scholar has observed, the Federation "was established essentially not because of ethnic or communal demands but rather to accommodate the legacy of the Malay States and the accompanying institution of the Sultanate."[188] Malays are mostly concentrated in the northern and eastern States of the peninsula. There are more Chinese present in the cities and towns than in rural areas. City-states such as Penang and Malacca have a significant Chinese population. The current demography is also a product of history, as Penang and Malacca were previously colonies of the British, and Chinese immigration was encouraged to suit colonial purposes. Other states remained British protectorates with the Sultans (traditional Rulers) remaining the heads of the State, and heads of Islam in the respective States. The special position of the Sultans is constitutionally preserved, and every 5 years, one of the Sultans takes his turn to occupy a unique constitutional position of the Yang di-Pertuan Agong (the King), acting as the Head of the Federation and Head of Islam for the Federal Territories and for those states not having a Sultan to fulfill that religious role. A Yang di-Pertua Negeri (a Governor), is appointed as the Head of the State in states that do not have Sultans. All Sultans and Yang di-Pertua Negeri occupy seats in the Conference of Rulers, a constitutional body that is empowered to elect future Kings from the pool of Sultans,[189] and that has to be consulted in such appointment as civil court judges, the auditor general, and members of election, public services and education service commissions. The consent of the Conference of Rulers must also be sought in such matters affecting the federation as alterations of boundaries of a state, and Islamic matters.[190] Federal initiatives towards a unified set of Islamic laws must have the consent of the Conference of Rulers.

Compared with the peninsular States, Sabah and Sarawak have a majority indigenous population comprising various ethnic groups. As part of the entry arrangement into the federation of Malaysia, the natives of Sabah and Sarawak are accorded special privileges similar to those enjoyed by the Malays.[191] No other communities, not even the aborigines in the peninsular States, are accorded such special privileges. Notwithstanding this, recent statements issued by Sabah and Sarawak politicians indicate an increased demand for a more prominent role in the central government as well as more autonomous powers to the state governments.

The minority Malaysian Indian community (comprising Hindus, Sikhs, Muslims and Christians) has the least political influence (that is, apart from the dire position

---

[188] Shafruddin, *supra* note 7, at p. xxiv.

[189] Only the rulers take part in the election and removal of the King to the exclusion of all the Yang di-Pertua Negeri. See paragraph 7, Fifth Schedule, Federal Constitution.

[190] Not being the head of Islam in their respective states, the Yang di-Pertua Negeri do not have say in the aspect of Islamic matters. See paragraph 7, Fifth Schedule, Federal Constitution.

[191] See Federal Constitution, articles 16A, 95B–95E, 112A–112D, and, in particular, Part XIIA, comprising arts 161-161H: "Additional Protections for States of Sabah and Sarawak" as well as 10th Schedule, part IV, "Special Grants to states of Sabah and Sarawak".

of the *orang asli* of peninsular Malaysia).[192] Yet robust public discussion of this fact can be seen as divisive and a challenge to Malay privileges, and recent Indian political leaders have been incarcerated for raising these issues.[193] Last but not least, as with any other economically vibrant country, there is a growing immigrant population (legal and illegal) that serves to meet the labor requirements in Malaysia.[194]

There are significant asymmetries in natural resources, development, wealth, education, and economic strength in Malaysia. Timber, plantation, oil and gas and mineral resources are concentrated in comparatively less developed East Malaysian States, and East Coast States in West Malaysia, whereas the dynamic capital Kuala Lumpur attracts wealth and financial investment. The different ethnic communities that comprise multi-cultural Malaysia will experience different levels of economic progress, education and so on. However tabulating such differences is a political exercise, for some a dangerous one, since public presentation of figures that challenge the official view of economic progress (and the race preference policies) can lead to censure.

The federal structure of fiscal and legal centralization makes it extremely difficult for a component State to address these asymmetries by itself, independent of assistance from the central government. This state of affairs partly explains the lack of economic development in Kelantan, a State that has since 1990 been under the control of PAS, a Malay-Muslim political party which vies with the ruling UMNO for the Malay vote by presenting itself as more Islamic, and the inability of rich States such as Selangor and Penang – also governed at the state level by political parties that are in opposition federally – to move forward alone without central assistance. Since the opposition parties won control of the State legislature following the general election in March 2008, the federal government has decided to defer several significant federal projects in Penang that had been previously approved.[195] The Penang government will not be able to implement these deferred projects without the federal government's financial assistance.

---

[192]Regarding which, see R.D.L. Jumper, *Orang Asli Now: the Orang Asli in the Malaysian Political World* (Lanham, NY: American University Press, 1999).

[193]For recent threatened use of the Sedition Act against a leader of the Hindu Rights Action Force (HINDRAF), see Fauwaz Abdul Aziz, "HINDRAF Leader faces fresh sedition charge" *malaysiakini*, 11 December 2007 – the charge is in relation to a letter sent to the British PM on 15 November (and currently accessible on the government run news service, Bernama, at www.bernama.com/bernama/v3/news.php?id=300857) accusing the Malaysian government of ethnic cleansing policies against Indians in Malaysia.

[194]Sajad Hussein, "70,000 More Bangladeshi Workers Coming To Malaysia", *Bernama Daily Malaysian News*, 8 March 2009; "Declining Birth Rate Affects 70 Mln Population Target". *Bernama Daily Malaysian News*, 4 July 2007 (this report states that as at March 2006, there was a total of 1.85 million registered foreign workers in Malaysia); Farrah Naz Karim and Patrick Sennyah, "Two-week amnesty for 1.2 m illegal immigrants", *New Straits Times*, 22 October 2004.

[195]Pauline Puah, "Guan Eng meets Abdullah on deferred projects" *The Edge* 16 July 2008. http://www.theedgedaily.com/cms/content.jsp?id=com.tms.cms.article.Article_2a6bf920-cb73c03a-11151520-d4fbdb32.

In what is perhaps a reflection of federal politics, royalties arising out of oil and gas resources occasionally become an issue between the federal government and the states within the boundaries of which the resources are mined.[196] These occasions usually coincide with the opposition being in power in these component states. Following the opposition's gaining control of the state of Terengganu in 1999, the national petroleum company stopped paying royalties to the state for petroleum exploited in the state. This led to legal action by the state against the company and the federal government which controlled the company.[197] After the federal government re-captured Terengganu in 2004, the royalties were subsequently re-instated.[198]

12.5 Conclusion

Amongst federal systems of the world, Malaysia is no doubt at the extreme end of the central-federal spectrum. There are many conclusions one can draw from this picture, but perhaps three broad ones will suffice to characterize the situation. First, in terms of social and economic development, it seems clear that the high degree of legal uniformity and centralized governance, including fiscal centralism and a national justice system, have been successfully deployed since independence by successive Malaysian Governments in their macroeconomic policies and state planning instruments to achieve rapid and sustained social and economic growth. Second, in terms of politics, the weakened position of the states *vis à vis* the centre in this federal arrangement has contributed to the dominance of the UMNO-led Barisan Nasional governing coalition over the opposition parties at all levels of government, thus perpetuating the semi-democratic nature of Malaysia's politics and governance and discouraging the kind of political and legal diversity and experimentation that might otherwise have flourished in a true federation.[199] Third, weakened as the states are, they have been able to retain some key areas of executive and legislative power: Sabah and Sarawak continue to enjoy greater administrative autonomy than the other constituent states through the special deals they struck when they joined the Federation; and, in the peninsular states, the special position of the Malay Rulers, and their constitutional role in safeguarding Islam (as religion

---

[196] In current litigation over oil royalties mounted by the State Government of Kelantan against Petroleum Nasional Bhd, a federal government corporation, the Federal Government has asserted that it should be joined as a party on the basis that petroleum in the continental shelf off the coast of Kelantan belonged to the Federal, and not the State, government. See "Kelantan Government loses appeal to stop Federal Government from Intervening Suit," *Bernama*, 26 May 2011.

[197] *Petroleum Nasional Bhd v Kerajaan Negeri Terengganu & Another Appeal* [2003] 4 CLJ 337.

[198] Andrew Ong, "T'ganu to withdraw oil royalty suit," *Malaysiakini*, 8 January 2009.

[199] William Case, "Semi-democracy and Minimalist Federalism in Malaysia" in Baogang He, Brian Gilligan, Takashi Honugochi (eds.) *Federalism in Asia* (Cornwall, UK: Edward Elgar Publishing, 2007).

and as *syariah*) is jealously guarded and considered beyond critical public scrutiny and comment. These combined factors (which are constitutionally, politically and socially entrenched) of East Malaysian distinctiveness and the "traditional" authority of the state monarchies and their association with Islam, will continue to shape the nature of Malaysia's federal system and any proposed changes to it.

Chapter 13
Federalism and Legal Unification in Mexico

Oscar Echenique Quintana, Nadja Dorothea Ruíz Euler,
and Ricardo Carrasco Varona

13.1 Overview

The Mexican federal system was born between 1823 and 1824, a few years after Mexico achieved its independence from Spain (1821). The first Mexican constitution, enacted in 1824, established the principle of the Mexican nation's supremacy, thus rejecting the supremacy of the component states.

In general outline, the form of federalism chosen was inspired by the American model. Mexican reality, however, was profoundly different from the conditions prevailing in the model country. While the United States of America's federal system was designed in light of the underlying social reality, federalism in Mexico was by and large a political ideal. In reality, Mexico, as a self-governing country, was born with a heritage of profound centralism (derived from the colonial Spanish government) whose effects can be felt even today.

Mexican history in the nineteenth century reflects the tension between centralism and federalism. It was marked by the struggle between two groups: conservatives and liberals. The former pioneered a centralized political regime, while the latter

---

Oscar ECHENIQUE QUINTANA, Mexican lawyer. Graduated from the International Tax LLM of the University of Michigan Law School, 2009. Currently works for the Supreme Court of Mexico.

Nadja Dorothea RUÍZ EULER, Mexican lawyer. Graduated from the *Instituto Tecnológico Autónomo de México* (*ITAM*). Currently works for the Mexican Revenue Service.

Ricardo CARRASCO VARONA, Mexican lawyer. Graduated from the *Escuela Libre de Derecho*. Currently works for the Mexican Revenue Service.

O. Echenique Quintana (✉)
Supreme Court of Mexico, Law Clerk to Alfredo, Gutiérrez Ortiz Mena, Mexico City, Mexico
e-mail: OEcheniqueQ@mail.scjn.gob.mx

N.D. Ruíz Euler • R. Carrasco Varona
Federal Revenue Service, Mexico City, Mexico
e-mail: nadja.ruiz@sat.gob.mx; ricardo.carrasco@sat.gob.mx

fought for the legal changes necessary to build a real federal structure. As a result of this struggle, Mexico experienced a variety of constitutional regimes which were based on both conservative and liberal views.

The early twentieth century was marked by the revolutionary movement, the outcome of which resulted in the adoption of the current Mexican political system. In 1917, a new Mexican constitution was enacted. It was based on a traditional model of a federal state, which included separation of powers and (limited) sovereignty for its component states. These states are endowed with some exclusive powers that, in principle, neither the federal authorities nor other component states can encroach upon. Furthermore, local constitutions and authorities shall respect the principle of separation of powers established in the federal constitution. A special regime exists in the Mexican Federal District (currently, Mexico City), which is the seat of the federal government.

Mexico's twentieth century was characterized by a strong presidential system and overall control by one political party. It was only during the last quarter of the century that power became more diversified and the long-awaited federalism became a serious political option. The crucial moment in this development was the defeat of the predominant political party in the presidential elections in 2000. From this moment onwards, political and economic processes have gradually brought Mexico closer to a real federal system.

13.2 The Federal Distribution and Exercise of Lawmaking Power

13.2.1 Central and State Legislative Powers

Besides the federal Mexican Constitution, each of the component states[1] has, as a (limited) sovereign, its own constitution. Based upon a *federal agreement* made in 1824, the constitution of the component states shall not infringe the substance of the federal Constitution.

The federal constitution allocates the legislative power to either the central government or to the component states. This is achieved by vesting the component states with general and residual legislative power and then assigning specific

---

[1] As mentioned above, the Mexican federal system includes a Federal District (Mexico City) where the central government has its principal residence. This District, however, does not have its own constitution since it is governed by a local statute. Nevertheless, the local government has been promoting a local constitution in order to turn the Federal District into a component state. Despite this fact, every reference hereinafter to the component states includes the Federal District, except as otherwise indicated.

legislative powers to the central government. In other words, the component states' legislative competence is limited only by the legislative power allocated to the federal level. Note that the opposite is true, however, with regard to Mexico City, i.e., the Federal District: here the residual power is given to the center and local authorities have only the competences expressly assigned to them.

The central government has the power to legislate in the matters specifically provided in Article 73 of the federal constitution. This enumerative approach is then somewhat modified by the last subsection of the article that provides for implied powers of the central government, opening up a potentially wide area for federal legislation.

The main areas exclusively reserved to the central government include the macroeconomic policy; currency; national debt; taxation of customs, oil, natural resources, financial institutions, electric energy, tobacco, and alcoholic beverages; foreign and interior policy; military defense; resolution of disputes among component states; labor; financial services; citizenship; communication; and national security.

There are certain subjects on which the central government has the power to issue general regulations distributing competences among its own jurisdiction, the component states, and the municipalities (e.g., in the fields of education, health, and the environment); the states may then legislate within the established federal framework. From a practical point of view, the most important areas of central government regulation are banking, financial law, commercial law (including the law of contracts which is thus uniform throughout Mexico), competition, and labor law.

The federal constitution allows both the federal and state levels to legislate in most of the remaining areas of law as long as they stay within their respective jurisdiction. For example, there are core areas of private law (including property, family, inheritance, torts) and criminal law, as well as procedure, in which both levels have their own legislation.

The federal constitution also establishes some guidelines that components states must follow with regard to their form of government, i.e., the basic structure of their executive, judicial and legislative branches. In addition, the federal constitution specifies certain matters of law in which local legislation is expressly forbidden, or at least confined to narrow limits, e.g., alliances with other states or countries, currency, taxation on the export and import of goods, or the printing of money.

It is also worth mentioning that federal legislation is not always passed by the same actors. As a rule, a federal statute must be passed by both houses of the Central Congress. Some legislation, however, can be made only by one of the houses. For example, the House of Representatives alone approves the Federal Expense Government Budget, and the Senate alone approves international treaties signed by the President.

13.2.2 Principles Relating to the Interaction Between the Central and State Legal Systems

It is important to highlight that there is no specific hierarchy rule between state and federal law. The Mexican Supreme Court jurisprudence has corroborated this principle. Thus, potential conflicts between state and federal legislation shall be primarily resolved according to the respective competences. If one level invades the sphere reserved to the other, i.e., where federal legislation intrudes upon matters reserved to the states or vice-versa, the conflict is solved by the Supreme Court by way of special constitutional procedures. Normally, federal and state law should thus not be applicable to the same situation. Where this is nonetheless the (exceptional) case, central law will prevail under the notion of federal supremacy. This can have a top-down unifying effect as will be explained in the next section.

Below the component states there is a third level of government: the "municipalities". They are the component states' territorial and administrative divisions and constitute a particular form of power decentralization. Furthermore, they can be conceived as *sui generis* entities because they have some statutory freedom but are also linked to the state to which they belong by strong and permanent ties.

Municipalities have legal personality and their own patrimony. They are exclusively in charge of certain services and functions and are also allowed to form associations with other municipalities. The highest level of governance of these entities it is a group of representatives headed by a municipal president. The municipal representatives have to approve administrative provisions regarding all the matters within the municipalities' jurisdiction.

Municipalities were introduced in the constitution of 1917 in order to strengthen federalism by returning some competences, previously absorbed by the central government, to the local level. Yet, despite the allocation of some powers to the municipalities, the central power of the states has prevented the development of real municipal independence.

13.3 The Means and Methods of Legal Unification

13.3.1 Legal Unification or Harmonization Through the Exercise of Central Power (Top Down)

Article 133 of the federal Constitution establishes the supremacy principle according to which all authorities at all government levels must observe the commands of that document. This means that the contents of laws made and applied by each government entity are roughly alike or at least not irreconcilable. In addition, the general supremacy of the federal Constitution has had the effect that, in practice, states have generally followed federal law. As a result, component states thus follow central federal law in two ways: they are required to comply with federal constitutional provisions, and they often voluntarily mimic the general model of federal law (both in constitutional and statutory matters). Indeed, frequently, local rules are merely copies of provisions enacted by the Central Congress. This is true for most of private and criminal law as well as for both civil and criminal procedure.

There is, however, no complete legal unification regarding matters that fall under the residual powers clause established in article 124[2] of the federal constitution, i.e., in areas that are reserved exclusively to the component states because they are not assigned to the federal government.

When it comes to the judiciary, it is noteworthy that in Mexico, the interpretation of law, both at the constitutional and the legislative level, strongly contributes to its legal harmonization. In particular, the federal constitution provides the judicial branch with various mechanisms to enforce constitutional provisions. The most important of these mechanisms is the *amparo* procedure. It allows the judicial branch to control the uniformity of the national law by deciding whether a federal or local provision infringes the federal Constitution. Given the importance of this procedure, its basic features and contributions to legal unification will be explained in greater detail below.[3]

Another fairly common "top-down" harmonization mechanism is the negotiation of agreements between the federal government and the states about the allocation of certain administrative duties. These agreements are commonly promoted by the executive branch with the goal to define the distribution of resources and to determine areas of competence. Most of these agreements are related to economic development, public security, health and education.

In addition, the three federal branches of government, i.e., the legislature, the executive, and the courts, are constantly sponsoring and promoting conventions, meetings, and publications related to the harmonization of national law. Local authorities, academic institutions from the whole country, and private sector organizations frequently participate in these efforts which thus provide a national platform for action.

These efforts are remarkable against the background of the traditional predominance of the executive in Mexico, which lasted from the beginning of the twentieth century until the 1990s. In its heyday, this predominance itself ensured considerable unification of law since the legislature, the judiciary, and the member

---

[2] The "residual powers clause" established in article 124 of the federal constitution is similar to the 10th amendment to the United States of America Constitution, which sets forth the following: "The powers not delegated to the United States by the Constitution, nor prohibited by it to the states, are reserved to the states respectively, or to the people."

[3] See below Sect. 13.4. Institutional and Social Background, 1. The Judicial Branch.

state authorities could rarely decide against the position and will of the executive. Over the last two decades, this situation has gradually changed. The other branches of the federal government as well as the member states have increasingly claimed their share in decision making and exercised their legal powers more freely. This spelled the end of the traditional authoritarian ways of legal unification that had prevailed for so many decades. The current path can thus be described as a gradual and moderate decentralization process, driven by the enactment of general (central) laws distributing institutional powers more widely among the federal authorities, state units, and even municipalities.

Overall, Mexican federalism is marked by considerable complexities and even contradictions. Witness, for example, that legislation on commerce is an exclusive power of the Central Congress but that controversies about commercial issues can nonetheless be brought before local authorities.

13.3.2 Legal Unification Through Formal or Informal Voluntary Coordination Among the Component States (Bottom Up)

Due to compliance with the central constitution and to a *de facto* weakly developed federalism, local legislatures commonly follow federal law when enacting state statutes.

On the judicial side, the supremacy of federal law – especially that of the constitution – expressly forces the local courts to keep their decisions within constitutional parameters. Likewise, decisions must also be in accordance with international treaties signed by the federal executive and any implementing legislation enacted by the Central Congress. Among the local courts, significant efforts have been made to build institutional frameworks for gathering and sharing experiences and for pursuing joint projects of nationwide scope. For example, the states' supreme courts have created the National Commission of Supreme Courts of the United Mexican States (CONATRIB). The Commission meets periodically in order to share ideas with the goal of improving the effective administration of justice. This Commission has pursued several projects pertaining to legal unification, such as the draft Model Criminal Procedural Code published in 2008.

The executive branches of the component states also play a role in the discussion of federal concerns and the relations between federal and the local policies. A noteworthy institution is the National Confederation of Governors (CONAGO), which was created in 2002. While its proposals of course do not bind federal authorities, local executives participating in the Confederation have been leading an important struggle to maintain the balance between powers on the federal and the state levels.

13.3.3 Legal Unification Promoted by Other State and Non-state Actors

Even though Mexico has traditionally been a clear case of top-down unification, today state and non-state local actors play a more significant role than in the past. Final outcomes of legislative disputes thus increasingly betray the influence of these actors.

In Mexico, there is nothing similar to the United States' "Restatements", a notion rather alien to the legislation-centered civil law tradition. Non-state actors do play an occasional role, however. For example, it is rather common in Mexico to publish law reform proposals issued by academic institutions and non-profit organizations. In addition, many private organizations promote legal standards and thus push for harmonization. For example, chambers of commerce, industries, or bankers constantly develop harmonization proposals for lobbying purposes. There are also various privately organized entities whose members belong to the local judiciary or the local administrative courts. Members of these organizations meet in order to promote the unification of criteria for judicial dispute resolution. An example is the Mexican Association of Judges (*Asociación Mexicana de Impartidores de Justicia*), a private organization whose members are judges representing courts in charge of law enforcement at both the central and local levels.

In addition, Mexican law – both federal and state – often generally follows models provided by international organizations. Examples include model rules generated by the Organization for Economic Co-operation and Development (OECD) and the Organization of American States (OAS), among others. These models concern areas such as international commerce, taxation, and arbitration.

13.3.4 The Role of Legal Education and Training in the Unification of Law

Generally speaking, the legal education that students receive at any institution in the country covers a combination of federal and local law. The common approach is that students learn federal law and the law of the component state where the institution is located. The resulting knowledge is thus a mixture of central and state law.

Yet, legal education particularly emphasizes the study of federal law and of the law of the Federal District. Moreover, where scholars discuss codified private law, they mostly refer to the Civil Code enacted in 2000 and applicable in the Federal District, particularly since it is highly similar to the Federal Civil Code.[4]

---

[4]Mexico has a Federal Civil Code (applicable to all areas subject to federal law) as well as civil codes on the local level, i.e., for the federal district and each of the member states; yet, due to the model function of the Federal Code, they are all highly similar.

There is no bar admission requirement in order to practice law in Mexico.[5] When an accredited law faculty has granted a student a law degree, the Ministry of Education issues a professional license. This is done simply on the basis of an application and requires no additional examination.

While there is no bar admission requirement, Mexico has several bar associations with voluntary membership. For example, the *Barra Mexicana Colegio de Abogados* and the *Ilustre y Nacional Colegio de Abogados de México* are important associations working as forums for the discussion of legal matters with other professionals and in an academic environment. Since these associations also exist in the component states, they serve as platforms for the encounter between groups from throughout the country, on the national as well as local level.[6]

Continuing legal education is currently a major concern of both government and private institutions. Government officials can find many educational programs sponsored by the institution they work for. In some contexts, especially in the judicial branch, enrolling in continuing education programs is required for appointment to certain positions.

Postgraduate programs play an important role in legal unification because many of them operate on a national basis. Frequently, students from all over the country gather in these educational contexts and thus receive instruction in the same material. Sometimes, this type of continuing education fosters the promotion of harmonization or unification of particular areas of law.

13.3.5 The Influence of International Law

In Mexico, the effects of both public and private international law significantly promote a high level of harmonization. Mexico has always been noted for accepting and complying with international obligations. There is also a broad tendency to resort to principles contained in international treaties, and some recent Supreme Court decisions regarding the supremacy of treaties over federal and state law have entailed a high level of national harmonization in matters regulated by international instruments. Examples include the Mexican membership in NAFTA as well as various treaties in civil and commercial matters, such as on child adoption, marriages, commercial arbitration, and commodities sales agreements.[7]

---

[5]Nonetheless, the Federal Judicial Power has been studying the matter and has come to the conclusion that it is necessary to establish a mandatory bar admission requirement in Mexico. The latter is part of a comprehensive and coherent reform regarding the Mexican justice system.

[6]In Mexico, joining the professional world generally begins before a student's graduation, e.g., by working part-time in a law firm. Mexican law students thus acquire practical experience at an early stage of their careers. It is also more common first to join law firms, companies, or government offices rather than to establish one's own practice right at the outset.

[7]Mexico is also a member of the Vienna Convention on the Law of Treaties of 1969 (in force 1980).

A very representative example can be found in the field of taxation. Mexico has frequently made tax treaties with foreign countries based on the Model Tax Convention on Income and on Capital issued by the OECD. Therefore, international tax matters, particularly the rules applicable to foreign taxpayers, have become increasingly unified in the last few years.

13.4 Institutional and Social Background

13.4.1 The Judicial Branch

In Mexico, the judicial branch acts as a standardizing agent, so to speak. This is because through its decisions (jurisprudence), it clarifies and establishes the meaning of the law. This is done with the objective of examining if the law is in conformity with the federal constitution, which is the supreme law of the nation.

Constitutional scrutiny is carried out through a special procedure known as *amparo*. In one very general sense, it constitutes a judicial review process as it is understood in many constitutional regimes around the world. Yet, having evolved from special circumstances, the *amparo* procedure is also marked by particular features that make it unique.

At the outset, the *Miguel Vega* case (1869) – roughly the Mexican equivalent of *Marbury vs. Madison* in the United States of America – created a groundbreaking precedent: it established that the federal constitution is above any other law or legal regulation and that the judiciary is the only branch entitled to decide whether any specific provision or any government decision is in accordance with the meaning of the federal constitution. This precedent and principle became the basis for the *amparo*.

Generally speaking, the *amparo* procedure's objective is to protect any person against infringements of constitutional rights by government authorities. It is regulated by a special code (*Ley de Amparo*), administrative provisions issued by the Supreme Court, and the jurisprudence of the judiciary.

In principle, any person (individuals or companies) may bring an *amparo* action, claiming that an authority has infringed his constitutional rights. Among the main claims that can be brought by means of the *amparo* are violations of personal freedom (a *habeas corpus* approach), and the unconstitutionality of a law in general (*judicial review* function) or of an administrative or judicial decision in particular cases (review of executive or judicial acts).

On the whole, the Mexican *amparo* is a complex institution which can be employed for a variety of purposes through roughly the same rules, as long as the infringement of constitutional rights is at stake, including human rights provided in international instruments.[8]

---

[8] As a result of major reforms to the Constitution, published on June 6th and 11th, 2011.

The action is presented before a federal *amparo* court. In some circumstances, the case goes to a court higher in the federal hierarchy. The Supreme Court receives appeals only when the case is considered innovative or particularly relevant to the judicial, political or social circumstances of the country.

One of the most debated and analyzed aspects of the *amparo* is the scope of its binding effect, i.e., the question of who benefits from an *amparo* decision. In principle, the decision of the court has merely a "relative effect", i.e., it works only *inter-partes*. It thus benefits only the party that brought the case to the court. The holding does not bind other courts, which may therefore issue contrary decisions in other cases. This explains why, in practice, the same legal provision or decision may be enforceable against one individual (or company) but not against another (i.e., the one who brought an *amparo* action and won the case).

This changes, however, once there is an established "jurisprudence". A decision becomes "jurisprudence" when its argument has been sustained at least five times in different cases, i.e., when at least five cases have been decided under the same rationale.

A decision can also be deemed "jurisprudence" when the Supreme Court decides a conflict between contradictory lower federal *amparo* court decisions and thus adopts one holding over others. In such a case, it is not necessary to wait for five decisions confirming the same rationale. The effect of becoming "jurisprudence" is that the rationale binds lower courts in the hierarchy when deciding similar cases; it thus becomes a more general rule which also no longer refers to the real parties and facts of the original case.

The normal lack of *erga omnes* effects notwithstanding, the *amparo* procedure functions as a powerful means of legal unification for a combination of reasons: (1) it can be raised in practically any case involving a claim of constitutional rights infringement; and (2) it is widely used by both individuals and companies in order to attack an allegedly unconstitutional decision of state authorities, so that (3) the meaning of the federal Constitution is constantly examined and enforced by the judicial branch. This exerts unrelenting pressure on all branches of government at all levels to act within the limits of the Constitution. According to recent changes to the Constitution,[9] however, decisions will have *erga omnes* effect when certain requirements are met. Tax legislation was not included for the latter purposes.

It has been argued that the resultant unification of law exceeds the competence of the *amparo* courts because this violates the independence and sovereignty of local authorities. Be that as it may, the procedure greatly promotes the uniformity and constitutional integrity of the Mexican legal system, albeit at the expense of local autonomy.

Moreover, as a consequence of recent changes to the Constitution mentioned above,[10] in some cases, *amparo* remedies are extended even to class actions.

---

[9] See note 9.

[10] See note 9.

13.4.2 The Relationship Between the Central and Component State Governments

The central government does not have the power to force component states to legislate in any area of law. Any coordination of state laws must thus be the outcome of a purely political process.

Only the central government may execute federal law. Yet, as mentioned before, it is common for federal and the local authorities to negotiate agreements about the distribution of competences and the allocation of resources to execute laws and regulations.

The component states participate in the central legislative process through the Senate. Members of this chamber are deemed to represent the component state in which they were elected. The senators fully participate in a bicameral legislative system and work with the House of Representatives in the production of federal law which must be passed by both chambers.[11] Most of the senators are chosen by direct election in which only the citizens of the respective state can vote. There are, however, other senators who are chosen according to the percentage of votes obtained by the political party to which they belong. As a result, the Senate is constituted by a mixture of direct election and proportional representation.

13.4.3 Taxation

The general principle in taxation is that both the central government and the component states may levy all taxes they deem necessary to cover public expenditures. Yet, as mentioned above, there is an enumeration of certain taxes that the federal constitution expressly assigns to the federal level, i.e., taxes on commerce, natural resources, oil products, financial services, alcohol, and tobacco.

In light of the fact that there is no constitutional prohibition of multiple taxation, the central government and the component states have entered into several agreements in order to avoid excessive burdens on the taxpayer. The legal expression of these negotiations is the Law of Tax Coordination. It establishes a system of distribution of competences pertaining to the collection and administration of taxes. The main purpose of the tax coordination system is the distribution of the revenue between the federal government and the component states.

On the administrative level, the tax coordination system works as the framework for bilateral agreements between the component states and the central government. Under the agreement, a component state accepts the amount of revenue it will receive from the central treasury. Municipalities can also participate in the scheme.

---

[11]The federal budget is an exception; it is passed by the House of Deputies alone.

The distribution is not equal for each state; instead, it depends on considerations of necessity (level of poverty in the state) and development (i.e., mainly the contribution to the national economy).

13.4.4 The Bureaucracy

The civil service of the central government is separate from the systems of the component states. Mobility between federal and local offices does exist but is not common. It occurs mainly when a local political group gains a federal position. On the whole, candidates usually prefer positions with the central government because the wages are higher.

Both at the federal and the state level, the need for civil service rules to provide governmental officials with certainty about their position has produced a lot of legislative activity. At the federal level, there is now a law setting forth the general rules for the central offices' civil service system (*Ley del Servicio Profesional de Carrera en la Administración Pública Federal*, 2003). Unfortunately, practice has not yet become entirely standardized since not all governmental offices have developed and implemented programs under this law. There is also no uniform set of rules for both the federal and state levels because political interests keep blocking the road towards a generally institutionalized practice. Still, civil service systems will gradually be regulated more and more under the current framework, making this area a coming example of legal harmonization, even though the process may require several years on the local level.

13.4.5 Social Factors

Mexico has a long heritage of social diversity. Its population is mainly a mixture of Hispanic immigrants and ancient indigenous groups. Some of the latter communities have tried to avoid integration; this has created unique ethnic cleavages within the country. These communities are highly heterogeneous, speaking many different languages, following various religious beliefs, and keeping diverse social institutions.

Indigenous populations are recognized by the federal constitution under the principle of "self determination" which is, however, limited by the principle of national unity. Their status does not directly affect the structure of the federal system as it is established by the Constitution.

While the indigenous communities are dispersed throughout the nation, there is a major concentration in the south. This has produced important political consequences. In the mid-1990s, a popular armed movement arose in the southern states, pioneering the recognition of indigenous rights. This ended up shaping the constitutional framework by giving it the pluricultural character that it has today.

The social situation in Mexico is marked by a variety of social asymmetries of which the ethnic diversity of the population is just one. Another important characteristic is the pronounced inequality of wealth distribution. Both features are connected: historically, the indigenous communities have not benefited from the economic growth of the country. As a consequence, there is currently an important correlation between the concentration of indigenous communities within certain states and local poverty.

In particular, this has entailed significant differences between the northern and the southern states: traditionally, the northern states have been more developed. This disparity in the economic situation has influenced the behaviour of local authorities, especially in that they have continuously fought for greater shares of the national resources. On the one hand, northern authorities usually claim a greater share of the national revenue, arguing that their economy is more efficient and productive than in the southern states. On the other hand, southern states argue they should receive more of the national revenue as they "need" it more given the high level of poverty prevailing there.

The federation constantly faces this struggle and tries to resolve the conflict. The pertinent legal provisions and administrative regulations reflect this situation.

13.5 Conclusion

The history of Mexico as an independent nation has been shaped by a permanent battle to realize its political aspirations. One of the most striking aspects of this journey has been the search for a federal way of life, with the centralist tradition presenting a constant obstacle to overcome. The evolution of Mexican law perfectly illustrates this situation. Even during the modernization process in the mid-twentieth century, the legal system still operated largely under the President's control, which blocked further development towards real democracy. As can be imagined, the strong presidential rule during that period fostered the unification of the legal system.

In addition to this political situation, the institutional mechanisms of the Mexican judicial system have also been a significant catalyst of legal unification. The power of the courts under the *amparo* procedure has enabled them to push for uniformity by forcing authorities in all branches and on all levels to stay within the boundaries drawn by the federal constitution.

The changes in the political environment that occurred in last quarter of the past century and particularly as a result of the presidential elections in 2000 (when the predominant party lost for the first time ever) have set Mexico on a new course towards becoming a real federalist nation. This emerging "real" federalism is already beginning to work against legal uniformity as local authorities are increasingly seeking to use their newly-gained political freedom.

Looking at the matter from an economic perspective, however, the new federalism may be more mirage than reality – or at least render federalism highly contingent on fiscal considerations. In the economic context, the inertia of the centralist tradition is especially hard to overcome. For example, even though the local authorities now vigorously demand greater freedom to shape the political, economic, and social features within their territories, most of them insist that the central government must continue to bear the responsibility for collecting the revenue and for distributing it among the component states. Also, the central authorities sometimes seem to fear losing the control and power they have had in the past.

Today, strong commercial interests, as well as some political interests, are pushing both federal and local authorities to maintain and promote the harmonization of law by pointing to the benefits of common and consistent rules throughout the nation. Yet, such efforts are merely one element in a complex mix of factors pulling in various directions, and the outcome of the resulting struggles is far from clear.

For any person interested in reading more about the topics of this report, the authors recommend the following bibliography:

AGUIRRE SALDÍVAR, Enrique, *Los retos del derecho público en materia de federalismo: Hacia la integración del derecho administrativo federal,* México, IIJ-UNAM, 1997.

ARTEAGA NAVA, Elisur, *Derecho constitucional*, México, Oxford, 1999.

BARRAGÁN BARRAGÁN, José, *El federalismo mexicano: Visión histórico constitucional,* México, IIJ-UNAM, 2007.

CABRERA ACEVEDO, Lucio, *El constituyente de Filadelfia de 1787 y la judicial review*, México, SCJN, 2005.

CARPIZO, Jorge, *Estudios constitucionales*, México, UNAM-Porrúa, 2003.

CARPIZO, Jorge, *Federalismo en Latinoamérica,* México, IIJ-UNAM, 1973.

COSSÍO, José Ramón, *Dogmática Constitucional y Régimen Autoritario*, México, Fontamara, 1998.

COSSÍO, José Ramón, *Cambio Social y Cambio Jurídico,* México, ITAM, 2001.

FIX-ZAMUDIO, Héctor, *Ensayos sobre el derecho de amparo*, México, UNAM-Porrúa, 2003.

GONZÁLEZ OROPEZA, Manuel, *La jurisprudencia: su conocimiento y forma de reportarla,* México, SCJN, 2005.

GONZÁLEZ OROPEZA, Manuel, *El federalismo,* México, IIJ-UNAM, 1995.

HÄBERLE, Peter, *El federalismo y regionalismo como forma estructural del Estado constitucional,* México, IIJ-UNAM, 2007.

HERNÁNDEZ, Antonio M. y VALADÉS, Diego *(coords), Estudios sobre federalismo, justicia, democracia y derechos humanos*, México, IIJ-UNAM, 2003.

ORTIZ AHLF, Loreta, *Derecho internacional público*, México, Oxford, 3ª ed., 2004.

PEREZNIETO CASTRO, Leonel, *Derecho internacional privado*, México, Oxford, 8ª ed., 2003.

SEPÚLVEDA, Cesar, *Derecho internacional*, México, Porrúa, 25ª ed., 2006.

SERNA DE LA GARZA, José M. *(coord), Federalismo y regionalismo*, México, IIJ-UNAM, 2002.

SUPREMA CORTE DE JUSTICIA DE LA NACIÓN, *La jurisprudencia: su integración,* México, SCJN, 2005.

TENA RAMÍREZ, FELIPE, *Derecho Constitucional Mexicano*, México, Porrúa, 2005.

ZALDIVAR LELO DE LARREA, Arturo, *Hacia una nueva ley de amparo,* México, IIJ-UNAM, 2002.

Chapter 14
How Federal Is the Russian Federation?

Jeffrey Kahn, Alexei Trochev, and Nikolay Balayan

14.1 Overview

It is undeniably true that in the last 8 years Russian law has experienced an extraordinary period of unification. Whether the Russian Federation (Russia) continues to operate a federal system of government, however, is a question on which reasonable minds differ. On the one hand, its constitution proclaims Russia to be a "federal, rule-of-law" state, divides the country into 83 component states of six different types, and appears to allocate separate spheres of both exclusive and shared jurisdiction to both the central government and to the component states. On the other hand, Russia's political system has grown increasingly centralized and the actual

---

This Report presents an accurate statement of Russian law as of the date of its submission for the Thematic Congress of the International Academy of Comparative Law held in Mexico City on November 13, 2008.

At the time the report was submitted, Jeffrey Kahn was Assistant Professor of Law, Southern Methodist University Dedman School of Law, Dallas, Texas, where he is now an Associate Professor of Law; Alexei Trochev was Lecturer, University of Wisconsin Law School and is now a professor at Nazarbayev University (Kazakhstan) in the School of Humanities & Social Sciences; Nikolay Balayan, a graduate of the Saratov State Law Academy, earned his LL.M. from the Dedman School of Law, Southern Methodist University, and is a member of the Bar of the State of New York.

J. Kahn (✉)
Dedman School of Law, Southern Methodist University, Dallas, TX, USA
e-mail: jkahn@smu.edu

A. Trochev
School of Humanities & Social Sciences, Nazarbayev University, Astana, Kazakhstan
e-mail: atrochev@hotmail.com

N. Balayan
LL.M., Dedman School of Law, Southern Methodist University, Dallas, TX, USA
e-mail: nikolay.balayan@gmail.com

implementation of the Constitution's division of jurisdiction between governments has resulted in such an extraordinary degree of central control that the *de facto* federal nature of the system is thrown into doubt.

The Russian Federation emerged from the rubble of its predecessors, the Russian Soviet Federated Socialist Republic (RSFSR), itself the largest component state of the Union of Soviet Socialist Republics (USSR). Soviet federalism, however, was a façade that did not mask a rigidly centralized system operating under the explicit control of the Communist Party.[1] Russia is not the Soviet Union. But the course of Russian federalism has been influenced by this past. It has become progressively more centralized in its first 15, post-Soviet years. This change has played an important role in the unification of law.

The first decade of Russian federalism was characterized by an economically and politically weak central government that struggled to maintain control over newly empowered, ethnically non-Russian, resource-rich component states. The Federation Treaty (signed March 1992) devolved considerable power to these components in an effort to preserve the state itself. The Russian Constitution (adopted December 1993, displacing the Federation Treaty) created a strong federal executive and the potential for a dominant central government. Nevertheless, political and economic considerations led the first Russian President, Boris Yeltsin (1991–1999), to negotiate scores of treaties and agreements with the executive leadership of many of the component states. These documents ceded substantial federal authority ranging from control over taxation and natural resources to cultural and linguistic policies. They were both a cause and effect of an extraordinary disharmony between the laws of the central government and those of the defiant component states. The mid-1990s were characterized by a so-called War of Laws, in which the central government asserted that thousands of component state-level laws and executive orders contravened the Constitution. Many component states routinely withheld taxes, refused conscripts, or otherwise defied the legal mandates asserted by the central government.

Russia's second president, Vladimir Putin (2000–2008), ended this shadowy bilateral treaty system and took as his first task the strengthening of federal executive power. The central government has reasserted the supremacy of the Constitution, accomplished a considerable unification of law, and blurred a previously clearer division of central and regional power (and the political constituencies for that power) into a so-called "unified system of executive power".[2] Most areas of law have been unified under a broad and strict rule of federal legal supremacy enforced by a centrally administered judiciary and by a variety of centrally controlled

---

[1] See Art. 6, USSR Constitution (1977) ("The leading and guiding force of the Soviet society and the nucleus of its political system, of all state organizations and public organizations, is the Communist Party of the Soviet Union.").

[2] Art. 77(2), Constitution of the Russian Federation (hereinafter "Ст. ___ Конст. РФ"). English translations of the Constitution are from the Kremlin's website (http://www.kremlin.ru/eng/articles/ConstMain.shtml).

bureaucracies. Russia's third president, Dmitrii Medvedev, has given no indication in the first ten months of his presidency that he will deviate from this approach.

14.2 The Federal Distribution and Exercise of Lawmaking Power

14.2.1 Which Areas of Law Are Subject to the (Legislative) Jurisdiction of the Central Authority?

Article 71 of the Constitution lists 18 subjects over which jurisdiction is allocated to the central government. Article 72 lists 14 subjects over which jurisdiction is allocated to the joint authority of the central government and component states. The chart appended to this report compares similar and overlapping subjects.

All of these subject areas are, for all practical purposes, under the control of the central government to the degree that the central government desires to exercise such control. Article 76(2) of the Constitution provides that all laws and normative legal acts of the component states in areas of joint jurisdiction must be issued in accordance with the federal law on the issue. The Constitutional Court has upheld the central government's view that in areas of joint authority (Article 72), the central government takes the leading role in establishing the space left for local law-making, even when that space is a null set. The central government has also been accorded a remarkable power of preemption by the Constitutional Court.

Federal law often operates throughout Russia directly, unmediated by the law of component states. Thus, the law of contracts, torts, property, business organizations, and other aspects of private and commercial law (subjects that other federal systems may leave to the jurisdiction of the component states) are all governed by federal law (largely to be found in the federal civil code). Alternatively, federal law may establish principles and standards that are then implemented by the law of component states. For example, the tax code establishes federal taxes but also establishes tax principles to be followed by component states and municipalities.

Thus, most law in Russia is federal law. Through a system of codification, the central government regulates all civil law, civil procedure, criminal law, criminal procedure, administrative law and procedure, and the procedure for use in the commercial courts. There are federal codes governing the use of land, air, water, and forests. Federal codes also govern all labor law and family law. There are codes for the citing and construction of towns, housing, collection of taxes and customs duties, and the regulation of government budgets.

Many other areas of law are also constitutionally allocated to the central government. These include the establishment of the basic legal principles of the marketplace, fiscal and monetary policies, and the establishment of federal banks (including the Central Bank). The judicial system in Russia is almost entirely federal. The same is true of law enforcement personnel.

14.2.2 Which Areas of Law Remain Within the (Legislative) Jurisdiction of the Component States?

Russia is comprised of 83 component states of six different types (see *infra* at 14.4.5). Although all component states are constitutionally defined as equal, they do not all possess the same constitutional power or jurisdiction. The 21 republics are organized under a constitution; the remaining 62 component states are organized under charters or fundamental laws.[3] Only republics (which are all named for non-Russian ethnic groups) are constitutionally entitled to establish their own official languages alongside Russian.[4]

The Constitution identifies 14 areas over which component states and the central government share joint authority. As noted above, this neither guarantees equal voice in the legislative process nor a capacious role in the regulation of these subjects. The central government is invariably the senior partner. Some areas of the law remain influenced by regionally specific legislation; among these are family law, tax law, real property law, and labor law. All local legislation in these areas must conform to federal codes establishing both general principles and specific requirements in these subject areas.

Even the form of government *within* the component state is not the exclusive prerogative of component states. Article 77 of the Constitution indicates that the organization of legislative and executive branches of component state government must conform to both the "fundamentals of the constitutional system of the Russian Federation" and "general principles … as envisioned by a federal law". In 2004, such a law ended elections for component-state executives.[5] The federal president now nominates candidates to be ratified by the component-state legislature.[6]

14.2.3 Does the Constitution Allocate Residual Powers to the Central Government, the Component States, or (In Case of Specific Residual Powers) to Both?

Article 73 of the Constitution states that "[o]utside the limits of authority of the Russian Federation and the powers of the Russian Federation on issues under the joint jurisdiction of the Russian Federation and constituent entities of the Russian Federation, the constituent entities of the Russian Federation shall enjoy full State power". Article 76(4) directs that component states "shall effect their own legal

---

[3]Ст. 5(2) и (3) Конст. РФ.

[4]Ст. 68(2) Конст. РФ.

[5]Федеральный закон от 11 декабря 2004 г. № 159-ФЗ.

[6]The president may dismiss the legislature and call early elections if it rejects his candidate three times. *Id.*, Ст. 1(2)(c).

regulation, including the adoption of laws and other normative legal acts," in the sphere of residual powers not otherwise allocated exclusively to the central government or jointly with the component states.

Exclusive and joint federal authority is so expansive that it is difficult to identify subjects left to the "full State power" of component states. Federal constitutional or statutory silence regarding a particular subject, for example, is no indication that it falls under the umbrella of Article 73. For example, the Constitutional Court declared that component states could not regulate advertising because only the federal legislature could establish the foundations of a single market; advertisements were seen to be a part of the free distribution of goods and fair competition protected under that rubric by Article 8 of the Constitution.[7]

14.2.4 What Is the Constitutional Principle According to Which Conflicts (If Any) Between Central and Component State Law Are Resolved (e.g. Supremacy of Federal Law)?

Regarding subjects in Articles 71 (exclusive federal authority) and 72 (joint authority), the Constitution unambiguously provides for the supremacy of federal law in the event of conflict with component-state laws or other normative legal acts.[8] The phrase "laws or other normative legal acts" includes component state constitutions or charters, treaties or agreements negotiated with the central government, and regular legislation. The Constitutional Court has permitted the passage of federal laws that have the practical effect of shifting jurisdiction from the joint authority envisioned by Article 72 to the exclusive jurisdiction of the central government.[9]

Regarding residual powers left by Articles 73 and 76(4) to component states, the constitutional principle is precisely the opposite of the one stated above: "[i]n the event of a conflict between a federal law and a normative legal act of a constituent entity of the Russian Federation ..., the normative legal act of the constituent entity of the Russian Federation shall prevail".[10] As noted above, however, it is not easy to identify substantial residual powers.

A sharp existential debate raged in the 1990s whether the country was a "constitutional-treaty" federation (i.e. based on a federal constitution, the preferred position of the central government) or a "treaty-constitutional" federation (i.e. a treaty-based confederation, in the opinion of several ethnic republics). As a result, numerous assertions of "sovereignty" in the Constitution acquired special

---

[7] Постановление Конституционного Суда РФ от 4 марта 1997 года № 4-П.
[8] Ст. 76(5) Конст. РФ.
[9] Постановление Конституционного Суда РФ от 9 января 1998 года № 1-П.
[10] Ст. 76(6) Конст. РФ.

importance.[11] These clauses, along with those allocating to the central government exclusive authority over the territory and structure of the country, have been read by the Constitutional Court (a strong proponent of the constitutional-treaty approach) as independent grounds to strike down legal acts by component states as unconstitutional in addition to more specific, sufficient grounds.[12]

14.2.5 Do the Municipalities – By Virtue of the Constitution or Otherwise – Have Significant Law-Making Power and If So, in What Areas?

Perhaps because of the Soviet legacy, the existence and independence of municipal government is constitutionally protected, presumably against encroachment by component states.[13] Municipal property is constitutionally entitled to the same protection as private and state property.[14] Municipalities are constitutionally authorized to "independently manage municipal property, form, approve, and execute the local budget, establish local taxes and levies, maintain public order and decide other questions of local importance".[15]

14.3 The Means and Methods of Legal Unification

14.3.1 To What Extent Is Legal Unification or Harmonization Accomplished by the Exercise of Central Power (Top Down)?

The Constitution establishes certain "fundamentals" in its first chapter (articles 1–16), and "rights and freedoms of the individual and citizen" in its second chapter (articles 17–64). These chapters are protected from amendment; they may only be changed by drafting a new constitution.[16] Among these fundamentals, as noted above, the Constitutional Court has invoked the sovereignty of the Federation to strike down component state legislation. Similarly, the equality of component states in their relations to the central government has been a means of unification and

---

[11] See, e.g., преамбула, Ст. 3(1) и 4(1) Конст. РФ.
[12] See, e.g., § 3.1 Постановления Конституционного Суда РФ от 7 июня 2000 г. № 10-П.
[13] Ст. 12 Конст. РФ.
[14] Ст. 8(2) Конст. РФ.
[15] Ст. 132(2) Конст. РФ.
[16] Ст. 135 Конст. РФ.

harmonization of law.[17] Other norms include the federal supremacy provisions of Article 15(1), and guarantees for a single economic space (Art. 8) and social welfare (Art. 7).

Similarly, individual rights norms influence unification efforts. The Constitution contains a highly detailed equal protection guarantee.[18] The power of the state to limit individual rights is also limited both substantively[19] and procedurally.[20] Notably, component states are not permitted to limit constitutionally protected individual rights for any reason, since such limitations are possible only by federal law.[21]

The number and specificity of rights guaranteed by the Constitution is such, however, that resort to more general norms is not always necessary. The Constitution grants the central government the exclusive authority over the "regulation and protection of human and civil rights and freedoms," a reference to the 47 articles on the subject in chapter two of the Constitution.[22] Thus, for example, although the Constitution provides generally for the independence of local self-government as a protection against encroachment by other state authorities, the more specific constitutional guarantee of voting rights was held to permit the central government to enact framework legislation to harmonize the timing of municipal elections.[23]

Central legislation, particularly the codes listed *supra* at 14.2.1, play a very significant role in legal unification and harmonization. Most law in Russia is federal law. To the extent that the law of component states occupies a particular subject area, it is most likely to have been guided by federally promulgated principles.

The unification and harmonization of law is also accomplished through the judicial creation of uniform norms. Russia has three central supreme courts.[24] The Supreme Court is the highest judicial organ for civil, criminal, administrative and other cases in the federal judicial system.[25] It also may determine the legality of the laws and regulations of component states. The Higher Arbitration Court hears

---

[17] Ст. 5(4) Конст. РФ; Постановление Конституционного Суда РФ от 14 июля 1997 г. № 12-П.

[18] Ст. 19(2) Конст. РФ.

[19] Some individual rights in this chapter may not be restricted for any reason. Ст. 56(3) Конст. РФ. Other rights may be restricted, but only for specified reasons and only by federal law. Ст. 55(3) Конст. РФ.

[20] Ст. 45–46 Конст. РФ (concerning defense of rights and judicial review).

[21] Ст. 55(3) Конст. РФ.

[22] Ст. 71(в) Конст. РФ. It should be noted that Article 72(b) assigns the "protection of human and civil rights and freedoms" to the joint authority of both the central government and component states. However, as noted above, the central government is *primus inter pares*.

[23] Постановление Конституционного Суда РФ от 30 мая 1996 г. № 13-П.

[24] Ст. 128 (1) Конст. РФ.

[25] Ст. 126 Конст. РФ.

commercial disputes and disputes between private businesses and governments.[26] The Constitutional Court's jurisdiction is described *infra*, at Sect. 14.4.1.

Since the early 1990s, these courts have actively exercised their authority to strike down laws and regulations of component states and municipalities that they determined to be in conflict with the Constitution and federal law. Since the Russian Constitutional Court began functioning in 1992, this tribunal declared unconstitutional more than a hundred component state legal acts.[27] In 1998, the Court ordered other federal courts to strike down analogous component state legal acts, which were previously found unconstitutional.[28] By mid-1998, federal courts of general jurisdiction, headed by the Russian Supreme Court, declared illegal 2,016 sub-federal legal acts, issued by sub-federal legislatures and executives.[29] For much of the 1990s, however, the central government lacked the means to carry out judicial decisions and force the compliance of sub-federal governments with federal standards.

When Vladimir Putin announced a crackdown in 2000 against component state laws that were not in line with federal standards, these courts largely approved his agenda and became major instruments of legal unification. Between 2000 and 2005, federal courts reviewed over 4,000 contested component state laws and regulations and struck down almost all of them.[30] Moreover, amendments made in 2001 to the federal constitutional law "On the Constitutional Court" provided that the judicial annulment of the provisions of a law enacted by one of the component states automatically annuls all laws of all component states that contain the same provisions.[31] By 2008, component states routinely accepted these court decisions, promptly repealed invalidated laws and regulations or brought them into compliance with federal law. Most often, top federal courts were involved in unifying laws in the areas of joint jurisdiction.

14.3.2 To What Extent Is Legal Unification Accomplished Through Formal or Informal Voluntary Coordination Among the Component States? (Somewhat Bottom Up, Coordinate Model)

Voluntary coordination by component state legislatures accounts for a rather small extent of legal unification in Russia. As noted *infra* at Sect. 14.3.3, restatements

---

[26] Ст. 127 Конст. РФ.

[27] This statistic is derived from the official, annual compilations of decisions of the Constitutional Court.

[28] Постановление Конституционного Суда РФ от 5 ноября 1998 г. № 147-О.

[29] Сухова С.С. Законный диспут // Сегодня. 2000. 16 Февраля. С. 2.

[30] Григорьева Е. Пять тысяч несоответствий // Известия. 2001. 30 июня. С. 2.

[31] Ст. 87 Федерального конституционного закона от 21 июля 1994 г. № 1-ФКЗ.

and uniform or model laws are unknown in Russia. Models for legislation typically come through the promulgation of federal guidelines regarding subjects within the joint authority of the central government and component states. Nevertheless, component state legislatures do seem to learn from one another. This has been evident in the past in the similarities (to the point of identity) of their declarations of sovereignty adopted between June 1990 and July 1991. It is likewise evident in the formulaic approach to constitution-drafting that component states undertook in the early 1990s.

As discussed in more detail at Sect. 14.4.3, the 83 component states have been grouped into seven "federal districts," each of which are comprised of 6–18 component states. Their legislatures may find opportunities to interact with each other through the office of the federal presidential envoy in charge of each district.

Russia has a unified judicial system in which federal courts overwhelmingly predominate.[32] The Supreme Court and Higher Arbitration Court, referenced *supra* at 14.3.1, rest atop a pyramid of lower courts of general jurisdiction and lower arbitration courts, respectively. Two types of courts may be found in the component states: constitutional or charter courts, and justices of the peace. Justices of the peace function in all component states except Chechnya. Constitutional or charter courts (depending upon the organic law of the component) function in only 16 component states: the republics of Adygei, Bashkortostan, Buriatiia, Chechnya, Dagestan, Kabardino-Balkariia, Kareliia, Komi, Mari El, North Osetiia-Alaniia, Sakha-Yakutiia, Tatarstan, and Tuva; the oblasts (provinces) of Kaliningrad and Sverdlovsk; and in the City of Saint Petersburg, which is one of two "cities of federal significance".

The constitutional courts of component states are primarily concerned with determining whether the laws and decrees of component states and the municipalities within them comply with the constitutions (charters) of the component states. They use both abstract (advisory) and concrete (i.e. concerning particular cases) constitutional review procedures. By mid-2008, these courts issued over 400 decisions.[33] Eight courts began working before 1996. Their hasty creation was driven by component states seeking to create judicial systems that were independent of the central judiciary. During this period, these courts by and large did not strive for legal unification.

This decentralizing trend came to a halt at the end of 1996 with the passage of a federal constitutional law that entrenched a unitary judicial system.[34] As a result of strengthening central power, the constitutional (charter) courts increasingly focused

---

[32] Ст. 118(3) Конст. РФ; Ст. 3 Федерального конституционного закона от 31 декабря 1996 года № 1-ФКЗ.

[33] Estimate calculated from legal databases, court websites, and decisions published in regional mass media. See also Боброва В. Конституционные (уставные) суды вынесли уже 250 решений // Российская юстиция. 2001. № 5.

[34] Федеральный конституционный закон от 31 декабря 1996 года № 1-ФКЗ. Many governors challenged this law, but the Constitutional Court upheld its constitutionality. Определение Конституционного Суда РФ от 12 марта 1998 г. № 32-О.

their attention on verifying the compliance with federal law of municipal and component state laws and regulations. In 2000, two-thirds of these court decisions concerned the compliance of such laws with federal laws.[35] The Russian Constitutional Court co-ordinated and directed this trend in formal and informal meetings with the judges of these courts and was particularly solicitous of the requests of component state courts to consider the constitutionality of federal laws. A concerted effort to expeditiously publish decisions of these tribunals also contributed to unifying and harmonizing trends. In 1999 and 2001, the Court organized (together with the RF presidential administration) two large-scale meetings to promote the contribution of these courts to legal unification.[36] Such meetings allowed judges to discuss their jurisprudence and exchange views on judicial practice with colleagues in other jurisdictions.

This shift in transforming the courts of the component states into active agents of legal unification coincided with the enactment of numerous federal statutes in areas of joint jurisdiction and pressure from the Putin Administration to uphold their supremacy over the laws of component states. This shift culminated in October 2002, when the St. Petersburg Charter Court rejected the attempt of the St. Petersburg governor to run for a third term.[37]

Historically, agreements between the executive-branch officials of component states aimed to bolster the negotiating position of the components *against* the federal center. Thus, they often promoted less unification and more legal conflict. Now, the chief executives of each component state are nominated by the federal president and confirmed by the regional legislature. By presidential decree, they also may work as part of the federal civil service (This is discussed in greater detail *infra* at 14.4.2). Therefore, as part of the "unified system of executive power" foreseen by Article 77 of the Constitution, legal unification may be increasingly advanced with the help of component state executive branches.

14.3.3 To What Extent Is Legal Unification Accomplished, or Promoted, by Non-state Actors?

Restatements and uniform or model laws (as these are known in the United States) are unknown in Russia. For the most part, private entities such as trade organizations and industrial associations do not yet possess the necessary political influence to

---

[35] Alexei Trochev, *Less Democracy, More Courts: A Puzzle of Judicial Review in Russia*, LAW & SOCIETY REVIEW 38: 513–548 (September 2004).

[36] The meetings led to publications summarizing their proceedings and conclusions. See Шуберт, Т. Э. Проблемы образования конституционных (уставных) судов субъектов Российской Федерации // Право и политика – 2000. – № 3. See Проблемы исполнения федеральными органами государственной власти и органами государственной власти субъектов Российской Федерации решений Конституционного Суда Российской Федерации и конституционных (уставных) судов субъектов Российской Федерации. М., 2001.

[37] Постановление Уставного суда Санкт-Петербурга от 2 октября 2002 года № 042-П.

exert pressure for legal unification either by exerting autonomous pressure on the central government or the component states. When they do act, it is often in concert with state actors according to procedures established by federal law. The primary source of input into the legislative process by non-state actors is through *ad hoc* involvement in either the process of legislative initiative (which is legally possible in the component states, although very rare) or through participation in parliamentary working groups and other committees of the State Duma (the lower chamber of the Federal Assembly). Such participation is governed by federal law.[38]

It is important to note that although freedom of association is constitutionally guaranteed, non-governmental organizations are subject to substantial state regulation.[39] Such associations take different forms but each type requires state registration and different levels of state intrusion into the activities of the association, with the consequences one would expect on the range of activities in which such organizations feel free to engage.[40] Recent amendments to this law further tightened registration requirements.[41] These sparked considerable international controversy by increasing state control over non-governmental organizations, including international human rights monitors, thus further limiting the independent growth of civil society.[42] Such state involvement necessarily affects the capacity of non-state actors to organize, represent their members' interests, and voice dissent.

Legislative Initiative. At the level of the central government, the right of legislative initiative is exclusively reserved to state actors.[43] In component states, however, a more direct role for non-state actors is possible.[44] Five component states appear to have granted the right of legislative initiative to non-governmental organizations.[45] Twenty-four component states have legislation extending the right of legislative initiative to Russian citizens residing in that component state.[46]

Parliamentary Working Groups. The general absence of a right of non-state actors to initiate legislation directly (although hardly unusual) has meant that non-state actors either must resort to their own lobbying efforts or seek *ad hoc* invitations to participate in the legislative committees and working groups of the relevant legislature.

---

[38] Ст. 27 Федерального закона от 19 мая 1995 № 82-ФЗ, «Об общественных объединениях».

[39] Ст. 30 Конст. РФ; Ст. 5 Федерального закон от 19 мая 1995 № 82-ФЗ.

[40] Ст. 7, 21 и 23 Федерального закона от 19 мая 1995 № 82-ФЗ.

[41] Федеральный закон от 10 января 2006 года № 18-ФЗ.

[42] The U.S. State Department repeatedly expressed its "serious concerns" about these amendments. See Press Statement # 2006/66, U.S. Dep't of State, January 19, 2006.

[43] Ст. 104(1) Конст. РФ.

[44] Ст. 6(1) Федерального закона от 6 октября 1999 г. № 184-ФЗ.

[45] Общественные организации Карелии - одни из немногих в России наделены конституционным правом законодательной инициативы, Закс.ру, 21 февраля 2007 (http://www.zaks.ru/new/archive/view/27301).

[46] Афиногенов Д.В. Народная законодательная инициатива в России: обзор регионального законодательства http://www.ecom-info.spb.ru/law/index.php?id=564

Because of the top-down emphasis on legal unification in Russia, the most effective locus of this activity is in the lower chamber of the Federal Assembly, the State Duma. The State Duma establishes committees and commissions to draft and evaluate legislation.[47] These are free to seek the involvement of both state and non-state actors for the "preparation of opinions, suggestions, and notes, and also to provide scholarly expertise[.]"[48] Duma regulations further provide for "working groups," which are essentially subcommittees.[49] Consultative (i.e. non-voting) participation in such working groups may be extended quite broadly and may include representatives of non-state organizations and "experts and specialists".[50] The responsible committee has the right to conduct its own, independent, expert analysis of the conformity of draft legislation with the Constitution and federal constitutional laws.[51]

Quasi-State Actors. Perhaps because of the highly regulated nature of civil society in the Russian Federation, an unusual feature is the role that *quasi*-state actors play in legal unification. These are organizations that are created by the state but are not part of the constitutional structure of the state. These organizations take different forms, the level of state influence in them varies, and they occupy different roles. The following play a significant role in the law-making process:

1. *The Public Chamber of the Russian Federation.* The Public Chamber was created in 2005 as a special body that "guarantees" the interaction of citizens of the Russian Federation with organs of state power at all levels of government.[52] The Chamber consists of 126 members chosen in three tranches.[53] One of its primary purposes is to evaluate draft legislation at both the central level and the component state level.[54] The Chamber possesses a variety of investigative and consultative powers, including a weak subpoena power for documents and

---

[47]Ст. 101(3) Конст. РФ. Currently there are 32 committees in the State Duma. Ст. 19(2) и 20, Регламента Государственной Думы (hereinafter Ст. ___ Регламента ГД) (available at: http://www.duma.gov.ru/).

[48]Ст. 112(1) Регламента ГД.

[49]Ст. 111(3) Регламента ГД.

[50]Ст. 111(4) и Ст. 113(2) Регламента ГД.

[51]Ст. 112(1) и 121(1) Регламента ГД. Public discussion of drafts is also possible. Ст. 119(6) Регламента ГД. The Legal Office of the State Duma is specially tasked with determining the conformity of proposed legislation with all existing federal law. Ст. 112(2) – (4) Регламента ГД. The participation of this office is required when a component state seeks to exercise its right of legislative initiative. See Ст. 114(2)(г) Регламента ГД.

[52]Ст. 1(1) Федерального закона от 4 апреля 2005 г. № 32-ФЗ.

[53]One-third of the membership (42 members) is chosen by the President of the Russian Federation. Nomination of civil servants is prohibited. Those members in turn select the next third (42 members) from competing all-Russian (i.e. nationally active) non-governmental organizations. The remaining third are chosen in a similar manner as representatives from inter-regional and regional public associations. Ст. 8(1), (5) – (6) Федерального закона от 4 апреля 2005 г. № 32-ФЗ.

[54]Ст. 2(3). Shortly after the establishment of the federal Public Chamber, component states founded their own chambers to assess regional legislation, with goals and authorities roughly similar to the federal chamber.

materials necessary to evaluate proposed legislation.[55] However, opinions of the Chamber are only advisory in nature.[56]

In 2006–2007, the Public Chamber sent opinion letters to the State Duma regarding 65 draft pieces of federal legislation.[57] Out of the 27 drafts that ultimately were passed into law by the end of 2007, 23 fully or partially took into account the Public Chamber's opinion letters.[58] The Public Chamber has recently sought to make receipt of its opinion letters mandatory for all federal legislation, an idea which received initial support from (then President-elect) Dmitrii Medvedev.[59]

2. *Russian Trilateral Commission for Social-Labor Relations.* When draft legislation is proposed on labor issues, the Duma's regulations require that the draft be submitted to the Russian Trilateral Commission for Social-Labor Relations.[60] The Commission is comprised of representatives of the Russian Government, the All-Russia Organized Labor Association and the All-Russia Employers' Association.[61] The latter two associations are non-state actors, although each association is formed on the basis of federal law.[62]

3. *The Chamber of Commerce and Industry of the Russian Federation.* The Chamber of Commerce and Industry of the Russian Federation and similar chambers in the component states are established and operate under federal law.[63] The Chamber is a "non-state, non-commercial organization, uniting Russian businesses, and Russian entrepreneurs".[64] Chambers of Commerce and Industry seek the creation of favorable conditions for entrepreneurial activity, the regulation of entrepreneurs' relations with their social partners, the development of all kinds of entrepreneurial activity and promote connections with foreign entrepreneurs. The Chambers should not be mistaken for wholly non-governmental organizations: these goals are established by federal law.[65] State authorities are required by law to render assistance to chambers in achieving these goals; even assistance as mundane as the provision of meeting places is established by law.[66] State

---

[55] Ст. 16(3) и 18(4).

[56] Ст. 17.

[57] О деятельности Общественной палаты Российской Федерации в 2006–2007 гг. – М., 2008. С. 16.

[58] *Id.* Thus, its recommendations were considered during the adoption of the fourth part of the Civil Code. *Id.*, at 19.

[59] Российская газета, № 4616. (20 марта 2008 года), 2.

[60] Ст. 108(1³), 114(2)(г²), и 122(1)(з) Регламента ГД.

[61] Ст. 1(1) Федерального закона от 1 мая 1999 № 92-ФЗ.

[62] Ст. 4(2) Федерального закона от 27 ноября 2002 года № 156-ФЗ; Федеральный закон от 12 января 1996 года № 10-ФЗ.

[63] Федеральный закон от 7 июля 1993 года № 5340-1.

[64] Ст. 1(1) Федерального закона от 7 июля 1993 года № 5340-1.

[65] *Id.* Ст. 3(1).

[66] *Id.* Ст. 4(1).

authorities also exercise control and oversight over the Chambers' observance of federal legislation.[67]

The Chambers "conduct independent expertise of the drafts of statutory acts in the sphere of economics, external economic relations, and also on other issues, touching interests of businesses and entrepreneurs".[68] Chambers participate in the evaluation of draft legislation, represent their interests in working groups and committees of the State Duma, and lobby for the introduction of draft legislation.[69] Between 2004 and 2007, the federal Chamber evaluated 181 draft laws, and promoted 47 draft amendments and 29 draft laws, including the Federal Law "About Development of Small and Medium Enterprises in the Russian Federation" of July 24, 2007.[70]

The Chamber also drafts a significant document called the "Conception of Legislation Development of Russian Federation," which reflects its view on the most urgent directions of legislative development for business needs.[71] The most recent (second) Conception concerns the period 2008–2011; the first Conception covered the period 2004–2007.[72]

4. *The Ombudsman of the Russian Federation*. The Ombudsman of the Russian Federation was created by statute in 1997.[73] The Ombudsman considers Russian legislation about human rights.[74] The Ombudsman has no right of legislative initiative. Therefore, the Ombudsman is limited to lobbying component states and the central government regarding proposed legislation. In 2007, the Ombudsman made such references 62 times and prepared 4 draft laws.[75]

14.3.4 What Is the Role of Legal Education and Training in the Unification of the Law?

The main law schools in Russia draw students from throughout the federal system. The overwhelming focus of legal education (which follows the Western European

---

[67]*Id.* Ст. 4(3). State interference with Chambers' activities is forbidden. Ст. 4(2).

[68]*Id.* Ст. 12(1)(a).

[69]ИнФКраткий отчет об участии ТПП России в законотворческом процессе Государственной Думы ФС РФ в период работы IV созыва (2004–2007 года) http://www.tpprf.ru/ru/activities/lawmaking/plan-result/results/

[70]*Id.*

[71]ТПП РФ: КОНЦЕПЦИЯ РАЗВИТИЯ ЗАКОНОДАТЕЛЬСТВА РОССИЙСКОЙ ФЕДЕРАЦИИ НА ПЕРИОД 2008–2011 гг. http://www.garant.ru/products/ipo/prime/doc/6285114/

[72]*Id.*

[73]Федеральный конституционный закон от 26 февраля 1997 г. № 1-ФКЗ.

[74]ЕЖЕГОДНЫЙ ДОКЛАД УПОЛНОМОЧЕННОГО ПО ПРАВАМ ЧЕЛОВЕКА В РОССИЙСКОЙ ФЕДЕРАЦИИ, 2007 г. http://ombudsman.gov.ru/doc/documents.shtml

[75]*Id.*

model as an undergraduate course of study) is on central or system-wide law. The Government of the Russian Federation has the authority to establish procedures for drafting and confirming educational standards for higher professional education.[76] Accordingly, standards in the area of legal education in Russia are established by the central government, in particular by the Ministry of Education of the Russian Federation.[77] A state diploma as a "specialist in law" requires a 5-year course of study. These national standards require 6,062 h of mandatory instruction in "general professional disciplines," out of which 4,744 h of instruction are required for the "federal component" and 658 h are recommended for the "national-regional" component.[78] Therefore, law schools in Russia are mainly oriented to teach system-wide law.

Under federal law, the Chamber of Advocates of each component state determines the award of advocate status (admission to the bar) and administers the qualifying examination.[79] It is the Federal Chamber of Advocates, however, that adopts the list from which questions on the exam may be drawn and establishes standards for the general procedure of bar admission.[80] The exam consists of both a written and an oral part.[81] The form of the written examination is determined by qualifications commissions of the Chamber of Advocates of the component state.[82] The oral examination is administered with the use of examination cards, containing at least four questions from the list adopted by Federal Chamber of Advocates.[83] The current list contains 588 questions.[84] The overwhelming majority are questions of federal law. The Chamber of Advocates of the component state has substantial discretion to determine bar passage rates.[85]

---

[76]Ст. 24(2)(8) Федерального закона от 22 августа 1996 года № 125-ФЗ.

[77]See Министерство образования Российской Федерации, Государственный образовательный стандарт высшего профессионального образования, Специальность 021100 – юриспруденция, квалификация – юрист (27 марта 2000 года).

[78]*Id*. The federal component includes 24 subjects. The national-regional component is recommended to include four subjects: criminal-executive law (i.e. the law of enforcing court orders, including punishment), prosecutorial supervisory review (надзор [*nadzor*]), the law of private enterprise, and commercial law. The remaining 660 h are "electives" left to the choice of the student from a range established by the component state. In addition, 1,620 h are required in a "discipline of specialization" (a "major").

[79]Ст. 9(3) Федерального закона от 31 мая 2002 года № 63-ФЗ.

[80]*Id*. Ст. 11(1).

[81]Ст. 2.2 Положения о порядке сдачи квалификационного экзамена на присвоение статуса адвоката (утв. решением Совета Федеральной палаты адвокатов от 25 апреля 2003 г.; в ред. решений от 25 августа 2003 г., 25 июня 2004 г., 6 сентября 2005 г. и 2 марта 2006 г.).

[82]*Id*.

[83]*Id*.

[84]Перечень вопросов в билеты для сдачи квалификационных экзаменов на приобретение статуса адвоката (Утвержден Советом ФПА РФ 6 апреля 2005 г. (протокол № 11)).

[85]Ст. 2.6 Положения о порядке сдачи квалификационного экзамена на присвоение статуса адвоката, *supra* note 81.

Federal law does not contain any territorial restrictions applicable to one admitted to the bar.[86] Thus, an advocate admitted to the bar of one of the component states can practice in all jurisdictions and in all levels of the court system. However, an advocate may not be admitted to more than one bar at the same time.[87] An advocate is free to move from membership in the bar of one component state to that of another by filing a petition.[88]

Graduates of the main law schools in Russia (Moscow State Legal Academy, Saint-Petersburg State University Law Department, Urals State Legal Academy, Saratov State Academy of Law, and others), especially those outside Moscow and Saint-Petersburg, tend to practice and take jobs throughout Russia. For obvious reasons, graduates of law schools located in Moscow and Saint Petersburg tend to remain in those cities. Graduates of less prestigious law schools also tend to practice in the location of their schools.

Institutions of legal education and training also play a unifying role. One of the most significant and successful of them is the Russian Academy of Justice, which was established in 1998 by the Russian Supreme Court and Russian Higher Arbitration Court.[89] Its primary goal is the training of candidates for judicial office and other court officials, as well as their continuing education.[90] An important goal of the further training program for judges, judicial candidates, and personnel of the courts of general jurisdiction is the promotion of a unified judicial system on the whole territory of the Russian Federation.[91]

Another prominent institution is the Russian Legal Academy under the Ministry of Justice of the Russian Federation. This institution provides professional training, higher qualification training, and internships for personnel from all agencies of the Ministry of Justice, the Federal Registrar's Service, and the Federal Bailiff's Service.[92] It has branches in 14 federal subjects.

In addition to these two prominent institutions, the Ministry of Internal Affairs of Russia operates numerous legal institutions throughout Russia, which train personnel for that Ministry.[93] The Public Prosecutor's Office of Russia also has a similar set of institutions in its structure, training personnel for the Public Prosecutor's

---

[86]Федеральный закон от 31 мая 2002 года № 63-ФЗ.

[87]*Id*. Ст. 15(4).

[88]*Id*. Ст. 15(5).

[89]Establishment of the Academy was greeted by specialists on the Russian judiciary as a very positive step in the development of competent judges. See Peter H. Solomon, Jr. and Todd S. Foglesong, *Courts and Transition in Russia*. A Challenge of Judicial Reform 99–107 (2000).

[90]Указ Президента РФ от 11 мая 1998 года № 528 «О Российской академии правосудия».

[91]See, e.g., the Russian Academy of Justice statement of goals: http://www.raj.ru/ru/training/cgs.html

[92]See the Academy's website: http://www.minjust.ru/ru/sub_institution/low_academy/

[93]See list of training institutions in the Ministry of Internal Affairs: http://www.mvd.ru/about/education/100019/

Office.[94] The fact that these are subordinated within their corresponding agencies of the central government and provide training for personnel throughout Russia necessarily promotes a higher degree of uniformity in the performance of these law enforcement bodies.

14.3.5 To What Extent Do External Factors, Such as International Law, Influence Legal Unification?

Compliance with international legal obligations plays a role in legal unification. Article 15(4) of the Constitution provides that generally recognized principles of international law, as well as international treaties of the Russian Federation, are a part of its legal system.[95] This clause continues: "If an international agreement of the Russian Federation establishes rules, which differ from those stipulated by law, then the rules of the international agreement shall be applied". This constitutional provision makes international obligations an important source of the unification of law in Russia.

In most cases, Russia honors the treaty obligations that it has undertaken, including those in the areas of legal unification and harmonization. Thus, the 1980 Vienna Convention on the International Sale of Goods has direct effect in the civil law relations in Russia.[96] The 1971 Berne Convention for the Protection of Literary and Artistic Works had a direct influence on the drafting of the Fourth Part of the Russian Civil Code.[97] It is worth noting that anticipation that Russia would join the World Trade Organization led to the drafting of particular provisions in the Fourth Part of the Russian Civil Code. That is, Russian domestic law took into account an international convention to which Russia was not a party, but hoped soon to be.[98]

Participation in international organizations also plays a role. Russia's entry into the Council of Europe substantially affected its legislation and led to the unification and harmonization of many laws. One of the conditions of the admission of Russia into the Council of Europe required that Russia will "pursue legal reform with a view to bringing all legislation in line with Council of Europe principles

---

[94] See list of training institutions in the General Procuracy, http://genproc.gov.ru/structure/scientific/district-7/

[95] See also Art. 7 of the First Part of the Civil Code, which restates the constitutional supremacy requirement and provides that international treaties act "directly" in the regulation of civil relations in Russia except when the treaty requires for its application the enactment of national law.

[96] Mikhail G. Rozenberg, *The Civil Code of the Russian Federation and International Agreements*, MCGILL LAW JOURNAL 475 (1999).

[97] Яковлев В.Ф., Маковский А.Л. О четвертой части гражданского кодекса России // Журнал россиийского права. – 2007 (http://www.juristlib.ru/book_3085.html).

[98] *Id.*

and standards".⁹⁹ The task of putting Russian law in accord with these standards required a considerable amount of unification or harmonization of law.¹⁰⁰

Russia is a party to or has signed five UNCITRAL conventions and enacted only one statute based on a UNCITRAL model law. UNCITRAL Model Law on International Commercial Arbitration was largely replicated in the Federal Law "About International Commercial Arbitration".¹⁰¹ Some specialists even argue that this Russian law, probably, as no other national law based on the Model Law, absorbed the provisions of the Model Law with the minimum amount of additions and divergences.¹⁰²

Russia is a member of UNIDROIT. Russia has signed two UNIDROIT conventions and is a party to one convention.¹⁰³ Russia is a contracting state to four international instruments that were adopted under the auspices of other organizations, but were based on UNIDROIT drafts or conventions. UNIDROIT has prepared only one model law: its Model Franchise Disclosure Law (2002). Russia does not have rules of law regulating this subject. Russian courts make frequent references to the UNIDROIT Principles of International Commercial Contracts as, for example, to its provisions on freedom of contract (article 1.1),¹⁰⁴ interest for

---

⁹⁹Section 10 subsection "xx" of European Parliamentary Assembly, Opinion on Russia's Request for Membership of the Council of Europe, 1996 Sess., Doc. No. 193 (1996); see also European Parliamentary Assembly, Invitation to the Russian Federation to Become a Member of the Council of Europe, Council of Ministers Resolution 96(2), 1996 Sess. (February 8, 1996).

¹⁰⁰See Jeffrey Kahn, *Vladimir Putin and the Rule of Law in Russia*, GEORGIA JOURNAL OF INTERNATIONAL AND COMPARATIVE LAW 36: 512, 531–552 (2008); J.D. Kahn, *Russia's "Dictatorship of Law" and the European Court of Human Rights*, REVIEW OF CENTRAL AND EAST EUROPEAN LAW 29: 1, 1–14 (2004); Ивлиев Г.П. Оценка законопроектов с учетом решений Совета Европы и Европейского Суда по правам человека // http://www.duma.gov.ru/index.jsp?t=pravupr/ocenka_zak/9.html; Никитенко Е.В. Влияние членства России в Совете Европы на становление иснтитута защиты прав российских граждан // В мире права. – 2001. – № 2; Воинов И. Разрешение коллизий норм европейского и российского права // Российская юстиция. – 2001. – № 6.

¹⁰¹William R. Spiegelberger, The Enforcement of Foreign Arbitral Awards in Russia: An Analysis of the Relevant Treaties, Laws, and Cases, *American Review of International Arbitration* 273–274 (2005).

¹⁰²Костин А.А. Типовой Закон ЮНСИТРАЛ и Российский Закон о международном коммерческом арбитраже: сравнительно-правовой анализ // Актуальные вопросы международного коммерческого арбитража: К 70-летию Международного коммерческого арбитражного суда при Торгово-промышленной палате Российской Федерации. М.: Спарк, 2002.

¹⁰³UNIDROIT (International Institute for the Unification of Private Law). Annual Report – 2007. pp. 33–41. The Soviet Union signed the Convention Providing a Uniform Law on the Form of an International Will (1973) in 1974 and the Russian Federation is identified by UNIDROIT as the current signatory. Russia signed the Convention on Stolen or Illegally Exported Cultural Objects (1995) in 1996. Russia became a party to the Convention on International Financial Leasing (1988) in 1998.

¹⁰⁴Решение арбитражного суда Краснодарского края от 4 мая 2007 года, Дело № А-32-12529/2006-12/252, стр. 10.

failure to pay money (article 7.4.9),[105] and force majeure (article 7.1.7).[106] Likewise, the International Commercial Arbitration Court under the Russian Chamber of Commerce and Industry also applies UNIDROIT Principles in cases in which the parties have identified it as the applicable law, as well as on its own initiative as rules that reflect international trade customs.[107]

Russia has been a member of the Hague Conference on Private International Law since 2001. Russia is a party to four of conventions adopted by the Conference and has signed one.[108]

Another organization, though not intergovernmental, which should be mentioned here is the International Chamber of Commerce and particularly its Incoterms (International Commercial Terms) – "standard trade definitions most commonly used in international sales contracts".[109] These terms were recognized by a decree of the Russian Chamber of Commerce and Industry as trade custom on the territory of Russian Federation.[110] The Chamber is not a public authority, so this decision is not legally binding. It indicates, however, the recognition of its importance in the light of certain Civil Code provisions about customs of business intercourse as one of the means of privity regulation.

14.4 Institutional and Social Background

14.4.1 The Judicial Branch

Article 125 of the Constitution authorizes the Russian Constitutional Court to police whether central legislation has exceeded the lawmaking powers allocated to the

---

[105] Решение арбитражного суда Белгородской области от 23 мая 2007 года, Дело № А08-1403/07-12, стр. 2–3.

[106] Решение арбитражного суда Камчатской области от 23 ноября 2007 года, Дело № А24-1138/07 (10), стр. 4.

[107] Интернет-интервью с А.С. Комаровым, Председателем Международного коммерческого арбитражного суда: «Международный коммерческий арбитраж в России: актуальные вопросы практики разрешения споров» (11 октября 2007 года) // http://www.consultant.ru/law/interview/komarov.html

[108] The Soviet Union signed the Convention on Civil Procedure (1954) in 1966. The Russian Federation indicated in a diplomatic note of 14 April 1992 that it desired to be considered as a party to this Convention. The Soviet Union signed the Convention Abolishing the Requirement of Legalisation for Foreign Public Documents (1961) in 1991 and the Russian Federation indicated in a similar note in 1992 its intention to be considered a party. The Russian Federation became a party to the Convention on the Service Abroad of Judicial and Extrajudicial Documents in Civil or Commercial Matters (1965) in 2001. The Russian Federation acceded to the Convention on the Taking of Evidence Abroad in Civil or Commercial Matters (1970) in 2001.

[109] http://www.iccwbo.org/incoterms/id3042/index.html

[110] Вилкова Н.Г. Применение ИНКОТЕРМС в практике МКАС при ТПП РФ // http://sklad-zakonov.narod.ru/Vlad_st/incoterms_com.htm

central government. Governors or legislatures of the component states can request that the Court review the facial constitutionality of federal statutes, decrees of the Russian President, and edicts of the Russian Cabinet (i.e. without requiring an underlying case filed in a trial court). Municipalities (and individuals) can request that the Court determine the constitutionality of federal statutes through a concrete judicial review procedure (i.e. when the contested law "has been or is subject to being applied" to them). Component state legislatures can also ask the Court to issue a binding official interpretation of provisions of the Constitution without challenging a specific federal statute. The Court issues such interpretations only in plenary meetings and by a two-third majority of votes of judges hearing the case.[111] Finally, the Court has the power to settle disputes between government bodies at the central and component state level over the scope of their authority. Government institutions can ask the Court to settle such disputes without challenging a specific federal statute.

Decisions of the Constitutional Court are final and binding on all government institutions at the federal, component state, and municipal levels. Increasingly, the Court issues a "constitution-conforming" interpretation of contested legislation without striking it down. Such an interpretation is also binding on all governments. Even when the Court declines to rule on the merits of a petition, the Court sometimes inserts a "constitution-conforming" interpretation of contested legislation and insists that such interpretation is also binding.[112]

Under the Russian Civil Procedure Code, the Russian Supreme Court handles complaints alleging the illegality of presidential decrees and edicts of the Federal Cabinet.[113] Governors or legislatures of component states may bring such complaints to the Supreme Court. In areas of joint jurisdiction, it remains unclear whether these decrees and edicts have a higher legal force than statutes of component states adopted on the same subject matter. The court deals with this uncertainty on an *ad hoc* basis and tends to rule in favor of the central government.

The Russian Supreme Court regularly addresses federalism questions.[114] The Court upholds the authority of the federal center in almost every case. The component states, after having lost their cases, often contest these judgments of

---

[111]Ст. 21 Федерального конституционного закона от 21 июля 1994 г. № 1-ФКЗ; see also ALEXEI TROCHEV, JUDGING RUSSIA: THE CONSTITUTIONAL COURT IN RUSSIAN POLITICS, 1990–2006 118–87 (2008).

[112]See, e.g., Определение Конституционного Суда Российской Федерации от 7 декабря 2006 г. № 542-О (reprinted in Российская газета от 2 марта 2007); see also Trochev, *supra* note 111 at 118–87.

[113]Ст. 27, Гражданский процессуальный кодекс РФ.

[114]This sub-section draws substantially from Trochev, *supra* note 111 at 139–155. This book, published by Cambridge University Press, is based on an extraordinary volume of primary sources and statistical data, including interviews with 15 Justices and 15 clerks on the Constitutional Court. To aid the reader of this report, footnotes are provided for the major decisions that are referenced here. Readers are invited to study Trochev's book for a more thorough statistical analysis of his data.

the Russian Supreme Court in the Russian Constitutional Court by challenging the constitutionality of the federal legislation that the Supreme Court applied in their cases.[115]

The Russian Constitutional Court also regularly reviews federalism questions. The Court accepts for review about 15–20 % of petitions coming from the component states. Moreover, the Chief Justice or the Judge-Rapporteur routinely meets in person with the petitioners from the component state governments to discuss their cases. According to the official statistics published by the Court, between 1995 and 2006 the Court received 627 petitions "on the issues of federalism" and issued over a hundred judgments accompanied by numerous dissents. Russia's component states continued to use the Court more actively under President Putin's centralizing regime (147 petitions) than under Yeltsin's presidency (113 petitions).

General federal relations. The Court has repeatedly allowed the component states to legislate in areas of joint jurisdiction "until the adoption of a federal statute on the matter".[116] This has gone hand in hand, however, with equally powerful limitations on component state legislation once the federal center chooses to be more active. In 1996, the Court expanded federal supremacy in the joint federal – regional jurisdiction enumerated in Article 72 of the Russian Constitution.[117] The Court has ruled that if the component states fail to legislate in the area of joint jurisdiction, then the federal center has the power to preempt responsibilities of the component state.[118] For example, the Court declared that the component states could not regulate advertising because only the federal legislature could set up the foundations of a single market, that is, free distribution of goods and fair competition.[119] These foundations, according to the Court, taken together with federal supremacy in fiscal

---

[115]It should be noted that the Supreme Court and the Constitutional Court have a long and troubled history of sparring over their respective jurisdictions. For an excellent analysis of this relationship, see William Burnham and Alexei Trochev, *Russia's War Between the Courts: The Struggle over the Jurisdictional Boundary between the Constitutional Court and Regular Courts*, AMERICAN JOURNAL OF COMPARATIVE LAW 55: 381 (2007).

[116]See, e.g., Постановление Коснтитуционного суда от 30 ноября 1995 № 16-П and Постановление Коснтитуционного суда от 9 июля 2002 № 12-П. For example, in 2001, the Constitutional Court upheld the right of component states to set up extrabudgetary funds and to determine their own revenue bases, even though the Federal Budget Code did not assign this power to the component states and the Russian Supreme Court had earlier ruled that the creation of subfederal extrabudgetary funds violated federal law. Определение Конституционного Суда от 6 декабря 2001 № 228-О. In another decision issued in 2002, the Constitutional Court refused to hear a petition by the federal Cabinet and reiterated that the delimitation of state property ownership between the federation and its parts should be achieved by balancing federal and sub-federal economic interests through the process of federal legislation. Определение Конституционного Суда от 14 мая 2002 № 112-О.

[117]Постановление Конституционного Суда РФ от 18 января 1996 года № 2-П.

[118]Постановление Конституционного Суда РФ от 3 ноября 1997 года № 15-П.

[119]Постановление Конституционного Суда РФ от 4 марта 1997 года № 4-П.

policy, do not permit the expansion of component state and municipal taxes and fees beyond those listed in federal law.[120]

Relations with ethnic republics. For much of the 1990s, the 21 ethnic republics within Russia demanded special privileges and status. The Court routinely repudiated these demands and upheld strong central government authority. In the 1995 *Chechnya Secession* case, the Court approved and legitimized the authority of the Russian President to use military force to quell rebellion in the component states and secession from the federation.[121] It has upheld the central government's prerogative to divide central and component state functions by adopting federal statutes instead of continuing the practice of signing bilateral intergovernmental treaties.[122] It has struck down the "sovereignty" clauses of constitutions of seven republics.[123] In the same decisions, the Court struck down numerous provisions on republican citizenship, and control over land use and natural resources. The Constitutional Court has upheld the constitutionality of a federal statute that permits the federal executive, through a rather complicated and lengthy procedure involving courts of general jurisdiction, to dissolve legislatures of the component states and to remove their governors.[124]

Fiscal federalism. The Court repeatedly rejected challenges to the power of the federal center to control component state fiscal policies. For example, the Court ruled that the constitutional requirements of a "social state" (Article 7) and a single-budget system limited the autonomy of the budgets of the component states and obliged them to provide federally-set guarantees of social protection, that is, the federal government could "commandeer" the component states to increase salaries and benefits

---

[120] Постановление Конституционного Суда РФ от 21 марта 1997 года № 5-П. This court-ordered fiscal centralization ran against President Yeltsin's 1993 decree and against an earlier decision of the Court issued in 1996, both of which allowed the component states to set up their own taxes. Постановление Конституционного Суда РФ от 4 апреля 1996 года № 9-П. Yeltsin promptly repealed his decree and chose not to interfere with component state fiscal autonomy. The component states continued to levy their own taxes and set up various trade barriers, particularly in the wake of the August 1998 financial crisis. As a result, it was impossible by the end of the decade to ignore the diversity of fiscal regimes in Russia's component states. Clearly, the widespread explosion of component state and municipal taxes, fees and trade barriers (and even customs duties!) worried judges concerned about the future of Russia's common market and of the Federation itself.

[121] Постановление Конституционного Суда РФ от 31 июля 1995 года № 10-П.

[122] Определение Конституционного Суда РФ от 4 февраля 1997 г. № 13-О. Articles 11(3) and 16(1) of the Constitution mention these agreements as part of the "foundations of constitutional order," and by 1998 the central government had signed bilateral treaties with 47 component states. JEFFREY KAHN, FEDERALISM, DEMOCRATIZATION, AND THE RULE OF LAW IN RUSSIA 159 (2002). Nevertheless, the Court ruled that federal statutes were superior to intergovernmental agreements, and that the component states could not require the federal center to sign such agreements.

[123] Постановление Конституционного Суда РФ от 7 июня 2000 № 10-П; Определение Конституционного Суда РФ от 27 июня 2000 года № 92-О.

[124] Постановление Конституционного Суда РФ от 4 апреля 2002 № 8-П.

for public employees.[125] In another decision, the Court ruled that the states (and municipalities) cannot even pick and choose banks in which to keep their budgetary accounts – they have to keep them in the branches of the Russian Central Bank.[126]

Appointments. The Court has concluded that the component states may not veto appointments of federal judges, procurators and police chiefs in their territories, as all such matters were a prerogative of the federal center.[127] The Court ruled that only the federal legislature could regulate the involvement of the component states in this process. The Court has also upheld legislation abolishing direct gubernatorial elections and granting the federal President the power to nominate and dismiss governors of the component states (overturning its own precedent set in 1996 that governors of the component states had to be directly elected).[128]

Recalling the weaknesses of Gorbachev's presidency in handling the break-up of the USSR, most judges of the Constitutional Court agreed that the federal center had to be stronger to save Russia from political, economic, and territorial collapse even if it meant the widespread use of coercion, commandeering and near-total federal preemption of the autonomy of component states. Numerous interviews with judges indicate that they perceived a strong (even authoritarian) federal center to be the lesser evil compared to the breakdown in center-regional relations that characterized the recent past. The judgments of the Court issued between 1995 and 1998 largely paved the way for President Putin's campaign of legal unification launched in 2000. Thus, the Court was effective in terms of shaping the recentralization of the Federation, but it was not effective in setting the limits of this centralization and legal unification.

The Russian Constitutional Court has the power to authoritatively interpret component state law. In its 2001 decision, the Court struck down the Moscow City land use law and declared that it is the court of last resort in any public law disputes in which all other courts failed to protect individual rights through the application of unconstitutional federal laws or laws of the component states. Thus, while the Russian Supreme Court and the Higher Arbitration Court have the statutory authority to interpret component state law, their interpretation can be challenged in the Constitutional Court. The case law of the Constitutional Court indicates that this tribunal often interprets component state law through:

1. The complaints of individuals against the laws of component states, such as laws on land use, elections, and taxation;
2. The petitions of the governments of the component states to confirm the constitutionality of their legislation, which had previously been invalidated by other federal courts as non-conforming with federal law, such as the structure of the civil service;

---

[125] Определение Конституционного Суда от 13 апреля 2000 № 43-О.
[126] Постановление Конституционного Суда от 17 июня 2004 № 12-П.
[127] Постановление Конституционного Суда от 7 июня 2000 № 10-П.
[128] Постановление Конституционного Суда РФ от 21 декабря 2005 № 13-П.

3. The petitions of the governments of the component states to settle separation-of-powers disputes at the component-state level; and
4. The petitions of the members of the federal parliament to declare component state laws unconstitutional.

Throughout the 1990s, most component states successfully defied the unfavorable judgments of the Russian Constitutional Court that interpreted component state law by openly or quietly refusing to implement them. However, by 2008, most component states reversed this stance and carried out constitutional court decisions interpreting component state law faster and in full. The only area in which component states continue to defy the Court remains the regulation by component states of migration, as numerous component states continue to impose unconstitutional restrictions on the freedom of movement, particularly in Moscow and in the North Caucasus. But they are able to resist largely because the federal center has no interest in relaxing the control over the migration flows across Russia.

Although the Russian version of federalism diffuses some lawmaking power, judicial power is largely unified. Federal courts include (1) the Russian Constitutional Court, (2) the Russian Supreme Court that crowns a hierarchy of almost 2,500 federal courts of general jurisdiction, of which there are 83 appellate courts and 2,400 trial courts, and (3) the Higher Arbitration Court that heads the hierarchy of arbitration courts, consisting of ten cassation courts, 20 appellate courts, and 81 trial courts. The federal courts apply not only federal law but also the laws enacted by the component states. Within the federal court system, the higher courts exercise the power to reverse judgments of lower courts for failure to correctly follow component state constitutions, charters, laws, and regulations.

The 1996 Federal Law "On the Judicial System of the Russian Federation" authorizes the component states to establish justices of the peace ("JPs") and their own constitutional or charter courts. The constitutional and charter courts have already been discussed. There are about 11,000 justices of the peace, and they exist on the level of political subdivisions of cities and regions. They are trial-level courts and form the lowest rung of the courts of general jurisdiction. These courts have limited civil and criminal jurisdiction as well as jurisdiction over minor administrative offenses, similar to misdemeanors in common-law systems, including traffic violations. Decisions of the justice of the peace courts can be appealed to the district-level federal courts of general jurisdiction, which conduct a complete *de novo* trial with live witnesses. Since 2000, the workload of the justice of the peace courts has grown dramatically, and in most component states they became overloaded. In 2007, they handled all administrative offenses, half of all criminal cases and two-thirds of civil cases.

These courts, however, are not under the complete control of the component states. The federal center determines the number of JPs, their general qualifications, their basic characteristics and jurisdiction. Their salaries are set by federal law and paid by the federal budget. The justices of the peace apply federal procedural law and substantive law, since federal law preempts the component state law in the areas of joint jurisdiction. The component state legislatures appoint JPs for the term of

5 years but the chairs of federal courts de-facto control judicial recruitment. The federal law requires component states to pay for the support staff of the JP courts and to provide logistical support to these courts.

There are no formal mechanisms for resolving differences in legal interpretation among central and/or component state courts. While the Constitution authorizes the Russian president to co-ordinate and reconcile relations among the top government institutions at both the federal and component state levels, no Russian president has greatly improved the thorny relations among the top three central Russian courts. A proposal to establish a "Higher Judicial Office" in charge of settling differences in judicial interpretation emerged during the 1993 constitution-making process and has resurfaced occasionally since the Constitution's adoption. But the judges of the RF Constitutional Court have repeatedly defeated these proposals, arguing that such an office is incompatible with judicial independence.

Differences are most often resolved via informal bargaining between judges of different courts. Sometimes, the Supreme Court and Higher Arbitration Court refer their differences in interpreting the same federal laws to the Constitutional Court through the abstract constitutional review procedure. Similarly, there are no formal mechanisms for resolving differences in legal interpretation among the Russian Constitutional Court and component state constitutional courts. Increasingly, the latter draw in their decisions on the legal interpretation offered by the former. When such differences arise, decisions of both courts containing conflicting interpretations of component state law stand valid. There are no formal mechanisms for resolving differences in legal interpretation among component state constitutional courts.

14.4.2 Relations Between the Central and Component State Governments

On the one hand, the recent history of the Russian Federation under its present Constitution indicates that truly recalcitrant component state governments can (and have) simply refused to take direction from the central government. The results of this obstinacy have on some occasions been extreme and violent (Chechnya), on some occasions strategic and partially successful (Tatarstan), but for the most part ultimately unsuccessful as a practical political matter. On the other hand, the central government now has the statutory power to use an array of inducements and threats to obtain component state compliance.

Among his first acts as president, Vladimir Putin succeeded in passing legislation to amend a 1999 federal law that had attempted to standardize baseline principles for the structure of the legislative and executive branches of the component states (e.g. terms of office, immunity of officeholders, etc.).[129] The amendments gave the federal president the power to dismiss regional legislatures and executives for

---

[129]Федеральный закон от 6 октября 1999 № 184-ф3.

continuing and/or gross violations of federal law. Thus, the central government does possess the power to force the component states to rescind regional legislation that contravenes federal constitutional or statutory law. This power has been upheld by the federal judiciary.[130] The dismissal process is cumbersome and lengthy, and requires the involvement of the federal judiciary to determine the existence of a violation sufficient to trigger the successive stages to dismissal.[131] This power was augmented (and rendered less likely to be used) by further legislation replacing direct election of governors and presidents by constituencies in their component states with the power of the federal president to nominate them for office.[132] The constitutionality of this statute was also upheld by the Constitutional Court.[133]

The execution of central government law depends upon the areas involved. In some areas, the central government itself executes the law. For example, all law enforcement personnel are part of the federal bureaucracy. The investigation and prosecution of crime, therefore, is entirely a function executed by the central government. Likewise, with the exception of Justices of the Peace and judges of the currently operating constitutional or charter courts of the component states, the judiciary is entirely a federal one.

In some cases, the executive branch of the component state may be conscripted (or entitled, depending upon one's point of view) to execute central government law through the federal civil service bureaucracy. This is the result of a recent law, signed in the final days of the presidency of Vladimir Putin, that provides an exception by presidential decree to the general rule prohibiting the appointment to the federal civil service of elected or politically appointed officials.[134] This change is in clear furtherance of the federal executive's interpretation of Article 77(3) of the Constitution, which has been viewed as providing for his leadership of a "unified system of executive power" in the Russian Federation.

The Federal Assembly of the Russian Federation is a bicameral legislature comprised of a lower chamber called the State Duma and an upper chamber called the Council of the Federation. The Duma is comprised of 450 deputies. The Council of the Federation is comprised of two representatives from each of the component states (thus, now comprised of 166 senators).

The autonomy of contributions by the component states in the Federal Assembly has been substantially reduced in recent years. Between 1993 and 2001, half of the deputies in the State Duma were selected proportionally via nationwide party lists and half were selected by a first-past-the-post system of territorially defined electoral districts. Each component state's two-person delegation to the Council

---

[130] Постановление Конституционного Суда РФ от 4 апреля 2002 № 8-П.

[131] Федеральный закон от 29 июля 2000 № 106-ФЗ. For a summary of the process, see Kahn, *supra* note 122, at 262.

[132] Ст. 1(4)(а) Федерального закона от 11 декабря 2004 г. № 159-ФЗ.

[133] Постановление Конституционного Суда РФ от 21 декабря 2005 № 13-П.

[134] Ст. 3 Федерального закона от 29 марта 2008 года № 30-ФЗ.

of the Federation was comprised *ex officio* of the head of the executive branch (the president, governor, or mayor) and the chairperson of the parliament of the component state.[135]

Today, neither chamber of the Federal Assembly is as reflective of the component states or their governments. The Council of the Federation was restructured in 2000 at the start of Vladimir Putin's first term as President.[136] The top executive and legislative officials in each component state no longer served *ex officio* in the upper chamber. This demotion cost them their senatorial immunity from prosecution and their direct influence over federal lawmaking. The chief executive of the component state now nominates senators, who must be approved by the regional legislature. Since the chief executive of each component is himself nominated by the President of the Russian Federation, there is reason to suspect a reduction in the independence of these representatives.

Legislation passed in Putin's second term changed the previous double-ballot approach in the State Duma. All territorial electoral districts have been eliminated. The State Duma is now filled entirely through a proportional system based on nationwide party lists.[137] By removing clear connections between Duma deputies and territorially based constituencies, this restructuring has also diminished the representation of component state interests in the federal legislature.

The division of taxing authority is made in the federal Tax Code. The central government collects a Value Added Tax, excise taxes, a tax on individual income, a "Uniform Social" tax paid by employers from the wages of employees, a tax on mineral extraction, a water tax, customs and duties.[138] The component governments collect taxes on business property, a tax on gambling businesses, and a tax on transportation.[139] Municipal governments collect taxes on land and personal property.[140]

Article 72(1)(i) provides that the central government and the component states shall have joint authority over the "establishment of common principles of taxation and levies in the Russian Federation". Both the central government and the component states have taxing powers, although the extent of power exercised by the component states is largely within the control of the central government. Article 75(3) of the Constitution states that "The system of taxes paid to the federal budget and the general principles of taxation and levies in the Russian Federation shall be determined by federal law". Again, because of federal control over most taxation and natural resources, revenue sharing is largely a top-down affair.

---

[135] Федеральный закон от 5 декабря 1995 года № 192-ФЗ.

[136] Федеральный закон от 5 августа 2000 № 113-ФЗ.

[137] Федеральный закон от 18 мая 2005 г. № 51-ФЗ.

[138] Ст. 13 Налогового кодекса РФ.

[139] Ст. 14 Налогового кодекса РФ.

[140] Ст. 15 Налогового кодекса РФ.

14.4.3 Other Formal or Informal Institutions for Resolving Intergovernmental Conflicts

The Constitution grants the President the power to "use conciliatory procedures to resolve disputes between State government bodies of the Russian Federation and State government bodies of constituent entities of the Russian Federation, and disputes between State government bodies of constituent entities of the Russian Federation".[141] If the agreed resolution cannot be reached the President can pass the dispute for consideration of the proper court.[142]

The State Council is one such institution. Under the presidential decree "About the State Council of the Russian Federation," one of the goals of the Council (which is comprised of the heads of the subjects of the Russian Federation) is to provide assistance to the President in the resolution of disagreements between public authorities of the Russian Federation and public authorities of the subjects of the Russian Federation, and also between the public authorities of the subjects of the Russian Federation.[143]

Another unusual federal institution is the Envoy of the President of the Russian Federation in the Federal District. This institution was established in May 2000 by decree of the President of the Russian Federation.[144] The decree and accompanying regulations divided Russia into seven federal districts. These districts coincided with existing military districts. The capital of each district was deliberately chosen not to coincide with the capital of one of the non-Russian ethnic republics, in an effort to deflate the leadership pretensions of the most powerful component states. Each district is under the charge of one of the President's "plenipotentiaries" (полномочные представители [polnomochnye predstaviteli, "polpredy" for short and commonly translated as envoys]). According to the decree, these *polpredy* are officially part of the Administration of the President and are charged with overseeing the President's constitutional authority in the districts.[145] The *polpredy* report directly to the President.[146]

Legal unification was among the primary objectives of the *polpredy* from their start. *Polpredy* were given extensive control over federal cadre policy in their districts and given wide access to participate in both federal government agencies operating in their districts and in the work of component state institutions. *Polpredy* and large numbers of federal inspectors set to work scouring component state

---

[141] Ст. 85(1) Конст. РФ.

[142] *Id.*

[143] Указ Президента РФ от 1 сентября 2000 года № 1602.

[144] Указ Президента РФ от 13 мая 2000 года № 849 «О полномочном представителе Президента Российской Федерации в федеральном округе».

[145] Положение «О полномочном представителе Президента Российской Федерации в федеральном округе», утверждено Указом Президента РФ от 13 мая 2000 года № 849.

[146] *Id.*

constitutions and laws, and the bilateral treaties signed with the central government, for conformity with federal legal norms.

Among the functions of the Plenipotentiary of the President of the Russian Federation in the Federal District is organization "by order of the President of the Russian Federation of carrying out of the conciliation for resolution of the disagreements between federal public authorities and public authorities of the subjects of the Russian Federation, located within the limits of the federal district".[147]

14.4.4 The Bureaucracy

The civil service in Russia is divided into a federal civil service and the civil service bureaucracies of the component states.[148] The legal regulation and organization of the federal civil service is within the exclusive jurisdiction of Russian Federation.[149] The legal regulation of the civil service of each component state is in the joint jurisdiction of the central government and the component state, while the organization of the component state civil service rests with that component state.[150] We do not have adequate data to assess the current extent of lateral mobility between the federal civil service and the civil service bureaucracies of the component states. However, federal law seems to contemplate such mobility, e.g. in provisions for determining the total length of government service.[151]

14.4.5 Social Factors

There are important racial, ethnic, religious, linguistic and other social cleavages in the Russian Federation. More than four-fifths of the population is ethnically Russian. A combination of Imperial Russian and Soviet history, however, has established substantial populations of non-Russian ethnic groups in different parts of the Federation. Turkic and Finno-Ugric peoples live in the Volga Region (Tatars, Bashkirs, Mariis, Udmurts, Chuvash, and Mordvins), North (Komi, Karelians), and Eastern Siberia (Tuvins, Buryats, Yakuts). The North Caucasus is home to scores of Slavic and non-Slavic ethnic groups, including Chechens, Kalmyks, Avars,

---

[147]*Id.*

[148]Ст. 2(2) Федерального закона от 27 мая 2003 года № 58-ФЗ «О системе государственной службы РФ».

[149]Ст. 71(т) Конст. РФ. This excludes personnel in the judicial and law enforcement organs of the state, which are within the joint jurisdiction of the central government and the component states. Ст. 72(л) Конст. РФ.

[150]Ст. 2(4) Федерального закона от 27 мая 2003 года № 58-ФЗ.

[151]Ст. 14 Федерального закона от 27 мая 2003 года № 58-ФЗ.

Ossetians, Ingush, and many others. Although Russian is the official language, all of these different ethnic groups speak different languages with varying degrees of linguistic overlap and mutual intelligibility.

Most religious Russians are Orthodox Christians. Most of the Turkic peoples of the Volga Region and many of the ethnic groups of the North Caucasus are Muslims. Kalmyks and Tuvins are Buddhists. There are also substantial populations of adherents to other forms of Christian Orthodoxy (e.g. the Georgian Orthodox Church), and Christianity (e.g. the Armenian Apostolic Church, Protestantism and Catholicism). Although adherents have dwindled in numbers, Judaism has a long history in Russia (as does anti-Semitism).

For these multi-cultural reasons, the Russian Constitution makes an important distinction that is often lost in translation. The state is identified by two names of equal validity: Russia (Россия) and the Russian Federation (Российская Федерация).[152] A citizen of Russia is not a *Russian* (русский [*russkii*]) – that adjective describes one of several Slavic ethnic groups – but a *Rossianin* (Россиянин or российский or [*rossiiskii*]) – a civic category that may include any of the over 100 ethnic groups that populate the country.

One need look no further than the two wars fought in Chechnya to imagine the violence into which Russian ethno-federal politics are capable of descending. These routes of ethnic conflict extend back centuries, but were subject to particular manipulation by early Bolshevik planners, who deliberately created "titular" ethnic republics (i.e. political units named for particular ethnic groups, whose indigenous languages and customs were also given privileged status) to secure support for their seizure of power.[153] Subsequent demographic trends resulted in minority status for several ethnic groups within their "own" republics or regions. According to the 1989 census, the titular ethnic groups in 15 of 20 ethnic republics within the boundaries of the RSFSR were a minority of the population.[154] These ethnically based divisions took a life of their own after the collapse of the Soviet Union. Forty-six provinces and two federal cities now have predominantly ethnic Russian populations, whereas the other component states are mostly named for non-Russian ethnic groups that in most cases comprise at least a plurality of their population.[155]

As of this writing, Russia is comprised of 83 component states.[156] There are 46 provinces, 21 republics, 9 territories, 4 autonomous districts, 1 autonomous

---

[152]Ст. 1(1) – (2) Конст. РФ.

[153]Kahn, *supra* note 122, at 72.

[154]Jeffrey Kahn, *The Parade of Sovereignties: Establishing the Vocabulary of the New Russian Federalism*, POST-SOVIET AFFAIRS 16: 58, 63 (2000).

[155]Kahn, *supra* note 122, at 11–12.

[156]The Russian Federation initially comprised 89 components. This change is the result of deliberate efforts to decrease the number of components by merging several in accordance with Article 66(5) of the Constitution.

province, and two "cities of federal significance," Moscow and St. Petersburg.[157] Some component states form part of the territory of other component states, and thus have special relationships with those components. The Constitution requires that all component states "shall have equal rights as constituent entities of the Russian Federation[,]" and "be equal with one another in relations with federal State government bodies".[158] This has not been interpreted to require identical structures of government in component states; indeed, the Constitution acknowledges a distinction in the organic law of republics (which have constitutions and are ruled by presidents) compared to other components (which have charters and are ruled by governors or mayors).[159]

There is substantial asymmetry in natural resource allocation, development, wealth and education that is more often exacerbated than ameliorated by the structure of the federal system. Russia is richly endowed with natural resources unevenly distributed among its component states. Considerable iron ore reserves are to be found in the European part of Russia, which is predominantly populated with ethnic Russians living in provinces (области [oblasti]). Timber stocks are largely found in remote parts of Siberia and in Northwest Russia (particularly the republics of Karelia and Komi). Coal, oil, and natural gas deposits are also predominantly found in Siberia and the Far East, which are sparsely populated with both ethnic Russian and various indigenous peoples. The Republic of Sakha-Yakutiia in the Far East sits atop almost all of Russia's substantial diamond reserves. In terms of development and financial wealth, there exists extreme disparities between the wealthiest component states (the federal cities of Moscow and St. Petersburg, Tatarstan, Bashkortostan, Sakha-Yakutia) and the poorest (Chechnya, Kalmykia, and the border republics of the North Caucasus, Marii El in the Volga Region, and the provinces of Ivanovo or Pskov).

Control over these resources was a leading cause of the struggle between the central government and the component states between 1990 and 1999. In their declarations of sovereignty, the component states almost universally asserted exclusive possession of everything of value in their territories. These declarations set the tone for newly drafted laws and constitutions, which also asserted complete control over natural resources and other valued property on the territory of the component state. These documents and this wealth were then used as bargaining chips to wrest concessions from the federal executive in the form of bilateral treaties and agreements.

In short, component states blessed with various forms of wealth sought to protect assets perceived to be "theirs," while component states lacking such resources grew

---

[157] Ст. 65(1) Конст. РФ. See also Указы Президента РФ от 09.01.1996 № 20; 10.02.1996 № 173; 09.06.2001 № 679; 25.07.2003 № 841; Федеральные конституционные законы от 25.03.2004 № 1-ФКЗ; от 14.10.2005 № 6-ФКЗ, от 12.07.2006 № 2-ФКЗ, от 30.12.2006 № 6-ФКЗ, от 21.07.2007 № 5-ФКЗ.

[158] Ст. 5(1) и (4) Конст. РФ.

[159] Ст. 5(2) Конст. РФ.

increasingly dependent on the largesse of the central government and increasingly resentful of the perceived selfishness of their wealthier neighbors. Much of this competition was crushed by Vladimir Putin. With the exception of republics that were both exceptionally wealthy and possessed sizeable non-Russian ethnic minorities, most component states were stripped of their claimed powers to tax and control "their" resources and forced to submit to federal policies.

14.5 Conclusion

As indicated by the across-the-board high scores on the "unification scorecard" and the more substantive analysis of this report, we believe that Russia is a highly centralized federal state with an extremely unified legal system. We also believe that plausible arguments can now be made – based on its new electoral system, "unified system of executive authority," and current division of jurisdiction between the central and component state governments – that Russia may have ceased to be a federal state in any meaningful sense of the term. Terms lose their meaning when stretched too far.

Nevertheless, we conclude that Russia remains federal because its legal processes (and political will) preserve the federal character of the state. Its current degree of centralization of power and unification of law was not inevitable and may not be permanent. The history of this very new federal state is one of substantial change in the relationship between the central government and the component states. It is worth noting that in the face of so much change, the federal Constitution remained virtually unchanged until the final days of 2008.[160] We do not think that this is evidence of the Constitution's irrelevance. To the contrary, we think that this indicates a degree of flexibility built into the Constitution (although we do not speculate whether this flexibility was intentional) that has given it the "play in its joints" that has led to its changing interpretation in changing times and circumstances.[161] However, it should be noted that this most recent amendment (which lengthens the terms in office for the President and members of the State Duma) is part of a trend of increasing power to the federal center, particularly the Executive Branch.[162] The day may come when the current trends

---

[160] Until December 30, 2008, only those passages concerning the number and identity of component states had been changed (always according to constitutionally established processes).

[161] Bain Peanut Co. v. Pinson, 282 U.S. 499, 501 (1931) (Holmes, J.) ("The interpretation of constitutional principles must not be too literal. We must remember that the machinery of government would not work if it were not allowed a little play in its joints".).

[162] Федеральный Конституционный Закон от 30 декабря 2008 г. № 6-ФКЗ. The law increases the term in office of the president to 6 years (from four) and of members of parliament to 5 years (from four). The amendment was accomplished with unusual haste following its proposal by President Medvedev in his address to the Federal Assembly on November 5, 2008. According to one respected national newspaper, the upper chamber of the parliament, the Council of the

of unification of law and centralization of authority are reversed, perhaps with little need for constitutional amendment to accomplish this altered course. For the present, however, we see problems from too much unification of law, rather than not enough.

Appendix A: Constitutional Division of Exclusive Federal Authority and Joint Federal-Constituent Subject Authority Organized by Subject Area

Subject area	Exclusive federal government authority (article 71)	Joint federal-constituent subject authority (article 72)
Constitutional and physical integrity of the state	(a) The adoption and amending of the Constitution of the Russian Federation and federal laws, control over compliance therewith	(a) Measures to ensure the correspondence of constitutions and laws of republics, the charters, laws and other normative legal acts of krays, oblasts, cities of federal significance, autonomous oblast and autonomous okrugs to the Constitution of the Russian Federation and federal laws
	(b) The federative structure and the territory of the Russian Federation	(m) Establishment of general principles of the organisation of the system of State government and local self-government bodies
	(m) Determination of the status and protection of the State border, territorial sea, air space, the exclusive economic zone and the continental shelf of the Russian Federation	

(continued)

Federation, required only 20 min to pass on the measure, which had already been approved by more than the two-thirds of regional legislatures required by Article 136 of the Constitution. Барахова, А. Президентский срок уложили в двадцать минут // Коммерсантъ. 2008. 23 декабря. On the eve of adoption, one liberal party (Yabloko) protested this haste as in violation of the federal law on constitutional amendments. Interfax, *Russian party says extension of presidential term approved unlawfully*, 22 December 2008 (available at Johnson's Russia List 2008 – # 232, 23 December 2008).

(continued)

Subject area	Exclusive federal government authority (article 71)	Joint federal-constituent subject authority (article 72)
Civil rights	(c) Regulation and protection of human and civil rights and freedoms; citizenship in the Russian Federation, regulation and protection of the rights of national minorities	(b) Protection of human and civil rights and freedoms, protection of the rights of national minorities, ensuring lawfulness, law and order, public security; border zone regimes (l) Protection of the traditional habitat and the traditional way of life of small ethnic communities
Property & natural resources	(e) Federal State property and administration thereof (f) Establishment of the basic principles of federal policy and federal programmes in the sphere of State, economic, ecological, social, cultural and national development of the Russian Federation	(d) Demarcation of State property (c) Issues of the possession, utilisation and management of land and of subsurface, water and other natural resources (e) Use of natural resources, protection of the environment and provisions for ecological safety; specially protected natural territories, protection of historical and cultural monuments (j) … land, water and forest legislation; legislation on subsurface resources and on environmental protection …
Fiscal & monetary policies	(g) Establishment of the basic legal principles for the unified market; financial, currency, credit and customs regulation; money emission; the basic principles of pricing policy, federal economic services, including federal banks (h) The federal budget, federal taxes and levies, federal funds of regional development	(i) Establishment of common principles of taxation and levies in the Russian Federation
Foreign affairs	(j) Foreign policy and international relations of the Russian Federation, international treaties of the Russian Federation, issues of war and peace (k) Foreign economic relations of the Russian Federation	(n) Coordination of international and foreign economic relations of constituent entities of the Russian Federation, observance of international agreements of the Russian Federation

(continued)

(continued)

Subject area	Exclusive federal government authority (article 71)	Joint federal-constituent subject authority (article 72)
Defence & national security	(l) Defence and security; military production; determination of the procedure for selling and purchasing weapons, ammunition, military equipment and other military hardware; production of poisonous substances, narcotic substances and the procedure for their use (i) Federal power-engineering systems, nuclear power, fissile materials, federal transport, railways, information and communication, activities in space	
Courts & judicial decision-making	(n) The judicial system, public prosecution, criminal, criminal-procedural and criminal-executive legislation, amnesty and remission, civil, civil-procedural and arbitration-procedural legislation, legal regulation of intellectual property (o) Federal choice-of-law	(k) Personnel of judicial and law enforcement bodies; lawyers, notaries
Social services		(f) General issues of upbringing, education, science, culture, physical education and sport (g) Coordination of health care issues; protection of the family, maternity, fatherhood and childhood, social protection, including social security (h) Carrying out measures against catastrophes, natural disasters, epidemics and rectification of their consequences (j) Administrative, administrative-procedural, labour, family, housing, ... legislation; ...

(continued)

(continued)

Subject area	Exclusive federal government authority (article 71)	Joint federal-constituent subject authority (article 72)
Bureaucracy	(d) Establishment of the system of federal legislative, executive and judicial bodies, the procedure for their organisation and activities, the formation of federal State government bodies	
	(r) Federal State service	
Other	(p) Meteorological service, standards, metric and time systems, geodesy and cartography, names of geographical units, official statistics and accounting	
	(q) State awards and honorary titles of the Russian Federation	

Chapter 15
Federalism and Legal Unification in South Africa

Karthy Govender

15.1 Overview

There was profound antipathy towards the notion of a federal state amongst the liberation organisations such as the African National Congress (ANC) and this manifested itself in positions assumed during the negotiations process of the South African constitution. As a consequence, the Constitution of the Republic of South Africa 1996 studiously avoids describing the system of governance in South Africa as federal. The 'grand design' of the Apartheid government involved the fragmentation of the country into self-governing, and later, independent entities based on ethnic groups or tribal affiliations. The ultimate goal was that African South Africans would be stripped of their South African citizenship and afforded the citizenship of one of these 'independent' entities in which they would exercise their civil and political rights.[1] The Apartheid government described this as a process of internal decolonisation. In reality, it was nothing other than denationalisation. These homelands were impoverished parcels of land cobbled together to create 'independent states'. They were totally dependent on the South African state for their financial survival and were provided with monthly grants. The ANC and its allies were concerned that a federal system would result in the resurrection of the despised homeland system in a different guise. There were also concerns that a

---

Karthy Govender, Professor of Law at University of KwaZulu-Natal and a former commissioner on the South African Human Rights Commissioner.

[1] The National States Citizenship Act 26 of 1970 provides that every black person would become a citizen of the tribal entity to which he or she had a tribal or cultural affiliation and would simultaneously cease to be a citizen of South Africa. The fact that they did not live in that entity nor desired the new citizenship was irrelevant.

K. Govender (✉)
Howard College School of Law, University of KwaZulu-Natal, King George V. Avenue,
4001 Durban, Republic of South Africa
e-mail: kgovender@ukzn.ac.za

rigid division of powers between the central government and the various component spheres would inhibit and frustrate the developmental and egalitarian objectives of the central state.

Prior to 1994, South Africa had a unitary system of government. While provincial and local spheres of government existed, they were subservient to and subject to the control of a strong central government where all meaningful decisions were made.[2] The legal system prior to 1994 was thus a unified one with little divergence in laws between the various provinces. Towards the end of the 1980s, most of the independent homelands had collapsed into military dictatorships and were dysfunctional. The Apartheid grand design had unravelled before formal negotiations began.

During the process of negotiations, the ANC leadership started seeing the benefit and advantages of strong regional government for the delivery of services and the political empowerment of the citizens. It seemed that exposure to models of federalism such as the German Constitution assisted in convincing the liberation organisations that effective regional government could be combined with strong central leadership.[3] Some of the political groups such as the predominantly Zulu party, the Inkatha Freedom Party (IFP), favoured a strong federal arrangement and advocated an asymmetrical arrangement with maximum devolution of original power to the KwaZulu-Natal (KZN) region. It was the inability to reach consensus on this and other issues that caused them to boycott the constitutional drafting process.

In South Africa, there was a two-stage constitutional drafting process. The unelected leaders of the various political groupings drafted the Interim Constitution,[4] which was in effect a cessation of hostilities. It was agreed that the Interim Constitution would last for 2 years and that during this period the Final Constitution would be drafted by the democratically elected representatives. An important aspect of the negotiated settlement was that the Final Constitution had to be consistent with 34 Constitutional Principles agreed to by the various parties and enshrined in schedule 4 of the Interim Constitution. The relevant principles dealing with structures of government provided that government shall be structured at national, provincial and local levels,[5] that the powers and functions of the various spheres be defined in the Constitution, that these powers not be substantially inferior to those provided for in the Interim Constitution[6] and that the functions of the national and provincial levels of government include exclusive and concurrent powers.[7]

---

[2] S. Woolman et al. 'Co-operative Government' in *Constitutional Law of South Africa* (2nd edition) at 14–1.

[3] N. Haysom 'Federal Features of the Final Constitution.' In P. Adrews and S. Ellmann (eds.) *The Post-Apartheid Constitutions: Perspectives on South Africa's Basic Law* (2001) 504.

[4] Constitution of the Republic of South Africa, Act 200 of 1993.

[5] Principle XVI of Schedule 4 of the Constitution of the Republic of South Africa, Act 200 of 1993.

[6] Principle XVIII.

[7] Principle XIX.

In addition, the allocation of a competence to either the national or provincial spheres had to be in accordance with listed criteria.[8] Further, the national sphere was precluded from exercising its powers so as to encroach upon the geographical, functional and institutional integrity of the provinces.[9] All the provisions of the Final Constitution had to comply with all the constitutional principles.

South Africa has a central government, nine provincial governments, six metropolitan local councils and various district councils and local municipalities. Having provincial spheres of government played a vital role in accommodating the aspirations of smaller political groupings that were strong regionally but insignificant at a national level. In the early and somewhat fragile days, having all the parties participating within the system enhanced its legitimacy and provided invaluable stability. After the elections in 1994, the IFP, despite boycotting the negotiations, won control of the KZN legislature and participated in the new process. This in turn resulted in a much more stable political environment within the province and contributed to ending the low intensity civil war between the IFP and ANC supporters in the province.

Presently eight of the nine provinces as well as the national government are controlled by the ANC. After the April 2009 elections, the Democratic Alliance won control of the Western Cape Province. There is a view within the ruling party that there should be a reduction in the number of provinces in order to facilitate effective delivery. The ANC's dominance of the various legislatures and its firm internal discipline has resulted in a very high degree of uniformity of laws.

15.2 The Federal Distribution and Exercise of Lawmaking Power

15.2.1 *Central Legislative Jurisdiction*

Chapter 3 of the Constitution lays down the principles of co-operative governance and provides that 'government is constituted at national, provincial and local spheres of government which are distinctive, interdependent and interrelated.'[10] It has been argued that the term 'sphere' conveys the impression of co-equals as opposed to a term such as 'level' which denotes a more hierarchical arrangement.[11]

The subject matter of the legislation or legislative functional area is the main criteria used in determining the allocation of legislative authority between the central and provincial spheres. The central legislature is situated in Cape Town

---

[8] Principle XXI.
[9] Principle XXII.
[10] Section 41(1) of the Constitution.
[11] S. Woolman, *supra* note 3 at 14–1.

and each of the nine provinces has its own legislative assembly. The central and provincial spheres share concurrent legislative competence over functional areas listed in Schedule 4 of the Constitution. Subject to a limited central override,[12] the provincial spheres have exclusive competence over functional areas listed in Schedule 5 of the Constitution.

15.2.1.1 Legislative Areas Formally Allocated to the Central Government

While Schedule 5 allocates exclusive powers to the provinces, it allows the central sphere to legislate over these matters in certain circumstances. Thus the only truly exclusive powers are those vested in the central sphere and which are not listed in either Schedules 4 or 5. Important functional areas such as defence, justice and foreign affairs are not listed either in Schedule 4 or 5 and thus fall within the exclusive competence of the central sphere.

In addition, section 44(2) of the Constitution permits the central legislature to pass legislation dealing with functional areas falling within Schedule 5 when it is necessary to maintain national security; to maintain economic unity; to maintain essential standards; to establish minimum standards required for the rendering of services or to prevent unreasonable action taken by a province which is prejudicial to the interests of another province or the country as a whole.

15.2.1.2 Concurrent Powers

The areas of concurrent legislative competence listed in Part A of Schedule 4 of the Constitution are: administration of indigenous forests; Agriculture; Airports other than international and national airports; Animal control and diseases; Casinos, racing, gambling and wagering, excluding lotteries and sports pools; Consumer protection; Cultural matters; Disaster management; Education at all levels except tertiary education; Environment; Health Services; Housing; Indigenous law and customary law; Industrial promotion; Language policy and the regulation of official languages to the extent permitted by section 6 of the Constitution; Media services directly controlled or provided by the provincial government subject to section 192; Nature conservation, excluding national parks, national botanical gardens and marine resources; Police subject to the provisions of Chapter 11; Pollution control; Population development; Property development; Property transfer fees; provincial public enterprises; Public transport; Public works; Regional Planning and development; Road traffic regulation; Soil conservation; Tourism; Trade; Traditional leadership subject to chapter 12; Urban and rural development; Vehicle licencing and welfare services.

---

[12]Section 44(2) of the Constitution.

The central sphere has concurrent competence over all functional areas listed in Schedule 4 and in respect of matters that are reasonably necessary for, or incidental to, the effective exercise of a Schedule 4 competence.[13]

15.2.1.3 Important Sources of Central Government Authority to Regulate

The source of the central legislative authority's law-making power is section 44(1)(a)(ii) of the Constitution, which allows it to pass laws with regard to any matter, including a matter within a functional area listed in Schedule 4, but excluding, subject to subsection (2), a matter within a functional area listed in Schedule 5. Since 1994, the central sphere has engaged in a programme of frenetic law making as it sought to transform the society. By way of contrast, very few acts are passed each year by the provinces.

15.2.1.4 Areas of Central Regulation of Practical Importance

The Central legislature during the first 13 years of democracy passed laws that impacted directly on most facets of life. Laws and legal norms had to be changed to make them consistent with the provisions of the Constitution. Laws that directly and indirectly discriminated had to be changed. Systematic patterns of discrimination had to be dismantled. The vision of a more egalitarian society had to be realised and the marginalised and previously disadvantaged sections of our community had to be provided with greater legal protection.

15.2.2 State Legislative Jurisdiction

15.2.2.1 Exclusive and Concurrent State Regulation

In addition to the areas of concurrent jurisdiction in Schedule 4, a list of exclusive functions is assigned to the provinces in terms of Schedule 5 of the Constitution. The following relatively minor areas are within the exclusive legislative competence of the provinces: – Abattoirs; Ambulance Services; Archives other than national archives; Libraries other than national libraries; Liquor Licences; Museums other than national museums; Provincial Planning; Provincial Cultural matters; Provincial recreation and amenities; Provincial sport; Provincial Roads and Traffic and Veterinary Services, excluding regulation of the profession. The central legislature can intervene and pass laws in respect of functional areas falling within Schedule 5 if the requirements of section 44(2) are satisfied.

---

[13] Section 44(3) of the Constitution.

The states may pass laws even if the central legislature has enacted a law in the specific functional area. The deadlock or dispute resolving mechanism comes into effect if there is an irreconcilable conflict between the central and provincial laws.

15.2.2.2 Important Areas of Exclusive State Regulation

As indicated earlier, laws regulating areas such as education, safety and security, social welfare, planning and development, culture, and sport are passed by the central legislature and supplemented and implemented at provincial level. The provincial implementation of education and dispensing of social welfare grants is particularly important.

15.2.2.3 Important Areas of Coexisting Regulation

When some of the provincial legislatures were not controlled by the ANC, there were areas such as education, social welfare, traditional authorities, and town and regional planning in which there were co-existing regulations which sometimes had to be reconciled.

15.2.3 Residual Power

The residual power is, in terms of section 44(1)(a)(ii) of the Constitution, allocated to the central sphere of government.

15.2.4 Resolving Conflicts Among the Spheres of Government

As stated earlier, Chapter 3 of the Constitution articulates the principles of co-operative governance which requires the various spheres to exercise their powers in a manner which does not encroach upon the geographical, functional or institutional integrity of other spheres. A positive duty is imposed on organs of state involved in disputes to make every reasonable effort to settle their disputes and avoid legal proceedings against each other. The Constitutional Court (CC) has held that the failure to make meaningful attempts to settle the matter would be sufficient grounds for refusing direct access to the court.[14] Direct access is a process where a litigant seeks a hearing directly before the CC as a court of first instance. It would appear that courts will require litigants to demonstrate that a genuine attempt

---

[14]*National Gambling Board v. Premier of KwaZulu-Natal and Others* 2002 (2) BCLR 156 (CC).

15 Federalism and Legal Unification in South Africa

had been made to comply with the prescripts of Chapter 3 before they will be entitled to litigate. In addition, section 150 of the Constitution directs that the courts must prefer any reasonable explanation that avoids a conflict between central and provincial laws over an interpretation that results in a conflict.

Conflicts between central and provincial laws are dealt with by reference to the following enquiries[15]:

- Does the central legislature have the legislative competence to pass its law?
- Does the provincial legislature have the legislative competence to pass its law?
- If the both legislatures have the legal competence to pass the laws then the issue would be whether the different laws can be reconciled.
- If there is an irreconcilable conflict then the central law will prevail if the provisions of section 146 of the Constitution are satisfied.
- If the provisions of section 146 of the Constitution are not met then the provincial law will prevail.

If any one of the criteria listed in section 146 is met, the national law will prevail.[16] Criteria permitting the central override are divided into two categories. If one of the criteria listed either in section 146(2) or (3) is satisfied, then the conflicting provincial law is rendered inoperative for the period of the conflict.[17] All the criteria listed in section 146(2) are subject to the additional requirement that the central legislation be applied uniformly to the country as a whole. Thus national law that targets a particular province will not prevail in terms of section 146(2).

In terms of section 146(2), central law will prevail if any one of the following three conditions is established:

- The central legislation deals with a matter that cannot be regulated effectively by legislation enacted by the respective provinces individually.[18]
- The central legislation deals with a matter that, to be dealt with effectively, requires uniformity across the nation, and national legislation provides that uniformity by establishing norms and standards, frameworks or national policies.[19]
- The central legislation is necessary for the maintenance of national security, the maintenance of economic unity; the protection of the common market in respect of the mobility of goods, services, capital and labour; the promotion of economic activities across provincial boundaries; the promotion of equal opportunities or equal access to government services; or the protection of the environment.[20]

---

[15] *Ex parte Speaker of the KwaZulu-Natal Provincial Legislature* 1996 (4) SA 653 (CC). Victoria Bronstein 'Conflicts' in *Constitutional Law of South Africa* (2nd edition) at 16–4.
[16] J Klaaren 'Federalism' in M. Chaskalson et al., *CLOSA* (1st edition) 5–12.
[17] Section 149 of the Constitution.
[18] Section 146(2)(a) of the Constitution.
[19] Section 146(2)(b) of the Constitution.
[20] Section 146(2)(c) of the Constitution.

In Mashavha,[21] the CC had to consider the constitutionality of the President assigning to the provinces the administration of the Social Assistance Act 59 of 1992 in its entirety. In terms of the Interim Constitution, the President could only assign the administration of the Act over to the provinces if the provisions of section 126(3) of the Interim Constitution[22] were not applicable. The court found that the assignment was invalid as the administration dealt with a matter that could not be regulated effectively by separate provincial legislation. In order for the administration of social welfare grants to be fairly and equitably administered, it needed to be regulated or coordinated by uniform norms or standards that applied throughout the Republic. To achieve equity and effectiveness, it was necessary to set minimum standards across the nation.[23] The primary objection of the court was that if the province of Gauteng, the richest in the country, paid a higher old age pension than Limpopo then the dignity of people in Limpopo would be offended as different classes of citizenship would be created. Thus in order to prevent inequality and unfairness in the provision of social assistance to people in need, there had to be uniform norms and standards that applied throughout the country.

In terms of section 146(2), central law will prevail over provincial law if it is aimed at preventing unreasonable action by a province that is prejudicial to the economic, health or security interests of another province or the country as a whole or impedes the implementation of national economic policy.

In the Liquor Bill[24] case, the CC provided useful guidance on how to navigate between and apply the various clauses that demarcate competencies and how to resolve conflicts. The central legislature passed the Liquor Bill, which sought to comprehensively regulate the liquor industry. The bill divided the economic activity of the liquor industry into three categories: manufacturing; distribution and retail sales. The bill treated manufacturing and distribution as national issues and retail sales as provincial issues to be dealt with by provincial liquor authorities. Yet, even in respect of retail sales, the bill prescribed detailed mechanisms as to how the provincial legislatures should establish their retail licensing systems. The Western Cape government, then controlled by the New National Party, challenged the constitutionality of the bill by arguing that it exhaustively regulated issues concerning manufacturing and distribution and that even in the retail sphere, it relegated the provinces to the role of funders and administrators. The central sphere contended that the bill primarily dealt with trade, economic and social welfare issues. These are competencies that fall within the functional areas of concurrent competence. The provincial government argued that the bill dealt with liquor licences, an exclusive competence of the province in terms of schedule 5. The bill in fact impacted on both concurrent and exclusive provincial competencies.

---

[21] *Mashavha v. President of the Republic of South Africa and others* 2005 (2) SA 476 (CC).

[22] This was the predecessor of section 146 of the Final Constitution.

[23] V. Bronstein *supra* note 15 at 16–19.

[24] *Ex Parte President of the Republic of South Africa: In Re Constitutionality of the Liquor Bill* 2000 (1) BCLR 1 (CC).

The court emphasised that under the post-apartheid constitutional developments, governmental power is not located in the national sphere alone.[25] Legislative authority is vested in the Parliament for the national sphere, in the provincial legislature for the provincial sphere and in municipal councils for the local sphere. Any interpretation must recognise and promote this new philosophy of cooperative governance at various levels. Yet given the breadth of the competencies listed in the various schedules, their parameters of operation will, of necessity, overlap. The Constitution allows for provincial exclusivity in respect of matters falling within schedule 5, subject to an intervention by the central sphere that is justified in terms of section 44(2) of the Constitution. The functional competencies in schedule 4 should be interpreted as being distinct from, and excluding schedule 5 competencies. The court found that the primary purpose of schedule 4 is to enable the national government to regulate inter-provincially. Conversely, the provinces, whose jurisdiction is confined to their geographical territory, are accorded exclusive powers in respect of matters that may be regulated intra-provincially.

The main substance and character of the legislation determines the field of competence in which it falls. A single piece of legislation may have various parts and more than one substantive character. On this reasoning, it was concluded that the central sphere has the power to regulate the liquor trade in all respects other than liquor licensing. The manufacturing and distribution segments of the legislation impact on inter- as opposed to intra- provincial competencies, and this would suggest that the competence of liquor licensing in Schedule 5 was not intended to encompass manufacturing and distribution of liquor. In any event, the court was prepared to conclude that even if the provincial competence in respect of liquor licences extends to licensing, manufacturing and distribution, 'its [the central sphere's] interest in maintaining economic unity authorises it to intervene under section 44(2) of the Constitution.'[26] Yet the court adopted a much stricter approach to the national regulation in respect of retail sales. A relatively uniform approach to liquor licensing in the country may be desirable but this did not amount to a necessity that justified an intrusion into the exclusive provincial competence. Thus, those aspects of the law that regulated manufacturing and distribution were deemed constitutional and the segment of the central law regulating the retail industry was deemed unconstitutional.

15.2.5 Municipal Law-Making Powers

Municipalities are assigned original law-making powers over defined areas by section 151 of the Constitution. Municipalities may legislate on and administer matters listed in Part B of Schedule 4 and Part B of Schedule 5. The following

---

[25]Ibid. at para 55 ff.
[26]Ibid. at para 76.

competencies are listed in Part B of Schedule 4: Air Pollution; Building regulations; Child Care facilities; Electricity and Gas reticulation; Fire-fighting services; Local tourism, Municipal airports; Municipal planning; Municipal health services; Municipal public transport; Municipal public works in so far as it applies to the needs of the municipality; pontoons, ferries etc; Storm water management systems in built up areas; Trade regulations and Water and sanitation. Part B of Schedule 5 lists the following competencies: Beaches and amusement facilities; Billboards; Cemeteries; Cleansing; Control of public nuisances; Control of undertakings that sell liquor to the public; Facilities for the accommodation, care and burial of animals; Fencing and fences; Licensing of dogs; Licensing and control of undertakings that sell food to the public; Local amenities; Local sport amenities; Markets; Municipal abattoirs; Municipal parks and recreation; Municipal roads; Noise pollution; Pounds; Public places; Refuse removal; Street trading; Street lighting and Traffic and parking.

Subject to section 151(4), a municipal by-law that conflicts with national or provincial legislation is invalid.[27] Section 151(4) provides that neither the national nor the provincial government may compromise or impede a municipality's ability or right to exercise its powers. Thus, while the municipalities have original legislative authority, this power cannot be exercised in a manner that conflicts with provincial or national laws. Nonetheless, the national and provincial legislatures must ensure that their laws do not compromise or impede a municipality's ability to exercise its powers or performs its functions.[28] It would thus appear that if the primary effect of the national or provincial law is to compromise or impede a municipality's ability to exercise its power, then those laws will not take precedence over conflicting by-laws. Both the national and provincial governments are required, by agreement, to assign to municipalities the administration of a matter listed in Part A of Schedule 4 or Part A of Schedule 5 which necessarily relates to local government.[29] Such assignments are to be made only if the matter could be most effectively administered locally and if the municipality has the capacity to do so. Municipalities are empowered to make by-laws for the effective administration of matters over which they have capacity to administer.[30]

The Constitutional Court has held that local governments under the democratic order are constitutionally entrenched and are therefore fundamentally different entities to the vulnerable local authorities of the past, which governed subject to central parliamentary control.[31] The Constitutional Court in City of Johannesburg v Gauteng Development Tribunal and Others considered the demarcation of responsibilities between the provinces and local authorities.[32] The Development Facilitation Act of 1995 created a provincial tribunal to hear applications involving the rezoning

---

[27] Section 156(3) of the Constitution.
[28] Bernard Bekink, *Principles of South African Local Government Law* (Lexis Nexis, 2006) 164.
[29] Section 156(4) of the Constitution.
[30] Section 156(3) of the Constitution.
[31] *Fedsure Life Assurance v. Greater Johannesburg TMC* 1999 (1) SA 374.
[32] City of Johannesburg v Gauteng Development Tribunal and others 2010 (6) SA 182 (CC).

of land and the development of townships. The Town Planning and Townships Ordinance gave the same power to the municipality of Johannesburg. There was a perception that the Gauteng Provincial Tribunal was more lenient in granting approval than the City which applied its town planning policy more vigilantly. This resulted in applicants engaging in forum shopping. The issue was whether the municipality or the provincial sphere had competence over these matters or whether it was a concurrent competence. The municipality argued that municipal planning is a competence assigned to local government in terms of Part B of Schedule 4 read with section 156 of the Constitution. The respondent argued that the law fell under urban and rural development which was a competence located under Part A of Schedule 4 and thus within the competence of the provincial legislature. The court considering the constitutional scheme emphasized that the various spheres of government were distinct, but interdependent. In addition each sphere was given authority to exercise its power within the parameters of competence and no sphere was permitted to intrude into the domain of another sphere except in circumstances permitted by the Constitution. The competences listed in Parts B of Schedule 4 and 5 fell within the executive competence of local government. The court held that municipal planning had acquired an established meaning which included the zoning of land and the establishment of township and declined to give the urban and rural development competence the broad interpretation contended for by the respondent. As section 151(4) of the Constitution precluded the provincial government from compromising or impeding the municipality's right to exercise its powers or perform its functions, the province could not give itself powers to exercise adjudicative powers over municipal planning. Consequently the law was deemed to be unconstitutional. This is an explicit recognition that the legislative and executive competence of local government must be recognised and respected and local government is not to be regarded as a subservient sphere of government. The City of Cape Town, one of the six metropolitan councils, is now controlled by the DA. These decisions could lay the foundation for successful and confident provincial and local spheres asserting their legislative and executive power and resisting national encroachment in their jurisdiction.

15.3 The Means and Methods of Legal Unification

15.3.1 Legal Unification Through the Exercise of Central Power

15.3.1.1 Unification via Applicable Constitutional Norms

The national Constitution is the most powerful source of legal unification and harmonisation. Section 2 of the Constitution recognises the Constitution as the supreme law of the land and provides that law or conduct inconsistent with it is invalid and that the obligations it imposes must be fulfilled. Thus, laws passed by both the central sphere and the various provincial spheres must be consistent with the national constitution. Inconsistent laws will be deemed invalid and set aside by the courts.[33] In Matatiele Municipality,[34] the CC set aside a constitutional amendment and law incorporating the municipality into another province on the basis that the provincial legislature had failed to facilitate public participation in the consideration and approval of the legislation and amendment.[35] The court emphasized that the Constitution entrenches both representative and participatory democracy and the views of the affected citizens ought to have been canvassed prior to the decision being made to incorporate the municipality into the Eastern Cape. Thus all organs of state function within the discipline of the national Constitution and can exercise no power or perform any function beyond that conferred upon them by law.[36]

In addition, section 8(1) of the Constitution is wide-ranging and provides that the Bill of Rights applies to all law and binds the legislature, the executive, the judiciary and all organs of state in all spheres. There is thus a constitutional imperative on all public entities to act in accordance with the provisions of the Bill of Rights.

The national Constitution allows the provinces to promulgate their own constitutions. Provincial constitutions must be adopted by a two-thirds majority of members of the provincial legislature. Before a province brings a constitution into effect, the CC must certify that the text of the provincial constitution is not inconsistent with that of the national Constitution.[37] Yet provincial constitutions may provide for legislative and executive structures and procedures different from that provided for in the national Constitution.[38] Thus far, only the Western Cape has successfully adopted a provincial constitution.[39] The space created for provincial constitutions is very limited; given the detailed regulation of the governance by the national constitution, their usefulness is therefore questionable.

Organs of state are defined widely to include a functionary or institution exercising a public power or performing a public function in terms of legislation.[40] This effectively means that the exercise of public power at both the central and provincial spheres must be in accordance with the provisions of the Bill of Rights and must be consistent with the other provisions of the Constitution.

---

[33] Section 172 of the Constitution.

[34] *Matatiele Municipality and Others v. President of the Republic of South Africa and Others* 2007 (1) BCLR 47 (CC).

[35] Section 118 of the Constitution was interpreted as requiring public participation in the process.

[36] *Fedsure supra* note 31 at para 58.

[37] Sections 142-144 of the Constitution.

[38] Section 143(1) of the Constitution.

[39] Constitution of the Western Cape, 1997 1 of 1998.

[40] Section 239 of the Constitution.

15.3.1.2 Unification via Central Legislation (or Executive or Administrative Rules)

(a) Creating Directly Applicable Norms or Mandating Conforming State Implementing Legislation

Much of the major restructuring of the legal order has occurred at the central sphere with the provinces then passing implementing legislation. As an illustration, reference will be made to education, which is a concurrent competence of both the central and provincial spheres. All the important laws regulating education first emanate from the national legislature. The National Education Policy Act[41] indicates how national education policy is to be determined: the national government must give regard to the relevant constitutional provisions and to a set of directive principles dealing with education. There must also be a prior consultation with a host of bodies, including the Council of Education MEC's[42] representative bodies of educators, students and other stakeholders before the policy is adopted.[43] Subject to the Constitution, section 3 of the Act provides that national policy shall prevail over the whole or part of any provincial policy on education in the event of a conflict. Thus the process, while consultative and inclusionary, is centrally driven. Once decided upon, it is binding on the entire country.

In order to deal with the legacy of segregated education, the central Parliament passed the South African Schools Act (SASA).[44] The primary objective of the Act is to set up a system that will redress past injustices and provide a high quality of education for all learners. It sets in place norms and practices to regulate the delivery of education in South Africa. The SASA envisages that the provincial legislatures will supplement aspects of the Act. For instance, SASA stipulates the processes that must be complied with before a learner can be suspended and expelled from state schools.[45] It then provides that the provincial MEC responsible for education must by notice in the provincial gazette determine the behaviour that would constitute serious misconduct and the procedure for determining culpability in individual cases.[46] SASA provides that every public school shall elect a governing body which is tasked with promoting the best interests of the school. The governing body is required to function in terms of SASA and any applicable provincial law.[47] Other central laws follow a similar pattern. Detailed legislation is enacted and the provinces are invited to implement the norms with supporting or implementing legislation after their input is obtained in respect of the national norms. This is the

---

[41] National Education Policy Act 27 of 1996 ("NEPA").
[42] MEC refers to the Member of the Executive Council of the Province. The Executive Council is the cabinet of the province.
[43] Section 5 of the NEPA.
[44] Act 84 of 1996.
[45] Section 9 of the South African Schools Act 84 of 1996.
[46] Section 9(3) of the South African Schools Act.
[47] Section 18 of the South African Schools Act.

pattern that is adopted in respect of most competencies. With the ANC controlling both the national and all the provincial legislatures, agreed national norms are enforced. In addition, a number of laws passed by the central legislature have been assigned to the provinces for implementation.

(b) Indirectly Forcing State Regulation by Threatening to Take Over the Field in Case of State Inaction

As indicated earlier, the central legislature can legislate over competencies listed in schedule 5 if the requirements of section 44(2) are satisfied.[48] In respect of concurrent competences listed in schedule 4, a national law predominates in the absence of any provincial law. The Constitution also allows national intervention in and the assumption of control over provincial administrations.

Such an intervention is permitted in terms of Section 100 of the Constitution if the province cannot or does not fulfil an executive obligation required of it. Prior to intervening, the province concerned must be put on notice that it is failing to fulfil its obligations and must be required to remedy the situation in a prescribed manner. Interventions must be justified on the basis that it is necessary to maintain essential national standards; maintain economic unity; maintain national security or prevent the province from taking unreasonable action that is prejudicial to the interests of another province or the country as a whole. Certain process requirements are also imposed on the central sphere.[49] Written notice must be given to the National Council of Provinces (NCOP) within 14 days of the intervention. The intervention will cease unless it is approved by the NCOP before the end of a period of 180 days of the intervention. Prior to that period, the NCOP may adopt a motion disapproving of the intervention, in which event the intervention must cease forthwith. In addition, section 139 of the Constitution permits provincial intervention in local government in instances where local government is failing to fulfil its constitutional or legal obligations. In the event of the provincial executive failing to exercise this authority, the central sphere may intervene on the same grounds and subject to the same procedural constraints.[50]

15.3.1.3 Unification via Judicial Creation of Uniform Norms by the Central Supreme Courts

South Africa has a unitary judicial system. The Constitutional Court is the highest court of the land in respect of constitutional matters and may decide issues connected with a constitutional matter.[51] The Supreme Court of Appeals has constitutional jurisdiction and is the highest appellate court in respect of all

---

[48]The contents of section 44(2) of the Constitution are discussed at *supra* note 13 and accompanying text.

[49]Section 110(2) of the Constitution.

[50]Section 139(7) of the Constitution.

[51]Section 167 of the Constitution.

non-constitutional matters.[52] Appeals from the various High Courts are generally heard by the SCA and if there are constitutional issues, a further appeal may be lodged with the Constitutional Court. The High Courts have jurisdiction within their territory of operation, but their legal rulings are applicable throughout the country. Thus an interpretation of the Constitution made by the Natal Provincial Division would be binding on state employees in Cape Town. A single judiciary contributes significantly to the high degree of harmonisation and uniformity of laws that presently exists in South Africa. Section 167(5) of the Constitution requires any declaration of invalidity of a national act, provincial act or conduct of the President made by the High Court and SCA to be confirmed by the CC before it has any force or effect. This confirmatory jurisdiction of the CC allows it to control declarations of invalidity made against the highest organs of state in the country.

15.3.1.4 Unification via Centrally Controlled Means

Over the last 14 years, intergovernmental institutions have been set up to facilitate and coordinate policy development amongst the various spheres of state. The central legislature comprises the National Assembly (NA) and the National Council of Provinces (NCOP). One of the important functions of the NCOP is to promote and protect the interests of the provinces at the central legislature. Different processes are prescribed for the passage of bills affecting the provinces (s76) and in respect of bills not affecting the provinces (s75). In respect of bills not affecting the provinces, the NCOP must consider and pass the bill approved by the NA. In the event that the NCOP rejects or amends the NA's version of the bill, then the NA is only required to reconsider the bill taking into account the version passed by the NCOP.[53] Much greater powers are given to the NCOP when considering bills that affect the provinces. If the version of the bill passed by the NCOP does not accord with the version passed by the NA, then the bill must be referred to a mediation committee comprising nine members of each house. If agreement cannot be reached, then the bill becomes law only if it is passed by a two-thirds majority of the NA.

Determining whether a bill should follow either the section 75 or 76 route is referred to as tagging by Parliament. In Tongoane v Minister of Agriculture, the Constitutional Court held that the test is whether the provisions of the bill substantially affect the interests of the province. This is a much wider enquiry than ascertaining whether the provincial legislatures have concurrent legislative power. A bill must be tagged as a section 76 bill if it substantially affects the provinces even if it deals with matters outside the legislative competence of the provinces.

The President's Co-ordinating Committee comprises the President, the Minister for Provincial and Local Government and the nine provincial premiers. The main function of the body is to develop provincial policy and ensure adequate

---

[52] Section 168 (3) of the Constitution.
[53] Section 75 of the Constitution.

provincial administration of the concurrent functions.[54] Intergovernmental Relations Committees of Ministers and Members of Executive Councils (MINMECS) are advisory executive structures that are concerned with drafting intergovernmental line-function policies and harmonising concurrent legislation. The Forum of South African Directors-General (FOSAD) comprises national and provincial Directors-General.[55] Its main function is to co-ordinate policy implementation between the central and provincial spheres and to advise the national Cabinet and the provincial Executive Councils.

Chapter 3 of the Constitution entrenches the notion of co-operative governance which recognises the distinctiveness, interdependence and interrelatedness of the national, provincial and local spheres of government. This chapter obliges the different spheres not to use their powers in a manner which undermines the effective functioning of another sphere and to co-operate with each other in mutual trust and good faith. The Intergovernmental Relations Framework Act 13 of 2005 was passed in order to establish structures to promote and facilitate intergovernmental relations and to provide mechanisms to settle intergovernmental disputes. The Act creates a number of forums such as the President's Co-ordinating Council, the Premier's Intergovernance Forums and the District Intergovernmental Forums and the purpose of these forums is to foster sound intergovernmental relations in respect of a particular competence or within a geographical area. In addition power exists to form optional forums. Thus the national minister of education can establish a forum dealing with this competence and the various political role-players from the various spheres would be members of this forum. The purpose of these forums is to facilitate effective consultations and they are not deemed to be executive decision making bodies. Finally the Act requires that intergovernmental disputes must be formally declared and attempts must be made to conciliate and mediate them before the parties have recourse to the courts.

15.3.2 Legal Unification Through Formal or Informal Voluntary Coordination Among the Component States (Bottom Up)

15.3.2.1 Unification via Component State Legislatures

The provincial legislatures have little influence on legal unification. As indicated earlier, South Africa was, prior to 1994, a unitary state; and since 1994, the central sphere's legislative enactments have provided the uniform law that has applied throughout the country. The process of legal unification has been most decidedly centrally driven.

---

[54]S. Woolman *supra* note 3 at 14–27.
[55]The director-general is the administrative head of the department.

15.3.2.2 Unification via Component State Judiciary

The concept of a state or provincial judiciary does not exist in South Africa. There is a single judicial system. Magistrates' courts are creatures of statutes with defined criminal and civil jurisdiction. The High Courts are courts of inherent jurisdiction and function within the boundaries of the provinces, but function as part of a national unified judicial system.

15.3.2.3 Unification via Component State Executive Branches

There does not appear to be a co-ordinating structure of the provincial executive branch that excludes the central structures.

15.3.3 *Unification Through Non-state Actors*

Restatements by non-state actors do not occur in South Africa. Model laws are generated by agencies of the central government such as the Law Reform Commission. There are also a number of labour bargaining councils comprising employers and the various recognised trade unions formed with the objective of reaching agreements in order to foster industry peace. These bargaining councils are structured at national and provincial levels and a fair amount of delegated power, especially in respect of resolving disputes, is afforded to the provincial entities. Yet in most instances, the substance and core provisions of the agreement are negotiated at central level.

15.3.4 *The Role of Legal Education and Training on Legal Unification*

Law schools draw students from all parts of the country. Because of South Africa's segregated history, some Law Schools are only able to attract students that reside in close proximity to it. Nonetheless, most of the leading schools attract students from the different provinces.

The focus of legal education is on teaching principles and norms that are applicable throughout the Republic. None of the leading law schools offer courses that focus exclusively on principles that are only applicable within a particular province. Reference may be made to supporting and supplementing provincial legislation in specific areas such as consumer affairs, the regulation of casinos, or planning legislation, but this would be considered as part of a broader reflection on norms that are applicable nationally.

The legal profession is divided into advocates and attorneys. After students graduate from Law School, they are required to do a period of articles (attorneys) and pupillage (advocates) and then write the professional examinations set by the respective professional body that they wish to join. Assessments and testing are centrally controlled with candidates being tested on general law applicable throughout South Africa. The Law Society of South Africa, the oversight body for the attorneys, sets and assesses the admission examinations. The Bar Council of South Africa performs the corresponding function for the advocates. While the examinations are set nationally, they are taken in various centres around the country. The distinction between attorneys and advocates replicates that between solicitors and barristers in the UK.

Law graduates work throughout the country, and both attorneys and advocates are deemed to be officers of the High Court of South Africa. Thus, once a person is admitted, they do not have to write any other examination to practice in another province. Nevertheless, they are required to belong to their provincial societies and to be formally admitted to the court in which they regularly practice. This facilitates oversight and ensures that there is better control of the profession. There is a rule of civil practice that a litigant must have a firm of attorneys based within a certain radius of the court in which he or she is litigating. This often means where attorneys are based beyond the radius of 8 km of the court, they will engage correspondents to serve and receive documents. Advocates appear in all courts in the country.

In addition, the Law Society of South Africa runs nine practical training schools throughout the country. While the schools are situated in the various provinces, the syllabi and examinations are agreed upon and set centrally. After completing their 4 year LLB degrees, students may register for a course of practical training lasting for a period of 6 months. Students that complete the professional training course need to undertake 12 months of articles of clerkship with a firm of attorneys. Those that do not complete the course or choose not to take it must complete a period of 24 months of articles. The tuition offered at the various Schools for Legal Practice prepares them for their practice and procedure examination, which is a necessary prerequisite to practice.

The Bar Council has a programme of lectures for pupil advocates and 1 year period of pupillage with a practising advocate. Upon the completion of the pupillage, candidates write the Bar examination, which is set nationally. Training of judicial officers occurs intermittently, but plans are being made for more co-ordinated training in the future.

15.3.5 *External Influences on Legal Unification*

The signing of international agreements is the responsibility of the national executive.[56] Agreements other than those of a technical nature must be approved by resolution in both the NA and NCOP. Agreements other than self-executing provisions

---

[56]Section 231 of the Constitution.

become law when they are enacted by the central legislature.[57] Customary international law that is consistent with the Constitution or an act of the central Parliament[58] is applicable in the country. Thus international law is absorbed through the central sphere. A conscious effort is made to ensure that laws passed by the central Parliament accord with binding international law principles. Reference is sometimes made in national laws to the need to comply with international obligations. One of the objectives of the Equality Act,[59] a national act which is applicable throughout the country, is to give effect to the obligations specified in the Convention on the Elimination of All Forms of Discrimination Against Women and the Convention on the Elimination of All forms of Racial Discrimination. International law also aids the courts in the interpretation of provisions of the Bill of Rights. Central laws, some of which incorporate principles of international law, are generally binding on provinces. This also contributes to the high degree of legal unification within the country

15.4 Institutional and Social Background

15.4.1 The Judicial Branch

There is a single judiciary which is empowered to declare any law or conduct inconsistent with the Constitution invalid to the extent of the inconsistency.[60] Thus the High Courts, the Supreme Court of Appeals (SCA) and the Constitutional Court (CC) have the power to ensure that lawmakers act within the powers allocated to them by the Constitution. Any challenge to the constitutionality of laws will normally commence in the High Court and declarations of invalidity of national and provincial laws have to be confirmed by the CC before it has any force or effect.[61]

The Constitutional Court has exclusive jurisdiction over disputes between organs of state in the National or Provincial sphere concerning the constitutional status, powers or functions of those organs of state.[62] If the President has concerns about the constitutionality of laws passed by the central legislature, he may refer it to the CC for a decision on its constitutionality.[63] The NA may also submit an application to the CC that is supported by at least one-third of its members to challenge a law within 30 days of being signed by the President.[64]

---

[57] Section 231(3) of the Constitution.
[58] Section 232 of the Constitution.
[59] Promotion of Equality and Prevention of Unfair Discrimination Act 4 of 2000.
[60] Section 172(1) of the Constitution.
[61] Section 172(2) of the Constitution.
[62] Section 168(4) of the Constitution.
[63] Section 79(4) of the Constitution.
[64] Section 80 of the Constitution.

A challenge to a provincial law will commence in the High Court situated within that province and the decision may then be appealed to the SCA and finally to the CC. There are no state courts and differences of interpretation by the various High Courts are resolved on appeal either to the SCA or to the CC. The SCA has both constitutional and non-constitutional jurisdiction and the CC is the highest court in the land in respect of constitutional matters and issues connected with decisions on constitutional matters. Finally, the CC decides whether a matter is a constitutional matter or not. Given the width and range of the Constitution, litigants wishing to convert a matter into a constitutional matter have ample scope to do so. Yet a non-constitutional interpretation of provincial law will be finally determined by the SCA.

15.4.2 Relations Between the Central and Component State Governments

15.4.2.1 Forcing Component States to Legislate

There is no constitutional provision enabling the central legislature to compel the provinces to legislate. Given its own exclusive competencies and the expansive list of concurrent competencies, the central legislature can legislate over all important matters and its law will be applicable and binding in the absence of any provincial law dealing with that subject matter. The executive co-ordination and the dominance of the ANC at both central and provincial levels results in greater co-operation in the respective legislative programmes of the central and provincial legislatures.

15.4.2.2 Execution of Central Government Law

All organs of state within the central sphere and provinces are required to execute central government law to the extent that the law is binding and applicable. For example, all the educators and managers of education in the province are required to execute and implement the South African Schools Act 1996. The Preferential Procurement Policy Framework Act[65] obliges all organs of state to adopt either the 80/20 or 90/10 formula in deciding and implementing their preferential procurement policies. This national law provides that organs of state can allocate no more than 10 points or 20 points out of 100, depending on the value of the contract, to affirmative action and black empowerment criteria in evaluating tenders to supply goods or services to the state. All provincial tender processes have to abide by and be within this national framework, even if the provinces would prefer a higher allocation of points to affirmative action criteria. There are many other similar national laws directly binding on central, provincial and local government officials.

---

[65] Act 5 of 2000.

15.4.2.3 Representation of the Component States at the Central Level

The NCOP, the second chamber of the central legislature, is meant to protect the interests of the provinces. The NCOP comprises a single delegation from each province and each delegation consists of ten delegates.[66] The composition of the delegation must reflect the political composition of the provincial legislature that it represents. The NCOP thus has 90 members as the country has 9 provinces.

15.4.2.4 Appointment of Component State Representatives to the NCOP

The percentage of seats that a party secures in the provincial legislature determines the number of delegates that it is entitled to in the provincial delegation to the NCOP. Thus if a party has 60 % of the seats in the KZN Provincial Legislature, it will be entitled to 6 of the 10 seats allocated to the delegation. The political parties determine who represents them in the NCOP. A formula is prescribed in the Constitution as to how the provincial delegation is to be composed.[67]

15.4.2.5 The Power to Tax

The power of the provinces to levy taxes is extremely limited. In terms of section 228 of the Constitution, the provincial legislature may impose taxes, levies and duties other than income tax, value added tax, general sales tax, rates on property or customs duties. Given these exclusions, provinces have very limited powers to raise taxes. In addition, they are prevented from imposing taxes if to do so may materially and unreasonably prejudice national economic policy, economic activities across provincial boundaries, or the national mobility of goods, services, capital or labour.[68]

Multiple taxation is not an issue in South Africa. Given the far-reaching constitutional limitation on the taxation powers of the provinces, taxes are in effect levied by the central sphere and conflicts have not arisen.

15.4.2.6 Revenue Sharing

The Constitution[69] requires that an Act of Parliament be enacted to provide for the equitable division of revenue raised nationally among the national, provincial and local spheres of government. Each province is entitled to an equitable share of the

---

[66] Section 60 of the Constitution.
[67] Part B of Schedule 3 of the Constitution.
[68] Section 228(2) of the Constitution.
[69] Section 214 of the Constitution.

revenue. In deciding on the allocation, a variety of factors are taken into account, including the national interest, the needs and interests of the national government determined by objective criteria, the need to ensure that provinces and municipalities are able to provide basic services and perform the functions allocated to them and the fiscal capacity and efficiency of the provinces and the municipalities. Parliament and each of provincial legislatures are required to appropriate money for each financial year for the requirements of the state and the province.[70] Each year, the central legislature enacts the Division of Revenue Act in order to equitably divide the revenue raised. The expenditure of funds is regulated by the Public Finance Management Act 1 of 1999.[71]

15.4.3 Other Formal or Informal Institutions for Resolving Intergovernmental Conflicts

In terms of chapter 3 of the Constitution, organs of state have a constitutional duty to foster co-operative governance. The essence of the duty is to avoid legal proceedings and, where possible, to resolve duties through political discussion rather than through litigation. If a court is not satisfied that the duty has been properly discharged, it may refer the matter back to the organs of State involved to exhaust the constitutional requirement to mediate and negotiate fully.

In Uthukela District Municipality,[72] the CC held that it 'will rarely decide an intergovernmental dispute unless the organs of state involved in the dispute have made every reasonable effort to resolve it at a political level.'[73]

15.4.4 The Bureaucracy

The Constitution provides for a public service for the Republic which is to be structured in terms of national legislation.[74] The Public Service Act 1994 is a single piece of legislation which applies to officers and employees employed in the public service by national, provincial and local governments.[75] The terms and conditions of service of the various ranks are determined nationally. Annual pay increments are negotiated nationally and are applicable to public servants employed in all three spheres. The provincial governments are responsible for the recruitment,

---

[70] Section 26 of the Public Finance Management Act 1 of 1999.
[71] The Public Finance Management Act 1 of 1999.
[72] *Uthukela District Municipality and Others v President of the RSA* 2003 (1) SA 678.
[73] Ibid. at page 684.
[74] Section 197(1) of the Constitution.
[75] Section 2 of the Public Service Act 1994.

appointment, promotion, transfer and dismissal of members of the public service.[76] This must be done within the terms of the Public Service Act. Thus an employee leaving a provincial position and assuming a position in national department and vice versa continues to be employed in the public service.

Given the integrated nature of the civil service, there is considerable movement of staff from provincial posts to national government. In my opinion, there is greater willingness for civil servants to move from posts within the provinces to posts in the national government than the other way around.

15.4.5 Social Factors

15.4.5.1 Important Racial, Linguistic, and Cultural Cleavages

During apartheid, white and black people resided in all provinces. Within each province, areas were demarcated for the exclusive use of a specific racial group. The consequence was that local residential and business areas were rigidly segregated. The geographical division of the country into nine provinces has resulted in some provinces having a disproportionate number of residents who identify themselves with a particular linguistic, cultural or tribal group. For instance, in the Eastern Cape, approximately 83.3 % of the residents speak isiXhosa, 9.3 % speak Afrikaans and 3.6 % speak English. By way of contrast, 80.9 % of the residents in KwaZulu-Natal speak isiZulu, 13 % speak English and just over 1 % speak Afrikaans.[77] Thus in the Eastern Cape and in KwaZulu-Natal, the vast majority of residents identify themselves as belonging to the Xhosa or Zulu cultural and tribal groupings.

15.4.5.2 Dispersion of Racial, Cultural and Tribal Groups

Many of the nine provinces have disproportionate percentages of specific cultural or tribal groupings within its boundaries. While whites are dispersed throughout the country, the largest percentage of Indians is found in KwaZulu-Natal and small numbers have settled in various parts of the country. There is a large coloured community in the Western Cape, giving them a significant political voice in the running of the province. People identifying themselves either as Xhosa or Zulu reside throughout the country. The population of the country is about 46 and a half million. Ethnically, the population is divided as follows: Africans 79.0 %; Whites 9.6 %; Coloureds 8.9 %; and Asians 2.5 %.[78] The Inkatha Freedom Party, whose membership is predominantly Zulu, argued for a maximum devolution of

---

[76]Section 197(4) of the Constitution.
[77]SA Yearbook 2006/2007 (GCIS) 8–26.
[78]*Africa South of the Sahara 2006* (36th edition) 1081.

power to the provinces during the constitutional negotiations. In addition to their political interests being best served by a strong federal system, they were concerned that a strong ANC government at national level would dominate the constituent provinces.

The fear that the provincial administrations will promote parochial tribal interests led to measures such as the national override provisions. Given the ANC's dominance of both the national and provincial governments, it is unlikely that racial, ethnic, religious or linguistic cleavages will become manifest in the foreseeable future as pivotal policy decisions are likely to be centrally driven for a while yet.

The lives of many South Africans are comprehensively regulated by norms and principles of African Customary law. Customary law applies in many rural or traditional areas within the various provinces. Aspects of customary law differ markedly from legal principles generally applicable in the country. Much of it is unwritten and is overseen by traditional leaders functioning within traditional structures, including courts. The Constitution recognises the institution, status and role of traditional leaders as a part of customary law, provided that these principles are in accordance with the Constitution.[79] Courts are obliged to apply principles of customary law provided that they are applicable and consistent with the Constitution and any relevant legislation. In Bhe,[80] the CC declared invalid customary norms that prevented intestate succession by women and extra-marital children on the basis that they were unfairly discriminated against. Much more dramatically, the CC recently held in Shilubana[81] that traditional authorities had the duty to develop their own law in line with the Constitution. In the past, the principle of male primogeniture prevented a woman from becoming chief of the tribe. The CC held that the tribal authority could develop the existing customary law in order to achieve equality and allow women to ascend to the chieftainship. Thus the process has started of testing customary law against the provisions of the Constitution. This will no doubt result in many of the more egregious customary norms that discriminate on the basis of gender or sex being changed. It will also result in the constitutional values having broader application and relevance.

15.4.5.3 Asymmetry in Resources

There is significant asymmetry in natural resources, development, wealth and education between the component provinces. Guateng, by far the richest province, is the site of the gold and diamond trade and is the industrial heartland of the country. Gauteng contributes 33.3 % to the total GDP while Mpumalanga, Limpopo, North-West and Northern Cape contribute 6.8, 6.7, 6.3 and 2.2 % respectively to the total

---

[79]Section 211 of the Constitution.

[80]*Bhe v. Magistrate, Khayelitsha* 2005 (1) BCLR 1 (CC).

[81]*Shilubana and Others v. Nwamitwa* CCT 3/07.

GDP.[82] This significant difference in wealth is reflected in the development levels of the various provinces. The poorest are heavily subsidized by the wealthier provinces. The better job opportunities, schools and universities are found in the wealthier provinces and it is often a challenge to secure able and competent personnel to fill administrative positions in the poorer and less developed provinces. There is thus more robust political discourse in the wealthier provinces. The ANC has initiated a debate on whether the number of provinces should be reduced in order to ensure better delivery of services.

15.5 Conclusion

Despite some federal features, South Africa exhibits a very high degree of uniformity of laws between the constituent parts. The present order emerged from a strong unitary system with complete uniformity of laws. The apartheid order was driven by the central legislature and the provincial and municipal components were indisputably subservient. The negotiating parties opted for a more balanced and nuanced division of powers between the central and provincial spheres of government. Real and defined power was given to the provincial sphere of government. In the early days of the new dispensation, the Western Cape was controlled by the New National Party and KwaZulu-Natal by the IFP. All the other provinces and the central government were firmly controlled by the ANC. On a number of occasions, both the Western Cape and the KZN provincial governments tested the boundaries of provincial power. It appeared that we were about to witness robust assertions of jurisdiction by the provinces for the first time. The ANC's subsequent electoral victories in the Western Cape and KZN, which saw it gaining control over these provincial legislatures, resulted in the embryonic assertion of provincial power being short lived.

Nevertheless, the DA's victory in the 2009 elections in the Western Cape will enable that province to assert its constitutional competences more robustly and it is likely that there will be more contestation between the spheres of government.

After the ANC gained control over the nine provincial legislatures, it sought to drive and achieve its vision of a developmental state from the central sphere. The rigid party discipline resulted in nationally agreed policies being implemented uniformly at both national and provincial levels. During this period South Africa was a de facto unitary state with the necessary constitutional basis, capacity and potential to develop federal features. Various administrative and executive mechanisms contributed to this uniformity. In addition, the national legislature engaged in a process of frenetic law making as it sought to transform the apartheid society into one which more accorded with the vision of the new Constitution. Correspondingly, very few laws were passed by the provincial sphere. Finally,

---

[82]Ibid.

the existence of a centrally structured judiciary interpreting a supreme constitution binding on all organs of state has further contributed to the high levels of uniformity in laws that we experience.

In the last few years some significant developments have occurred. At a political level, the opposition has gained control of the Western Cape and the City of Cape Town. There have also been judgments of the Constitutional Court affirming the importance of respecting the jurisdictional integrity of the various spheres. It seems that this nascent federal system is beginning to stir and awaken.

Chapter 16
The Trend Towards Homogenization in the Spanish 'State of Autonomies'

Aida Torres Pérez

16.1 Overview

The current system of territorial allocation of powers in Spain was established by the 1978 Constitution. In the aftermath of Franco's dictatorship, the territorial model of political decentralization became one of the most controversial issues in the process of constitution drafting. Self-government claims voiced from several regions, mainly the Basque Country, Catalonia, and Galicia, could not be ignored. The 1978 Constitution set up an open-ended model. The Constitution did not define the component states, or their powers.[1] The Constitution recognized the right to autonomy and established basically two proceedings for enacting the corresponding Autonomy Statute, and thus for achieving the status of "Autonomous Community" (hereinafter component states).[2] The Autonomy Statute is the foundational norm of the component states and hence the supreme norm within the state legal

---

Professor of Constitutional Law at Pompeu Fabra University (Barcelona). My thanks go to Dolors Feliu, Victor Ferreres, Maribel González Pascual, Rafael Jiménez Asensio, Hèctor López Bofill, Ramon Riu, and Alejandro Saiz Arnaiz for our discussions on these topics. The usual disclaimers apply. This work was submitted for publication in December 2009.

[1] Cruz Villalón, P., "La estructura del Estado o la curiosidad del jurista persa", *Revista de la Facultad de Derecho de la Universidad Complutense*, núm. 4, 1982; Fossas, E., "Asimetría y plurinacionalidad en el Estado autonómico", en Fossas, E. y Requejo, F., *Asimetría federal y Estado plurinacional*, Trotta, Madrid, 1999.

[2] These two proceedings are known as "fast-track" and "slow-track" proceeding to autonomy, because the level of autonomy that could be achieved at the beginning depended on the proceeding that was followed. Ruipérez Alamillo, J., *Formación y determinación de las Comunidades Autónomas en el ordenamiento constitucional español*, Tecnos, Madrid, 1991; López Guerra, L.,

A. Torres Pérez (✉)
Law Department, Pompeu Fabra University, Barcelona, Spain
e-mail: aida.torres@upf.edu

system.[3] After the Constitution's approval, the model of political decentralization was extended to the whole territory, which became organized in 17 Autonomous Communities[4] (and two autonomous cities).[5]

The Spanish Constitution contains the list of powers reserved to the central government. Beyond this list, component states may assume the powers they choose by listing them in the respective Autonomy Statute. Although this model is potentially asymmetrical regarding the allocation of powers among the component states, in practice the states have tended to assume equivalent levels of power.[6] The allocation of powers between the central government and the component states follows two criteria: subject matter and function.[7] The central government and the states might be granted exclusive or concurrent powers. In case of exclusive powers, the corresponding level of government enjoys all functions over a specific subject matter. In case of concurrent powers, each level of government is allocated a specific function with regard to the same subject matter: legislation, basic legislation, or execution. For example, regarding labour law, the central government has legislative power, while execution is left to the states; regarding environmental law, the central government has the power to pass basic legislation, while the states have the power to develop basic legislation and to execute the laws.

One can identify four main periods regarding the development of the Spanish territorial model.[8] Over the first period (1979–1985), the Statutes of Autonomy of each component state were enacted. Public institutions were set up and began to function. The 1981 "Autonomy Agreements" brought homogeneity regarding the states' institutional design. Second, between 1985 and 1999, there was a trend towards homogenizing state powers. The 1992 Autonomy Agreements led

---

Derecho Constitucional. Los poderes del Estado. La organización territorial del Estado, Tirant lo Blanch, Valencia, 2007, pp. 315–319.

[3] Aguado Renedo, C., *El Estatuto de Autonomía y su posición en el ordenamiento jurídico*, Centro de Estudios Constitucionales, Madrid, 1996; Torres Muro, I., *Los Estatutos de Autonomía*, Centro de Estudios Políticos y Constitucionales, Madrid, 1999; Castellà Andreu, J. M., *La función constitucional del Estatuto de Autonomía de Cataluña*, Institut d'Estudis Autonòmics, Barcelona, 2004.

[4] Andalucía, Aragón, Asturias, Baleares, Canarias, Cantabria, Castilla-La Mancha, Castilla y León, Cataluña, Extremadura, Galicia, Madrid, Murcia, Navarra, País Vasco, la Rioja, Comunidad Valenciana.

[5] Ceuta and Melilla.

[6] AA.VV., *Uniformidad o diversidad de las Comunidades Autónomas*, Institut d'Estudis Autonòmics, Barcelona, 1995.

[7] Viver Pi-Sunyer, C., *Materias competenciales y Tribunal Constitucional. La delimitación de los ámbitos materiales de las competencias en la jurisprudencia constitucional*, Ariel, Barcelona, 1989; Carrillo, M., "La noción de materia y el reparto competencial en la jurisprudencia del Tribunal Constitucional", *Revista Vasca de Administración Pública*, núm. 36, 1993.

[8] Argullol Murgadas, E. (dir.), *Federalismo y autonomía*, Ariel, Barcelona, 2004, p. 91; AJA, E., *El Estado autonómico. Federalismo y hechos diferenciales*, Alianza Editorial, Madrid, 1999, pp. 58–78.

to the transfer of new powers to the states and to the amendment of several Autonomy Statutes to incorporate these new powers. The result was a considerable homogenization of the model of political development.[9] Third, from 1999 to 2004, there was a tendency towards centralization, particularly since 2000, when the Popular Party achieved an absolute majority. Finally, from 2004 to the present, several component states have amended their Autonomy Statutes in order to improve the level of self-government. This last wave of amendments has elicited a profound debate about the territorial model of political decentralization as well as much political tension. Shortly after Catalonia amended its Autonomy Statute in 2006, the Statute was challenged before the Constitutional Court by the representatives of the Popular Party in Congress, arguing that a significant number of provisions clashed with the federal Constitution.[10] The decision by the Constitutional Court was for long awaited and finally issued in June 2010 (STC 31/2010). Regarding the definition of the several types of competences, the Constitutional Court mainly applied previous case-law without taking up the challenge of rethinking how competences are functionally defined.[11]

The Spanish system is sometimes regarded as a federal state. Hardly anybody in Spain, however, would characterize it as a true federation. Several reasons militate against such a characterization; among others, they are: the component states cannot amend the respective Autonomy Statutes without the approval by the central Parliament; component states may not intervene in the process of constitutional amendment; the Senate does not actually represent the states, and hence the states do not fully participate in the legislative process at the central level; and the judiciary is not decentralized.[12] In sum, the Spanish "autonomous" system is a *sui generis* model in comparative law.

---

[9] Aja E., *El Estado autonómico...*, *op. cit.*, pp. 69–74; Álvarez Conde, E., "El ejercicio del derecho a la autonomía y la configuración del Estado autonómico", en *El funcionamiento del Estado autonómico*, MAP, Madrid, 1999.

[10] The Autonomy Statute of Catalonia has been challenged by the parliamentary representatives of the Popular Party and the *Defensor del Pueblo* (the Spanish Ombudsman). Other amended Autonomy Statutes, such as the Statute of Andalucía, which have included identical or very similar provisions, have not been challenged before the Constitutional Court.

[11] The Constitutional Court decision was rendered after the submission of this work. Since then many articles have been published commenting upon this. Among others, see the monographic issued by *Teoría y Realidad Constitucional*, núm. 27, 2011, and by the *Revista d'Estudis Autonòmics i Federals*, núm. 12, 2011.

[12] Fossas, "Asimetría y plurinacionalidad...", *op. cit.*, pp. 284–285; Requejo, F., *Multinational federalism and value pluralism*, Routledge, London, 2005, pp. 82–83.

16.2 The Federal Distribution and Exercise of Lawmaking Powers

16.2.1 Central Government Legislative Powers

The Constitution contains the list of powers allocated to the central government in article 149.1. Pursuant to this article, the central government's *exclusive* powers extend to the following subject matters, among others: nationality, immigration, the right of asylum; international affairs; defence and the Armed Forces; administration of justice; customs, tariffs, and foreign trade; monetary system, general finance and public debt; external health; harbours of general interest, airports of general interest, control of the aerial space, transit and transport, meteorological service and aircrafts' registration; railroads and land transportation through the territory of more than one state; postal services and telecommunications; aerial and submarine wires, and radio-communication; public works of general interest; protection of the cultural, artistic, and monumental heritage of Spain against exportation and exploitation; museums, libraries, and archives belonging to the central government without prejudice to their management by the states; public security, without excluding the creation of state police bodies according to the respective Autonomy Statute; statistics for national purposes; and authorization for convoking popular consultations via referendum.

The Constitution also allocates *concurrent* powers to the central government with respect to several subject matters. It allocates to the central government either general legislative power or the power to pass basic legislation. Firstly, *legislative* power includes the competence to pass parliamentary legislation and the power to enact executive regulations to develop legislation. The central government holds legislative powers over subject matters such as: commercial, criminal, procedural, and labour law; intellectual and industrial property, pharmaceutical products, forcible expropriation, regulation and concession of water resources and projects when waters run through more than one state, the authorization of electrical installations when their use affects more than one state or when the transportation of energy goes beyond the borders of one state, and the conditions for obtaining, issuing, approving, and standardizing academic and professional degrees.

Secondly, the Constitution may grant to the central government the power to pass *basic legislation* on several subject matters. The concept of "basic legislation" is elusive and has been interpreted through constitutional case law in an expansive way. Basic legislation should set a common floor for all component states in order to secure the general interest. Basic legislation includes parliamentary acts, but also, by way of exception, executive regulations when they are necessary to complement the basic legislation.[13] The Constitution grants the central government powers to enact basic legislation concerning a number of subject matters: contractual obligations, credit, banking, and insurances; the general planning of the economic activity; promotion and general coordination of scientific and technical research; health; social security; administrative contracts and concessions; the regime of responsibility of all public administrations; environmental protection, without prejudice to the states' capability to establish additional standards of protection; woodlands, forestry projects, and livestock trails; mining and energy systems; press, radio, and television, and all means of social communication in general; and education.

The most frequently used constitutionally specified source authorizing central regulation is the clause regarding "the bases and coordination of the general planning of economic activity" (art. 149.1.13). The practical use of this clause is similar to the so-called "commerce clause" in the US. Article 149.1.13 has been interpreted broadly by the Constitutional Court. As a result, this clause has allowed the central government to regulate subject matters within state powers, as long as there is a connection with the economic activity, such as housing, tourism or agriculture, among others.

16.2.2 State Legislative Powers

The Spanish Constitution does not expressly allocate powers to the component states. States may take all powers that have not been reserved to the central government by the Constitution (*principio dispositivo*).[14] Hence, state powers are those listed in the respective Autonomy Statute.

The Constitution includes a list of competencies that all states may have assumed at the foundational moment, according to article 148.1.[15] Depending on the proceeding followed to enact the Autonomy Statute, certain states could only acquire the powers included in the list of article 148.1. These states needed

---

[13]Tornos Mas, J., "La delimitación constitucional de las competencias. Legislación básica, bases, legislación de desarrollo y ejecución", en *El funcionamiento del Estado autonómico*, MAP, Madrid, 1999.

[14]Fossas, E., *Principio dispositivo en el Estado autonómico*, Marcial Pons, Madrid, 2007.

[15]Article 148.1 includes, for instance: the organization of self-governing institutions; regulation of the territory, zoning, and housing; public works of interest to the Autonomous Community in its own territory; railways and highways whose itinerary runs completely within the territory of the Autonomous Community; refuge harbours, recreational harbours, airports, and generally those which do not carry out commercial activities; agriculture and livestock woodlands and forestry; activities in matters of environmental protection; museums, libraries, and music institutions of interest to the Autonomous Community; monuments of interest to the Autonomous Community; promotion of culture, research, and, when applicable, the teaching of the language of the Autonomous Community; promotion and regulation of tourism within its territorial area; social assistance.

to wait for 5 years to expand this list.[16] These were the so-called "slow-track" states (art. 146).[17] "Fast-track" states could assume all powers not reserved to the central government from the very beginning (art. 151.1).[18] At present, article 148 is irrelevant, as all the "slow-track" states have extended their powers after waiting the requisite 5 years.

Component states may only acquire *exclusive* powers, including legislative and executive powers, over subject matters that are not reserved to the central government.[19] Component states have tended to assume the following exclusive powers: organization of their self-governing institutions; regulation of the territory, zoning, and housing; railways and highways whose itinerary runs completely in the territory of the state; public works of interest to the state in its territory; and social assistance, among others. In general, subject matters listed in article 148 of the Constitution were taken as exclusive powers by the states.

With regard to *concurrent* powers, when the central government has jurisdiction to legislate, component states may assume the power to *execute* central government legislation. It should be recalled, as mentioned above, that the central legislative power includes parliamentary acts and developing governmental regulations. Therefore, the states may only execute central norms and adopt self-organizing regulations.[20] Component states have tended to assume executive power, for instance, over the following subject matters: prisons, labour law, or intellectual and industrial property.

When the central government holds the power to pass basic legislation, component states may assume the power to pass *developing legislation* and to *execute* central basic legislation. They have tended to do so in fields such as credit, banking, and insurance; mining and energy systems or environmental protection.[21]

The exercise of central power cannot prevent the states from exercising their concurrent powers. Thus there is no pre-emptive effect. Each level of government

---

[16] According to article 148.2: "After five years, through the reform of their Statutes, the Autonomous Communities may expand their competences within the framework established in Article 149".

[17] Most of the states followed the "slow-track" proceeding (Aragón, Asturias, Baleares, Canarias, Cantabria, Castilla-La Mancha, Castilla y León, Extremadura, Madrid, Murcia, la Rioja, and Comunidad Valenciana).

[18] The states that followed this proceeding, which was more complex, were: Andalucía, Cataluña, Galicia, and País Vasco. Navarra followed a specific procedure (Additional Disposition 1 of the Constitution).

[19] Jiménez Asensio, R., *La Ley autonómica en el sistema constitucional de fuentes del derecho*, Marcial Pons, Madrid, 2001.

[20] Jiménez Asensio, R., *Las competencias autonómicas de ejecución de la legislación del Estado*, IVAP, Madrid, 1993.

[21] The 2006 amendment to the Autonomy Statute of Catalonia partly redefined the types of concurrent and executive powers (articles 111 and 112). These clauses have been challenged before the Constitutional Court claiming that they clash with the Constitution and previous Constitutional Court case-law.

has specific functions with regard to concurrent subject matters, and the central government cannot go beyond its attributed functions. In other words, the central government may not infringe functions allocated to the component states or prevent the states from exercising their powers.

In practice, however, the concept of "basic legislation" has been interpreted broadly. As a result, the central government might intrude in fields of state power when enacting basic legislation. The line separating "basic legislation" from "developing legislation" is not clear. As a result, the expansive exercise of the power to pass basic legislation can have the effect of preventing the states from fully exercising their developing powers in practice. The Constitutional Court has jurisdiction to police the central government to ensure that it respects the limits of basic legislation. The Court has recognized, however, that the central government has considerable leeway in this context. At the same time, component states do not need to wait for the central government to enact basic legislation to exercise the respective powers to pass developing legislation. Yet, once the central government legislates, component states must adapt their legislation to central basic laws.[22]

In practice, the fields in which states have passed a greater number of laws are the following: public institutions, education, culture, agriculture, livestock and fishing, social assistance, environment, zoning and housing, public works, industry, commerce, media, health, and tourism. One might say that the most productive and innovative states have been Catalonia (which holds an undisputed first place in this regard), Galicia, Madrid, Valencia, Andalucía, and Canarias.[23] Also, states that enjoy specific powers have legislated on the linguistic system and on private law. The most important areas in which central and component state regulations coexist are those in which the central government holds the power to pass basic legislation and states have jurisdiction to develop and execute central legislation; environmental law, or education are examples. Also, central and state legislation coexist when economic activity is somehow involved and the central government invokes the constitutional clause authorizing it to act in this field.

---

[22]Fernández Farreres, G., "El sistema de distribución de competencias entre el Estado y las Comunidades Autónomas en la jurisprudencia constitucional: cuestiones resueltas, problemas pendientes", *Asamblea. Revista Parlamentaria de la Asamblea de Madrid*, núm. 2, 1999.

[23]See Porras, A., Gutiérrez, F., y Morillo, M. L., "La actividad legislativa de los parlamentos autonómicos, 1980–2000: Agenda legislativa y mapa normativo", en Subirats, J., y Gallego, R., *Veinte años de autonomías en España*, CIS, Madrid, 2002, p. 170, 194–195. The "Instituto de Derecho Público" publishes since 1989 a report on the Autonomous Communities (*Informe Comunidades Autónomas*), which includes information about the legislative activity of each Autonomous Community.

16.2.3 Principles Relating to the Interaction Between Central and State Legal Systems

The Constitution allocates residual powers to the central government (art. 149.3). The system works as follows: the Constitution lists the powers reserved to the central government in article 149.1. In their respective Autonomy Statutes, component states may take any powers not reserved to the central government. Then, the remaining powers not taken by the component states belong to the central government by virtue of the residual clause (art. 149.3). In practice, this clause is of very little use because, over time, component states have tended to assume all powers not reserved to the central government.

The constitutional principle to resolve conflicts between central and component state law is the "competence principle." There is no hierarchy between central government and component state legislation. Hence, in case of conflict, the question is whether the competence corresponds to the central government or to state authorities, according to the Constitution and the respective Autonomy Statute.

The Constitution is the supreme norm of the land and thus it is hierarchically superior to the Statutes of Autonomy. At the same time, Statutes of Autonomy complement the Constitution regarding the system of allocation of powers in Spain. In order to have the whole picture of how power is vertically allocated, both the Constitution and the respective Statute of Autonomy need to be taken into account.

16.3 The Means and Methods of Legal Unification

16.3.1 The Exercise of Central Power (Top Down)

The Constitutional Court has interpreted several *constitutional principles* as, in some way, reinforcing the powers of the central government and thus limiting the exercise of state powers. These constitutional principles are the following: unity (art. 2), solidarity (art. 2, 138.1), free movement of people and goods throughout the territory (art. 139.2), subordination of all wealth to the general interest (art. 128.1), and economic order and market unity (art. 131.1, 138.2, 139.2).[24] In addition, constitutional norms protecting rights must be interpreted and applied in the same way throughout the country. The central government has powers to legislate on the basic conditions guaranteeing the equality of all Spaniards in the exercise of their rights and fulfilment of their constitutional duties (art. 149.1.1).[25]

---

[24] Viver Pi-Sunyer, C., *Materias competenciales y Tribunal Constitucional*, op. cit., pp. 106–120.

[25] Pemán Gavín, J., *Igualdad de los ciudadanos y autonomías territoriales*, Civitas, Madrid, 1992; Cabellos Espiérrez, M. A., *Distribución competencial, derechos de los ciudadanos e incidencia del derecho comunitario*, Centro de Estudios Políticos y Constitucionales, Madrid,

The most common means of legal unification is central government legislation, including both legislative acts and governmental regulations. The central government, however, may not mandate that component states pass implementing legislation. In particular, when the central government enjoys the power to pass *basic legislation*, developing state legislation must abide by it, but the states are free to decide how and when to exercise their developing power. In any event, through basic legislation, the central government can establish the goals that must be achieved by developing state legislation. This is an important way of harmonization because the Constitutional Court has broadly interpreted the scope of "basic" legislation.

In addition, according to the Constitution, several subject matters need to be regulated through "*organic law*". The difference between organic laws and ordinary laws is that the former need to be approved by the absolute majority of Congress. Formally, organic laws are not a means of allocating powers to the central government. However, since this kind of law may only be passed by the central Parliament, the subject matters reserved to organic laws are ultimately reserved to the central government. This is true, for instance, for the general electoral regime and the development of fundamental rights. In addition, any powers that states may take regarding these fields must comply with the respective organic laws enacted by the central government.

The use of the *spending power* by the central government has turned out to be a very controversial issue. The Constitutional Court has held that it cannot be a mechanism to take over state power. In the 1990s (STC 13/1992), constitutional case law curtailed the central government's traditional policy of using the spending power to induce state policy-making. Through the exercise of its spending power, the central government had tended to regulate the conditions to obtain public funds in fields under state jurisdiction. The Constitutional Court argued that the spending power does not grant new powers to the central government over subject matters allocated to the states. Thus, the capacity to intervene through the spending power on a certain field must be limited to the specific functions enjoyed by the central government in that field. Yet, the Constitutional Court has admitted that even when the subsidized field corresponds to the exclusive power of the states, the central government may still grant public funding. In those cases, the central government shall limit itself to assigning an amount of money to a certain activity in a general way, without setting specific goals, conditions, or processes to obtain those funds. In practice, however, even exclusive state powers have been conditioned by the central government spending power.[26]

2001; González Pascual, M. I., *El proceso autonómico ante la igualdad en el ejercicio de los derechos constitucionales*, IVAP, Oñati, 2007.

[26]Fernández Farreres, G., "La subvención y el reparto de competencias entre el Estado y las Comunidades Autónomas", *REDC*, núm. 38, 1993; Fernández Farreres, G. (dir.), *El régimen jurídico de las subvenciones. Derecho español y comunitario*, Consejo General del Poder Judicial, Madrid, 2007; Carrasco Durán, M., "Repercusión de los Estatutos de Autonomía en la actividad de fomento estatal", a Agudo Zamora, M., *El desarrollo del Estatuto de Andalucía*, Centro de

The central government may not take over a field that is reserved to the component states, even in the case of state inaction or state action that does not conform to centrally specified standards. It is for the Constitutional Court to resolve the conflicts regarding the allocation of powers. First, with regard to state inaction, the central government can bring an action before the Constitutional Court, but the central government cannot force the states to regulate by threatening to take over the field. In the past, it was admitted that the central government could pass legislation as "supplementary" law, which would apply in case of lack of state legislation. In the mid-1990s (STC 118/96, 61/97), however, the Constitutional Court held that the central government could only legislate in those fields over which it had specific powers. Thus, the central government was prevented from passing developing legislation by arguing that it would only apply as supplementary law, if all states had assumed the power to develop basic legislation regarding that specific field. Second, with regard to state action clashing with centrally specified standards, the central government can bring an action before the Constitutional Court. The Constitutional Court will decide whether the state has unduly infringed central legislation.

Exceptionally, the Constitution establishes that if a component state does not comply with its constitutional or legal obligations, or if its action seriously impinges upon the general interest, the central government may take the *necessary measures to force the state* to comply with its obligations and to protect the general interest (article 155). Before it can do so, however, the central government should require the non-complying state's President to abide by the law. Furthermore, the Senate is required to approve any necessary measures by absolute majority. In practice, this provision has never been used.

The Constitutional Court has the ultimate authority to interpret the Constitution and the Statutes of Autonomy. Through its case law, the Court has delineated the scope of central government and state powers. Its interpretation of constitutional clauses allocating powers is binding upon all judges and public authorities. Constitutional interpretation might allow for a broader or narrower scope of action for the central government to pass uniform legislation. For instance, the appeal to the "general interest" has allowed for a broad interpretation of the power to enact "basic legislation", narrowing the scope of state powers in crucial areas such as education. Also, the broad interpretation of article 149.1.13 (general planning of economic activity) has allowed the central government to act in fields under state power such as housing, tourism, or agriculture (STC 152/88, 75/89, 14/89). This has been an avenue for furthering harmonization among the states.[27]

Estudios Andaluces, Sevilla, 2008; Sánchez Serrano, L., "Ayudas comunitarias y distribución de competencias entre el Estado y las Comunidades Autónomas", *Noticias de la Unión Europea*, núm. 118, 1994; Torres Pérez, A., *La projecció de la potestat subvencional sobre la distribució competencial*, Institut d'Estudis Autonòmics, Barcelona, 2011.

[27] Fernández Farreres, G., "El sistema de distribución de competencias entre el Estado y las Comunidades Autónomas en la jurisprudencia constitucional", *op cit*.

In several fields, the Constitution allocates to the central government a *coordinating power*. This term has been interpreted by the Constitutional Court as the competence to establish mechanisms for integrating the multiple state systems within the central system. These integration mechanisms seek to secure a degree of homogeneity in the face of potential diversity of state regulations over the same field, such as regulations of health or scientific and technical research. In practice, these mechanisms take on a number of forms: they may mandate disclosure of certain information, establish forums for sharing information, set criteria that component states must follow, or create public central registries. The Constitutional Court has also admitted that the power to legislate might include the power to coordinate.[28]

16.3.2 Formal or Informal Voluntary Coordination Among the Component States (Bottom Up)

State legislators are likely to follow each other. Since the states have tended to take the same kind of powers, they are also prone to look to one another when acting upon them. As a result, the degree of state diversity in practice is lower than could be expected. There is a clear *trend towards harmonization* in the fields under state power. In particular, after one state decides to innovate in a certain field, the others tend to follow suit. Hence, momentary diversity produced when certain states pass innovative legislation is diluted in a bottom up homogenizing process.[29] State legislation is not identical, but the degree of similarity is high. This phenomenon is known as "*isomorfismo*." For instance, state power over zoning is exclusive. In this area, states have tended to emulate previous regulations, except where the central government has invoked its authority to legislate. Still, some differences regarding terminology and procedures remain.

At the same time, component states might pursue different agendas: Catalonia, Andalucía, Valencia, and Canarias tend to legislate more profusely on education and culture. The Basque Country, Navarre, Asturias, and Cantabria are more prone to legislate on public works, zoning, housing, and industry. Galicia, Castilla y León, and Extremadura tend to regulate agriculture, livestock, and fishing. In general, there is a tendency to expand legislation on social assistance and issues related to the welfare state.[30]

The *collaboration* among component states, both bilateral and multilateral, is minimally regulated by the Constitution (art. 145.2), which refers to the Autonomy Statutes for further details. The Constitution establishes two kinds of agreements: "collaborating conventions" and "cooperation agreements". The main difference between them is that the latter require the central Parliament's authorization while

---

[28]López Guerra, L., *Derecho Constitucional . . .*, *op. cit.*, pp. 384–386.
[29]Porras, Gutiérrez y Morillo, "La actividad legislativa . . . ", *op. cit.*, pp. 168–169, 191 y ss.
[30]Porras, Gutiérrez y Morillo, "La actividad legislativa . . . ", *op. cit.*, pp. 195–201.

the former only require that information be provided to the central Parliament. Generally, state governmental officials handle state-to-state collaborative negotiations. Yet, pursuant to the respective Autonomy Statutes, the adoption of collaborating conventions or cooperation agreements might also require the participation of the state Parliament. In that case, parliamentary participation might take several forms: information-sharing, authorization, approval, ratification, or supervision.[31] In any event, state parliaments only become involved at the end of the process.[32]

In practice, it is rare for the component states to formally subscribe to state-state collaborating conventions. Until 2006, only 25 had been published, and they relate to fields such as forest fires, road planning and construction, or environmental protection.[33] Most of the existing agreements are bilateral (rather than multilateral) and they are aimed at solving specific problems between neighbouring component states, limiting any unifying effect they might otherwise have. An explanation for the reluctance to subscribe to multi-state collaborative agreements might also lie in the lack of political will or in the lack of a tradition of state multilateral negotiation.[34] States have tended to make use of informal means of collaboration to avoid central parliamentary control, but these agreements are not published.[35] In any event, horizontal collaboration does not seem to be a relevant way of unification.

By contrast, bilateral conventions between the central government and component states have been much more frequent (numbering more than 8,000), even though they lack constitutional recognition. In practice, the central government tends to sign the same model-convention with several component states bilaterally. The predominance of bilateral relationships between the central government and component states over agreements between the member states themselves has been regarded as a flaw from the standpoint of state self-government.[36]

The most common means of voluntary cooperation are the so-called *sectorial conferences*, which are not regulated by the Constitution. These bilateral conferences are composed of a ministry of the central government and the respective state authorities, depending on the subject matter under discussion, such as transportation, science and technology, healthcare, environmental protection, etc. Since these bodies lack decision-making powers, they are fora for exchanging

---

[31] González García, I., *Convenios de cooperación entre Comunidades Autónomas. Una pieza disfuncional de nuestro Estado de las Autonomías*, Centro de Estudios Políticos y Constitucionales, Madrid, 2006, pp. 107–111.

[32] Analysts are very critical of how horizontal collaboration is regulated. See García Morales, M. J., "Las relaciones intergubernamentales en el Estado Autonómico: estado de la cuestión y problemas pendientes", en AA.VV., *Las relaciones intergubernamentales en el Estado autonómico*, Centro de Estudios Políticos y Constitucionales, Madrid, 2006, pp. 41–44, 84–89.

[33] González García, *Convenios de cooperación... op. cit.*

[34] González García, *Convenios de cooperación... op. cit.*; AJA, *El Estado autonómico... op. cit.*, p. 207; García Morales, "Las relaciones intergubernamentales...", *op. cit.*, pp. 33–40.

[35] García Morales, "Las relaciones intergubernamentales...", *op. cit.*, pp. 44–47.

[36] Aja, *El Estado autonómico... op. cit.*, pp. 199–204.

information, reaching agreements about common lines of action, or discussing formal conventions. They are weakly institutionalized and their effectiveness varies considerably.[37] The ultimate productivity of sectorial conferences may also vary depending on which central government ministry has responsibility for convoking and presiding over the conference.[38] In 2004, the Conference of Presidents, a reunion of the central government and state Presidents, met for the first time. Since then, it has met three times, but the experience has been rather disappointing.

The field in which voluntary coordination among component states has been most productive is matters involving the European Union. The Conference for European Communities Affairs has functioned in practice since 1988, and it was formally established in 1997. During 2005, it held 11 horizontal meetings without the participation of the central government. There is no actual legal regulation of these "horizontal sectorial conferences," which are very common in federal states, such as Germany.

16.3.3 The Influence of EU Law on Legal Unification

The process of European integration plays a central role in legal unification. With the accession to the European Union (EU), Spain transferred sovereign powers to a supranational organization. Powers transferred to the EU included powers previously allocated to both the central government and the states. Consequently, EU legislation has the general effect of enhancing unification in areas previously under the domain of the states.

At the same time, the need to comply with obligations coming from the EU can also promote legal unification in practice. The Constitutional Court has held that EU integration cannot be a way to circumvent the domestic allocation of powers. Thus, implementation of EU law must correspond to the level of government constitutionally established for regulating the subject matter at stake. In particular, the central government cannot claim the power to implement EU law merely on the basis of its international responsibility vis-à-vis the EU. The Constitutional Court has admitted, however, that the central government may assume a coordinating function to secure compliance with EU law. Therefore, in practice, the transfer of powers to the EU and compliance with EU legislation has had a considerable unifying effect.[39]

---

[37] García Morales, "Las relaciones intergubernamentales...", *op. cit.*, pp. 89–92.

[38] Aja, *El Estado autonómico... op. cit.*, pp. 140, 211–215.

[39] Albertí Rovira, E., *Las Comunidades Autónomas en la Unión Europea*, Centro de Estudios Políticos y Constitucionales, Madrid, 2005; Bustos Gisbert, R., "La ejecución del derecho comunitario por el gobierno central", *Revista Vasca de Administración Pública*, núm. 67, 2003.

16.4 Institutional and Social Background

16.4.1 The Judicial Branch

The Constitutional Court is vested with the power to monitor whether the central government or the component states have exceeded the lawmaking powers allocated by the Constitution or the Autonomy Statute, respectively. Indeed, the Constitutional Court holds the ultimate power to interpret both the Constitution and the Statutes of Autonomy. Autonomy Statutes belong to the so-called "constitutionality block" (*bloque de constitucionalidad*), which is the group of norms that the Constitutional Court must take into consideration when deciding about the allocation of powers.

Both the central government and the component states can bring an action before the Constitutional Court complaining that another unit exceeded its powers.[40] Case by case, the Constitutional Court has delineated the content and limits of central government and component states' competencies.[41] Over time, the number of cases before the Constitutional Court regarding the allocation of powers has fluctuated. In the first years under the 1978 Constitution, both the central government and component states were particularly belligerent; this is especially true for Catalonia and the Basque Country. Between 1984 and 1988, an average of over 100 cases a year were brought before the Constitutional Court. During the 1990s, the conflicts notably diminished (30–40 cases per year). At that time, the Socialist Party (PSOE) in government did not have an absolute majority in Congress and needed the support of national minority parties. Conflicts increased again from the end of the 1990s until 2004, which is the period of time (1996–2004) governed by the Popular Party (PP). Aside from a fluctuating caseload, it sometimes takes the Constitutional Court up to 8 years to issue a decision.[42] The backlog of cases, and the long delays in resolving them, is one of the main problems facing this Court.

Before filing an action before the Constitutional Court, the central and the state government involved may meet in a so-called "bilateral commission of cooperation" in order to reach an agreement. The law regulating the Constitutional Court acknowledges this mechanism and extends the period of time to file a constitutional challenge against a legislative act (*recurso de inconstitucionalidad*) if the conflicting parties have previously attempted to reach an agreement through this bilateral commission. When the conflict involves a governmental regulation (*conflicto de competencias*), prior to bringing the case before the Court, component state governments must, and the central government may, require from the other that the norm or act allegedly exceeding powers be derogated or annulled. Around

---

[40]García Roca, J., *Los conflictos de competencia entre el Estado y las Comunidades Autónomas (una aproximación desde la jurisprudencia constitucional)*, Centro de Estudios Políticos y Constitucionales, Madrid, 1993.

[41]Aja, *El Estado autonómico*... *op. cit.*, p. 135.

[42]Aja, *El Estado autonómico*... *op. cit.*, pp. 131–133.

40–45 % of the conflicts are solved through these extra-procedural mechanisms of negotiation and hence they do not reach the Constitutional Court.

The territorial decentralization of power does not affect the structure of the judiciary, which is unitary. As a result, there are no state courts. "Superior Courts of Justice" (*Tribunales Superiores de Justicia*), one sitting in each component state, have specific functions regarding the application and interpretation of component state law, but they are integrated with the unitary judicial system.

16.4.2 The Senate

The Spanish Parliament is composed of two houses: Congress and Senate. The Senate is defined by the Constitution as the house of territorial representation (art. 69). Nevertheless, neither its composition nor its functions allow the Senate to actually represent the component state governments. The system for electing the senators is hybrid. First, there are four senators for each province.[43] These senators are directly elected by the citizens of each province. Second, component states shall appoint one senator, plus an additional one for each one million people living in that state. These senators are appointed by state parliaments. As a result, only around 20 % senators represent the states. The rest are elected by the citizens on the basis of the provinces. Hence, the Senate fails to deliver state territorial representation.[44]

In addition, only exceptionally does the Senate hold specific functions regarding the territorial allocation of powers, such as the approval by absolute majority of measures to force the component states to fulfil their constitutional obligations (art. 155 Constitution). Moreover, the Senate has a secondary role in the legislative process. Even though the Senate can amend or veto legislative texts, Congress may reject these amendments by simple majority, and may override the Senate's veto by absolute majority (or simple majority after 2 months from the first vote). Therefore, Congress always has the last word. The role of the Senate has been the object of a long-standing debate. Analysts are very critical of the current situation and many have advocated for the Senate's reform.[45] Yet, there is no political consensus to amend the Constitution in this regard.

16.4.3 The Bureaucracy

The central government's civil service is separate from that of each state. Since the Statutes of Autonomy were approved, it has taken several years to build civil service

---

[43]There are 50 provinces in Spain.

[44]Aja, *El Estado autonómico... op. cit.*, pp. 144–145.

[45]Aja, *El Estado autonómico... op. cit.*, pp. 145–147, 215–221; AA.VV., *La reforma del Senado*, Senado-CEC, Madrid, 1994; Alberti Rovira, E., *La reforma constitucional del Senado*, Barcelona, 1996.

systems within the states.[46] The Constitution allocates to the central government the power to pass basic legislation regarding the public administration system and the civil servants' statutory regime, which shall secure a common treatment for all citizens. The central government has legislated extensively in this field, with the goal of unifying the systems and guaranteeing a homogeneous position to all civil servants.[47] Component states may assume powers to regulate the state civil service regime, but state legislation must abide by the central government basic legislation.[48] In the first years, the creation of state civil services was based upon the transfer of civil servants from the central government system.[49] The Law 12/1983 on the autonomous process designed the general framework for the transfer of civil servants. This legislation secured the recognition of rights and other benefits that civil servants had at the moment they were transferred.[50] Beyond these transfers, there is little lateral mobility in practice.

16.4.4 Tax Power

Both the central government and component states enjoy tax power. The Constitution recognizes the principle of state financial autonomy, which means that the states need to have sufficient financial resources to develop their powers (art. 156.1). The same constitutional clause holds that state financial autonomy must be understood according to the principle of coordination with the central government treasury and the principle of solidarity among all Spaniards. The tax system is minimally regulated by the Constitution and developed by the Organic Law on the Financial System of the Autonomous Communities (LOFCA). The Constitution lists the financial resources of the component states in article 157.1:

(i) "State taxes". Component states may create their own taxes. States are, however, banned from taxing the same events already taxed by the central government, and they must respect constitutional principles such as the principle of economic capability. The Constitutional Court has distinguished between the object and the event being taxed: the object is defined as the source of wealth; the taxable event is a more restricted concept referring to the specific circumstances that justify creating the tax. The same object might be the basis of different taxable

---

[46]Castells Arteche, J.M., *Proceso de construcción y desarrollo de la función pública autonómica*, Madrid, 1987.

[47]Albertí Rovira, E., *Manual de Dret Públic de Catalunya*, Marcial Pons, Barcelona, 2000, pp. 350–357

[48]Mauri Majós, J., "La distribució de competències en matèria de funció pública", *Autonomies*, núm. 24, 1999; Lliset-Tornos, *La funció pública de les Comunitats Autònomes*, Barcelona, 1985.

[49]Castells Arteche, *Proceso de construcción..., op. cit.*

[50]Albertí Rovira, *Manual de Dret Públic... op. cit.*, pp. 351-354; AJA, *El Estado autonómico... op. cit.*, pp. 234–235.

events. Hence, states may tax the same object as the central government, as long as they do it for different reasons. For instance, the Constitutional Court ruled that Andalucía's tax on "under-used lands"[51] did not infringe the principle prohibiting multiple taxation. Although this state tax and the central government tax on property target the same object (the land), the taxable event is different: the central government taxes ownership of all kinds of goods, whereas the state taxes the insufficient use of the land in terms of the profits that could be obtained.[52]

(ii) "Taxes transferred by the central government in total or in part; extra-charges upon state taxes and other forms of participation in the central government revenue". Over time, the central government has transferred to the states the revenue of central taxes, either completely or in part. Moreover, in several cases, regulative powers have also been transferred to the states, for instance, regarding income tax, property tax, and inheritance and donations tax.[53]

(iii) "Transfers from the central budget, taking into consideration the public services provided by each component state and the need to secure a minimum level of essential services throughout the whole territory". Indeed, one of the most controversial issues regarding the financial system is how to determine the criteria to calculate the percentages of participation of each state in the national budget.

(iv) "Transfers from the "Interterritorial Compensation Fund" (*Fondo de Compensación Interterritorial*)". Resources from this Fund are distributed by the central Parliament among the component states. These resources are aimed at neutralizing economic divergences among the states, and giving effect to the principle of solidarity.

(v) Other resources coming from state properties or operations of credit.

In practice, component states have not created truly separate tax systems, and their main financial resources come from central government revenue sharing. Although the Constitution establishes that states may create their own taxes, increasing the tax pressure has a political cost and thus it is not common.[54] Among state taxes, one can mention the following: Extremadura's tax on under-used irrigation lands, Asturia's tax on under-used agrarian lands, Andalucía's tax on under-used land, Islas Baleares' tax on premises affecting the environment, and Valencia's tax on residual waters.

---

[51]This tax targets the insufficient use of rural lands in terms of the failure to obtaining the profits considered to be optimum for that region by the legislator.

[52]Checa Gonzalez, C., *Los impuestos propios de las Comunidades Autónomas*, Aranzadi, Navarra, 2002.

[53]Ruiz Almendral, V., *Impuestos Cedidos y corresponsabilidad fiscal*, Tirant lo Blanch, Valencia, 2004; Mora Lorente, M.D., *Impuestos cedidos: implicaciones internas y comunitarias*, Tirant lo Blanch, Valencia, 2004; Villarin Lagos, M., *La cesión de impuestos estatales a las Comunidades Autónomas*, Lex Nova, Valladolid, 2000.

[54]Zornoza, J., *Los recursos de las CCAA*, Madrid, 1996.

The Basque Country and Navarra enjoy a different tax system based on their "historical rights": the so-called "economic agreement" (*concierto económico*). According to the "economic agreement", these component states collect their own taxes, and later they transfer a specific amount to the central government to compensate for the services they receive.[55]

16.4.5 Social and Legal Asymmetries

In Spain, there are important historical and linguistic cleavages among the component states. Several states enjoy a distinct national identity on the basis of their particular history, culture, and language. These component states are the Basque Country, Catalonia, and Galicia. During Franco's dictatorship, public power was totally centralized and languages other than Spanish were banned. In the transition to democracy, these regions claimed for self-government. The territorial model was one of the most controversial issues during the Constitution-drafting process. Two options were on the table: either recognizing a certain degree of autonomy of these regions, or designing a general decentralized model for the whole country. The latter option prevailed.

At the same time, the Constitution acknowledged some distinct elements regarding specific states, such as different official languages and the power to keep, modify, and develop historically rooted private law.[56] At present, Euskera, Catalan, and Galician are co-official languages in the respective state territories, as it is established by the respective Autonomy Statute. Euskera is official in the Basque Country and Navarra (only in some areas), Catalan in Catalonia, Valencia, and the Balearic Islands, and Galician in Galicia.[57] These states have legislative powers to regulate the linguistic regime within their territories. In addition, Aragón, Catalonia, Navarra, Islas Baleares, Galicia, and, in the Basque Country, Vizcaya and Álava have kept and developed their respective historical private legislation regarding fields such as family law, inheritance, donations, and specific contracts.[58]

In some of these states, there are political parties that do not exist in the rest of the territory, and claim a higher level of self-government, such as *Convergència i Unió* (*CiU*) and *Esquerra Republicana* (*ERC*) in Catalonia, and the *Partido Nacionalista*

---

[55]Lambarri, C. and Larrea, J. L., *El Concierto Económico*, IVAP, Oñati, 1995.

[56]López Aguilar, J. F., *Estado autonómico y hechos diferenciales*, Centro de Estudios Políticos y Constitucionales, Madrid, 1998; AA.VV., *Asimetría y cohesión en el Estado autonómico*, MAP, Madrid, 1997; García Roca, F. J., "Asimetrías autonómicas y principio constitucional de solidaridad", *Revista Vasca de Administración Pública*, núm. 47, 1997.

[57]Sigúan, M., *España plurilingüe*, Alianza Editorial, Madrid, 1992; MILIAN, A. (coord.), *El plurilingüisme a la Constitució española*, Institut d'Estudis Autonòmics, Barcelona, 2009; AJA, *El Estado autonómico... op. cit.*, pp. 162–169.

[58]Martínez Vázquez de Castro, L., *Pluralidad de derechos civiles españoles*, Civitas, Madrid, 1997., Aja, *El Estado autonómico... op. cit.*, pp. 169–172.

Vasco (*PNV*) in the Basque Country. Some of these parties include among their goals the independence of the state territory, such as *Esquerra Republicana* and *Partido Nacionalista Vasco*.

In addition, there are asymmetries in wealth and economic development among the component states.[59] The Basque Country, Catalonia, and Madrid are more economically developed and industrialized than other states. These economic asymmetries are relevant for the redistribution of wealth pursuant to the solidarity principle and revenue sharing in general. One of the most important asymmetries acknowledged by the Constitution relates to the tax system, as mentioned before. The Basque Country and Navarra enjoy an asymmetrical tax system, the so-called "economic agreement", on the basis of their "historical rights". In contrast to the general system, these component states collect taxes and pass on a specific amount of money to pay for the services provided by the central government.[60] The tax system in Canarias also shows some peculiarities. Catalonia has for a long time demanded a system close to the Basque "economic agreement", which would allow for greater autonomy over its financial resources.

From a territorial standpoint, the insular character of two component states introduces some asymmetries. The territories of Baleares and Canarias are each composed of a group of islands. The Constitution recognizes the *Cabildos* and *Consejos insulares* as specific public institutions for local government in Canarias and Baleares, respectively (art. 141.4).[61] Also, the historical territories of the Basque Country have their own institutions, which have exclusive powers to regulate the local electoral system.[62] Finally, there are two autonomous cities on the African continent: Ceuta and Melilla. They hold a particular status within the system of political decentralization.

16.5 Conclusion

Generally, the Spanish system of political decentralization shows a significant trend towards harmonization. This is due to several factors at the supranational, central, and state level. Diversity is mainly found in those fields in which the Constitution accommodates asymmetries within specific states, such as language, the tax system, some areas of private law, and public institutions.

The tendency towards legal harmonization has been bolstered by the process of European integration. Both central and state powers have been transferred to the EU. Thus, subject matters that could have been regulated differently across the states

---

[59] Agranoff, R., "Asymmetrical and Symmetrical Federalism in Spain. An Examination of Intergovernmental Policy", in de Viliers, B., *Evaluating Federal Systems*, Martinus Nijhoff Publishers, the Netherlands, 1994, pp. 75–78.

[60] Aja, *El Estado autonómico... op. cit.*, pp. 172–180.

[61] Aja, *El Estado autonómico... op. cit.*, pp. 180–184.

[62] Saiz Arnaiz, A., "La competencia de los territorios históricos del País Vasco en materia de régimen electoral municipal", *Revista Española de Derecho Constitucional*, núm. 82, 2008.

are now under EU jurisdiction. At the same time, although the implementation of EU law corresponds to either central or state authorities according to the domestic allocation of powers, the central government retains a coordinating power to secure compliance with EU law. In addition, EU law tends to leave little discretion to the member states for its implementation, and even directives have tended to be more and more detailed.

In addition, the central government has furthered unification through several mechanisms. First, the broad interpretation of "basic legislation" has allowed the central government to expand its action over areas under concurrent state power. Also, the broad interpretation of the clause on the general planning of economic activity has allowed the central government to intrude on fields of otherwise exclusive state jurisdiction. The power of the central government to pass organic laws is a further source of legal unification. Finally, in practice, the central government's spending power constitutes a mechanism to influence state policy-making.

There is potential for diversity in fields regarding both the powers taken by the states and the powers that they choose to exercise. In practice, however, there is a clear trend towards harmonization in both fields. As explained, states are free to take all powers not reserved to the central government by the Constitution. When the first Statutes of Autonomy were enacted, the degree of diversity among the states was considerable. Yet, since the 1992 Autonomy Agreements, the reform of several Statutes led towards homogenizing state powers across the component states. In 2006, Catalonia amended its Autonomy Statute to improve the level of self-government. Soon thereafter, other states followed suit. Thus, the degree of diversity introduced is being partly diluted. Still, some differences remain, regarding, for instance, the power to create a state police body or the regulation of language.

Although there are no big differences regarding component state powers, diversity could come from dissimilar legislation across the states. Nevertheless, when certain states innovate, the others tend to emulate them. Thus, the degree of diversity momentarily introduced tends to diminish over time. As a result, even in areas of exclusive powers, there is a tendency towards legal harmonization.

The highest degree of diversity is found in those fields in which the Constitution accommodates asymmetries among the states regarding language, tax, distinct public institutions, or private law. Such asymmetries tend to be found in those states with a distinct national identity. These states aim at deepening the legal recognition of asymmetric powers as a translation of their *de facto* asymmetry.[63] Admittedly, the model for the territorial allocation of powers designed by the 1978 Constitution pursued a double goal: decentralizing political power and accommodating self-government claims by national territories. The system has worked particularly well at decentralizing power, but it has proven not to be fully satisfactory for those regions with a distinct national identity. Basically, the Basque Country and Catalonia have been pressing to change the *status quo*. The proposals from nationalist

---

[63]Fossas, "Asimetría y plurinacionalidad...", *op. cit.*

parties range from a true federal (asymmetrical) system to the independence of specific states. The amendment of Catalonia's Autonomy Statute in 2006, which was challenged before the Constitutional Court, and the surrounding tensions have brought about a heated debate over the need to rethink the current constitutional design.

Chapter 17
Federalism and Legal Unification in Switzerland

Eleanor Cashin Ritaine and Anne-Sophie Papeil

17.1 Overview

The Swiss Confederation is a rather young state. Even though the foundation of Switzerland took place as far back as 1291,[1] the Swiss Confederation as such was only established much later. In 1648, following the treaty of Westphalia, Switzerland became independent from the Roman-German Empire. In 1803, the name "Swiss Confederation" was definitely adopted,[2] and the country was given full international status following the 1815 declaration of "perpetual neutrality of Switzerland".[3] From 1815 to 1848, however, the Swiss Confederation was not truly a sovereign state but rather only a community of Cantons, each of which had its own sovereignty. The legal basis for a federal state was created in 1848 with the adoption of the first federal Constitution (September 12th, 1848). This federal structure is maintained

---

[1] Pacte fédéral (August 1st 1291) uniting the Cantons of Uri, Schwyz, Nidwald to be found at: Quellenwerk zur Entstehung der Schweizerischen Eidgenossenschaft Abt. 1, Urkunden Bd., 1 Aarau 1933 and http://www.admin.ch/org/polit/00056/index.html?lang=fr (last visited on 06.03.09).

[2] Mediationsakte 19 February 1803, "Act of Mediation" by Napoleon Bonaparte, see J. Biedermann, "Chartes, pactes et traités de la Suisse", Lausanne 1915.

[3] «Acte de reconnaissance et garantie de la neutralité perpétuelle de la Suisse et de l'inviolabilité de son territoire» drafted by Charles Pictet de Rochemont (November 20th, 1815), CPJI, série C, n. 17–1, vol. II, 1929, pp. 1190ss.

E. Cashin Ritaine (✉)
Ducrest and Heggli Law Firm, Geneva, Switzerland
e-mail: eleanor.cashin-ritaine@wanadoo.fr

A.-S. Papeil
University of Neuchâtel, Rue du Rocher 20, 2000 Neuchatel, Switzerland
e-mail: anne-sophie.papeil@unine.ch

today under the 1999 Constitution[4] and is reflected in three tiers of government: The *Confederation* or federal government, the *Cantons* and the *Communes*.

The highest governmental tier of the Swiss Confederation is the central, i.e., federal government. The term "Confederation" is misleading: a confederation, in modern political terms, is usually limited to a permanent union of sovereign states for common action in relation to other states.[5] However, the denomination of "Confederation" has been maintained due to translation difficulties,[6] even though Switzerland technically is a federal state.[7] In German, the Confederation is called "*Schweizerische Eidgenossenschaft*" which does not relate to a similar word in French, Italian or even English. The term *Eidgenossenschaft* could be translated as a "*sworn brotherhood*" and describes the historical foundation of Switzerland as it was created in 1291 by the representatives of three Cantons swearing their allegiance to a common State.[8]

The 26 Swiss Cantons are the middle tier of government. They are the component states of the Confederation. The Cantons did not emerge out of a central state due to decentralisation; on the contrary, the Cantons were sovereign and independent states which decided in 1848 to create the Confederation.[9] The Cantons thus transferred their sovereignty to the Confederation in a bottom-up manner. Article 3 of the 1999 Constitution states that "[t]he Cantons are sovereign insofar as their sovereignty is not limited by the Federal Constitution; they shall exercise all rights which are not transferred to the Confederation". In this context, the meanings of the words "sovereignty" and "sovereign" are not the classical ones, e.g., Cantons do not have what German authors call the "*Kompetenz-Kompetenz*",[10] meaning the right to

---

[4]Federal Constitution of the Swiss Confederation of 18 April 1999 (RO 1999 2556, modified as of 16 December 2005 FF 2005 6793).

[5]The Oxford English Dictionary, vol. II-C, Oxford reprinted 1978. "A permanent union of sovereign States for common action in relation to externals".

[6]T. Fleiner, "Switzerland: Constitution of the Federal State and the Cantons", in Lidija R. Basta Fleiner/T. Fleiner (eds.), *Federalism and Multiethnic States, The Case of Switzerland*, 2ᵉ ed., Bâle/Genève/Munich 2000, p. 103.

[7]A confederation is most likely to feature three differences from a federation: There are no real direct powers of the Confederation in comparison to a federal government: many confederate decisions are only implemented by member-state legislation. Decisions are not taken by simple majority but by special majorities or even by consensus or unanimity (every member has a veto). Changes of the constitution, which usually takes the form of a treaty, require unanimity.

[8]A citizen of each Canton swore on August, 1st 1291 on a small mountain called "Grütli": *"we will be a one and only nation of brothers ... "* This leads to the term confederation ("*Eidgenossenschaft*").

[9]To be complete, the joining of Cantons came in stages: 1291: Uri/Schwyz/unterwalden (split up into: Obwald/Nidwald); 1332: Luzern; 1351: Zurich; 1352: Zug/Glarus; 1481: Freiburg/Solothurn; 1501: Basel (1833 split up into: Basel Stadt/Basel Land)/Schaffhausen: 1513: Appenzell (1597 split up into: Appenzell Ausserrhoden/Appenzell Innerrhoden); 1803: Sankt-Gallen/Aargau/Thurgau/Ticino/Vaud; 1815: Valais/Neuchâtel/Genève; 1979: Jura.

[10]Schweizer in, St. Galler Kommentar zu Art. 3 BV, Rz. 7, Schulthess 2008.

define in their constitutions the distribution of tasks between federal government and themselves. Cantons therefore only have a subsidiary or indirect competence.[11]

The Cantons have kept their intrinsic nature of a sovereign state (*statehood*),[12] their own constitutions, and most of their political autonomy, yet only the federal state is a sovereign in respect to international law. As a result, the study of the Swiss federal system is different from the study of other federations throughout the world, the Cantons still exercising sovereign powers within the Confederation in relation to each other, whereas only the Confederation, as such, has full and direct international sovereignty.[13]

On the final and lowest tier of government, one finds the Municipalities (*Communes*) which compose the Cantons.

Like most modern states, Switzerland has enacted a strict separation of powers between the executive, the legislative, and the judicial branches of government. This separation exists within each tier of government, up from the Municipalities to the central level.

17.2 The Federal Distribution and Exercise of Law-Making Power

The Swiss main legislative body is the Federal Assembly (*Assemblée Fédérale*) which is composed of two Chambers: the National Council (*Nationalrat* or *Conseil National*) and the Council of States (*Ständerat* or *Conseil des Etats*).[14] When the two Chambers are united for a common session, they form the United Federal Assembly (*Assemblée Fédérale Unie*). However, many legislative acts are also enacted at the cantonal level.

The National Council has 200 members. In this Council, the representation of the Cantons is proportionate to the size of their population. However, according to Article 149 al. 4 of the Constitution, each Canton has a right to at least one seat. Zurich with its large population has 34 seats, whereas Uri and Glarus, Obwalden, Nidwalden, Appenzell Outer Rhodes, and Appenzell Inner Rhodes are entitled to just one representative each.[15]

---

[11]T. Fleiner-Gerster, "Problèmes de la souveraineté intérieure et extérieure", in T. Fleiner-Gerster/S. Hutter (eds.), *Federalism and Decentralization*, Fribourg 1987, p. 64; T. Fleiner/A. Misic, "Föderalismus als Ordnungssprizip der Verfassung", in D. Thürer/J.-F. Aubert/J.-P. Müller (eds.), *Verfassungsrecht der Schweiz*, Zürich 2001, p. 436.

[12]Comp. "République de Genève", "Etat de Vaud", "République de Neuchâtel"... A similar system can be found in Germany: "Freistaat Bayern", "Freistaat Sachsen-Anhalt"...

[13]Even though the Cantons may, in certain fields, notably in taxation matters, conclude international treaties with neighboring states (Cst., *art 56*).

[14]The National Council represents the overall population and the Council of States, the member states of the Confederation, i.e. the Cantons.

[15]See the document "legislative power" on the website www.admin.ch (last visited on 06.03.09).

In this legislative organ, the election of the members is based on proportional representation in respect to the population of each Canton. This results in giving smaller parties a higher chance of being elected than they would have if the election system were a winner-take-all majority system.[16]

The Council of States (*Ständerat, Conseil des Etats*) has 46 members.[17] Each Canton elects two representatives, except for Obwalden, Nidwalden, Appenzell Outer Rhodes, Appenzell Inner Rhodes, Basle-Land and Basle-City which only have one representative.[18] The rules governing the election of the members of the Council of States is purely a cantonal matter (Cst., *Art. 150 al. 3*).

The process leading to the adoption of a new law is complex and often lengthy. This is a fundamental characteristic of the Swiss law making process which seeks, above all, *consensus* at all stages. It takes at least 12 months to enact legislation, but in extreme cases, the procedure has lasted as long as 12 years,[19] typically if the case is contested. The law making procedure[20] can encompass up to 15 steps. Yet, this is only the case when the opinions of the two Chambers of Parliament differ.

The Constitution provides for the general law making powers of the Confederation but also for the powers of the Cantons. Title III of the Constitution deals with the structure of the Federation and the relationship between its components. About 50 very detailed articles of the Constitution relate to the distribution of power. This great number of articles can be explained by the complex system of direct democracy, which requires the consent of each Canton for each new federal competence.[21]

It is a basic principle of the relationship between the Confederation and the Cantons "to divide before to collaborate".[22] Yet often the distinction between Federal and cantonal matters cannot be clearly drawn.[23]

As a general rule, the Confederation has authority in all areas in which it is empowered by the Federal Constitution. Article 42 provides that "*The Confederation shall accomplish the tasks which are attributed to it by the Constitution*".

---

[16]W. Linder, "Swiss Democracy: Possible Solutions to Conflict in Multicultural Societies", 2nd ed., London/New York 1998, p. 45.

[17]Cst., art. 150 al. 1.

[18]Cst., art. 150 al. 2.

[19]Typically, the law providing national and regional development was initiated in 1972 and entered into force in 1980 (LAT, RS 701). The law on civil liability has been under discussion since 1988.

[20]T. Fleiner/A. Misic/N. Töpperwien, "Swiss Constitutional Law", The Hague 2005, p. 101; see the figure 3.4 in W. Linder, op. cit. p. 123.

[21]T. Fleiner, "Swiss Confederation", in R. Blindenbacher/A. Ostien (eds.), *Dialogues on Distribution of Powers and Responsibilities in Federal Countries*, Global Dialogue on Federalism Booklet Series # 2, Montreal 2005, p. 270.

[22]J. F. Aubert/P. Mahon, "Petit Commentaire de la Constitution fédérale de la Confédération suisse du 18 avril 1999", Zurich 2003, p. 382.

[23]B. Knapp, "Kompetenzverteilung und Zusammenwirken der Kantone", in D. Thürer/J.-F. Aubert/J.-P. Müller (eds.), *Verfassungsrecht der Schweiz*, Zürich 2001, §29, pp. 457–472.

Numerous articles of the Constitution grant specific powers to the Confederation, yet the content and the scope of each of these powers can vary from one field to another, as in some fields the Cantons may also have competing powers. The division of powers is mandatory so that the Cantons and the Federation cannot agree to change it. There are four different kinds of powers in Switzerland: exclusive powers, competing powers, powers limited by principles, and parallel powers.

Exclusive powers are the competences which plainly exclude cantonal action whenever this competence is allocated to the Confederation, even before any laws are enacted in that field. This kind of competence is less important today because the domains in which it applies have already been legislated, e.g., money, customs, and postal services. The Confederation thus has competences in the fields of economy,[24] agriculture,[25] defence,[26] social and health issues,[27] supply of energy and other essential goods,[28] media and communication,[29] immigration,[30] civil and criminal law.[31] Additionally, the organization of the federal courts is determined exclusively by federal legislation.[32]

Competing competences between Cantons and the federal government are the rule in Switzerland. Cantonal competence, however, ends when the Federation enacts laws in a specific field.

Powers limited by principles (or guidelines) are a variety of competing competences where the Confederation provides for broad principles that the Cantons must respect. For example, the Federation establishes the principles for energy and the Cantons must comply with those principles even if they are competent in this matter.[33] Some principles enacted in the Constitution are thus directly imposed on

---

[24]Private economic activity (art. 95); Competition Policy (art. 96); Banking and Insurance (art. 98); Monetary Policy (art. 99); Policy on Economic Development (art. 100); Foreign Trade (art. 101); Gambling (art. 106).

[25]Agriculture (art. 104); Production, importation, refining and sale of Alcohol (art. 105).

[26]Weapons and Military Material (art. 107).

[27]Consumer Protection (art. 97); Promotion of Construction and Ownership of Housing (art. 108); Landlord and Tenant (art. 109); Labour (art. 110); Social Security (art. 111); Old age, Survivors' and Disability Insurance (art. 112); Employee Pension Plans (art. 113); Unemployment Insurance (art. 114); Family Allocations and Maternity Insurance (art. 116); Health and Accident Insurance (art. 117); Protection of Health (art. 118); Medical Assistance to Procreation and Gene Technology in the Human Field (art. 119); Medical Transplantation (art. 119 a); Gene Technology in the Non-Human Field (art. 120); Residence and Domicile of Foreigners (art. 121).

[28]Transportation of Energy (art. 91); Supply of Essential Goods and Services (art. 102); Weights and Measures (art. 125).

[29]Postal and Telecommunication services (art. 92); Radio and Television (art. 93).

[30]Residence and Domicile of Foreigners (art. 121).

[31]Civil Law and Civil Procedure (art. 122); Criminal Law and Criminal Procedure (art. 123).

[32]The most important legal sources are the Federal Supreme Court Act (LTF 17/06/2005, RS 173.110, RO 2006 1205.), the Federal Criminal Court Act (LTPF 04/10/2002, RS 173.71, RO 2003 2133) and the Federal Administrative Court Act (LTAF 17/06/2005, RS 173.32, RO 2006 2197).

[33]FF 1997 I 253.

the Cantons, e.g., the cantonal laws must respect the principle of proportionality, the principle of equality, and they must not restrict personal liberties such as the freedom of expression.[34]

Competences are parallel when there is no exclusion of either the Confederation or the Cantons, e.g., in the matter of direct taxes.[35]

Each article of Title III of the Constitution is used to regulate different fields of law and thus empowers the federal government to enact federal legislation. Important federal acts in the area of constitutional law include: the Federal Act on the Organization of the Federal Judiciary of 16 December 1943[36]; the Federal Swiss Citizenship Act of 29 September 1952[37]; the Federal Act on the Proceedings of Federal Parliament and the Form, Publication, and Entry into Force of Its Acts of 23 March 1962[38]; the Federal Administrative Procedure Act of 20 December 1968[39]; the Federal Political Rights Act of 17 December 1976[40]; and the Federal Act on the Organization of the Federal Council and the Federal Administration of 21 March 1997.[41]

Public law is the most important area of regulation for the central government. More specifically, important matters within its competence are the matters of public transportation, communications, and economic issues. In private law, intellectual property is an important matter of legislation. Yet, depending on the political objectives of the Federal Council, the fields of law-making can change drastically from one legislative period to another.

For example, in 2006 and 2007, many regulations concentrated on school and education, on telecommunications, on environmental law, and on the transfer of cultural property. The 2007–2008 legislative period, by contrast, focused on corporate governance, company law, and implementation of the Schengen-Dublin Agreement on the free movement of citizens into Switzerland. In 2009, due to the recession and the banking scandals involving banking major UBS (originally for Union Bank of Switzerland), the focus was on regulating financial services.

Despite the great number of powers of the federal state, the Cantons still have autonomous legislative power as well the right to self-organisation.[42] According to Article 3 of the Constitution, the sovereignty of the Cantons is exercised to the extent it is not limited by the federal Constitution. This provision gives the residual powers to the Cantons, which in turn often confer these powers on the Municipalities (*Communes*).

---

[34] Cst., arts. 5, 8, 10 and 16.
[35] Cst., art. 128 and 129.
[36] RS 171.11.
[37] RS 141.0.
[38] RS 171.111.
[39] RS 172.021.
[40] RS 161.1.
[41] RS 172.010.
[42] Cst., art. 47.

17 Federalism and Legal Unification in Switzerland

Each Canton has its own constitution, but in order to ensure the democratic nature of these constitutions and their conformity with federal law, the Federal Assembly has to approve any amendments to cantonal constitutions.[43] Yet, there is no uniform model law of the Confederation in this respect.

The following matters are in the exclusive power of the Cantons: the implementation of federal law (Cst., *art. 46*); the drafting of cantonal constitutions (Cst., *art. 51*); determination of the power of Communes (Cst., *art. 50*); education at all levels (Cst., *art. 62*); culture (Cst., *art. 69*); languages (Cst., *art. 70*); and church and state relationship (Cst., *art. 72*). In many Cantons,[44] main regulations focus on public law, principally on the organisation of local authorities, schools, telecommunications, and land use planning. Cantons administer their finances, and make decisions regarding their development based on their specific cultural heritage.

The Cantons are allowed to act even within those areas that are in the competence of the central government as long as the latter has not made use of its power.[45] Nevertheless, when the federal government begins to legislate in such an area, the powers of the Cantons are totally or partially restricted retroactively.[46]

As mentioned, in some areas, both cantonal and federal powers coexist. The most important areas of this nature include telecommunications and land use planning, schools, and culture in general. Moreover, the Confederation and the Cantons have competing powers in the areas of personal income tax, corporate income, and capital tax.

In the field of their competences, the Cantons are, in principle, free to accomplish their tasks however they wish.[47] They must, nevertheless, comply with all sorts of federal, constitutional or legislative mandates, e.g., Article 62 II on education or Article 72 II on maintaining public peace between religious communities.

A special feature of Swiss law pertains to the organisation of cantonal justice. As of now, cantonal courts are essentially organized in accordance with cantonal law. The Cantons regulate the appointment and remuneration of judges, the partitioning of the Canton into judicial districts, the rules on admittance to the bar and to many legal professions, etc. Nevertheless, the Cantons must observe the requirements of federal law on a variety of organizational issues.

A number of principles have been developed to avoid or solve conflicts between federal and cantonal authorities. Typically, Article 44 para. 1 of the Swiss Constitution provides that the Confederation and the Cantons "shall collaborate, and shall support each other in the fulfilment of their tasks".

---

[43]Cst. art. 51; see A. Auer/G. Malinverni/M. Hottelier, "Droit constitutionnel suisse", vol. 1 "l'Etat", 2ᵉ ed., Berne 2006, pp. 63–66.

[44]According to the study of the different official cantonal registers, principally BE, FR, VD, NE, GE.

[45]U. Thalmann, "Die Verfassungsrechtliche Stellung der Kantone", in P. Hänni (éd.), *Schweizerischer Föderalismus and europäischer Integration: die Rolle der Kantone in einem sich wandelnden internationalen Kontext*, Zurich 2000, p. 85; M. Arefaine, "Federalism and Accommodation of Diversities: With Special Reference to Divided Societies", Fribourg 2005, p. 163.

[46]U. Thalmann, ibid.

[47]Cst. art. 43.

As a general rule, however, Article 49 states the supremacy of federal law[48]: "federal law breaks the cantonal law".[49] Thus, the Cantons cannot enact a rule contrary to the federal law.[50] Yet, this principle must be tempered, and the Federal Supreme Court (*Tribunal fédéral, Bundesgericht*) has decided that this supremacy only exists if the division of powers is respected. Thus when the Constitution gives a specific competence to the Cantons, the cantonal regulation is superior to the federal regulation on the same matter.[51]

In addition, Article 189 of the Constitution provides that the Federal Supreme Court "shall judge public law disputes between the Confederation and the Cantons". However, the idea is that the Cantons and the Confederation should not view each other as rivals but as partners working toward common goals. Thus, Article 44 para. 3 of the Constitution holds that in case of conflict between the Confederation and the Cantons, such conflict shall be resolved as much as possible through negotiation or mediation. Yet, there is no federal mediator to resolve those kinds of conflicts, nor is there a special commission within the federal parliament that specializes in questions of distribution of powers. As a result, if there is a conflict, it is usually too late for mediation. To avoid such conflicts, a certain number of principles are laid down by the Constitution, and the Federal Supreme Court has jurisdiction to decide such conflicts (Cst., *Art. 189, 1d*).[52] As a result, the Federal Supreme Court can defend a constitutional cantonal provision that conflicts with a federal provision.[53]

Another principle is subsidiarity[54] which is based on Articles 3, 42 and 46 of the Constitution. According to this principle, the powers should, as much as possible, be allocated to the lowest level of government that is able to properly fulfil the task in question.[55]

Under Articles 3 and 42, the federal government only has those powers that are specifically allocated to it by the federal Constitution, and the federal government shall only assume those tasks which require uniform regulation. As a result, tasks that do not require uniform regulation throughout Switzerland are left to the Cantons.[56]

---

[48] Cst. art. 49.

[49] "Bundesrecht bricht Kantonales Recht".

[50] ATF 120 Ia 299.

[51] FF 1997 I 218; ATF 128 II 112.

[52] ATF 117 Ia 221.

[53] G. Zaccaria, "Das Staatsrecht der Schweizerischen Kantone", Zurich 1979, p. 57.

[54] On the principle of subsidiarity see: U. Thalmann, "Subsdiaritätsprinzip und Kompetenz-Verteilung", in T. Fleiner/P. Forster/A. Misic/U. Thalmann (eds.), *La nouvelle Constitution suisse. Fédéralisme, droits fondamentaux, droit économique et structure de l'Etat*, Bâle/Genève/Munich 2000, pp. 149–170; A. Epiney, "Subsidiarität als verfassungsrechtlicher Grundsatz", in *Rapports suisses présentés au XIVe Congrès international de droit comparé* (Athènes), Zurich 1994, pp. 9–33.

[55] M. Arefaine, "Federalism and Accommodation of Diversities: With Special Reference to Divided Societies", Fribourg 2005, p. 163. See also Cst., Art. 5a.

[56] U. Thalmann, "Die Verfassungsrechtliche Stellung der Kantone", op. cit. pp. 73–74.

Merely one article of the Constitution is dedicated to the Municipalities (*Cst., Art 50*). The Constitution doesn't grant them law making powers, as the *Communes* are an institution of cantonal law. Yet, some federal laws also enlist the help of the *Communes* to implement federal legislation, as in the case of the Federal Act on Military Organisation[57] or the Federal Act on Civil Protection.[58] Additionally, the Constitution provides that the Confederation shall pay attention, in its activities, to the special situations of the cities, urban conglomerations, and mountainous regions.[59] The degree of autonomy granted to the *Communes* is thus determined by the individual Cantons[60] and therefore varies considerably between them.[61]

As a rule, the Cantons control the Municipalities. This control is more extensive than the one applied by the Confederation over the Cantons.[62] However, in general, Municipalities have the right to self-administration. They also have the legislative and administrative powers in areas that directly concern the local level, such as municipal citizenship, primary education, and municipal police.[63] Moreover, they have the right to raise their own taxes.

The federal courts have held that Municipalities are autonomous in areas where they have a relatively important decision making power.[64] It has also been decided that the Municipalities are competent to interpret their own regulations. In other words, the Cantons cannot arbitrarily impose a specific understanding of a municipal legal act,[65] and the Confederation must remedy any violation of municipal autonomy committed by Cantons.

17.3 The Means and Methods of Legal Unification

The unification of law has been, and still is, a long process in Switzerland. Even if federal law appears to be predominant, because of its territorial scope, cantonal law still remains voluminous. Typically, when the Confederation legislates, the Cantons generally still have the right to fill in the details, thus creating legal diversity.

---

[57] Art. 11, 131 ss. Laam.

[58] Art. 46 al. 2 LPPCi.

[59] Cst. art. 50 al. 2 et 3.

[60] Cst. art. 50 al. 1.

[61] T. Fleiner/A. Misic/N. Töpperwien, op. cit. p. 137: "It can be said that the more important the Municipalities have been in history of the Canton the more powers they are attributed".

[62] A. Auer/G. Malinverni/M. Hottelier, op. cit. p. 84.

[63] A. Auer/G. Malinverni/M. Hottelier, op. cit. pp. 83–84.

[64] ATF 101 Ia 259.

[65] ATF 108 Ia 74; ATF 103 Ia 468.

These rules are set down in the Constitution, but the Constitution can be revised by a majority of the votes of Swiss citizens and the Cantons.[66] This has occurred many times to ensure the unity of the law within the Confederation.

Unification of private law is a main political topic in Switzerland. The central unification of law by the Confederation is balanced by increasing opportunities for the Cantons to participate in the decision-making process at the central level. Abolishing the Cantons' differing regulations in favor of nationwide legislation has improved the equality of laws as well as legal certainty.[67]

The most recent project of unification of the law relates to the unification of criminal procedure. The draft bills for a Swiss Code of Criminal Procedure and for a Swiss Code of Juvenile Criminal Procedure, of 21 December 2005, replace Switzerland's 26 cantonal codes of criminal procedure, as well as the corresponding regulations at federal level. As a result, since January 1 2011, criminal offenses are defined in a standard way in the Swiss Penal Code and they will be prosecuted and judged according to the same procedural rules. This unique procedural code helps defense counsel and makes it easier for prosecuting authorities to deploy staff across cantonal borders. It will also facilitate international cooperation.[68]

In addition, the erstwhile multitude of civil procedure codes has now been overcome: as of January 1, 2011, Switzerland has a federal, and thus uniform, Code of Civil Procedure, although, again, in some matters Cantons still fill in the details.

There are no directly applicable constitutional norms which unify a field of law. However, the unification of law is mainly based on the Articles 122 and 123 of the Swiss Constitution. Additionally, Article 42 al. 2 provides that the Confederation shall assume the tasks which require uniform regulation. This entails a top-down approach. Yet according to the interpretation of the principle,[69] and to the statements of commissioners and representatives of the government, the Article doesn't mean that the Confederation may legislate with no other constitutional basis than this Article. In other words, the Confederation may not use Article 42 in a circular fashion every time it considers that one task shall be regulated uniformly.[70]

Most of the unification of law is achieved by a directly applicable norm: that is to say, by a federal act. Important examples include the Federal Act on the Organization of the Federal Judiciary; the Federal Act on the Proceedings of Federal Parliament and the Form; the Federal Administrative Procedure Act; the Federal Act on the Organization of the Federal Council and the Federal Administration

---

[66]Cst. art. 140 al. 1 let. A; Cst. art. 142 al. 2; Cst. art. 195.

[67]See the Explanatory Report "*Message*" 21/12/2005, FF 2006 1057.

[68]Ibid.

[69]U. Thalmann, "Subsidiaritätsprinzip und Kompetenzverteilung", op. cit. pp. 165–166; R. J. Schweizer, "Die neue Bundesverfassung: die revidierte bundesstaatliche Verfassungsordnung", PJA 1999, p. 672.

[70]See on www.admin.ch (last visited 6.3.09): the statements of commissioners and representative of the government, PV 4687–4688 (commission of the Council of States) and 1386–1388 (commission of the National Council).

of 21 March 1997; the Civil Code; the Code of Obligations; the Federal Act on Private International Law; the Federal Act on Cartels and Other Restrictions of Competition, and, as of recently, the federal Codes of Criminal and Civil Procedure.

The powers of the Confederation and of the Cantons to legislate and to implement the law do not necessarily overlap. Sometimes the central government is empowered to implement unified law, i.e., concerning taxes, postal service, and customs. But more often, the task to apply federal acts is allocated to the Cantons, and the Confederation only supervises such implementation. In some cases, the Constitution explicitly provides for the cantonal enforcement of federal law, e.g., in the fields of environmental protection,[71] the protection of animals,[72] and of national highways.[73]

As a result, most federal laws are implemented by the Cantons and even by local and municipal authorities. Executing a federal law thus usually requires a cantonal law or at least an ordinance. The adverse consequence is that federal laws are not always implemented uniformly.

The distribution of the federal budget sometimes induces the Cantons to regulate certain matters. For example, in the field of social protection, the fact that the Confederation pays part of the allowance for poor retired citizens will have an influence on the Cantons' decisions to run complementary social programmes in order to obtain a share of the federal funds.

The spending power under the federal budget is granted to the Federal Council according to Article 183 of the Constitution: "The Federal Government shall prepare the financing plan, draft the budget and establish the federal accounts. It shall ensure correct financial management". Also, according to Article 167 of the Constitution, "the Federal Parliament shall decide on federal spending, shall adopt the budget, and shall approve the federal accounts".

Federal financial influence on cantonal legislation is also found in the field of education, particularly in respect to universities.

The Confederation cannot force Cantons to regulate by threatening to take over the field in case of cantonal inaction or if cantonal action does not conform to centrally specified standards. However, according to Article 186 al. 2 of the Constitution, the Confederation shall approve cantonal legislation where the implementation of federal law requires it.

The Confederation cannot influence legislation through the judicial creation of uniform norms by the Federal Supreme Court (*Tribunal fédéral*). Swiss law belongs to the civil law family, which, in contrast to the common law tradition, is based on abstract rules, which judges must then apply to the cases coming before them. In other words, laws are first enacted by the legislature and then applied by the judges. Yet, there is frequently a consistent line of court decisions. Judicial «precedents» thus play a very significant role in Switzerland despite their non-binding nature. The uniform interpretation of law is given by the Federal Supreme

---

[71] Cst. article 74 al. 3.
[72] Cst. art. 80 al. 3.
[73] Cst. art. 83.

Court when the provisions of law or of the Constitution have a very general meaning. Courts also deduce new rules from existing legislation by way of analogy or legal analysis (Art. 1 of the Swiss Civil Code).

There is no centrally managed coordination and information exchange system among the Cantons, but there are mechanisms to coordinate action and to prevent conflicts. For example, the procedure required for the adoption of every federal law leaves much room for coordination and information exchange between the Cantons. The Constitution states that the adoption of federal legislation is preceded by a consultation procedure and by political debate.[74] Moreover, Switzerland is a small country which means that people in important positions often know each other; thus they try to resolve problems by informal talks.

In addition, a Conference of the Cantonal Executives has been established. This institution meets at regular intervals and allows direct influence by the Cantons on the Confederation. It is also a good tool for the collective and coordinated resolution of problems. This institution is seen today as a successful and strong lobby group for the Cantons, and as an important partner for discussions with the Confederation.[75]

Yet, legal unification is not accomplished through formal or informal voluntary coordination among the Cantons. Typically, cantonal legislatures differ and there is little harmonisation. Nor is there any unification of case law between the Cantons as legislation is often different from one Canton to the next.

There are nevertheless a number of horizontal instruments of cooperative federalism that enable the Cantons to take collective action without the involvement of the Confederation.

There are inter-cantonal organizations and agencies, and the traditional legal instrument of cooperation is the so-called *concordat*.[76] *Concordats* are inter-cantonal treaties functioning as a form of regional cooperation.[77] These treaties can regulate the unification of legislation and even create common institutions.

A major example can be found in the field of education that is within the jurisdiction of Cantons. A special institution called the Swiss Conference of Cantonal Ministers of Education[78] was established in order to help to coordinate action. The *Conference* is a joint endeavour of the 26 cantonal government ministers, who are responsible for education, training, culture, and sport. It shapes the cooperation among the Cantons through a series of inter-cantonal agreements: e.g., the Agreement on Education Coordination, various Agreements on Financing and on Freedom of Access to Education. A new inter-cantonal agreement to harmonise compulsory education is currently under consideration.

---

[74]Cst., art. 147.

[75]N. Schmitt, "Swiss Confederation", in J. Kincaid/G. A. Tarr (eds.), *Constitutional Origins, Structure, and Change in Federal Countries*, Global Dialogue on Federalism, Series number 1, Montreal 2005, p. 358.

[76]See Auer/G. Malinverni/M. Hottelier, op. cit. pp. 565–580.

[77]Cst., art. 48.

[78]See the website of the Conference: http://www.edk.ch (last visited 6.3.09).

In respect to higher education at the universities, the Swiss University Conference (*Conférence Universitaire Suisse*)[79] established the Inter-cantonal Convention on Coordinating University Policies. The main goal of this Convention is to strengthen the cooperation between the Cantons and the federal government.

Legal unification can also be accomplished, or at least promoted, by non-state actors. In Switzerland, the work of legal scholars helps to provide uniform interpretation of laws. Swiss judges often base their decisions on the works of legal scholars, both Swiss and foreign. Article 1 al. 3 of the Civil Code provides specifically that the judge "shall be inspired by the solutions (...) contained in the writing of legal scholars". Legal scholars can also draft model laws which contribute to the unification of law at a later stage. Standards and practices of industry, trade organizations or other or private entities can create rights and obligations. This is particularly true in the banking and financial industry.

Legal education and training is diverse in Switzerland, as it is a matter of cantonal competence, but the Swiss University Conference aims to ensure a better cooperation between the universities. Additionally, law schools draw students from throughout the federal system, yet the linguistic differences (especially between German and French speaking parts) limit student mobility. There is no law school in the Italian-speaking part of the country. Italian-speaking students thus often study in Italy and their diploma is recognized in Switzerland. Some federal institutions play a unifying role in legal education, e.g. by offering internships to graduates at central courts or in the federal administration, such as the Federal Office of Justice. Still, the linguistic diversity of Switzerland remains an important differentiating factor among lawyers.

Swiss legal education focuses on federal law. Yet, bar admission is organised by the Cantons, and each maintains a register of lawyers who have a business address within the Canton and who fulfil the professional requirements[80] and personal qualifications.[81] In practice, graduates tend to set up their offices or take jobs in the Cantons in which they qualified.

---

[79] http://www.cus.ch/wFranzoesisch/index.php (last visited 6.3.09).

[80] Art.7 LCCA 23/06/2003 Professional requirements: 1 To be inscribed in the register, the lawyer must be in possession of a lawyer's license that has been granted on the basis of the following conditions: a. course of studies in law leading to a graduate degree awarded by a Swiss university or to an equivalent diploma awarded by a university from one of the States that has concluded an agreement of reciprocal recognition with Switzerland; b. at least one year of practical experience in Switzerland that has been concluded with an examination of juridical knowledge in theory and in practice. 2 Cantons in which Italian is the official language may recognise a foreign diploma, acquired in the Italian language that is equivalent to a graduate degree.

[81] Art 8 LCAA 23/06/2003 Personal qualifications: 1 To be inscribed in the register, lawyers must fulfil the following personal qualifications: a. they must have the capacity to act; b. there can be no criminal conviction against them for acts that are incompatible with the legal profession and that have not yet been deleted from the register of convictions; c. there can be no deeds of loss; d. they must be capable of practising law independently; they may be employed only by persons who themselves are inscribed in one of the cantonal registers of lawyers. 2 Lawyers who are employed by recognised charitable organisations can be registered as long as conditions, according

According to Article 4 of the Federal Act on the Freedom of Movement for Lawyers, "all lawyers who are listed in a cantonal register of lawyers can represent parties before judicial authorities in Switzerland without additional authorisation".[82]

External factors, such as international law, exercise considerable influence on legal unification in Switzerland. Typically, as Switzerland has a monistic approach, compliance with international legal obligations plays a major role. In other words, international treaties that are self-executing have to be applied directly by the competent authorities, i.e., without need to transform them into domestic statutes.[83] Treaties are thus part of the Swiss legal system. Switzerland is also member of various institutions pursuing international legal unification, such as the Hague Conference on Private International Law, and it has signed a number of international conventions in the field of private international law. These conventions are also reflected in the Federal Act on Private International Law (PILA) of 18th December 1987, a federal act unifying the field. Thus, Article 49 PILA directly refers to the Hague "Maintenance" Convention. It provides that "Maintenance obligations between spouses shall be governed by the Hague Convention of October 2, 1973 on the Law Applicable to Maintenance Obligations". Similar reference is made in chapter 9a of the PILA to The Hague Convention on the Law Applicable to Trusts and on Their Recognition of 1st July 1985.

Further international influence can be found in the field of arbitration where, in order to promote institutional arbitration in Switzerland and to harmonise the existing rules of arbitration, the Chambers of Commerce and Industry of Basel, Bern, Geneva, Ticino, Vaud and Zurich have adopted the "Swiss Rules of International Arbitration", in force since January 1st 2004.[84] These provisions are based on the UNCITRAL Arbitration Rules and replace the former rules of the six chambers.

17.4 Institutional and Social Background

17.4.1 The Judicial Branch

In Switzerland, the Federal Supreme Court (Federal Tribunal) is the highest court.[85] It covers a wide spectrum of litigation as it rules on disputes concerning private law, criminal law, public and administrative law. At the same time, the Federal Tribunal is also a constitutional court. It decides on the constitutionality of acts and laws within the country.

---

to paragraph 1, letters a-c, have been fulfilled and their representation of parties is strictly limited to mandates within the context of the purpose as defined by the organisation concerned.

[82] Loi fédérale sur la libre circulation des avocats (Loi sur les avocats, LLCA) of 23rd June 2000.

[83] ATF 127 II 177; ATF 120 Ib 360.

[84] YCA 2004 pp. 447ss; ASA, spec. Series, n°22, pp. 131ss; www.swissarbitration.ch (visited 6.3.09).

[85] Cst., art. 189 al. 4.

The Federal Supreme Court thus has a variety of tasks such as providing those seeking justice with legal redress in specific cases, ensuring the uniform application of federal law, and contributing to the further development of the law. On appeal, it reviews the decisions of the highest cantonal courts and other authorities of the Confederation to ensure they are in compliance with the law. It is also responsible for ensuring that the rules governing the making, application and interpretation of law are adhered to.

The Federal Tribunal has its seat in Lausanne.[86] This geographically demonstrates the independence of the judiciary from the federal government and parliament in Berne, and it also expresses an accommodative spirit and federal solidarity with regions of linguistic minorities by allocating to the French-speaking part of the country an important element in the constitutional system.[87]

Even though the Federal Tribunal acts as constitutional court, its power to overturn federal laws is considerably restricted. Article 190 of the Constitution requires the Court, as well as all other cantonal and federal authorities, to apply federal laws and ratify international law. The Federal Tribunal can interpret federal laws and define their meaning. Furthermore, the Federal Tribunal can identify gaps in the legislation and will, on occasion, criticise certain regulations. The interpretation of Article 190 in legal scholarship is somewhat contradictory: the Article is interpreted as not forbidding the Federal Supreme Court from stating its opinion on the constitutionality of federal laws, but at the same time it obliges the Federal Supreme Court and other bodies to apply federal laws, even if they are considered unconstitutional.[88]

In recent years (1996 and 2000), the Federal Council tried to introduce concrete review under the Constitution. Two arguments were put forward: first, that the lack of constitutional review of federal laws creates a gap in the system of legal protection; and second, that the Federal Tribunal has changed its jurisprudence to comply with the European Convention of Human Rights.[89] These arguments for introducing concrete review failed to find a majority in parliament. Thus, the proposal to expand the jurisdiction of the Court to include concrete review of federal laws and acts having general effect on the federal assembly was defeated. As a result, there is presently no control of the constitutionality of federal law whereas there *is* control on the constitutional competence of the Cantons.

---

[86] Except the social division which is in Lucerne, but this division is integrated to the Federal Supreme Court.

[87] O. SIGG, "Switzerland's Political Institutions", English translation F. M. Blackwell/D. N. Roscoe/M. Mettler, Zurich 1991, p. 34.

[88] A. Auer/G. Malinverni/M. Hottelier, op. cit. pp. 685–791.

[89] The Federal Supreme Court is willing to verify the harmony of federal law with the European Convention of Human Rights (ECHR). Moreover, in the case of a conflict between federal law and the ECHR, the Federal Supreme Court has refused to apply federal laws that violate the ECHR in some recent cases, on the condition that the parliament did not wilfully legislate against international law.

Surprisingly, Article 95 of the Federal Supreme Court Act (LTF),[90] which defines the types of actions brought before the Federal Supreme Court, does not mention cantonal legislation. As a result, the application and judicial control of cantonal law are cantonal competences. This competence follows from Articles 3 and 47 of the Constitution, which obliges the Confederation to respect cantonal autonomy. In exceptional cases, however, the Federal Supreme Court may examine the application and the interpretation of cantonal law. Such is the case, for example, when there are serious restrictions of liberty. The Federal Supreme Court also judges the compatibility of cantonal acts with superior federal norms.

The Swiss system of justice is complex. There are administrative, civil and criminal courts at both the cantonal and federal levels. The judicial system is constructed as a pyramid. At the base, there are the courts of first instance, i.e., the trial courts, which are followed by the courts of appeal. Both first and second instances are cantonal. Trial courts and courts of appeal apply federal and cantonal civil and criminal law.

At the top of pyramid is the Federal Tribunal. It has power to decide appeals from cantonal courts. It also rules on appeals lodged against decisions by federal agencies. The Federal Tribunal decides conflicts between the Confederation and the Cantons as well as conflicts among the Cantons. It is empowered to review legislative and executive acts of the Cantons and thus to guarantee the (cantonal) constitutional rights of the citizens.

17.4.2 Relations Between the Federal and Cantonal Governments

The Central government has no (constitutional) power to force the Cantons to legislate in the field of their exclusive powers. Yet, under the interpretation of Articles 173, 182, and 187 of the Constitution, the Confederation has such power indirectly. The Confederation must ensure the implementation of federal law and thus can oblige the Cantons to act.

In spite of this rule, there is no sanction if the Cantons do not respect their obligation to legislate. Legal scholarship has frequently discussed this matter, but no solution has been found. In practice, however, there are no cases in which the Cantons did not respect their obligation.

As mentioned, the implementation of federal law is largely performed by the Cantons.[91] Federal law binds the Cantons with regard to how they implement federal legislation. However, as a general principle, the Confederation must leave the Cantons as much freedom of action as possible. It must also take the financial burden of the Cantons created by the execution of federal law into account.[92]

---

[90] Federal Tribunal Act of 17 June 2005, RS 173.110.

[91] Cst., Art. 46 al. 1: "The Cantons shall implement federal law in conformity with the Constitution and the statute".

[92] Cst., Art. 46 al. 2.

The relationship between the Cantons and Confederation is very close as the composition of the central government is decided by the parliament, where cantonal representatives play a major part. Both chambers of the Parliament are directly elected by the people: the National Council (representing the Swiss People) is elected in accordance with federal rules, and the Council of States (representing Cantons) according to provisions varying from one Canton to another. In both cases, the Cantons form the constituencies.

The government of Switzerland in the sense of the executive power consists of the seven members of the Federal Council, as well as the Federal Chancellor, and is elected by the United Federal Assembly for a 4-year term. The President of the Swiss Confederation is elected each year and is considered *Primus inter pares* (first among equals) during that time.[93]

Competing power of the Confederation and Cantons is exercised over taxes on income of individuals and on income of corporations. The Swiss tax system is not centralized and is therefore particularly complicated. The three levels of government may raise taxes, i.e., the citizens pay taxes to each level. The consequence of this system is that the total tax burden differs considerably among the Cantons.

Article 127 al. 1 of the Constitution provides that "[t]he general principles of taxation, particularly the population of taxpayers, and the object of the tax and its calculation, shall be established by statute"; that is to say, submitted to a referendum. The Federal Constitution[94] provides for the various taxes that are the Confederation's competence. The Confederation has exclusive power to levy a withholding tax on income from capital investment and certain insurance payments (federal anticipatory tax), a compensatory tax for the exemption of civil and military service, customs duties, federal stamp duties, a tax on commodities such as alcohol, beer and tobacco, a value-added tax, and a special tax on gambling houses.

The power of the Confederation to tax is limited to 11.5 % on the income of natural persons by Article 128 of the Constitution (direct taxes) and to 8 % on the supply of goods and services by Article 130 of the Constitution (value added taxes).

According to Article 46 al. 3 of the Constitution, the Confederation shall take into account the financial burden that is associated with implementing federal law by leaving sufficient funds to the Cantons, and by ensuring an equitable financial equalization. Article 135 of the Constitution states that that the Confederation shall promote fiscal equalization among the Cantons. When granting subsidies, it shall take into account the financial capacity of the Cantons and the special situation of the mountainous regions. Article 128 al. 4 provides that, concerning the direct taxes, at least one sixth of this amount shall be used for financial equalization among Cantons.

---

[93] For details on the executive power, see the document of executive power on www.admin.ch (last visited 6.03.09); Auer/G. Malinverni/M. Hottelier, op. cit. pp. 49–56.

[94] Cst., art. 134.

The harmonization of direct taxes is provided by Article 129 of the Constitution which states:

> "The Confederation shall establish principles on the harmonization of direct taxes of the Confederation, the Cantons and the Municipalities; it shall take into account the efforts of the Cantons to harmonize their taxes. Harmonization applies to tax liability, tax object, taxation period, and procedural and criminal law on taxation. Harmonization shall not cover tax scales, tax rates, and tax-exempt amounts."

17.4.3 The Bureaucracy

The civil service of the central government is separate from the civil services of the Cantons.

The Post and Telephone Service (*La Poste Suisse*) and the Federal Railways (CFF) belong to the main federal services which deal directly with the general public. Most federal programs are implemented by the Cantons and the Municipalities, and there is no parallel federal administration.

There is no organized lateral mobility or career advancement between the civil services of the Cantons and of federal government. Still, it is not unusual for civil servants to move between central and federal civil service positions. Experience in cantonal administration is considered an asset when applying for leading positions in the federal administration.

17.4.4 Social Factors

Switzerland is a multi-ethnic, multilingual and multi-confessional nation shaped by the will of its people. Switzerland is said to be an "artificial aggregate of pieces of Eastern France, Southern Germany, Western Austria and Northern Italy".[95] There is no "nationalism" based on ethnic, religious or linguistic factors. Instead, nationalism comes from a sense of common political values.[96] The elements of national identification are the legendary and symbolic tales of William Tell and *Helvetia* (the mother of the nation), and the Alps. The picture of a nation, basically composed of farmers and shepherds living in isolated mountain chalets or small villages (like the well-known figure of Heidi), distinguishes Switzerland from other countries despite the large-scale industrialisation since the nineteenth century.[97]

---

[95] N. Schmitt, "Switzerland", in J. Kramer/H.-P. Schneider (eds.), *Federalism and Civil Societies: An International Symposium*, Föderalismus-Studien, vol.14, Baden-Baden 1999, p. 335.

[96] N. Schmitt, ibid.

[97] U. Im Hof, "Die historische Dimension der nationalen Identität", *National Forschungsprogamm 21, Kulturelle Vielfalt und nationale Identität*, Bâle 1991, p. 14.

From the beginning, Swiss identity has relied not only on what its people shared together but on Swiss specificities,[98] such as a tradition of hard work, cleanliness, humanitarian organizations (the Red Cross being a mirror of the Swiss flag), a sense of peace (neutral state) and plurilingualism.[99]

In Switzerland, language and religion are the major causes of diversity. The country has four national languages: German, French, Italian and Romansch,[100] of which only the first three are official. According to the report of the Federal Statistical Office, 63.7 % of the population speak German as their main language, 20.4 % speak French, 6.4 % speak Italian, 0.5 % speak Romansch, and 9 % speak other languages.[101]

Cantons determine their official language.[102] German is the official language of 19 Cantons,[103] French of six,[104] and Italian is the language of merely one.[105] Some Cantons are bilingual (e.g., Freiburg) and one of them (Grison) is trilingual. Article 2 of the Constitution states that the Confederation shall "promote the common welfare, the sustainable development, the inner cohesion, and the cultural diversity of the country" and the Cantons have the requisite competences in the fields of culture, education, and religion in order to maintain the diversity of culture between Swiss citizens. According to Article 70 al. 3 of the Constitution, the Confederation and the Cantons shall encourage understanding and exchange among the linguistic communities.

Linguistic differences remain, however, very important throughout Switzerland, even within the same linguistic region. A special feature of the German part of Switzerland is the diversity of the dialects spoken: the Basel, Berne, or Zurich dialects are so diverse that understanding, even between the inhabitants of the German part of Switzerland, may be difficult.

In respect to linguistic differences, the French-speaking people are mainly in the west of Switzerland, the Italian- and Romansch-speaking in the east and southeast and the German-speaking people prevail in all other parts of Switzerland.

---

[98] B. Ruckstuhl, "Die Schweiz, ein Land der Bauern und Hirten", in S. Ferrari/ D. Siegrist, *Aus wen schoss Wilhelm Tell? Beiträge zu einer Ideologiegeschichte der Schweiz*, Tagung vom 13.-19. January 1991 in Salecina/Maloja, Zurich 1991, p. 136.

[99] F. Grin, "Gestion "à la suisse" de la diversité linguistique: un succès menacé par l'économie?", in H. Guillorel et G. Koubi (dir.), *Langues et droits – Langues du droit, droit des langues*, Bruxelles, Bruylant, 1999, p. 251 (253 et 254), D. Froidevaux, "Construction de la nation et pluralisme suisses: idéologies et pratiques", *Revue suisse de Science politique*, 1997, n. 3, p. 29–58.

[100] Cst., art. 4.

[101] Statistical Yearbook 2008 by the Federal Statistical Office, see www.statistique.admin.ch (last visited 6.03.09).

[102] Cst., art. 70 al. 2.

[103] Aargau, Appenzell Outer Rhodes, Appenzell Inner Rhodes, Basle-Land, Basle-City, Bern, Grisons, Glarus, Lucerne, Nidwalden, Obwalden, Saint-Gallen, Schaffhausen, Schwyz, Solothurn, Thurgau, Uri, Zug, Zurich.

[104] Fribourg, Geneva, Jura, Neuchâtel, Valais, Vaud.

[105] Ticino.

Switzerland is also diverse in terms of religions. The country has been marked by the civil war between Catholics and Protestants and then by a strong "*Kulturkampf*".[106] This situation explains the important constitutional provisions on religion. Articles 8 and 15 of the Constitution prohibit religious discrimination among the various denominations: there are Protestants, Roman Catholics, Orthodox Christians, Muslims, and Jews. Article 72 of the Constitution provides that "The regulation of the relationship between Church and State is a cantonal matter". That is to say that each Canton develops its relationship with religious institutions in different ways. Cantons may have any one of these three kinds of relations: union of church and state,[107] separation of church and state,[108] or autonomy of churches within a public law status.

In the process of interpretation of law by courts, the difference of religion can have an influence. For example, the decisions concerning divorce or abortion prevailing in Catholic Cantons differ from those in Protestant ones.

Religious divisions throughout Switzerland are now, however, not necessarily cantonal any more. At present, only the Roman-Catholic group can pride itself on being a majority in some Cantons.

There are also differences between cities and rural areas. Some of the Cantons are generally urban, such as Basel-City, Geneva, or Zurich, and most of them are located to the west and north of Switzerland. The smaller Cantons of central Switzerland and Appenzell are rural. But most of the Cantons do not belong to either group because industry, handicrafts, and small businesses are widespread throughout the Country. Nevertheless, tensions between rural states and cities persist. "[I]t is a problem of mentality, a feeling that the cities may acquire too much influence and democratic power. (. . .) The Swiss especially fear that Zurich will become too big and have too much weight".[109]

To conclude, "The Swiss case is clearly one of cross-cutting cleavages, a society in which alignments on values, party alignments, religious alignments, linguistic alignments, and territorial alignments of the Cantons all cut across each other".[110]

Political consensus and political commitment by the citizens are key elements of the Swiss political system. Strong federalist principles highly influence the legal and administrative environments for regulatory reform. The composition of the federal government reflects the principles of accommodation of linguistic, religious, or

---

[106] *Kulturkampf* describes the strong reaction of the Protestants against the Catholics and the Church in general.

[107] None of the Swiss Cantons has this sort of relation with the church. However, the Canton of Vaud experiences a certain form of union: Its Cantonal Constitution at Article 13 provides that the Protestant Church is a "national institution" which is organised by the Canton itself. By contrast, the Catholic churches are not corporations of public law but constitute a private law organisation.

[108] Geneva, Neuchâtel.

[109] O. K. Kaufmann, "Swiss Federalism", in R.A. Goldwin/A. Kaufman/W.A. Schambra (eds.), *Forging Unity out of Diversity*, Washington, DC, 1989, p. 214.

[110] J. Linz, "Discussion on the Swiss Federalism", in R.A. Goldwin/A. Kaufman/W.A. Schambra (eds.), *Forging Unity out of Diversity*, Washington, DC, 1989, p. 256.

topographic diversity,[111] although minorities have a strong voice in the country. That is the reason why differences of culture are an important factor in the law making process: For example, the popular initiative is an original weapon for minorities to introduce new ideas into the political debate.[112] Yet, the unity of the country is maintained while at the same time the diverse identities of the Cantons are preserved.

In addition, the equitable representation of minorities is also perceptible in the composition of the country's supreme judicial body: the Federal Court. Article 107 of the Constitution provides that in electing the Federal Court judges and their substitutes, the Federal Assembly shall ensure that the three official languages of the Confederation are represented. In practice, the composition of the Federal Court also reflects the various political tendencies in Switzerland, and judges are elected in such a way that all regions of the country are represented.

An interesting example of coordination and cooperation between federal and cantonal authorities, and thus of the virtue of federalism, can be found in the field of education. This is a main element of national cohesion, and also an essential feature that measures the success of federalism.

The Cantons have the basic responsibility for education.[113] Yet, the federal government can run technical universities and grant subsidies to the Cantons for scholarships, and it can also take measures to encourage education.[114]

There is a variety of compulsory educational systems. At present, "there are two, three or four different types of lower secondary schools to match performance requirements, and teaching hours for the nine compulsory years of schooling vary between 7100 and 8900 per child".[115] Teachers at primary schools are nominated and paid by the *Communes* and they receive an almost equal salary throughout each Canton. Less affluent *Communes* receive subsidies for the salaries of their teachers and for the building of schools. However, the differences between schools have not all been eliminated. The Curricula are inadequately coordinated and that creates difficulties for children when they move and change schools between Cantons.

17.5 Conclusion

The Swiss Federal system is an original design. Its peculiarities result in a complex legislative system. The unification of law has been a long process, which is still ongoing.

---

[111]M. Arefaine, op. cit. p. 166. The composition of the Federal Council is a compromise of all parties enabling the representation of all political tendencies, religions, genders, and all linguistic parts of Switzerland.

[112]Auer/G. Malinverni/M. Hottelier, op. cit. pp. 258–261.

[113]Cst., art. 62.

[114]J.-F. Aubert/P. Mahon, op. cit. pp. 512–515.

[115]Statistical Yearbook 2008 p. 519.

It is not appropriate to speak of centralization with respect to Switzerland because of the relatively strong autonomy of the Cantons. Even under modern conditions, one must not forget that the Cantons, and before them the Municipalities, created the Confederation.

Certain fields of law, such as successions and real rights are strongly harmonized thanks to the Civil Code. But Cantons still have adjunct competences which are expressed in different provisions, e.g., Article 499 of the Constitution which states that the Cantons must determine the authorities competent for establishing a public will (testament). Moreover, some provisions of the Constitution, such as Article 56 al. 1, which states that within their scope of powers, the Cantons may conclude treaties with foreign countries, lend credibility to the view that the Cantons are still sovereign, even if their power is concurrent and described as "subsidiary" to the federal treaty-making power.

Nevertheless, only few areas of law show a low level of unification. At present, only police law, inheritance taxes, education and some kinds of procedures are not unified. As mentioned, unification in these fields is on-going, and differences between the laws of the Cantons are less important than first impressions would lead one to conclude. In addition, the internationalisation of law, globalisation, and a growing influence of institutions such as UNCITRAL, UNIDROIT, and the Hague Conference on Private International Law promote harmonization as well. As a result, therefore, law in Switzerland is fairly uniform, in spite of the intrinsic diversity of the Swiss population and of the strong federalism which marks the political systems.

Chapter 18
The United Kingdom: Devolution and Legal Unification

Stathis Banakas

18.1 Overview

The United Kingdom is a unitary, not a federal state. The UK experience is, therefore, not that of a federal state. Indeed, a UK National Report on the present theme would have had much less to contribute only a few years ago.

Today, however, there are four relatively distinct separate components of the UK, England, Wales, Scotland and Northern Ireland, with devolved legislative powers to the Scottish Parliament, the Welsh Assembly and the Northern Ireland Assembly, while the UK Parliament at Westminster in London retains its overall sovereignty over the whole of the UK, and continues to legislate directly for England on all matters, and for Wales, Scotland and Northern Ireland on reserved matters. This devolution of legislative power is *sui generis*, being neither a purely legislative delegation of secondary rule-making power by the Westminster Parliament, as, for example, in the case of local authority by-laws and regulations, nor a purely independent primary law making power granted under a common constitution, as in the case of US State laws; An exception are certain sovereign powers of the Scottish parliament. Additionally, the centuries-old judicial plurality in the UK, in which England and Wales, as one common jurisdiction, and Scotland and (to a lesser extent) Northern Ireland, traditionally enjoyed independent and separate systems of

---

Ptycheion Nomikis (Athens), PhD (Cantab.), Advocate (Greece), Reader in Law, University of East Anglia, United Kingdom; Fernand Braudel Senior Fellow, European University Institute (Autumn 2008).

S. Banakas (✉)
UEA Law School, University of East Anglia, NR4 7TJ Norwich, UK
e-mail: e.banakas@uea.ac.uk

administration of justice and common law sources, a plurality in itself unique and fascinating, was recently substantially reshaped in a major Constitutional reform of the judiciary in the UK. Therefore, the current UK experience, although not that of a federal state, may still be valuable from a comparative perspective, especially in the light of the absence of a detailed written Constitution and the special nature of judicial common law making in the UK component parts. An important early *caveat* must be entered: The devolution of legislative powers and the Constitutional reforms of the judiciary are recent developments and just barely fully operative and it is too early to know what the effect will be of the diverse new institutions and legal regimes, on legal uniformity in the UK.

This chapter will look at two distinct forms of plurality of legal sources in the UK[1]:

- Legislative plurality, recently reshaped by the devolution reforms, and
- Judicial plurality in common law making, also recently reshaped by the Constitutional reform of the UK judiciary.

The chapter will address the unification and harmonization processes and influences underpinning UK law as a whole:

- The multi-layered Constitutional framework
- The effect of European Courts and Institutions, the uniform development of the common law by UK courts under the stare decisis doctrine, and the transnational development of English common law.
- The role of legal doctrine and legal culture.
- The role of the Law Commissions, entrusted with law review and legal reform in the UK's constituent parts.

This report has not followed the principal authors' questionnaire as closely as its author might have wished to, because the questionnaire does not fit the emerging situation in the UK as well as it fits other, more truly federal systems.

18.2 Central Distribution and Exercise of Lawmaking Power

18.2.1 Legislative Plurality in the UK-Devolution of Legislative Power

A significant development in the UK in the last years of the twentieth century has been political, economic and legal devolution, first of Scotland, and then of Wales

---

[1] Constraints of time and space prevent me from discussing in this paper at any length the allocation and effect of secondary or delegated legislative powers in different parts of the UK.

and Northern Ireland. The debate for further devolution of powers within the English counties continues but with no concrete results of any importance to date.[2]

Primary law making for the whole of the UK has been in the hands of the Westminster Parliament in London (hereafter the UK Parliament), since the union of England and Scotland at the beginning of the eighteenth century, with the Union with Scotland Act 1706 and the Union with England Act 1707.[3] The UK Parliament is constitutionally composed as the Monarch, the House of Lords and the House of Commons. The Monarch remains the UK Head of State after the devolution, and appoints the UK Prime Minister, who selects his cabinet with a free hand, subject, of course, to the consent of Parliament. The House of Lords remains an unelected body, despite recent major reforms, and the way its members should be selected is still hotly debated in the evolution of this reform process. Suffice to note here that the House of Lords functions entirely as a UK legislative chamber and its members do not represent regions in the way that the US Senate represents States or the German *Bundesrat* represents German *Länder*. The House of Commons members are elected in UK-wide general elections, representing their individual constituencies that are dotted all over the UK, without any regional deviations of any kind. Both the members of the House of Lords and the House of Commons are not representing regions and are not in any way connected with devolved bodies, with the exception of House of Commons members from Northern Ireland that can be, simultaneously, members of the Northern Ireland Assembly or, indeed, the Northern Ireland executive.

For legislation to be properly enacted, all three branches of the UK Parliament, i.e., the Monarch, the House of Lords and the House of Commons must assent, in reverse order. The House of Commons decides first, the House of Lords must then assent and the Monarch's assent is the last one before the Act of Parliament can be promulgated. However, after a second rejection of a Bill by the House of Lords, following a complicated procedure, the House of Commons can proceed without the consent of the Lords, under the terms of the Parliament Acts of 1911 and 1949. The second of these Acts, further curtailed the power of the Lords by reducing the time that they could delay bills voted by the House of Commons to a maximum time of 1 year.

---

[2]The current debate about devolution for English regions cannot be entered into here. It is often linked to the so-called 'East Lothian' question, i.e. Scottish members of the Westminster Parliament having a vote on laws passed by that Parliament exclusively for England. There are, however, eight English Regional Assemblies, besides London, but with no primary legislative powers, described on the official UK government site as follows: 'Voluntary, multi-party and inclusive Regional Assemblies have been established in each of the eight English regions outside London, building on the partnership working arrangements that already existed in some regions between local authorities and regional partners. Assemblies operate within the same boundaries of the Government Offices in the regions and the RDAs. Their constitutions vary from region to region'. See http://www.communities.gov.uk/citiesandregions/regional/regionalassemblies/ (last visited 4.9.2008).

[3][1706 c. 11]; [1707 c. 7(S)].

Before the devolution process, which is analyzed below, came into effect, the UK Parliament would legislate in all areas of law for the whole of the UK, i.e., England, Wales, Scotland and Northern Ireland. Although the separateness of the Scottish legal system from English common law, and the separate and largely independent judicial system in Scotland, were preserved after the union in the eighteenth century, all new legislation for Scotland before the recent devolution had to pass through the UK Parliament. The separateness of Scottish (or Scots) law was, however, always acknowledged in that legislation for Scotland was passed separately from legislation for England and Wales, often with different provisions of a procedural and technical nature to fit it with the special features of Scots law and often with different commencement dates.[4] This practice is likely to continue after the devolution with regard to all legislative measures for Scotland that have been reserved for the UK Parliament (see below).

Primary law making for England and Wales remains in the hands of the UK Parliament, for the time being. As far as Wales is concerned, the Welsh devolution process, analyzed below, may 1 day in the future lead to greater law-making autonomy for Wales, but Wales remains and is likely to remain firmly integrated into the judicial structure of the English legal system.

Northern Ireland is a special case. Several attempts at devolution of law-making powers to Belfast were made and failed during the province's turbulent political history in the second half of the twentieth century, culminating in the devolution process actually in progress and described below. And unlike Wales, Northern Ireland always enjoyed a separate court system. But, like in Wales, the common law in Northern Ireland has always being essentially English in sources and style, with limited exceptions often imposed by the special political problems facing the province.

18.2.1.1 The Scottish Parliament

> Most important in terms of actual significance and impact in the UK has been the Scottish devolution, with the creation of the new Scottish Parliament, which now sits in its splendid new building in Scotland's elegant capital City, Edinburgh. The main legislation is contained in the Scotland Act of 1998.

This Act gives to the Scottish Parliament sovereign powers to legislate in Scotland, and to confer or remove functions exercisable in Scotland, except in areas reserved for legislation exclusively by the Westminster Parliament.[5] But the

---

[4] As an example, the Human Rights Act 1998 came immediately into effect in Scotland but only 2 years later, i.e. in 2000, in England and Wales.

[5] Section 29 of the Scotland Act 1998 entitled 'Legislative competence', provides the following on the legislative competence of the new Scottish Parliament (1) An Act of the Scottish Parliament is not law so far as any provision of the Act is outside the legislative competence of the Parliament. (2) A provision is outside that competence so far as any of the following paragraphs apply—(a) it would form part of the law of a country or territory other than Scotland, or confer or remove

ambit of these exceptions can be modified, increased or decreased, by the UK executive, acting as Her Majesty by Order of Council, under a special provision in the Act.[6] Importantly, the independence of Scots Private law and Scots Criminal law is preserved and enhanced by the Scotland Act, as the Scottish Parliament is given powers over these matters even in areas reserved for Westminster, unless the rule in question is special to a reserved matter.[7]

Matters of Constitutional importance reserved for Westminster include freedom of trade in the UK guaranteed by the Union with Scotland Act 1706 and the Union with England Act 1707[8]; certain provisions of the European Communities Act 1972[9]; the provisions of the Local Government, Planning and Land Act 1980 on designation of enterprise zones[10]; the provisions of the Social Security Administration Act 1992 on rent rebate and rent allowance subsidy and council tax benefit[11]; the Human Rights Act 1998, which implemented in the UK the European Convention of Human Rights, which first came into force in Scotland.[12]

Other reserved matters, on which the Scottish Parliament has no legislative powers, are defined by Schedule 5 of the Scotland Act. These include, first, several aspects of the UK constitution, namely, the Crown, including succession to the Crown and a regency, the Union of the Kingdoms of Scotland and England, the Parliament of the United Kingdom, the continued existence of the High Court of Justiciary as a criminal court of first instance in Scotland and of appeal, and the continued existence of the Court of Session as a civil court of first instance and of appeal. Even the determination of the remuneration of judges[13] of the

---

functions exercisable otherwise than in or as regards Scotland, (b) it relates to reserved matters, (c) it is in breach of the restrictions in Schedule 4, (d) it is incompatible with any of the Convention rights or with Community law, (e) it would remove the Lord Advocate from his position as head of the systems of criminal prosecution and investigation of deaths in Scotland.

[6] Section 30 of the same Act entitled 'Legislative competence: supplementary' provides: (1) Schedule 5 (which defines reserved matters) shall have effect. (2) Her Majesty may by Order in Council make any modifications of Schedule 4 or 5 which She considers necessary or expedient. (3) Her Majesty may by Order in Council specify functions which are to be treated, for such purposes of this Act as may be specified, as being, or as not being, functions which are exercisable in or as regards Scotland. (4) An Order in Council under this section may also make such modifications of (a) any enactment or prerogative instrument (including any enactment comprised in or made under this Act), or (b) any other instrument or document,—as Her Majesty considers necessary or expedient in connection with other provision made by the Order.

[7] Or the subject-matter of the rule is interest on sums due in respect of taxes or excise duties and refunds of such taxes or duties, or the obligations, in relation to occupational or personal pension schemes, of the trustees or managers.

[8] Articles 4 and 6 of the Union with Scotland Act 1706 [1706 c. 11] and the Union with England Act 1707 [1707 c. 7(S)].

[9] [1972 c. 68]—Section 1 and Schedule 1, Section 2, Section 3 (1) and (2), Section 11 (2).

[10] Paragraphs 5(3)(b) and 15(4)(b) of Schedule 32 [1980 c. 65].

[11] Sections 140A to 140G [1992 c. 5].

[12] [1998 c. 42].

[13] Head L, Schedule 5.

Court of Session, sheriffs principal and sheriffs, members of the Lands Tribunal for Scotland, and the Chairman of the Scottish Land Court is a reserved matter. This shows that, despite the traditional independence of the Scottish legal system recognized in the devolution legislation, all matters relating to the tenure and remuneration of judges, important for judicial independence from party politics, are reserved as matters of UK Constitutional importance. Significantly, however, Her Majesty's prerogative and other executive functions, functions exercisable by any person acting on behalf of the Crown, or any office in the Scottish Administration are not reserved,[14] showing the extent of devolved executive power to the Scottish executive. Other reserved matters include the registration and funding of political parties, foreign affairs, such as international relations, including relations with territories outside the United Kingdom, the European Communities (and their institutions) and other international organizations, regulation of international trade, and international development assistance and co-operation. But observing and implementing international obligations, obligations under the Human Rights Convention and obligations under Community law, are tasks for the devolved Parliament, showing the significant extent to which the new Scottish Parliament can legislate in these areas.[15] Public service reserved matters include the Civil Service of the State, but exclude amending the Sheriff Courts and Legal Officers (Scotland) Act 1927, on the appointment of sheriff clerks and procurators fiscal etc., allowing the Scottish Parliament powers to change the way frontline judicial offices are designed and fulfilled. Defense matters are also reserved.

In relation to financial and economic matters, besides fiscal, economic and monetary policy, including the issue and circulation of money, taxes and excise duties, UK government borrowing and lending, the currency, other reserved matters include the regulation of financial services, investment business, banking and deposit-taking, collective investment schemes and insurance, the financial markets, including listing and public offers of securities and investments, the transfer of securities and insider dealing as well as the law on money laundering. The law of business associations i.e., the creation, operation, regulation and dissolution of all types of business associations,[16] is also reserved. The definition of "business association" includes 'any person (other than an individual) established for the purpose of carrying on any kind of business, whether or not for profit'; and "business" includes the provision of benefits to the members of an 'association'.[17] All aspects of insolvency law are also reserved, such as the modes of, the grounds for and the general legal effect of winding up, and the persons who may initiate winding up, liability to contribute to assets on winding up, powers of courts in

---

[14] Section 2 (1) of Schedule 5.

[15] Always, however, *praeter* and not *contra* the Constitutionally entrenched European Convention: see *infra*, in the text.

[16] Excluding particular public bodies, or public bodies of a particular type, established by or under any enactment, and, significantly, charities.

[17] Section C1.

relation to proceedings for winding up, arrangements with creditors, and procedures giving protection from creditors. Competition law remains in the province of the UK Parliament, regarding the regulation of anti-competitive practices and agreements, abuse of dominant position, monopolies and mergers.

Regulations of professions such as architects and auditors is also reserved for the Westminster Parliament but, significantly, not the regulation of particular practices in the legal profession for the purpose of regulating itself or the provision of legal services. This exception recognizes the historical independence and differences of the legal professions in the constituent parts of the UK. Central UK legislative competence is further reserved in another important area of commercial law, i.e., intellectual property law, and, perhaps inevitably, in the light of wide EU harmonization, consumer protection law, including product liability, product standards and safety.[18] Telecommunications, postal services and internet services law, including electronic encryption are also reserved. In the field of energy supply, legislative regulation of nuclear energy, electricity, coal, and more controversially, oil and gas is largely reserved. The same is true for road, rail, air, and marine transport.

In the sphere of general private law and social policy, and against a background of the historically distinct evolution and independence of Scottish private law already mentioned, a number of significant issues are matters reserved for the Westminster Parliament. The list begins with social security law, including national insurance, provision of benefits, pensions, allowances, grants, loans and any other form of financial assistance, child support, occupational and personal pensions. Other significant reservations are employment law, employment rights and duties and industrial relations, and equal opportunities. Health and safety law is also reserved, with several important aspects of modern medical law, such as regulation of medicines, abortion and xenotransplantation, embryology, surrogacy and genetics.

18.2.1.2 The Welsh Assembly

With the Government of Wales Act 2006, the Welsh Assembly was granted power to make laws, which, at the present stage, and before a constitutional referendum envisaged by the Act is held to strengthen devolution, are called 'Measures of the National Assembly of Wales'.[19] An Assembly Measure 'may make any provision

---

[18]Excluding food, agricultural and horticultural produce, fish and fish products, seeds, animal feeding stuffs, fertilizers and pesticides, in relation to which Scottish self-regulation was long established before the devolution.

[19]Section 93 (1), entitled 'Assembly Measures', provides: 'The Assembly may make laws, to be known as Measures of the National Assembly for Wales or Mesurau Cynulliad Cenedlaethol Cymru (referred to in this Act as "Assembly Measures")'. After the referendum envisaged in section 103 is held and shows a positive result, the Assembly may (Section 107 (1) entitled 'Acts of the Assembly'') 'make laws, to be known as Acts of the National Assembly for Wales or Deddfau Cynulliad Cenedlaethol Cymru (referred to in this Act as "Acts of the Assembly")'.

that could be made by an Act of Parliament'[20] However, the power of the United Kingdom to make laws for Wales is retained,[21] and, as in the case of Scotland, it is made clear in the 2006 Act that a provision of an Assembly Measure applies only in relation to Wales.[22]

Unlike in the case of the Scottish Parliament, which, as already shown, has a residual legislative competence in all matters other than those reserved for the UK Parliament, the areas of legislative competence of the Welsh Assembly are set out in Part 1 of Schedule 5 of the Act,[23] mainly covering areas that are usually left to local government regulation, with the addition of powers in relation to the distinct cultural and linguistic heritage of Wales. As there never was a separate legal system in Wales like there was in Scotland, and as English Private and Criminal Law always applied in Wales, and as English Law Courts always had common jurisdiction over England and Wales, there was no scope for granting to the Welsh Assembly any general competence over private or criminal law matters.

Besides, however, the areas of competence set out in the list in Schedule 5, Part 1 of the 2006 Act, the Welsh Assembly may submit to Her Majesty a draft Legislative Competence Order (LCO) for approval in Council, after the consent is obtained of both UK Houses of Parliament, adding a new area of competence to the list, in a procedure laid down by Section 95 of the Act, entitled 'Legislative competence: supplementary'. The power to submit a draft LCO adds a certain dynamic to Welsh devolution as it allows the Welsh Assembly to actively engage in new areas of legislative policy in Wales. This is already pursued with a certain enthusiasm by Welsh political leaders in the Assembly.

18.2.1.3 The Northern Ireland Assembly

In the troubled history of Northern Ireland, devolution finally arrived when, in 2007, the Northern Ireland Act of 1998 was given effect by the election of members of the Northern Ireland Assembly, established by the Act. In September 2007 they sat for the first time in their Chamber in Belfast and assumed their legislative powers.

---

[20]Section 94 (1).

[21]Section 93 (5).

[22]Section 94 (4) (b).

[23]They are the following: Field 1: agriculture, fisheries, forestry and rural development; Field 2: ancient monuments and historic buildings; Field 3: culture; Field 4: economic development; Field 5: education and training; Field 6: environment; Field 7: fire and rescue services and promotion of fire safety; Field 8: food; Field 9: health and health services; Field 10: highways and transport; Field 11: housing; Field 12: local government; Field 13: National Assembly for Wales; Field 14: public administration; Field 15: social welfare; Field 16: sport and recreation; Field 17: tourism; Field 18: town and country planning; Field 19: water and flood defense; Field 20: Welsh language.

According to the Northern Ireland Act 1998, 'the Assembly may make laws, to be known as Acts'.[24] But it shall be the Secretary of State for Northern Ireland, a UK Government minister, who submits Bills passed by the Assembly for Royal Assent.[25] The usual caveats apply, with regard to European Convention rights, European Community law and, a particularly sensitive issue in Northern Ireland, discrimination against any person or class of person on the ground of religious belief or political opinion.[26] Furthermore, there are lists of excepted[27] and reserved[28] matters. The consent of the Secretary of State is required in relation to a Bill containing a provision which deals with an excepted matter and which is ancillary to other provisions (whether in the Bill or previously enacted) dealing with reserved or transferred matters, or a provision which deals with a reserved matter.[29] In these matters, where consent is given, a Bill to which the Secretary of State has consented cannot be submitted by him for Royal Assent unless he has first laid it before the UK Parliament for information and possible debate.[30] The Secretary of State may decide not to submit for Royal Assent a Bill containing a provision which he considers incompatible with any international obligations of the UK, with the interests of defense or national security or with the protection of public safety or public order; or which would have an adverse effect on the operation of the single market in goods and services within the United Kingdom.[31]

The list of excepted matters in Schedule 2 of the Act starts with the integrity of the status and property of the Crown, the UK Parliament, international relations, including relations with territories outside the United Kingdom, the European Communities (and their institutions) and other international organizations, and international development assistance and co-operation; the defense of the realm; trading with the enemy; the armed forces of the Crown, war pensions; the Ministry of Defense Police, control of nuclear, biological and chemical weapons and other weapons of mass destruction, dignities and titles of honor, treason (but, significantly, not powers of arrest or criminal procedure), nationality; immigration, including asylum and the status and capacity of persons in the United Kingdom who are not British citizens; free movement of persons within the European Economic Area

---

[24] Section 5 (1); section 5 (6) contains the usual proviso 'This section does not affect the power of the Parliament of the United Kingdom to make laws for Northern Ireland, but an Act of the Assembly may modify any provision made by or under an Act of Parliament in so far as it is part of the law of Northern Ireland'. And section 6 (2) (a) provides that the Assembly has no legislative power to make laws that 'would form part of the law of a country or territory other than Northern Ireland, or confer or remove functions exercisable otherwise than in or as regards Northern Ireland'.

[25] Section 14.

[26] Section 6 (2) c, d, e. Also section 7, 'Entrenched enactments', (1), provides that these include the European Communities Act 1972, and the Human Rights Act 1998.

[27] Schedule 2.

[28] Schedule 3.

[29] Section 8.

[30] Section 15.

[31] Section 14 (5).

and issue of travel documents. The list also includes taxes or duties under any law applying to the United Kingdom as whole, and national insurance contributions. The appointment and removal of judges of the Supreme Court of Judicature of Northern Ireland, other holders of judicial offices, county court judges, recorders, resident magistrates, justices of the peace, members of juvenile court panels, and coroners; elections, including the franchise, in respect of the Northern Ireland Assembly, the European Parliament and district councils, the registration of political parties, coinage, legal tender and bank notes; nuclear energy and nuclear installations, including nuclear safety, and regulation of activities in outer space.

The list of reserved matters in Schedule 3 includes the conferral of functions in relation to Northern Ireland on any Minister of the Crown, property belonging to Her Majesty in right of the Crown or belonging to a department of the Government of the United Kingdom or held in trust for Her Majesty for the purposes of such a department, navigation, including merchant shipping, but not harbors or inland waters, civil aviation but not aerodromes, the foreshore and the sea bed and subsoil and their natural resources, submarine pipe-lines, submarine cables, domicile, the Post Office, posts (including postage stamps, postal orders and postal packets) and the regulation of postal services. Significantly, it also includes disqualification for membership of the Assembly; privileges, powers and immunities of the Assembly, its members and committees, the criminal law, the creation of offences and penalties, the prevention and detection of crime and powers of arrest and detention in connection with crime or criminal proceedings, prosecutions, the treatment of offenders (including children and young persons, and mental health patients, involved in crime), the surrender of fugitive offenders between Northern Ireland and the Republic of Ireland and compensation out of public funds for victims of crime, the maintenance of public order, including the conferring of powers, authorities, privileges or immunities for that purpose on constables, members of the armed forces of the Crown and other persons, the establishment, organization and control of the Royal Ulster Constabulary and of any other police force (other than the Ministry of Defense Police), the Police Authority for Northern Ireland, and traffic wardens. Also firearms and explosives, civil defense; additionally, all matters, other than those specified in Schedule 2 (above), relating to the Supreme Court of Judicature of Northern Ireland, county courts, courts of summary jurisdiction (including magistrates' courts and juvenile courts) and coroners, including procedure, evidence, appeals, juries, costs, legal aid and the registration, execution and enforcement of judgments and orders, but not bankruptcy, insolvency, the winding up of corporate and unincorporated bodies or the making of arrangements or compositions with creditors, and the regulation of the profession of solicitors; import and export controls and trade with any place outside the United Kingdom, financial services, including investment business, banking and deposit-taking, collective investment schemes and insurance, financial markets, including listing and public offers of securities and investments, transfer of securities and insider dealing; regulation of anti-competitive practices and agreements; abuse of dominant position; monopolies and mergers; intellectual property; units of measurement and United Kingdom primary standards; telecommunications, wireless telegraphy, Internet services, electronic encryption;

xenotransplantation, surrogacy arrangements, human fertilization, human genetics; consumer safety in relation to goods; technical standards and requirements in relation to products in pursuance of an obligation under Community law but not standards and requirements in relation to food, agricultural or horticultural produce, fish or fish products, seeds, animal feeding stuffs, fertilizers or pesticides; environmental protection (emission limits), the environmental protection technology scheme for research and development in the United Kingdom, and data protection.

18.2.2 Plurality of Judge-Made Law

The account, above, of the plurality of legislative powers in the recently devolved systems of the United Kingdom does not give a complete picture of legal pluralism in this country. What needs to be added is a note on the plurality of judge-made law because that continues to play a very important role as a primary source of law in all parts of the UK. In most fields of private law, both substantive and procedural, as well as constitutional and administrative law (to a lesser extent), traditional legislative lethargy has surrendered detailed development of the law to the courts of record, under the doctrine of *stare decisis*. Broadly speaking, judge-made law in the UK shows a sharp dividing line between, on the one hand, English common law, applicable in England and Wales and also, despite its separate courts system, in Northern Ireland, and, on the other hand, Scots law, applicable only in Scotland. Origins, tradition, sources, precedent, literature and legal culture of these two are clearly distinct and different, so much so as to make Scots law terra incognita for lawyers in England, Wales and Northern Ireland[32] (although this cannot be said about English common law in Scotland).

The devolution process has arguably consolidated this divide to the extent that, as detailed below, the recently inaugurated UK Supreme Court will have to wear different hats when deciding appeals from different regions. Still, the fact that, for the first time in the UK's legal history, all appeals now converge in London (except Scottish Criminal law appeals that are now firmly domesticated in Edinburgh), where the UK Supreme Court, staffed, as it is, with judges from every part of the UK, deals with them as one, central, last resort jurisdiction is bound to counterbalance this devolution. This could develop into a showcase of how the goal of *e pluribus unum* can be achieved in practice.

---

[32] As an example of a personal experience, I can reveal that my English law students have consistently failed throughout the years of teaching generations of them to identify the Scottish Supreme Court, the name of the legal profession in Scotland, or a single Scots law author or legal journal. They are more likely to have more knowledge of French or Australian law.

18.2.3 Concluding Remarks: What Is Ruled in the Province and What Stays in the Centre?

There is no easy and quick way out of the labyrinth of devolved and non-devolved legal powers to a landscape, where who has legal powers for what is clearly mapped. But the broad lines of what powers are allocated to the parts and what are reserved for the centre could be drawn as follows:

A. All matters of constitutional, administrative, European and international law are reserved for the UK Parliament and the UK Government. Included are areas of private law that are regulated by European or international law transposed into domestic UK law, such as commercial law, company law and competition law, human rights, and criminal law unified or harmonized in Europe or by international treaty. Employment law is also the responsibility of the Centre, as is pensions law.

In other areas of public law, such as social security law and taxation, Scottish, Welsh and Northern Irish legal bodies are allowed a certain degree of local autonomy, as detailed above. Essentially, income tax is central, UK-wide, and Inland Revenue is the UK Government's agency that collects it. The Scottish parliament can raise some additional taxes for services in Scotland, such as education, health, police and social security. And local authorities all over the rest of the UK raise so-called local council taxes to fund local services, such as schools, the police, roads, and garbage collection. The UK Government does allocate substantial funds to the regional executives and local authorities, and there is a controversy over the size of the Scottish grant from Westminster. To put it rather crudely, the power of the purse certainly lies with the Centre.

B. It is in areas of private law, broadly defined, that devolved parts of the UK have greater competence, provided they are areas not affected by EU legislation, which would be reserved for the Centre.

The Scottish Parliament has competence in areas such as health, education, industry, local government, social work and housing, economic development and transport, criminal and civil law and home affairs, environment, agriculture, forestry and fishing, sport and the arts, unless matters are specifically reserved for the UK Parliament, as detailed above. Scottish private law within the competency of the Scottish Parliament includes the general principles of private law, private international law, the law of persons, the law of obligations, as well as the law of property and succession,[33] and the law of actions. Similar competencies in private law areas have been granted to the Northern Ireland Assembly. The Welsh Assembly has more restricted powers in these areas, depending often, as detailed earlier in this section, on a Legislative Competence Order granted by the Westminster Parliament.

---

[33]Characteristically, Scots law has only relatively recently caught up with the rest of the UK in important areas of Property and Succession law: The Conveyancing and Feudal Reform (Scotland) Act 1970 modernized heritable securities and created new ways of changing land conditions. The Land Tenure Reform (Scotland) Act 1974 allowed for the redemption of feu duty and the Land Registration (Scotland) Act 1979 provided for a new Land Register where titles to land are given a government-backed indemnity. Many of these matters were already dealt with by a series of major codifications in the rest of the UK in the mid-1920s.

18.3 The Means and Methods of Legal Unification

18.3.1 The Multi-layered Constitutional Framework

As a preliminary, it should be recalled that even before the recent devolution reforms, there were in the United Kingdom three separate legal systems, with distinct sources and court systems.

- English law, applicable in England and Wales;
- Scots law, applicable in Scotland
- The law of Northern Ireland, essentially identical with English law, but often with important divergences enacted by Parliament in view of the special political circumstances of the Northern Ireland provinces.

According to fundamental Constitutional principles, the main sources of the law in the whole of the UK are:

- Acts of Parliament, i.e. statutes enacted by the Westminster Parliament in London for England and Wales, Scotland, or Northern Ireland, as the case may be. Following the devolution reforms, competent legislative acts of the devolved bodies must be added as sources of law exclusively in the devolved region (see details above).
- Statutory Instruments and subordinate (delegated) legislation, again, issued for England and Wales, Scotland, or Northern Ireland, as the case may be; these are ministerial orders issued under the authority of an Act of Parliament.
- Judicial Precedents, i.e., final decisions of courts of record (known as the common law). The authority of this judge-made law is equal to that of legislation, except that, by reason of the fundamental Constitutional principle of the Sovereignty of Parliament (see also below), the common law gives way to Acts of Parliament that expressly, or by implication, govern a specific matter. The supreme court of record, with authority to change its own precedent and overrule any other court in the land, is the new UK Supreme Court, which since 1 October 2009 has replaced the House of Lords as the supreme appellate jurisdiction in the UK. Yet, and in matters of European law and Human Rights law, the supreme courts of record are the European Court of Justice and the European Court of Human Rights in Strasbourg respectively (the final decisions of which are now binding on UK courts after the introduction of the Human Rights Act 1998)

The UK's constituent legal parts are subject to a multi-layered unification and harmonization process, under principles of UK Constitutional law, EU treaties and the European Convention of Human Rights, which has been fully incorporated into domestic UK law since the enactment of the Human Rights Act 1998.

It is a special feature of UK Constitutional law that there is no written Constitutional text that can be used for the constitutional control of devolved legislative power, in the way that it is in other jurisdictions such as the USA or Germany. The doctrine of sovereignty of the UK Parliament vitiates against the formal recognition of superior legislative authority to a preexisting legislative text. The degree to which this doctrine has been affected by important transfers of sovereignty from Westminster to the EU and the European Convention of Human Rights is hotly debated by scholars and judges. But to the extent that judges as the ultimate arbiters of legality accept, in a Kelsenian sense, the supremacy of certain principles embedded in UK legislation, namely, those that stem from the EU Treaty, the European Convention of Human Rights and European legislation protecting individual rights such as non-discrimination, data protection, consumer safety and the like, or policies such as environmental protection, these principles acquire de facto a superior legislative authority and are increasingly used as Constitutional parameters of legality of legislative and executive action. Formally, the courts in the UK have no jurisdiction to review the constitutionality of Acts of the UK Parliament, because of the doctrine of parliamentary sovereignty. But, as already noted, after the devolution process, the UK Supreme Court has jurisdiction to review the compliance of legislation passed by the devolved law-making bodies with the devolution Acts. The UK Supreme Court, which is, unlike the Judicial Committee of the House of Lords that it replaced, clearly detached from the Upper House of the UK Parliament, could, however, enhance the process of a gradual de facto judicial review of constitutionality of legislative acts, both of the UK Parliament, and of the devolved legislative bodies, as far as respect for the basic individual rights and policies, described above as embedded into UK law, is concerned. It is not impossible to imagine the growth of a UK Supreme Court jurisprudence establishing practices of interpretation of rights and principles of constitutional import, reminiscent of the work of the US Supreme Court in interpreting the US Constitutional amendments to develop a constitutional control of State legislation. This new constitutional reality is already to some extent reflected in a common theme emerging from the devolution legislation, in the lists of matters reserved or excluded from the legislative power of devolved legislative bodies, or the enumeration of entrenched UK legislation that cannot be abrogated or modified, or in provisions that legislative acts of devolved bodies must not be incompatible with any of the Convention rights, or Community law, or must not discriminate against any person or class of persons on the ground of religious belief or political opinion. In a historical perspective, these new developments are a significant advance towards a consolidation of the fragmented sources of the UK Constitution into a modern charter of constitutional principles. Let us now take a closer look at those sources.

Formally, and in the absence of a written constitution, the primary sources of constitutional law in the United Kingdom continue to be the same as the sources of legal rules in general, namely:

A. Legislation, i.e., Acts of Parliament, legislation enacted by Ministers and other authorities upon whom Parliament has conferred power to legislate, exceptionally, legislative instruments issued by the Crown under its prerogative powers, and, since 1973, legislation enacted by competent organs of the European Communities. Many Acts of Parliament have been enacted which relate to the system of Government.

Most topics of Constitutional law have been affected by legislation; constitutional law, unlike, for example, the private law of contract and tort, is mainly statutory law. But the numerous statutes enacted throughout the centuries, from medieval charters to present day Acts of Parliament, can by no means be seen as forming a constitutional code. They do not form part of a systematic exposition of principles or rules, and, unlike in most other contemporary legal systems, they can be formally repealed or altered by another Act of Parliament, under normal Parliamentary legislative procedure. But there are a few statutes, which, although of no different formal status than the other Acts, have special Constitutional significance in the field of civil liberties and individual rights:

The Magna Carta first enacted in 1215, long before the formation of the present state of the United Kingdom, and confirmed on numerous occasions thereafter. It is a Charter setting out the rights of various classes of the medieval communities according to their needs. Famous clauses guarantee judgment by the law of the land or one's peers (jury trial) and that to none justice should be denied (habeas corpus). Today, the Magna Charter is more of symbolic value than actual legal force.

Petition of Right, enacted by the English Parliament in 1628; most important contents include protests against taxation without consent of Parliament and against arbitrary imprisonment.

Bill of Rights and Claim of Right. The first was enacted by the English Parliament in 1689, laying the foundations of the modern constitution by disposing of the more extravagant claims of the Monarchy to rule by prerogative right. Its articles are still part of English law and guarantee that the Monarchy cannot legislate without Parliament's consent. The Claim of Right was enacted by the Scottish Parliament in 1689, with similar provisions.

The Act of Settlement passed by the English Parliament in 1700, providing for the succession to the throne and the independence of the judiciary.

The European Communities Acts implementing the various EU Treaties have introduced a variety of new individual rights into English law, of a constitutional nature. It must be noted that these two Acts are viewed by the British judiciary as having, unofficially, a higher status than ordinary legislation, although, in theory, of equal formal authority with any other Act of Parliament.

The consolidating Treaty of Lisbon, made the Charter of Fundamental Rights of the European Union an integral part of EU law, under a special Protocol attached to the main text of the Treaty. This was considered potentially dangerous to the independence of the common law system of British justice. Accordingly, a separate Protocol has been agreed, under which the Charter has no binding force on any court, and the European Court of Justice no jurisdiction to enforce the Charter in the UK (or Poland, which raised similar concerns). Since the Human Rights Act of 1998 has incorporated into UK law the European Convention of Human Rights (see below), the exclusion of the EU Charter mainly avoids the binding effect of so-called 'social' or 'economic' rights. To that extent, UK Fundamental Rights might not be harmonized with such rights in the rest of Europe. Furthermore, since 1999, the UK and Ireland have had an opt-out right to choose on legislation in the field of civil judicial co-operation – essentially, measures that relate to cross-border civil litigation and family law. So far, the UK has taken part in most civil litigation measures, including small claims and cross-border legal aid, but not measures that deal with divorce and family law. Under the Treaty of Lisbon, this opt-out has been extended to cover police and judicial co-operation, essentially measures that deal with the fight against organized crime and terrorism, cross-border prosecution, and investigation and rights for the individual. Essentially, the UK kept the choice to opt in to measures, such as these, which will bolster individual rights and procedural guarantees, or to adopt only measures which will expand cross-border police powers and investigative activity.

The Human Rights Act (HRA) 1998, incorporating into UK domestic law the European Convention of Human Rights, and other important legislation concerning equality and non discrimination that are regarded as implying an obligation of legislative compliance with fundamental rights now embedded in the UK Constitutional order.

The HRA 1998 was endowed by the UK Parliament with a provision that primary and secondary legislation must be compatible with its provisions. Courts are given the power to review and declare the incompatibility of primary legislation with the HRA, although the doctrine of the sovereignty of Parliament is preserved by an express provision that a judicial declaration of incompatibility is not binding on the parties and does not undermine the validity of the legislation. However, even if these declarations cannot bind the UK Parliament, or the executive as a party to judicial proceedings, recent experience has shown that they carry a lot of weight as expressions of the power of the courts to defend fundamental democratic values of the country. In the words of the UK's greatly respected former Senior Law Lord, Lord Bingham, '[T]he 1998 Act gives the courts a very specific, wholly democratic, mandate' in this connection.

It is noteworthy that this legislation is declared as entrenched in the devolved legislative competences in all the devolution reforms, as is also the legislation establishing the EC Treaties (see above). Also, decisions of the UK Supreme Court on devolution issues arising from action incompatible with either the Human Rights Act or the EC Treaties will be binding on both the legislative and the executive of the devolved parts of the UK.

B. A second important source of UK Constitutional law is judicial precedent, i.e., decisions of the courts expounding the common law or interpreting legislation. This includes, since 1973, the decisions of the European Court of Justice in relation to European Community law, and since 2000 the decisions of European Court of Human Rights in Strasbourg in relation to Human Rights law. An important judicial task is the interpretation of enacted law. Although courts do not have the authority to rule on the validity of an Act of Parliament, they can do so in the case of subordinate legislation, and are always expected to interpret statutes.

Secondary sources of the U.K. constitution are:

(a) Custom or constitutional convention, i.e. rules of conduct based upon political, social or commercial custom and recognized by the courts as having binding force.
(b) *Lex et consuetudo Parliamenti*, i.e. the law and custom of both Houses of Parliament, the House of Commons and the House of Lords, which both have the inherent power to regulate their own affairs.
(c) Doctrinal Writings, of writers of constitutional works of authority (more below).

Where does this wonderful UK mix of constitutional law sources take us? For a conclusion in this brief survey of the UK constitutional landscape, it must first be observed that written constitutions make it possible for the legal structure of government to assume a variety of different forms. They allow the protection of certain rights of the citizen by placing these rights beyond the reach of the organs of government created by the constitution. Such rights become fundamental or basic rights, which, as in the case of the German Basic Law (*Grundgesetz*), may be designated as being in essence unalterable. A further important goal that can be achieved by a written constitution is that of the separation of powers, legislative, executive, and judicial. The United Kingdom has no written constitution that can implement these tasks and serve as a higher fundamental law. As there is no single written document to serve as the fundamental law of the country and the foundation of the legal system, the position of *Grundnorm* in present day U.K. law is occupied by the legal doctrine of the legislative supremacy of Parliament. What is meant by this doctrine is that there are no legal limitations upon the legislative competence of Parliament. No present Parliament can formally bind its successors. The doctrine of sovereignty of Parliament clearly distinguishes the United Kingdom from those countries in which a written constitution imposes limits upon the legislator and vests ordinary courts or a special constitutional court with the power to decide whether legislative acts are in accordance with the constitution. U.K.'s membership of the European Community, however, has led to a restriction of this doctrine, as Community law must prevail over inconsistent legislation passed by the U.K. Parliament, whether before or after the enactment of the European Community Act 1972. This principle, affirmed by the European Court of Justice with regard to the national law of all member states, was also accepted by U.K. courts. The introduction of the Human Rights Act 1998 has further undermined the traditional supremacy of the doctrine, as already pointed out and as evident in the devolution legislation. Whereas it will be hard for the UK Parliament to act in a way contrary to fundamental legislation, which it has itself declared as entrenched in the legislative powers of devolved legislative bodies, in theory, it still retains absolute sovereignty and power to do so.

18.3.2 The Effect of European Courts and Institutions, the Uniform Development of the Common Law by UK Courts Under the Stare Decisis Doctrine, and the Transnational Development of English Common Law

The recent major Constitutional reforms in the UK, both in the devolution process and with regard to the system of administration of justice, have not affected the centuries-old stare decisis rule that ensures a strict adherence to the precedent laid down by a superior court, in a hierarchy currently topped by the new UK Supreme Court. Indeed, the inauguration of the UK Supreme Court has removed the last remaining ambiguity as to whether the top UK Court has absolute power to lay down precedent for all UK courts from which it can hear an appeal, as the former separate jurisdiction of the Privy Council on matters of UK law, including devolution matters, has now been abolished.

Stare decisis ensures the maximum effect of at least three different layers of forces of uniform development exercising their gravitational pull on the UK as a whole, at the present time.

A. First, there is the crucial, centralized supervision by the UK Supreme Court of a strictly uniform application of the common law across the UK (except Scots Criminal law), and equally uniform interpretation of statutory law and the exercise of judicial review of administrative action.

Before the inauguration of the new UK Supreme Court, the grip of the House of Lords on the interpretation of all legislation, the judicial review of administrative action and the development of the common law by UK courts in all parts of the UK had already been tightened, after the so-called Practice Statement of 1966, in which the then Lord Chancellor, Lord Gardiner LC, announced that the House of Lords in its judicial capacity would no longer be bound by its own precedent, and concluded with the words that '[T]his announcement is not intended to affect the use of precedent elsewhere than in this House'.

Thus, the courts below, in all parts of the UK, are bound by the House of Lords' and now the UK Supreme Court's precedent, and cannot change their own. This applies equally to the two major appeals courts in the UK, the (English) Court of Appeal and the (Scottish) Court of Session. The Court of Appeal, the highest court in what the legislation abolished when the new UK Supreme Court became operational, designated as 'The Supreme Court of Judicature', traditionally exercised an important role in consolidating precedent and ensuring discipline in the development of English common law, with a considerable influence also in other jurisdictions in the British Commonwealth. This role had increased in significance after the reforms in the nineteenth century that finally ended the judicial separation of law and equity, integrating the chancery jurisdiction into the system of a Supreme Court of Judicature, with a single High Court and a Court of Appeal. Focusing exclusively on English law, unlike the House of Lords that had a wider UK remit, the Court of Appeal grew in authority. When Lord Denning returned from a brief spell in the House of Lords to preside over it as Master of the Rolls, he inaugurated a debate on stare decisis in the Court of Appeal, supporting the view that the court ought to have power to review and depart from its own precedent, without House of Lords authority. But in the important case of Davis v Johnson,[34] the House of Lords put beyond any doubt the hierarchical application of the doctrine of stare decisis also to decisions of the Court of Appeal, confirming the authority of the Court of Appeal's own more orthodox judgment in Young v Bristol Aeroplane Co Ltd.[35]

Several judges and observers of the debate on the power of the Court of Appeal to depart from its own precedent without the authority of the House of Lords had concentrated on the implications of such a departure from the doctrine of stare decisis for English law, but the affirmation of the absolute authority of House of Lords to control and alone change precedent had obvious implications for the uniformity of the law in all constituent parts of the UK. Had the Court of Appeal, which, as the sole Appeal Court in England and Wales and Northern Ireland, pronounces exclusively on English law, and which has no jurisdiction whatsoever in Scotland, been granted power to change English law without the intervention of House of Lords, English law would have been allowed to proceed entirely separately from the law of Scotland. By affirming its authority on the Court of Appeal the House of Lords put a stop to this possibility. As the final arbiter of all appeals from all parts of the UK, the House of Lords had always been a fertile forum of exchange of concepts and techniques of English and Scots law. Whenever general principles of significant importance were under consideration, the House would rarely distinguish between the two, although care was always taken to have enough Scots Law Lords on a panel and give them appropriate authority, when hearing a Scottish appeal. But English Law Lords were never prevented from judging a Scottish appeal, and vice-versa. Indeed, some of the most influential developments of English common law have been the work of Scottish Law Lords and Lord Chancellors, of which there were always aplenty in Westminster. In establishing or changing precedent across the UK, the House of Lords had always used indiscriminately appeals from any part of the UK, rarely, if ever, confining its effect to the UK part from which the appeal originated. Characteristically, one of the more celebrated House of Lords judgments, creating the modern law of negligence and one of the most important principles of English tort law, came from a Scottish appeal.[36] Only occasionally, exceptional results would be explained as caused by a special doctrine of Scots law, but even then they would retain their influence on English law.

Will there be an important change now that the new UK Supreme Court has come into existence? As already noted, according to the Constitutional reform legislation passed by the UK Parliament, and in order to avoid a conflict with the aspirations of the devolution process, a decision of the UK Supreme Court, 'on appeal from a court

---

[34] 1979 AC 264.
[35] [1944] KB 718 CA.
[36] Donoghue v Stevenson [1932] AC 562.

of any part of the United Kingdom, other than a decision on a devolution matter, is to be regarded as a decision of a court of that part of the United Kingdom'. This may imply that, technically, any such decision should be regarded as having no overall UK effect. In reality, however, it is hard to contemplate that the Supreme Court judges will not use their power, inherited from their predecessors in the House of Lords, to change the law in any part of the UK in a way that allows a common pursuit of an optimal development. Additionally, devolutions issues, in which the Supreme Court will officially decide as a UK court, include important entrenched and reserved matters (described in Part I above), in which UK law as a whole must remain uniform.

B. A second layer of transnational uniformity operating on all UK law exists in the already emphasized superior authority of the EU Court of Justice in Luxembourg (ECJ), and other empowered EU Institutions such as the EU Commission, to make or interpret EU law, on all matters of EU Law; and the superior authority of the European Court of Human Rights in Strasbourg (ECHR), on all matters of the European Convention of Human Rights. ECJ and ECHR precedent is binding on all courts in the UK.

C. A third layer of transnational uniformity affects all UK law as a result of the remarkable extent to which English common law is developed transnationally in all jurisdictions within the British Commonwealth, where close attention and respect is still being paid to important developments in different jurisdictions, even after the almost complete eclipse of the Privy Council's power to hear appeals from the member states of the Commonwealth.

18.3.3 The Role of Legal Doctrine and Legal Culture

Whereas the sources of the UK's legal systems, especially that of Scotland, after the devolution, are different, legal culture, an important factor of uniformity, is largely the same in all of its parts: it is the common law culture. In this culture, supreme authority in the interpretation of the law is vested with judges, as the leading juris prudentes, not with doctrinal writers. Doctrinal writing is, admittedly, held in greater esteem in Scotland, where the systematic collection of the Institutions of Scottish law by Lord Stair (published in 1683) is an important depository of Scottish law institutions and doctrines. But even in Scotland authority is sought in precedent rather than scholarly opinion.

This fact has affected seriously the extent to which textbook writers and others writing on the development of the law by legislators and courts can influence that development. It has been noticed in other jurisdictions, for example, the US, that textbook writers have exercised great influence in creating and safeguarding the perception of uniformity in American common law, despite the jurisdictional fragmentation into State laws, which escapes to a considerable extent any central federal judicial control. In the UK textbook writers do not have the same impact. However, they are cited across jurisdictional borders. But, usually, these are only writers writing on 'English' law (rather than 'Scottish') or, simply, 'law'.

As already noted above, it is the judges of the UK Supreme Court and of the other courts of record, rather than the scholars, that exercise the greatest influence in the uniform development of the law in the UK. However, judges increasingly cite non-judicial sources in their reasoning, and this enhances the indirect influence of scholarly writing on the development and interpretation of the law. Indeed, the House of Lords had recently even cited the jurisprudence of foreign jurisdictions, common law and European, as well as doctrinal writers from such foreign jurisdictions. Moreover, the integration into all the legal systems of the UK of the jurisprudence of the European Court of Justice and the European Court of Human Rights has increased the indirect authority of scholars writing in these fields. In this way, the unifying influence of these two European courts (and also of the EU Commission legislating or interpreting EU law) is enhanced.

All judges in the UK are recruited from the ranks of experienced practitioners. This applies equally north and south of the English/Scottish border. And while it is true that the legal professions in England, Wales and Northern Ireland (barristers and solicitors) are completely separate from the legal profession in Scotland (advocates), with separate historical development and traditions, the reality on the ground is that legal culture is remarkably similar all over the different parts of the UK. In practice, the training, skills and organization of lawyers are generally identical, the only major difference being that in the south, in London, one finds large law firms that do not exist in Scotland. As judges of all jurisdictions across the UK are drawn from the ranks of practitioners, they share a common culture of pragmatism, social and economic awareness and aversion of theoretical and dogmatic constructions. They are also immune from party political pressure since they are not elected, as some judges in the US, for example, are, but are selected on merit by their peers. This culture is conducive to similarity of judicial reasoning and alertness to developments in all parts of the UK and beyond, enhancing uniformity of solutions at the point of delivery of justice, despite the plurality of formal sources of legislative and judge-made law.

18.3.4 *The Role of the Law Commissions, Entrusted with Law Review and Legal Reform in the UK's Constituent Part*

The Law Commissions Act 1965 created 'a body of Commissioners, to be known as the Law Commission, consisting ... of a Chairman and four other Commissioners appointed by the Lord Chancellor', for the purpose of 'promoting the reform of the law' of England and Wales. The Act provides that the person to be appointed as Chairman shall be a person who holds office as a judge of the High Court, or Court of Appeal, in England and Wales. This Law Commission, with a remit only to review English law, is accompanied by a Scottish Law Commission, created by the same Act, for the purpose of promoting the reform of the law of Scotland.

The function of both Commissions is described by the Act as follows:

'It shall be the duty of each of the Commissions to take and keep under review all the law with which they are respectively concerned with a view to its systematic development and reform, including in particular the codification of such law, the elimination of anomalies, the repeal of obsolete and unnecessary enactments, the reduction of the number of separate enactments and generally the simplification and modernization of the law'. Significantly, the Act provides that the Commissioners' have a duty 'to obtain such information as to the legal systems of other countries as appears to the Commissioners likely to facilitate the performance of any of their functions'.

The work of both Commissions has had a significant effect on preserving the coherence and uniformity of English and Scottish law respectively. And although the two Commissions work separately, it can be safely assumed that in their duty to reform the law in the light of the experience of 'other countries' they take into account the current position in the other part of the UK, when making proposals of law reform. Admittedly, and by reason of its broader use in several overseas jurisdictions, it will be more often the case that English law will inspire recommended reforms of Scots law, such as in the law trusts, than vice versa. It remains true that harmonizing the two separate legal systems of England and Scotland is clearly not within either Commissions statutory remit. Still, in the end, the work of these two independent statutory bodies, with membership drawn from eminent academics and practitioners in the two countries, is bound to contribute to the congruence of the two legal systems, as the Law Commissioners are less susceptible to national politics and genuinely concerned with improving the state of the law, if necessary, with the adoption of a foreign idea.

18.4 Institutional and Social Background

18.4.1 The UK Supreme Court

The UK Supreme Court is the final court of appeal in the United Kingdom of Great Britain and Northern Ireland, except for Scottish criminal cases. There are 12 judges in the UK Supreme Court. The Court will normally only be engaged in appeals on points of law that are not settled but disputed, or if there is a clear need to review and possibly change existing law. The UK Supreme Court hears appeals from any order or judgment of the Court of Appeal in England and Wales, and subject to certain statutory restrictions, directly from a decision of the High Court of Justice in England and Wales. It also hears appeals from any order or judgment of the Court of Appeal in Northern Ireland and again subject to statutory restrictions, direct from a decision of the High Court of Justice in Northern Ireland, as well as, finally, from judgments or certain orders of the Inner House of the Court of Session in Scotland. Criminal appeals are only heard from judgments or orders of the Court of Appeal

Criminal Division in England and Wales or the Court of Appeal in Northern Ireland on an appeal to that court, the Courts-Martial Appeal Court on an appeal to that court and the High Court of Justice in England and Wales or of the High Court of Justice in Northern Ireland. Generally, leave to appeal must be granted by the court below or, if refused, by the UK Supreme Court. There are no automatic rights of appeal under UK law.[37] The UK Supreme Court has, significantly, taken over from what was formerly the Judicial Committee of the Privy Council the adjudication of "devolution issues", under the Scotland Act 1998, the Government of Wales Act 1998 and the Northern Ireland Act 1998. The three devolution Acts contained a significant new rule of precedent with respect to the relative authority of judgments of the Appellate Committee of the House of Lords and the Judicial Committee of the Privy Council, which now applies to the judgments of the UK Supreme Court. The Scotland Act 1998, provided,[38] as do the other two Acts in similar provisions, that '[A]ny decision of the Judicial Committee in proceedings under this Act.... shall be binding in all legal proceedings (other than proceedings before the Judicial Committee).' But the number of appeals heard by the Judicial Committee of the Privy Council on devolution issues has been low.[39]

The Constitutional Reform Act 2005 was an overhaul of the UK constitutional order in which a clear separation of powers between the executive, the legislature and the judiciary was created for the first time in British constitutional history. The Act also modified the ancient office of the Lord Chancellor, and provided that the Lord Chancellor, who now carries also the title of Secretary of State for Justice, other Ministers of the Crown and all persons with responsibility for matters relating to the judiciary, or otherwise to the administration of justice, must uphold the continued independence of the judiciary.[40] This independence is strengthened in the Act by granting the chief justice of any part of the United Kingdom' the right to lay before Parliament (or the Scottish parliament, as appropriate) written representations on matters that appear to him to be matters of importance relating to the judiciary, or otherwise to the administration of justice, in that part of the United Kingdom. It is specified that in relation to England and Wales or Northern Ireland, the right belongs to the Lord Chief Justice of that part of the United Kingdom, and in relation to Scotland, to the Lord President of the Court of Session. Under the Act, the appellate jurisdiction of the House of Lords, together with the devolution jurisdiction of the Judicial Committee of the Privy Council, was transferred to the new Supreme Court of the United Kingdom on 1st October 2009.[41] The first

---

[37] Unlike the civil law tradition of the right 'to be heard twice'.

[38] Section 103 (1).

[39] In 2000, when the jurisdiction began, there were 3 such appeals, 10 in 2001, 4 in 2002, 1 in 2003, 4 in 2004 and only 2 in 2005, all from Scotland.

[40] Section 3 (1).

[41] Under Section 23 of the Act, the Court will comprise 12 judges (to be known as "Justices of the Supreme Court"), including a President and Deputy President, appointed by the Queen (the number can be increased by Order in Council).

members of the Court were 11 of the 12 Lords of Appeal in Ordinary,[42] in office when section 23 of the Constitutional Reform Act came into effect. All judges appointed to the Supreme Court in the future will not be members of the House of Lords and will be called 'Justices of the Supreme Court', and the current Law Lords have ceased to be members of the House of Lords. Significantly, the method of appointment of future members of the Supreme Court is transformed. A special selection commission is established, which must consult senior judges, the Lord Chancellor and, importantly, the devolved executives.[43] The selection "must be on merit"[44] and the commission must ensure that the judges of the Supreme Court between them have knowledge and experience of practice in the law of each part of the United Kingdom.[45] The Lord Chancellor may accept, reject or request the reconsideration of the selection of an individual candidate,[46] not only for lack of merit, but also on the ground that there is not enough evidence that if the person were appointed the judges of the Court would between them have knowledge of, and experience of practice in, the law of each part of the United Kingdom.[47] Thus the Lord Chancellor, this most ancient office of the realm, becomes the guardian of legal plurality in the UK at the highest level.[48] Furthermore, it is declared[49] that the creation of the Supreme Court must not '[to] affect the distinctions between the separate legal systems of the parts of the United Kingdom' and that a decision of the Supreme Court 'on appeal from a court of any part of the United Kingdom, other than a decision on a devolution matter, is to be regarded as a decision of a court of that part of the United Kingdom'.[50] These two provisions are intended to safeguard the existing autonomy of the separate legal systems of different parts of the United Kingdom. The UK Supreme Court will make decisions as a national UK court only on appeals on devolution matters. Indeed, in doing so, it will be the only national UK court of any jurisdiction or level.

From a comparative perspective, these two provisions are particularly interesting. Unlike Supreme Courts elsewhere, e.g., the US Supreme Court, the German *Bundesverfassungsgericht* and *Bundesgerichtshof*, the Swiss *Bundesgericht*, which

---

[42] One did not accept the appointment, creating a vacancy.

[43] Section 27 (2).

[44] Section 27 (5).

[45] Section 27 (8).

[46] Section 29.

[47] Section 30 (2) (c).

[48] In an official statement released on 08 October 2007, Jack Straw MP, the current Lord Chancellor and Secretary of State for Justice, announced that he would adopt the new appointments process for Justices of the new UK Supreme Court with immediate effect, stating: "I believe that it is sensible to adopt the new process from now on. This is because those newly appointed to the Appellate Committee of the House of Lords will spend the majority of their career in the Supreme Court. I will therefore adopt Section 8 of the Constitutional Reform Act on a voluntary basis, as any new appointments made will help to determine the character of the Court".

[49] Section 41 (1).

[50] Section 41 (2).

are visibly guardians of national legal unity, the UK Supreme Court is designed to safeguard the separateness of the legal systems in the country. These other courts are, however, all in countries of a federal structure, whereas the UK, despite the devolution and other current constitutional reforms, remains a unitary state. It appears that while the emphasis in a federal state may need to be placed on a national Supreme Court with visible wide nationwide jurisdiction in order to safeguard fundamental federal unity, the emphasis in a unitary state such as the UK, restructured after extensive devolution of lawmaking power to several constituent parts, needed to be placed on a Supreme Court that safeguards the independence of the legal systems of these parts, preempting federalist demands created by concerns about the Court's impact on such independence. Additionally, it must be taken into account that so-called devolution issues, on which the UK Supreme Court will decide as a national UK court, include fundamental legal principles of national UK law and legislative texts declared by the devolution acts as entrenched in any acts of the devolved legislative bodies in different parts of the UK.[51]

The UK Supreme Court has inherited the power of the House of Lords, since the Practice Statement of 1966, to overrule existing precedent and lay down new law, also in Scotland, except in criminal matters. It is the only court in the land that can do so. All other courts in the UK must abide by authority laid down by the UK Supreme Court; otherwise their judgments may be held to be *per incuriam* and be reversed. The UK Supreme Court has, in other words, inherited an important function of unifying the law and keeping it uniform across the land. If its final pronouncements must be regarded, officially, as judgments of a court of the part of the UK from which the appeal originated, this function may have been significantly undermined by the Constitutional reform, except in the case of the all too important devolution issues. But the reality on the ground is likely to be different.

18.4.2 Courts in England and Wales, Scotland and Northern Ireland

The legal landscape in the UK has become richer since the recent Constitutional reforms. By far the greatest diversity exists between Scotland and the other constituent parts of the United Kingdom. Whereas both Wales and Northern Ireland have been granted significant legislative autonomy under the devolution programme of the present Government, Wales is integrated into English common law and the English judicial system, and Northern Ireland, although with a separate judicial system as explained below, is also a jurisdiction where English law applies.

---

[51] See, extensively, supra in the text.

18.4.2.1 England and Wales, Northern Ireland

In the birthplace of the common law, the Royal Courts of Justice in London have supervised over the centuries a tightly centralized system of administration of justice in England and Wales. Formerly known as the Supreme Court of Judicature for England and Wales, there is one general court of first instance for civil, commercial and chancery matters, the High Court, one Criminal Court, and the Court of Appeal. But while the courts in Scotland are not affected, after the inauguration of the UK Supreme Court, the Supreme Court of England and Wales is renamed the 'Senior Courts of England and Wales'.[52] This change of name may be explained as based on the need to avoid confusion but can also be seen as removing a certain historical symbolism, and, combined with the statutory requirement that the justices of the UK Supreme Court must between them have knowledge of, and experience of practice in, the law of each part of the United Kingdom, can also be seen as establishing formal parity between the three legal systems of the country.

In Northern Ireland, the formerly named 'Supreme Court of Judicature of Northern Ireland' is renamed to "Court of Judicature of Northern Ireland".[53]

18.4.2.2 Scotland

Scotland traditionally possessed its own 'mixed' legal system, of a civil law and common law origin, distinct legal institutions and separate courts. The Court of Session is Scotland's supreme court in civil and criminal matters. It is both a court of first instance and a court of appeal, with a further appeal to the UK Supreme Court in civil matters only. Its origins can be traced to the early sixteenth century. The court presently consists of judges who are designated 'Senators of the College of Justice' or 'Lords of Council and Session'. The court is headed by the Lord President, the second in rank being the Lord Justice Clerk. The Court of Session is divided into the Outer House and the Inner House. The Outer House consists of 24 Lords Ordinary sitting alone or, in certain cases, with a civil jury. They are a first instance court on civil matters, including cases based on delict (tort) and contract, commercial cases and judicial review of administrative action. The Inner House is the appeal court, but it also has a small range of first instance business. It is divided into two Divisions of equal authority, and presided over by the Lord President and the Lord Justice Clerk respectively. Judges are appointed to the Divisions by the UK Secretary of State for Scotland, not the devolved Scottish executive, after consulting the Lord President and Lord Justice Clerk. Each division is made up of five Judges,

---

[52]Section 59 of the Constitutional Reform Act 2005.
[53]Section 59.

and the quorum is three. The two Divisions of the Inner House hear cases on appeal from the Outer House, the Sheriff Court and certain tribunals and other bodies.[54]

The High Court of Justiciary hears criminal appeals and serious criminal cases. Trials are held before a judge and jury. The principal judge of this Court is the Lord Justice-General. The Court is based in Edinburgh, but trials can be held in towns and cities all over Scotland. There is no further appeal to the UK Supreme Court in criminal cases, meaning that Scottish criminal law is not subject to a central UK overview.

Finally, the first instance courts of general jurisdiction in Scotland, and civil courts of first appeal, are the Sheriff Courts. For purposes of jurisdiction, Scotland is split into six regions called Sheriffdoms. Each Sheriffdom has a Sheriff Principal who manages the Sheriff courts in his area and hears appeals in civil matters. Within the six Sheriffdoms there are a total of 49 Sheriff Courts, with a single judge conducting trials, who is called a Sheriff. Sheriff Courts are trial courts for both civil and criminal matters.

18.4.3 Legal Education and Training

It is not possible to study Scots law in a Law School anywhere in England, Wales or Northern Ireland. But in Scotland, at least one Law School, at the University of Dundee, offers joint honours degrees in both Scots and English law, and this does attract a small number of students from England and Wales. It would be fairly accurate to state that in the United Kingdom there is no exchange of law students between England and Scotland.

The training and access to the legal profession is clearly separate in Scotland and in the rest of the United Kingdom. But legal practitioners in the two parts of the UK, despite their different professional titles (advocates in Scotland, barristers and solicitors everywhere else), education, training and qualification credentials, are fairly mobile across the border. Significantly, a number of very distinguished House of Lords judges in the recent history of the UK, very influential in the development of English law, have been Scottish Advocates-QCs, sitting with their English, Welsh and Northern Irish brethrens Barristers-QCs, with great ease. This does, of course, imply that the reality on the ground, in terms of the judicial development of core areas of the law across the UK, with the exception of purely domestic Criminal law, is much more one of uniformity rather than separateness, although the tradition wants Scotland to be a separate jurisdiction with no historical or cultural ties with English common law.

---

[54]The decisions of the Court of Session are reported in Session Cases (cited as 1999 S.C. 100), Scots Law Times (cited as 1999 SLT 100) and Scottish Civil Law Reports (cited as 1999 SCLR 100).

18.4.4 Officials and Other Enforcement Agencies[55]

The UK has only one, UK civil service, run from London. Enforcement authorities (e.g. police) are not run by central government (an exception is the London Metropolitan Police), nor by regional executives, but by local authorities (e.g. Cambridgeshire, Strathclyde), but they all have, of course, a duty to apply UK law. There is no equivalent to the US Federal systems of civil servants and enforcement agencies. Armed forces are national, and there are no local auxiliary military bodies (such as the US National Guards), and the Territorial Army is a national UK body.

18.5 Conclusion

At a time when the devolution process and historic constitutional reforms of the entire UK system of justice at the highest level have barely been fully implemented, it is hard to predict how the new constitutional and legislative rules, central mechanisms and structures put in place to preserve the separateness of the UK's legal systems, but also to safeguard the basic unity of UK state law, will perform. More political uncertainty lurks beyond the not so distant horizon with the ruling Scottish National Party's pledge in Scotland to hold a referendum on Scottish complete independence from the United Kingdom. However, and until such a dramatic rupture takes place, it can be safely assumed that the long tradition of centralized legal power and delivery of justice initiated in the British Isles by William the Conqueror, coupled with an equally long common legal culture of all legal professions in the UK, will not easily change, despite constitutional and political reforms. Despite the recently institutionalized, with the devolution processes, plurality of formal sources of legislative and judge-made law in the different parts of the UK, the decisive role of judges, who are more empowered than judges in the civil law tradition as well as more independent from party and community politics than judges in the US and some other jurisdictions is likely to keep the UK ship steady in the potentially turbulent seas of devolved legal development lying ahead. Judicial selection strictly on merit and a common legal culture uniting lawyers in all parts of the UK will shield legal evolution from any atavistic fragmentation on grounds of regional nationalism, as it has always done, even before the Acts of Union in the eighteenth century. Additionally, large chunks of the law are out of bounds for devolved legislators and judges, including the basic core of fundamental rights, European law, public law and the entire private law, commercial and civil, Scottish Criminal law remains the only historical regional preserve that will continue to escape any check of uniformity.[56]

---

[55]On the appointment of judges see *supra*.
[56]See the detailed lists of entrenched statutes and reserved matters in Part I, above.

The challenge for the new UK Supreme Court in deciding appeals on devolution issues will be to map the territory of reserved 'UK Law', a challenge similar to that faced by the US Supreme Court since its inception, to define the boundaries of federal law in the US. In deciding other matters, the challenge for the UK Supreme Court will be to preserve uniformity based on pragmatism and common sense in meeting the legitimate aspirations of the nascent devolved legal systems of the UK, to have their own distinct identities and styles. It will be helped considerably by the fact that the authority, and unifying influence, of the two European courts, the ECJ and the ECHR, has been enhanced by the devolution reforms.[57] And its task will be further facilitated when the English and Scottish Law Commissions continue to produce increasingly converging proposals for law reform in the two countries. So, hopefully, like in the ancient Roman recipe, celebrated by Virgil in his poem,[58] the success of which depended on the masterful mix of the different ingredients into one pleasant sauce,[59] the UK's mix of legal systems will continue to set into a miraculously uniform blend, provided, of course, the master chefs, scholars, practitioners and judges, do not forget their centuries-old cooking skills.

---

[57]Powder to the guns of those campaigning for a 'Europe of the Regions', instead of the present Europe of sovereign nation-States. Among them was one of the most prominent Scottish intellectuals and politicians, the late Professor Sir Neil McCormick, who had also served as an MEP of the Scottish National Party, which advocates 'Independence within Europe' for Scotland.

[58]*it manus in gyrum: paulatim singula vires deperdunt proprias, color est e pluribus unus, nec totus viridis, quia lactea frusta repugnant, nec de lacte nitens, quia tot variatur ab herbis* (*Moretum*, by Virgil).

[59]That (probably) still survives today in the artisan pesto sauce of Genoa.

Chapter 19
United States Federalism: Harmony Without Unity

James R. Maxeiner

19.1 Historical Background

Uniformity of law figured prominently in the first century of American federalism. Just 13 years after the Declaration of Independence of 1776, the United States of America abandoned its first constitution and adopted a new one that provided for more uniform law. The Constitution of 1789, however, recognized and perpetuated a non-uniform law of slavery. To abolish that non-uniform law of slavery the country fought the bloody Civil War (1861–1865). With abolition of slavery, the United States rejected the idea that component states might have fundamentally different social, economic, or political systems.

Until 1865 division over slavery obscured a general need for uniform law that was growing parallel to the development of modern means of transportation and communication. In 1776 travel was rare; commerce among component states was of minor importance. Within a century, all that had changed. Merchants carried on trade in every state; citizens of all states established relations with each other. The founding in 1878 of the American Bar Association well marks the national need: the first article of the Association's constitution made a first purpose of the association "uniformity of legislation throughout the Union".

Before the Civil War, representatives acting for component states negotiated political solutions to slavery, this one great national issue of disharmonious legislation. They left largely unattended other issues of uniform law. The principal role

---

© 2008, James R. Maxeiner, J.D., Cornell; LL.M., Georgetown; Ph.D. in Law, Ludwig Maximilian University (Munich, Germany). Associate Professor of Law and Associate Director, Center for International and Comparative Law, University of Baltimore School of Law.

J.R. Maxeiner (✉)
University of Baltimore, Baltimore, MD, USA
e-mail: jmaxeiner@ubalt.edu

of the national United States Supreme Court was to preserve against particularistic state intrusion areas for federal legislation. Political realities ruled out political solutions to national needs for uniform law.

Prior to the Civil War, Supreme Court Justice Joseph Story despaired that the nation was "perpetually receding farther and farther from the common standard".[1] The divisive issue of slavery in effect required seeking uniform law through means that were less-overtly political. Story himself used a variety of ways to promote uniform law. He authored important court decisions that gave uniform federal law preëminence. He wrote commentaries that formed the basis of harmonized state law.[2] He chaired one of the first major reports on codification. And he taught at the first truly national law school.

After the Civil War, with the issue of slavery resolved, the nation could give attention to the importance of uniform law for the rapidly growing commerce among the states. No longer, however, did representatives acting for component states negotiate political solutions to these needs. Instead, shifting coalitions of interested parties persuaded the central government or the individual component states to adopt uniform or harmonized legal rules. No longer was the principal role of the national United States Supreme Court in legal unification to determine what states could do without infringing federal prerogatives; it became to decide what the central government might do without violating states' rights.

Two post-Civil War developments mightily furthered this more expansive federal role. The post-Civil War amendments to the Constitution, especially, the 14th amendment of 1868 assuring rights of citizenship and due process throughout the Union, resulted in new, expansive powers for the federal government. Meanwhile, the ever growing commerce among the component states led the central government to seek to satisfy those needs with greater federal involvement. At first slowly, and then decisively with the development of the administrative state in the "New Deal" of the 1930s, the Supreme Court acquiesced in an expanded role of the central government.

Today, the picture of federalism remains much the same as that which developed in the century following the Civil War: consensus based approaches that do not involve governments negotiating with each another. These approaches are principally three:

1. The central government, relying on pre-existing federal powers, adopts laws that apply nationwide. These federal laws usually do not displace state law completely. The component states, to the extent necessary, adjust their laws to coordinate with national laws.

---

[1] Joseph Story, Progress of Jurisprudence, An Address Delivered Before the Members of the Suffolk Bar, at Their Anniversary, at Boston (Sept. 4, 1821), in *The Miscellaneous Writings of Joseph Story* 198, 213, 224 (William W. Story ed., 1852).

[2] And this American legal writers did from the earliest of publications. See, e.g., *American Precedents of Declarations* iii–iv (1802) ("the work, though more immediately applicable to the practice of New-England, may be considered as adapted by form, and qualified by authority, to invite the attention and meet the necessities of every State in the Union.").

2. The component states, either in imitation of the law of one leading state or of the federal government or following uniform and model laws proposed principally by the National Conference of Commissioners of Uniform State Law (founded by the states in 1892) or the American Law Institute (founded by academic and practicing lawyers in 1923), adopt substantially similar laws.
3. Both the central government and the component states, in the interest of national harmony, rely on third party harmonization through "Restatements" of law and other academic and non-binding interpretations of laws as well as on decisions of private, national-standards setting bodies (*e.g.,* trade associations).

In all of this, the national Supreme Court plays what sometimes seems a capricious role: generally it accepts those consensus decisions, but from time-to-time, at the request usually of private parties and rarely of component state representatives, it determines that the nationally-agreed upon federal rule impermissibly infringes on state authority.

19.2 The Federal Distribution and Exercise of Lawmaking Power

The location of lawmaking powers is rightly the first question in reporting on uniform laws in federal entities. Unification of laws is needed only if lawmaking powers rest with more than one entity. If lawmaking powers are reserved to the central government, laws are perforce uniform. But if states enjoy lawmaking power, uniformity of law is challenged. Absent concerted efforts to make laws uniform, anything like uniformity is apt to be the result of accident.[3]

Americans assume that extensive lawmaking powers are essential to every level of a multi-governmental entity. How can an entity be federal if its component states do not have independent law making authority? How can a locality have home rule if it cannot write its own laws? Foreign examples challenge this assumption. An entity can properly be seen as federal, even though some, or perhaps all, lawmaking powers are concentrated with the central government. Component states are no less independent and decentralization is no less furthered by different models where lawmaking is a cooperative endeavor of the component states at the central level and law applying is devolved upon the component states. It is well to remember that there is no unitary form of federalism and that different forms may use different admixtures of these models.

This Sect. 19.2 addresses distribution of lawmaking powers in American federalism. The following Sect. 19.3 considers approaches used to bring uniformity when those powers are exercised in applying law. Section 19.4 deals with the institutional and social background of uniform law while Sect. 19.5 is a conclusion.

---

[3]*Cf.*, Timothy Walker, Introduction to American Law § 144, at p. 149 (1837).

19.2.1 The Limited Legislative Jurisdiction of the Central Authority

19.2.1.1 Federal Powers

The Constitution of the United States of America creates a federal government of limited powers. Article I, section 8 sets out the lawmaking powers of Congress. It is the principal source of federal legislative authority. Article VI prescribes that where the federal government has legislative power, federal law is supreme. Article 1, section 10, proscribes certain conduct by the states. The tenth amendment, adopted in 1791, reserves powers not delegated to the federal government to the states.

Article 1, section 8 bestows upon the federal legislature (Congress) powers: 1. "To lay and collect Taxes, Duties, Imposts and Excises, to pay the Debts and provide for the common Defence and general Welfare of the United States; ... " (the *"General Welfare Clause"*); 2. to borrow money; 3. "To regulate Commerce with foreign Nations, and among the several States, and with the Indian Tribes" (the *"Commerce Clause"*); 4. "To establish an uniform Rule of Naturalization, and uniform Laws on the Subject of Bankruptcies throughout the United States;" 5. to coin Money and fix the standard of weights and measures; 6. To punish counterfeiting; 7. To establish post offices and post roads; 8. To secure to authors and inventors the exclusive right to their respective writings and discoveries (the "Patent and Copyright Clause"); 9. To constitute Tribunals inferior to the Supreme Court; 10. To define and punish offences against the Law of Nations; 11. To declare war; 12. To raise and support Armies; 13. To provide and maintain a Navy; 14. To make rules for the same; 15. To call forth the Militia to execute the Laws of the Union, suppress Insurrections and repel Invasions; 16. To make rules for the same; 17. To exercise exclusive Legislation over the Seat of the Government; and, 18. "To make all Laws which shall be necessary and proper for carrying into Execution the foregoing Powers, and all other Powers vested by this Constitution in the Government of the United States, or in any Department or Officer thereof" (the *"Necessary and Proper Clause"*). Article II, section 2 bestows upon the President, with "the advice and consent of the Senate" (*i.e.*, the upper house of the legislature), "the power to make treaties" (the *"Foreign Affairs Power"*). Article III, section 2, provides that national judicial power shall extend to "all cases arising under this Constitution, the laws of the United States, and treaties made ... under their authority" as well as certain other controversies involving the United States or parties from different states or nations.

While all lawmaking powers are in principle enumerated, some are so general that a power is available if the political will is present. Often it is. The federal government need not wait for states to take action. That it does take action, does not, however, as we shall discuss below, oust the states of lawmaking jurisdiction completely.

Education law is an example of how quickly leadership can change when political will is present. For a long time any federal involvement in this area, other than in funding higher education, met with substantial resistance. States, often following the lead of national accrediting and testing bodies, determined the law. But in the 2000s the central government sought to set national standards for local education.

19.2.1.2 Few Federal Lawmaking Powers Are Exclusive; Most Are Concurrent with Lawmaking Powers of Component States

Were federal powers all exclusive—as was argued by some in the early years of the country[4]—federal law would be uniform and this report could be limited to areas outside federal lawmaking authority. But that view did not prevail. The Supreme Court rejected it in 1819 in the case of *Sturges v. Crowninshield*,[5] where it held that federal power to create uniform laws on the subject of bankruptcy is not exclusive so long as Congress is not currently exercising that power.

In those early years, the Supreme Court followed the approach laid out in the Federalist, No. 32, which identifies three categories of exclusive federal powers in the Constitution.[6] The first category consists of those powers that the Constitution expressly designates "exclusive." The only such power is the power over the national seat of government (no. 17 above). In the second category are those powers that the Constitution grants to the federal government and expressly denies to the states (principally in article I, section 10). These include powers to enter into treaties, coin money, impose duties on imports or exports, maintain armies, and conduct war. The Federalist's third category cannot be linguistically, but only politically, defined. It consists of those powers that the Constitution grants the federal government, where, according to the Federalist, "a similar authority in the states would be absolutely and totally *contradictory* and *repugnant*".[7]

Few federal powers fall into the Federalist's first and second categories; most are in the third. Since the Supreme Court has hesitated to find federal powers broadly exclusive, most federal lawmaking powers are concurrent with the powers of the states.

Concurrency conflicts with the objective of uniformity of law and is a catalyst for uniform lawmaking. For where federal legislative jurisdiction is concurrent with that of the states, absent uniform laws, and perhaps even then, law is anything but uniform. As we shall see, in this "interjurisdictional gray area" there is a "conflict and confusion."[8]

---

[4] See, *e.g.,* Sturges v. Crowninshield, 17 U.S. (4 Wheaton) 122 (1819) (arguments of Daggett and Hopkinson for plaintiff). See also Joseph Story, 1 *Commentaries on the Constitution of the United States* § 444, p. 428 (1833); David P. Currie, *The Constitution in the Supreme Court: The First Hundred Years*, 1789–1888, at 145–150 (1985).

[5] 17 U.S. (4 Wheaton) 122.

[6] Joseph Story, Constitution, *supra* note 4, § 437, at 422.

[7] 1 The Federalist: A Collection of Essays Written in Favour of the New Constitution No. 32 (1788) [emphasis in original].

[8] So called by Ryan, Erin. 2007. Federalism and the tug of war within: Seeking checks and balance in the interjurisdictional gray area. *Maryland Law Review* 66: 503.

19.2.1.3 The Most Important Federal Powers

The most important constitutionally specified sources authorizing central government regulation are the General Welfare Clause, the Commerce Clause, the Patent and Copyright Clause, the various clauses related to the national defense, the Foreign Affairs Power, and the Necessary and Proper Clause.

Where potential legislation does not clearly fall under one of the powers specifically stated, the most likely basis for federal regulation is either the Commerce Clause alone or the Commerce Clause in conjunction with the Necessary and Proper Clause.

Federal regulation is often piecemeal. State law is, in theory, organic. Federal law is to supplement state law to deal with specific issues that require national treatment. This is just the reverse of providing a general federal rule from which component states are permitted to deviate. It means that federal regulation is often neither comprehensive nor systematic.[9]

The Commerce Clause by its terms authorizes the federal government "To regulate commerce ... among the several States." Some people at the time of its adoption thought that this was a power to regulate commerce generally among the states.[10] Instead, the Supreme Court viewed the power more narrowly. It sought to distinguish commerce that it saw as properly concerning the federal government and commerce that concerned only the component states. The task of drawing clear lines proved impossible to achieve. In the very case where the Supreme Court first attempted to measure state statutes against federal legislative power, *Gibbons v. Ogden*, Justice Johnson presciently warned that the competing powers "meet and blend so as scarcely to admit of separation".[11]

In nearly two centuries of interpreting the Commerce Clause the Supreme Court has vacillated from expounding it expansively to reading it restrictively. The Court has prescribed one test or another to judge whether a particular exercise of federal authority is proper (*e.g.*, "channels or instrumentalities of commerce," "in commerce," "affecting commerce").

In deciding this question, the Supreme Court has little political legitimacy on which to rely, since its members are not elected. Faced with demands for federal action in response to the Great Depression of the 1930s, the Court largely ceded this issue as a political decision to Congress. Only more recently, in the boom economic times of the 1990s, did the court—to general consternation—revisit the issue and

---

[9]The approach is reminiscent of how common law courts construe statutes in derogation of the common law.

[10]See., *e.g.*, James Sullivan, The History of Land Titles in Massachusetts 352–355 (1801); *see generally* William W. Crosskey, *Politics and the Constitution in the History of the United States* (3 vols., 1953, 1980).

[11]6 U.S. (9 Wheaton) 1, 32 (1824). The Court did not accept the argument that whenever Congress "declines to establish a law, it is to be considered a declaration that it is unfit that such a law should exist".

invalidate a federal law based on the Commerce Clause.[12] The law in question prohibited carrying firearms in school zones; it regulated "non-economic activity" and therefore, in this Court's view, fell outside the legislative authority of the federal government. The result of the Supreme Court's Commerce Clause jurisprudence is to complicate federal legislation and to inhibit, but not prohibit, broader national solutions to problems.

19.2.1.4 Important Practice Areas of Federal Regulation

In American legal practice, a common expression is "don't make a federal case out of it." While coined with litigation in mind, it speaks to the division in legal practice of federal and state matters. Commercially and politically important matters are largely issues of federal law; day-to-day mundane matters are typically issues of state law. Large law firms tend to deal with the former; solo practitioners are more likely to handle the latter. So matters of traditional private law, *e.g.*, contracts, family law, inheritance, real property, are largely state law. Major commercial matters, other than corporate organization itself, are often federal law.

Some areas in which federal law has a strong or dominant role include:

Competition law. It consists of antitrust, unfair competition and trademark law. Although it is principally federal law, there are significant state and even municipal laws that also regulate the field. Moreover, local authorities not infrequently enforce federal laws.

Employment and labor law. Although the federal involvement is high, states still set the basic tenor. In practice, most states adhere to an employment-at-will doctrine which permits employers (and employees) largely unlimited freedom to sever the employment relationship. Federal law overlays this state law with many particular regulations governing such disparate topics as discrimination among employees based on personal characteristics (such as age, gender, national origin, race and religion), sexual harassment, equal pay, and labor unions.

Environmental law. Basic property law, including land-use planning, is quintessentially state law. Yet there is an overlay of all manner of federal law from A for Asbestos School Hazard Detection and Control, 20 U.S.C. §§ 3601 *et seq.*, to T for Toxic Substance Control, 15 U.S.C. §§ 2601 *et seq.*

Securities law. The laws under which business organizations are formed are state laws, but the principal laws under which large public corporations are regulated, pursuant to which obligations to shareholders are determined, and especially the regulation of the securities markets are federal.

Tax law is based on authority other than the Commerce Clause, namely on the General Welfare Clause. While the component states have extensive taxes of their own, excepting taxes on real estate and on turnover, federal tax law is the most important and largely sets the rules *de facto* by which state taxes are assessed.

---

[12]United States v. Lopez, 514 U.S. 549 (1995).

19.2.2 The Organic Legislative Jurisdiction of the Component States

19.2.2.1 State Powers

The component states are the organic sources of government authority in the United States. Each state has its own constitution from which authority to legislate arises. The federal Constitution assumes the existence of the component states. The federal government can not abolish the states or fundamentally alter the nation's composition. Article IV, section 3, while allowing Congress to admit new states, provides that "no new State shall be formed or erected within the Jurisdiction of any other State; nor any State be formed by the Junction of two or more States, or parts of States, without the Consent of the Legislatures of the States concerned as well as of the Congress".

The Constitution, with a minor exception relating to the state militia, contains no explicit grant of exclusive legislative jurisdiction to the component states; its tenth amendment, however, reserves powers not delegated to the central government, to the component states.

Since the federal government is a government of limited authority, and the states maintain the organic law-giving competence, to this day state law dominates core areas of public and private law, including most criminal and civil law. The latter includes contracts, family, inheritance, property, tort and corporate law. States determine the organization of, and the procedures used by, their courts.

Areas where state law is dominant, but shares authority with federal law include consumer protection, criminal law, education law, gambling law, as well as traffic and driving law.

19.2.3 Conflicts and Coordination of State and Federal Law

19.2.3.1 Supremacy of Federal Law

Article VI, section 2 provides that federal law is supreme (the "Supremacy Clause").[13] The lowest of federal laws is superior to conflicting provisions of state laws, including state constitutions.

The Supreme Court has given federal law a greater priority than the Supremacy Clause strictly requires. It has not limited the Supremacy Clause to being a mere

---

[13]"This Constitution and the Law of the United States which shall be made in Pursuance thereof; and all Treaties made, or which shall be made, under the Authority of the United States; shall be the supreme Law of the Land; and the Judges in every State shall be bound thereby, any Thing in the Constitution or Laws of any State to the Contrary notwithstanding."

choice-of-law rule that determines which law applies in the case of a conflict.[14] Instead, it has held that in certain situations, federal legislation preempts state legislation entirely. This happens most easily, when a federal statute states that it preempts state law. In such cases, a court has only to determine whether state law is inconsistent with federal law. But federal law may also implicitly preempt state law if it "stands as an obstacle to accomplishment and execution of the full purposes and objectives of Congress".[15] The Supreme Court may find this to be the case when there is "conflict preemption" or there is "field preemption." The former is the case where state law contravenes federal purposes or requires action that *conflicts* with federal law. The latter occurs when federal regulation of a particular *field* is "so dominant" that state laws on the same subject should not operate.[16]

In areas of concurrent state/federal legislative competency, state, and even municipal, governments sometimes adopt legislation that is inconsistent with federal laws. This legislation is presumptively valid until such time as a court, acting in a concrete case or controversy, determines that the state legislation is invalid as preempted by federal legislation or by a grant of federal legislative authority.

19.2.3.2 Non-exercise of Federal Powers and State Law

Non-exercise of federal powers in the early years of the country made it more difficult to determine when a power should be exclusive. For some things, the country could not wait. For example, for more than 50 years after the constitutional convention, Congress did nothing about setting national standards for weights and measures. So the "common understanding" was, that until Congress should fix a general standard for the states, each state was "at liberty to fix one for itself".[17]

The difficulty non-exercise made for interpretation is well illustrated by the Supreme Court's contrasting treatment of the two powers the Constitution grants in clause 4 of article I, section 8: "4. To establish an uniform Rule of Naturalization, and uniform Laws on the Subject of Bankruptcies throughout the United States." Although the Constitution uses virtually the same language for both powers and combines them in the same clause, the Court held the former exclusive[18] and the latter concurrent.[19]

---

[14]*Cf.* Joseph Story, 1 *Commentaries on the Constitution of the United States* § 441, p. 425 ("Are the state laws inoperative only to the extent of the actual conflict; or does the legislation of congress supersede the state legislation, or suspend the legislative power of the states over the *subject matter?*").

[15]Hines v. Davidowitz, 312 U.S. 52, 67 (1941).

[16]*See* English v. General Electric Company, 496 U.S. 72, 79 (1990).

[17]Walker, *supra* note 3.

[18]Chirac v. Chirac, 15 U.S. (2 Wheaton) 259 (1817).

[19]Sturges v. Crowninshield, 17 U.S. (4 Wheaton) 122 (1819).

In the case of the Naturalization Power, the Court followed the argument of the Federalist: the Naturalization Power falls within the third category "because if each state had power to prescribe a *distinct rule*, there could be no *uniform rule*".[20] Of course, the same argument seems to be true equally for the Bankruptcy Power, which the Federalist did not address. But the Court held otherwise. The principal difference between the two cases is that Congress had always exercised the Naturalization Power while it had only intermittently exercised the Bankruptcy Power.[21]

The Supreme Court does not, however, allow state legislation in every instance of unexercised federal power. For example, in the case of state regulation of commerce, it applies the doctrine of the "dormant Commerce Clause." Under this doctrine it may invalidate state or local laws that "discriminate against"[22] or impose an "undue burden"[23] on "interstate commerce."

19.2.3.3 Coordination of State and Federal Law

Unlike more modern federal constitutions, the American Constitution of 1789 does not address directly how state and federal governments should coordinate their laws. It does not well demark areas where federal legislative jurisdiction is exclusive and where it is shared with the states. It does not define what exclusive and what concurrent might mean. But it does allow a high level of concurrency in lawmaking.

The combination of these two factors—lack of constitutional coordination and a high incidence of concurrent jurisdiction—contributes mightily to non-uniformity and uncertainty. It creates a certain competition between state and federal law.

Competition between state and federal law need not lead to substantial legal uncertainty, if conflicts between state and federal authority are determined before laws take effect.[24] For this, coordination prior to litigation is essential. It is not enough to say that one government level has authority to legislate, and to the extent that it does, its law governs and supersedes competing laws.

A particular weakness of American federalism is that questions of legislative competency are often decided not beforehand, but only as a legal rule is applied, and therefore at the risk and expense of those trying to comply with the law, whichever is applicable. The issue of legislative competency may even be an element of a party's case. For example, to apply a federal law may require proof that this particular instance of application has a specific connection to "interstate commerce," such as

---

[20]1 *The Federalist*: supra note 7 [emphasis in original].

[21]Sturges v. Crowninshield, 17. U.S. (4 Wheaton) 122 (1819).

[22]City of Philadelphia v. New Jersey, 437 U.S. 617, 628 (1978).

[23]Dean Milk Co. v. City of Madison, 340 U.S. 349, 353 (1951).

[24]*See* Maxeiner, James R. 2007. Legal certainty: A European alternative to American legal indeterminacy? *Tulane Journal of International & Comparative Law* 15: 541, 596 (discussing German federalism).

an "effect" on "interstate commerce"[25] or use of an "instrumentality of interstate commerce, or of the mails".[26] Conversely, to apply state law may require a showing that this specific application does not infringe on a possibly not yet adopted federal law.[27]

There is a point of view that such case-by-case review is work worth doing notwithstanding the obvious greater efficiency of an *ex ante*, generalized decision. Some see that "the challenge faced by the new commercial federalism [is] in establishing and policing the limits on federal power".[28] This approach would "enable redress whenever a plaintiff with standing shows that regulatory activity in the gray area unduly threatens Our Federalism [with tyranny]".[29]

19.2.4 Municipalities

The Constitution makes no provision for municipalities. As a matter of state law, municipalities have only such authority as the states grant them. Originally, the states strictly limited municipal authority. Beginning in the latter part of the nineteenth century, however, states began extending "home rule" to municipalities. Often, in addition to authority to administer their own affairs, states granted municipalities authority to legislate. Today municipalities are seen as the intrastate analogue of federalism. Most states apply a rule that all powers are granted until retracted. This includes authority to issue laws as significant as creating criminal offenses, imposing requirements on employment, prohibiting trade practices and controlling construction through zoning laws. There are approximately 40,000 sub-state government entities in the United States.

19.3 The Means and Methods of Legal Unification

The means and methods of legal unification are the same as the means and methods of lawmaking and law applying in general. Thus unification takes place, or does not take place, within the context of existing approaches to legal methods. In this regard, the United States operates within its own peculiar version of the common law.

---

[25]For example, the antitrust laws. *See, e.g.*, Summit Health, Ltd. v. Pinhas, 500 U.S. 322 (1991).

[26]For example, the securities laws. *See, e.g.*, Rule 10b–5, 17 CFR 240.10b–5.

[27]Some American law professors now see this "*competitive federalism,*" i.e., non-uniformity of law, as a good thing! See, *e.g.*, Johnson, Bruce and Moin A. Yahya. 2004. The evolution of Sherman act jurisdiction: A roadmap for competitive federalism. *University of Pennsylvania Journal of Constitutional Law* 7: 403.

[28]*See* Overby, A. Brooke. 2003. Our new commercial law federalism. *Temple Law Review* 76: 297, 356.

[29]Ryan, Erin. 2007. Federalism and the tug of war within: Seeking checks and balance in the interjurisdictional gray area. *Maryland Law Review* 66: 503, 648.

The common law heritage is both blessing and bane for American legal unification. It is a blessing, because it brings a strong central court and a tradition of consistent case law. But it is a bane, because conditions in the United States are different from those in eighteenth century England, when the common law methods adopted by the United States developed. American courts are less centralized than were their eighteenth century English counterparts; the limitations of a law of precedents are much greater in a modern economy of 300 million people than they were in a pre-industrial economy of fewer than ten million people.[30]

In its Supreme Court the United States shares the common law benefit of a strong court at the seat of national government. Insofar as the Supreme Court is competent—both legally and practically—its pronouncements in Washington can have much the same salutary effect for legal unification as those of its counterparts in Westminster had in the eighteenth and nineteenth centuries.

As we have seen, however, for most of American law, the Supreme Court is not legally competent. It therefore often is not able to contribute substantially to legal unification. In most areas of law, the Supreme Court of the United States is not the highest tribunal, instead the highest courts of the states have the last word. There are 50 such courts. There are no formal and only limited informal means for coordinating the decisions of those 50-plus supreme courts.

Moreover, the precedents of the United States Supreme Court share the deficiencies of case law generally. Precedents decide single cases; they find a rule applicable to one case. They are not designed to decide abstractly and consistently a generality of cases. More precedents in theory clarify the law, but they also muddy it by increasing exponentially the number of "authoritative" texts. Most American precedents these days descend from the federal appellate courts or the state courts, and are not decisions of the Supreme Court. They have binding effect only on subordinate courts and do not bind coordinate courts or their respective subordinate courts. Only the Supreme Court can bind all courts and then only in matters of federal law. But it renders full opinions in only about 80 cases a year.

Statutes have long been the principal source of American law. Yet the United States has difficulty adopting and implementing statutes. The American legal system has yet to develop efficient and effective methods of legislation.[31] The United

---

[30] According to the first British census, in 1801 the population of England was 8,331,434. Abstract of the Answers and Returns, Made Pursuant to the Act, Passed in the Forty-First Year of His Majesty King George III, Intituled, 'An Act for Taking an Account of the Population of Great Britain, and the Increase or Diminution Thereof', Enumeration 4 (1802), *available at* online historical population reports, http://www.histpop.org/ohpr/servlet/PageBrowser?path=Browse/Census%20(by%20date)&active=yes&mno=2&tocstate=expandnew&tocseq=100&display=sections&display=tables&display=pagetitles&pageseq=first-nonblank

[31] See Maxeiner, James R. 2006. Legal indeterminacy made in America: U.S. legal methods and the rule of law. *Valparaiso University Law Review* 41: 517, 528.

States, says Judge Richard A. Posner, has no "overall theory of legislation".[32] An overall theory of legislation requires accepted methods of drafting and methods of statutory interpretation. While the American legal system has methods of statutory interpretation, these are, according to Justice Antonin Scalia, unintelligible.[33] It has no method of legislative drafting, which it has long neglected.[34] Individual Congressmen, not government ministries, are responsible for drafting legislation. Coalitions of Congressmen must negotiate with each other and strike deals with the President to get laws adopted. The consequences for legal unification are substantial and negative: new legislation is difficult to adopt and[35]; its technical quality is apt to be poor.

19.3.1 Legal Unification and Harmonization by Exercise of Central Power

19.3.1.1 Through Constitutional Norms

The Constitution as adopted in 1789 had few norms directly applicable to component states. Most of these concern establishing state recognition of the laws and legal acts of other states and of the federal government or prohibiting certain state conduct (*e.g.*, imposing customs duties, making treaties with foreign countries). Among those few designed to create uniform norms, perhaps the most important and surely the most controversial, was article IV, section 3, the nefarious "Fugitive Slave Clause." It requires (*requires*, for it has never been repealed), that persons "held to service or labor in one State under the laws therefore, escaping into another," shall not be freed, "but shall be delivered up on claim of the party to whom such service or labor may be due."

The Bill of Rights (the first ten amendments), adopted in 1791, also did not create norms directly applicable to the states; it applied only to the federal government.[36] That changed, however, following the adoption of the fourteenth amendment in 1868. While the amendment did not itself apply the Bill of Rights to the states, the Supreme Court has interpreted the fourteenth amendment Due Process Clause, which does apply to the States, to incorporate the most important protections of the Bill of Rights.

---

[32]Posner, Richard A. 1983. Statutory interpretation—In the classroom and in the courtroom. *The University of Chicago Law Review* 800, 800.

[33]Antonin Scalia, *A Matter of Interpretation, in A Matter of Interpretation: Federal Courts and the Law* 14 (Amy Gutmann ed., 1997).

[34]Mary Ann Glendon, "Comment", *A Matter of Interpretation, supra* note 33, at 96.

[35]*See* Smythe, Donald J. 2007. Commercial law in the cracks of judicial federalism. *Catholic University Law Review* 56: 451, 459–461.

[36]Barron v. Baltimore, 32 U.S. (7 Pet.) 32 (1833).

The Supreme Court can and does—albeit infrequently—use the protections of the Bill of Rights to create uniform law throughout the land. The advantage of this approach is that one Supreme Court decision instantly brings legal unification. For example, on January 21, 1973, first-trimester abortion was legal in some states and illegal in others. On January 22, 1973, when the Supreme Court decided the case of *Roe v. Wade*, 410 U.S. 113 (1973), it became legal in all states.

Necessarily only the Supreme Court can create such national unity. Since its authority extends only to deciding specific cases, it can not promulgate comprehensive legislative-like solutions to problems. As a consequence the Court is better able to harmonize law than it is to unify law. What the Court does best is prohibit contradictory legislation. Less well can it prescribe positive legislation, although it does occasionally prescribe specific rules. Where the Court does prescribe such national norms, typically these norms overwhelm any state rules. Most commonly they are procedural. Typically they take their names from the cases that promulgated them. Two examples are:

"*Brady materials*".[37] In criminal procedure, prosecutors must disclose certain information that may exculpate defendants or may impeach the testimony of witnesses against the defendant (*e.g.*, deals in exchange for testimony).

"*Miranda warnings*".[38] In criminal investigations, before questioning a suspect, the police must inform the suspect of his or her fifth amendment right not to make self-incriminating statements. In the decision itself the Court prescribed specific language.[39]

While this approach has the virtue of immediate applicability, it has serious drawbacks. Constitutionalizing an issue largely eliminates legislative solutions. Legislative solutions can be political compromises. They can change as political temperaments change. They can draw bright lines that are easy to apply, even if they are not always easy to justify. Constitutional solutions are, by the nature of American constitutional decision-making (see below), judge-made solutions normally devoid of bright lines. They invite litigation to change them or just to determine what they mean, for there is no other way to obtain an authoritative interpretation.[40]

---

[37] Brady vs. Maryland, 373 U.S. 83 (1963). *See* California Commission on the Fair Administration of Justice, Report and Recommendations on Compliance with the Prosecutorial Duty to Disclose Exculpatory Evidence, available at http://www.ccfaj.org/documents/reports/prosecutorial/official/OFFICIAL%20REPORT%20ON%20BRADY%20COMPLIANCE.pdf (March 6, 2008) (noting at 2 that "The prosecutor's *Brady* duty to disclose exculpatory evidence under the due process clause of the United States constitution is wholly independent of any statutory scheme. It is self-executing and needs no statutory support to be effective").

[38] Miranda v. Arizona, 384 U.S. 436 (1966).

[39] *Id.* ("You have the right to remain silent. Anything you say can and will be used against you in a court of law. You have the right to speak to an attorney, and to have an attorney present during any questioning. If you cannot afford a lawyer, one will be provided for you at government expense.")

[40] See, *e.g.*, Mary Ann Glendon, *Abortion and Divorce in Western Law* 45 (1987) ("But if the courts unnecessarily decide such controversies on constitutional grounds, these potentially creative and collaborative processes are brought to a halt.")

19.3.1.2 Through Directly Applicable Central Legislation (or Executive or Administrative Rules)

In a few areas of law, *i.e.*, where the Constitution gives Congress a clear grant of power, or where the courts hold that grant to be exclusive, federal legislation brings uniform law. These areas include naturalization, patents and copyrights.[41]

In those areas where Congress shares legislative authority with the states, it has been hesitant to oust states of concurrent jurisdiction and timid even in asserting its own. The working assumption is that the federal role should be limited unless there is a compelling reason to assert federal leadership.[42]

Congress has usually resisted requests that it occupy systematically a distinct field of law to the exclusion of the states. Indeed, unless one defines a distinct field narrowly, it may never have done so.

For example, many have long looked to Congress for a national commercial law but for more than two centuries, all such expectations have been disappointed. Already in 1801, James Sullivan, then attorney general and later governor of Massachusetts, urged that "[t]here ought to be one uniform rule throughout the nation, on bills of exchange, promissory notes, policies, and all personal contracts [for these] all arise from commerce, and the regulation of them is the regulation of commerce itself".[43] Other equally distinguished jurists and well-placed advocates made similar proposals in the 1880s and again in the 1920s and 1930s. Their calls induced not national commercial law, but did contribute to efforts to find state alternatives. They were catalysts for the creation of the National Conference of Commissioners of Uniform States Laws in 1892 and for the drafting of the Uniform Commercial Code in the 1940s and 1950s.[44]

Congress, when it does act, often does not cover a whole field but only sections of it, or even only specific problems within a section. An example is data protection, which is also known as privacy law. The United States was among the first countries to adopt a data protection law, but applied it only to consumer credit reports.[45] Since then many countries have adopted data protection laws; most have adopted what are referred to as "omnibus" laws that apply to personal data generally. The United States, even as it slowly followed the lead of other countries in expanding data protection, stayed true to what is called a "sectoral" approach. The sectoral approach made the United States something of a laughing-stock in international discourse in

---

[41] To promote uniform interpretation and application of patent and copyright law, in 1982 Congress created a new appellate court to decide all such appeals. It is an unusual creature in a system that prefers generalist to specialist courts.

[42] *See, e.g.*, Buzbee, William W. 2005. Contextual environmental federalism. *New York University Environmental Law Journal* 14: 108, 110.

[43] Sullivan, *supra* note 10, at 353.

[44] *See* Taylor, E. Hunter. 1980. Federalism or uniformity of commercial law. *Rutgers-Camden Law Journal* 11: 527, 529–530.

[45] Fair Credit Reporting Act, adopted in 1973, 15 U.S.C. § 1681 *et seq.*

the 1990s, when the United States protected video tape rental and sale records[46] long before it protected financial[47] and health records.[48]

The protection of health records is an example of Congress delegating authority to create uniform rules through administrative rule rather than federal statute.

Federal direct legislation is thus paradoxical: federal law can be found in nearly every aspect of life, yet there are surprisingly few areas of practice based exclusively on federal law.

19.3.1.3 Through Central Legislation Inducing State Legislation

The federal government cannot compel states to adopt legislation. Such measures are considered an infringement of the sovereign prerogatives of the component states.[49] Thus the United States is not able to adapt the directive approach of the European Union or the erstwhile framework laws approach of Germany.

While Congress hesitates to preempt state lawmaking power, it practically rushes to use federal legislation to induce states to adopt laws that coordinate with federal policies and thereby harmonize with one another. Congress uses approaches far too numerous to detail here. Most go under the name of "cooperative federalism." That the result is cacophony rather than harmony is not an unusual judgment.[50]

A mundane example suggests the problematic nature of such cooperation. The *Consumer Patient Radiation Health and Safety Act of 1981*[51] directed the Secretary of Health and Human Services to develop minimum standards for state certification and licensure of personnel who administer ionizing or nonionizing radiation in medical and dental radiologic procedures. The Act does not require adoption of the standards and does not sanction non-adoption. Only 35 states developed standards. According to the professional organization behind such licensing, these standards

---

[46] Video Privacy Protection Act, adopted in 1988, 18 U.S.C. § 2710. The Act does not cover DVDs, since they had yet to be commercialized.

[47] Gramm-Leach-Blilely Privacy of Consumer Financial Information, adopted in 1999, 15 U.S.C. § 6801, *et seq.*

[48] The *Standards for Privacy of Individually Identifiable Health Information* ("Privacy Rule"), *45 CFR Part 160 and Subparts A and E of Part 164,* implementing the requirements of the Health Insurance Portability and Accountability Act of 1996 ("HIPAA"), Public Law 104–191.

[49] Printz v. United States, 521 U.S. 898 (1997).

[50] *See, e.g.*, Adler, Jonathan. 2005. Jurisdiction mismatch in environmental federalism. *New York University Environmental Law Journal* 14: 130 ("The division of authority and responsibility for environmental protection between the federal and state governments lacks any cohesive rationale or justification."). *See also* Fischman, Robert L. 2005. Cooperative federalism and natural resources law. *New York University Environmental Law Journal* 14: 179; Overby, A. Brooke. 2003. Our new commercial law federalism. *Temple Law Review* 76: 297.

[51] 42 U.S.C. §§ 10001–10008.

"vary dramatically" from state-to-state. The remaining 15 states, the professional organization reports, essentially have no standards (requiring 2 weeks, not 2 years of training).[52]

This lack of success of the law illustrates the limits of the cooperative federalism approach. Without compulsion, *i.e.*, either binding law or a practically equivalent fiscal measure, not all states go along; those that do, do not do so uniformly. The result, at best, is harmonized law; it is not uniform law.

It is sometimes suggested that the threat of federal legislation leads to states adopting legislation as a lesser evil. This seems to have been an explanation for the creation of the Uniform Commercial Code. But in most instances, where legislation does not go through the NCCUSL process, if there is such a reaction, *i.e.*, if it leads to legislation, that legislation is likely to be disparate and not uniform, and is likely to be adopted by some, but not by all states.

This approach is less likely to come out of the central government than from local constituencies. What is more likely to happen is that one constituency, with greater or lesser access to legislative influence, suggests a need for a national rule. It or other constituencies then seek state legislation as an alternative to federal legislation.

19.3.1.4 Through Information Exchanges Among the Component States

Information exchanges among component states are an important source of coordination, but these are rarely managed by the central government. More commonly, national organizations, *e.g.*, the National Association of Attorneys General, the National Center for State Courts, or national trade associations, do the managing.

19.3.2 Legal Unification Through Formal or Informal Voluntary Coordination Among Component States

19.3.2.1 By Component State Legislatures Imitating Others

Imitation, which is a form of informal coordination, is one of the most important methods for attaining harmonization, if not unification, in American law. Uniform and model laws promote this imitation, but do not exhaust it. Success with formal uniform laws voluntarily adopted has been limited. See Sects. 19.3.3.1 and 19.3.3.2 below.

---

[52]American Society of Radiologic Technologists, Background Information on State and Federal Licensure Issues, https://www.asrt.org/content/GovernmentRelations/LegislativeGuidebook/LicensureBackgroundInfo.aspx

19.3.2.2 By Component State Judiciaries, e.g., Through State Court Consideration of Practice of Sister States

This is essentially the restatement approach, considered below, but without the validation of the precedents reviewed by the American Law Institute. Little can be expected of this approach. It cannot possibly be systematic or comprehensive, nor can it be uniform or universal. Owing to the vagaries of litigation, a court can consider only issues that arise in a specific case. Owing to limitations of case law, a court can decide only issues on the facts of this case. Owing to the proliferation of precedents, a court can hardly review all those precedents that might possibly come into play. No longer is it reasonable to expect a judge—especially a trial judge—to review decisions around the country.[53] Owing to the irregularity of litigation, it should not be expected that the same issue would even come before the highest courts of all 50 states, not to mention be decided in the same way.

19.3.2.3 By Agreements Among Component States

Component states in the United States may agree with each other to legislation or administrative rules. Article I, section 10, clause 3 of the Constitution requires that the federal government approve such "interstate compacts." While use of interstate compacts has become more common in recent years, the focus of most compacts is usually not on creating uniform law. Typically interstate compacts are regional and concerned with matters of administration rather than of legislation.

19.3.3 Legal Unification Promoted by Non-state Actors

Two non-state actors play a prominent role in promoting legal unification: the Uniform Law Commission (until recently called the National Conference of Commissioners of Uniform State Law) and the American Law Institute ("ALI"). The two bodies differ in their basic approach, but both depend on voluntary adoption of their products. Besides these two law reform organizations, a host of other private organizations, ranging from associations of government officials to university think tanks, offer model laws to the nation's legislatures for possible adoption.[54]

---

[53] *See* Maxeiner, *Legal Indeterminacy, supra* note 31, at 543.

[54] *See, e.g.,* United States Ombudsman Association, Model Ombudsman Act for State Governments (1997), available at http://www.usombudsman.org/documents/PDF/References/USOA_MODEL_ACT.pdf; *Centers for Law and the Public's Health:* A Collaborative at Johns Hopkins and Georgetown Universities, The Model State Emergency Health Powers Act (2001), available at http://www.publichealthlaw.net/Resources/Modellaws.htm

19.3.3.1 Uniform Laws and the Uniform Law Commission

The Uniform Law Commission was founded in 1892 by the states themselves. The states are represented in the Commission by state delegations. The Commission drafts and proposes uniform laws for state legislatures to adopt. The ideal goal is that all states will adopt all uniform laws without changes. The Commission began work with commercial and divorce law.

The optimism of the founders of the Uniform Law Commission was palpable; its first report asserted: "It is probably not too much to say that this is the most important juristic work undertaken in the United States since the adoption of the Federal [C]onstitution".[55] While uniform laws have had some success, it has not matched these hopes. In the first century of its existence, the Commission proposed approximately 200 uniform acts. Only about 10 % of these acts were adopted by as many as 40 states; more than half were adopted by fewer than 10 states.[56]

Uniform laws encounter a host of problems some of which are inherent in the task and some of which are peculiar to the American form. These problems range from the political to the technical. They include:

(i) *A perception that they lack drafting legitimacy*. Legislation is normally subject to political compromise. But there is no democratic representation in the drafting of uniform laws. While drafting sessions are open to the public, not surprisingly, the industries most immediately concerned are best represented. There is a perception by many members of the bar and public that the uniform laws projects are "captured" by those industries. (*E.g.*, Article 9, bankers; UCITA/proposed Article 2B, software).

(ii) *A perception that they are supportive of the status quo*. This perception is often reality. Uniform laws are sold to state legislature as mere technical matters that rationalize existing law and acknowledge industry practices. They should not launch off in the direction of law reform. Even the perception that they are new can lead to defeat. Many of the provisions attacked in UCITA/proposed Article 2B UCC were challenged by consumer groups even though they did not go beyond existing law. Already approved amendments to Article 2 UCC were cut back to garner support.

(iii) *Non-universal adoption*. If uniform laws are to provide legal unification, all 50 states should adopt them. There is no political base that can help bring that about; the sponsoring organization must rely principally on good will. It is thus no wonder that so few uniform laws have been adopted universally.

(iv) *Non-uniform adoptions*. Since they are laws of the individual states, the adopting states may vary the uniform laws as they see fit. Many do. Indeed,

---

[55]*See* Leonard A. Jones, "Uniformity of Laws Through National and Interstate Codification", in *Report of the Sixth Annual Meeting of the Virginia State Bar Association* 157, 169 (1894), *reprinted in American Law Review* 28: 547 (1894).

[56]White, James J. 1991. One hundred years of uniform state laws: Ex Proprio Vigore. *Michigan Law Review* 89: 2096, 2103–05.

some of the uniform laws (*e.g.*, Article 2 of the U.C.C.) even offer legislatures alternative provisions. Insofar as there are interest groups that care about those laws, those groups get 50 chances to get changes made in the law that they could not get made at the drafting stage.

(v) *Non-uniform interpretation.* No statute is perfect nor can any statute anticipate all issues that are likely to arise under it. Judicial interpretation has a critical role in keeping uniform law current. Yet, since uniform laws are by definition laws of the several states, there is no court that can authoritatively interpret them. Until there is such a court—as was proposed as long ago as 1917—no uniform law that has been the subject of judicial interpretation is likely to be uniform.[57]

(vi) *Not amendable.* Recent experiences with the Uniform Commercial Code call into question whether uniform laws can be effectively amended. In the late 1990s the Uniform Law Commission spent a great deal of time drafting changes to Article 2 (sales) and Article 2A (leasing) and creating a new Article 2B (software). After objections from the American Law Institute to proposed Article 2B and from business to changes in Articles 2 and 2A, the Commission removed Article 2B from the Code, made it into a separate law, the Uniform Computer Information Transactions Act ("UCITA"), and reduced the scope of amendments to Articles 2 and 2A. Nonetheless, nearly a decade later, no state has adopted the amendments to Article 2 and only two states have adopted UCITA. The Commission is no longer actively promoting the latter.

19.3.3.2 Restatements and the American Law Institute

The American Law Institute was founded in 1923 by practicing jurists and academics. Its membership consists of individual jurists and is self-selecting. Its initial project was the creation of a "Restatement" of American law. As originally conceptualized, the Restatement was to define scientifically legal terminology and through the intellectual strength of its system, to be relied upon by courts in deciding lawsuits. What was originally to be a single restatement turned into restatements of particular areas of the law. Most commonly these are areas where state law dominates. The American Law Institute branched out from restatements to develop "model laws" and to join the NCCUSL in the Uniform Commercial Code project. Model laws differ from uniform laws in that there is no expectation that a model law will be adopted by all states verbatim.

Restatements have as their audience principally the judiciary. They are not adopted by legislatures as a whole but by judges piecemeal. While they help to

---

[57]*See* Pope, Herbert. 1919. The federal courts and a uniform law. *The Yale Law Journal* 28: 647, 651 (proposing entrusting federal courts of appeal with the task of reviewing uniform legislation with a newly established federal court to review their decisions).

systematize legal analysis, they have not brought about unification. They do promote harmonization and often (but not always) ward off worst cases of conflicting rules.

The founders of the American Law Institute were no less optimistic about their work than were the founders of NCCUSL about theirs. The ALI founders compared their task to that faced by the lawyers of Justinian's day who "produced the codification and exposition of that law which has been the main foundation of all the law of the civilized world except the law of the English speaking people".[58]

Top down or coordinate involvement in (a) restatements, (b) uniform law and (c) private standard setting appears both to be possible and yet rare. Its rarity is fairly easily accounted for. On the one hand, the federal and state authorities do not have the political interest required for continued involvement. On the other hand, the level of continued involvement required is great while the effect of that involvement is uncertain and indirect. Restatements, uniform laws and private standards do not have the force of law by themselves, but require action by other players to attain that status. Constituencies with particular interests are more likely to be able to rouse themselves to participate in such activities. In such cases, proposed legislation can become identified with those constituencies and then fail to be adopted (*e.g.*, Uniform Computer Information Transactions Act).

19.3.4 The Role of Legal Education and Training in the Unification of Law

Legal education has been a major force for harmonization, if not unification of law, through law schools, their professors, and bar examinations. Professional legal training has not been a force for harmonization, but neither has it been a force promoting non-uniformity of law, because it no longer exists in institutionalized form. While apprentice training was once the exclusive path to the bar, it largely disappeared in the course of the nineteenth century. The United States is almost alone among the world's major legal systems in not having a system of formal practical training corresponding to "articling" in other Common Law countries, similar apprenticing in other civil law countries or to government-organized training known in Germany and Japan.

19.3.4.1 Law Schools

Law school began as supplement for law office training and, in the course of the nineteenth century, became their substitute. Before the Civil War (1861–1865), there

---

[58]Report of the Forty-Sixth Annual Meeting of the American Bar Association 90 (1923); Lewis, William Draper. 1943. The American Law Institute. *Journal of Comparative Legislation & International Law* 25: 25, 28.

were few law schools. All were private and some were independent of institutions of higher learning. From their earliest days, law schools, for financial self-preservation, sought students from outside their immediate states of location. Law students, having few schools to choose from, attended schools outside their home states.

Today, nearly all American law schools draw significant numbers of students from states outside their states of location. Not all law schools, however, draw from throughout the federal system to the same extent. Some do so nationally, some regionally and some locally. Over the last century all have tended to expand the areas from which they draw. To similar extents, graduates practice outside the states of their law schools' locations.

Today, and for a very long time, most American law schools have not focused on teaching the law of their states of location. They concentrate on federal law in areas where federal law predominates, such as bankruptcy, constitutional law, intellectual property, antitrust, securities regulation and taxation, as well as in other areas where federal law serves as a model, such as civil and criminal justice and administrative law. In areas where state law predominates, such as contracts, property, torts, family law and inheritance law, they concentrate not on the law of specific component states but on a hypothetical law of an amalgam of all states.

American legal methods tend to support this homogenizing approach. American law schools stress the skill of arguing specific points in issue rather than skills of interpreting and applying systematic statutes to facts. Since argument takes priority, skill at identifying the precedents needed to make the argument are more important than systematic understanding of a specific body of law.

American law schools have a positive effect for harmonization of law. That effect is widely recognized. When they teach state law, they teach an homogenized law the basics of which applies equally well in all states. When they teach federal law, they teach a presumptively superior regime on which states ought to model their laws.

Oddly, American law schools do not have such a positive effect on unification of law. Indeed, they may have a negative effect. This effect is scarcely noticed. Uniform law by its nature cannot be case law—at least, not where there is a multitude of case-law making courts. It must be statutory law; that is, it must consist of, ideally, a single authoritative text. But law schools generally give statutes short shrift. The issue-focused nature of American litigation tends to prefer study of case law based solutions. For example, to this day, some American law school first year contracts classes study only the common law of contracts and do not give the Uniform Commercial Code ("UCC") much attention. Those which do include it, are forced to alert their students to the inconsistencies that exist among the states in interpreting the text. In general, the technique of teaching a non-existent national law, means that there is no single authoritative text for state law. Students do not study a single authoritative text for one state with a mind toward determining whether the state where teaching is occurring ought to adopt that law.

When law schools address federal law, teaching does tend to promote a single national interpretation of that federal law either. But federal law is, as we have seen, often only an overlay on state law. Yet it is an overlay that sometimes focuses on problems that are quite different from the same problems in state courts. For example, federal courts in so-called diversity jurisdiction cases consider only cases of at least $75,000. Procedures suitable for such larger cases are not necessarily suitable for smaller cases that the state systems address.

19.3.4.2 Law Professors

Three of the nation's first law professors, James Wilson, James Kent and Joseph Story, were also leading judges of their era and leading promoters of uniform national law. All three conceptualized—and Kent and Story actualized—plans for law commentaries designed to bring certainty and uniformity to law in America.

For most of the nation's history, through such commentaries, law professors have contributed positively to increasing harmony and uniformity in law. They typically played the leading role in third party legal harmonization through uniform laws, restatements and model laws. They typically serve as principal "reporters" for these projects.

In recent years, however, many, if not most, law professors have turned away from activities that promote unification and towards more particularist pursuits. At elite law schools professors now prefer social science scholarship about law and rarely engage in doctrinal writing that might contribute to unification of law. At non-elite schools professors prefer clinical and other practical education to legal scholarship. Focused as this education is on local practice, it does little to promote unification of law.

19.3.4.3 Admission to Practice

Admission to practice is by component state. While some federal courts have their own procedures and some have special rules, the states are responsible for issuing licenses to practice law.

Testing for admission to practice is, however, only partly by component state. To a degree that varies among the states, they incorporate into their own testing procedure tests developed by a third-party, independent, non-governmental body, the National Conference of Bar Examiners.

All but two states, Washington and Louisiana, use the Multistate Bar Exam, for 1 day of their 2-or-3 day state bar exams. The Multistate Bar Exam consists of 200 multiple choice questions on the topics of contracts, torts, constitutional law, criminal law, evidence, and real property. These questions are not jurisdiction-specific but test issues that should have the same solutions in all states.

Louisiana does not participate, presumably, because its own legal heritage, while much influenced by the common law, has a predominantly civil law origin. As a result, in core private law areas of contracts, torts and real property, its legal approaches differ from those of other states and are non-uniform.

19.3.4.4 Post-graduate Legal Education and Post-admission Legal Training

The United States has no independent legal research institutes comparable to the renowned Max Planck Institutes in Germany. American law schools do not have a tradition of scientific study of law and do not offer American law students as a matter of course the opportunity to do doctoral work in law.[59] They do offer American and foreign law students alike many opportunities for a fourth year of legal education in the form of studies for masters' degrees. Often, these degrees have a particular subject matter focus.

While practical training is not required for admission to practice, most jurisdictions now require that practitioners participate in what is called "continuing legal education" ("CLE") following admission to practice. Requirements vary state-by-state. Most CLE programs are independent of the law schools and are offered by bar associations, other lawyer associations or proprietary bodies. While directed generally by practitioners with practice in mind, they are not apprentice-type programs. They take place in classroom settings.

Graduate and continuing legal education in their relationship to unification of law tend to mirror law school education. Graduate education tends more toward central, while continuing legal education tends more toward component state law.

19.3.5 Influence of International Law on Legal Unification

Where the federal government enters into a treaty obligation, that obligation can create uniform domestic law. This can occur where the federal government may otherwise not have authority to act.[60] There is no need for the states to take separate action. Thus when the United Nations Convention on the International Sale of Goods took effect, it became uniform law for all 50 states.

Such cases are rare and are likely to be all the rarer in the future. Since ratification of CISG, the Congress has shown increased hostility to treaties, such as CISG, that are self-executing, *i.e.*, that require no further legislation by Congress. Still, insofar as Congress adopts law, either through a self-executing treaty or through legislation implementing a non-self-executing treaty, the international law will become a uniform American law.

Compliance with international legal obligations plays a role in unification only rarely and then only a minor one.

Voluntary international coordination can matter but usually only in a very attenuated way. Although the United States participates in such voluntary coordination, American legal institutions not infrequently ignore or even rebuff actual cooperation.

---

[59] The J.S.D., or S.J.D. (doctorate of juridical science), is not routinely offered or granted to others besides foreign jurists and American academics already holding teaching positions.

[60] *See, e.g.*, Missouri v. Holland, 252 U.S. 416 (1920).

19.4 Institutional and Social Background

19.4.1 The Judicial Branch

19.4.1.1 Judicial Review of Federal and State Action

The United States Supreme Court polices whether either Congress or the states have impermissibly exceeded their respective lawmaking powers. The procedure and substance of that review, however, contribute substantially to making American law non-uniform and uncertain.

(a) The Court cannot review legislation before it takes effect; it has no authority of *abstract* review. Early in its history it created the "case or controversy" requirement. That doctrine demands that the courts may review the constitutionality of a law only when the law is applied in a concrete case. This delays resolution of these questions. Until overturned, laws are presumptively valid; the law-abiding must comply with them if they can.

(b) The Court does not have a monopoly of judicial review of constitutionality; review is not *concentrated*. Lower and state courts may also determine the issue of constitutionality. The Supreme Court reviews exercises of lawmaking powers only in the ordinary course of appellate decision making. Parties must raise constitutional questions in the first instance of proceedings. First-instance courts cannot refer the questions to a constitutional court. The court of first instance may try to avoid the constitutional issue. If it does reach the issue, the disappointed party must then appeal the decision. Since most cases raising an issue of distribution of power end up in an intermediate federal or state appellate court, an exercise of lawmaking authority may be upheld in one jurisdiction and not in another.

(c) The subject of the Court's review—perhaps because of the case or controversy requirement—tends to be application of the law to an individual case, rather than a validation or invalidation of the law as a whole.

19.4.1.2 Judicial Review and Harmonization of State Legislation

The United States Supreme Court is not authorized to interpret state law authoritatively. Only exceptionally—and then against substantial criticism—does it do so.[61]

No single court has authority to interpret authoritatively the uniform laws that the states adopt. This is possibly the biggest deficiency of the Uniform Commercial Code and of other uniform laws. It has long been recognized. Issues of interpretation remain unresolved decades after the Uniform Commercial Code first became law.

---

[61] *See, e.g.*, Bush v. Gore, 531 U.S. 98 (2000); West Virginia ex rel. Dyer v. Sims, 341 U.S. 22 (1951).

19.4.1.3 Dual Court Structures

There are parallel state and federal courts in both first and appellate instances. The Constitution did not require, but it does authorize, such dual structures[62] out of fear that state courts would not enforce federal law. This system of competing competencies complicates coordination and wastes judicial and private resources. This waste is by and large accepted as a necessary evil.

Most states now permit federal courts of appeals and some other courts[63] to "certify" to their state's highest court questions of state law that may determine a cause and for which there is no controlling state law precedent. In New York, the procedure has been available since 1986. From 1986 through the end of 2005 federal courts certified 71 cases to New York's highest court, of which the court accepted 66. While there are reasons peculiar to New York that explain this very low rate of referral, New York's experience tends to confirm this Reporter's impression that this procedure has not become a measure used routinely to promote uniformity and coordinate judiciaries.[64]

19.4.2 Relations Between the Central and Component State Governments

The central government cannot compel states to adopt legislation. Such compulsion would be considered an infringement of the sovereign prerogatives of the component states. Nor, on the same ground, can the central government compel component states to execute central government law.[65]

The component states as such and their governments are not represented at the central level. They have not been since 1913 (amend. XVII). Until 1912 each of the legislatures of the component states (art. 1, § 3, cl. 1) selected two senators in the United States Senate. Since 1913 the people of those states have elected the senators directly.

---

[62]U.S. Const. art. III, § 1.

[63]Whether other courts are allowed to certify questions varies by state. Other courts that may certify are federal district courts, federal bankruptcy courts and the highest courts of sister states.

[64]Advisory Group to the New York State and Federal Judicial Council, *Practice Handbook on Certification of State Law Questions by the United States Court of Appeals for the Second Circuit to the New York State Court of Appeals* (2nd ed. 2006), available at http://www.nycourts.gov/ctapps/Cert.pdf. The New York procedure is available only to the federal courts and may be used by them *sua sponte* only after a case has been fully-briefed and argued. At that point, certification is not a time-saver, but a time waster.

[65]Printz v. United States, 521 U.S. 898 (1997). The *Printz* decision is at odds with earlier federal practice. The first Congress, in providing for implementation of the Congressional power "[t]o establish a uniform rule of naturalization" art. 1, § 2, cl. 4, provided for state court application of that uniform law. An Act to establish a Uniform Rule of Naturalization of March 26, 1790, Statutes at Large, 1st Cong., 2nd Sess., 103.

Component state representatives at the central level are elected by the people of the component states: senators by all the people in the state, representatives by districts.

19.4.3 The Bureaucracy

The civil service of the central government is separate from the civil services of the component states. There is no formalized mobility between the separate civil service systems.

The lack of continuity in the upper levels of the bureaucracies—both of the central government and of the component states—is a significant hindrance to unification of law.

19.4.4 Social, Regional and Environmental Factors

19.4.4.1 Social Factors

In contemporary America, social factors do not contribute greatly to the disharmony of law. Federal law affirmatively prohibits laws that discriminate based on race or ethnicity, which thus largely assures harmony in these areas.

The social factor with the greatest present potential for disharmony is gender-orientation. Although the Supreme Court in 2003 in *Lawrence v. Texas*[66] invalidated state criminal laws prohibiting consensual sexual conduct among same sex couples, states continue to vary—often dramatically—in their legal treatment of civil relationships among same sex couples.

In the past, social factors were much more productive of disharmony. Historically race was the most important. Even after the Civil War put an end to the non-uniform law of slavery, former slave states sought to preserve *de jure* social separation of people through laws requiring segregation of races in public accommodations and prohibiting marriages among people of different races. In contrast, northern states generally did not require *de jure* segregation; some even prohibited *de facto* segregation. The result was substantial disharmony from state-to-state. Some states prohibited people of one race from attending school with people of another race; other states did not. Some states prohibited people of one race from marrying people of another race; other states did not. Some states prohibited innkeepers from housing people of different races in the same facilities; other states prohibited innkeepers

---

[66] 539 U.S. 588.

from housing people of different races in different facilities.[67] The Supreme Court's decision in *Plessy v. Ferguson*,[68] which validated separate ("but equal") treatment of people based on race as consistent with the equal protection clause of the fourteenth amendment, is today nearly as infamous as the Supreme Court's *Dred Scott* decision, which held that Negros were not citizens of the United States.[69] Not until nearly a half-century later, in 1954, in an equally famous decision, *Brown v. Board of Education*,[70] did the Supreme Court overturn *Plessy*. Subsequent to *Brown,* the Court invalidated other state laws making racially-based distinctions. For example, not until 1967 did it invalidate prohibitions on inter-racial marriages (anti-miscegenation laws).[71] While the *Brown* decision is widely regarded as a triumph of American (litigation- and case law-based) constitutional jurisprudence, it took a federal statute, the Civil Rights Act of 1964, to impose national uniformity.[72]

While most state laws distinguishing people by race were directed against persons of African descent, many found applicability to persons of Asian descent as well as to Native Americans (American Indians). Some states also adopted laws specifically directed against persons of Asian descent. These too, of course, worked against uniformity of law.

Federal laws that made distinctions based on race principally involved immigration. They did not create non-uniformity of law, since immigration law is exclusively federal law. The national government's responsibility for native Americans tended to minimize state legislation and hence non-uniform treatment of that group.[73]

Formerly, ethnicity played a significant role in creating disharmony in law among the states. Different states reacted to immigrants with different laws. Some states supported immigrants by facilitating immigrants' use of their mother tongues; others sought to suppress such use.[74] Political considerations of the day often played a part. During World War I there was a wave of legislation prohibiting use of German and other languages. In 1923 in *Meyer v. Nebraska,* the Supreme Court invalidated a state statute that prohibited teaching students in languages other than English.[75]

---

[67]For a listing of the disparate laws as they stood in 1950, see *States' Laws on Race and Color* (Pauli Murray, ed., 1950). American race and nationality legislation was of particular interest in Nazi Germany as a precedent for its own racist laws.

[68]163 U.S. 537 (1906).

[69]Scott v. Sanford, 60 U.S. (19 How) 393 (1857).

[70]347 U.S. 483 (1954).

[71]Loving v. Virginia, 388 U.S. 1 (1967) (overturning Pace v. Alabama, 106 U.S. 583 (1883)).

[72]Pub. L. 88–352. *See* Carrington, Paul D. 1999. Restoring vitality to state and local politics by correcting the excessive independence of the supreme court. *Alabama Law Review* 50: 397, 440.

[73]Although even here, there was some non-uniformity. In 1950 thirteen states prohibited sales of liquor to Native Americans, five prohibited marriages of Native Americans to white persons, and three provided for separate schools. *States Laws on Race and Color, supra* note 67, at 19.

[74]For a catalogue and analysis of such legislation, see Heinz Kloß, *Das Volksgruppenrecht in den Vereinigten Staaten von Amerika* (2 vols., 1940–1942).

[75]262 U.S. 390. Justice Holmes would have upheld the prohibition. See William G. Ross, *Forging New Freedoms. Nativism, Education, and the Constitution*, 1917–1927 (1994).

The Civil Rights Act of 1964 put an end to laws discriminating on the basis of an individual's place of national origin. But different states and jurisdictions still treat differently the extent to which public services are to be provided in English only or in additional languages.

The election of Barack Obama to the presidency of the United States well demonstrates that racial and ethnic differences are of declining importance. It also demonstrates, however, that race remains more important than ethnicity. He is usually identified as a "black" president and only rarely as a "second generation Kenyan or African" person.

19.4.4.2 Regional Factors

That different groups settled the United States at different times and places has led to regional variations in law. These variations go back to the earliest days of the country. Massachusetts was settled initially by Puritans from England, while Pennsylvania was settled by Quakers from England and Germans from the Palatinate. Maryland was settled as a refuge for Roman Catholics. Other southern states were settled by second sons of the English aristocracy and the enslaved African-Americans they brought to tend their properties. In the Middle West, Missouri, Illinois, Iowa, Ohio and Wisconsin were much settled by Germans, while Scandinavians settled Minnesota. Utah was founded by Mormons fleeing persecution in New York, Illinois and Missouri. California was settled by Mexicans and by Americans seeking gold.

These different patterns of settlement have played a role in the uniformity and in the disharmony of the nations' laws. Before the Civil War, northern states were seen to prefer settling disputes by law, while southern states were thought to prefer duels pursuant to "codes of honor." Massachusetts has long been considered to have creditor-friendly laws, while Texas and Florida are seen to favor debtors.[76] Missouri is widely considered to have stayed in the Union in the Civil War because of the strong hostility of the new German immigrants to slavery. Utah was admitted to the Union only when the Mormon inhabitants agreed to outlaw bigamy, which was permitted by their religion.

How much these different patterns of settlement continue to contribute to disparate law is well beyond the scope of this report. It is a matter of social science. In terms of continuing day-to-day influences on law, regional environmental variations, with only a few exceptions, are of more significance than are differences in ethnic or religious make-ups of the inhabitants of different states. Only in areas of recent immigration is there a noteworthy possibility of material disharmony in law based on population characteristics. Even then, disharmony among the states is likely to be limited to the availability of services in non-English languages.

---

[76] As we have seen in considering the homestead exemption in bankruptcy.

19.4.4.3 Environmental Factors

Both the nature of the land and the patterns of settlement contribute to significant differences among the laws of the states. In most of the West land is plentiful, but desert. In a desert, issues of water rights take center stage. On some western highways, livestock enjoy the right-of-way ("open range country"), while on eastern roads the owner is strictly liable for damage they may cause. Rights to the seashore vary from state-to-state.

More densely-settled areas were quicker to institute zoning controls. But Houston, a large and sprawling Texas city of about two million people, still has no formal zoning code.

19.5 Conclusion

"Unification" does not well describe the legal system of the United States. Unification is found only when law is exclusively federal. In most areas of the law there are significant non-uniformities between state and federal law and among laws of states and of municipalities. The government presents the people not with one law, but with a multitude of laws. The people are left to sort out the various laws at their peril.

Yet if law in the United States is not uniform, it is largely harmonized.[77] While there are numerous inconsistencies in law, only rarely are these inconsistencies substantive at a societal level (*e.g.,* death penalty in some states, but not others). Usually inconsistencies are matters of detail only. These details can, however, be extremely important in individual cases (*e.g.,* death penalty, statutes of limitation).

In everyday life, the devil is in the detail. Thus inconsistencies, while only in detail, nonetheless have very real societal costs. American lawyers spend inordinate amounts of time worrying which law applies and determining what that law is. For half a century, if not longer, American jurists have accepted these inefficiencies as "the price we pay for our federalism."[78]

This price is so-well recognized, that most lawyers simply assume that the system could not exist without it. In blissful ignorance of alternative solutions, they and the public at large do not regularly challenge this enormous waste.

---

[77] *Accord*, Taylor, E. Hunter. 1980. Federalism or uniformity of commercial law. *Rutgers-Camden Law Journal* 11: 527, 531 ("In sum, likeness rather than exactness—harmony rather than uniformity—has been the history of the "Uniform" Commercial Code, as will inevitably be the result of any code or model act which must depend for its uniformity on state-by-state enactment.").

[78] Knapp v. Schweitzer, 357 U.S. 371, 380 (1958) (opinion by Frankfurter, J.).

Less-well recognized, are other costs that some may debate, but that seem real to this Reporter:

1. Undermining respect for law. Law is realized when people abide by and enforce it. Numerous inconsistencies in law complicate abiding by law and enforcing it. Law-abiding begins to look like a game that only suckers play. In short, they strike at the efficacy of law.[79]
2. It is little recognized that disparate laws are deficient laws. When all solutions are equally valid, none is preferred. When each component state goes its own way willy-nilly, no way is identified as the best way. Instead of one law being subject to careful consideration in drafting and improvement in application, many laws are haphazardly drafted and carelessly applied.
3. Disparate laws invite undue influence or particularist interests.

To this Reporter, neither the recognized nor the unrecognized costs seem worth paying. The cacophony of non-uniform law should long ago have been replaced by the harmony of uniform or better national law. The legal system is indeed a lagging indicator. More than a century and a third ago one critic rightly noted:

[A]s the country has grown older, the people of the United States as a whole—in their personal relations—have become far more united and harmonious than have the various systems of State law by which their commercial and domestic interests are largely governed. For this reason the constant conflict of law which daily arises in the affairs of our national life, with its consequent uncertainties, is becoming an evil so serious that it must soon pass from the hands of the theorist to those of the practical statesman.[80]

---

[79]Taking a similar view, see Pope, Herbert. 1919. The federal courts and a uniform law. *The Yale Law Journal* 28: 647.

[80]Hannis Taylor, *An Inter-State Code Commission* (1881), reprinted in Report of the Organization and of the First, Second and Third Annual Meetings of the Alabama State Bar Association 210 (1882).

Chapter 20
Venezuela: The End of Federalism?

Allan R. Brewer-Carías and Jan Kleinheisterkamp

20.1 Overview of the History and Development of the Federal System in Venezuela

Venezuela was the first Latin American country to gain independence from the Spanish Crown in 1810. A general congress of representatives of the former colonial provinces of the *Capitanía General de Venezuela* enacted on 21 December 1811 the Federal Constitution for the States of Venezuela, the first constitution on the South American continent. This Constitution followed the general principles of modern constitutionalism derived from the North American and French Revolutions, such as the republican system; supremacy of the constitution paired with constitutional judicial control; organic separation of powers; territorial distribution of power; and declaration of fundamental rights. The 1811 Constitution established a federal form of government. Venezuela was thus the second country after the United States of America to adopt a federal system, which enabled the construction of an independent state that united the former colonial provinces. Today, the territory of the republic is divided into 23 states, a Capital District (that covers parts of the

---

Allan R. BREWER-CARÍAS, Professor, Central University of Venezuela; former Simón Bolívar Professor, University of Cambridge UK; former Vice President of the International Academy of Comparative Law.

Jan KLEINHEISTERKAMP, Senior Lecturer, Department of Law, London School of Economics; Visiting Professor at the University Panthéon-Assas – Paris II.

A.R. Brewer-Carías
Law Faculty, Central University of Venezuela, Caracas, Venezuela
e-mail: allan@brewercarias.com

J. Kleinheisterkamp (✉)
Department of Law, London School of Economics, Houghton Street, WC2A 2AE London, UK
e-mail: j.kleinheisterkamp@lse.ac.uk

city of Caracas), and federal dependencies that comprise the islands located in the Caribbean Sea. The municipalities with jurisdiction in Caracas are organized in a Metropolitan District (*Distrito Metropolitano*), with a two tier municipal government.

Following a period of dissolution in Simón Bolívar's *Gran Colombia* as of 1821, the "State of Venezuela" re-emerged as a separate country in 1830 with a rather mixed (centralized-provincial) form of government, but lived intense struggles between the central region and provincial forces. This period ended three decades later with a 5-year "Federal War" (1858–1863), from which the Federation re-emerged with the establishment of the United States of Venezuela (1864). From that moment on, the form of government in Venezuela has always been federal, at least on paper. During the second half of the nineteenth century, successive civil wars led to various constitutional reforms in which the federal system of government was kept, yet with a progressive tendency of centralization regarding numerous elements that historically had characterized the federal system. For instance, regarding unification of laws, the states accepted in the 1864 Constitution, as part on the "Basis of the Union", "to have for all of them one same substantive legislation on criminal and civil matters".[1] In 1881, the words "the same laws on civil and criminal procedure" were added.[2] Accordingly, the Civil, Criminal, and Commercial Codes, but also the Codes of Civil and Criminal Procedure have always been federal laws.

During the first half of the twentieth century, dominated by autocratic regimes, Venezuela saw a continued process of centralization in the fields of the military, administration, taxation and legislation. The territorial distribution of power and territorial autonomy of the component states had almost disappeared, in spite of the Constitutions' continuing formal proclamations of federalism.[3] The second half of the twentieth century was characterized by democratization,[4] especially under the constitution of 1961, which upheld the federal form of government, albeit with highly centralized powers at the national level. A political decentralization process sparked by the democratic practice began in 1989 with the transfer of powers from the central government to the federal states.[5] For the first time since the nineteenth

---

[1] Article 13 n° 22 *Constitución de los Estados Unidos de Venezuela* of 22 April 1864. The texts of all the Venezuelan Constitutions are published in A.R. Brewer-Carías, 1–2 *Las Constituciones de Venezuela* (Caracas 2008).

[2] Article 13 n° 19 *Constitución de los Estados Unidos de Venezuela* of 27 April 1881.

[3] *See also* J. de Galíndez, "Venezuela: New Constitution", *American Journal of Comparative Law* 3: 81–82 (1954): "Only in theory does Venezuela continue to be a federal republic".

[4] See M. Kornblith, "Constitutions and Democracy in Venezuela", *Journal of Latin American Studies* 23: 61, 63 (1991).

[5] For the political background of this decentralization reform and its impact on the political scene in Venezuela, see M. Penfold-Becerra, "Federalism and Institutional Change in Venezuela", in: E.L. Gibson (ed.), *Federalism and Democracy in Latin America* 197–225 (Baltimore 2004). See also Point 20.2.2.1, below.

century, the governors of the federal states were elected directly,[6] and regional political life began to play an important role in the country.

Hugo Chávez, a former military officer whose *coup d'état* had failed in 1992 and who was elected as the President of the Republic in 1998, convened a National Constituent Assembly that sanctioned today's Constitution, which was submitted to a referendum in 1999.[7] This 26th Constitution of Venezuela has caused the pendulum to swing back. Instead of undertaking the changes needed for reinforcing democracy, namely the effective political decentralization of the federation and the reinforcement of state and municipal political power, it re-launched the centralization process under an authoritarian government.[8]

20.2 Federal Distribution and Exercise of Lawmaking Powers

20.2.1 Areas of Law Subject to (Legislative) Jurisdiction of the Central Authority

20.2.1.1 Matters Attributed to the Central Government

Article 156 of the Constitution of 1999 enumerates all the areas of jurisdiction of the *Poder Público Nacional*, i.e., the central public power in Venezuela. As regards the legislative jurisdiction, Article 165 n° 32 explicitly provides that the central authority (National Assembly) has jurisdiction for the legislation in the areas of:

- Constitutional rights, obligations and guarantees;*
- Civil law, commercial law, criminal law, the penal system, procedural law and private international law;*
- Electoral law;*
- Expropriations for the sake of public or social interests;*
- Public credit;*
- Intellectual, artistic, and industrial property;*
- Cultural and archeological treasures;*
- Agriculture;*

---

[6] See *infra* note 30.
[7] See on the 1999 constitution-making process: A.R. Brewer-Carías, "The 1999 Venezuelan Constitution-Making Process as an Instrument for Framing the development of an Authoritarian Political Regime," in: L.E. Miller (ed.), *Framing the State in Times of Transition. Case Studies in Constitution Making*, 505–531 (Washington 2010).
[8] *See* A.R. Brewer-Carías, *Dismantling Democracy. The Chávez Authoritarian Experiment* (Cambridge 2010).

- Immigration and colonization[9];*
- Indigenous people and the territories occupied by them;*
- Labor and social security and welfare[10];*
- Veterinary and phytosanitary hygiene[11];*
- Notaries and public registers;*
- Banks and insurances;*
- Lotteries, horseracing, and bets in general;*
- The organization and functioning of the organs of the central authority and the other organs and institutions of the state.[12]*

Article 156 n° 32 also specifies that the central authority also has legislative jurisdiction for all matters of "national competence", i.e., for the implementation of all other matters enumerated in Article 156 n°s 1–31. In this list, the power to legislate is explicitly attributed to the central authority (National Assembly) for the following matters[13]:

- Those related to the armed forces (n° 8)* and civil protection (n° 9)[14];
- Monetary policies (n° 11);*
- The coordination and harmonization of the different taxation authorities; the definition of principles, parameters, and restrictions, and in particular the types of tributes or rates of the taxes of the states and municipalities; as well as the creation of special funds that assure the inter-territorial solidarity (n° 13);
- Foreign commerce and customs (n° 15);*
- Mining and natural energy resources (hydrocarbon)[15];* fallow and waste land; and the conservation, development and exploitation of the woods, grounds, waters,[16] and other natural resources of the country (n° 16)[17];
- Standards of measurement and quality control (n° 17);*

---

[9]*See also* Article 156 n° 4: "the naturalization and the admission, extradition and expulsion of foreigners"; Article 38.

[10]*See also* Article 156 n° 22: "the regime and organization of the social security system".

[11]*See also* Article 156 n° 23: "the legislation in matters of … public health [and] food safety … "

[12]*See also* Article 156 n° 31: "the national organization and administration of justice, the *Ministerio Público* and the *Defensoría del Pueblo*".

[13]See TSJ Sala Constitucional, decision n° 565 of 15 April 2008, file n° 07-1108, where the Supreme Tribunal interpreted the word "regimen" found in some of the provisions in Article 156 as indicating the power to legislate. See in 114 *Revista de Derecho Público*, 154–170 (2008).

[14]*See also* Articles 328–332.

[15]For the exclusive nature of the central authority's legislative power over the natural energy resources see in more detail the text accompanying note 37, below.

[16]See also Article 304, which provides that all waters are property of the Republic and that the law establishes the necessary provisions in order to guarantee their protection, exploitation, and recovery.

[17]Contrast with n° 23 (environment and water in the context of public health, housing and food safety).

- The establishment, coordination, and unification of technical norms and procedures for construction, architecture, and urbanism, as well as the legislation on urbanism (n° 19);*
- Public health, housing, food safety, environment,[18] water, tourism,[19] and the territorial organization (n° 23);
- Navigation and air transport, ground transport, maritime and inland waterway transport (n° 26)[20];
- Post and telecommunication services and radio frequencies (n° 28);*
- Public utilities such as especially electricity, potable water, and gas (n° 29).[21]

Furthermore, the Constitution attributes to the central authority the powers to:

- Conclude, approve, and ratify international treaties (Article 154);*
- Legislate on antitrust and the abuse of market power (Articles 113 and 114).*

20.2.1.2 Nature of the Jurisdiction Attributed to the Central Government

The Constitution does not expressly specify whether the central authority (National Assembly) has exclusive powers in these areas or whether the legislative powers are shared with the component states and the municipalities. The exclusive character of legislative powers has to be determined by interpretation for each of them separately. All of the areas of "general legislation" enumerated in Article 156 n° 32 can be considered to be of the exclusive power of the central authority, together with those other areas mentioned above that are marked with an asterisk (*), or those others where the central authority has already legislated.[22] Neither the component states nor the municipalities may legislate in these areas.[23] In all other areas that belong to the concurrent powers shared between the central government and the component states and the municipalities, the National Assembly always retains the power to enact "basic laws" ("*leyes de base*"), which establish the framework that must be respected by the component states when enacting local "laws of development" ("*leyes de desarrollo*"), Article 165(1).[24]

---

[18]See also the concurrent power in this area of the municipalities, Article 178 n° 4.

[19]For the concurrent nature of this power, see TSJ Sala Constitucional decision n° 826 of 16 May 2008, file n° 08-0479.

[20]*See also* Article 156 n° 23: "the national policies and the legislation in matters of navigation".

[21]See Article 164 n° 8, which attributes "exclusive" power to the states for "the creation, regulation, and organization of public utilities of the states".

[22]Cf. A.R. Brewer-Carías, "La descentralización política en la Constitución de 1999: federalismo y municipalismo (una reforma insuficiente y regresiva)", 7 *Provincia* 7, 29–31 (2001).

[23]See, e.g., for the exclusivity of the federal jurisdiction for matters related to retirement and pensions on the basis of Article 156 n° 32, TSJ Sala Constitucional, decision n° 518 of 1 June 2000, file n° 00-0841; decision n° 1452 of 3 August 2004, file n° 02-2585.

[24]*See also Exposición de Motivos de la Constitución* (the official justification of the 1999 Constitution): "As regards to the concurrent powers, the Constitution adopts the experience of

Article 156 can be considered the most important source specified in the Constitution that authorizes central government regulation. On its basis, practically all important areas of government are covered by central legislation. In summary, it seems fair to say that the central authority (National Assembly) has legislative jurisdictions in all areas of law, either for enacting central legislation or for enacting framework laws.

20.2.2 Areas of Law Remaining to the (Legislative) Jurisdiction of the Component States

20.2.2.1 Overview

Article 164 enumerates a list of matters that are formally designated to be of the "exclusive jurisdiction" of the component states. This designation, however, is misleading since none of these matters can be regarded as truly exclusive,[25] especially not as concerns the legislative powers.

Article 164 partially integrates the provisions of the "Decentralization Law" of 1989,[26] which already provided for the transfer of powers to the states. But different from Article 164 of the 1999 Constitution, Article 11 of the Law of 1989 had provided explicitly that the states would have the power to legislate on these matters.[27] With the entry into force of the 1999 Constitution, the states' pretensions to legislate in their areas of exclusive powers have been rejected and subordinated to national legislation.[28] The constitutional provision in Article 158, which establishes

---

comparative law on decentralization and it provides that national laws have the nature of basic laws, in which general, basic, and guiding concepts are laid down; and that state laws are laws developing these basic principles, which allows for better conditions for the delimitation of competences"; G.O. n° 5908 Extra of 19 February 2009.

[25]Cf. Brewer-Carías, *supra* note 22 at 29.

[26]*Ley Orgánica para la Descentralización, Delimitación y Transferencia de Competencias del Poder Público*, G.O. n° 4153 of 28 December 1989. See on this law see A.R. Brewer-Carías, "Bases legislativas para la descentralización política de la federación centralizada (1990: El inicio de una reforma)", in *idem* (coord.) et al., *Leyes para la Descentralización Política de la Federación* 7–53 (Caracas 1990).

[27]Article 11, sole paragraph, of the Law of 1989 reads: "Until the states assume these powers through specific legislation, enacted by the respective legislative assemblies, the presently existing legislation continues in force".

[28]See, e.g., *Dictamen de la Procuraduría de la República*, Oficio N° D.A.G.E. 000019 of 20 October 2000, available at http://www.pgr.gob.ve/PDF/Dictamenes/CONSTITUCIONAL1.pdf, which rejects the possibility that the states can establish the legislative basis for the conservation, administration and exploitation of the national highways on the basis of Article 164 n° 10, and suggesting that, until a national law is enacted, the states and the federal government should conclude cooperation agreements. On these matters, the TSJ, Sala Constitucional Decision n° 565

that decentralization is a national policy, has been ignored by the central government and the "Decentralization Law" despite having been reenacted with virtually no changes in 2003 and again in 2009,[29] and can be considered dead letter.[30]

20.2.2.2 Nature of the Jurisdiction Attributed to the Component States

The only true legislative power of the component states is to organize their own constitutional structure by adopting their own constitutions (Article 164 n° 1) "in accordance with this [federal] Constitution". This provision limits this power of self-organization, since the federal constitution imposes a general organizational structure on the component states and establishes uniform rules for the state governors (Articles 159–163, and 166).[31] Moreover, the 1999 Constitution deprives the component states of establishing in their respective state constitutions the rules of organization and functioning of their legislative assemblies, which are instead governed by a federal law of the central authority (Article 162 *in fine*)[32] as well as the basic legislation on public Administration and public servants, which has also been enacted by the central authority.[33] The only exclusive legislative powers remaining with the component states thus concern the specific legislation on the details of the organization and functioning of the governors' office and states' administrative organization.[34]

---

of 15 April 2008, has eliminated the "exclusive" character of the states' jurisdiction, transforming it into a "concurrent" jurisdiction, available at http://www.tsj.gov.ve/decisiones/scon/Abril/565-150408-07-1108.htm

[29]G.O. n° 37753 of 14 August 2003; G.O. n° 39140 of 17 March 2009.

[30]J. Sánchez Meléan, "Pasado, presente y futuro de la descentralización en Venezuela", 9 *Provincia* 20, 26 (2002); A.R. Brewer-Carías, "La descentralización política. Un modelo de Estado," in: F. Otamendi Osorio, T. Straka, & Grupo Jirahara (eds.), *Venezuela: República democrática* (Barquisimeto 2011), 645–673.

[31]Cf. TSJ Sala Constitucional, decision 1182 of 11 October 2000, file n° 00-1410: "It is therefore clear that the states are constitutionally privileged by the principle of autonomy for the organization of their public power; however, it has to be understood that this autonomy is relative and therefore subject to numerous restrictions established by the Constitution and the Law". See also note 23 above. For the central regulation of the state governors see also Articles 22–32 of the "Decentralization Law" of 1989 and 2003, according to which, *inter alia*, state governors can be removed for "repeated disobedience of orders or decisions by the President of the Republic" (Article 31); for harsh criticism see A. Hernández Becerra, "Nivel territorial intermedio en Colombia y Venezuela", 15 *Provincia* 95, 105 (2006), but it has to be noted that prior to 1989, state governors were directly appointed by the President.

[32]*Ley Orgánica de los Consejos Legislativos de los Estados*, G.O. N° 37282 of 13 September 2001.

[33]*Ley Orgánica de la Administración Pública*, G.O. N° 5890 Extra of 31 July 2008; *Ley del Estatuto de la Función Pública*, G.O. N° 37522 of 6 September 2002.

[34]Cf. Brewer-Carías, *supra* note 22 at 27.

The two other items of Article 164 which make reference to legislative powers by referring to the component states' right to enact a *"régimen"*, which could be understood as conferring legislative powers,[35] are:

- The exploitation of non-metallic minerals that are not reserved to the central authority, salt mines and oyster beds (n° 5);
- The public utilities of the component states (n° 8).

The first of these two areas is – despite being labeled as an "exclusive power" of the component states by Article 164 – by and large only a concurrent power, since the central authority retains the power over "the mines and natural energy resources (hydrocarbon) ... and the conservation, development and exploitation of the ... grounds ... and the other natural treasures" according to Article 156 n° 16.[36] It follows from this provision, read in conjunction with Article 164 n° 5, that especially the exploitation of natural energy resources (hydrocarbon) – i.e. gas and petrol, the dominant source of income of Venezuela – are of exclusive jurisdiction of the central authority and subjected to the legislation enacted by the National Assembly.[37] Only the administrative procedures for the exploitation of non-precious stone, salt mines and oyster beds thus seem to fall under a genuine exclusive legislative jurisdiction of the states.[38] Furthermore, the second of the areas enumerated above (public utilities) is also merely a shared competence, since Article 156 n° 29 provides that the "general legislation" on the public utilities (at least those offered to the citizens at home) falls within the power of the central authority.

In summary, there are no relevant areas of law making that are reserved to the states.[39] If at all, they only have exclusive administrative powers in some areas. The states possess merely concurrent powers for some few areas in which they may enact

---

[35]For the meaning of *"régimen"* in the constitutional catalogues of jurisdictions see note 13 above.

[36]This constitutional provision thus undermines Article 11 n° 2 of the 1989 Decentralization Law (note 26 above), which provided that "in order to promote the administrative decentralization and according to the provision of Article 137 of the Constitution [of 1961] the following matters are transferred to the exclusive jurisdiction of the States: ... the legislation, administration and exploitation of stones for construction and decoration or of any type other than precious ... of the earthy substances, the salt-mines and the pearl producing oyster banks".

[37]The total control of the central authority over gas and petrol resources is complemented by Article 156 n° 16(3), which provides that a federal law will establish a system of special economic attributions to the states in whose territory the exploited resources are found, yet without prejudice to the possibility to also establish special attributions in favor of other states, which means that the central authority has broad discretion in its decisions regarding at least gas and petrol.

[38]For the exclusivity of the jurisdiction over salt mines, albeit only in a conflict between a state and a municipality see TSJ Sala Constitucional, decision n° 78 of 30 January 2001, file n° 00-1556 ("una competencia originaria de los [Estados] ... una competencia natural y exclusiva"). For such a state law see *Ley de Régimen, Administración y Aprovechamiento de Salinas y sus Productos del Estado Sucre, Gaceta Oficial Extraordinaria del Estado Sucre* n° 10 of 29 November 1993.

[39]Brewer-Carías, *supra* note 22 at 29; K.S. Rosenn, "Federalism in the Americas in a Comparative Perspective", *University of Miami Inter-American Law Review* 26: 1, 16 (1994).

legislation (see those items not marked with an asterisk (*) above Sect. 20.2.1).[40] In any event, all state legislation in matters of concurrent powers, which takes the form of "development laws" (*leyes de desarrollo*), is contingent upon the prior enactment of federal "basic laws" (*leyes de base*) (Article 165(1)). The latter set a binding framework for the former.[41] Article 165(1) commands that such federal "basic" framework laws have to respect the principles of interdependency, coordination, cooperation, shared responsibility and subsidiarity.[42] Yet this will not prevent the federal authority from also regulating specific details, at least as long as such detailed federal regulation can be justified under the principle of subsidiarity, i.e., if a need for centralized and thus uniform legislation can be shown. Articles 164 and 165(1) therefore only guarantee a kind of minimum core of legislative power of the states in the areas of shared competences.[43] This minimum core is rather restricted in the light of the constitutional case law which tends to interpret the powers of the central authority broadly.[44]

---

[40] See also Article 15 of the *Ley Orgánica de los Consejos Legislativos de los Estados*, G.O. 37282 of 13 September 2001, whose enumeration of the powers of the state parliaments, other than the power to enact and amend a state constitution and (restricted) budgetary laws, essentially mentions only the legislative power to enact "development laws" within the framework of federal "basic laws".

[41] For a case in which a state claimed to be unable to legislate on matters of concurrent powers because the National Assembly had not yet enacted the necessary federal laws see TSJ Sala Constitucional, decision n° 3203 of 25 October 2005, file n° 02-2984. See also A.R. Brewer-Carías, "Centralized Federalism in Venezuela", 43 *Duquesne Law Review* 629, 639 (2005).

[42] Cf. TSJ Sala Constitucional, decision 843 of 11 May 2004, file n° 03-1236, where the Supreme Tribunal affirms *obiter* that "the concurrent powers ... have to be previously delimitated by a basic national law; ... only the national legislator has the power for enacting basic regulatory laws (according to the principles of interdependency, coordination, shared responsibility and subsidiarity) in the areas of concurrent powers"; this is reaffirmed in TSJ of 15 April 2008, *supra* note 13, on the relation between Articles 156 n° 26 and 164 n° 10 regarding highways.

[43] See, e.g., TSJ Sala Constitucional, decision n° 2495 of 19 December 2006, file n° 02-0265, where the State of Carabobo claimed that Article 42 of the *Ley General de Puertos* (G.O. n° 73589 of 11 December 2002) violated its powers resulting from Article 164 n° 10 of the Constitution (which grants states the "exclusive" powers for the conservation, administration, and exploitation of commercial ports "in coordination with the national government") because the federal law obliges the States either to establish an autonomous entity for the administration of each port or to grant concession to private entities for that task. The Supreme Tribunal rejected this argument, and interpreted Article 164 n° 10 as conferring merely concurrent powers, with the reasoning that such obligation is "justified" (it follows from the preceding discussion of federalism in general that this justification is made with regards to the principle of subsidiarity, although it is not specifically invoked) "by the general interest, which the Republic has to protect, in the effective and also efficient administration of decentralized public services... The reservation of the administration to a specialized entity safeguards that services are rendered optimally and it is in this line of reasoning that said provision is justified".

[44] See note 46 below and note 28 above, and also Point 20.4.1.1, below.

20.2.3 Allocation of Residual Powers

In line with the previous constitutions, the 1999 Constitution generally allocates residual powers with the states. Article 164 n° 11 provides that the states have "exclusive" powers "for everything that, according to this Constitution, is not allocated to the national or municipal power". This general residual power is, however, undermined by two inverse attributions of residual power to the central authority. Article 156 n° 12 grants the central authority full control over all "other taxes, excises, and revenues not attributed to the states or the municipalities by this Constitution or the law". Furthermore, Article 156 n° 33 provides for the jurisdiction of the central authority "in all other matters that correspond to it [the federal government] due to their nature or kind". This provision has been copied from the 1961 Constitution, which was intended as an implicit powers clause in favor of the federal government.[45] The federal government's power is further strengthened by the Supreme Tribunal's willingness to accept inherent powers in favor of the national level.[46] In summary, the general residual power allocated to the states is a rather theoretical one.[47] In practice, it seems that – in case of doubt – the presumption in favor of federal powers will virtually always prevail.

20.2.4 Conflicts Between Central and Component State Law

As mentioned above, the component states do not have any exclusive legislative powers. Any legislative activity by the states can thus only take place within the framework established by the "basic laws" (Article 165) that must have been enacted by the central government prior to the state's legislation.[48] By definition, these

---

[45] Cf. C. Ayala Corao, "Naturaleza y Alcance de la Descentralización Estadal", in: A.R. Brewer-Carías et al. (eds.), *Leyes para la Descentralización Política de la Federación* 94 (Caracas 1990), referring to the *Exposición de Motivos* of the 1961 Constitution.

[46] Cf. TSJ Sala Constitucional 15 April 2008 (note 13 above), affirming, with reference to Constitutional provisions on some public services of national interest, "that the central government [the "Administration"] has an implicit general power or general clause of public order to condition, limit, or interfere with the rights or liberties on the basis of the doctrine of inherent or implicit rights ... that allows [the interpreter] ... to review the spirit of the provision attributing powers in such manner as to accept the existence of a power when this is the logical consequence of the legal provision and of the nature of the main activity exercised by the organ or entity".

[47] A.R. Brewer-Carías, *La Constitución y sus Enmiendas* 28 (Caracas 1991); *idem*, "El Sistema Constitucional Venezolano", in D. García Belaunde et al. (eds.), *Los Sistemas Constitucionales Iberoamericanos* 771, 778 (Madrid 1992); Rosenn, *supra* note 39 at 16; *see also* J.M. Serna de la Garza, "Constitutional Federalism in Latin America", *California Western International Law Journal* 30: 277, 286 (2000): "the peculiar manner in which implicit powers have been understood, has created an additional instrument that can be used by the federal government to expand its powers".

[48] See text accompanying note 41 above.

central "basic laws" must be superior to the state laws, since the latter have to remain within the framework of the former. Accordingly, in case of conflict between federal law and state law, the former will prevail.[49] The only – rather theoretical – hypothesis in which a state law could prevail over a federal law is when it can be shown that the central government did not respect the constitutional limits to its legislative powers, such as in particular the principle of subsidiarity of Article 165(1).[50]

20.2.5 Law-Making Powers of Municipalities

According to Article 178 "[t]he powers of the Municipality are the governance and the administration of its interests and the management of the matters attributed to it by this Constitution and the national laws with respect to local life". For such purpose, Article 174 provides that the government and administration of the municipalities is attributed to the mayors; and Article 175 assigns the legislative function to the *Consejos Municipales* (municipal councils), which they exercise through "municipal laws" in the form of *ordenanzas* in the matters attributed to them in Article 178.[51] These "own" areas of the municipalities are, according to Article 178, matters related to zoning, historic monuments, social housing, local tourism, public space for recreation, construction, local transport, public entertainment, local environmental protection and hygiene, local public utilities, funerals, child care and other community matters. Only the matters related to local public events (n° 3) and funerals (n° 6) can be regarded as exclusive powers of the municipalities, while the other areas are concurrent and thus limited to the framework of federal and state laws.[52] According to the Law on Municipalities of 2010, the lack of federal legislation (and by logical extension also of state legislation) is supposedly no obstacle to the legislative activity of the municipalities in concurrent matters.[53]

Nonetheless, it has to be pointed out that the Municipality as the "primary political unit of the national organization" (Article 168) has been virtually rendered

---

[49] *See, e.g.*, TSF Sala Constitucional, decision n° 1495 of 1 August 2006, file n° 05-2448 in which the Supreme Tribunal, upon request by the national *Defensoría del Pueblo* (Ombudsman) suspended temporarily the *Ley de Defensa y Seguridad Ciudadana* of the State of Zulia, G.O. of the State of Zulia n° 659 Extra of 24 May 2004, due to the potential incompatibility with the *Código Orgánico de Procedimiento Penal* and the constitutional guarantees of freedom by allowing police forces to arrest suspect persons for 48 h; a final decision is not yet published. For the legal analysis of constitutionality by the *Defensoría del Pueblo* see http://www.defensoria.gob.ve/detalle.asp?sec=160104&id=110&plantilla=1

[50] See text accompanying notes 42–44.

[51] For the definition of *Ordenanzas* see Article 54 n° 1 of the *Ley Orgánica del Poder Público Municipal*, G.O. n° 6015 Extra of 18 December 2010.

[52] *See, e.g.*, for tourism TSJ Sala Constitucional, decision n° 826 of 16 May 2008, file n° 08-0479.

[53] Article 57 *in fine* of the *Ley Orgánica del Poder Público Municipal* (note 51 above).

moot since 2006 by the creation of a parallel structure of *Consejos Comunales* ("communal" councils), which are elected by local "assemblies of the citizens", *Asamblea de Ciudadanos y Ciudadanas*,[54] which can be formed by interested citizens. These *Asambleas de Ciudadanos y Ciudadanas* have been attributed jurisdiction to "approve the rules of the communal living of the community",[55] the scope of which is not further defined.[56] Although these structures that have been extensively regulated in 2010,[57] and are supposed to allow "self-governance" of local communities and are therefore a potential source of diversity,[58] their members are not elected by popular, direct and secret suffrage, thus violating the constitutional principle of representative democracy. Also, it can be doubted that they will balance the high degree of centralization of the country. These community structures, understood as vehicles for the advancement of socialism, are directly coordinated, supervised, and financed by the *Ministry for the Popular Power for the Communes and Social Protection* of the National Executive. Their leaders are appointed directly by the President[59] without the participation of the states or the municipalities.[60]

---

[54]The possibility to create such *Asamblea de Ciudadanos y Ciudadanas* is mentioned in Article 70 of the Constitution as one of the "means of participation and protagonism of the people in the exercise of its sovereignty", "whose decisions have binding character". The proposed reform of the Constitution, rejected in the Referendum of 2 December 2008, would have added "as long as they do not contradict the Constitution and the laws", which is probably the interpretation that has to be given to the present Article 70 anyway.

[55]Article 6 n° 1 of the *Ley Orgánica de los Consejos Comunales*, G.O. n° 39335 of 10 April 2009. "Community" is defined in Article 4 n° 1 as "the social conglomerate of families and citizens which live in a specific geographic area, which share a common history and interests, know each other and have relations with each other, use the same public utilities and share similar economic, social, urbanistic, and other necessities and potentials".

[56]It is worth noting that Article 6 n° 5 of the same law provide that Assembly of Citizens "exercises the social control". See in this regard the *Ley Orgánica de Contraloría Social*, G.O. n° 6011 Extra of 21 December 2010. Articles 9 and 16 of the *Decreto con Rango, Valor y Fuerza de Ley Orgánica del Servicio de Policía y del Cuerpo de Policía Nacional*, G.O. n° 5880 Extra del 9 April 2008 require the police only to inform and to consult the "communities", the *Consejos Comunales*, or the other "communitarian" organs, without mentioning the municipalities. Furthermore, Articles 47–48 provides "communities" with the possibility to create their own police force "committed to the respect of values, identity and the own culture of each community", with "the task to guarantee and ensure social peace, cohabitation, the exercise of rights and the fulfillment of the law". The National Police Law has been declared constitutional by TSJ Sala Constitucional, decision n° 385 of 15 March 2008, file n° 08-0233.

[57]See in particular, *Ley Orgánica del Poder Popular*, G.O. n° 6011 Extra of 21 December 2010; *Ley Orgánica de las Comunas*, G.O. n° 6011 Extra of 21 December 2010.

[58]*But see* note 54 above *in fine*.

[59]Articles 28 to 32 of the *Ley de los Consejos Comunales* (note 55 above).

[60]On this reform in general see A.R. Brewer-Carías, "El inicio de la desmunicipalización en Venezuela: La organización del Poder Popular para eliminar la descentralización, la democracia representativa y la participación a nivel local", *Revista de la Asociación Internacional de Derecho Administrativo* 49–67 (Mexico 2007); A.R. Brewer-Carías, "Introducción General al Régimen del Poder Popular y del Estado Comunal (O de cómo en el siglo XXI, en Venezuela se decreta, al

20.3 The Means and Methods of Legal Unification

In view of the above sketched centralization of virtually all relevant law-making activity as well as the weakness of federalism in the country's history, legal unification is not an issue in Venezuela. The legal unification has been achieved exclusively through the central power of the federal government (top down). Attempts to decentralize the powers by transferring powers to the component states and municipalities have failed so far and have practically become obsolete. Voluntary coordination among component states or an impact of non-state actors on legal unification do not seem to have played a role and are rather unlikely to play one in the future in view of the tendencies to reduce federalism further more.

The curricula of the Venezuelan faculties of law, half of which are located in Caracas, are focused exclusively on federal law and are rather similar irrespective of their location.[61] In the absence of legislative diversity in Venezuela, legal education and training can be considered a factor that supports the centralization of the making and application of the law. The absence of legislative diversity also suggests that external factors are irrelevant for maintaining the high degree of centralization.

20.4 Institutional and Social Background

20.4.1 The Role of the Judicial Branch

20.4.1.1 The Role of the Supreme Tribunal

The Constitutional Chamber of the Supreme Tribunal of Justice (*Sala Constitucional del Tribunal Supremo de Justicia*) is the court with jurisdiction over all disputes over the constitutionality of statutes and acts resulting from the direct application of the Constitution and over all disputes between the central government, the states and the municipalities ("*acción de resolución de conflictos entre órganos del Poder Público*") (Articles 266 n° 4 and 336 n° 9). Yet, the jurisdiction of this court has to be put into a larger political context created by the 1999 Constitution and subsequent laws that have put into question the impartiality of the court, which

---

margen de la Constitución, un Estado de Comunas y de Consejos Comunales, y se establece una sociedad socialista y un sistema económico comunista, por los cuales nadie ha votado)," in: idem (coord.) et al. (eds.), *Leyes Orgánicas sobre el Poder Popular y el Estado Comunal* (*Los consejos comunales, las comunas, la sociedad socialista y el sistema económico comunal*) 9–182 (Caracas 2011).

[61] *For a list of, and internet links to, most of the law faculties in Venezuela see* http://venezuela.justia.com/recursos/universidades/

since 1999 has been dominated by the followers of the President.[62] It is therefore little surprise that conflicts over powers between the central government and the states are systematically decided to the detriment of the latter.[63]

The only known recent case in which the Supreme Tribunal effectively declared that a federal law violated the legislative powers of a state under the new constitution concerns a case in which no federal interests were at stake. The presidential *Decreto con fuerza de Ley General de Puertos* of 2002[64] provided, among other things, that the entities created by the states for the administration of commercial ports are obliged to transfer 12.5 % of their gross income to the municipality in which the port is located. The Supreme Tribunal declared this provision unconstitutional, *inter alia*, because it would violate the states' exclusive right to dispose of the "exploitation" of the ports according to Article 164 n° 10, and thus of the revenues obtained thereof.[65]

Examples for the Tribunal's bias in favor of the central government may be found in its refusal to hear cases in which the Central Government in 2003, after significant tensions between the President and states governed by the opposition had cut off payment of the constitutionally guaranteed share of the *Situado Constitucional*, the federal financial transfer to the states (Article 167 n° 4).[66] The Tribunal justified its refusal by stating that the alleged lack of payment is merely a question of the application of ordinary law and therefore not of constitutional nature, thus forcing the states to restart their claims before the Administrative Chamber.[67]

Another illustration is a case concerning the disarmament of the state police by the national armed forces after violent clashes between followers of the President and state police force.[68] *Inter alia*, the National Armed Forces, which are under the control of the President (Article 156 n° 8, 236 n° 5), confiscated in 2003 the assault rifles of the state police of Zulia, who had bought them in 2001 with the authorization of the federal Minister of the Interior and with federal funds for

---

[62]*See, e.g., Decreto de la Asamblea Nacional Constituyente sobre la Reorganización del Poder Judicial y el Sistema Penitenciario*, G.O. n° 36805 of 11 October 1999 (intervening in the Supreme Tribunal and allowing the removal of justices by a Special Commission created by the Constituent Assembly); Human Rights Watch, "Rigging the Rule of Law: Judicial Independence Under Siege in Venezuela", 16/3b *HRW Reports* 17–20 (2004), available at http://www.hrw.org/reports/2004/venezuela0604/venezuela0604.pdf. *See also* A.R. Brewer-Carías, *supra* note 8 at 226–244.

[63]Other than the following examples, for the bias of the Supreme Tribunal in favor of the federal government see also A.R. Brewer-Carías, "El juez constitucional vs. la supremacía constitucional", *mimeo*, available at http://www.allanbrewercarias.com, on the systematic rejection of all constitutional actions against the reform of the Constitution, which was eventually rejected in the referendum of 2 December 2007.

[64]G.O. n° 73589 of 11 December 2002.

[65]TSJ Sala Constitucional, decision n° 2495 of 19 December 2006, file n° 02-0265, *see also* note 43 above.

[66]See below Point 20.4.2.2.

[67]TSJ Sala Constitucional, decision n° 1682 of 18 September 2003, file n° 03-0207 (State of Monagas); and decision n° 1109 of 8 June 2004, file n° 03-0725 (State of Apure).

[68]See TSJ Sala Constitucional, decision n° 1140 of 9 June 2005, file n° 03-0969.

decentralization.[69] The State of Zulia requested the Supreme Tribunal to declare that the action violated the State's powers to organize the state police and to guarantee the protection of public order (Articles 164 n° 6 and 332(3)), justifying the need for armory with the fact that the central government had not yet established the national police as required by the 1999 Constitution.[70] The Supreme Tribunal simply rejected the request with the argument that there was no conflict of power because the Armed Force has the powers to regulate the possession of "war weapons", which a law of 1939 defines as "all those which are used or could be used by the Army, the National Guards and the other security agencies for the defense of the Nation and the protection of public order",[71] which effectively covers all type of weapons.

20.4.1.2 Component States' Law Applied by Courts

Since 1945 Venezuela has had no state courts, since the judicial system falls within the exclusive jurisdiction of the central government (Article 156 n° 31). The only exception is the *justicia de paz*, a local system of judges for the conciliatory proceedings in neighborhoods that falls under the jurisdiction of the municipalities (Articles 178 n° 8 and 285).

All courts have jurisdiction to interpret state laws just as any another law and the recourse of cassation against their decisions eventually leads to the Supreme Tribunal's *Sala de casación* (Article 266 n° 8). The different chambers of the Supreme Tribunal can also decide on requests for the interpretation of laws (Article 266 n° 6). These interpretations are, in principle, not actually binding. Formally, only the interpretations of constitutional provisions made by the Constitutional Chamber (*sala constitucional*) of the Supreme Tribunal, which is the ultimate guarantor for the uniform interpretation and application of the constitution, are "binding on the other Chambers and the other courts of the Republic" (Article 335).[72] In practice, however, the interpretations of national, state and municipal laws made by the other chambers of the Supreme Tribunal are *de facto* highly persuasive for the lower instances due to the Tribunal's authority and the system of recourses.

---

[69]For the parallel case of the destitution of the head of the metropolitan police of Caracas by the Armed Forces see TSJ Sala Constitucional, decision n° 3343 of 19 December 2002, file n° 02-2939.

[70]Transitional Provision 4 n° 9 of the Constitution, according to which this law should have been enacted within 1 year after the entry into force of the new Constitution. The *Ley Orgánica del Servicio de Policía y del Cuerpo de Policía Nacional* was only enacted in 2008 through a presidential decree, G.O. 5880 Extra of 9 April 2008.

[71]Article 3 of the *Ley de Armas y Explosivos*, G.O. 19900 of 12 June 1939.

[72]On this point see also A.R. Brewer-Carías, "Instrumentos de justicia constitucional en Venezuela (acción de inconstitucionalidad, controversia constitucional, protección constitucional frente a particulares)", in: J. Vega Gómez & E. Corzo Sosa (eds.), *Instrumentos de Tutela y Justicia Constitucional* 75–99 (Mexico City 2002); and A.R. Brewer-Carías, "Judicial Review in Venezuela", *Duquesne Law Review* 45: 439–465 (2007).

The Constitutional Chamber, when deciding actions on unconstitutionality regarding (national, state, and municipal) laws and regulations, has the exclusive power to review and to annul any kind of legislation – including state law and municipal statutes (Article 336 n° 2)[73] – with *erga omnes* effect (Article 334(3)). Lower courts may declare the unconstitutionality of national, state and municipal statutes and regulations in particular cases and controversies; but this will only have effect *inter partes* (Article 334(2)). In these latter cases, an extraordinary recourse for revision can be brought before the Constitutional Chamber of the Supreme Tribunal so as to obtain a binding interpretation of the Constitution on the question of constitutionality of the challenged legal provision (*stare decisis* principle) (Article 334(4)).[74]

20.4.2 Relations Between the Central Government and Component States

20.4.2.1 The Component States and Federal Law

Although deprived of most exclusive legislative powers, the states are nevertheless declared to be politically "autonomous" (Article 159). Accordingly, the central government cannot force the states to legislate, such as to enact "development laws" within the framework of central "basic laws" in matters of concurrent powers. So long as the states have not assumed their responsibility to legislate, the existing legislation will continue to apply,[75] and, in case of lacunae, courts will apply federal law by way of analogy.

Central government law is applied not only by the central government through specific federal agencies located and functioning in any part of the country, but also by the states and the municipalities when deciding on matters therein regulated.

Prior to 1999, Venezuela always had a bicameral Congress. In the Senate, the federal chamber of Congress, each state and the Federal District were represented by two directly elected senators, and additional senators represented minorities.[76] The 1999 Constitution eliminated the Senate and, in consequence, component states and municipalities are no longer represented in law-making at the central level. The

---

[73] See, e.g., TSJ Sala Constitucional, decision n° 843 of 11 May 2004, file n° 03-1236, whereby a law by which the State of Guárico intended to decentralize to the municipalities more areas than provided for in Article 165(2) was annulled.

[74] See Brewer-Carías, *supra* note 72 at 84: "Accordingly, any interpretation by the Constitutional Chamber of any law or any other legal provision of the rank of a law or regulation does not have binding effect".

[75] Article 11, *Parágrafo Único*, of the 1989 and 2003 Decentralization Law (see notes 26 and 29 above).

[76] Article 148 of the 1961 Constitution.

component states' influence on the central legislative process is retained, according to the Constitution, by the National Assembly's obligation to consult the States' Legislative Council before passing laws on matters which could be of interest to the states (Article 206). Unfortunately, this provision has been systematically ignored in practice.[77]

Furthermore, the 1999 Constitution required the creation of an intergovernmental entity called the Federal Council of Government for the purpose of planning and coordinating the policies and actions for the development of the decentralization process and transfer of powers from the central government to the components states and municipalities. The Federal Council of Government was to be headed by the Vice President of the Republic and integrated by Ministers, governors of the component states and one mayor from each component state, as well as of representatives of the civil society (Article 185). Such entity was finally created in 2010, but rather as an instrument designed to reinforce the centralization process through a central planning system.[78]

20.4.2.2 Public Finances

Virtually everything concerning the taxation system has been centralized even more in the 1999 Constitution, so that the powers of the component states in tax matters have been basically eliminated. The Constitution lists in detail all the central government powers with respect to basic taxes (income tax, inheritance and donation taxes, taxes on capital, production, value added, taxes on hydrocarbon resources and mines, taxes on the import and export of goods and services, and taxes on the consumption of liquor, alcohol, cigarettes and tobacco) (Article 156 n° 12), and also expressly attributes to the municipalities some taxation powers with respect to local taxes (Article 179). In addition, as mentioned above, the Constitution gives to the national government (not to the states) residual competencies in tax matters (Article 156 n° 12). The Constitution does not grant the component states any power on matters of taxation, except with respect to official stationery and revenue stamps

---

[77]The 2003 law on the reform of the 1989 Decentralization Law was allegedly never submitted to the States' Legislative Council, see TSJ Sala Constitucional, decision n° 1801 of 24 August 2004, file n° 04-0331; and decision n° 966 of 9 May 2006, file n° 04-0331 (recourse of nullity eventually rejected due to inactivity of the claimants for more than 1 year). See also the allegations made by the State of Carabobo in its action against the *Decreto con Fuerza de Ley General de Puertos* (G.O. 37589 of 11 December 2002), which were rejected by the Supreme Tribunal with the argument that, in the meantime, the Decree had been substituted by a law for which the states allegedly have been consulted; TSJ Sala Constitucional, decision n° 2495 of 19 December 2006, file n° 02-0265.

[78]See *Ley Orgánica del Consejo Federal de Gobierno*, G.O. n° 5963 Extra of 22 February 2010. See the comments of Penfold-Becerra, *supra* note 5 at 220: "If this Federal Council is not properly regulated by the law, it could be used by the central government as a means to divide the governors through the political use of resources accumulated in [the Intergovernmental Fund for Decentralization]". *See also* Sánchez Meleán, *supra* note 30 at 26.

(Article 164 n° 7). Thus, the component states can only collect taxes when the National Assembly expressly transfers to them, by statute, specific taxation powers (Article 167 n° 5), which has never happened so far.

Therefore, due to the state's lack of resources from taxation, their financing is basically provided by the transfer of national financial resources through three different channels. First, it is done by means of the so-called *Situado Constitucional*, (Constitutional Contribution by the Federal Government) provided in the national Constitution, which is an annual amount within the National Budget Law equivalent to a minimum of 15 % and a maximum of 20 % of total ordinary national income, estimated annually (Article 167 n° 4). Second, a national law has established a system of special economic allocations for the benefit of those component states where mining and hydrocarbon projects are being developed. According to this statute, these benefits have also been extended to include other component states (Article 156 n° 16).[79] And third, financing for states and municipalities also comes from national funds such as the Inter-Territorial Compensation Fund, which was created by the Federal Council of Government Law of 2010 and substitutes the former Intergovernmental Fund for Decentralization (FIDES), created in the Decentralization Law of 1993 (Article 167 n° 6). According to the Constitution, this Fund is administered by the Federal Council of Government (Article 185(2) *in fine*) and wholly controlled by the central authorities.[80] In fact, the central government has repeatedly and over some period of time retarded the transfer payments, thus causing serious financial problems to some states.[81]

20.4.3 Other Institutions for Resolving Intergovernmental Conflicts

Except the Constitutional Chamber of the Supreme Tribunal of Justice, which has jurisdiction to resolve constitutional and administrative conflicts between the central government and the component states and the municipalities, and the Federal Council of Government, which is called to plan and coordinate policies and actions for the process of decentralization and transfer of competencies, there are no other institutions (political, administrative, judicial) to help resolve conflicts between component states or between the central government and component states.

---

[79] *Ley de Asignaciones Económicas Especiales para los Estados y el Distrito Metropolitano de Caracas Derivadas de Minas y Hidrocarburos*, G.O. 37086 of 27 November 2000; substituted by *Ley de Asignaciones Económicas Especiales Derivadas de Minas y Hidrocarburos*, G.O. 5991 Extra of 29 July 2010. See A. Vigilanza García, *La Federación descentralizada. Mitos y realidades en el reparto de tributos y otros ingresos entre los entes políticos territoriales de Venezuela* (Caracas 2010).

[80] See note 78 above.

[81] Sánchez Meléan, *supra* note 30 at 28-2; see also text accompanying note 67 above.

20.4.4 The Role of Bureaucracy

Even though national legislation on public servants was enacted in 2002,[82] which is applicable to all levels of civil servants, each level of government has its own civil service system. Thus, the civil service of the central government is separate from the civil services of the component states and of the municipalities. Being separate civil service systems, there is no formal lateral mobility (or career advancement) between them. Yet for retirement purposes (pensions), a matter falling under exclusive federal jurisdiction,[83] the length of time worked in any of the three levels of government counts for the purpose of retirement.

20.4.5 Social Factors

Venezuela is a multicultural and mixed (*mestizo*) country where no important racial, ethnic, religious, linguistic or other social cleavages in the federation exist. There is a very small population of indigenous peoples (approximately 1 %), whose rights have been expressly recognized in the Constitution (Articles 119–126). The most important indigenous peoples group is located in the southern State of Amazonas, and its members have actively participated in the political process of the state and its municipalities. The Constitution also guarantees that in addition to the members of the National Assembly elected in each state, three separate members must be elected by the indigenous peoples (Article 186).[84]

There are very significant asymmetries in natural resources, development, wealth and education between the component states. The main oil exploitation (the main source of income of Venezuela) is located in the States of Zulia and Anzoategui, and the main mining exploitations in the State of Bolívar. Since the component states are dependent on national financial allocations, one of the factors established in the Constitution for the distribution of the resources from the *Situado Constitucional* is related to the population of each state. Yet, the Constitution allows the assignation of special economic advantages to the states in whose territory the natural resources are located (Article 156 n° 16).[85]

---

[82]*Ley del Estatuto de la Función Pública, supra* note 33.

[83]*Ley del Estatuto Sobre el Régimen de Emolumentos, Pensiones y Jubilaciones de los Altos Funcionarios y Altas Funcionarias del Poder Público*, G.O. N° 39592 of 12 January 2011; *see also* note 23 above.

[84]See also note 76 above.

[85]*Ley de Asignaciones Económicas Especiales Derivadas de Minas y Hidrocarburo* (note 79 above).

20.5 Concluding Remarks

Federalism has always been a most sensitive and controversial topic in Venezuela and accordingly has developed in a rather particular way, often described as "centralized federalism".[86] Already the *Exposición de Motivos* of the 1961 Constitution reflected the peculiarity of the Venezuelan conception of federalism:

"'Federation' in Venezuela, properly speaking, represents a peculiar form of life, a bundle of values and feelings that the Constituency is obliged to respect to the degree that the interests of the people allow. Therefore, the following definition has been adopted: 'The Republic of Venezuela is a federal state in the terms established by this Constitution' . . . In other words, it is a federation to the degree and with the particular form in which this idea has been lived by the Venezuelan society".[87]

The decentralization process initiated in 1989 had brought about – probably for the first time – some new dynamism into the political landscape of Venezuela by granting new opportunities at state level to counterbalance the power of the central government. Yet the 1999 Constitution and especially the political evolution since 2002 have more or less dried out the buds of living federalism created by the 1989 decentralization process.[88] Some go as far as affirming that, *de facto*, Venezuela is no longer a federation.[89]

As concerns the legislative powers, the finding that the component states of Venezuela do not have any significant legislative powers outside the restricted framework of federal laws also has to be put into the broader picture of legislative activity in Venezuela in general. In 2007, the National Assembly enacted a total of 19 laws, not including 62 approvals of treaties concluded by Venezuela with foreign

---

[86] See Brewer-Carías, *supra* note 41.

[87] *Exposición de Motivos de la Constitución de la República de Venezuela* (1961), cited by M. Arcaya, *Constitución de la República de Venezuela* 35–36 (Caracas 1971). This passage is partially also cited by M. Kornblith, "The Politics of Constitution-Making: Constitutions and Democracy in Venezuela", *Journal of Latin American Studies* 23: 61, 86 (1991).

[88] Sánchez Meleán, *supra* note 30 at 27 (citing the President himself as having declared in his weekly television show "Aló Presidente" that Venezuela is a "unitary republic"); J. Biardeau R., "El proyecto de reforma y la destrucción del Estado Federal Descentralizado", *mimeo* (20 October 2007), available at http://www.aporrea.org/ideologia/a42897.html (criticizing the planned reform of the Constitution [failed due to the negative referendum on 2 December 2007] as "not containing any elaboration of the principles of the decentralized federal State in the new geometry of power. Much is being said about popular power [*poder popular*], but the cruel reality is that it is born as an appendix of the national executive power and without any autonomy". More optimistic in 2002 was Penfold-Becerra, *supra* note 5 at 221: "Venezuela's federal system might help counterbalance presidential power, continue to modify legislators' behavior, and even undermine the coalition that keeps Chávez in power. It is still too early to tell the impact of federalism on the eventual shape of Venezuelan democracy, but evidence indicates that federalism remains a critical source of political change in the country".

[89] Serna de la Garza, *supra* note 47 at 283.

countries.[90] The first of these laws was enacted by unanimous vote; it empowered the President in Article 203(4) to regulate a significant number of matters by way of "decree with force of law" for periods of 18 months.[91] The same occurred in 2010 with the approval of another enabling law authorizing the President for 18 months to regulate another significant number of matters by way of the same "decree with force of law".[92] Taken together with the broad legislative powers attributed to the central government, this means that the country is primarily governed directly by the President through decree. All in all, the discussion about federalism in Venezuela is by now virtually meaningless.

---

[90] Asamblea Nacional, *Informe de Gestión 2007 – Balance Legislativo* (18 December 2007), available at http://www.asambleanacional.gov.ve/uploads/biblio/Balance_Legislativo%202007%20.pdf

[91] *Ley que Autoriza al Presidente de la República para Dictar Decretos con Rango, Valor y Fuerza de Ley en las Materias que se Delegan*, G.O. n° 38617 of 1 February 2007. See on the Decree Laws enacted according to this 2008 enabling law, 115 *Revista de Derecho Público* (2008). Previously, the President had been given fast track powers for one year by the *Ley Habilitante* of 2000, G.O. n° 37077 of 14 November 2000; on this law see A.R. Brewer-Carías, "Apreciación general sobre los vicios de inconstitucionalidad que afectan los Decretos Leyes Habilitados" in: Academia de Ciencias Políticas y Sociales (ed.), *Ley Habilitante del 13-11-2000 y sus Decretos Leyes* 63–103 (Caracas 2002).

[92] *Ley que Autoriza al Presidente de la República para Dictar Decretos con Rango, Valor y Fuerza de Ley en las Materias que se Delegan*, G.O. n° 6009 Extra of 17 December 2010.

Contributors

Principal Authors:

Daniel Halberstam. Eric Stein Collegiate Professor of Law, University of Michigan.

Mathias Reimann. Hessel E. Yntema Professor of Law, University of Michigan.

Argentina National Reporters:

Alfredo M. Vítolo. Professor of Constitutional Law and Human Rights, University of Buenos Aires; Treasurer, Argentine Association of Comparative Law.

Australia

Cheryl Saunders. Professor of Law, University of Melbourne.

Michelle Foster. Associate Professor of Law, University of Melbourne.

Austria

Bernhard A. Koch. Professor of Civil and Comparative Law, University of Innsbruck.

Anna M. Gamper. Professor of Public Law, Constitutional Theory and Comparative Constitutional Law, University of Innsbruck.

Belgium

Alain-Laurent Verbeke. Professor of Law at the Universities of Leuven , Tilburg & UCP Lisboa Global School of Law; Visiting Professor of Law Harvard Law School; Professor of Psychology at the University of Leuven; Attorney-at-Law, Brussels; Member of the Bar of Brussels and Kortrijk (Belgium).

Brazil

Jacob Dolinger. Professor of Private International Law at State University of Rio de Janeiro (ret.), Visiting Professor at the Universities of Sao Paulo, Loyola of Los Angeles and Miami, FL., Lecturer at the Hague Academy of International Law.

Luís Roberto Barroso. Professor of Constitutional Law, Rio de Janeiro State University (UERJ).

Canada

Aline Grenon. Professor of Law, University of Ottawa, Faculty of Law, French Common Law Program; member of the Law Society of Upper Canada and of the Barreau du Québec.

European Union

Jan Wouters. Jean Monnet Chair, Professor of International Law and International Organizations, Director of the Leuven Centre for Global Governance Studies and Institute for International Law University of Leuven, Belgium.

Hanne Cuyckens. Assistant, Institute for International Law, Research Fellow, Leuven Centre for Global Governance Studies, University of Leuven, Belgium.

Thomas Ramopoulos. Research Fellow, Leuven Centre for Global Governance Studies; Doctoral Researcher, Institute for International Law, University of Leuven, Belgium.

We thank Walter van Gerven, who was a co-author of an early draft report on the European Union.

Germany

Jürgen Adam. District Judge, Freiburg, Germany, Human Resources Officer at the Ministry of Justice of Baden-Württemberg, Stuttgart, Germany.

Christoph Möllers. Professor of Constitutional Law, Humboldt-University, Berlin.

India

Sunita Parikh. Associate Professor, Department of Political Science, Washington University, St. Louis, Missouri.

Italy

Louis Del Duca. Edward N. Polisher Distinguished Faculty Scholar, Penn State Dickinson School of Law; *laurea in giurisprudenza*, Università di Roma.

Patrick Del Duca. Professor of Law from Practice, UCLA Law School; Partner, Zuber, Lawler & Del Duca, LLP; *laurea in giurisprudenza*, Università di Bologna.

Malaysia

Hean Leng Ang. Advocate and Solicitor, High Court of Malaya; Sessional Lecturer, School of Arts and Sciences, Monash University (Sunway Campus), Selangor, Malaysia.

Amanda Whiting. Associate Director, Malaysia, Asian Law Centre, the University of Melbourne, Australia.

Mexico

Oscar Echenique Quintana. Law Clerk, Justice Alfredo Gutiérrez Ortiz Mena, Supreme Court of México.

Nadja Dorothea Ruíz Euler. Attorney, Federal Revenue Service, Mexico City.

Ricardo Carrasco Varona. Attorney, Federal Revenue Service, Mexico City.

Netherlands

Arjen van Rijn. Attorney and partner at Pels Rijcken & Droogleever Fortuijn, The Hague.

Russia

Jeffrey Kahn. Associate Professor of Law, Southern Methodist University Dedman School of Law, Dallas, Texas.

Alexei Trochev. Professor, Nazarbayev University (Kazakhstan) School of Humanities & Social Sciences.

Nikolay Balayan. a graduate of the Saratov State Law Academy, earned his LL.M from the Dedman School of Law, Southern Methodist University, Dallas, Texas, and is a member of the bar of the State of New York.

South Africa

Karthy Govender. Professor of Law at University of KwaZulu-Natal, Durban; former Human Rights Commissioner; former acting Judge, High Court of South Africa.

Spain

Aida Torres Pérez. Professor of Constitutional Law at Pompeu Fabra University, Barcelona.

Switzerland

Eleanor Cashin Ritaine. formerly Director, Swiss Institute of Comparative Law; Attorney, Geneva.

Anne-Sophie Papeil. Lawyer for the unemployment insurance fund of Neuchâtel.

United Kingdom

Stathis Banakas. Reader in Law, University of East Anglia.

United States

James R. Maxeiner. Associate Professor of Law, University of Baltimore, Maryland.

Venezuela

Allan R. Brewer-Carías. Professor, Central University of Venezuela.

Jan Kleinheisterkamp. Senior Lecturer, Department of Law, London School of Economics.

Index

A

Aborigine (also Aboriginal), 170, 171, 179, 180, 264, 301, 328, 334. *See also* Indigenous peoples

Academic writings, 3, 20–22, 42, 48, 113, 138, 297, 299, 300, 333, 453, 454, 459, 471, 513
    influence on legal unification, 20, 187, 406, 452

Administrative law
    administrative courts, 104, 105, 112, 115, 116, 119, 245, 247, 248, 284–286, 291, 345, 443
    administrative procedure (*see* Procedure)
    generally, 49, 162

Age of federations, 47–48, 50

Amendment (also Constitutional amendment), 11, 75, 79–82, 84, 85, 97, 111, 112, 119, 185, 189, 238, 242, 256, 257, 260, 261, 269–274, 278, 279, 283, 287–289, 298, 302–304, 309–311, 314, 326, 331, 343, 360, 362, 365, 368, 379, 386, 387, 402, 419, 422, 431, 437, 445, 474, 492, 494, 498, 503, 504, 510, 518

Apartheid, 391, 392, 413, 415

Argentina, 4, 5, 9, 10, 17, 21, 24, 33, 36, 37, 39, 42, 52, 72–77, 83, 85

Asymmetry (also Asymmetric), 4, 8, 100, 123, 149–150, 171, 234, 254, 385, 392, 414–415, 418, 435–437

Australia, 5, 9–11, 13, 14, 16–19, 23–25, 28, 29, 33, 38, 39, 42, 44, 90–100, 102, 184, 320

Austria, 5, 9, 11, 14, 16, 17, 19, 21, 23, 26, 29, 33, 37, 39, 42, 47–119, 193, 229, 456

Authoritarian, 5, 47, 344, 377, 525

Autonomy
    Autonomy Statute (also Statue of autonomy, Statutes of autonomy), 418–424, 426, 427, 430, 431, 434, 436, 437
    economic (also fiscal autonomy, financial autonomy, budgetary autonomy), 122, 143, 145, 275, 277, 284, 376, 432
    generally, 136
    judicial, 41, 452
    legislative, 157, 238, 485
    linguistic and cultural, 142
    municipal (also autonomy of municipalities), 243, 293, 447, 449, 501
    policy, 215
    political, 268, 441
    state (also autonomy of states, autonomy of component states, Regional autonomy, provincial autonomy, Länder autonomy), 9, 75, 80, 85, 118, 157, 159, 270, 272, 273, 291, 294, 377
    tax, 41, 250

B

Banks, 31, 35, 89, 91, 105, 133, 158, 172, 173, 204–205, 215, 239, 300, 304, 314, 317, 341, 357, 377, 388, 421, 422, 443, 444, 451, 466, 470, 526, 530

Bar, 21–26, 57, 83–84, 96, 114, 139, 162, 165, 181, 186, 188, 221, 226, 246, 259, 268, 281, 285, 318–324, 327, 346, 355, 369, 370, 408, 445, 451, 492, 509, 511, 513, 514, 521

Basic law, 252, 392, 423, 477, 527, 528, 531–533, 538. *See also* Constitution

Belgium, 4, 5, 9, 10, 16, 17, 23, 25, 26, 33, 39, 42, 46, 47, 50, 121–151, 191–193, 292
Bijural legislation, 6, 23, 24, 179–182, 186, 188–190
Bill of Rights
 amparo, 343, 347–348, 351–353
 due process, 503
Bottom-Up Unification (also bottom up coordination), 15, 55, 93–94, 137, 216–220, 258–259, 344, 362–364, 406–407
Brazil, 4, 5, 9, 10, 13, 14, 16, 17, 33, 36, 37, 39, 42, 72, 153–167
Bureaucracy, 15, 58, 100, 146, 233, 263, 290, 291, 315–317, 331–332, 350, 380, 383, 390, 412–413, 431–432, 456, 517, 541. *See also* Civil service

C
Canada, 5, 6, 103–14, 16–19, 21, 23–26, 28, 33, 36, 38, 39, 42, 44, 46, 50, 52, 169–190, 292
Cantons, 5, 19, 25, 47, 148, 439–460
Cassation, 83, 135, 136, 141, 284, 285, 287, 378, 537
Central court jurisprudence, 12–13
Central government, 8, 75, 91, 116, 124, 157, 173, 231, 249–250, 256, 274–275, 297, 340, 356, 392, 418, 444, 488, 492, 524. *See also* Federal government
Centralization, 9, 15, 17, 22, 34–39, 41, 43, 46, 47, 50, 52, 87–102, 118, 238, 255–265, 267, 268, 281, 329, 376, 377, 386, 387, 419, 524, 525, 534, 535, 539
Central legislation, 114–12, 18, 34, 41, 56, 57, 97, 135, 140, 205–213, 257, 311, 325, 361, 373, 397, 403–404, 426, 437, 505–507, 528
Central takeover. *See* Takeover
City (also cities, autonomous cities), 4, 14, 16, 23, 26, 72, 73, 76, 81, 83, 84, 100, 154, 170, 201, 218, 237, 257, 270, 274–276, 280, 287, 309, 313, 314, 322, 326, 334, 340, 341, 355, 363, 370, 377, 378, 384, 385, 400, 401, 416, 418, 435, 442, 457, 458, 464, 487, 500, 520, 537. *See also* Municipal
Civil law (also Legal traditions, Civil law systems), 5, 6, 10, 12–15, 17, 18, 20, 21, 23, 24, 37, 41–46, 48, 50, 66, 104, 105, 108, 155, 169, 170, 179–183, 185, 186, 188–190, 239, 248, 274, 276, 313, 314, 317, 345, 357, 371, 443, 449, 472, 483, 486–488, 498, 511, 513, 525. *See also* Common law
Civil procedure, 3, 27, 37, 45, 55, 161, 174, 176, 241, 257, 258, 262, 270, 357, 373, 374, 443, 448, 449. *See also* Codes, code of civil procedure; Procedure
Civil service (also Civil servants), 19, 58, 100, 117, 146, 163, 232, 233, 240, 242, 250, 253, 263, 291, 297, 331, 332, 350, 364, 366, 377, 380, 383, 413, 421, 423, 431, 432, 456, 466, 488, 517, 541. *See also* Bureaucracy
Civil war, 73, 393, 458, 491, 492, 519, 524
Cleavages
 ethnic, 335, 350
 linguistic (also language), 138, 147, 148, 414, 434
 social, 34, 45, 46, 58, 118, 146–148, 253, 332, 383, 541
 territorially bounded cleavages, 46–47
Codes (also Legal codes, Codification)
 civil code, 21, 161, 170, 181, 185, 189, 190, 219, 221, 241, 248, 256, 270, 276, 291, 345, 357, 367, 371, 373, 449–451, 460
 code of civil procedure, 161, 241, 448
 commercial code, 22, 246, 505, 507, 510, 512, 515, 520, 524
 criminal code, 77, 97, 315
 generally, 245, 258
Colony (also colonial, colonize), 42, 72, 74, 169, 255, 256, 258, 259, 261, 296, 297, 334
Commerce
 commerce clause, 9, 35, 43, 52, 55, 421, 494, 496, 497, 500
 regulation of commerce, 500, 505
Commercial law, 16, 52, 108, 133, 138, 174, 184, 185, 190, 246, 341, 357, 369, 467, 472, 501, 503, 505, 506, 520, 525
Common law, 5, 10, 12, 13, 17, 20, 22–24, 34, 41–46, 48, 66, 93, 94, 96, 97, 155, 169, 170, 179–183, 185, 188–190, 256, 307, 313, 315, 317, 321, 378, 449, 462, 464, 471, 473, 475, 476, 478–481, 487, 496, 501, 502, 511–513. *See also* Civil law
Commonwealth government, 95, 101. *See also* Central government, Federal government
Communities, 55, 58, 72, 79, 122–124, 126–132, 134–137, 140–147, 149, 150, 171, 192–194, 196, 197, 203, 205, 225, 232, 233, 256, 328, 334, 335, 350, 388, 418, 421, 423, 432, 445, 457, 463, 465,

Index 553

466, 469, 474, 475, 534. *See also* Regions
Component states (also Member States, cantons, provinces, member units, component units). *See also* Länder
  component state bureaucracy, 100, 146, 233, 253, 263, 331–332, 350, 383, 412–413, 431–432, 456, 517
  component state executive, 57, 318, 358, 364, 404, 406, 407
  component state judiciaries, 17–18, 29, 56, 58, 66, 97, 141, 245, 364, 379, 508
  component state law, 12–14, 24, 41, 48, 56–58, 66, 79, 80, 85, 91, 97, 113, 114, 125, 138–139, 141, 163, 175, 176, 179, 181–183, 185, 188–190, 200–203, 224, 229, 248, 316, 359–360, 362, 364, 377–379, 398, 400, 403, 404, 409, 410, 424, 431, 524, 532–533
Confederation, 344, 359, 440–450, 453–457, 459, 460
Conflicts
  of competences, 127
  of law, 20, 521
  of powers, 537
Congress, 14, 35, 43, 44, 75–81, 121, 164, 261, 262, 265, 341, 343, 355, 419, 425, 430, 431, 494–496, 498–500, 503, 505, 506, 514–516, 538. *See also* Legislature
Constitution (also constitutional)
  constitutional interpretation (*see* Interpretation)
  constitutional law, 4, 31, 32, 49, 71, 103, 109, 110, 138, 169, 172, 192, 200, 238, 249, 273, 276, 280, 287, 289, 296, 299, 311, 362, 363, 366, 392, 397, 417, 442, 444, 473–477, 501, 512, 513
  federal constitution, 8, 74, 103, 154, 238, 283, 296, 340, 359, 419, 440, 498, 529
  generally, 36, 49, 154, 219, 252–253, 496
  state constitution, 31, 154, 249, 303, 312, 326, 328, 332, 359, 378, 379, 498, 529, 531
Constitutional court, 104, 121, 158, 196, 238, 268, 357, 396, 419, 452, 477, 515. *See also* Supreme court; High court
Constitutional interpretation, 88, 159, 163, 410, 426. *See also* Interpretation
Constitutional monarchy, 103, 121, 254, 268, 290, 475
Contract law, 21, 22, 57, 137–138, 219, 221, 222, 245
Cooperation
  generally, 15–19
  judicial, 17, 18
  legislative, 15, 16, 145, 157, 160
  principle of sincere cooperation (eu) (also Duty of cooperation), 201, 202
Coordinate Unification
  component unit executive, 15, 18–19
  component unit judiciary, 17–18, 516
  component unit legislatures, 15–17
Corporate law, 133, 175, 216, 498
Courts. *See* Judiciary; Constitutional Court; High Court; Supreme Court
Criminal law
  criminal jurisdiction, 173, 174, 176, 260, 315, 378
  criminal procedure, 37, 48, 86, 155, 162, 239, 241, 242, 258, 270, 314, 343, 357, 443, 448, 469, 504, 524 (*see also* Procedure; Codes, code of criminal procedure)
  generally, 38–39
Culture, 18, 36, 49, 130, 131, 146, 156, 177, 199, 234, 242, 245, 247, 267, 281, 292, 293, 300, 315, 328, 330, 389, 396, 421, 423, 427, 434, 445, 450, 457, 459, 462, 468, 471, 480–481, 488, 534
  power over culture of component states, 495, 498, 539
Currency, 77, 89, 91, 111, 172, 173, 193, 198, 300, 303, 341, 388, 466, 495, 500
Customary law, 38, 296, 313, 314, 394, 414

D

Decentralization, 3, 4, 9, 38, 46, 49, 82, 126, 155, 262, 263, 265, 273, 294, 342, 344, 419, 431, 434, 435, 441, 493, 524, 525, 528–531, 535, 537–540, 542
Decisions. *See* Judicial decisions, Stare decisis
Defense. *See* Military
Democracy (also democratic), 72, 89, 111, 112, 146, 268, 298, 333, 336, 351, 364, 395, 402, 434, 442, 524, 525, 534, 542
Development (also economic development), 28, 55, 59, 72, 77, 79–76, 96, 100–101, 105, 112, 118, 132, 145, 149–150, 155, 162, 166, 171, 189, 193, 199, 203, 204, 212–215, 217, 219, 220, 224, 225, 228, 235, 247, 248, 256, 257, 268, 269, 292–294, 298, 304, 308, 311, 315, 326, 329, 333, 335, 336, 340, 342, 343, 345, 351, 367, 368, 385, 396, 400, 414, 415, 445, 462, 478–482, 488, 491, 526, 527, 530, 539, 541

Devolution (also devolutionary, holding-together), 4, 47, 48, 50, 122, 124, 126, 137, 150, 287, 292, 392, 413, 461–489
Direct application of central law (also Directly applicable, or Direct application), 205, 206, 209, 249, 283, 535
Directive (also Council directive, EC directive), 10, 11, 17, 26, 56, 81, 82, 135, 139, 140, 162, 202, 205, 208–212, 216, 220, 223, 226, 227, 231–233, 246, 250, 258, 262, 290, 403, 436, 506
Discrimination (also non-discrimination, anti-discrimination), 27, 92, 122, 140, 146, 200, 319, 324, 395, 409, 458, 469, 474, 476, 497

E

Education law, 259, 494, 498. *See also* Legal education
Elections (also Electoral System), 74, 90, 98, 102, 103, 105, 111, 116, 124, 125, 142, 143, 150, 164, 171, 239, 242, 244, 256, 270, 280, 285–287, 297, 298, 300, 301, 305, 309, 326, 330, 333–335, 340, 342, 349, 351, 358, 361, 377, 380, 383, 386, 393, 415, 435, 442, 463, 468, 470, 484, 488, 519
  direct election (also direct vote), 154, 329, 349, 380
Employment law, 467, 472. *See also* Labor law
Energy (law or policy), 467
Enumerated powers, 126–127, 174
Environmental law (or policy), 44, 55, 108, 132, 139, 308, 311, 319, 418, 423, 444, 497, 505, 506
Equality
  of component states, 356
  gender equality, 22, 319
  generally, 145
  law of equality, 122
Ethnicity, 5, 46, 50, 58, 118, 146–148, 166, 170, 234, 253, 256, 264, 297, 299, 314, 320, 333–335, 350, 351, 358, 359, 376, 382–386, 388, 414, 456, 517–519, 541. *See also* Race
European Union, 4, 6, 8, 11, 14, 17, 18, 20, 21, 23–30, 32, 33, 35–36, 45, 47–49, 104, 108, 111, 112, 114, 116, 117, 126, 133–135, 138, 139, 150, 191–235, 238–240, 242, 246, 247, 251, 252, 269–271, 276, 277, 280, 282–284, 290, 293, 294, 429, 435, 467, 472–475, 480, 481, 506

Execution (of laws), 124, 250–251, 380, 410, 454
Executive (Branch), 15, 18–19, 57, 154, 164, 245, 261, 318, 343, 344, 358, 364, 379–381, 386, 407. *See also* President

F

Family law, 21, 37, 56, 66, 78, 134–135, 155, 174, 200, 241, 254, 269, 306, 307, 314, 316, 317, 320, 326, 357, 358, 434, 476, 497, 512
Federal city, 384, 385
Federal district, 4, 14, 154–156, 158, 159, 163–166, 340, 341, 345, 363, 382, 383, 516, 538
Federal enclaves. *See* Federal establishments
Federal establishments (also Federal territories, Federal enclaves), 79–80, 301, 305, 307, 311, 313, 314, 316, 317, 321–323, 326–328, 332, 334
Federal government, 4, 9, 11, 14–16, 36, 38, 47, 72, 75, 76, 78–82, 85, 108, 109, 111, 112, 114–116, 122, 129, 131–135, 145, 147, 150, 172, 175, 177–179, 181–184, 187, 239, 241, 249–251, 298, 300, 302, 312, 313, 319, 325, 329, 331, 335, 336, 340, 343, 349, 362, 376, 382, 387–390, 393, 440, 441, 443–446, 449, 451, 453, 456, 458, 459, 492–498, 500, 503, 506, 514, 528, 532, 535, 536, 540. *See also* Central government
Federal powers
  concurrent (powers) (also shared or parallel powers), 35–37, 55, 56, 79, 89, 91, 128–129, 135, 142, 144, 175–177, 200, 239–241, 252, 257, 258, 272, 307, 392, 394–395, 418, 420, 422, 443, 527, 530, 531, 538
  exclusive (powers), 36, 90, 109, 123, 127–128, 130, 144, 172, 174, 238–239, 252, 256–258, 344, 385, 394, 399, 418, 420, 422, 425, 435, 436, 443, 445, 454, 455, 527, 528, 530–533, 538
Federal takeover. *See* Takeover
Federation, 4, 73, 87, 104, 124, 154, 170, 191, 238, 264, 296, 344, 355, 419, 440, 524
Finanzausgleich. *See* Taxation; Fiscal equalization
Freedom of speech (also Freedom of expression), 101, 303, 444

Index

G
Germany, 4, 5, 9–13, 15–18, 23, 24, 26, 28, 29, 33, 36, 39, 43, 47, 48, 52, 192, 193, 209, 229, 237–254, 267, 283, 429, 441, 456, 473, 491, 506, 511, 514, 518
Guarantee clause (also Republican form of government clause), 9, 74

H
Harmonization, 4, 6, 8, 16, 17, 21, 27, 29, 35, 48, 55–57, 59, 63, 64, 80–85, 92–95, 97, 101, 102, 113–115, 118, 134, 137, 138, 171, 179–182, 184, 185, 187, 188, 199, 203–216, 218, 235, 243–245, 256, 258, 259, 271, 302, 310, 314, 317–319, 342–346, 350, 360–362, 371, 372, 425–427, 435, 436, 456, 460, 462, 467, 473, 493, 503–507, 511–513, 515, 526,
Health (law, policy), 131, 472
High Court, 17, 83, 87, 88, 90, 91, 93, 96–99, 101, 104, 115, 255, 257–260, 262, 295, 303, 322, 326, 327, 405, 407–410, 465, 478, 481–483, 486, 487. *See also* Supreme Court; Constitutional Court
Horizontal integration, 4
House of Representatives, 95, 98, 99, 133, 143, 164, 251, 329, 341

I
Implementation (also conforming rules, implementing rules), 10, 14, 93, 94, 108, 114, 116, 118, 125, 145, 150, 204, 206, 207, 209, 214, 216, 220, 223, 225, 231, 249, 250, 257, 258, 274, 280, 283, 290, 292, 314, 396, 398, 404, 406, 429, 436, 444, 445, 449, 454, 516, 526
Independence (also independent). *See also* Autonomy
 generally, 309
 judicial, 83, 379, 466, 536
India, 5, 9, 11, 13, 14, 17, 23, 24, 28, 33, 36, 37, 39, 40, 42, 44, 46, 47, 171–173, 255–265, 292, 296, 311, 333–335, 413, 494, 518
Indigenous peoples (Indigenous Groups, Native Americans, Aboriginals), 36, 155, 169–171, 179, 180, 264, 314, 319, 333, 350, 385, 518, 526, 541
Inequality, 351, 398
Inheritance law, 32, 37, 512
Institutional and social background, 5, 54, 57, 97–100, 115–118, 140–150, 162–166, 229–235, 247–254, 260–265, 284–293, 325–336, 343, 347, 373–386, 409–415, 430–434, 452–459, 482–488, 493, 515–520, 535–541
Insurance law, 183, 219
Integration (also integrative, coming-together), 4, 48, 50, 117, 148, 151, 157, 192, 193, 199, 203, 220, 223, 230, 234, 235, 350, 427, 429, 435, 445, 481
Intellectual property law, 133, 467
International Law (also International norms, External influences)
 mandatory compliance (also self-executing), 26–28, 85, 135, 408, 452, 514
 private international law, 27, 28, 32, 45, 49, 57, 97, 161, 187, 228, 284, 346, 373, 449, 452, 460, 472, 525
 voluntary participation, 26, 28, 97
Interpretation (also constitutional interpretation), 6, 80, 88, 109, 126, 157, 175, 202, 243, 279, 311, 343, 374, 397, 426, 448, 474, 493, 527
Islamic law. *See Syariah*
Italy, 4, 5, 9, 10, 12–14, 16, 17, 19, 21, 23, 25, 26, 28, 33, 36, 37, 39, 47, 52, 192, 193, 267–270, 274–276, 281, 283–287, 289–294, 451, 456

J
Judicial decisions, 12, 84, 161, 162, 178, 220, 247, 362, 370. *See also* Stare decisis
 binding on component states, 374
 persuasive authority in component states, 537
Judicial review, 9, 12, 85, 140, 196, 261, 283, 321, 326, 347, 352, 361, 364, 374, 474, 478, 486, 515, 537
Judiciary
 federal judiciary, 17, 18, 76, 83, 96, 98, 182, 183, 188, 239, 241, 244, 246–248, 255, 310, 314, 319, 325, 326, 330, 342, 362, 363, 377–380, 443, 444, 447, 448, 459, 503, 510, 513, 516, 521
 generally, 163, 182, 213, 229, 362, 363, 370, 376, 378, 486, 487
 state judiciary, 17–18, 28, 56–58, 66, 67, 85, 92, 94, 97, 98, 115, 139, 141, 230, 243, 246, 248, 249, 314, 317, 326, 364, 379, 407, 410, 431, 502, 507, 508, 513, 515, 516, 537
 unitary judiciary, 13, 17

Jurisdiction
  federal court(s), 17, 18, 76, 83, 96, 98, 182, 183, 188, 239, 241, 244, 246–248, 255, 310, 314, 319, 325, 326, 330, 342, 362, 363, 377–380, 443, 444, 447, 448, 459, 503, 510, 513, 516, 521
  state court(s), 17–18, 28, 56–58, 66, 67, 85, 92, 94, 97, 98, 115, 139, 141, 230, 243, 246, 248, 249, 314, 317, 326, 364, 379, 407, 410, 431, 502, 507, 508, 513, 515, 516, 537

L

Labor law, 55, 155, 159, 162, 167, 239, 254, 341, 357, 358, 497. *See also* Employment Law

Länder (Germany and Austria), 27, 110, 114, 118, 120. *See also* Component states

Language (also linguistic), 5, 14, 16, 23, 25, 26, 36, 46, 49, 50, 55, 58, 118, 122, 123, 130, 131, 133, 136, 138, 142, 146–149, 170, 177, 218, 224, 225, 234, 253, 254, 256, 264, 268, 273, 287, 292, 295, 297, 302, 303, 314, 316, 333, 350, 356, 358, 359, 383, 384, 394, 413, 414, 421, 423, 434–436, 445, 451, 453, 456–459, 468, 495, 499, 504, 518, 519, 541
  language, culture, and education, 36

Law-making Power (also law-making), 92, 112, 115, 172, 220, 243, 275, 309, 357, 360, 366, 395, 399–401, 441–447, 464, 474, 533–535, 538

Law professors, 281, 285, 501, 513

Law reform commission (also law commission), 14, 15, 20, 95, 101, 102, 182, 259, 318, 407, 462, 481–482, 489, 508–510

Legal education. *See also* Legal practice
  bar admission, 25–26, 57, 83–84, 114, 139, 246, 320, 346, 369, 451
  law school, 23–25, 96, 138, 185–186, 246, 259, 319, 320, 368–370, 407, 451, 487, 492, 511–514
  legal training, 138–139, 224–227, 259, 319–324, 345–346, 368–371, 407–408, 487, 511–514

Legal practice, 8, 22–26, 29, 43, 49, 84, 227, 320, 321, 408, 497

Legal profession, 26, 29, 185–186, 225, 227, 239, 260, 269, 281, 307, 316, 317, 320–322, 407, 445, 451, 467, 471, 481, 487, 488

Legal traditions. *See* Civil law; Common law

Legislative centralization, 35–40, 43, 52–53
Legislature, 10, 11, 14–16, 19, 21, 22, 41, 43, 46, 49, 53, 76, 77, 80, 98, 100, 109, 123, 159, 160, 170, 173, 201, 228, 249, 251, 257, 300, 306, 309–312, 315, 325, 335, 343, 344, 358, 362–365, 374–381, 387, 393–406, 409–412, 415, 449, 450, 483, 494, 498, 507–510, 516. *See also* Congress; Parliament
  bicameral, 98, 349, 380
  generally, 420, 421, 527, 530

M

Malaysia, 4, 5, 9–14, 17, 21, 25, 27, 33, 36, 37, 41, 42, 295–337

Market (also Law of the Market), 31, 32, 35, 38, 45, 49, 94, 147, 150, 187, 192, 197, 198, 214, 216, 218, 222, 230, 232, 240, 270, 275, 290, 291, 305, 357, 359, 375, 376, 388, 397, 400, 424, 466, 469, 470, 497, 527

Member States (EU), 55, 74, 134, 192, 240, 344, 428, 440, 479. *See also* Component states

Mexico, 4, 5, 9, 11, 13, 14, 16, 17, 19, 21, 23–25, 28, 29, 33, 36–39, 42, 44, 54, 292, 339–351, 355, 534, 537

Military (also defense), 35, 72, 76, 81, 85, 90, 91, 107, 141, 153, 155, 156, 163, 172, 175, 256, 257, 263, 270, 341, 361, 376, 382, 389, 392, 443, 447, 448, 455, 466–470, 488, 496, 524, 525, 537

Minorities (also Minority), 10, 12, 29, 36, 37, 118, 122, 123, 131, 133–134, 149, 170, 234, 254, 258, 268, 273, 287, 289, 292, 297, 328, 334, 384, 386, 388, 430, 453, 459, 538

Mobility (also geographic mobility), 23, 26, 58, 146, 186, 224–227, 233, 246, 247, 253, 263, 332, 350, 383, 397, 411, 432, 451, 456, 517, 541

Model laws, 16, 18, 29, 56, 57, 94, 95, 113, 138, 187, 190, 315–317, 363, 364, 372, 407, 445, 451, 493, 507, 508, 510, 513

Municipal (also municipality). *See also* City

N

Natural resources (also Minerals, Oil), 59, 79, 118, 149, 155, 156, 166, 174, 175, 177, 234, 254, 257, 305, 335, 336, 341, 349, 356, 376, 381, 385, 388, 414, 467, 470, 506, 526, 530, 541. *See also* Water

Index

Non-State (Actors), 8, 19–22, 29, 57, 84, 95, 137–138, 161, 219–224, 235, 245–246, 259, 318–319, 323, 345, 364–368, 407, 508–511, 535. *See also* Private organizations

O

Ombudsperson (also Ombudsman, Ombud), 368, 419, 508, 533

P

Parliament. *See also* Congress; Legislature
  component state representatives, 58, 142–143, 411, 493, 517
  lower house (also House of Representatives), 95, 98, 99, 133, 143, 164, 251, 329, 341
Pension (also Pension law), 35, 89, 132, 165, 175, 176, 290, 309, 332, 398, 443, 465, 467, 469, 472, 527, 541
Pluralism (also legal pluralism, plurality), 75, 205, 308, 313, 384, 419, 434, 457, 461–467, 471, 481, 484, 488
Political parties, 15, 34, 45, 103, 119, 142, 164, 264, 296, 333, 335, 411, 434, 466
Preemption (also pre-empt, preempt), 114, 198, 200, 203, 213, 235, 242, 357, 375, 377, 378, 385, 422, 499, 506. *See also* Supremacy
President, 4, 14, 19, 41, 47, 50, 94, 124, 154, 195, 215, 257, 261, 272, 279, 280, 284–286, 340–342, 351, 356–358, 363, 364, 366, 367, 374–377, 379–383, 385–387, 398, 402, 405, 406, 409, 412, 426, 429, 455, 483, 486, 494, 503, 519, 523, 525, 529, 534, 536, 537, 539, 542, 543. *See also* Executive
Private law, 7, 8, 20–22, 24, 27, 28, 31, 32, 37, 38, 43–45, 48, 97, 121, 133, 138, 170, 174, 179, 180, 184, 186, 189, 190, 216–223, 239, 241, 314, 341, 345, 372, 423, 435, 436, 444, 448, 452, 458, 465, 467, 471, 472, 475, 488, 497, 498, 513
Private norm generation (also private norm setting), 6, 19, 20
Private organizations (also private entities), 57, 138, 161, 223–224, 345, 364, 451, 508, 531. *See also* Non-state actors
Procedure (also Procedural law). *See also* Civil procedure; Criminal procedure
  administrative procedure, 38, 108, 176, 250, 279, 421, 448, 530

  civil procedure, 3, 27, 37, 45, 55, 161, 174, 176, 241, 257, 258, 262, 270, 357, 373, 374, 443, 448, 449
  criminal procedure, 37, 48, 66, 155, 162, 239, 241, 242, 258, 270, 314, 343, 357, 443, 448, 469, 504, 524
Provinces (also Provincial), 5, 71, 115, 123, 170, 255, 268, 344, 363, 392, 420, 464, 523. *See also* Component states

R

Race (also racial), 58, 90, 118, 146–148, 253, 298, 299, 328, 332, 333, 335, 383, 409, 413–414, 497, 517–519, 541
Referendum, 119, 268, 280, 287, 289, 290, 420, 455, 467, 488, 525, 534, 536, 542
Regions, 55, 75, 100, 113, 122, 155, 171, 212, 246, 261, 268, 352, 356, 392, 407, 442, 463, 508, 524. *See also* Communities
Regulation, 10, 75, 91, 105, 128, 157, 172, 199, 239, 256, 271, 306, 341, 357, 394, 420, 444, 461, 496, 527
  administrative regulation, 10, 19, 106, 351
Religion, 100, 244, 297–300, 302, 307, 310, 312, 314, 321, 325–327, 332, 333, 336, 457–459, 497, 519
  freedom of religion, 244, 310, 327
Religious Courts, 306
Republic (also republican), 9, 37, 73–75, 78, 80, 82, 103, 111, 116, 117, 153, 154, 166, 193, 209, 210, 215, 244, 248, 253, 268, 270, 272, 273, 285–287, 290, 292, 356, 358, 359, 363, 376, 382, 384–387, 391, 392, 398, 402, 407, 412, 434, 435, 470, 523–526, 528, 529, 531, 537, 539, 542
Reserved powers, 88, 127, 272
Residual powers, 36, 56, 110, 125, 127, 131, 157, 173, 200, 241, 257, 258, 308, 341, 343, 358–359, 396, 424, 444, 532
Restatement, 8, 20, 21, 29, 49, 57, 113, 137, 161, 186, 219–223, 345, 362, 364, 407, 493, 508, 510–511, 513
Revenue sharing, 58, 117, 143–145, 177, 252–253, 288–289, 293, 381, 411–412, 433, 435. *See also* Fiscal transfer; Fiscal equalization
Rights
  civil rights, 38, 169, 170, 174, 175, 178–182, 341, 388, 518, 519
  constitutional rights, 103, 159, 347, 348, 525

Rights (*cont.*)
  fundamental rights, 9, 27, 101, 128, 134, 135, 140, 158, 167, 204, 218, 258, 261, 439, 475, 476, 488, 523
  human rights, 27, 84, 85, 92, 97, 101, 111, 126, 134, 196, 197, 217, 218, 243, 247, 298, 315, 318, 319, 323, 324, 347, 365, 368, 372, 391, 453, 464–466, 469, 472–477, 480, 481, 536
Russian Federation (also Russia), 14, 355–390

S

Securities law (also Securities regulation), 91, 175, 190, 497, 501, 512
Senate, 98, 100, 124, 143, 145, 154, 164, 248, 286, 287, 328, 331, 349, 419, 426, 431, 463, 494, 516, 538. *See also* Upper house
Separation of powers, 41, 92, 101, 111, 159, 238, 340, 441, 477, 483, 523
Sharia, 13, 17, 37, 256, 260. *See also* Syaria
Social cleavages (also social differences, social factors). *See* Cleavages
Social security, 35, 77, 78, 89, 91, 131, 133, 149, 150, 156, 157, 164, 165, 239, 241, 247, 251, 270, 271, 279, 300, 304, 389, 421, 443, 465, 467, 472, 526
South Africa, 5, 9, 10, 13, 14, 17, 23, 28, 32, 33, 36, 38, 39, 42, 391–416
Sovereignty
  generally, 72, 296, 363, 376, 474
  sovereignty of component states, 340, 359, 363, 376, 385
Spain, 4, 5, 9, 10, 14, 16, 17, 19, 21, 25, 26, 29, 33, 37, 39, 42, 46, 47, 52, 72, 73, 193, 292, 339, 417, 419, 420, 424, 429, 431, 434, 435
Spending power, 90, 178, 179, 425, 426, 436, 449
Standards (also Standard practices, Standard setting), 11, 20, 31, 52, 55, 57, 75, 79, 81, 84, 92–95, 105, 106, 111, 113, 131, 135, 136, 138, 155, 158, 161, 166, 179, 187, 212, 213, 223, 224, 234, 244–246, 256, 279, 292, 295, 308, 313, 316–319, 321, 323, 324, 345, 347, 350, 357, 362, 369, 372, 379, 390, 394, 397, 398, 404, 420, 421, 426, 448, 449, 451, 467, 470, 471, 492–495, 499, 506, 507, 511, 526
Stare decisis (also binding effect), 83, 104, 136, 163, 205, 247, 248, 462, 471, 475, 478–480, 502, 538

State powers
  concurrent (powers) (also shared or parallel powers), 35, 37, 55, 79, 89, 91, 128–129, 135, 142, 175–177, 239, 252, 257, 258, 272, 392, 394–395, 418, 420, 422, 443, 527, 530, 531, 538
  exclusive (powers), 36, 90, 109, 127–128, 130, 144, 172–175, 238–239, 252, 256–258, 340, 344, 394, 399, 418, 420, 422, 425, 435, 436, 443, 445, 454, 455, 527, 528, 530–533, 538
Statutory law, 29, 155, 246, 248, 293, 380, 475, 478, 512
Structural centralization, 34, 40–41, 46, 50
Subsidiarity, 112, 195, 231, 232, 235, 272, 274, 276, 446, 531, 533
Supranational law, 26, 30
Supremacy, 27, 56, 79, 83, 91, 110, 125, 157, 200–203, 217, 242, 282, 283, 310, 325, 339, 342–344, 346, 356, 359–361, 364, 371, 375, 446, 474, 477, 498–499, 523
Supreme Court, 12, 75, 92, 104, 135, 159, 174, 201, 246, 256, 311, 342, 361, 404, 443, 470, 491. *See also* Constitutional Court, High Court
Switzerland (also Swiss), 4, 5, 10, 13, 14, 17–19, 23–27, 33–36, 42, 47, 48, 292, 439–460, 484
Syaria (*Syariah*), 296, 304, 306, 307, 310, 314–319, 321–323, 326, 327, 337
Symmetry (Symmetric), 59, 100, 104, 118, 149–150, 158, 159, 171, 234, 254, 385, 414–415, 435, 436

T

Takeover, 6, 313
Taxation (also Taxes, Taxing power, Tax)
  fiscal equalization, 99, 100, 455
  income tax (also personal income tax), 99, 101, 144, 150, 159, 165, 252, 257, 288, 411, 433, 445, 472, 539
  VAT or Sales Tax, 67, 144, 150, 165, 232, 257, 305, 329, 411
Territorially bounded cleavages. *See* Cleavages
Top-down unification, 92–15, 345
Transportation (also transport)
  power to regulate, 35, 98, 254, 399, 477, 496
  public transport, 159, 394, 400, 444
Treaty, 27, 28, 30, 84, 96, 112, 134, 135, 169, 192–197, 199–204, 207, 208, 214, 215, 217, 228, 229, 232, 240, 250, 268,

282–284, 289, 356, 359, 360, 371, 439, 440, 460, 472, 474–476, 514
Tribe (also Tribal), 254, 257, 264, 391, 413–414
Tribunal. *See* Judiciary

U

UNCITRAL, 28, 29, 57, 161, 187, 284, 372, 452, 460
UNIDROIT, 28, 57, 97, 161, 187, 284, 372, 373, 460
Unification, 3–67, 92, 103–119, 153–167, 169–190, 237–254, 256, 258–260, 276–285, 292, 295–337, 339–353, 355, 356, 360–373, 377, 382, 386, 387, 391–416, 424–429, 436, 439–489, 492, 493, 501–514, 517, 520, 524, 527, 535
Uniformity of law
  comparative by area of law, 31, 52, 96, 349
  comparative by federation, 47, 55, 66, 316, 491, 495
  comparative by legal tradition, 5, 14, 41, 45, 46, 180–182
Union, 4, 25, 36, 38, 39, 45, 47–49, 132, 153–159, 161, 163–167, 191–235, 238, 256, 258, 260–262, 264, 269, 270, 293, 294, 296, 315, 356, 372, 373, 426, 458, 463–465, 475, 488, 491, 492, 494, 506, 519, 524. *See also* Central government
Unitary
  judicial system (also unitary judiciary), 13, 17, 218, 244, 247, 258, 351, 357, 361, 363, 370, 378, 389, 404, 407, 431, 454, 464, 485, 537
  state, 153, 267, 269, 294, 296, 406, 415, 485
United Kingdom (also UK), 4, 5, 7, 9, 13, 14, 17, 23, 26–28, 33, 36, 38, 39, 42, 46, 50–48, 50, 52, 90, 121, 206, 215, 292, 320, 321, 461–489
United States (also US, American), 4, 5, 9–13, 15, 17–26, 28, 33, 36, 38, 39, 41, 43, 45, 47, 49, 55, 71, 73, 95, 153, 154, 159, 161, 210, 279, 293, 339, 343, 345, 347, 364, 491–521, 523, 524
Upper House (also Senate, Federal Council)
  generally (also Upper House Composition), 41, 50, 98, 100, 164, 262, 328, 474, 494
  uniform laws, 41, 494
  upper house veto (also Veto power), 41, 111, 116, 377, 431, 440

V

Venezuela, 5, 8, 10, 17, 32, 33, 37, 39, 42, 47, 523–543
Vertical integration, 4, 28, 127–129, 142, 212, 238, 252, 424
Veto, 41, 111, 116, 293, 301, 377, 431, 440

W

Water (also water resources), 52, 92, 106, 109, 118, 132, 144, 155, 171, 196, 250, 257, 300, 301, 305, 307, 308, 311, 313, 357, 381, 388, 400, 420, 433, 468, 470, 520, 526, 527
Welfare law (also social assistance, social welfare), 35, 107, 108, 112, 131, 134, 165, 171, 174, 239, 251, 272, 300, 301, 361, 394, 396, 398, 421–423, 427, 457, 468, 494, 496, 497, 526
World War I (also First World War), 103, 518
World War II (also Second World War), 149, 192, 268, 292, 296